# A SISTERHOOD OF SCULPTORS

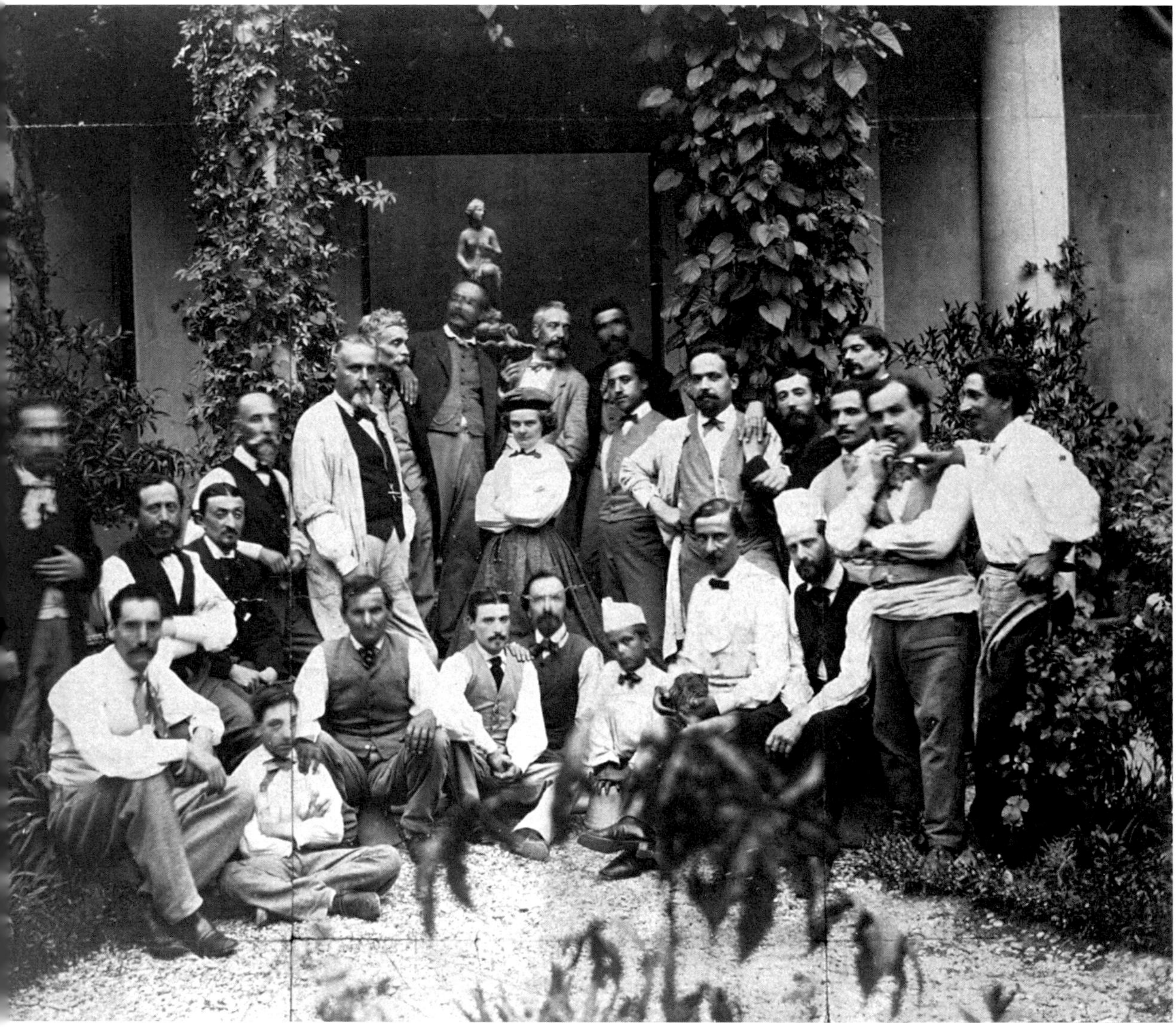

MELISSA DABAKIS

# A Sisterhood of Sculptors

## AMERICAN ARTISTS IN NINETEENTH-CENTURY ROME

THE PENNSYLVANIA STATE UNIVERSITY PRESS
UNIVERSITY PARK, PENNSYLVANIA

Publication of this book has been aided by grants from the Wyeth Foundation for American Art Publication Fund of the College Art Association and from the Terra Foundation for American Art.

Library of Congress Cataloging-in-Publication Data

Dabakis, Melissa, author.
A sisterhood of sculptors : American artists in nineteenth-century Rome / Melissa Dabakis.
p. cm
Summary: "Explores mid-nineteenth-century American women sculptors who developed successful professional careers in Rome. Draws from feminist theory, cultural geography, and expatriate and postcolonial studies to investigate the gendered nature of creativity and expatriation"—Provided by publisher.
Includes bibliographical references and index.
ISBN 978-0-271-06219-8 (cloth : alk. paper)
1. Expatriate sculptors—Italy—Rome—History—19th century.
2. Women sculptors—United States—History—19th century.
3. Sculpture, Neoclassical—Italy—Rome.
4. Sculpture, American—Italy—Rome—19th century.
5. Rome (Italy)—Intellectual life—19th century.
6. Rome (Italy)—Politics and government—19th century.
7. Feminism and art.
I. Title.

NB210.D33 2014
730.82'0973—dc23
2013046864


Printed in the United States of America
Published by The Pennsylvania State University Press,
University Park, PA 16802-1003

The Pennsylvania State University Press is a member of the Association of American University Presses.

It is the policy of The Pennsylvania State University Press to use acid-free paper. Publications on uncoated stock satisfy the minimum requirements of American National Standard for Information Sciences—Permanence of Paper for Printed Library Material, ANSI Z39.48–1992.

# Contents

*List of Illustrations* / *vii*
*Acknowledgments* / *xiii*

Introduction / *1*

PART I: FEMININE PROFESSIONALISM IN BOSTON AND ROME

1 The Boston-Rome Nexus / *15*
2 Neoclassicism in Cosmopolitan Rome / *37*
3 "A Woman Artist Is an Object of Peculiar Odium" / *63*

PART II: WOMEN SCULPTORS AND THE POLITICS OF ROME

4 Rome in the Colonial Imagination / *93*
5 Reimagining Italy / *117*

PART III: THE CIVIL WAR, RECONSTRUCTION, AND THE SUFFRAGE DEBATES

6 Antislavery Sermons in Stone / *149*
7 Women Sculptors, Suffrage, and the Public Stage / *181*

Postscript / *207*

*Notes* / *213*
*Selected Bibliography* / *257*
*Index* / *271*

# *Illustrations*


*Maps*

1 Map of Rome, from Edward Hutton, *Rome* (New York: Macmillan, 1909), frontispiece. Photo: Daniel P. Younger. / *xvi*

2 Map of the Italian peninsula, April 1859, from Bolton King, *A History of Italian Unity: Being a Political History of Italy from 1814 to 1871* (New York: Charles Scribner's Sons, 1899), vol. 2, frontispiece. Photo: Daniel P. Younger. / *121*

3 Map of the Italian peninsula, November 1860, from Bolton King, *A History of Italian Unity: Being a Political History of Italy from 1814 to 1871* (New York: Charles Scribner's Sons, 1899), vol. 2, frontispiece. Photo: Daniel P. Younger. / *122*

*Figures*

1 Harriet Goodhue Hosmer, ca. 1855, photograph, salt print. National Portrait Gallery, Smithsonian Institution, Washington, D.C. Photo: National Portrait Gallery, Smithsonian Institution / Art Resource, N.Y. / *16*

2 Thomas Hicks, *Margaret Fuller,* 1848, oil on canvas. National Portrait Gallery, Smithsonian Institution, Washington, D.C., lent by Constance Fuller Threinen (great-grandchild of Margaret Fuller's brother Arthur B. Fuller). Photo: National Portrait Gallery, Smithsonian Institution / Art Resource, N.Y. / *21*

3 Harriet Hosmer, *Hesper,* 1852, marble. Watertown Free Public Library, Mass. Photo: Daniel P. Younger. / *23*

4 Charlotte Cushman and Matilda Hays, ca. 1851, daguerreotype. Harvard Theatre Collection, Houghton Library, Harvard University, TCS38. / *30*

5 Emma Stebbins, *Angel of the Waters,* 1862, Bethesda Fountain (cast 1870), Central Park, New York, N.Y. Gelatin silver print. Museum of the City of New York, N.Y. Photo: The Museum of the City of New York / Art Resource, N.Y. / *34*

6 Charlotte Cushman and Emma Stebbins, ca. 1859, cabinet card. Harvard Theatre Collection, Houghton Library, Harvard University, TCS2. / *34*

7 *Apollo Belvedere,* ca. 120–40, marble. Photograph ca. 1870. Museo Pio-Clementino, Vatican Museums, Vatican City. Photo: Alinari / Art Resource, N.Y. / *38*

8 *The Vatican by Torchlight,* from Jacob Abbott, *Rollo in Rome* (Boston: Brown, Taggard & Chase, 1858), frontispiece. Photo: Daniel P. Younger. / *39*

9 Thomas Crawford, *Orpheus and Cerberus,* 1843, marble. Museum of Fine Arts, Boston, museum purchase with funds by exchange from a gift of Mr. and Mrs. Cornelius C. Vermeule III, 1975.800. Photograph © 2014 Museum of Fine Arts, Boston. / *39*

10 Antonio Canova, *Triumphant Perseus,* ca. 1800, marble. Museo Pio-Clementino, Vatican Museums, Vatican City. Photo: Scala / Art Resource, N.Y. / *43*

11 John Gibson, *Tinted Venus,* ca. 1851–56, tinted marble. Courtesy National Museums Liverpool (Walker Art Gallery). / *45*

12 Harriet Hosmer, *Daphne,* 1854, marble. Mildred Lane Kemper Art Museum, Washington University in St. Louis, gift of Wayman Crow Sr., 1880. / *47*

13 Harriet Hosmer, *Medusa,* 1854, marble. Detroit Institute of Arts, Founders Society Purchase, R. H. Tannahill Foundation Fund. Photo: The Bridgeman Art Library. / *48*

14 Gian Lorenzo Bernini, *Apollo and Daphne,* 1622–25, marble. Galleria Borghese, Rome. Photo: Alinari / Art Resource, N.Y. / *50*

15 Gian Lorenzo Bernini, *Bust of Medusa,* 1636, marble. Musei Capitolini, Rome. Photo: Andrea Jemolo / Scala / Art Resource, N.Y. / *52*

16 Antonio Canova, *Triumphant Perseus* (fig. 10), detail of the head of Medusa. / *52*

17 Door knocker, home of Harriet Hosmer, via Gregoriana, Rome. Photo: author. / *54*

18 Door handle, home of Harriet Hosmer, via Gregoriana, Rome. Photo: author. / *54*

19 Doorway with initials "H. H.," home of Harriet Hosmer, via Gregoriana, Rome. Photo: author. / *54*

20 Harriet Hosmer, *Oenone,* 1854–55, marble. Mildred Lane Kemper Art Museum, Washington University in St. Louis, gift of Wayman Crow Sr., 1855. / *56*

21 Harriet Hosmer, *Oenone* (fig. 20), view of the back. / *58*

22 Harriet Hosmer, *Puck,* 1856, marble. Smithsonian American Art Museum, Washington, D.C., gift of Mrs. George Merrill. Photo: Smithsonian American Art Museum / Art Resource, N.Y. / *60*

23 *Harriet Hosmer in Her Studio,* n.d., engraving (clipping from an unidentified periodical). The Schlesinger Library, Radcliffe Institute, Harvard University, A-162-82. / *64*

24 Louisa Lander, *Virginia Dare,* 1859–60, marble. The Elizabethan Gardens, Manteo, N.C. Photo courtesy of the Elizabethan Gardens and Daniel P. Younger. / *66*

25 Harriet Hosmer, *Zenobia in Chains,* 1861, marble. © Courtesy of the Huntington Art Collections, San Marino, Calif. Photo: Daniel P. Younger. / *68*

26 Hiram Powers, *The Greek Slave,* modeled 1841–43, carved 1846, marble. Corcoran Gallery of Art, Washington, D.C., gift of William Wilson Corcoran. / *70*

27 Erastus Dow Palmer, *The White Captive,* 1857–58, carved 1858–59, marble. The Metropolitan Museum of Art, New York, bequest of Hamilton Fish, 1894, 94.9.3. Image © The Metropolitan Museum of Art. Photo: Jerry L. Thompson. Image source: Art Resource, N.Y. / *71*

28 Louisa Lander, *Nathaniel Hawthorne,* 1859, marble. Courtesy of the Concord Free Public Library, Concord, Mass. Photo: author. / *74*

29 Louisa Lander, *Virginia Dare* (fig. 24), view of the back. / *79*

30 *The Prince of Wales at Miss Hosmer's Studio,* from *Harper's Weekly,* May 1859. Photo: Daniel P. Younger. / *82*

31 Harriet Hosmer, ca. 1867, photograph. Harriet Goodhue Hosmer Papers, The Schlesinger Library, Radcliffe Institute, Harvard University, A162-72-7. / *87*

32 *Hosmer and Her Men,* 1864, photograph. Harriet Goodhue Hosmer Papers, The Schlesinger Library, Radcliffe Institute, Harvard University, A162-74-2. / *88*

33 Margaret Foley, *Pascuccia,* 1866, stone. Museum of Fine Arts, Boston, gift of The Prince Company, Inc., 1987.472. Photograph © 2014 Museum of Fine Arts, Boston. / *90*

34 Albert Bierstadt, *Roman Fish Market, Arch of Octavius,* 1858, oil on canvas. Fine Arts Museums of San Francisco, gift of Mr. and Mrs. John D. Rockefeller 3rd, 1979.7.12. © Fine Arts Museums of San Francisco. / *95*

35 *Resting Satyr,* copy of a fifth-century B.C.E. Greek statue by Praxiteles, formerly at the Villa D'Este, Tivoli, now in the Hall of the Galatian, Palazzo Nuovo, Musei Capitolini, Rome. Photo: Album / Art Resource, N.Y. / *98*

36 Thomas Crawford, *The Indian: The Dying Chief Contemplating the Progress of Civilization,* 1856, white marble and wood. Collection of The New-York Historical Society, negative #8035; object #1875.4. / *100*

37 *The Sister Sculptresses Taking a Ride,* early to mid-1850s, pen and ink on paper. Harriet Goodhue Hosmer Papers, The Schlesinger Library, Radcliffe Institute, Harvard University, A-162-82. / *102*

38 Paul Akers, *Dead Pearl Diver,* 1858, marble. Portland Museum of Art, Maine, museum purchase with support from Mrs. Elizabeth Akers Allen, John M. Adams, F. R. Barrett, John M. Brown, Philip H. Brown, Abba H. Burnham, A. W. H. Clapp, Nathan Cleaves, Francis Cushing, William G. Davis, Henry Deering, John E. DeWitt, Mark P. Emery, Francis Fessenden, S. C. Gordon, Charles M. Gore, J. H. Hamlin, George S. Hunt, James H. McMullan, W. F. Milliken, Edward A. Noyes, Lewis Pierce, William L. Putnam, Thomas B. Reed, H. W. Richardson, Henry St. John Smith, A. A. Strout, D. M. Sweat, W. W. Thomas, Payson Tucker, George P. Wescott, 1888. / *103*

39 Emma Stebbins, *The Lotus Eater,* 1857–60, now lost. Photograph, Emma Stebbins Scrapbook, 1858–82, Archives of American Art, Smithsonian Institution, Washington, D.C. Photograph courtesy of Elizabeth Milroy. / *105*

40 Harriet Hosmer, *Sleeping Faun,* after 1865, marble. Museum of Fine Arts, Boston, gift of Mrs. Lucien Carr, 12.709. Photograph © 2014 Museum of Fine Arts, Boston. / *107*

41 Harriet Hosmer, *Sleeping Faun* (fig. 40), detail of the base. / *108*

42 *Barberini Faun,* Roman copy after Hellenistic original, ca. 220 B.C.E., marble. Glyptotek, Staatliche Antikensammlung, Munich. Photo: Vanni Archive / Art Resource, N.Y. / *109*

43 Harriet Hosmer, *The Waking Faun,* 1866–67, now lost. Photograph, Harriet Goodhue Hosmer Papers, The Schlesinger Library, Radcliffe Institute, Harvard University, A162-175f-6b. / *110*

44 Anne Whitney, *The Youth* (*Dream of Love* or *Boy with a Palm*), ca. 1862–63, now lost. Photograph dated ca. 1862–67, courtesy of the Wellesley College Archives, Papers of Anne Whitney. / *112*

45 Anne Whitney, *Chaldean Shepherd,* 1862, first version now lost. Photograph courtesy of the Wellesley College Archives, Papers of Anne Whitney. / *113*

46 Anne Whitney, *Lotus Eater,* 1868, plaster. Collection of The Newark Art Museum, gift of Mr. and Mrs. Hugh S. Hince, 1963, 63.75. / *114*

47 Anne Whitney, *The Chaldean Shepherd,* ca. 1868, plaster. Smith College Museum of Art, Northampton, Mass., gift of Mrs. Hugh Stratton Hince (Marion L. Stone, class of 1913), SC1967:50. / *115*

48 Martin Johnson Heade, *Roman Newsboys,* 1848, oil on canvas. Toledo Museum of Art, purchased with funds from the Florence Scott Libbey Bequest in memory of her father, Maurice A. Scott, 1953.68. Photo: Photography, Incorporated (Ray Sess and Carl Schultz), Toledo. / *118*

49 *"Thos. Nast, Esq., Our Special Artist, Now Attached to Garibaldi's Staff, in His Calabrian Costume,"* from the *New York Illustrated News,* November 3, 1860, 405. Photo: author. / *123*

50 Giuseppe Martegana, *Giuseppe Garibaldi,* 1882–ca. 1887, marble. U.S. Senate Collection, U.S. Capitol, gift of members of the Italian Society of Washington, Citizens of Italian Descent, 1888. / *123*

51 Harriet Hosmer, *Beatrice Cenci,* 1856, marble. From the collections of the St. Louis

Mercantile Library at the University of Missouri–St. Louis. / 126

52 *Beatrice Cenci,* postcard printed in Italy. Courtesy of the author. Photo: Daniel P. Younger. / 127

53 Harriet Hosmer, *Beatrice Cenci* (fig. 51), detail of hand with rosary. / 128

54 Harriet Hosmer, *Zenobia in Chains* (fig. 25), detail of the bodice. © Courtesy of the Huntington Art Collections, San Marino, Calif. / 133

55 Harriet Hosmer, *Zenobia in Chains* (fig. 25), detail of Medusa head. © Courtesy of the Huntington Art Collections, San Marino, Calif. / 133

56 *Minerva,* second century B.C.E., marble. Palazzo Nuovo, Capitoline Museums, Rome. Photo: author. / 135

57 *Minerva* (fig. 56), detail of Medusa head. Photo: author. / 136

58 Anne Whitney, *Roma,* 1869, bronze. Davis Museum and Cultural Center, Wellesley College, Wellesley, Mass., gift to the college by the class of 1886. / 139

59 Anne Whitney, *Roma* (fig. 58), detail of hand with coins. Photo © 2013 Joshua Touster. / 140

60 Anne Whitney, *Toussaint L'Ouverture in Prison,* 1869–71, now lost. Photograph courtesy of the Wellesley College Archives, Papers of Anne Whitney. / 142

61 John Quincy Adams Ward, *The Freedman,* 1863, this cast 1891, bronze. The Metropolitan Museum of Art, New York, gift of Charles Anthony Lamb and Barea Lamb Seeley, in memory of their grandfather, Charles Rollinson Lamb, 1979, 1979.394. Image © The Metropolitan Museum of Art. Image source: Art Resource, N.Y. / 143

62 *Mars (Ares) Ludovisi,* Hellenistic sculpture. Museo Nazionale Romano (Palazzo Altemps), Rome. Photo: Scala / Art Resource, N.Y. / 143

63 William Wetmore Story, *Cleopatra,* modeled 1858, carved 1860, marble on polychrome wood platform. Los Angeles County Museum of Art, Los Angeles, Calif., gift of Mr. and Mrs. Henry M. Bateman, 78.3. Digital image © 2014 Museum Associates / LACMA. Licensed by Art Resource, N.Y. / 151

64 William Wetmore Story, *The Libyan Sibyl,* 1860, this version 1861, marble. The Metropolitan Museum of Art, New York, gift of Erving Wolf Foundation, in memory of Diane R. Wolf, 1979, 1979.266. Image © The Metropolitan Museum of Art. Photo: Jerry L. Thompson. Image source: Art Resource, N.Y. / 152

65 Michelangelo Buonarroti, *The Libyan Sibyl,* detail of the Sistine Chapel ceiling, fresco, after restoration. Sistine Chapel, Vatican Palace, Vatican City. Photo: Erich Lessing / Art Resource, N.Y. / 154

66 Attributed to Frederick Christian Lewis, *Sartjee, the Hottentot Venus,* 1810, etching and aquatint. © The Trustees of the British Museum. / 154

67 Edmonia Lewis, *The Bust of Robert Gould Shaw,* 1867, marble. Museum of African American History, Boston and Nantucket, Mass. / 157

68 Anne Whitney, *Ethiopia Shall Soon Stretch Out Her Hands to God, or Africa,* 1862–64, plaster, destroyed. Photograph courtesy of the Wellesley College Archives, Papers of Anne Whitney. / 158

69 Sojourner Truth, carte de visite. Courtesy of the Wellesley College Archives, Papers of Anne Whitney. / 159

70 Antonio Canova, *Paolina Borghese as Venus Victorious,* 1803–6, marble. Galleria Borghese, Rome. Photo: Luciano Romano. Photo source: Scala / Art Resource, N.Y. / 161

71 Anne Whitney, *Ethiopia Shall Soon Stretch Out Her Hands to God, or Africa,* reworked 1865–66, plaster, destroyed. Photograph courtesy of the Wellesley College Archives, Papers of Anne Whitney. / 163

72 Anne Whitney, *Ethiopia Shall Soon Stretch Out Her Hands to God, or Africa,* 1862–64 (fig. 68), detail of the head. / *164*

73 Anne Whitney, *Ethiopia Shall Soon Stretch Out Her Hands to God, or Africa,* reworked 1865–66 (fig. 71), detail of the head. / *165*

74 Henry Rocher, *Edmonia Lewis,* ca. 1870, photograph, albumen silver print. National Portrait Gallery, Smithsonian Institution, Washington, D.C. Photo: National Portrait Gallery, Smithsonian Institution / Art Resource, N.Y. / *167*

75 Edmonia Lewis, *Preghiera,* 1866, marble. Collection of Kathryn Chenault, courtesy of Conner-Rosenkranz, New York, and Peg Alston Fine Arts. Photo: Helga Photo Studio. / *168*

76 Edmonia Lewis, *Forever Free,* 1867, marble. Howard University Gallery of Art, Washington, D.C. / *170*

77 *Am I Not a Woman and a Sister?,* 1845, from *Specimen of Modern Printing Types, Cast at the Letter Foundry of the Boston Type and Stereotype Company* (Boston: White, Lewis & Potter, 1845). Photo: author. / *171*

78 *Am I Not a Man and a Brother?,* 1837, woodcut. Library of Congress Rare Book and Special Collections Division, Washington, D.C. / *171*

79 Edmonia Lewis, *Forever Free* (fig. 76), detail of the kneeling woman. / *172*

80 Final masthead of the *Liberator,* by Alonzo Hartwell after Hammett Billings. First used May 31, 1850. Boston Athenaeum. / *174*

81 Harriet Hosmer, *Freedman's Memorial to Abraham Lincoln,* 1866, plaster, now lost. Photograph in the collection of the Watertown Free Public Library, Watertown, Mass. Photo: Daniel P. Younger. / *177*

82 Thomas Ball, *Emancipation Monument,* 1876, Lincoln Park, Washington, D.C. Photographic print on stereo card, Library of Congress Prints and Photographs Division, Washington, D.C. / *179*

83 Harriet Hosmer, *African Sibyl,* design for a portion of the Lincoln Monument, ca. 1890, now lost. Watertown Free Public Library, Watertown, Mass. Photo: Courtesy of Kirk Savage. / *179*

84 Vinnie Ream, *Abraham Lincoln,* 1870, marble. U.S. Capitol Rotunda. Photo: Architect of the Capitol. / *183*

85 Sarah Fisher Clampitt Ames, *Abraham Lincoln,* 1868, marble. U.S. Senate Collection, Washington, D.C. / *183*

86 Sarah Fisher Clampitt Ames, *Abraham Lincoln,* 1865, plaster cabinet bust. The Lynn Museum and Historical Society, Lynn, Mass. Image courtesy of the Lynn Museum and Historical Society. Photo: Daniel P. Younger. / *185*

87 Alexander Gardner, *Abraham Lincoln,* 1865, albumen silver print. National Portrait Gallery, Smithsonian Institution, Washington, D.C. Photo: National Portrait Gallery, Smithsonian Institution / Art Resource, N.Y. / *186*

88 Vinnie Ream at work on her Lincoln bust, ca. 1865, photograph. Library of Congress Prints and Photographs Division, Washington, D.C. / *187*

89 Vinnie Ream, *Abraham Lincoln,* ca. 1865–66, carte de visite. Research Division of the Oklahoma Historical Society. / *188*

90 Della Valle, Vinnie Ream as a *contadina* (Italian peasant girl), ca. 1869–70, photograph. Library of Congress Prints and Photographs Division, Washington, D.C. / *194*

91 George Peter Alexander Healy, *Vinnie Ream,* ca. 1870, oil on canvas. Smithsonian American Art Museum, Washington, D.C., gift of Brigadier General Richard L. Hoxie. Photo: Smithsonian American Art Museum / Art Resource, N.Y. / *194*

92 Henry Kirke Brown, *Lincoln Monument,* 1869, bronze. Prospect Park, Brooklyn, N.Y. Library

of Congress Prints and Photographs Division, Washington, D.C. / *196*

93 Henry Kirke Brown, *Model for a Monument to Lincoln,* 1866–67, plaster, now lost. Library of Congress Prints and Photographs Division, Washington, D.C. / *196*

94 Anne Whitney, *Samuel Adams,* 1876, marble. U.S. Capitol. Photo: Architect of the Capitol. / *201*

95 Anne Whitney, *Charles Sumner Memorial,* 1876, plaster model. Watertown Free Public Library, Watertown, Mass. Photo: Daniel P. Younger. / *202*

96 Anne Whitney, *Le Modèle,* 1875, bronze. Museum of Fine Arts, Boston, gift of Mrs. Maria Weston Chapman, 85.423. Photograph © 2014 Museum of Fine Arts, Boston. / *203*

97 Anne Whitney, *Charles Sumner Memorial,* 1900, bronze. Cambridge Commons, Cambridge, Mass. Photo © 2014 Joshua Touster. / *204*

98 Vinnie Ream at work on the *Farragut Memorial,* ca. 1879, photograph. Library of Congress Prints and Photographs Division, Washington, D.C. / *209*

99 Harriet Hosmer at work on the clay model of Thomas Hart Benton, ca. 1862. Harriet Goodhue Hosmer Collection, Schlesinger Library, Radcliffe Institute, Harvard University, A162-72-11. Photo: Marianecchi, Rome. / *210*

100 Vinnie Ream in wedding dress, ca. 1878, photograph. Library of Congress Prints and Photographs Division, Washington, D.C. / *211*

# Acknowledgments

This book has benefited from the assistance of many people and institutions in the United States and Italy. I apologize in advance for the inevitable omissions that will occur as I try to give thanks to so many. Short-term fellowships from the United States Capitol Historical Society and the Smithsonian American Art Museum provided research opportunities early in this project; to the staffs of both institutions, I am deeply indebted. Kenyon College kindly underwrote a Faculty Development Grant, a Summer Stipend, and a Senior Faculty Leave at different stages of this endeavor. The resources of the Fellows Office at the Smithsonian American Art Museum and the AAPG Library helped me finalize the last details of the book; my warm appreciation goes to Amelia Goerlitz and Anne Evenhaugen for their tireless assistance.

In Italy, this project was furthered in significant ways. I was privileged to serve as a Visiting Scholar twice at the American Academy in Rome; I also participated in an NEH Summer Seminar on New Perspectives on Italy in the Age of the Risorgimento, housed at the American Academy. To my colleagues at the academy, and the directors and participants of the seminar, I owe an enormous debt. It was with their assistance that I first comprehended the vast complexity of Rome, its people, and its history. The Centro Studi Americani; the Museo Centrale del Risorgimento, Vittoriano; the French Academy Library; and the Bibliotheca Hertziana generously opened their archives to me. With each visit, I came to love the city more and more. For two semesters, I served as resident director of the Kenyon in Rome program; indeed, teaching art history in the Eternal City has become one of the most satisfying experiences of my professional career. This book is possible, in part, because of these extraordinary scholarly and pedagogical opportunities.

Over the past ten years, I have enlisted the aid of many friends and colleagues, who shared information with me, gave me useful feedback, and in myriad ways lent their support to this project. To them I am extremely thankful: Joseph Adler, Susan Ashbrooke, Beth Belanger, Pina Benadetti, Sarah Blick, Norma Broude, Emily Burns, Jennifer Clarvoe, Jacqui Clinton, Serena Colasanti, Cynthia Burns Coogan, Wanda Corn, Miriam Dean-Otting, Erika Doss, Karen Drazen, Eugene Dwyer, Judy Fagan, Betsy Fahlman, Christine Fernando, Vivien Green Fryd, Yvonne Garcia, Cathy Geffen, Gregory Gibson, Wendy Greenhouse, Barbara Groseclose, Patricia Hills, Erica Hirshler, Patricia Johnston, Paul Kaplan, Deborah Laycock, Theresa Leininger-Miller, Karen Lemmey, Joanne Lukitsch, Patricia Mathews, Angela Miller, Cynthia Mills, Elizabeth Milroy, Eve Moore, David O'Brien, Kimberly Orcutt, Joel Rosenkranz, Peter Rutkoff, Howard Sacks, Kirk Savage, Marta Sierra, Erin Sutherland, Thayer Tolles, Joshua Touster, Kristen Van Ausdall, Tom Willette, Ruth Woehr, Barbara Wolanin, and Rebecca Zurier. I appreciate the careful attention that the Pennsylvania State University Press readers gave to this manuscript. I hope that I responded sufficiently to their wise counsel. I also wish to thank my many students in Gambier and Rome, who will always remain an inspiration to me.

Special acknowledgments are always due to special people. Helen Langa read various versions of this manuscript and advised me wisely over the years. Ellen Todd and Cécile Whiting read complete and, at times, multiple drafts; their intelligent suggestions and close friendship were essential to every phase of this project. Judy Sacks pondered every word of the manuscript and challenged me to write the best book that I possibly could. Her professional guidance and warm companionship will always be appreciated. Ellie Goodman at the Pennsylvania State University Press believed in this book and was its enthusiastic champion. Charlee Myranda Redman provided technical support; I am especially thankful for her help with photographs and permissions. Keith Monley took enormous care to clarify the text and correct inconsistencies. I am grateful to the Wyeth Foundation for American Art Publication Fund and the Terra Foundation for American Art publication grant for helping to defray costs associated with the production of this book.

And finally, much gratitude goes to my husband, Dan Younger, who patiently cheered me on, through thick and thin, at home and abroad. Many of his superb photographs illustrate this book; however, his contribution to this project is beyond measure.

Washington, D.C.
November 4, 2013

Portions of this book have previously appeared in abridged and revised form in the following venues:

Melissa Dabakis, "Sculpting Lincoln: Vinnie Ream, Sarah Fisher Ames, and the Equal Rights Movement," *American Art* 22 (Spring 2008): 78–101. © 2008 Smithsonian Institution.

Melissa Dabakis, "'Ain't I a Woman?': Anne Whitney, Edmonia Lewis, and the Iconography of Emancipation," in *Seeing High and Low: Representing Social Conflict in American Visual Culture,* edited by Patricia Johnston, 84–102. © 2006 by the Regents of the University of California. Published by the University of California Press.

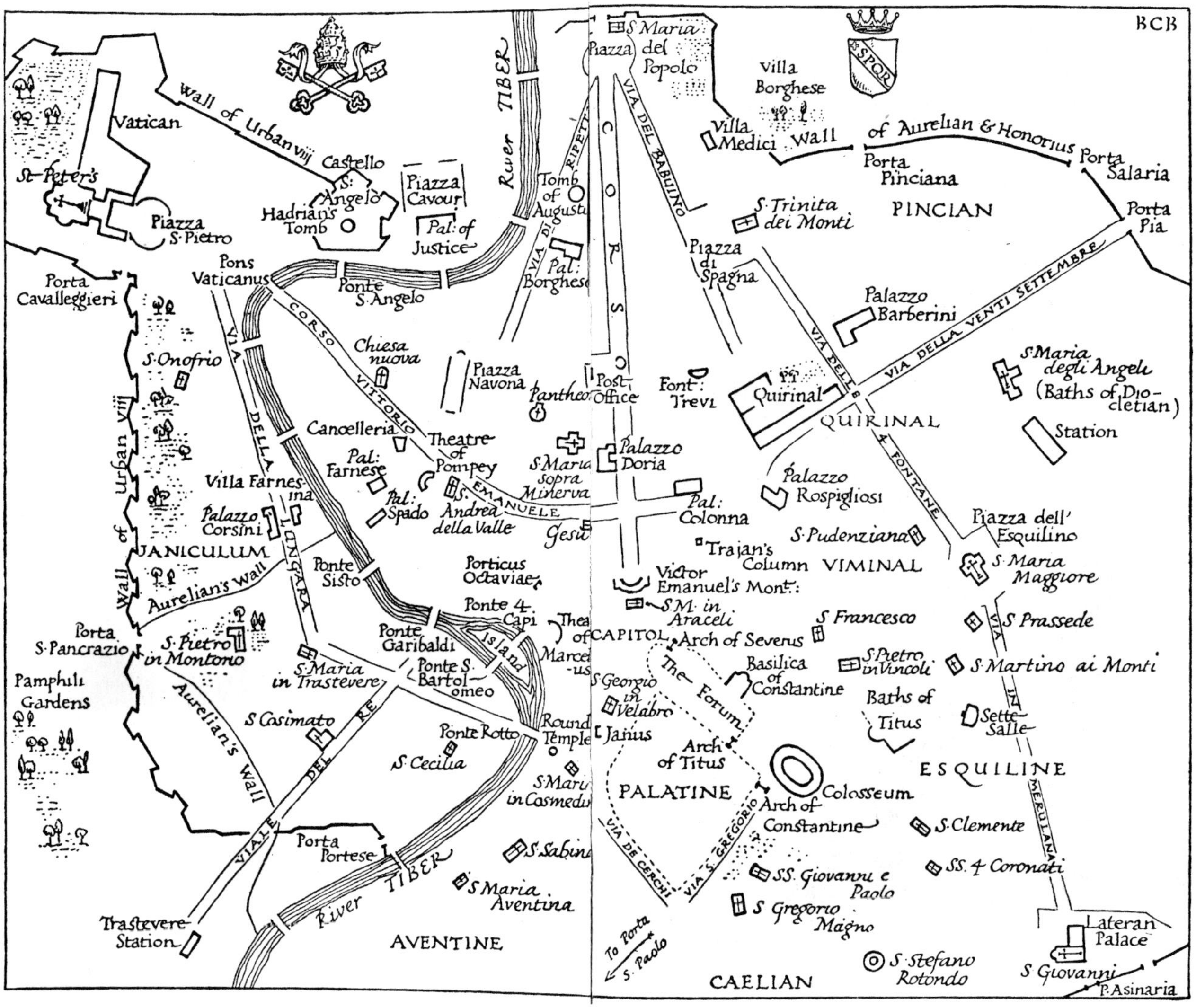


MAP 1

Map of Rome, from Edward Hutton, Rome (New York: Macmillan, 1909), frontispiece. Photo: Daniel P. Younger.

# *Introduction*

On a brilliant sunny day in the historical center of Rome, the fictional heroine Corinne is crowned poet laureate on the steps of the ancient Capitoline. The most famous woman in Rome, Corinne is lauded as a poetess, writer, improviser, and intellectual in Madame de Staël's (Germaine Necker's) popular novel *Corinne, or Italy* of 1807. Clad in a white tunic with an exotic turban wound round her head, the great beauty improvises verses while playing the lyre: "Italy, empire of the Sun; Italy, mistress of the world; cradle of literature; I salute you," her performance begins. While paying homage to Italy and its talented poets, she is interrupted by a large crowd chanting, "Long live Corinne! Long live genius! Long live beauty!"[1] As the novel opens, Corinne's fulfilling life in Rome personifies an ideal of feminine creativity coveted by ambitious nineteenth-century Anglo-American women.

Rome had welcomed talented European and American women artists into its cultural fold since the late eighteenth century. It was also home to many famous literary and artistic institutions, like the Arcadian Academy, to which the German poet Johann Wolfgang von Goethe and de Staël earned membership. Located on the slopes of the Janiculum Hill in Rome, the Arcadians allowed women unprecedented creative authority. The Swiss history painter Angelika Kauffmann, a close colleague of Goethe's, was invited to join the academy and eventually rose to leadership of the neoclassical school in Rome. Further, the Arcadians celebrated native Italian *improvisatrice* (female poetic improvisers), like Corilla Olimpica, upon whose life the fictional Corinne was based. *Improvisatrice* performed for literate Italian and foreign audiences through the mid–nineteenth century. Destinations of note for many Anglo-American visitors, these events were recorded in contemporary guidebooks with the specific dates and times of each performance carefully listed.

Spurred on by Rome's embrace of feminine creativity, Anglo-American women were enthralled with the mythic territory inhabited by Corinne. The moniker "American Corinnes" described many talented women who traveled to Rome, such as the erudite writer and journalist Margaret Fuller, the young and beautiful sculptor Vinnie Ream, and the writer and painter Sophia Peabody Hawthorne. In her feminist epic *Aurora Leigh* of 1856, the British poet Elizabeth Barrett Browning, an expatriate living in Italy, imagined her heroine in the mold of a modern Corinne. Chronicling their dreams and disappointments, adventures and struggles, this book focuses upon the talented women artists, writers, and social reformers who assembled in Rome in the mid-nineteenth century.

In absorbing the spirit of Corinne, a group of American women artists sought creative refuge in the Eternal City between 1850 and 1876. These neoclassical/realist sculptors developed successful professional careers in Rome, as they competed for and won public commissions, created ideal statuary (with mythological, historical, or biblical subjects), modeled portrait busts, and sold "fancy pieces" (garden sculpture and the like). This community of talented women included artists whose lives and works have become well known in art-historical circles: Harriet Hosmer (1830–1908), Edmonia Lewis (1844/46–1907), Anne Whitney (1821–1915), and Vinnie Ream (Hoxie) (1847–1914); and those whose reputations have remained (until now) buried in the historical record: Emma Stebbins (1815–1882), Margaret Foley (1820–1877), Sarah Fisher Ames (1817–1901), and Louisa Lander (1826–1923). At midcentury, they were among the first women artists to attain professional stature in the American art world while achieving international fame in Rome, London, and other cosmopolitan European cities. In the 1850s and 1860s, their independent lives charted new territory for feminine professionalism. In their invention of modern womanhood, these artists served as models for a younger generation of women who adopted artistic careers in unprecedented numbers in the years following the Civil War.[2] Indeed, their extraordinary lives still resonate with meaning, as contemporary women are emboldened by their example to seek new challenges and achieve new successes.[3]

## The White Marmorean Flock

In 1903, Henry James immortalized this community of American women sculptors in Rome by characterizing them as "that strange sisterhood of American lady sculptors who at one time settled upon the seven hills [of Rome] in a white marmorean flock."[4] Since James penned this phrase, it has come to define and delimit our understanding of the lives and careers of women artists active in Rome. Over the past several decades, feminist art historians have begun successfully to deconstruct the moniker "white marmorean flock." This book contributes to these endeavors.

James's terminology demands scrutiny. The term "flock" refers to the animal kingdom—either to birds or to sheep—certainly not to intelligent women. Art historian Jane Mayo Roos deftly questioned this language in 1983: "While [James's] sentence is a highly evocative one, it is also a killer: the inevitable implication is that these birds are women—tiny, anonymous, hapless creatures who traveled *en masse* and whose accomplishments were diminutive in scale."[5] Furthermore, the term "marmorean" (relating to marble), in its subtle aural association with "mammalian" (relating to female mammary glands or breasts), positioned women sculptors firmly in a feminized world of nature, sexuality, and childbearing rather than the masculinized world of culture and artistic production. At the same time, a "marmorean flock" that "settled" in Rome was an oxymoron, art historian Nancy Elizabeth Procter argues. A flock of stone birds cannot fly, and a flock of marble sheep remain immobile in their pastures. Thus the phrase referenced the ideological impossibility of a woman as an autonomous, creative artist and disavowed the historical productivity of American women sculptors in Rome.[6]

In referring to this heterogeneous group of women as a "flock," James refused to acknowledge the specificity of each artist's circumstances, denying them any sense of individuality. The phrase homogenized their experience into a monolithic womanhood, erasing class status, age difference, social background, sexual positionings, and even race. In fact, the artists hailed from widely divergent social and economic backgrounds: Louisa Lander grew up in an elite Boston Brahmin household, Harriet Hosmer was raised in a middle-class professional family, and Margaret Foley came from working-class circumstances. A generation separated the women in age: Anne Whitney, the oldest of the group, was born in 1821; Vinnie Ream, the youngest, was born in 1847. Edmonia Lewis was of mixed-race heritage, African-American and Chippewa Indian. This book takes difference between women artists as a central tenet, displacing the idea of a unitary category of woman artist envisioned by James's characterization.

At its core, this book is concerned with the gendered nature of creativity and expatriation. Although indebted to a host of scholarly and popular publications that have documented the lives and careers of individual sculptors, this book is thematic rather than monographic and provides a detailed investigation of the historical phenomenon of women's sculptural production in Rome in the mid–nineteenth century.[7] It takes its guidance from feminist theory, cultural geography (the historical and social dimensions of place), and expatriate and postcolonial studies. As an interdisciplinary examination of femininity and creativity, *A Sisterhood of Sculptors* provides models for viewing and interpreting nineteenth-century sculpture and for analyzing the gendered status of the artistic profession. As such, it complements several recent histories of women artists.[8]

More broadly, the book expands the ground upon which the art and careers of women artists have been studied and situates it firmly within the frame of nineteenth-century transatlantic studies. Paris has received the closest scrutiny from scholars of American art due to its alliance with modernist art practices. This book, in arguing for the significance of Rome as a site of nineteenth-century creative endeavor, examines the art and touristic economies that guided the careers of American artists and considers the cultural and political currents that framed their artistic practice.

## *The Lure of Rome*

Until 1876, Rome served as a central destination for American artists, journalists, social reformers, and tourists who were enchanted by Italy's mythic arcadian past and fascinated by its classical legacy.[9] Artists held center stage in the Eternal City, respected and admired by prominent people of the day, from statesmen and authors to businessmen and royalty. "Rome is the very home of art," one American writer espoused. "In no city in the world are collected so many of the finest works of the greatest artists." With much optimism, this writer concluded: "If a young artist cannot succeed here, he must be destitute of talent."[10]

The artist's life in Rome was consumed with studying, modeling, casting, copying, and visiting museums and ruins, in short, what was called the "Art-Life." In all, about thirty-eight American artists were living in the city in the 1850s. Among the sculptors were William Wetmore Story, Thomas Crawford, Harriet Hosmer, Louisa Lander, Emma Stebbins, Joseph Mozier, Chauncey Ives, and Benjamin Paul Akers.[11] In fact, sculptors were the most highly regarded among American artists in Rome, a fact that the landscape painter Thomas Cole grudgingly acknowledged in 1847: "It seems to me that sculpture has risen above par, of late: painters are [considered] but an inferior grade of artists."[12] In Italy, American sculptors found not only access to Roman antiquities but also the aid of skilled Italian carvers, proximity to Carrara and Seravezza marble, and the inspiration of an international coterie of artists, which numbered more than a thousand in 1851.[13]

Middle-class and elite American women imagined Rome as a hospitable zone for artistic practice. The city's mythic character (a land of romantic freedom) and its historical resonance (as home for both expatriate artists and *improvisatrice*), beckoned women artists, writers, and social reformers. Hosmer, Lander, Stebbins, and Foley, under the mentorship of the thespian Charlotte Cushman, formed a close-knit and supportive community (though not without personal and professional jealousies) that the author Nathaniel Hawthorne rendered with some sympathy in his romantic account of American artists in Rome, *The Marble Faun* (1860).[14]

The American colony of women sculptors, together with other *stranieri* (foreigners) from the United States and northern Europe, inhabited a defined area in Rome that stretched from the Piazza del Popolo (the northernmost entrance to the historic city) through the Piazza di Spagna, with its beautiful Spanish Steps, to the Piazza Barberini, at the foot of the famed via Veneto (map 1). These neighborhoods contained artists' studios, international art academies, photography studios, and public and private art collections that catered to the growing population of artists in the city. In addition, residential apartments and *palazzi,* English bookshops, circulating English-language libraries, and banks serviced the Anglo-American community in these quarters. In the Piazza di Spagna, the American banker's office of Pakenham and Hooker (where the American Express office is currently housed) prepared lists of "Artists in Rome," complete with the addresses of their studios and private residences. Notably, it also boasted a list of "Female Artists [in Rome]."[15]

Anglo-American travelers regularly visited the studios of women sculptors in Rome. As the American transcendentalist poet, journalist, and editor of the *New York Evening Post* William Cullen Bryant explained in 1859, Rome was "a better place for obtaining orders from their own countrymen than any of the American cities. Men [*and women,* I would add] who would never have thought of buying a picture or a statue at home, are infected by the contagion of the place the moment they arrive."[16] Bryant's choice of words, "infected by the contagion of the place," astutely characterized Rome and implied several layers of meaning. Travelers were both mesmerized by the cultural climate of the Eternal City and haunted by the fear of malaria (*mal aria,* or bad air), which infected the city and its surrounding area, the Campagna, in the warmer months. Both a physical plague (now understood as contracted from mosquitoes) from which travelers regularly died and a moral condition that mysteriously suffused the city, the contagion of malaria became synonymous with Rome in the nineteenth century. Henry James brought popular attention to this physical and moral "contagion" in his 1878 novella in which his eponymous protagonist Daisy Miller dies of malaria after socializing with a male suitor in the Colosseum late at night.[17]

Rome offered women sculptors vital opportunities both to imagine and to re-create themselves as professional artists, using travel and expatriation as means to strengthen a sense of themselves as emboldened actors on an international stage.[18] The moral contagion that James employed, however, served as a warning to ambitious women: Rome was a potentially hostile place where a woman's career and reputation could be destroyed if she did not comport herself properly, that is, with appropriate deference to domesticity and the cultural norms of true womanhood. This book traces both the pleasures and perils of Rome for nineteenth-century women sculptors.

## *Neoclassicism*

The American women sculptors who arrived in Rome in the 1850s and 1860s adopted the international art style known as neoclassicism and reconfigured it to give voice to feminine experience. Neoclassicism was a product of Enlightenment thinking in its fascination with the antique past, and specifically with the ideal nude. The concept of the ideal has been central to Western culture since the Greeks, serving as the means by which humans acknowledge, and redress, their limited comprehension of the cosmos, that is, their inability to apprehend the absolute.[19] In claiming to embody universal and eternal values, the ideal nude mediates the historical opposition between the transcendent and the material, thus giving visual form to pure idea through the perfected human body.[20]

In the eighteenth century, Enlightenment philosophers—Denis Diderot, François-Marie Voltaire, and Jean-Jacques Rousseau—argued that the figuration of ideal beauty had the capacity to express a universal moral good and, by extension, to suggest the human potential for a more perfect society. In an age of political revolutions—both in the United States and France—the creation of a better world depended upon the sovereign will of the individual. No longer subject to the higher authority of the king, the modern citizen acted as an autonomous agent in the world, free to pursue his own interests. Neoclassicism celebrated the newly won freedoms of the male citizen in the form of the ideal nude. In its association with the moral good of society, the nude exemplified the ideology of liberalism, a core principle of the Enlightenment.

The first generation of American neoclassical sculptors to arrive in Italy in the 1820s and 1830s included Hiram Powers (1805–1873), Horatio Greenough (1805–1852), and Thomas Crawford (1814–1857). Powers and Greenough chose Florence as their home; Crawford settled in Rome. They saw themselves as international citizens and recognized parallels between the Italian struggle for independence and unification, the *Risorgimento,* and the founding of their young republic. Italian nationalists, in turn, looked to the United States as a model for an enlightened republican government. Through the language of neoclassicism, the Americans voiced sympathy for the Italians' quest for sovereignty while simultaneously communicating political ideals resonant with the sculptors' new nation. This book embeds neoclassical sculptural practice in the material and ideological conditions of its production in Italy and provides a more expansive gendered and politicized reading of neoclassicism than is normally encountered in studies of nineteenth-century American culture.

In its association with liberty, freedom, and republicanism, neoclassicism revived the political ideals associated with antiquity. Educated Americans were well aware that knowledge of the classical past was necessary to the development of a free and civilized society. Commonly they embarked upon European tours as occasions for self-improvement. In traveling to Rome, middle-class and elite tourists gained firsthand knowledge of the classical world by walking through the Forum, the Palatine, and the Colosseum. In the Vatican Museum, they admired examples of the great artworks of Western civilization. Through contact with antique statuary, such as the *Apollo Belvedere* (fig. 7), understood at the time as the highest manifestation of antique genius, they acquired a cultural refinement and intellectual sophistication unavailable to them at home.

Standing in front of the *Apollo Belvedere,* viewers felt that they had come into contact with timeless truths that were embodied within the sculpture's ideal form. When the American writer Herman Melville visited Rome in 1857, he noted that antique marble sculptures, "the work of visionaries and dreamers," served as "realizations of the soul." He continued, "Governments have changed; empires have fallen; nations have passed away; but these mute marbles remain—the oracles of time, the perfection of art."[21] In the antebellum period, literate Americans, like Melville, imagined antique civilization as inhabiting a superior moral realm. Classical sculptures, like the *Apollo Belvedere,* which embodied eternal and universal principles, became icons of a modern enlightened consciousness.

Through an expanding body of printed material—newspapers, woodcuts, broadsides, and pamphlets—classical history, literature, and sculpture served a broad literate public. Indeed, this "culture of classicism" was much more populist than normally characterized in the art-historical literature. As a cultural movement, classicism claimed a unique position in antebellum America, serving as "the central intellectual project" (after Christianity) of the young nation, historian Caroline Winterer has argued. Widely read publications, such as the *Penny Magazine* and *Godey's Lady's Book,* regularly referenced classical literature, such as Virgil, and illustrated famous antique sculpture, such as the *Laocoön.*[22] In these diverse ways, antiquity and classicism had entered the American popular imagination, inculcating notions of civic virtue and patriotism into its male and female readers.

Classical culture was an intellectual province open to American women. Considered morally superior to men in Victorian society, women claimed unquestioned access to the virtue of the ancients and demonstrated a selfless concern for the common good.[23] With its high-minded morality, neoclassicism offered a seemingly safe path into the profession of sculpture, mitigating, in part, the dangers posed to women artists who were successful in the public sphere. Rejecting the patriarchal bias of the Enlightenment, women artists consistently chose feminine themes for their neoclassical sculptures and imbued their subjects with an individual agency usually reserved for the male citizen.

## *The* Risorgimento*: Italian Political Life, 1820–1870*

Through the language of neoclassicism, American women artists produced sculptures that engaged with Italian political life in ways that have been only tangentially explored in the art-historical literature. Like their predecessors, they were inspired by the political events that unfolded on the Italian peninsula. European imperial powers continued to rule the peninsula into the 1850s, when American women artists arrived in Rome. Austria governed Venice and the Veneto, Florence, and Milan; the Spanish Hapsburgs controlled Naples and the southern Italian provinces; and the Vatican ruled the Papal States, including Rome.

Americans aided the Italian nationalist cause in any way they could. The American sculptor Horatio Greenough donned the uniform of the Florentine Civic Guard when Florence rebelled against Austrian rule in 1847.[24] His wife, Louisa, sewed the flag under which he and Hiram Powers demonstrated for liberal reforms. "*We* Italians have been doing something in the way of revolution," Powers proudly asserted. Espousing the Republican cause, he proclaimed, "In short, we Italians . . . proved to the world that we are worthy to be trusted with liberty."[25] In a triumphant sign of unity, he repeated the phrase "we Italians" on several occasions in his correspondence. In Rome, Thomas Crawford helped defend the Porta San Pancrazio on the Janiculum Hill, where most of the fighting took place during the Roman Republic, a five-month period in 1849 when Giuseppe Mazzini and other radical Republicans governed the city. In all, 268 foreigners joined in the defense of Rome.[26] The cultural, political, and artistic transactions between Italy and the United States are a central focus of this book.

Italy generated complicated and often contradictory responses from Anglo-American expatriates and visitors in the mid–nineteenth century. The Italian peninsula served as a cultural mecca for tourists, who sought the spectacle of an antique arcadian past, presented to them in guidebooks and cheaply sold prints and photographs. Exotic in its old-world traditions, intriguing yet dangerous in its Catholic pomp and ritual, and timeless in its dereliction, the imagined Italy beckoned nineteenth-century tourists to its shores. Many travelers approached this imagined antiquity as a spiritual home, an ideal past independent of Italy's current history. In other words, this notion of an arcardian past stood in conflict with Italy's contemporary political circumstances and its goals of independence, unity, and republicanism.[27]

In the late eighteenth century, Enlightenment thought asserted the superiority of northern Europe as the new center of Western civilization, heir to the legacy of the classical tradition.[28] As art historian Matthew Craske explains, "Northern European culture found its self-esteem much enhanced by the oft-repeated contention that Rome was 'the tomb' of old Europe." The "accounts of the shabbiness and decadence of modern life south of the Alps," he continues, only served to reinforce northern Europe's "sense of cultural vitality."[29] With the peninsula divided into intra-European colonies, Catholic powers dominated these regions, which, as colonized territories, remained industrially backward and economically undeveloped until years after the unification of the country in 1861. The Austrian prince Klemens von Metternich, for example, contemptuously referred to the peninsula as a "mere geographical denomination," without centralized political power or a unified identity of its own.[30] Northern Europe and the United States represented modern entities—technologically progressive, economically productive, and democratically governed.[31] Under colonial rule, the Italian peninsula appeared frozen in time, its colonial subjects viewed as a racialized other—idle, dependent, and childlike.

American women artists inhabited Italy at a unique political moment—at the historical juncture between colonialism and independence. Negotiating their roles as travelers and expatriates with caution, they were caught between the privileges of colonialism, the professional limitations of patriarchy, and the political ideology of republicanism. When the British journalist and radical Republican Jesse White Mario met Harriet Hosmer in 1854, for example, she found the sculptor "perfectly indifferent" to contemporary Italian culture and concluded that the American expatriate community regarded Rome "as their personal property, the exclusive heritage of art and artists."[32] In unwittingly adopting a mentality of racial superiority, Anglo-American women experienced the freedoms of Roman life from an empowered political perspective. At the same time, most envisioned and supported a free Italian nation. These living contradictions demonstrated a type of transculturation whereby American women artists were transformed by their contact with a colonized Italy. Moreover, such contact informed their artistic production in Rome.

## *The Modern Woman Artist*

In 1848, when Elizabeth Cady Stanton penned the "Declaration of Sentiments" for the First Women's Rights Convention, held in Seneca Falls, New York, she unleashed a powerful force in contemporary American society. Modeling her rhetoric upon that found in the Declaration of Independence, she opened her remarks with the familiar phrase: "We hold these truths to be self-evident," then argued "that all men *and women* are created equal; that they are endowed by their Creator with certain inalienable rights; that among these are life, liberty, and the pursuit of happiness."[33] Ratified and adopted by the convention, this document, with its explicit goal of instituting equal rights for women, had a resounding impact upon a young generation of professional women artists.

Simultaneously, the popular notion of "true womanhood" served as an ideal for middle-class and elite women.[34] The "true woman" was defined by home and family and idealized as selfless, sentimental, nurturing, and pious. Nonetheless, professional women maintained a dialogue with this powerful nineteenth-century belief system. In essence, the ideology of true womanhood characterized white bourgeois femininity as irrefutably different from masculinity. In the "Declaration of Sentiments," Stanton acknowledged and validated this widely held belief when she wrote that "man, while claiming for himself intellectual superiority, does accord to woman moral superiority."[35] In a seemingly contradictory move, she deferred to a belief in true womanhood as an empowering strategy that defined women as essentially different from and morally superior to men. At the same time, she argued for parity with men, that women had an absolute right to their labor and to autonomy in the public sphere.[36] In her remarkable document, Stanton encouraged women to occupy what appeared to be competing subject positions—domestic angel of the home and professional actor in the world.

Recent feminist scholars have embraced such paradox as a way of understanding nineteenth-century women's lives. Concerning middle-class and elite professional women, literary critic Cathy Davidson asks, "How do we mark where power ends and resistance . . . to this ideology of true womanhood [begins]?"[37] In other words, when do women appeal to domesticity and other avenues of sexual difference as beneficial options for personal and professional survival? How do women subvert the potentially oppressive nature of this ideological structure? Nineteenth-century professional women, it seemed, negotiated a delicate balancing act between the two ideological poles of difference and equality.

Like the experience of gender and sexuality, definitions of the public and private spheres are culturally constructed, historically specific, and central to the ways in which modern social and psychic worlds have been structured. Rather than static and unchanging, these domains are better understood as dynamic and flexible fields that require the adaptation of certain learned behaviors. To challenge male domination in public was to challenge proper notions of femininity itself, with its norms of appropriate comportment. Considered impudent, women in public were deemed indiscreet, and at times immoral.[38] The effort among women artists in Rome to balance interests private and public, domestic and professional, constitutes a central theme of this book.

Most of the women artists under study here distanced themselves from the vexed world of heterosexuality. Many had grown up in a sex-segregated sphere where "romantic friendships" between elite and middle-class women, universally perceived as chaste and spiritual in nature, had been the norm. The "romantic friendship" sentimentalized strong female bonds into a spiritualized love. In these same-sex relationships, desire was not denied, literary theorist Martha Vicinus has explained, but it certainly was sublimated. Reinforcing notions of sexual difference, romantic friendships between women were deemed "morally superior" as desire's "bodily nature was subsumed to its spiritual potential."[39] This form of morally pure, sexually passionless, and domestically bound womanhood emerged in Europe and North America in the eighteenth century. The model woman in the new American republic, for example, was the virtuous mother whose purity remained perpetually unsullied within a secure and private domestic realm.[40]

Meanings attached to same-sex love and sexuality were (and are) fluid, changeable, and impossible to define absolutely. In studying the lives of women artists and writers in Rome, we can imagine these intimate experiences within a continuum of sexual behaviors—ranging from the lesbian or lesbian-like to the normative heterosexual activities of marriage and childbearing. The heterosexual/homosexual binary is overly simplistic and even misleading. In many instances, these two polarities coexisted within women's lives. Sexuality never constituted an either/or proposition but manifested itself differently in various social and historical settings.[41] Many different types of same-sex relationships emerged in Rome.

We will never know for sure the nature of such varied female desire. How important is the discussion of female sexuality to our understanding of this women's community in Rome? From the fragmentary evidence that exists, same-sex sexuality, together with rituals of homosocial bonding, was a significant aspect of nineteenth-century women's lives in Rome.[42] Before same-sex desire and practice were medicalized—that is, made unnatural—at the end of the nineteenth century, women who felt strong emotional attachments to each other and acted out erotic behavior did not perceive themselves as different from the normative definition of woman.[43]

By 1869, Dr. Carl von Westphal, a German psychiatrist, had been among the first to identify this different category of womanhood: women who loved other women in a carnal way. He described these women as "inverts," "the third sex," or as simply "unsexed." When this new category of woman was linked with economic and/or professional independence, "the invert" became a dangerous being, potentially threatening to a social order defined by a normative belief in separate spheres, female dependency, and a proper subordination to male authority.[44] As an independent and ambitious entity, the women's colony in Rome engendered much criticism from male colleagues. This book chronicles the ways in which women sculptors negotiated these tensions in the male-dominated field of art making.

Women artists were constantly renegotiating the character of true womanhood in order to accommodate contemporary notions of creativity and genius that had largely been gendered masculine. They embraced the domestic realm but reshaped it with their all-female households; simultaneously they led autonomous public lives as accomplished professional sculptors. They inhabited numerous public personas, developed divergent sexual identities, and experienced varied same-sex relationships. They enacted the guises of the "mannish woman," the "tomboy," the "true woman," and the "lobbyist" (a hypersexualized female) according to their strategic needs. No one "true" feminine artistic self emerged in Rome.[45]

During the years 1850 to 1876, women entered the public realm as writers, artists, and reformers, providing various models of professional and political engagement for future generations of women. The sculptors who traveled or expatriated to Rome composed the first truly professional class of women artists and, as such, participated in a modern egalitarian moment in American history. Maturing in a social, cultural, and political environment that encouraged feminine professional pursuits, they lived lives that we now consider quite modern. This book illustrates that the American women artists who pioneered careers in Rome between 1850 and 1876 were exemplars of modern womanhood. Their personal lives and professional experiences, though distant in time, share much with the contemporary struggles of women today.

Following a historical sequence, *A Sisterhood of Sculptors* has three thematic sections. It is not, however, an exactly chronological narrative, as the works discussed in each chapter are linked to specific ideas and arguments. Part I, "Feminine Professionalism in Boston and Rome" (chapters 1 through 3), outlines the conditions under which American women sculptors developed professional careers in Boston, appropriated the subject and style of neoclassicism as their own, and mediated the gendered terrain of artistic production in Rome. Part II, "Women Sculptors and the

Politics of Rome" (chapters 4 and 5), addresses American responses to the political environment in Rome, specifically the unification of Italy as a nation state in 1860 and the inauguration of Rome as the nation's capital in 1870. This section makes clear the ideological linkage between Italy's political liberation and an Anglo-American vision of a feminist utopia abroad. Part III, "The Civil War, Reconstruction, and the Suffrage Debates" (chapters 6 and 7), focuses upon American women sculptors in the public sphere in Rome and at home. Witnessing events in the 1860s that led to the liberation of the Roman people, they produced sculptures that drew parallels between the Italian political struggle and the momentous events simultaneously transpiring in the United States. During the progressive (even perhaps utopian) political environment of Reconstruction, women sculptors attained professional success at home by participating (albeit fleetingly) in the growing public-monument industry. The book closes in 1876, with the end of Reconstruction, the loss of the suffrage battle, and the close of the heady moment of women's sculptural successes in Rome and the United States.

# Part One

## Feminine Professionalism in Boston and Rome

# One

## The Boston-Rome Nexus

Boston's community of reform-minded professional women created a fertile environment for female accomplishment in the mid–nineteenth century. They developed their voices as political activists and served as accomplished mentors and models for a younger generation of ambitious female artists like Harriet (Hatty) Hosmer (fig. 1). It was these women whom the young sculptor sought out, gravitating toward such pioneering figures as the writer and abolitionist Lydia Maria Child and later the successful thespian Charlotte Cushman. Child was an active member of the Boston Female Anti-Slavery Society, one of the most influential of the antebellum women's associations that established the first organized women's rights movement in the United States. Uncompromising in her struggle for the immediate emancipation of slaves, Child was stalwart in her concern for the lives of all women, white and black.[1]

Ridiculed as a "petticoat politician," Child endured harassment and even financial ruin for her radical positions on abolition and women's rights. In 1833, she wrote *An Appeal in Favor of That Class of Americans Called Africans,* one of the earliest American abolitionist tracts. In this extended essay, she had initially intended to respond to objections regarding the immediate emancipation of the slaves; in the end, she produced a full-fledged analysis of America's "peculiar institution." In no uncertain terms, she argued for the right of blacks to attain full citizenship. Between 1841 and 1843, she edited the *National Anti-Slavery Standard,* the official weekly of the American Anti-Slavery Society and one of the most progressive abolitionist publications in the country. Relentless in her pursuit of social justice, she served as a strong and indomitable model for the young Hosmer, living in close proximity in the Boston suburb of Watertown. Attracted to ambitious and powerful women all her life, Hosmer may possibly have sought surrogates for her own mother, whom she had lost to tuberculosis at the age of six.[2]

Unfettered by the strict rules of feminine decorum, the young Hosmer developed into a lively and precocious "tomboy," originally a term of social disparagement for little girls. Her father, Dr. Hiram Hosmer, raised her in what was then considered a healthy manner—encouraging physical exertion in an outdoor environment. As a child, she owned a horse, a dog, and a gun and was free to roam the hills and fields of her Watertown neighborhood. She swam, boated, and skated on the Charles River, growing up to become an expert horsewoman, a vigorous

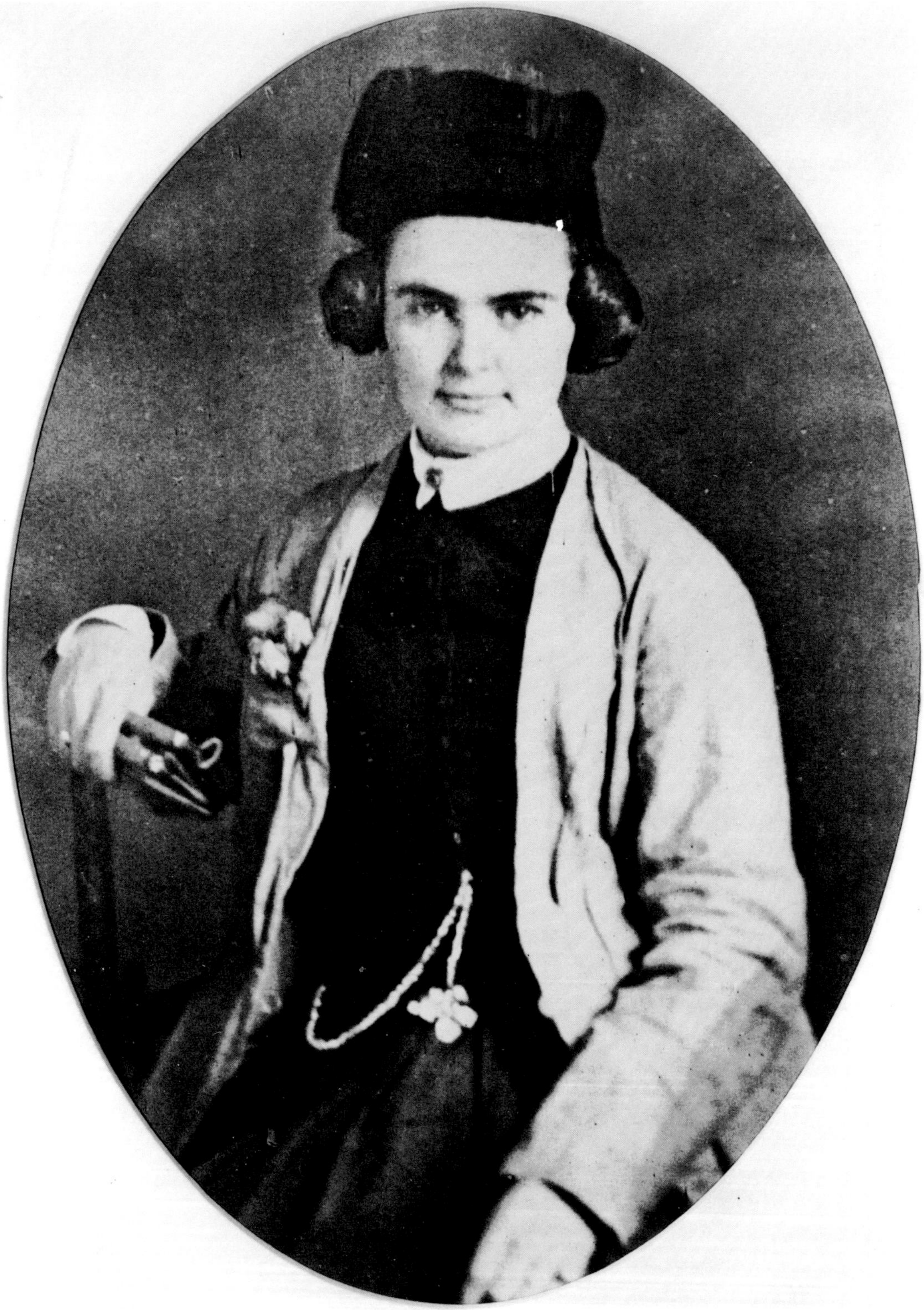

FIG. 1
Harriet Goodhue Hosmer, ca. 1855, photograph, salt print. National Portrait Gallery, Smithsonian Institution, Washington, D.C.

swimmer, and an enthusiastic hiker. Hosmer's tomboyish spunk and childhood pranks were somewhat notorious in her hometown. Considered eccentric by many of her neighbors, she daringly rode her horse to Boston all alone one night to win a bet. On a whim, she decoupled railroad cars from an engine to strand passengers in the Watertown train station. Apprehended for this stunt, she had to be bailed out of police custody by her father.[3]

Encouraging Hosmer's independence, Child had recognized something special in the young girl. Hatty had "refused to have her feet cramped by the little Chinese shoes, which society places on us all," Child later wrote in an article on the aspiring young artist. This "feeble tottering," she concluded, was misunderstood as "feminine grace."[4] Child knew that the "tomboy" stereotype had the effect of limiting the life experience of girls, coercing them to act within the bounds of conventional decorum. Indeed, in her critique of traditional feminine proprieties, she encouraged the tomboy in Hosmer (and in all girls) rather than the debilitating torture of "feminine grace."

The famous actress Charlotte Cushman, to whom Hosmer would soon become emotionally attached, had also been considered a tomboy as a child. The sculptor Emma Stebbins, in Cushman's defense, commented upon the label as it "applied to all little girls who showed the least tendency toward thinking and acting for themselves." The term served as "the advance-guard of that army of opprobrious epithets," Stebbins continued, "lavished so freely upon the pioneers of woman's advancement."[5] In 1868, the author Louisa May Alcott championed this type of invigorating childhood in her popular novel *Little Women,* based largely upon her own reform-minded family, in which she recorded the escapades of four sisters growing up in Concord, Massachusetts. Alcott imagined an active girlhood for her character Jo, who claimed to be terribly disappointed "in not being a boy."[6] In their boyish dress and sporting behavior, nineteenth-century tomboys, like Hosmer, disrupted traditional gender categories in middle-class society.[7]

Most likely at Child's urging, Dr. Hosmer enrolled his daughter at Elizabeth Sedgwick's Lenox Academy, a progressive boarding school in the Berkshires for audacious girls. At the Lenox Academy, Hosmer experienced an educational program in which girls were given opportunities to nurture their individual talents. Charles and Elizabeth Sedgwick had moved to Lenox in 1821 and were soon joined by Charles's sister, the feminist author Catharine Sedgwick. In the 1840s and 1850s, the Berkshire town served as a cultural center for Boston-based writers and intellectuals, including Herman Melville, Oliver Wendell Holmes, Henry Ward Beecher, and Nathaniel Hawthorne. It was also a magnet for an international coterie of progressive women reformers, among them Frances Ann (Fanny) Kemble, the British actress turned abolitionist; Harriet Martineau, the British writer on women's rights; Frederika Bremer, the Finnish feminist; and Anna Jameson, the British feminist and historian—all of whom engaged the young minds at the Lenox Academy.[8]

Hosmer came into contact with these powerful women while in Lenox. She developed a lifelong attachment to Catharine Sedgwick, who had traveled to Europe in 1840, publishing *Letters from Abroad to Kindred at Home* in 1841. Like other thoughtful reformers, she understood Italy in sophisticated terms, following the pressing political events of the *Risorgimento* and responding to Italy as a potential nation-state, rather than as an imagined mythic arcadia.[9] She was committed to women's rights, writing in 1857 that marriage was a woman's prerogative, not a social or moral imperative: "We believe that [the single woman] has an independent power to shape her own course, and to force her separate sovereign way."[10] There is little doubt that Sedgwick's progressive beliefs guided Hosmer, who maintained a close bond with the writer throughout her life.

At Catharine Sedgwick's invitation, Kemble first visited Lenox in 1838. In her youth, Kemble had inherited the mantle of her famous thespian aunt, Sarah Siddons. A reluctant performer, she pursued a theatrical career for a short time before marrying the Southern American aristocrat Pierce Butler and retiring from the stage in 1834. The marriage proved disastrous; the couple became estranged in 1842 and finally divorced in 1849, at which time she settled in Lenox.[11] Characterizing her "sisterhood" with Kemble in the strongest of terms, Sedgwick wrote: "I do not believe that men can ever feel so pure an enthusiasm for women as we can feel for one another—ours is nearest to the love of angels."[12] In Lenox, Sedgwick, Kemble, and the young Hosmer formed a close bond. A few years later, Hosmer would attribute her decision to pursue a sculptural career to her friendship with Kemble.[13]

Demonstrating an intrepid independence, Kemble became Lenox's most conspicuous resident. She caused quite a stir by adopting the revolutionary dress of pantaloons, thus participating in the short-lived yet quite radical Dress Reform Movement promoted by Amelia Bloomer. Kemble loved to ride her horse through the countryside, her riding habit consisting of a black velvet jacket and cap and a wide white riding skirt with man's trousers beneath. Writing in the journal the *Lily,* Bloomer noted that "male attire" had become prevalent among certain women in Lenox: "Several ladies of Lennox [*sic*] with Mrs. Kemble at their head, had actually paraded the streets, equipped in coats, vests and pantaloons, and all the other paraphernalia of a gentlemen's dress." Conservative critics attacked not only the outfit, which they considered sexually transgressive, but also the woman who wore it. Letters to the local newspaper complained that Kemble was corrupting the youth by encouraging what was considered a subversive (or tomboyish) wardrobe for women.[14] Indeed, Hosmer learned quickly the power and practicality of such dress, understanding the symbolic value of clothing that identified men with active, independent behavior and women with a weak, dependent, and immobile demeanor.

Hosmer was the product of a new philosophy of education that developed in New England schools in the antebellum period. Young women were taught independence and autonomy at the same time that they looked to one another for emotional and moral support. The atmosphere at the Lenox Academy encouraged a world of female intimacy as it nurtured the professional aspirations of its young students. Segregated within the cloistered world of the home or academy, women pursued personal relationships that were always assumed to be appropriately chaste, oftentimes alongside their traditional marriage and family attachments. At the same time, young women were encouraged to participate in professional pursuits, melding a female-centered domesticity with feminine professionalism. The writer and historian Elizabeth Ellet codified this ideology in 1859 by legitimizing the accomplishments of women artists, like Hosmer, Margaret Foley, and Louisa Lander, whose practice would otherwise have appeared deviant.[15] She imagined a template that bound true womanhood with feminine professionalism and thus lent a protective aura to women's artistic creativity in Boston and Rome.

## *Margaret Fuller: A Feminist Leader in Boston and Rome*

Margaret Fuller, journalist, political thinker, reformer, and editor of the Transcendentalist magazine the *Dial,* shared a desire for equal opportunity and self-determination with Boston's progressive women's community. Her father had schooled her in history, literature, mathematics, and biblical scholarship. She knew several languages and had become a leading Goethe scholar. Her education went far beyond that of many privileged young men. At first finding abolitionists a bit shrill for her liking, Fuller focused her intellectual energies upon the rights of women. By 1845, however, when she published her *Woman in the Nineteenth Century,* she concurred with the tenets of the radical abolitionist movement by positing parallels between the status of women and that of slaves. Throughout her career as a writer, she examined the intersecting plights of America's oppressed communities: women, slaves, and Indians.[16]

As one of the great intellects of her time, Fuller asserted leadership among Boston feminists by instituting her "Conversations" in 1839.[17] For five years she led a "gifted and extraordinary circle" of feminine colleagues in conversation.[18] Progressive women of all stripes attended these meetings, including Child and others active in the Boston Female Anti-Slavery Society. Elizabeth Peabody, a Boston-area educator and reformer, hosted the meetings at her bookstore on West Street in Boston. Her sister Sophia Peabody, future wife of Nathaniel Hawthorne and artist in her own right, also appeared at these meetings. It is likely that the sculptor Sarah Fisher Ames participated as well.[19] Attending the Conversations for three years, Ednah Dow Cheney, the future director of the School of Design for Women in Boston, wrote that Fuller "did not make us her disciples, her blind followers. She opened the book of life and helped us to read it for ourselves."[20]

In the first of thirteen Conversations, Fuller introduced Greek mythology and classical thought to twenty-five to thirty women. With her Transcendentalist leanings, she believed that the realm of ideas articulated in Greek mythology transcended even that of Christian revelation.[21] "Grecian mythology," Elizabeth Peabody remarked, "embodie[d] the highest intellectual action of the most cultivated nation on earth . . . [and was] commensurate with the thoughts of Genius."[22] To this elite American community, mythological heroes and heroines served as moral exemplars; Graeco-Roman sculpture signified human potential; and neoclassical sculptures reinstated ancient ideals in the contemporary world.[23]

Fuller blazed a path for many intellectual and creative women when she traveled to Europe in 1846 as the first female journalist to cover foreign affairs for Horace Greely's *New York Tribune,* one of the most progressive newspapers of its day. In London, she met the exiled Italian Republican leader Giuseppe Mazzini, with whose political cause she was deeply engaged. Her first dispatch from Rome, "Art, Politics, and the Hope of Rome," was dated May 1847. In her capacity as journalist, she covered with much sympathy the events leading up to and culminating in the Roman Republic and saw herself as the official historian of this momentous event.[24]

With the death of Pope Gregory XVI, in 1846, Rome had been freed from a despotic regime. His successor, Pius IX (Pio Nono) promised a more liberal government and immediately granted freedom of the press and amnesty to all political prisoners.[25] Fuller wrote home to the American people, "This cause is OURS, above all others."[26] By November 1847, however, it became clear to her and others that Pius "meant only to improve, not to *reform*."[27] On February 8, 1849, Mazzini issued a Proclamation of the Republic that resounded throughout the Papal States. In Rome, this revolutionary act was attended by parades in the Piazza di Venezia, the city's central square.

At the request of Pope Pius, Louis Napoleon sent the French army to restore social order and papal sovereignty in Rome. On April 30, 1849, the French troops entered the city, and the battle for the Republic commenced. To secure their safety, Fuller, together with the American sculptor Thomas Crawford and his family, evacuated to the American consul's residence, the Casa Dies on via Gregoriana, near the top of the Spanish Steps.[28] On May 6, Fuller informed her readership at home that she wrote "from barricaded Rome."[29] Actively supporting the Republican cause, the American sculptor William Wetmore Story and his wife, Emelyn, collected money from Americans for relief of the wounded and supplied food to the troops defending the city on the slopes near the Vatican.[30]

Lieutenant Colonel Giuseppe Garibaldi led the Republicans in their fight against the French and papal troops. The Romans fought bravely and defeated the French in early battles. Fuller, together with other brave women—Italian and foreign—tended to the wounded. She was appointed director (*regolatrice*) of the Hospital of the Fatebenefratelli in May and dedicated herself full-time to these duties.[31] Rome remained under siege by the French from late April until July 2, 1849, when the Roman Assembly suspended all military engagements and Garibaldi and his troops vacated the city.[32]

With her daringly independent life, Fuller puzzled many of the male sculptors and writers whom she knew in Boston and Rome. Several members of Boston's literary community, most notably Ralph Waldo Emerson and Nathaniel Hawthorne, considered Fuller desexed and "manly" for her intellectual brilliance. However, she surprised the Roman expatriate community and her friends at home with her unleashed passion in a world where proper women were not expected to seek or enjoy sexual pleasure. At Easter Sunday evening vespers at St. Peter's in 1847, Fuller met Giovanni Angelo Ossoli, a strikingly handsome Italian marquis who was ten years her junior. An aristocrat by birth, he held Republican sympathies and served with Garibaldi's forces in Rome.[33] Her male colleagues in Rome believed that she had flaunted her femininity by falling in love with Ossoli, who many considered her intellectual inferior. It is unclear to this day whether Fuller and Ossoli married; the birth of their child remained secret until shortly before their departure from Italy in January of 1850.[34] Upon their return to the United States, Fuller and her family died tragically in a shipwreck off Fire Island, New York.

In 1848, Thomas Hicks painted his portrait *Margaret Fuller* while both were in Rome (fig. 2). He represented Fuller in a pensive moment,

FIG. 2
Thomas Hicks, *Margaret Fuller,* 1848, oil on canvas, 16 ½ × 12 ½ in. National Portrait Gallery, Smithsonian Institution, Washington, D.C., lent by Constance Fuller Threinen (great-grandchild of Margaret Fuller's brother Arthur B. Fuller).

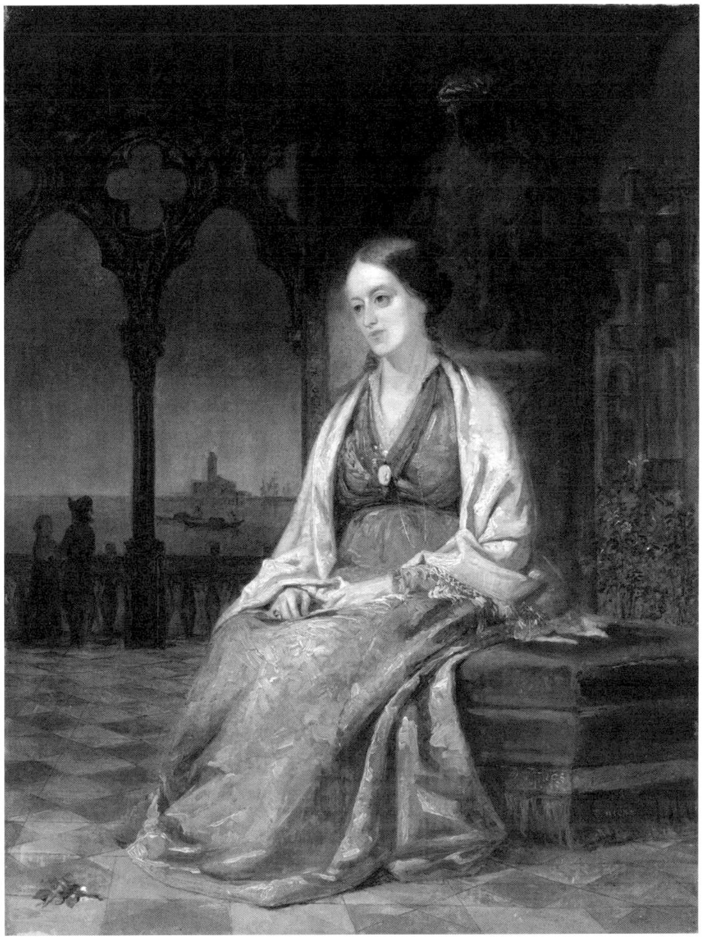

seated on a terrace surrounded by a Venetian Gothic arcade. A trysting couple appears in the midground of the painting; a canal with gondola fills the background. Fuller wears a purple satin dress with a fashionable cameo at her bosom. A white flower and gold chain further adorn her bodice. Behind her in shadow, a nude male torso, the *Eros of Centocelle,* stands upon a pedestal. Provocatively located behind her head, this idealized male nude appears as a ghostly reminder of her transgressive sexual pleasure in Rome. Before her on the ground lies a wilted red rosebud, suggestive of her deflowering. Hicks structured the image with a strong diagonal that located Fuller between the darkened image of the sexualized male nude and the red rose in the foreground, a symbol of her desire. In this portrait, the sculpture, amorous couple, and flower signify the embodied carnality that was absent in her persona of a proper bourgeois woman.

In Italy, Fuller refused the strictures of true womanhood. To her male friends and Transcendentalist colleagues in New England, her behavior was considered scandalous—so much so that Emerson, in his posthumous biography of Fuller, felt compelled to domesticate her, that is, mold her into a "proper" woman, by omitting her love affair and maternity from the narrative.[35] Despite her supposedly scandalous life in Italy, her powerful legacy lived on after her premature death. As her biographer Caroline Healy Dall explained, "In no way was Margaret's supremacy so evident as in the impulse she gave to the minds of younger women."[36] Years later, Henry James pointedly wrote that "the Margaret-ghost" continued to haunt "the old passages" of Rome.[37] For Boston's young women sculptors the "Margaret-ghost" rallied their ambitious spirits and guided their professional careers.

## *Boston's Sisterhood of Sculptors*

Little opportunity for sculptural training existed in Boston in the antebellum period. In the 1840s and 1850s, Harriet Hosmer, Margaret Foley, and Louisa Lander faced rigorous impediments to their study, most notably exclusion from life-drawing classes because of perceived threats to their modesty. Indeed, conventional wisdom at the time deemed women's emotions so unpredictable that contact with a live model would prove aesthetic disinter est impossible. Some even believed that women's reproductive capacities would fail with excessive mental stimulation. As a result, Foley and Lander taught themselves basic carving skills at home.[38]

Hosmer had access to more opportunities. As the daughter of a physician, she received some anatomical training from her father. In 1849, she studied for a short time with the British-born sculptor Peter Stephenson in Boston. By the fall of 1850, she had traveled to St. Louis to study anatomy with Dr. Joseph Nash McDowell at the Missouri Medical College. She lived with Cornelia Crow, an intimate friend she had met at the Lenox Academy, and her family. While in St. Louis, she developed a lasting relationship with Cornelia's father, Wayman Crow, a leading citizen and philanthropist who would later become one of her primary benefactors.[39]

Returning to her Watertown home in the summer of 1851 with an ambitious agenda, she began work on two marble pieces: a medallion portrait of Joseph McDowell and an ideal bust of *Hesper* (fig. 3). Mastering the marble medium with ease, she first made a clay model of *Hesper.* After a workman chopped the corners off the marble block for her, she carved the sculpture herself.

A personification of the evening star, *Hesper* was the first of several busts of female mythological figures she would produce in the next few years. The poem "In Memoriam A. H. H." by Alfred, Lord Tennyson, a lament to a departed young friend, may have been her inspiration. Tennyson wrote: "Sad Hesper o'er the buried sun / And ready, thou, to die with him, / Thou watchest all things ever dim / And dimmer, and a glory done." With this beautiful stanza in mind, Hosmer carved *Hesper*'s eyelids heavy with sleep and her head tilted slightly downward. In the figure's demeanor and expression, she suggested a somnolent state traditionally associated with death.[40]

As her first major sculptural work, the bust deserved commendation. Hosmer chose to depict *Hesper* with classicized features—longish face, aquiline nose, and small mouth. Her

FIG. 3
Harriet Hosmer, *Hesper,* 1852, marble, height 24 in. Watertown Free Public Library, Mass.

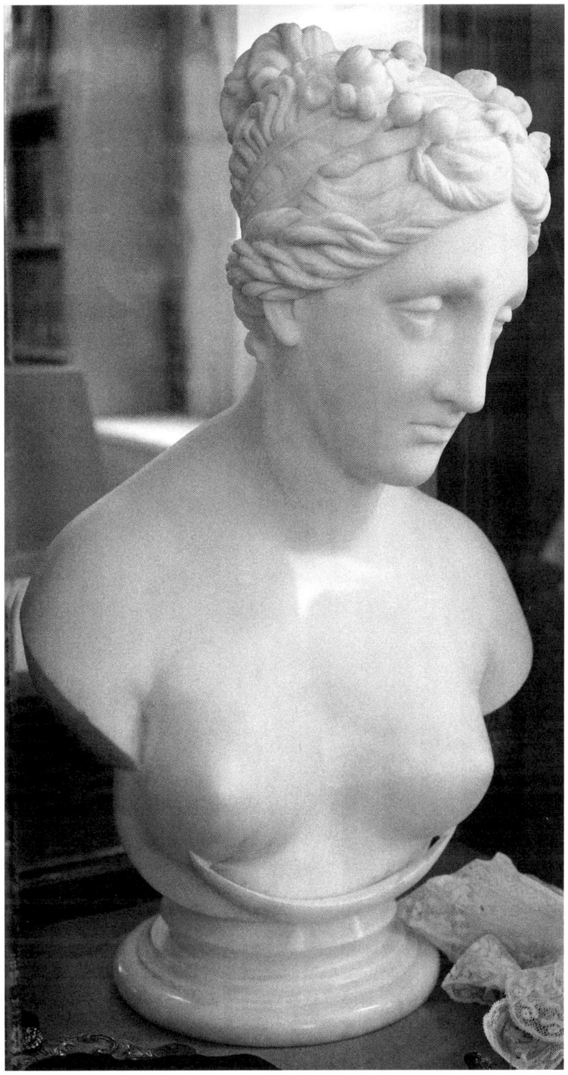

hair was ornately carved, with capsules of poppies (another symbol of death) entwined among the curls and the evening star ornamenting her crown. The crescent moon outlined the lower line of the sculpture, forming a transition from figure to base. The overly decorative design of the hair compensated, in part, for Hosmer's lack of success rendering the body. The figure's shoulders sloped as if without an underlying bone structure, and her arms terminated in an awkward manner. Nevertheless, this ideal bust would serve Hosmer well in giving her entry to one of the most prestigious studios in Rome—that of the neoclassical sculptor John Gibson.

Unlike Hosmer, who had a privileged training as a young sculptor, Foley and Lander were autodidacts. Little or none of their early work remains extant, except in written descriptions. Margaret (Peggy) Foley grew up in rural Vermont and at the age of fourteen left her family to work as a mill girl in Lowell, Massachusetts, before opening a sculpture studio in Boston. "The obstacles she has already overcome in following her profession," one Boston journalist noted in 1857, "would long ago have discouraged a less persevering and energetic mind."[41]

Foley was one of thousands of young single women, many from the rural regions of New Hampshire and Vermont, who sought employment in expanding factory towns. She toiled for perhaps a year or more in the early 1840s as an operative in the spinning room of the Merrimack Corporation, carving figures and faces on wooden bobbins in her spare time.[42] While living and working in Lowell, she contributed to the *Lowell Offering,* a literary magazine started and run by the operatives. Catharine Sedgwick's letters and the writing of Lydia Maria Child served as literary models for these young authors, who, as one contemporary source put it, could "be called the poetic element of factory life."[43] Foley's impressive writing skills would later aid her in Rome when she would write art reviews for newspapers and magazines back home.

Ambitious and liberally educated, Foley used her experience in Lowell as a springboard for her sculptural career. By the mid-1840s, she had established herself as a professional cameo carver, a skill she maintained for most of her life despite the fact that cameo dust was troubling to her health. When Ednah Dow Cheney opened her School of Design for Women in 1850, Foley enrolled in classes. According to Cheney, hordes of young women applied to attend her school in search of practical means of earning a living. With the number of unmarried women in the eastern United States growing in the 1840s, design schools were one avenue in which single women gained occupational training. Inspired by the Philadelphia School of Design for Women, founded by Sarah Worthington King Peter in 1844, Cheney's school offered classes in the domestic arts, such as textile and wallpaper design, wood engravings, and lithography.[44]

Creative women, like Foley, were often relegated to careers in the decorative arts. Presumed to have limited power of reason, they were thought incapable of working in higher, intellectual and didactic art forms. Cameo carving, considered a "beautiful pastime" for a "refined lady," was the type of profitable yet respectable endeavor that Cheney's School of Design offered young women. Related to miniature painting, which occupied many women artists in the first half of the nineteenth century, cameos were considered "a matter of fashion" because of their ornamental nature. Providing an intimate view of the subject, both miniatures and cameos were associated with preciousness and sentimentality, attributes identified with femininity. Because of their diminutive size, these objects could be produced within a domestic setting, thus maintaining a female artist's modesty.[45]

Foley was only one of a group of cameo carvers already at work in Boston. Using both shell and lava as her materials, she gained fame in this profession, selling her pieces for thirty-five dollars each. Cameos had come into vogue in the first decade of the nineteenth century, after the French resumed archaeological excavations at Pompeii. Around this time, the first school for cameo engraving opened in Rome, funded by Pope Leo XII. The popularity of the cameo was enhanced even more by Queen Victoria, who often wore these gems and gave them as gifts.[46] Margaret Fuller, as noted above, prominently displayed a cameo upon her bodice when posing for her portrait in Rome (fig. 2).

In 1857, after exhibiting three cameos at the store of Edwin Smith on Tremont Row, Foley was heralded in the Boston press as the most successful female cameo cutter in the United States.[47] When she exhibited her cameos in 1860 at the Boston Athenaeum, one reviewer raved that they "were the best things in the exhibition. Better likenesses could not be made, and every line of her execution tells of abundant untouched resources of genius."[48] Her reputation and career had been launched.

Foley produced a small cameo portrait of Theodore Parker (1858, now missing), the Unitarian minister, abolitionist, and feminist reformer. In 1860, the year Parker died in Florence, she completed a plaster cabinet bust (also missing) of the minister. Serving a populist audience, this plaster bust held "a place in many a negro cabin in America," the *St. Louis Globe* reported.[49] One can imagine Foley, a reform-minded artist, listening intently to Theodore Parker's famous sermons in Boston. Controversial for his religious and political views, Parker preached about America's social ills, focusing upon slavery, the plight of the urban poor, and the degradation of women. Between 1846 and 1852, attendance at his church services grew to two thousand, including such luminaries as the abolitionist William Lloyd Garrison, the women's rights activist Elizabeth Cady Stanton, the poet and reformer Julia Ward Howe (whose bust Foley would carve in Rome in 1865), and author Louisa May Alcott.[50]

Many in Boston's progressive reform community championed Foley's work ethic and recognized the challenges under which she labored. To offer financial support to the young artist, one Boston journalist urged "Mr. Parker's admirers . . . who know the value of an independent life in woman" to order busts at a cost of ten or twelve dollars.[51] The unlikely story of a working-class mill girl rising in social stature to become a professional artist certainly captured the imagination of many Boston reformers.

Contrasting starkly with Foley's working-class background was Louisa Lander's privileged Salem, Massachusetts, family. She was the great-granddaughter of a wealthy colonial merchant whose fortune had been passed down through the family. On her mother's side, she was a distant relative of the famous painter Benjamin West; her father had been a ship captain; and her brother was Colonel Frederick W. Lander, the explorer of America's western frontier. She grew up in comfortable circumstances in an Oak Hill mansion in the town of Danvers, just outside Boston. She studied firsthand the carved wooden sculptures by the famed Skillin brothers and Samuel McIntire that decorated her home. From all indications, Lander was a serious child, perhaps even driven in her ambitions. Rarely showing emotion and displaying an uncanny "self-control" at a young age, she exhibited a personality different from that of the riotously active and fun-loving Hosmer. For Lander, it was "art alone," Elizabeth Ellet wrote, that "could arouse the full ardor and energy of her spirit."[52]

Lander was born into an Essex County society that demonstrated a growing enthusiasm for the fine arts. As a young girl, she visited Tilden's Book Shop in Salem, where she viewed expensive works of art commissioned from Boston or New York artists before they were retired to the private domiciles of leading area families. She began carving wood and alabaster and modeling sealing wax at the age of thirteen. Using the alabaster from an old clock, she carved her first bas-relief portraits with a penknife. Soon a friend gave her some shell, with which she learned to make cameos. Like Foley, she began her professional career as a cameo carver, producing likenesses of her mother, father, and friends, one of which she exhibited at the Boston Mechanics Association in 1847.[53]

By 1855, she had opened a studio in Salem, carving portraits and ideal busts. By all indications, her sculptural career had a successful start. She was only the second woman to exhibit in the Annual Sculpture Exhibition of the Boston Athenaeum, an important institutional patron of the arts, where she showed the marble bust of her father, *Edward Lander* (now lost), and an *Ideal Head of the Water Nymph, Galatea* (also lost).[54] Amazed that Lander had had no training in the visual arts, an art critic for the *Boston Evening Transcript* described the bust at the Athenaeum as a "remarkable first effort" by "a young lady sculptor of marked genius and great promise."[55]

The Boston Athenaeum, founded in 1807, played a dominant role in the city's cultural life, introducing residents to current developments in the visual arts.[56] At the center of the New England art world in the nineteenth century, the Athenaeum provided women limited opportunities for the study of art and the exhibition of their own work. Lander exhibited two pieces in 1855; Hosmer showed *Puck* in 1857 (fig. 22); and Foley displayed her cameos in 1860. The artists took full advantage of what the Athenaeum had to offer. Shortly before her departure for Rome, Hosmer wrote, "Fridays are my Sabbaths, really my days of rest, for I go first to the Athenaeum and fill my eyes and mind with beauty."[57]

The institution owned a significant collection of sculptural casts, an invaluable resource for male artists, who had been allowed access to the collection since 1826.[58] Augustus Thorndike donated the first plaster casts of ancient sculptures in 1822. Selected by the internationally renowned neoclassical sculptor Antonio Canova, the Thorndike casts raised the cultural profile of the city by tangibly linking Boston with its classical heritage. The original collection consisted of eleven pieces, eight full figures and three small-scale works, the most important of which were the *Apollo Belvedere* (fig. 7), *Laocoön, Venus de' Medici,* and *Capitoline Venus.*[59]

The directors of the Athenaeum prohibited women artists from studying the collection of plaster casts, because they believed that it was indecorous for a woman to stare at a male body. Women gained access to the sculpture galleries as visitors, not as practicing artists. In fact, they formed the majority of museum visitors, indicating both the advantages and limitations of Boston's cultural environment. For example, they could view, but not draw, Thomas Crawford's *Orpheus and Cerberus,* the first life-size male nude in American sculpture, when it was exhibited in a special annex off the Athenaeum library in 1843 (fig. 9).[60] In 1851, Cheney's School of Design for Women requested and received free admission to the galleries for its female students, who could view, but not draw, the works on display.

Hosmer voiced her frustration with the city, both in its paucity of exhibition venues and its restrictions on women artists. In a witty poem of 1850 titled "Boston and Boston People," she complained that Bostonians "passed amid the joust of trade, / Dwelling on happy bargains made, /

. . . Such, O Bostonians! is your case. / Deplore the arts in such a place!"[61] Instead, she looked to Italy for professional opportunities.

## *Corinne and the Arcadian Academy in Rome*

When American women artists, writers, and intellectuals arrived in Rome in the 1850s, they discovered a social and cultural space that had traditionally affirmed feminine participation in creative endeavors. Among eighteenth-century *illuministi* (Enlightenment thinkers), women contributed to liberal thought as *cittadine* (modern female citizens) and were considered "the soul of modern society." Roman cultural institutions offered elite, educated Italian women the opportunity for literary expression at the same time as they welcomed talented European expatriates, such as the painters Angelika Kauffmann and Élisabeth Vigée-Lebrun, into their fold.[62]

The Arcadian Academy, fostering personal, creative, and intellectual networks among Romans and foreigners, allowed women unprecedented creative authority in the literary and visual arts from its incarnation in 1690 through the mid–nineteenth century.[63] Embracing the idea of poetry and painting as sister arts, the academy created a cultural environment where the literary and visual artistic spheres commingled. It promoted *conversazioni* (polite social conversations) for their members: artists with theoretical concerns; scholars committed to letters, science, antiquarianism, and religion; and writers who were entranced by the visual arts. Increasingly, Italian and foreign-born women participated in these conversations and appeared in public performances.

Rome's late eighteenth-century cosmopolitan community heralded Angelika Kauffmann as one of its most talented artist-intellectuals. Hosting a salon in her studio atop the Spanish Steps, she brought together a group of international literary and artistic figures and generously promoted new talent, especially that of women. The Arcadian Academy welcomed her as a member in 1789. After the death of the painter Anton Raphael Mengs, Kauffmann led the neoclassical community in Rome, gaining entry to and earning public legitimacy within the male preserve of history painting.[64]

More than any other institution in the eighteenth century, the Arcadian Academy opened its doors to creative women and publicly recognized their talents. In the literary field, the Italian *improvisatrice,* or female poetic improvisers, were renowned for their performances and conversations, to which the fashionable Roman and expatriate world flocked. Among the most famous was Corilla Olimpica (Maria Maddalena Morelli), court poet to the Grand Duke of Tuscany. Crowned poet laureate on the steps of the Capitoline in Rome on August 31, 1776, she was the only woman to share this honor with the Renaissance masters Tasso and Petrarch. Her crowning, while controversial for political reasons, revealed a celebration of feminine genius and creativity that would be recalled by Americans and Europeans well into the following century.[65]

By the mid–nineteenth century, Anglo-American guidebooks noted the times and places of literary performances by *improvisatrice.*[66] Isabella Pellegrini, Teresa Bandettini Landucci, and Fortunata Sulgher attracted much attention for their readings; Giannina Milli and Elena dei Conti Guoli held well-publicized public performances.[67] The American poet Julia Ward Howe noted with delight that she had attended an "Accademia," a public recitation by the *improvisatrice* Rosa Taddei, while in Rome.[68]

In 1807, Madame de Staël (Germaine Necker) championed Rome's female literary heritage in her extraordinarily popular novel, *Corinne, or Italy.* A novelist, feminist, and political thinker, she arrived in Italy with her children in 1804, a refugee from Napoleon's France. In Rome, she attended the salons of Angelika Kauffmann and became a member of the Arcadian Academy.[69] In her novel, de Staël imagined the beautiful Corinne, of Italian and British parentage, as the most creative and erudite woman in Rome.[70] Despite her eventual downfall after the loss of her British lover, the fictional character Corinne became a model of feminine liberation for many American and British women, including New England's elite community of women artists, writers, and intellectuals.[71]

American women artists and writers understood Italy in mythic as much as historic terms. The imaginary Italy was conceived as "feminine," a land devoted to culture rather than to material and political affairs. In popular Romantic literature, such as Lord Byron's *Childe Harold's Pilgrimage,* Italy represented a land where one could be free to be oneself.[72] With its legendary character as a land of romantic freedom and its historical resonance as a creative site for both expatriate artists and native *improvisatrice,* Italy beckoned many educated American women who envisioned Corinne's Rome as an enlightened center of female creative activity. Among the first women artists to visit Rome was Harriet Hosmer, who traveled to the Eternal City under the guardianship of her friend and mentor Charlotte Cushman.

### *Rome's New Sisterhood*

On November 12, 1852, Harriet Hosmer arrived in Rome, accompanied by her father, Dr. Hiram Hosmer; Sarah Jane Clarke Lippincott, the journalist known professionally as Grace Greenwood; Virginia Vaughn, a girlhood friend from Lenox; Charlotte Cushman; Sallie Mercer, Cushman's African-American maid and "right-hand woman"; and Matilda Hays, Cushman's partner, a feminist reformer and translator of George Sand's novels. The socially well-connected Vaughn had introduced Hosmer to Cushman in 1850 after a performance in Boston. Hosmer was immediately taken with this strikingly independent woman and developed a lifelong attachment to her. In a letter to her childhood friend Cornelia Carr (née Crow), she wrote: "Miss Cushman and Miss Hays (her friend and companion) have left Boston, and I can't tell you how lonely I feel. I saw a great deal of them during the three weeks that they were in the city. . . . Isn't it strange how we meet people in this world and become attached to them in so short a time?"[73]

Cushman and Hays represented models of creative freedom for Hosmer, who shared their residence at via del Corso 28 in Rome. In the neighborhood between the Piazza del Popolo and the Piazza di Spagna, where the Anglo-American community congregated, the young artist, at the age of twenty-two, resided under Cushman's watchful eye. Hosmer appreciated the heady environment in Rome, where independent women flourished. Within a month of her arrival, she felt completely content, explaining to Wayman Crow that Rome was a "delightful place which I now consider my home."[74] Teasingly, she referred to the Corso residence as "Old Maids' Hall."[75]

Cushman remained the matriarch of the Anglo-American community of women in Rome until her departure from the city in 1870. As a successful actress, she used her professional acumen to advocate for women artists, such as Hosmer, Margaret Foley, Emma Stebbins, and later Edmonia Lewis. An extraordinary woman who rose to theatrical prominence in the 1840s, she gained fame by playing unorthodox theatrical parts. As Meg Merrilies in *Guy Mannering,* she portrayed a withered crone whose hideous demeanor shocked audiences; as Romeo in Shakespeare's *Romeo and Juliet,* she assumed a male persona and wooed the beautiful Juliet with persuasive affection. By 1849, she was considered an equal to the highest-paid men in the field.[76] At the age of thirty-six, her success was such that she contemplated retirement in Rome; in reality, she returned to the stage intermittently throughout her life.

In both her theatrical roles and personal life, Cushman challenged the borders of traditional femininity. By shedding the veneer of womanhood on stage and at home, she assumed the guise of an "active, mannish woman." A recognizable gendered type by the 1820s, this masculinized persona was associated with women who transgressed into traditionally male professional arenas, like literature, art, and theater. She was joined in this daring endeavor by other women artists. The controversial writer George Sand, for example, dressed as a man, spoke at political meetings, traveled the world, and walked the streets day and night. The renowned French painter Rosa Bonheur donned trousers in her studio and had several lifelong relationships with women. Like these other gifted women, Cushman resisted any conventional gender positioning.[77]

Cushman and Hays dressed alike, wearing skirts with tailored shirts and jackets. In an 1851 photograph (fig. 4), both women dress almost identically, down to the cravat each wears around her neck. Cushman is seated in a three-quarter pose with a watch-fob chain dangling from her breast and a book in her lap; she gazes dreamily out of the picture plane. Hays stands in profile behind her, leaning one arm upon a column-like pedestal adorned with a book. In a protective gesture, her other arm seems to surround and support Cushman's figure. Adopting a pose traditionally associated with the heterosexual couple, Cushman and Hays openly performed the role of same-sex partners.[78]

In Rome, Cushman and Hays had the freedom to dress as they pleased, in what they considered a practical rather than unfeminine manner. Instead of a revealing décolletage, which represented the height of fashion, they wore tailored clothing that hid their bosom beneath a tight armature, which bespoke androgyny or a "female masculinity," as theorist Judith Halberstam suggests. This type of dress, which appropriated masculine sartorial forms for the female costume, served as a visual code for feminine independence from social convention, a code that, after meeting Cushman and Hays in 1848, the poet Elizabeth Barrett Browning recognized. "I understand that [Cushman] and Miss Hays have made vows of celibacy and of eternal attachment to each other—they live together [and] dress alike," she reported. "[I]t is a female marriage."[79]

Barrett Browning was taken with the household at via del Corso 28: "There's a house of what I call emancipated women," she wrote to a friend.[80] She met Hosmer in 1853; the two were drawn to one another until the poet's untimely death in

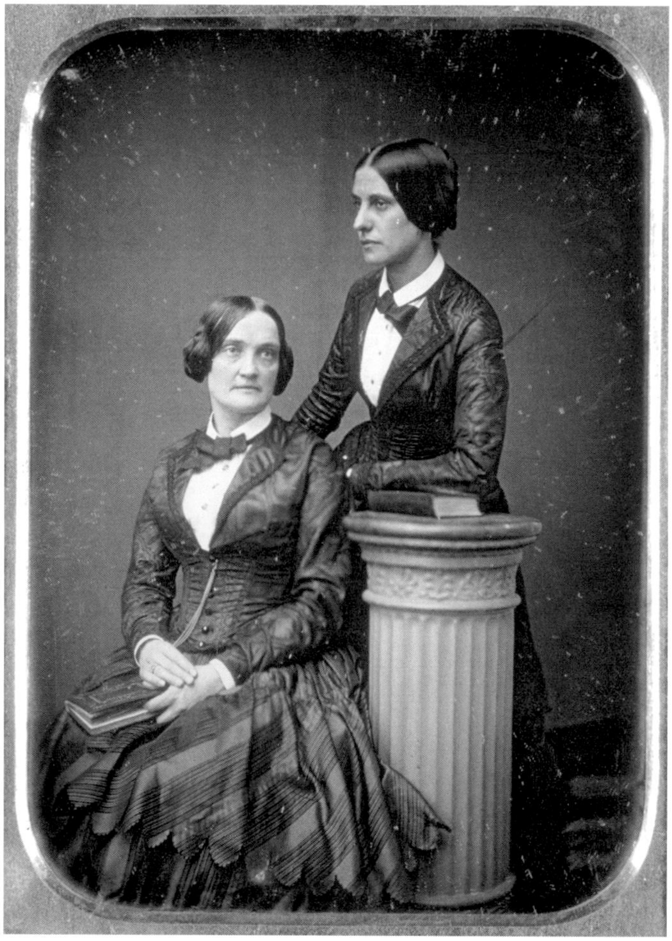

FIG. 4
Charlotte Cushman and Matilda Hays, ca. 1851, daguerreotype. Harvard Theatre Collection, Houghton Library, Harvard University, TCS38.

1861. They both had lost their mothers at an early age and had enjoyed active childhoods, despite Barrett Browning's bouts of illness. As a young girl, she had been trained in Greek and, like Fuller, was an avid reader of the classics. In London, she was for all intents and purposes trapped by her notoriously tyrannical father. At the age of forty, she fled, eloped with the younger Robert Browning, took up residence in Italy, and bore one son.[81]

In her semiautobiographical verse novel, *Aurora Leigh,* of 1856, Barrett Browning, using her popularity as a poet, gave voice to women's struggles and championed the talented women who surrounded her in Italy. Her protagonist, Aurora, is based in part upon the fictional character Corinne and the young Hosmer. The heroine first rejects marriage in favor of intellectual and personal independence; she then adopts the role of creative woman as androgyne; finally she finds success as both writer and woman within the ideal of a loving marriage.[82]

Barrett Browning touted Hosmer's liberated lifestyle in Rome, writing that she "emancipates the eccentric life of a perfectly 'emancipated female.'" But the poet anticipated the dangers of such an emancipated life, which, she explained, must be shielded "from all shadow of blame" by the artist's moral "purity." She continued, "[Hatty] lives here all alone (at twenty-two); dines and breakfasts at the *cafés* precisely as a young man would; works from six o'clock in the morning till night, as a great artist must, and this with an absence of pretension and simplicity of manners which accord rather with the childish dimples in her rosy cheeks than with her broad forehead and high aims."[83] In this extraordinary statement, Barrett Browning reveals much about Hosmer's strategies for negotiating her professional life. Hosmer had sworn to celibacy, renounced (at least traditional) marriage, and lived an independent and active life, safely absorbed in a homosocial female world.

Hosmer deliberately presented an androgynous appearance (fig. 1). She was of small stature, kept short-cut hair, and wore studio garb of beret, jacket, and waistcoat replete with watch fob. In figure 1's photograph, the artist addresses the viewer with confidence, holding her clay modeling tools visibly in her right hand, clearly asserting her identity as a sculptor. Like her friends—from Kemble in Lenox to Cushman and Hays in Rome—she dressed in a practical fashion that encoded her independent lifestyle. However, unlike her older mentors, who openly challenged the patriarchal structures of Roman society with their "active, mannish" guises, Hosmer fashioned herself as a "child-woman," according to Grace Greenwood.[84] She deliberately cultivated a childlike, almost impish demeanor that mitigated the challenges she posed to masculine artistic dominance. Instead, she concealed her professional aspirations behind a youthful façade of "childish dimples" and "rosy cheeks."

Hosmer and others in Cushman's circle in Rome provoked anxiety among Anglo-American men, who saw them as interlopers in their city.[85] The Cushman household soon became engaged with a group of expatriate women who took up residence in Rome for weeks, months, and occasionally years. Fanny Kemble's sister, Adelaide Sartoris, who had lived in Rome for two years, led a salon on Wednesday and Sunday nights in her apartment atop the Spanish Steps. Trained as an opera singer, she performed regularly at these cosmopolitan gatherings, which Hosmer attended with regularity. Kemble soon followed her sister to Rome, arriving in January of 1853. Hosmer, enamored with the city and its community of independent women, wrote that the two Kemble sisters were "like two mothers to me."[86]

Crafting identities in dialogue with "true womanhood," Kemble, Sartoris, Cushman, and Hosmer refashioned domesticity to suit their own ends. Cushman revised and adapted terminology usually linked to heterosexual families. Most commonly, she evoked models of marriage or of family—wife (*sposa*)/husband or mother/daughter/children. By enacting such domestic rituals, she positioned herself both within and against the dominant cultural narratives of gender and sexuality while nurturing intimate relationships between women.[87]

Cushman was fiercely protective of her young female charges in Rome and quickly made enemies with the influential American sculptor William Wetmore Story. Writing to his friend the poet James Russell Lowell shortly after the women's arrival in Rome in 1853, Story described the "furore at 28 Corso," with its "harem (scarem) as I call it . . . [of] emancipated females who dwell there in heavenly unity; namely, the Cushman,

Grace Greenwood, H[osmer]," and others.[88] The all-female household on the Corso unsettled him and caused a "furore" among the male artists. Story exoticized their residence by referring to it as a "harem." At the same time, his rhyming play on "harum-scarum"—"harem (scarem)" ("scare him/them")—possibly revealed his fear of this feminine collective. With an ironic tease, he knew that these "emancipated females" were a far cry from a choir of domestic angels living in "heavenly unity."

Story addresses Hosmer directly in his missive. "Miss Hosmer," he fumes, is "very wilful, and too independent by half." She "is mixed up with a set whom I do not like, and I can therefore do very little for her." He grudgingly admits that Hatty "is doing very well and shows a capital spirit, and I have no doubt will succeed." However, at this point, he subsumes the artistic process within a discourse of sexual difference: "But it is one thing to copy and another to create. She may or may not have inventive powers as an artist, but if she [has, will she not] be the first woman?"[89] This reluctance to ascribe originality to Hosmer's work (or to that of any woman artist) will appear many times in Rome, haunting all the women sculptors discussed in this book. Although Story would eventually become one of Hosmer's strongest supporters, his words affirmed an almost universal distrust of female creativity at the time.

By 1858 Cushman had secured a welcoming environment for female writers, artists, and intellectuals who passed through her orbit. Hosmer, the sculptor Emma Stebbins (who had arrived in Rome in 1856), and Cushman moved into their new residence in November, after extensive renovations were completed. Stebbins and Cushman inhabited the second-floor suite, with its bright sunny windows. Sallie Mercer had quarters on the floor below. Hosmer had the third floor to herself.[90] From the front windows of the three-story building at via Gregoriana 38, "the eye ranged over a wide prospect," Stebbins wrote. In the beautiful neighborhood off the Piazza di Trinità, high atop the Spanish Steps, one could take in "most of the picturesque outlines of the city, [with] St. Peter's looming large and grand in front, . . . a limitless expanse of open Campagna, and the marvellous sky of Rome for background."[91]

Cushman held her first reception in her new home in January of 1859, beginning a tradition that would continue for many years. As a female-centered space, the Saturday-evening receptions were always crowded, with many progressive and creative women in attendance.[92] Mingling at this festive event were the feminist art historian Anna Jameson, Kemble, Sartoris, and the British author and reformer Mary Howitt, to name just a few. When the Irish feminist Frances Power Cobbe came to town, she noted: "There was a brightness, freedom and joyousness among these gifted Americans, which was quite delightful to me."[93] Cushman "had the gift of drawing out the best from all who came," explained Emma Crow, the youngest daughter of the philanthropist Wayman Crow.[94]

The via Gregoriana household became known for its feminine refinement, erudition, and creativity. The interior exuded an "air of hominess"; the walls were covered with "choice pictures and such sculpture as there was space for." The apartment was filled with palms and flowers, cages of twittering birds, an "abundance of books," and beautiful antique cabinets that the

American art critic James Jackson Jarves helped Cushman purchase in Florence.[95] Upon entering, visitors often proclaimed, "O, this is like home!"[96] Despite personal and professional squabbles among the women in Rome—and there were many—this household served as a safe haven for feminine endeavors of all kinds.

The writer and historian Elizabeth Ellet followed the lives of the expatriate sculptors Hosmer, Lander, Foley, and Stebbins in her book *Women Artists in All Ages and Countries,* published in 1859. In this fascinating study of nineteenth-century feminine artistic practice, Ellet compiled the first histories of women artists. Her aim was populist, intending to reach as large an audience as possible. In the preface, she explained: "Should the perusal of my book inspire with courage and resolution any woman who aspires to overcome difficulties in the achievement of honorable independence, or should it lead to a higher general respect for the powers of women and their destined position in the realm of Art, my object will be accomplished."[97] She pictured the female artist with the capacity for self-motivation, self-reliance, and professional success, challenging the conventional narrative of the male artistic genius.[98]

Possessing "culture and refined taste," Stebbins embodied the perfect blend of "true womanhood" and "feminine professionalism" that Ellet heralded.[99] "Modest and gentle" by reputation, she was in 1856 the newest member to join Rome's women's community. Hosmer took Stebbins under her wing, escorting her to famous sites and introducing her to members of the artistic community; the two rode their horses together on the Campagna. Hosmer curiously described Stebbins as her "wife" and as a *scultrice* (woman sculptor), perhaps using these feminine appellations to allude to Stebbins's passive and dependent nature.[100] At the age of forty-one, she appeared shy and vulnerable, posing little threat to patriarchal dominance in the Roman art world. Hosmer addressed the Roman professional world with more bombast than Stebbins, who, self-effacing by nature, advanced her professional career judiciously.[101] Born to a prominent New York banking family, she remained free of the material worries that haunted Hosmer and other sculptors in Rome.

In New York, Stebbins had been trained in the genteel arts of pastel drawing, clay modeling, and copying European old-master paintings. She studied with the portrait painter Henry Inman and between 1839 and 1841 worked under the tutelage of the sculptor Edward Brackett before he moved to Boston.[102] By the early 1840s, she had become an active participant in the New York art world, had joined the American Art Union, and had been admitted as an associate member to the National Academy of Design, where she exhibited portrait drawings in 1843 and 1844. She also exhibited at the Pennsylvania Academy of the Fine Arts in 1845 and again in 1847.[103] After traveling to Rome with her sister and mother in 1856, she decided within six months to settle permanently in the city.[104]

Stebbins was one of the pathbreakers among this group of talented women artists working in Rome. She produced a male nude as her first sculpture, *The Lotus Eater* of 1857–60 (fig. 39).[105] At the same time, she moved American sculpture in a new, modern realist direction with her series of statuettes of workers, the first sculptural expression of industrial labor in American art history.[106] Moreover, she was among the first women awarded public projects in the United States when in 1860 she received the commission for the Horace Mann monument, to be located on the Massachusetts State House grounds. Her most well-known public sculpture, *Angel of the Waters* for Bethesda Fountain (1862, cast 1870), is located in Central Park (fig. 5).[107]

Cushman and Stebbins built a life together in Rome, using the trope of domesticity to emulate the heterosexual nuclear family. In March of 1857, they traveled to Naples, a sojourn that cemented their romantic attachment. At the time, Cushman was still involved with Hays. In April, Hays fled Rome after an emotional confrontation with Cushman.[108] By July, Stebbins and Cushman had formalized what would become a lifelong partnership.[109] "The current of [our] two lives ran, with rare exceptions, side by side," Stebbins would later write. "We were in Rome, as 'travellers and pilgrims' to the famous city."[110] Although theirs was not an untroubled relationship, they exchanged vows of love and fidelity in 1859.[111] Cushman described their relationship as a marriage: "Do you not know," she wrote to Wayman Crow, "that I am already married and wear the badge upon the finger of my left hand?"[112] In Rome, their domestic arrangement was not a secret. In New York, however, Stebbins's elite family grew more and more suspicious of Cushman's influence. Henry Stebbins, Emma's brother and money manager, openly disapproved of their same-sex relationship.[113] Although Stebbins suffered barbs from her family, the "marriage" lasted until 1876, the year Cushman died of breast cancer.

Cushman did not resist the performance of traditional bourgeois femininity after meeting Stebbins, whose social prominence and

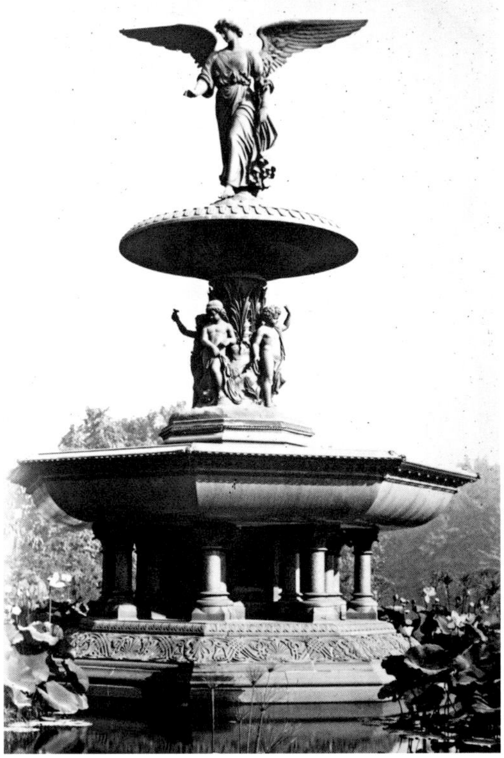

FIG. 5
Emma Stebbins, *Angel of the Waters*, 1862, Bethesda Fountain (cast 1870), Central Park, New York, N.Y. Gelatin silver print, 4 × 6 in. Museum of the City of New York, N.Y.

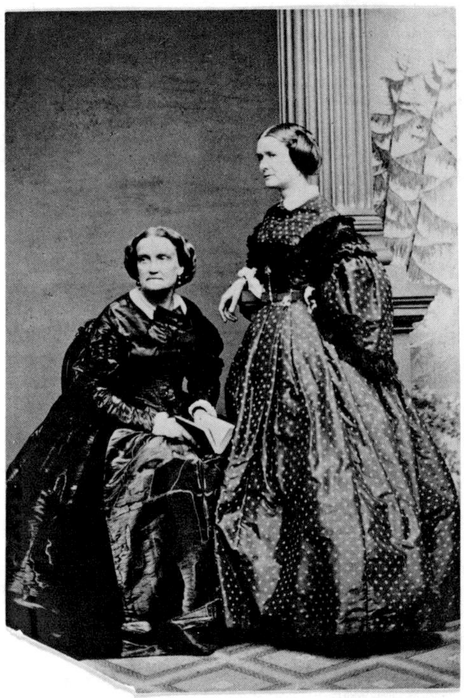

FIG. 6
Charlotte Cushman and Emma Stebbins, ca. 1859, cabinet card. Harvard Theatre Collection, Houghton Library, Harvard University, TCS2.

impeccable pedigree enhanced the actress's respectability and social standing in the Roman community. "She is high, true, noble and self-sacrificing," Cushman wrote of Stebbins. "I love her dearly."[114] In a photograph of 1859, both Cushman and Stebbins appear in lovely Victorian gowns; the seated Cushman holds an open book and wears a satin dress with white collar and cuffs (fig. 6). The cravat ornamenting her collar serves as the only visual reminder of her once "manly" costume (fig. 4); the dangling pearl earrings temper any challenge to femininity the bow tie may have posed. Stebbins stands with one arm resting on her waist, the other leaning upon a half column. Attention is drawn to the full crinolined dresses, especially the decorative polka-dotted gown that Stebbins wears. To be sure, yards of decorative clothing dominates this image of bourgeois propriety. Cushman no longer assumes the guise of an "active, mannish woman," as she had earlier in her life when involved with Hays. Both Stebbins and Cushman thrived within this woman-centered domesticity in Rome.

Cushman and her household understood the subversive potential of domesticity as a feminist strategy. In Rome they established a homosocial world that preserved the appearance of feminine propriety, despite the audacity and unconventionality of their lives. Often referring to herself as *mia madre,* she served as a model of female empowerment and self-sufficiency for her younger charges. She was Hosmer's champion, believing in the young sculptor's abilities and providing her with the means to pursue a successful career.[115] With Cushman's support, Hosmer became one of the most prominent American sculptors working abroad within five short years of her expatriation. She was happy in Rome: "It never entered my head that anybody could be so content on this earth, as I am here. I wouldn't live anywhere else but Rome," she exclaimed in a letter to Cornelia Carr. "I can learn more and do more here, in one year, than I could in America in ten."[116] She produced relatively few portrait busts and statues, instead dedicating herself to ideal statuary with mythological and literary associations. In her sculpture, Hosmer mobilized the language of myth to characterize women's place in the world and adapted neoclassical style and iconography to feminist purposes.

# Two

## *Neoclassicism in Cosmopolitan Rome*

Central to any Roman experience was a visit to the Vatican Museum. Daytime excursions were common, although little sunlight penetrated the eighteenth-century galleries, even the niches of the Belvedere Courtyard that housed the famous *Apollo Belvedere* (fig. 7) and *Laocoön*. As a result, torchlight viewings of ancient masterpieces became legendary. The soft glow of the flame accentuated the finer qualities of the marble carving while allowing viewers to focus upon one discrete work of art at a time (fig. 8).[1] After one such visit, the poet and reformer Julia Ward Howe explained that the marble sculptures "were rendered so lifelike by the artful illumination that when I saw them afterward in the daylight, it seemed to me that they had died."[2] The distilled light imposed an effect of smooth, sensual fleshiness upon the hard marble surfaces. The myth of Pygmalion, which describes the coming to life of the statue of Galatea, was a perfect metaphor for this viewing experience.[3] As Howe explained, the sculptures seemed to come to life, indeed transcend a quotidian reality, when animated in this dramatic way.

The twenty-first-century perception of marble's cold white stoniness could not differ more from the nineteenth-century viewing experience. In fact, Jacob Abbott's *Rollo in Rome*, one of the most popular tour books of the mid–nineteenth century, depicts an evening excursion to the Vatican on its frontispiece (fig. 8). Nocturnal visits to the Vatican were strictly regulated; parties were limited to twelve people. Because of the expense of nighttime visits—especially the cost of the torch and its bearer—small parties assembled, as demonstrated by Abbott's frontispiece, to defray the nearly twenty-dollar fee. This type of illumination, the guidebook advised, "brings out the expression of the statues in a very striking manner, so as to produce sometimes a most wonderful effect."[4]

In Boston, the American expatriate sculptor Thomas Crawford exhibited his neoclassical sculpture *Orpheus and Cerberus* under similar conditions (fig. 9).[5] When it was first installed, Crawford viewed his sculpture by torchlight, claiming that he had finished the work under similar subdued lighting in Rome.[6] In 1844, the Boston Athenaeum showcased the work in a specially built gallery equipped with soft lighting, brown walls, a red carpet, and windows veiled with thin pink curtains and crimson gauze. Under these circumstances, the male nude appeared warm and sensual, with the browns and reds of the gallery environment softly reflecting off its polished white surfaces.[7]

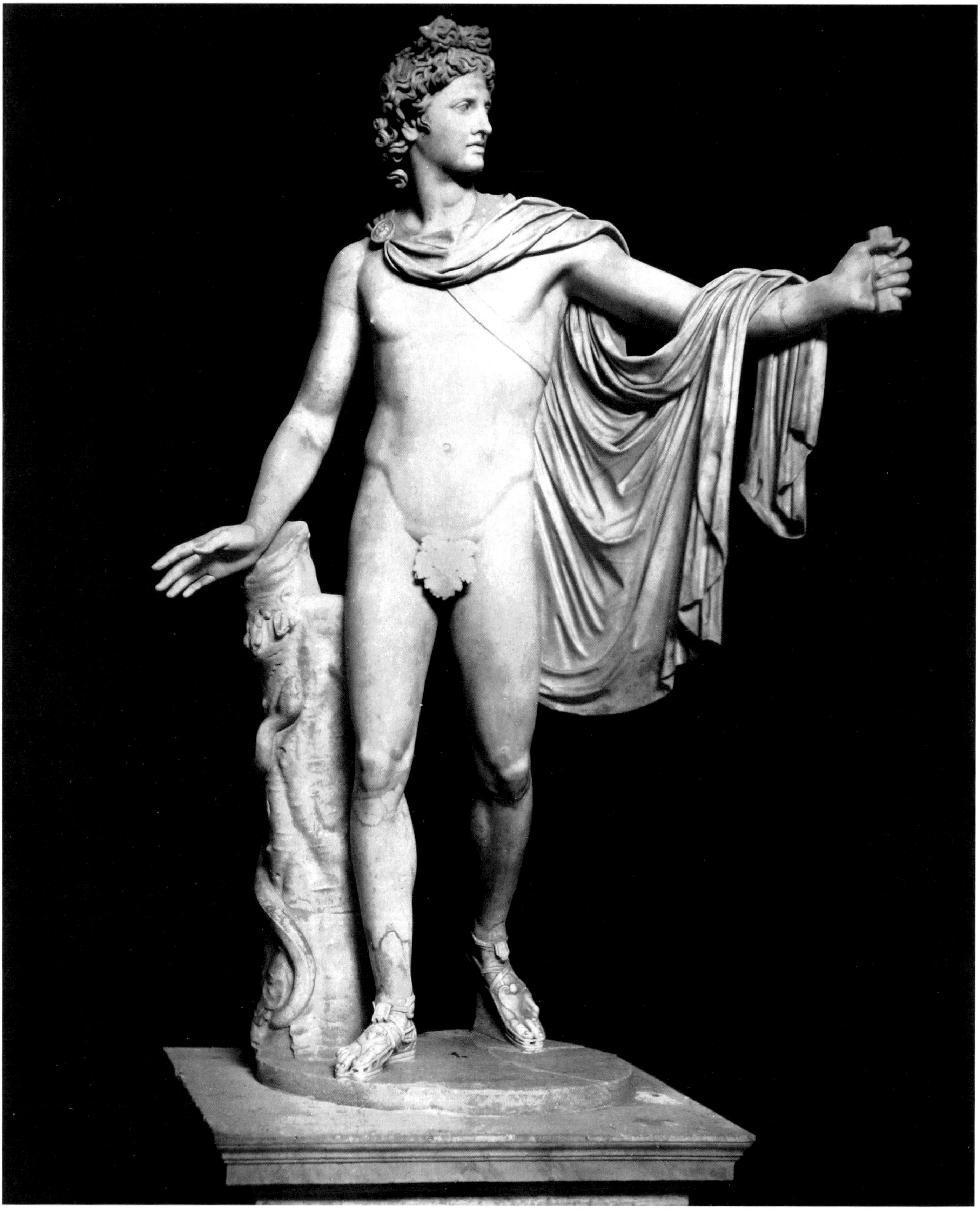

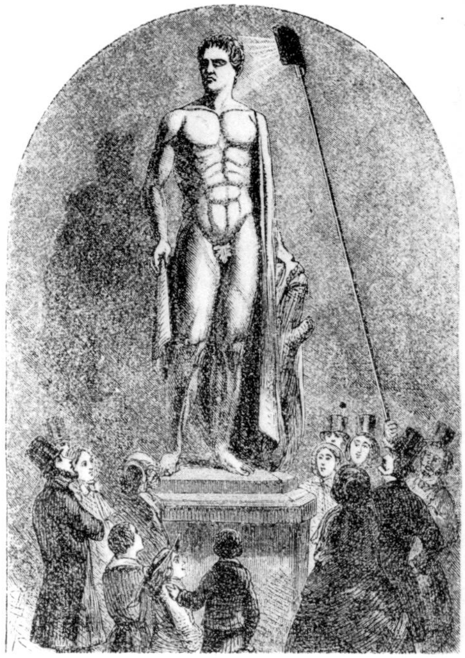

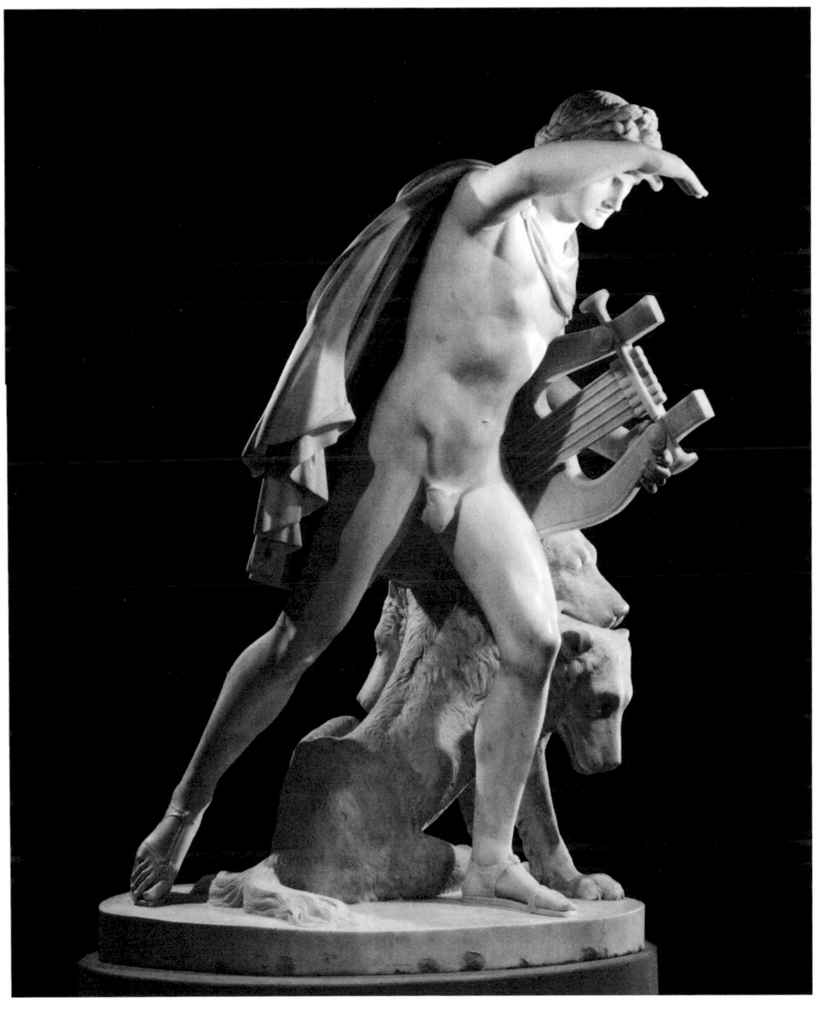

FIG. 7 *(opposite)*
*Apollo Belvedere,*
ca. 120–40, marble. Photograph ca. 1870. Museo Pio-Clementino, Vatican Museums, Vatican City.

FIG. 8
*The Vatican by Torchlight,* from Jacob Abbott, *Rollo in Rome* (Boston: Brown, Taggard & Chase, 1858), frontispiece. Photo: Daniel P. Younger.

FIG. 9
Thomas Crawford, *Orpheus and Cerberus,* 1843, marble, 171.5 × 91.4 × 137.2 cm. Museum of Fine Arts, Boston, museum purchase with funds by exchange from a gift of Mr. and Mrs. Cornelius C. Vermeule III, 1975.800. Photograph © 2014 Museum of Fine Arts, Boston.

The poet Orpheus, son of Apollo, was among the most popular figures in the American classical repertory.[8] According to myth, Orpheus fearlessly entered Hades to recover his beloved wife, Eurydice, who had died at an early age from a snake bite. In response to his heroism, Pluto, god of the underworld, freed Eurydice but forbade the poet to look at her until they had reached the terrestrial realm. In a moment of forgetfulness, Orpheus turned and glanced at Eurydice, who was immediately taken from him.[9] Imagining the poet's desperation, Crawford depicted the romantic hero lunging forward with billowing cape, having tamed the three-headed dog Cerberus, the guardian of Hades, with the music of his lyre.

In an essay published in 1843 Charles Sumner infused the pagan subject of Orpheus with the Christian virtues of chastity and fidelity.[10] Orpheus was one of those "rare husband[s]," the feminist Catharine Sedgwick wrote, who would follow his wife into the depths of hell.[11] In a special catalogue of the following year, Sumner included an additional testimony by Sedgwick, who praised the physical grace and moral purity of the figure.[12] Borrowing the figure's proportions from the famed *Apollo Belvedere,* Crawford was among the first sculptors to introduce this Greek ideal of "manly beauty" to American audiences.[13]

In writing to Sumner from Rome, the sculptor noted the troubled history of the nude in contemporary American culture. He recalled the uproar surrounding Horatio Greenough's *Chanting Cherubs* (now lost), which caused a furor in the United States because the little *putti* (the baby angels) were depicted nude. To assuage an outraged audience, the naked infants were forced to wear little aprons for the sake of modesty. In his letter, Crawford feared that "Sunday school mistresses" would do their bidding once more by making "poor Orpheus wear a shirt" in Boston. Or worse, Crawford continued, they would "make up a cargo of diapers after the latest fashion of the cherubs in Heaven so that modesty may not be shock'd upon arriving at the divine abode." Ultimately, the sculptor supplied *Orpheus* with a fig leaf to mollify any moral objections.[14] Veiled in its bourgeois morality, protected by its Christian virtues, and clad in a modest fig leaf, the male nude was thus introduced to Boston society.

The sculpture delicately communicated both propriety and sensuality. Its marble surface revealed a dry, matte finish that emphasized the properties of the hard cold stone. Moreover, the body demonstrated a simplified musculature and idealized physique. Indeed, when viewed in daylight, the figure of *Orpheus* appeared far removed from the contingencies of daily life (as if it had "died," as Howe had earlier stated). When exhibited in the warmly lit setting of the Athenaeum gallery, however, the sculpture's appearance was softened, "rendered so lifelike" by its "artful illumination." Under highly orchestrated and morally sanitized conditions, American museum visitors, often offended by the sight of the male nude in art, were free to appreciate the sculpture's sensuality.

In the special catalogue that accompanied the showing of the work in Boston, Sumner described the *Orpheus* as an "allegory of the artist seeking the ideal that always eludes him." Thomas Hicks, the American painter who would later eulogize Crawford, explained that the figure of *Orpheus* served as "the artist's [own] aspiration for the ideal—his search for the perfect beauty that forever allude[d] him."[15] Sumner and Hicks echoed Crawford's sculptural intention. "I am trying . . . to give an air of antique beauty to the whole composition," the sculptor wrote, "working as nearly as possible in the spirit of the ancient masters."[16] With these words, Crawford articulated the immense challenge that classical sculpture posed for contemporary artists.

Indeed, the stakes were quite high for neoclassical sculptors, who produced artwork that vied with antique perfection. As spokesman for the European academic tradition, Joshua Reynolds instructed artists to base their sculptural study on ancient art. In his *Discourse VI*, he intoned, "All the inventions and thoughts of the Antients [*sic*], whether conveyed to us in statues, bas-reliefs, intaglios, cameos, or coins, are to be sought after and carefully studied." At the same time, he insisted that these sculptures be "original" works of art.[17] This conundrum haunted late eighteenth- and nineteenth-century artists who chose to emulate antiquity. Referring to their art as the "true style," they balanced their desire for invention with the necessity of imitation. Only later did the term "neoclassical" come into use as an epitaph that decried the style's lack of originality to modern artists.[18]

Reynolds encouraged artists both to imitate antiquity and to be inventive, a conundrum that art historian Jonah Siegel described as the "unstable circularity of neoclassicism." Artists were required to work from antique models, but these very models were "by definition and common agreement impossible to reproduce." Neoclassicism remained intrinsically in crisis as it demanded a distant gazing at an object that could never be recovered, like a beloved that had been lost forever.[19] Like Orpheus, who traversed the netherworld in search of his lost love, only to gaze upon her and lose her, Crawford's sculpture allegorized the central challenge of neoclassicism—the sculptor's distant gazing at antiquity and the near futility of recovering the perfection of this aesthetic ideal.

Women artists reconfigured the dilemma of neoclassicism in significant ways. Knowledge of classical mythology played an important role in this endeavor and was particularly useful for those "who travel[ed] and visit[ed] museums and galleries of art" and who "interpret[ed] . . . paintings and sculptures."[20] Moreover, popular handbooks on mythology, like Bulfinch's *Age of Fable*, were often addressed to women and schoolchildren. The American sculptor Harriet Hosmer saw mythological stories as inspirational in their potential to articulate an alternative feminist reality. In both subject and style, her neoclassical work communicated directly with a progressive female audience in Rome, London, and the United States. Her mythic narratives associated the historical contingencies of daily life with the archetypal qualities of the feminine.[21] In so doing, her sculptures addressed the conundrum of neoclassicism by reconciling the universal claims of mythology with the immediacy of a sensual and naturalistic sculptural style.

## *Neoclassicism in Rome*

Neoclassical sculptors in Rome responded in a variety of ways to the challenge of antiquity. On the one hand, they understood that ancient art served as a creative stimulus to their work. On the other hand, they saw it, with its unattainable perfection, as a burden. The foremost practitioners of neoclassicism in Rome, Antonio Canova

(1757–1822) and Bertel Thorwaldsen (1770–1844), provided different aesthetic approaches to this dilemma. Canova pursued a sensuous style with careful attention to surface texture, which most closely approximated the fourth-century B.C.E. classical ideal of Praxiteles.[22] Perceiving an illicit danger in its "feminized grace and seductiveness," some Americans were quick to reject this sensual style. Alternatively, Thorwaldsen adopted the classical purity and formal restraint of the early fifth-century B.C.E. Severe style. For the most part, American viewers favored the more abstracted manner of Thorwaldsen, what art historian Alex Potts considered "a true male austerity," that is, a cerebral response to the artwork that denied the excesses of sensual pleasure.[23]

By 1792, Canova, a Venetian by birth, was arguably the most famous neoclassical sculptor in Europe.[24] His studio off via del Corso became one of the major tourist sights of Rome, especially after 1815, when Napoleonic rule of the peninsula had come to an end.[25] He often displayed his sculpture by torchlight to dramatic effect.[26] In de Staël's novel *Corinne,* when the fictive heroine visits Canova's studio with her lover, Oswald, Lord Nevil, they are shown around by torchlight: "[T]he more pronounced darkness dims the uniform dazzling whiteness of the marble, and the statues seem pale forms with more touching qualities of gracefulness and life."[27]

Canova was among the very few contemporary artists whose work was considered equal to that of the ancients. His sculptures were (and still are) exhibited alongside the Graeco-Roman masterpieces in the famous Belvedere Courtyard of the Vatican Museum. In fact, Pope Pius VII acquired Canova's *Triumphant Perseus* (fig. 10) in 1801 to replace the *Apollo Belvedere* (fig. 7), which Napoleon had spirited away to Paris in 1797.[28]

Canova's sculptural process, which consisted of five steps, had been in use at least since the Renaissance, when codified by Leon Battista Alberti, Giorgio Vasari, and Benvenuto Cellini. The artist first worked out the sculptural composition in a rough small-scale clay sketch, called the *bozzetto,* in which the sculptor strove to realize the *concetto,* the idea or conceit behind the work. Next, he produced a full-size clay *modello,* which he reinforced with an iron armature. From the *modello,* the plaster cast was taken. Italian workmen, highly trained artists in their own right, transferred the dimensions of the plaster to the marble with the aid of a pointing apparatus. After a workman (*lustratoro*) polished and cleaned the marble with a pumice stone, the sculptor usually "finished" the marble, demonstrating a virtuoso refinement in his carving.[29]

Like many busy sculptors, Canova employed an army of workmen to help produce the marble sculptures. These highly talented artisans often specialized in carving particular aspects of the figure, from drapery to hair and flesh. Sculptors and patrons alike often preferred the vitality of the original clay model (the *bozzetto*), abhorred the deathlike quality of the plaster, and celebrated the sculpture when "resurrected" in marble.[30] For the most part, sculptural works would remain in plaster unless commissioned in marble. Many different marble "originals" could be made from the same plaster statue. Once a patron ordered a work in marble, he or she usually paid one-half the cost of the sculpture in advance and the remainder upon completion of the sculpture. The entire process of producing a marble sculpture

FIG. 10
Antonio Canova, *Triumphant Perseus,* ca. 1800, marble. Museo Pio-Clementino, Vatican Museums, Vatican City.

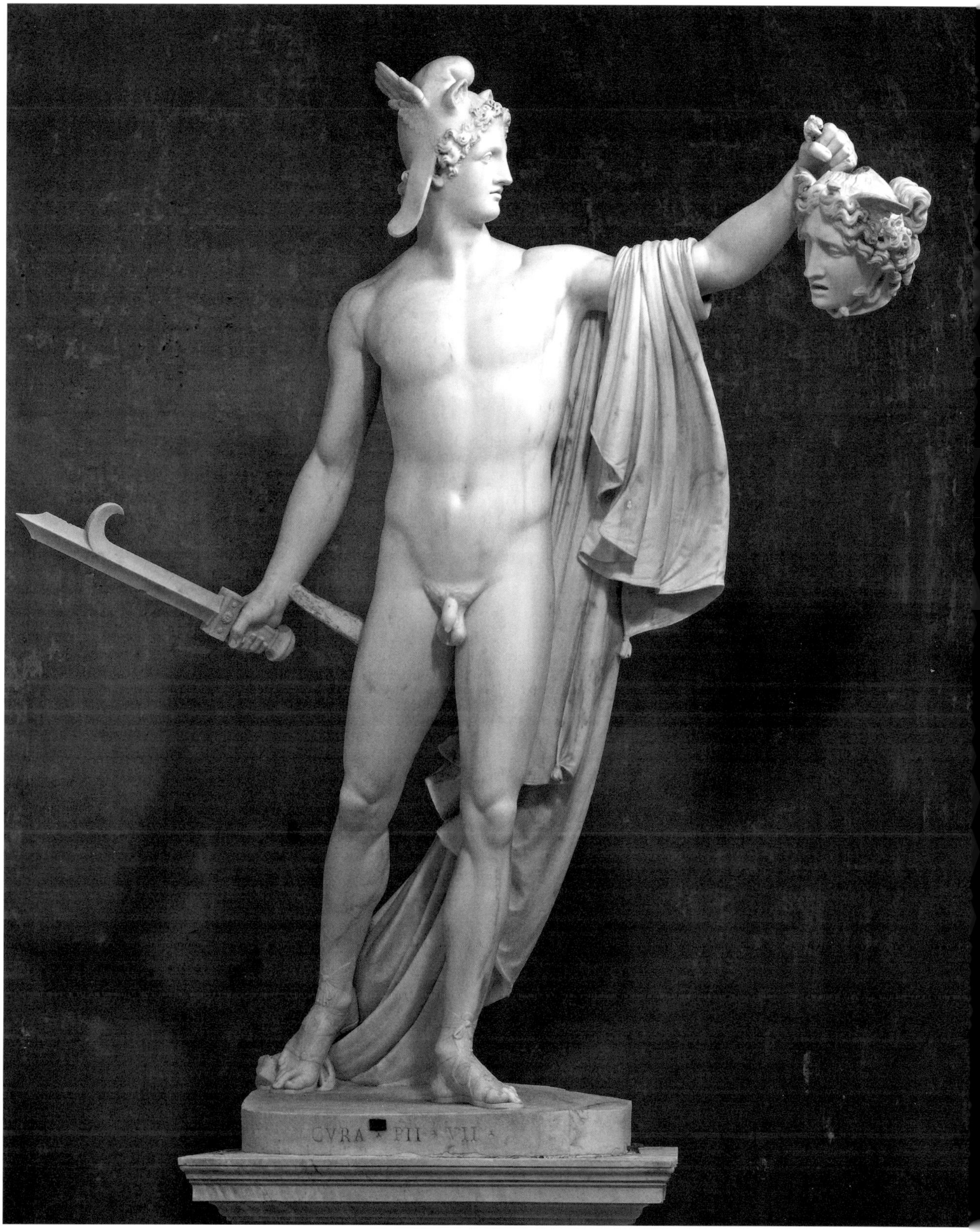

could take on average anywhere from six months to one year.[31]

Canova departed from traditional academic practice by refusing to copy classical masterworks.[32] In the nineteenth century, academic training led students through a discreet process, from imitation, where they learned practical skills, to invention, where the originality of the conceit triumphed over the craft of carving. In less talented students, this technique often resulted in a practice of mere copying and repetition. Canova offered an alternative approach to the study of the antique. He regularly completed his sculpture by candlelight rather than under the bright Italian sun. At times, he applied coloring to the marble that would reduce its glaring whiteness. Like the ancients, he tinted the surfaces, at times staining them with wax and grind-water, to simulate human warmth in the cold stone.[33] By coupling his interest in classical art with an attention to naturalistic detail and sensuous surface texture, he asserted the physicality of his sculpture. The sensual presence of the marble put many American viewers ill at ease and made them dangerously aware of the pleasures of viewing the neoclassical nude.[34]

Arriving in Rome in 1796, the Danish sculptor Thorwaldsen enjoyed an international celebrity, operating large work spaces on via Sistina.[35] After Canova's death in 1822, he became the ranking neoclassical sculptor in Rome. Thorwaldsen's purified surfaces denied any suggestion of sensuality and retained a hard flat finish as he refrained from polishing the marble in the manner of Canova. His figures lacked specific detail, referencing an ideal form. The generalized surfaces invited an unfocused viewing, which provided an emotional distance between viewer and work of art.[36] Adhering to Lutheran suspicion of aestheticism, Thorwaldsen's sculptures denied the viewer the pleasure of looking at the sensual body.

After his arrival in Rome in 1835, the American sculptor Thomas Crawford studied with Thorwaldsen for nearly one year. To the young sculptor, Thorwaldsen was the only living artist in Rome who "caught the spirit" of the ancients. Under Thorwaldsen's direction, his sculptural training consisted in drawing from live models at the French Academy and the Academy of Saint Luke, copying antique statuary in the Vatican and Capitoline collections, and even dissecting and drawing corpses in the Roman mortuary. According to Crawford, a young artist "will find everything he can possibly require for his studies [in Rome]; he lives among artists, and every step he takes in this garden for the arts presents something which assists him in the formation of his taste."[37]

Crawford opened his first studio on via del Orto di Napoli, which consisted of "three obscure, small and sunless apartments, so cold and damp that they strike a chill through you," Catharine Sedgwick explained.[38] Thorwaldsen visited him regularly to dispense criticism and advice. By 1837, Crawford's career was well under way in Rome. Accepted as a member of the prestigious Academy of Saint Luke, he became one of the leading lights of American neoclassicism. Showered with public commissions, he eventually occupied a studio with twelve rooms located in the ancient ruins of the Baths of Diocletian (today near Rome's Termini Railroad Station).[39] Tragically, the sculptor would be dead of a brain tumor by 1857.

The cosmopolitan city of Rome invited American sculptors to look at antiquity in disparate ways. For the most part, they adopted Thorwaldsen's ascetic sculptural style, which denied the sensual touch. However, under specific conditions of viewing, the soft torchlight of the Vatican Museum or the dimly lit environment of the Athenaeum gallery, neoclassical sculpture appeared less inert. American viewers experienced the sculptural figure corporeally, that is, in direct relation to his or her body. It was the effect of the light, rather than the sculptural surface itself, that suggested a lifelikeness, or the illusion of flesh and blood. In these circumstances, American neoclassical sculpture came closest to attaining antique perfection and a sensual originality.

The young Harriet Hosmer understood well the aesthetic challenges posed by the classical world. She studied with the foremost British neoclassical sculptor in Rome, John Gibson (1790–1866), who had been a student of both Canova and Thorwaldsen.[40] Despite his fame, Gibson confessed that his "artistic ambition" would become "depressed" when touring the sculptural collection in the Vatican Museum. For "the Greeks were gods" in the art of sculpture, he argued; their "eminence . . . beyond our reach."[41] Conceding the limits of neoclassicism, he shifted his aesthetic emphasis from the ideal to the human.

In 1850, Gibson produced his most controversial sculpture, the *Tinted Venus,* which surpassed even Canova in its sensual lifelikeness (fig. 11). The figure stood in *contrapposto,* with arms folded modestly around her abdomen and drapery cascading to the ground, partially concealing the nude torso. She held the golden apple, the prize in Paris's judgment of beauty. Using antique recipes, Gibson applied a thin layer of hot

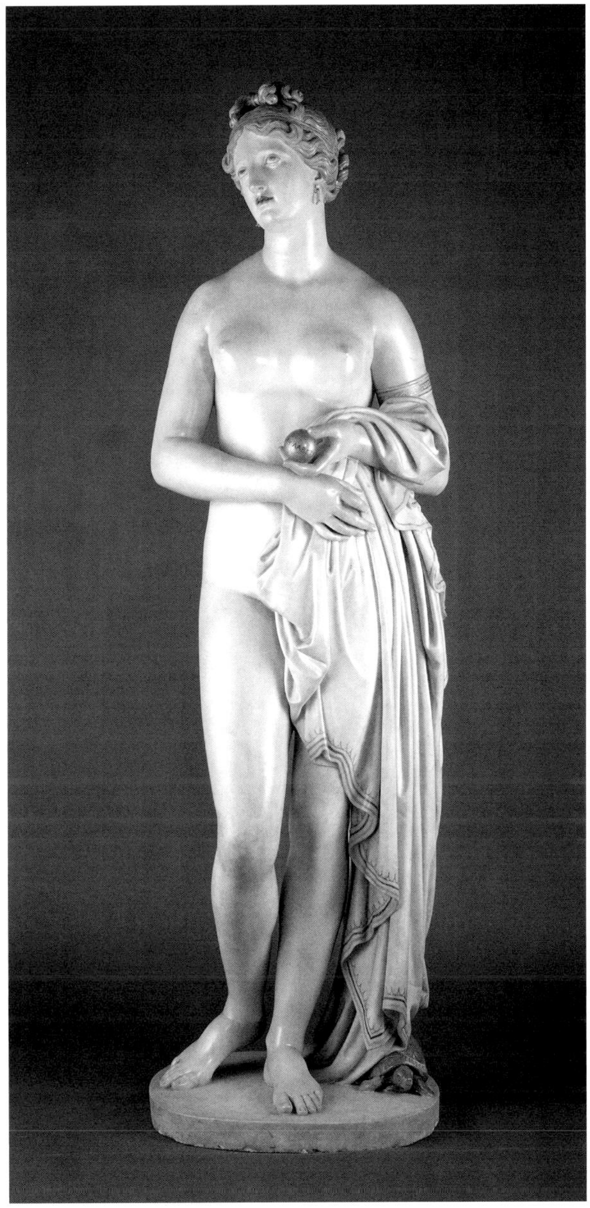

FIG. 11
John Gibson, *Tinted Venus,* ca. 1851–56, tinted marble. Courtesy National Museums Liverpool (Walker Art Gallery).

wax mixed with paint to the sculptural surface. He tinted the lips a rosy hue, painted the irises blue and the hair blond, and outlined the drapery in a colorful linear patterning, arguing that this technique was historically authentic as the Greeks had also added color to their marble statuary.[42] Defying the properties of stone—the figure wore gold earrings and a golden armlet—the female nude accosted the viewer with its fleshlike properties.[43]

The controversy did not prevent the touring classes from visiting his studio and viewing, with rapt attention, the sculptural nude.[44] The *Tinted Venus* "that everybody was talking about," one American visitor noted, "was making a great sensation in the art world. . . . It was colored so like life that . . . the creature really seemed to be alive." Quite disingenuously, the writer concluded that "it must have been an awful thing!"[45] The expatriate poet Elizabeth Barrett Browning saw the sculpture at London's Great Exhibition of 1851. A few years later, after viewing the *Tinted Venus* in Gibson's studio, she wrote to the British art historian Anna Jameson about the piece. She complained that the classical figure "has come out of her cloud of the ideal." With the sculpture's blatant humanity—its naturalistic coloring and specific decorative jewelry—the female body no longer evinced the ideal and thus, to Barrett Browning, eluded common decency.[46]

Hosmer studied with Gibson when the *Tinted Venus* was on view in his Roman studio. One of the few students he accepted, she set up shop under his supervision on the second floor of his studio in 1852. She sat by him for hours, watching him model his figures.[47] In her first year of study, much of her time was occupied with copying antique statuary, such as the head of the *Venus de Milo* and the *Cupid* of Praxiteles.[48] After five years, Gibson encouraged Hosmer to open her own workplace on via Margutta (just around the corner from his via Fontenella studio) in order to create an independent professional identity for herself. That she did quickly, but she continued to study with Gibson until 1860, learning to create sensuous neoclassical sculptures from her teacher. Their close personal and professional camaraderie ended with his death in 1866.[49]

## Daphne *and* Medusa

Gibson's biographer, Lady Eastlake, opined that in his talented student (Hosmer) he had "raised a living monument to himself."[50] There was no doubt that the young sculptor had indeed learned the lessons of her teacher. She matured into an independent and original artist—one of the most talented sculptors in Rome. Early on, while still working in Gibson's studio, she produced her first significant works, *Daphne* (fig. 12) and *Medusa* (fig. 13), both of 1854, creating sensuous heroines that appealed to female viewers. Gibson praised both works. In the naturalism of the flesh, he "had never seen [her sculpture] surpassed and seldom equaled." They "do her great honor."[51] Like the work of her teacher, these sculptural busts exuded a sensuality in their handling of the marble, regardless of their environment—the bright Roman sunshine or the torchlit gallery.

FIG. 12 *(opposite)* Harriet Hosmer, *Daphne*, 1854, marble, 26 1/2 × 19 1/2 × 13 1/2 in. Mildred Lane Kemper Art Museum, Washington University in St. Louis, gift of Wayman Crow Sr., 1880.

Hosmer was unique in depicting the mythological figures of *Daphne* and *Medusa* as pendants (intended to be viewed and interpreted as a pair). With her selective recovery of ancient heroines—and she almost always represented women in her sculpture—she chose her protagonists carefully.

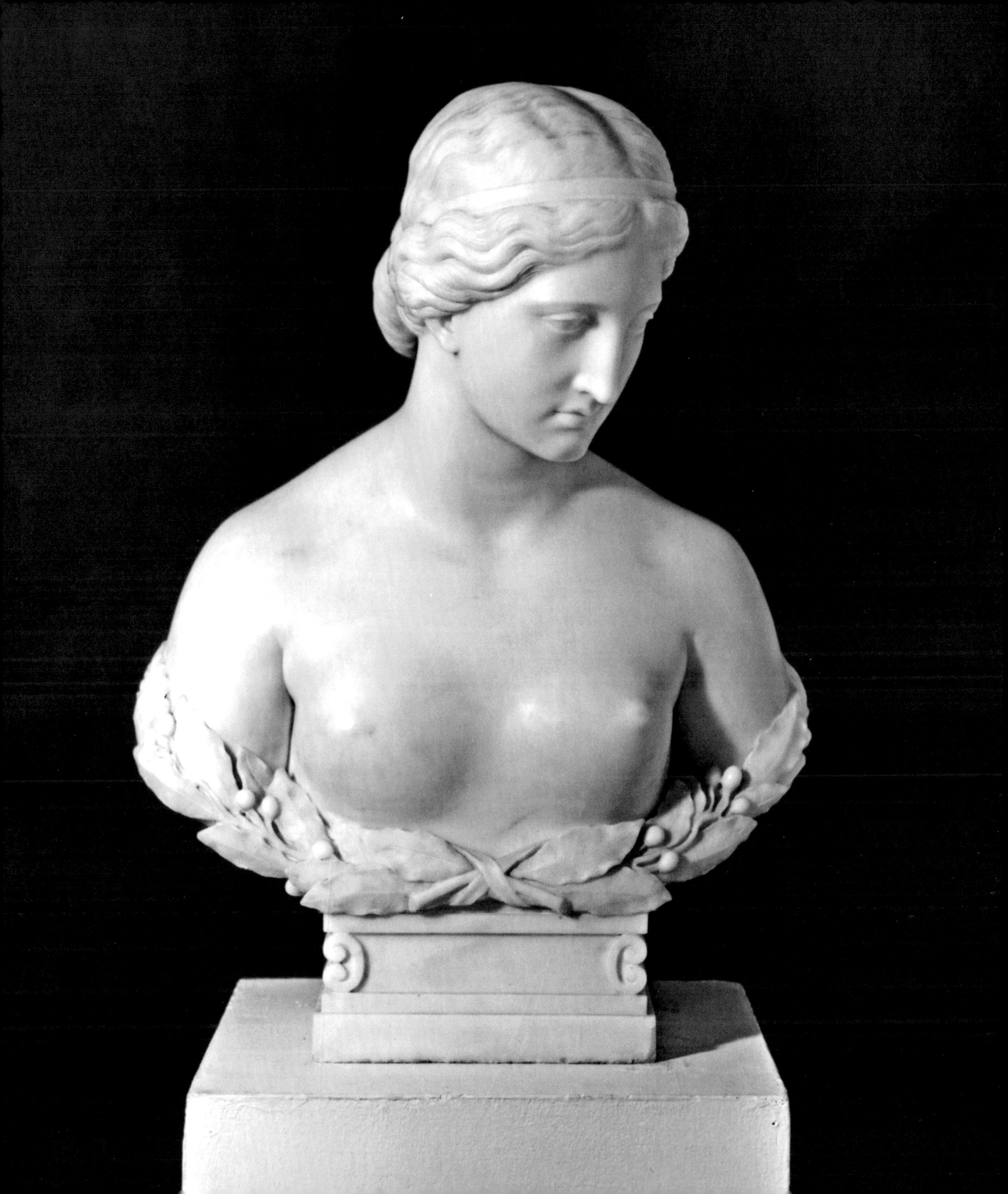

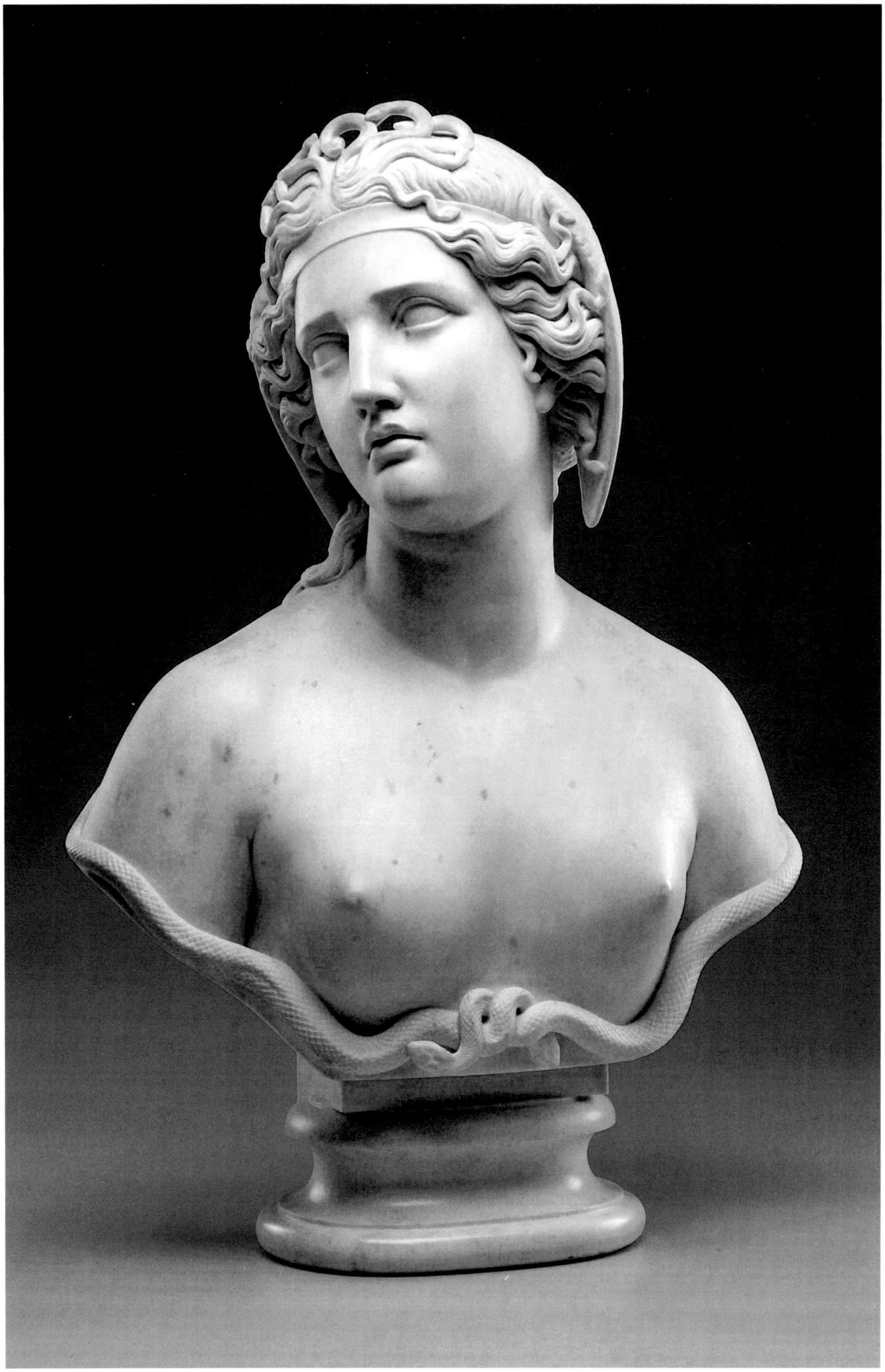

FIG. 13
Harriet Hosmer, *Medusa,* 1854, marble. Detroit Institute of Arts, Founders Society Purchase, R. H. Tannahill Foundation Fund.

By highlighting certain aspects of their narrative and ignoring others, she expanded and transformed the cultural meanings assigned to these figures. Sharing the theme of metamorphosis, *Daphne* and *Medusa* embody the possibilities of a fluid feminine identity rather than a static subjectivity defined by patriarchal norms.[52]

In selecting the nymph Daphne, who preferred running freely in the forest to the bonds of matrimony, Hosmer chose a mythological subject that was close to her heart. The beautiful Daphne became the unwitting target of Apollo's affections after Cupid mischievously shot him with an arrow. He pursued the virginal nymph relentlessly, "like a hound pursuing a hare, with open jaws ready to seize." Daphne ran on "the wings of . . . fear" and prayed to her father, the river god Peneus, for salvation: "Dearest Father, grant me this favor, that I may always remain unmarried, like Diana." Peneus consented, transforming his daughter into a laurel tree just moments before her capture.[53] In her devotion to celibacy, Daphne, like the goddess Diana, represented feminine purity and chastity. To modern nineteenth-century women like Hosmer, she resembled a tomboy, a young woman who insisted upon an active (boyish) life instead of surrendering to matrimony. Daphne's rejection of marriage no doubt constituted a heroic act for Hosmer and her feminine audience. Readers of mid-nineteenth-century novels by Charlotte Brontë, for example, were familiar with unmarried heroines, whose "virgin freedom" signified a liberating feminine autonomy.[54] The nymph Daphne and goddess Diana often served as models for this new type of womanhood.

In her sculptural style, Hosmer combined a sensuous naturalism with the geometric clarity of the fifth-century B.C.E. classical ideal. She rendered the proportions of the bust quite naturally, the shoulders and arms appearing fuller than in *Hesper* (fig. 3). The softened and naturalized breasts were carefully modeled from life. The face, however, inspired by Greek Severe-style sculpture, stands in sharp contrast to the naturalism of the body.[55] The idealized geometry of the visage, with its distant gaze, offers a visual counterpoise to the dangerously lifelike body. Outlining the lower edge of the sculpture, a delicate festoon reveals interlacing laurel leaves and berries that subtly suggest the nymph's imminent transformation.

Daphne's travail is not encoded in Hosmer's bust; rather, the figure demonstrates a serene and contemplative manner, evoking a somewhat surprising sense of autonomy and control. The classical ideal required a type of self-possession, or state of "blissful self-sufficiency," as Alex Potts would have it, that exemplified an untroubled relationship to the surrounding world. As a general rule, this attitude of independence from the contingencies of modern life suggested an eighteenth-century ideology of liberalism in which the universal male subject appeared in control and as master of his world.[56] Women by nature were considered passive and emotional beings, dependent upon their male protectors. Hosmer's *Daphne,* by contrast, gives visual form to an alternative feminine experience, one that expresses a cool and detached psychic autonomy and offers a strikingly refreshing commentary upon female consciousness.

Stylistically, Hosmer's bust is far removed from the dynamic excitement of Bernini's famed *Apollo and Daphne* (fig. 14), which she probably knew from her visits to the Borghese Gallery.

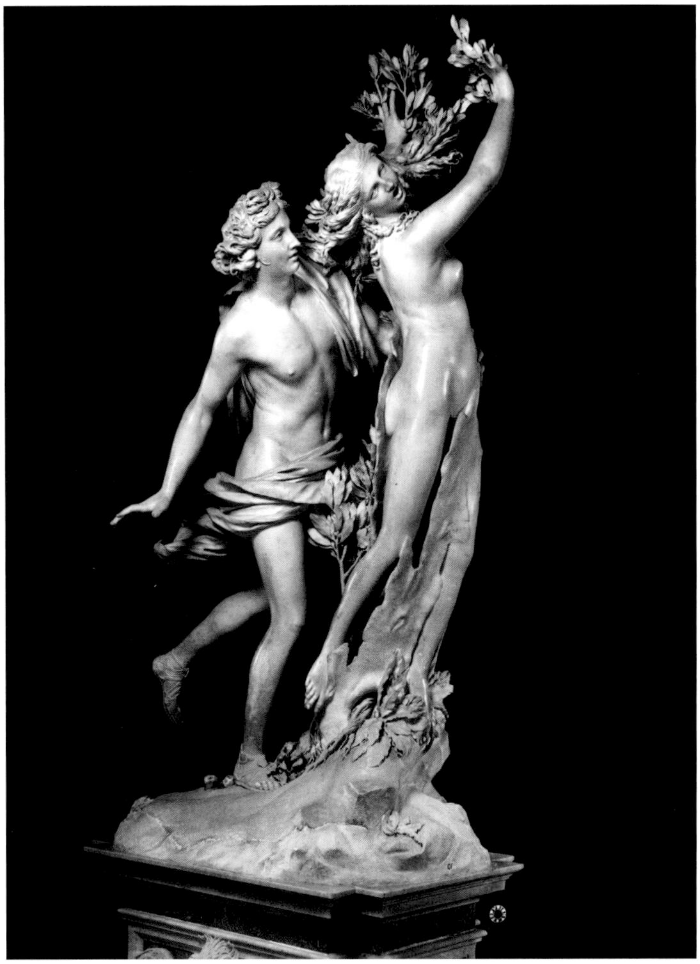

FIG. 14
Gian Lorenzo Bernini, *Apollo and Daphne,* 1622–25, marble. Galleria Borghese, Rome.

While Bernini's female protagonist expresses fear and dread through her facial features and posture, Hosmer's sculpture expresses a quiet calm. Hosmer understood that Graeco-Roman statuary differed from the Baroque in its lack of theatricality, that is, its psychic distance from the surrounding world. Like many artists working at the time, she was repulsed by Baroque emotionalism, seeing it as anathema to the self-containment of the classical ideal.

Hosmer reworked the popular myth of Apollo and Daphne to suggest female agency. As one critic has explained, the artist "reads Greek fable with an eye of her own."[57] Hosmer's nymph, rather than submit to her fate, chooses it. In representing the moment of transformation, the artist recast a story conventionally associated with victimhood into a potent tale of resistance. *Daphne* communicates a feminine independence. The simplified and austere facial features reference the masculine ideology of liberalism. Moreover, her refusal to engage the viewer signals a masterly disengagement from the world around her. Simultaneously, the sensuality of the torso and breasts celebrates the female body. In her first work produced in Rome, Hosmer created a neoclassical bust that telegraphed a new type of female subjectivity.

After completing the *Daphne,* Hosmer turned to the mythological subject of Medusa, a beautiful woman whom Neptune ravished in the Temple of Athena. Jealous of her loveliness, the goddess Athena transformed Medusa into a Gorgon, a terrifying female creature with entangled snakes for hair. One glance at her hideous face would turn a male viewer to stone. Of the three sister Gorgons, Medusa was the only mortal. The hero Perseus slew Medusa while she slept by safely looking upon her reflection in his bronze shield. He triumphantly cut off her head and presented it to Athena, who placed it on her shield to ward off evil and subdue her foes. Hosmer chose also to present Medusa in a moment of transformation: her beauty still intact yet her hair turning irrevocably into a serpentine mass. Slender snakes coil into decorative arabesques and form an aureole around her full face. Her graceful shoulders and torso terminate in a simple ribbon of serpents.

Hosmer's *Medusa* attracted more attention than her bust of *Daphne,* as the former represented both a dangerous monster and a desirable beauty to nineteenth-century audiences. The Romantic poet Shelley, for example, cast Medusa as the embodiment of "the tempestuous loveliness of terror."[58] Rather than picture the monstrous Gorgon, as had Bulfinch, "with huge teeth like those of a swine, brazen claws, and snaky hair,"[59] Hosmer depicted Medusa with pathos, humanity, and self-possession, characteristics rarely allowed her in visual representation. The figure's facial features and softly modeled neck and torso resist ideal abstraction. Moreover, the body exudes a quiet sensuality that denies the Gorgon's monstrousness. The naturalism with which Hosmer sculpted this bust references Medusa's humanity. Moreover, the narrative imaginatively captures Medusa's state of mind, as the young maiden turns away from the viewer with an expression of profound melancholy.

Hosmer knew of at least two other sculptural versions of the Medusa myth in Rome: Canova's *Triumphant Perseus* (fig. 10) and Gian Lorenzo Bernini's *Bust of Medusa* (fig. 15). The famous *Perseus* by Canova inhabited a privileged location in the Vatican galleries, where it was viewed by a legion of Anglo-American artists, tourists, and expatriates. The figure stands in *contrapposto* with arms extended laterally, head in profile, and drapery gently cascading behind the nude torso. The hero extends his sword to the side, offering a formal and psychic balance to the head of Medusa, which he grips with his other hand (fig. 16). Perseus stares at the severed head, his gaze redoubling the victory that his sword had earlier delivered. The extended saber reinforces the hero's phallic power, which he has demonstrated through his conquest of the dangerous female monster.

Compared with Bernini's *Bust of Medusa* (ca. 1636) in the Capitoline Museum, Canova's *Medusa* is more humanized, her mouth emitting a desperate cry, her eyes appearing to weep, and her head crowned with two symmetrical serpents' heads. Writing to his patron the Polish countess Valeria Tarnowska, who purchased an 1808 replica of the famous *Perseus,* Canova advocated animating the Medusa head by inserting a candle into the hollow marble form. It seemed that Canova imagined the Medusa as a flickering phantasm, emitting an independent life source distinct from that of Perseus.[60] By contrast, Bernini depicted the

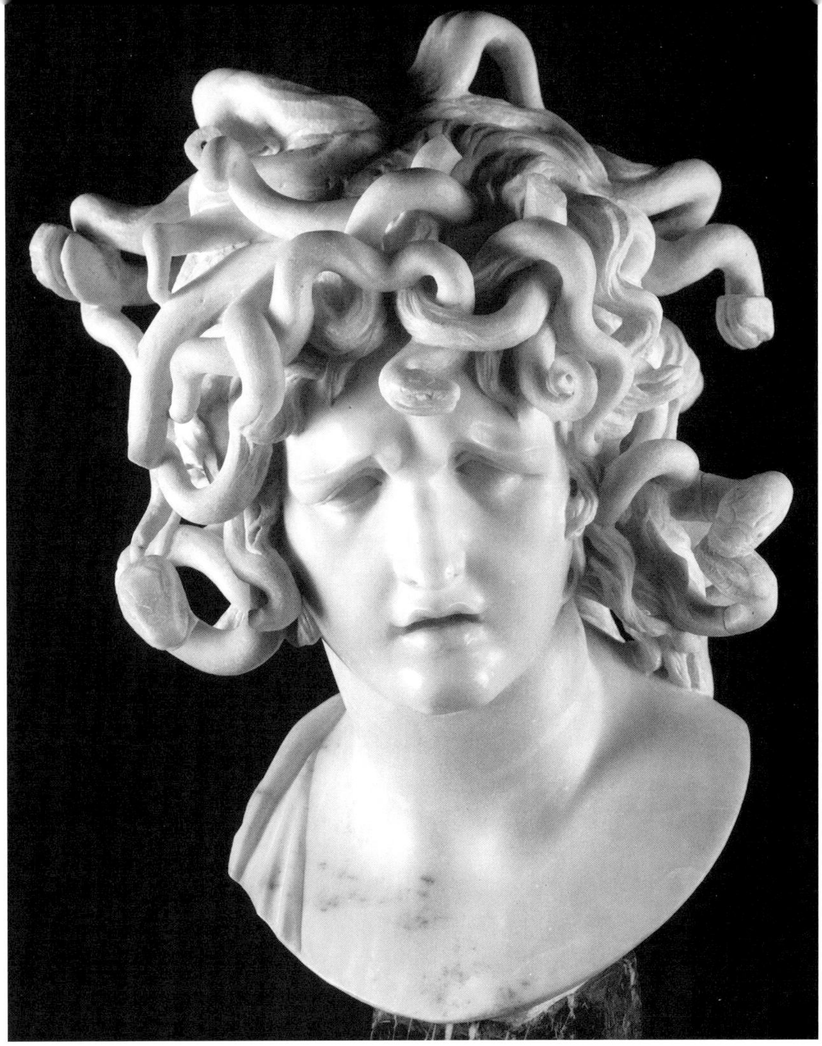

FIG. 15
Gian Lorenzo Bernini, *Bust of Medusa,* 1636, marble. Musei Capitolini, Rome.

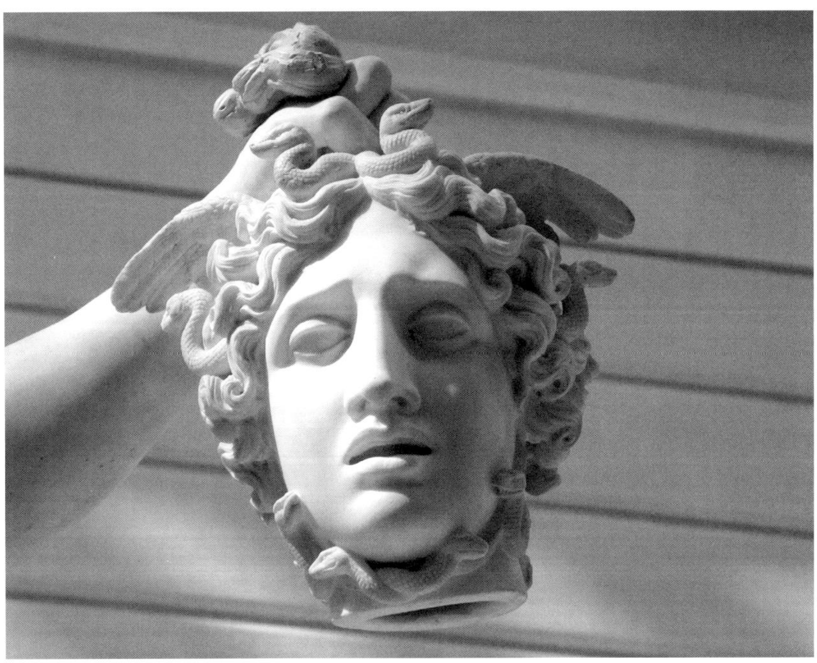

FIG. 16
Antonio Canova, *Triumphant Perseus* (fig. 10), detail of the head of Medusa.

once beautiful Medusa with a tortured grimace and large active snakes roiling about her head and face. The more-than-life-size bust was monstrous, instilling fear in those who viewed it.[61]

The head of Medusa demonstrated an alluring intensity for nineteenth-century viewers, both male and female.[62] As Canova's biographers explained, "The countenance of Medusa possesses at once a beauty and a horror which . . . exercises a sort of fascination over us."[63] Although not a particularly common theme in mid-nineteenth-century American art, the Medusa myth represented, according to art historian Sarah Burns, a dark, uncontrollable, and all-consuming energy that lay hidden below the smooth surfaces of the classical ideal.[64] This powerful theme played an important role in Freud's theory of psychoanalysis, which offers a symbolic model of the workings of the Victorian mind. Feminists, in particular, find psychoanalytic theory enlightening because it provides a means of understanding sexual difference (the symbolic presence or absence of the phallus, that is, masculine power or agency) that goes beyond social and ideological considerations. Psychoanalytic theory invites an investigation of the precarious psychic nature of gendered subjectivity and attempts to dismantle the patriarchal norms by which masculinity and femininity are socially constructed.[65]

Freud variously interprets the mythological figure of Medusa, but always from the perspective of the male psyche. The snakes encircling her head imply to the male viewer the presence of false penises, unconsciously calling to mind the image of a powerful masculinized woman. Only Medusa's death by decapitation resolves the anxiety caused by such unleashed feminine power.[66] The sight of the decapitated head of Medusa, as in Canova's *Perseus,* reassures male spectators that the masculinized/manly woman no longer poses a threat to the autonomy and independence of the privileged male sphere.

The Medusa myth also signifies castration anxiety on several contradictory levels.[67] Freud does not consider the act of castration as a physical reality, but as a symbolic experience tethered to the visual:[68] "The terror of Medusa," he wrote, "is thus a terror of castration that is linked to the sight of something." The snakes signal the pubic hair around the castrated sex of the mother, thus invoking anxiety in the male viewer. Simultaneously, the "sight of Medusa's head makes the spectator stiff with terror, turns him to stone," Freud concluded. "For becoming stiff means an erection. Thus . . . it offers consolation to the spectator."[69] Alternatively, the plenitude of snakes mollify the psychic fear of castration. Within this patriarchal universe, Medusa poses both a threat and a comfort to male viewers alone. To Freud, the female viewer is invisible.[70]

The female viewer, however, was present; she saw Hosmer's *Medusa* when exhibited in Rome, Boston, and elsewhere. To this audience, the sculpture subverted traditional patriarchal meanings associated with the myth. Hosmer's *Medusa* looks down and away from the viewer, refusing to engage the male psychic trauma. Indeed, women have read the Medusa story differently through history: her decapitated head often serving as a symbol of "the mannish woman" and thus signifying feminine empowerment. From the writings of Christine de Pizan in the fifteenth century to those of the poststructuralist feminist Hélène Cixous in the twentieth century, the mythological figure of Medusa functions as a sign of women's emancipation.[71]

In keeping with this tradition, the Anglo-American women's community in Rome understood *Medusa* as a feminist emblem. Hosmer herself posited Medusan imagery at the entrance to her home on via Gregoriana, adjacent to the domicile of Charlotte Cushman and the sculptor Emma Stebbins. The door knocker on the *portone* (the heavy exterior door) depicted the head of Medusa, whose hair showed only the first suggestion of turning into snakes, serpentine forms emerging on the left edge of the curls and on the forehead (fig. 17). The door handles comprised intertwining serpents (fig. 18), not unlike those near the base of Hosmer's bust of *Medusa*. In the ironwork directly above the doorway, the initials "H. H." proudly announced the sculptor's residence, where she moved in 1864 (fig. 19).[72]

Hosmer used Medusan imagery in many different contexts, all of which refused the Gorgon's monstrousness. The bust of *Medusa*, with

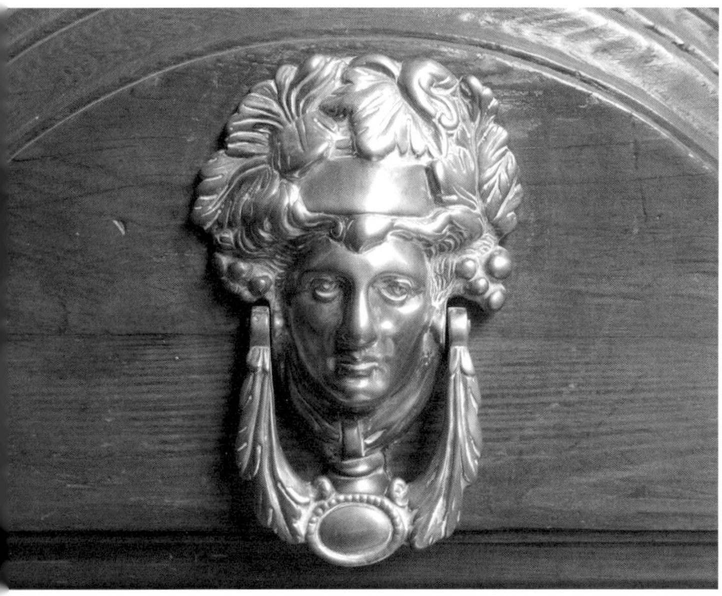

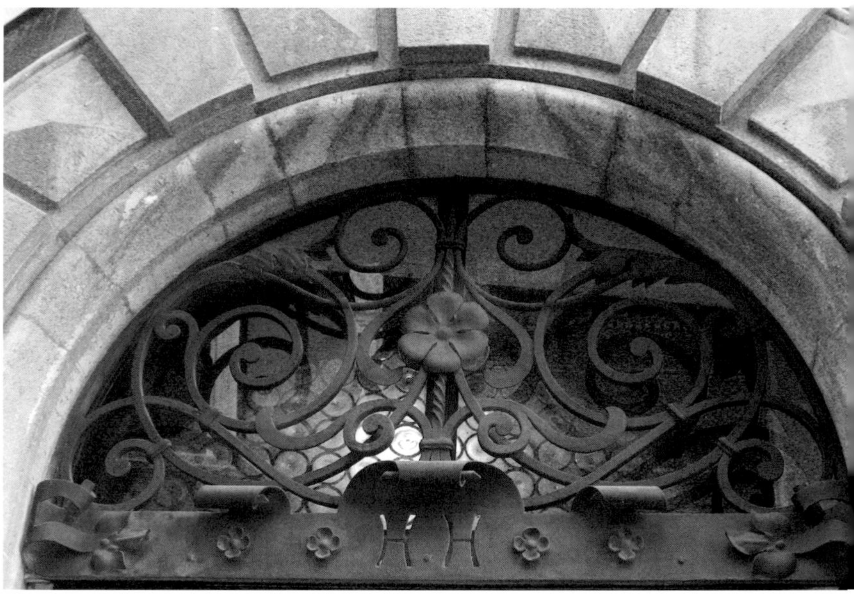


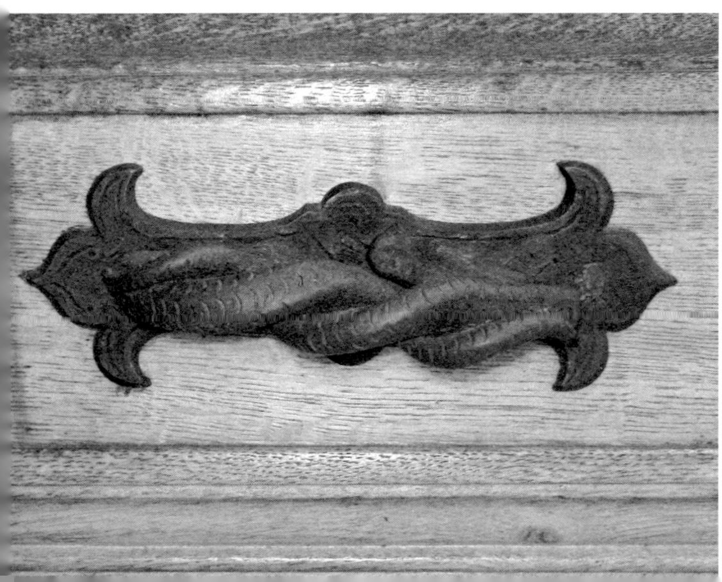

FIG. 17 *(above left)*
Door knocker, home of Harriet Hosmer, via Gregoriana, Rome.

FIG. 18 *(left)*
Door handle, home of Harriet Hosmer, via Gregoriana, Rome.

FIG. 19 *(above right)*
Doorway with initials "H. H.," home of Harriet Hosmer, via Gregoriana, Rome.

its sensuous naturalism, emblematized a new feminine emancipated life in Rome. The image appears not only on the breast of plate of the *Minerva* (figs. 56 and 57), a plaster cast of which stood in Hosmer's studio, but also on the belt worn by Hosmer's *Zenobia in Chains* (figs. 25 and 55). Moreover, the Medusa image may have served as a conceptual self-portrait of the artist. Like the Gorgon who metaphorically turned male viewers to stone, the sculptor literally transformed her subjects into marble. Reversing the Pygmalion myth, the female artist rendered eternal the Enlightenment ideals normally gendered masculine within a neoclassical paradigm.

Anglo-American women in Rome heralded Medusa as a symbol of a powerful "masculinized" woman who openly resisted the qualities associated with true womanhood. Cushman and her partner Matilda Hays, for example, openly enacted the guise of the "mannish woman"; similarly, Hosmer displayed the traits of the "tomboy." The Medusan emblem offered symbolic shelter in Rome to expatriate women sculptors and writers who transgressed into traditionally male professional arenas.

## *Hosmer and the Female Nude*

Living the artist's life in Rome was not always easy. After two years, Hosmer found herself in financial difficulties; she had bills coming due for marble and had to pay for ongoing work by studio assistants.[73] Her father, with economic troubles of his own at home, was no longer able to support her Roman sojourn. In fact, Dr. Hosmer was convinced that his daughter would soon return to Watertown when her money ran out. He was wrong. "My father says that of all places in the world, Watertown is the place for him, and I say that of all places in the world, Rome is the one for me." The sculptor was committed to living in Rome, no matter the cost. As a sign of her determination, she even sold her beloved horse.[74] At the age of twenty-four, she was resolute: "Nothing this side of Eternity will induce me to go to America to live for the next twenty-five years."[75]

During this challenging time, the young sculptor gained business acumen. Although the expenses associated with the sculptural profession were high, she admitted to Wayman Crow, her future benefactor, that she had "spent money with too little thought."[76] After counseling Hosmer about her finances, Crow offered support to the sculptor in 1854, when she created her first (and only) female nude, *Oenone* (figs. 20 and 21). She was grateful for the support of her "Pater/patron," as she called Crow, and was ready to tackle a new artistic problem: "After all, busts are not so satisfactory to make as statues," she explained, "for one is so limited in the power of expressing one's thoughts." She wrote to Crow regularly, describing her progress on the sculpture. She repeated again and again how hard she worked, detailing the difficulties an artist had to surmount. "It is work, work, work," she wrote, when complaining that others did not understand "the length of time one must study."[77] Despite her youthful indiscretions, she wanted Crow to know that she was worthy of his support, both financial and emotional.

In beginning the new project, she turned to her teacher, John Gibson, for guidance. She most likely knew his *Oenone,* which had been inspired by a shepherd girl he had seen on a walk in the

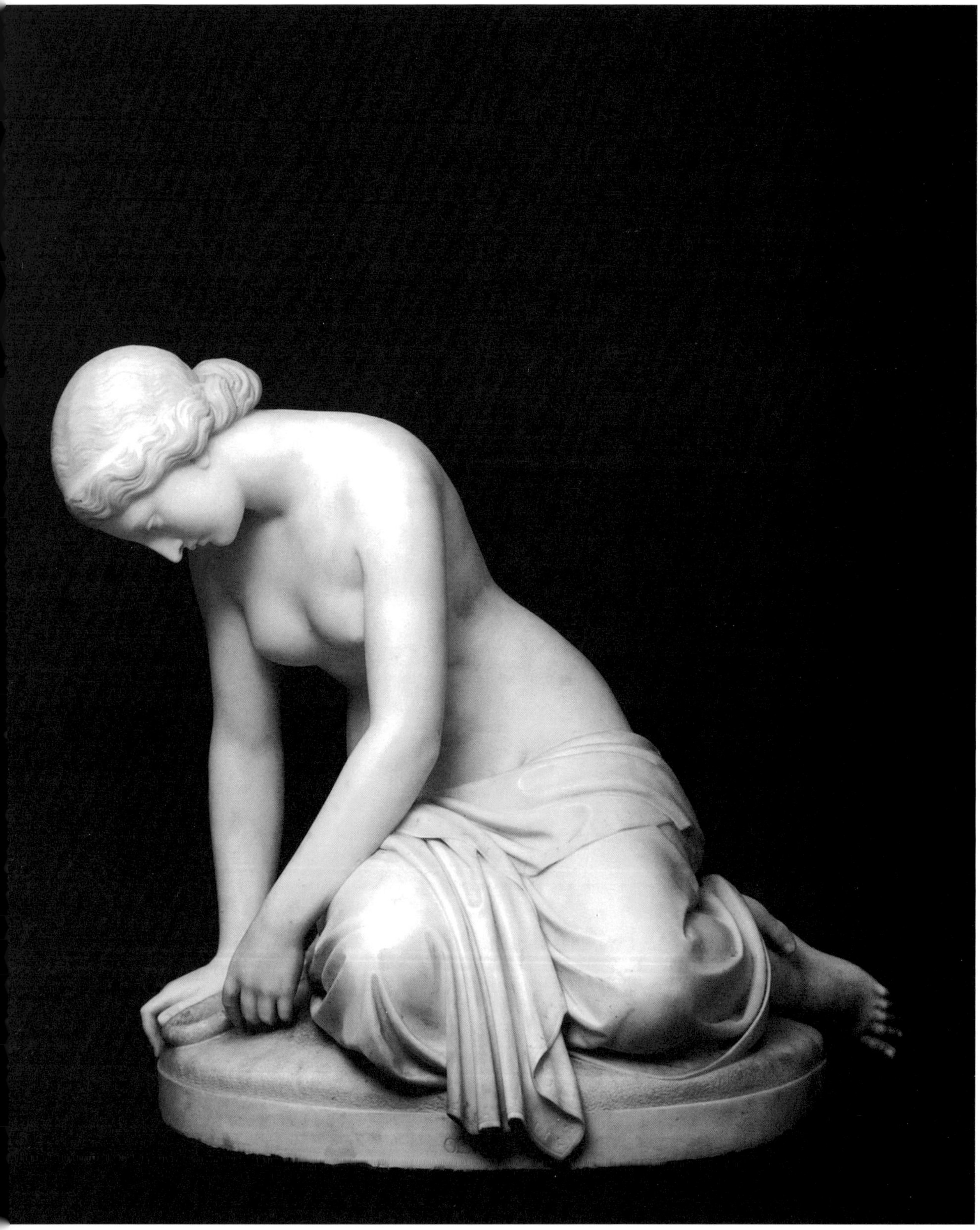

FIG. 20
Harriet Hosmer, *Oenone*, 1854–55, marble, 33 3/8 × 34 3/4 × 26 3/4 in. Mildred Lane Kemper Art Museum, Washington University in St. Louis, gift of Wayman Crow Sr., 1855.

Campagna, the rolling fields outside the city walls of Rome. Moreover, she had carefully studied his *Narcissus,* which he modeled from life, a cast of which remained in his studio in the 1850s.[78] Hosmer created a rather sensual rendering of Oenone, a naiad, or nymph of fountains and streams, who resided on Mount Ida. She was the beloved of Paris before he deserted her for the Trojan queen Helen. Borrowing the pose and contemplative manner of Gibson's *Narcissus,* she depicted the nymph less than life-size, collapsed with grief after having been abandoned by her lover.[79] She no doubt responded to the lament in Tennyson's poem "Oenone": "My eyes are full of tears, my heart of love, / My heart is breaking, and my eyes are dim, / And I am all aweary of my life."[80]

While at work on this sculpture, Hosmer caused quite a stir among the Anglo-American community in Rome. Following Gibson's example, she modeled her figure from life.[81] Outraged by Hosmer's "impertinence," Thomas Crawford wrote to his wife: "Miss H[osmer]'s want of modesty is enough to disgust a dog." He decried in the strongest of terms the "casts of the *entire female* model" that she "exhibited in a shockingly indecent manner" to all visitors to her studio.[82] Even Elizabeth Barrett Browning chafed upon entering Hosmer's studio in 1854, where she found the artist working from the nude model. We already know that Barrett Browning felt uncomfortable in the presence of Gibson's *Tinted Venus* (fig. 11). However, she was much more disturbed by this studio visit, where the sight of the nude model offended her "womanly instincts." She actually "preferred the company of Mr. Gibson's painted Venus," she wrote to her friend Ilsa Bragdon, which was "*nearly* as bad . . . as any natural nudity." She continued, "I would rather see a nude male model in the company of a man (though my husband) than a nude female model—and I would rather *not* see either."[83] What was particularly galling to Crawford—and disturbing to Barrett Browning—was that a professional female sculptor would have the same access to the nude as a male sculptor. In fact, the availability of live models in Rome was a great boon to American sculptors, especially women. In the United States of the 1850s, life classes were for the most part closed to female art students.

With *Oenone,* Hosmer entered into a long-lived controversy regarding the female nude in American art. Most commonly realized in mythological imagery, the neoclassical nude visualized transcendent ideas when embodied in the perfected human form. For an American audience, however, modesty remained an essential condition of the female nude. The strategic placement of drapery or hands was essential to a sculpture's success, as seen in Hiram Powers's *Greek Slave,* the most famous American neoclassical sculpture of the nineteenth century (fig. 26). *Oenone* far surpasses Powers's work in terms of modesty, as she wears a drape that covers her lower body. Her head and upper torso lean to the left over Paris's abandoned shepherd's crook. Her gaze and posture are turned inward in a sorrowful lament, a self-contained pose that shields the body from prying eyes. *Oenone* enacts a private moment of mourning from which the viewer is excluded. Her closed posture refuses engagement with the world.

When viewed from the rear, however, the sculpture expresses a soft sensuousness that elicits the pleasurable gaze (fig. 21). The female body displays a warm eroticism typical of Gibson's nudes. The nymph's left foot slides off

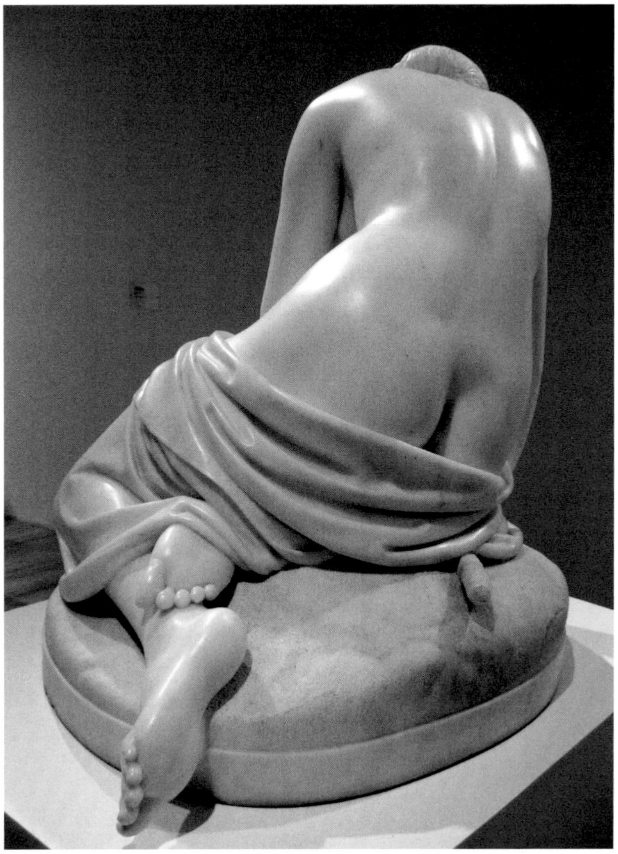

FIG. 21
Harriet Hosmer, *Oenone* (fig. 20), view of the back.

the pedestal, as if refusing its stony perch. The drapery slips down over the nymph's buttocks, offering a titillating view of the swelling hips and soft, curvaceous back. With the suggestiveness of the drapery, Hosmer emulated the sensuality of the *Venus de Milo,* attributed to Praxiteles in the nineteenth century, which she saw in the Uffizi Gallery in Florence. Following in the aesthetic footsteps of Canova and Gibson, Hosmer imbued her sculpture with a lifelike sensuality that at once ensured the sculpture's originality and inspired heated controversy.

Hosmer's sculpture appears to speak two sculptural languages. From the primary vantage point, the figure is modest, demure, and withdrawn, subverting the conventional pleasures of spectatorship. The face and hair are rendered with the geometric simplicity of the Severe style: her hair held back in a tight chignon and her idealized features solemn. However, from the rear, the sculpture yields its secret desires as the fleshy buttocks delight the viewer. With this multivalent sculptural style, Hosmer articulated a language of desire available to both male and female viewers.

As Julia Markus has suggested, *Oenone* may have held a special personal significance for Hosmer. Produced the year after her dear friend Cornelia Crow married Lucien Carr, the sculpture expresses a warm sensuality redolent of Hosmer's and Crow's "romantic friendship" in Lenox, an experience that remained central to both their lives.[84] In fact, the sculptor gave a bust of *Daphne* (fig. 12) to Cornelia as a "love gift" in the fall of 1854.[85] "When *Daphne* arrives, kiss her lips and then remember that I kissed her just before she left me," Hosmer wrote.[86] This language was quite common in the nineteenth century; kissing, hugging, and sharing a bed were activities in which women frequently engaged. Consistent with contemporary mores, these behaviors were certainly evidence of women's emotional intimacy, and perhaps also of a carnal sexuality.[87] Like the nymph Daphne, who had chosen a life outside of matrimony, the artist remained pure and chaste within the nineteenth-century imagination. Her emotional bond with Cornelia was considered proper, even morally superior to that of marriage. It was a spiritualized love, like "the love of angels."[88] However, with its peekaboo sensuality, *Oenone* transgressed into the carnal world, suggesting a blatant sexuality. The sculpture was never shown publicly in the nineteenth century, remaining instead in the residence of Hosmer's patron, where it was readily available for Cornelia's private viewing.

Hosmer used the language of domesticity to mitigate the dangers posed by her openly erotic sculpture. "I want you so much to receive my first child (*Daphne*)," the sculptor wrote to Cornelia. "At the same time I shall send another daughter [*Medusa*] to Boston, which you must make a point of visiting this summer."[89] Referring to her sculptures as her children, Hosmer entered into a chaste domestic compact with Cornelia that was as significant as a traditional marriage vow.

In Rome, Hosmer created for herself an alternative domesticity. The via del Corso apartment was never a lonely place. She lived a life that revolved around women: she adored her mentors, Cushman and Hays; visited often with her friend Barrett Browning; and welcomed old acquaintances from Lenox, Fanny Kemble and her sister, Adelaide Sartoris. Indeed, as a young sculptor in Rome, Hosmer remained both committed to her professional career and devoted to her female circle of friends. Writing to Cornelia Crow in 1854, the sculptor exclaimed, "Never have eighteen months gone by so swiftly and happily, since I was born. . . . [T]here is something in the air of Italy," she wrote. "In America, I never had that sense of quiet, settled content such as I now have from sunrise to sunset."[90] Hosmer's "quiet, settled content" indicated a new confidence and maturity. By 1856 she had attained a professional stature in Rome unprecedented for an American woman sculptor, having "surmounted all the difficulties of her position as woman and artist," Hays optimistically (and unrealistically) noted.[91]

As an active participant in Rome's international art community, she grew savvy about the market. She probably knew that busts sold more easily than full figures and that busts with both breasts exposed sold better than those draped.[92] Her heroic female figures, like *Daphne* and *Medusa,* were purchased almost exclusively by female patrons. *Medusa,* her first commissioned sculpture, was bought by Mrs. Samuel Appleton, wife of the prosperous Boston merchant and philanthropist, who later owned its pendant, *Daphne.*[93] In the early 1860s, the Duchess

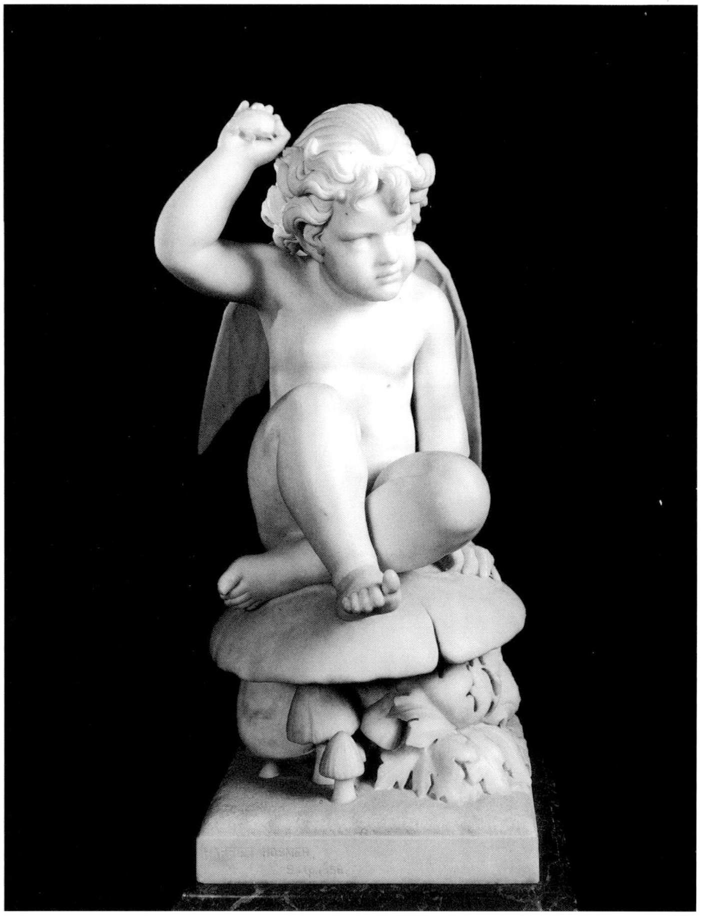

FIG. 22
Harriet Hosmer, *Puck,* 1856, marble, 30 1/2 × 16 5/8 × 19 3/4 in. Smithsonian American Art Museum, Washington, D.C., gift of Mrs. George Merrill.

of St. Albans, Lady Sibyl Mary Grey, and Lady Marian Alford, art patron, amateur painter, and intimate of Hosmer, purchased busts of *Medusa.*[94] Hosmer became a favorite of British aristocratic women, welcomed them to her studio in Rome, and regularly visited their palatial residences in England.

In addition to cultivating wealthy patrons, Hosmer assured her financial independence by producing fancy pieces, or conceits—imaginative works intended to amuse and delight. In *Puck* (fig. 22), she depicted the impish character from Shakespeare's *Midsummer Night's Dream.* The little boy—a playful and mischievous sprite, replete with bat wings—sits cross-legged on a toadstool. He raises his right arm, about to toss a giant beetle at an unsuspecting passerby, while with his left hand he traps a chameleon. With its compact dimensions, *Puck* was ideally suited for a domestic setting, and Hosmer produced fifty versions for American and British tourists.[95]

In 1857, Hosmer received the commission for the Judith Falconnet memorial, a tomb sculpture permanently installed in the church of Sant'Andrea delle Fratte in Rome. Located in close proximity to her new residence on via Gregoriana, which she shared with Cushman, the church was centrally situated in the expatriate neighborhoods of Rome. The recumbent effigy of Judith Falconnet quietly reposes in one of the church's chapels, the only such monumental commission given to an American sculptor.[96]

Although happy and successful in Rome, Hosmer confirmed a dilemma faced by nineteenth-century women artists. Writing to Wayman Crow in 1854, she noted: "Everyone is being married but myself. I am the only faithful worshipper of Celibacy." Bemoaning the difficult life of the woman artist, she continued, "An artist has no business to marry. For a man, it may be well enough, but for a woman, on whom matrimonial duties and cares weigh more heavily, it is a moral wrong, I think, for she must either neglect her profession or her family, becoming neither a good wife and mother nor a good artist. My ambition is to become the latter, so I wage eternal feud with the consolidating knot."[97] In this letter, she articulated a paradox of nineteenth-century femininity first put forward by Elizabeth Cady Stanton in 1848. Ambitious women were forced to occupy what appeared to be competing subject positions—domestic angel and professional agent—yet these two identities were often at war. In Rome, Hosmer, Louisa Lander, Margaret Foley, and Emma Stebbins pursued complex careers in which creativity, womanhood, and commercial success were balanced in divergent and, at times, perilous ways.

# Three

## "A Woman Artist Is an Object of Peculiar Odium"

The artist's studio was the popular face of female professionalism in Rome, a space in which women artists actively fashioned their identities. With its public character, the studio served as a site of both production and display where artists showcased themselves as well as their work. With its attendant mercantile interests, it witnessed commerce and financial negotiations and was a morally perilous zone that held the potential of tarnishing a woman artist's reputation.[1] Considered curiosities for the public lives they led, Harriet Hosmer and Louisa Lander attracted much attention in Rome. Visitors to the city obtained their addresses and calling hours at the American banker's office of Pakenham and Hooker in the Piazza di Spagna. At the intersection of artistic production, femininity, and the market, their studios were popular destinations; the artists and their sculptures, commodities to be consumed by the touristic eye.

Visited by patrons, critics, and tourists alike, the Roman studios of American male sculptors were treated as a kind of sacred precinct in which the artist's temperament and genius were revealed.[2] For women sculptors, the dynamic was different. Hosmer and Lander found that visitors to their studios examined their work environment, dress, and hairstyles more carefully than the sculpture they hoped to market. In the published engraving *Harriet Hosmer in Her Studio,* Hosmer is as much the center of attention—a spectacle for the touring classes—as her sculptural work (fig. 23). A bourgeois couple, attended by son, daughter, and dog, stare at the sculptor with fascination. Illuminated by a spotlight as she carves a female bust, Hosmer appears to pose on a stagelike podium. A curtain is pulled aside—as if part of a theatrical ensemble—to reveal a perfunctory wooden worktable, a set of steps to elevate the artist's short stature, and two busts: the female bust upon which she works and a male bust on the floor.

Hosmer was famous for her warm and welcoming studios, although this particular engraving does not convey this impression. In 1857, she opened her own workplace on via Margutta, at the base of the Pincian Hill, just down the street from the Palazzo Patrizi, a lovely old Renaissance palace that housed the studios of the American sculptors Randolph Rogers, Joseph Mozier, Chauncey Ives, and later Margaret Foley. According to Nathaniel Hawthorne, Hosmer occupied "a lofty room, with a sky-light window; it was pretty well warmed with a stove; and there was a small orange-tree in a pot, with the oranges growing on it, and two or three flower shrubs in

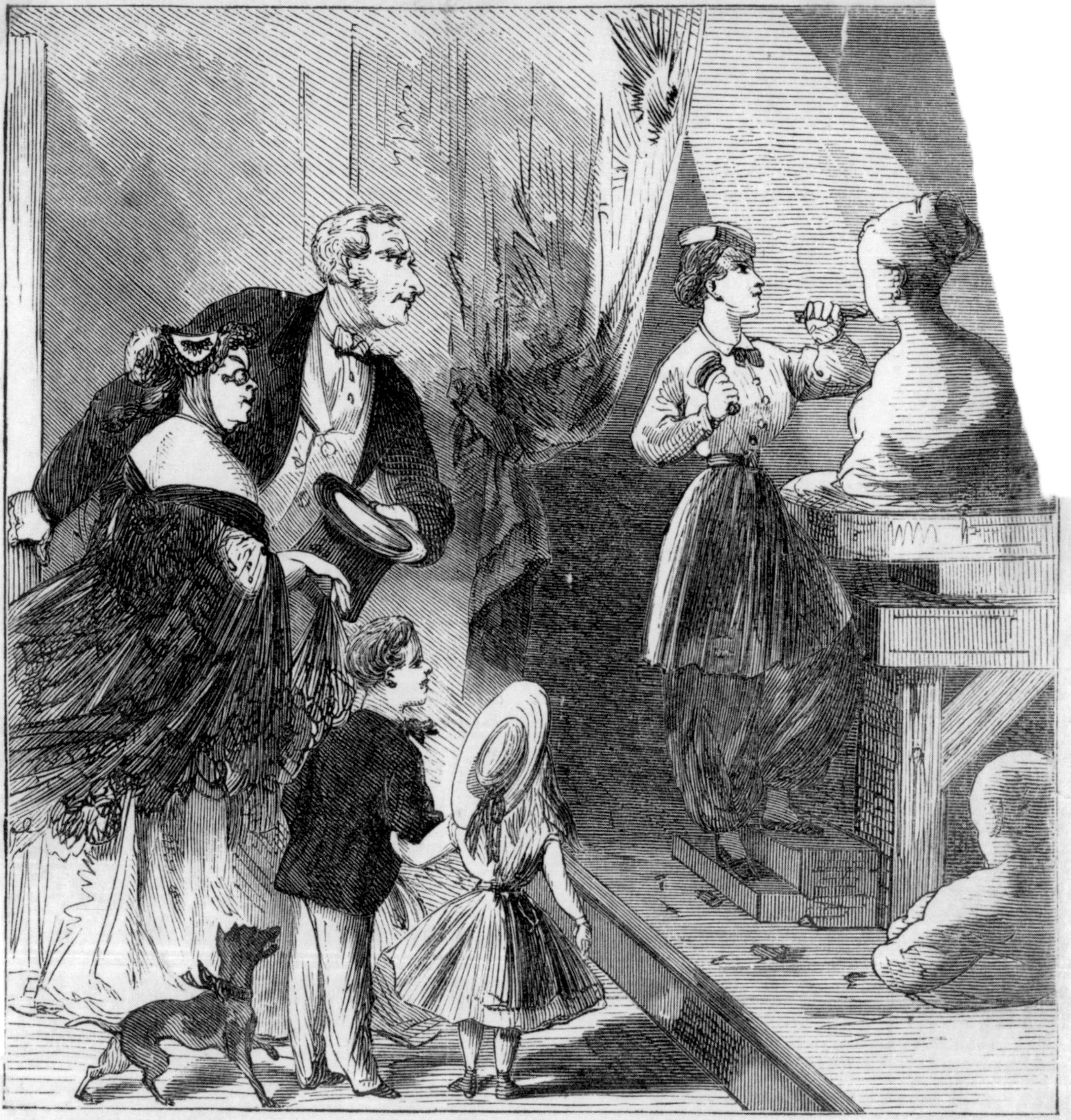

MEMORABLE WOMEN OF AMERICA: HARRIET HOSMER.—HARRIET HOSMER IN HER STUDIO.

bloom."[3] Brightly lit, warmed by the sun, and fecund with vegetation, the studio appeared as a nurturing space where Hosmer tended to her sculptures as if her children. Conflating the idea of home with her professional workplace, Hosmer legitimized her artistic practice by associating it with a feminized domesticity.

In the engraving, Hosmer wears a shirtwaist blouse with cravat, a beret atop her head, and a skirt covering her bloomers as she stands with mallet and chisel in hand. Rather than sport a "boyish" demeanor, she appears more feminized—read "sexualized"—with her hourglass figure and large bosom. The pantaloons are more exotic than practical in their appearance. In her book *Women Artists in All Ages and Countries,* Elizabeth Ellet insisted that Hosmer was "unmistakably" a woman, with "trim waist and well-developed bust."[4] These characterizations of the artist—both visual and verbal—stressed Hosmer's femininity and allayed fears of sexual inversion that dogged many professional women in Rome.

When Hawthorne visited Hosmer's studio in 1858, he was clearly troubled by the nature of her femininity. "She had on petticoats, I think; but I did not look so low," the author offered with feigned modesty. "She had on a male shirt, collar, and cravat," a manly outfit, which she modified with a feminized "brooch of Etruscan gold; and on her curly head was a picturesque little cap of black velvet; and her face was as bright and funny, and as small of feature, as a child's." Hawthorne thought her "very queer, but she seemed to be her actual self, and nothing affected nor made-up; so that . . . I give her full leave to wear what may suit her best, and to behave as her inner woman prompts." In the end, his suspicion of the manly woman became clear: "I shook hands with this frank and pleasant little woman—if woman she be, as I honestly suppose, though her upper half is precisely that of a young man."[5]

FIG. 23 *(opposite) Harriet Hosmer in Her Studio,* n.d., engraving (clipping from an unidentified periodical). The Schlesinger Library, Radcliffe Institute, Harvard University, A-162-82.

Louisa Lander dressed like Hosmer. "In her studio," Hawthorne tells us, she "wears a sort of pea-jacket, buttoned across her breast, and a little foraging-cap, just covering the top of her head."[6] Like Hosmer, she presented a public persona that was at odds with the ideology of true womanhood. She lived an independent life, residing alone rather than in a female household. Despite this fact, she remained loyal to the women's community in Rome and maintained close ties with those in Charlotte Cushman's orbit.

Opening her own studio in Rome in 1857, Lander refused to court domesticity as a protective mantle. As opposed to the "homely" workplace that Hosmer cultivated, Lander worked in an unadorned, commercialized space. The building had previously housed Antonio Canova's studio and currently boasted that of the American sculptor Paul Akers. Off the via del Corso, this little street, now called via Antonio Canova, was just a few blocks from Hosmer's studio on via Margutta. Lander's workplace, according to Hawthorne, was "large, high, and dreary, from the want of carpet, furniture, or anything but clay and plaster. A sculptor's studio [or, at least, *this* sculptor's studio] has not the picturesque charm of a painter's, where there is color, warmth, [and] cheerfulness."[7] With neither twittering birds nor potted plants, it was an unwelcoming place, devoid of a feminine touch.

Two nude female figures stood on display in her new work area: a nearly life-size sculpture of *Evangeline* (now lost) and a small-scale statuette of *Virginia Dare* (now lost; see fig. 24).

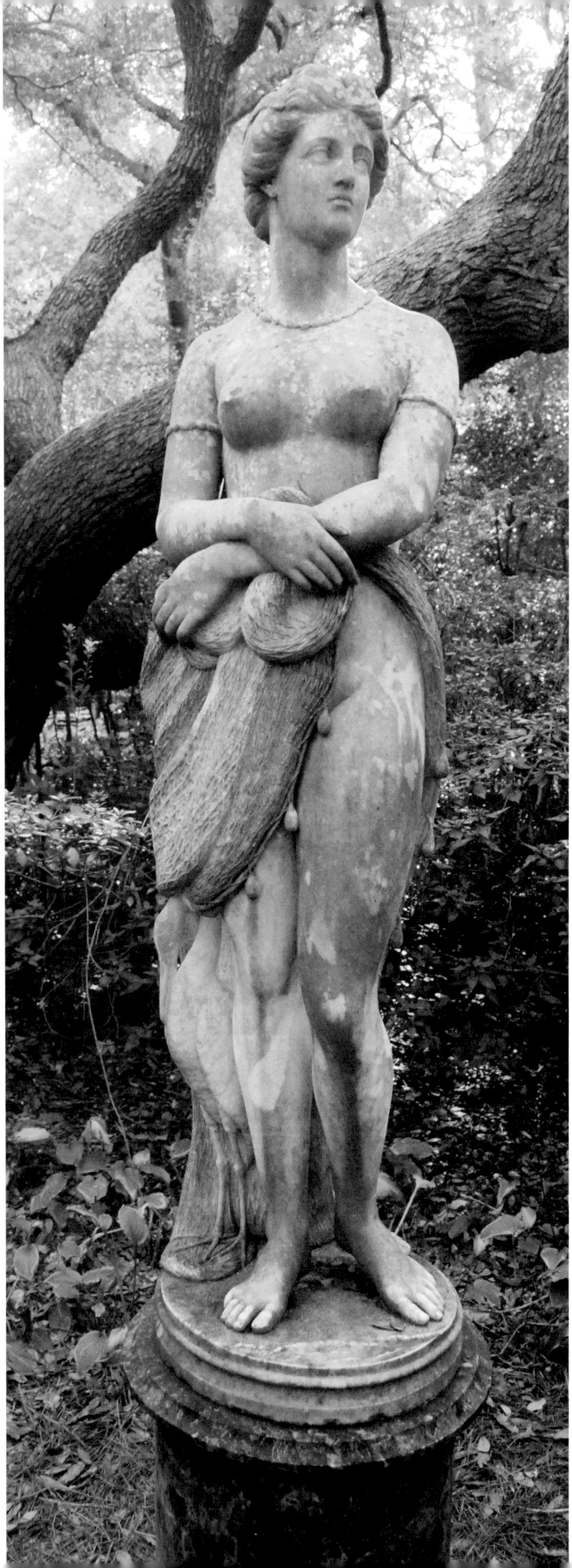

FIG. 24
Louisa Lander, *Virginia Dare,* 1859–60, marble. The Elizabethan Gardens, Manteo, N.C.

Both sculptures prompted discomfort on the part of Hawthorne and other visitors to her studio.[8] In displaying these seminude sculptures, she defied the standards of feminine decency at play in Rome, as her professional demeanor and sculptural ambition challenged the limits of bourgeois womanhood. As a result, her moral temperament, aligned with her controversial nudes, was sorely defiled.

Both Lander and Hosmer chafed under Rome's strict social codes, but only Lander was forced to evacuate the city due to rumors of moral profligacy. Hosmer had also responded to the challenge of the female nude with her *Oenone* of 1854–55, a three-quarter-life-sized figure with which Lander was most certainly familiar (fig. 20). Whereas *Oenone* was modest in her inward pose—her sensuality subtly communicated—*Virginia Dare* stood tall and proud, clad only in a fishnet and radiating an illicit sexuality. Both artists risked accusations of moral impropriety by publicly displaying nudes in their studios.[9] Elizabeth Barrett Browning and Thomas Crawford, to one degree or another, repudiated Hosmer's sculpture in private. Crawford's complaints served to shore up masculinity and its privileges—in this case, access to the female body.

Furthermore, authorial crises routinely affected women sculptors in Rome. Hosmer had been subject to doubts about her creative potential immediately upon her arrival in Rome. By 1858, rumors challenging the authenticity of her *Zenobia in Chains* (fig. 25) began to circulate. By 1863, these slanderous comments found their way into print—accusations that Hosmer vehemently fought. The response of the progressive women's community in Rome to Hosmer's monumental *Zenobia,* however, was drastically different (a subject addressed in chapter 5). Nonetheless, a mistrust of feminine artistic abilities would never fully disappear in nineteenth-century Rome.

### *Louisa Lander's Career in Rome*

When Louisa Lander arrived in Rome in 1855, she sought out Thomas Crawford as a teacher, as she knew his *Orpheus and Cerberus* (fig. 9) from her many visits to the Boston Athenaeum.[10] Crawford had married Louisa Ward, sister of the poet and reformer Julia Ward Howe, both of whom had attended Margaret Fuller's famous Conversations in Boston. The Ward sisters were regular participants in the newly expanded women's community in Rome.

Lander showed Crawford an ambrotype of her bust *To-day* (now lost) as soon as she arrived in Rome. According to written reports, the sculpture conveyed a nationalist message by personifying westward expansion. The figure wore a crown of morning glories and was clad in an American flag that fastened at the shoulder with stars. Serving as a patriotic emblem, it signified national progress to an American public hungry for unifying metaphors in a decade of growing sectionalism. Suitably impressed with Lander's bust, Crawford invited her to study with him in his famous Roman studio in the Baths of Diocletian. He guided her in modeling from antique statuary and drawing from plaster casts, but not, one would suspect, from the live model.[11] Clearly a double standard was in place: Crawford had studied from life at the French Academy and the Academy of Saint Luke; Hosmer and Lander, however, did not have access to such privileges as

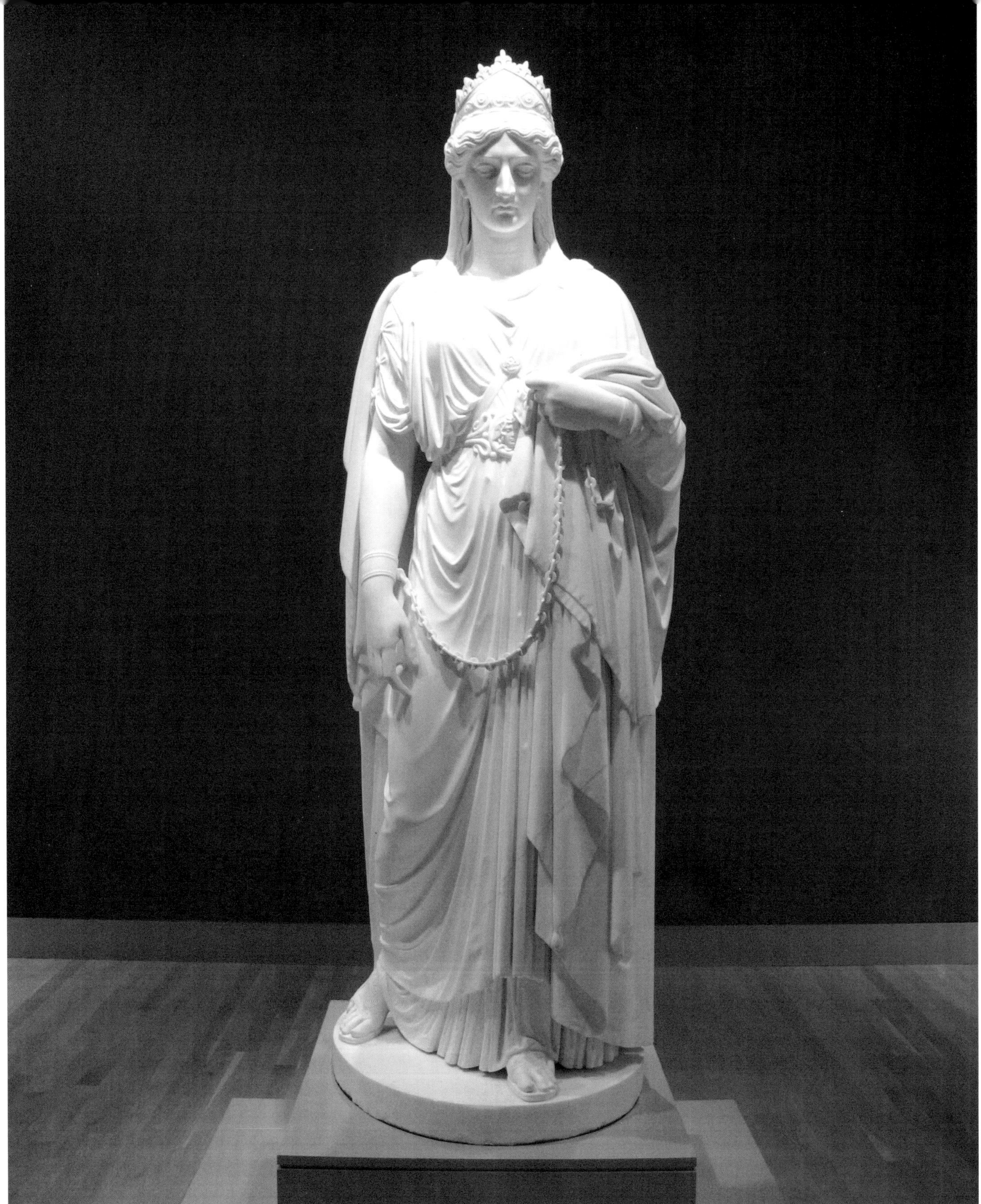

their modesty and reputation were presumed to be at risk.

All in all, Lander had a little more than one year of study with Crawford before his untimely death, in the fall of 1857. One newspaper noted that she "display[ed] much talent in the studies she ha[d] been pursuing" in Rome.[12] One of the first works that she produced was the recumbent figure *Evangeline* (now lost), begun in 1856 under Crawford's tutelage. Inspired by one of Henry Wadsworth Longfellow's most famous poems, she depicted a young woman who traveled south and west in futile search of her lover. Contemporary descriptions indicate that the figure was gracefully reclining, having fallen asleep after her lengthy wandering. A large-scale sculpture, it measured between two-thirds life-size and fully life-size, depending upon the source.[13] Completed in marble in 1858, the sculpture sold to a "wealthy and liberal gentleman in Salem."[14] When shown in Boston the following year, one critic disparaged the work, complaining that the figure must have suffered terribly from mosquitoes "if she really *did* sleep on the river's edge in . . . scanty drapery."[15] Despite the challenge to propriety, Lander focused much of her sculptural attention upon the problem of the female nude.

FIG. 25 *(opposite)* Harriet Hosmer, *Zenobia in Chains*, 1861, marble. © Courtesy of the Huntington Art Collections, San Marino, Calif.

Lander completed the full-scale plaster version of *Virginia Dare* in 1859; the marble was finished in 1860.[16] The sculpture memorialized the first child born in the Lost Colony on Roanoke Island, all of whose settlers had mysteriously vanished in 1587. It was suspected that the infant Virginia Dare and her mother were carried into captivity by Indians. Although no evidence exists that the child survived, Lander imagined the adult Virginia Dare as an Indian princess, a nationalist image that had symbolized the North American continent since the eighteenth century. In the 1850s, for example, the Indian-princess motif appeared in the decorations of the U.S. Capitol, as in Constantino Brumidi's fresco for the Committee on Agriculture Room.[17]

Lander's Anglo-Indian princess stands proud and tall as she looks out over the distant ocean before her. Her nearly nude body and facial features reveal a classicized idealism. She is clad only in a fishnet wrapped modestly around her waist and legs. The figure wears a necklace and arm bracelets of wampum beads, and her hair is bound with eagles' feathers. A beach crane stands beside her. She is not enchained, but her crossed wrists suggest captivity. The fishnet was of English manufacture, Lander explained in 1865, and together with the accoutrements of Indian culture "united the civil with the barbaric life" within the sculpture.[18]

Captive women intrigued the Victorian mind and served as a common theme in American art and literature at midcentury. As part of a national mythology, captivity narratives recorded the fates of victimized white Euro-American heroines who were forced into confinement among Indians. Caught between two worlds, they inhabited a transitional space that implied an elicit passage from virginity to sexual experience and from domesticity to wilderness. Uncontrolled by the rules of bourgeois femininity, these captives maintained lives that were potentially outside the bounds of true womanhood.[19]

Hiram Powers's *Greek Slave* (fig. 26), first created in 1843 and one of the most famous sculptures of its time, references the Greek War of Independence. The sculpture depicts a vulnerable Greek woman abducted by Turks and sold into slavery. With her locket and cross hanging upon her abandoned drapery, she represents a pious, faithful woman, absolved of the responsibility of her public nudity. Responding to the popularity of the *Greek Slave,* Erastus Dow Palmer produced his *White Captive* in 1859, which portrays a young American girl as an Indian captive (fig. 27). Active in Albany, New York, and one of the few American sculptors who did not travel to Rome, Palmer was greatly admired for his nationalistic themes. In *The White Captive,* a nude girl is tethered to a tree trunk by the remains of a night dress that had been torn from her body. Although causing an outcry in some circles because of its blatant nudity, the sculpture was generally hailed as a "thoroughly American subject." Her "virgin purity and Christian faith assert themselves" in the young girl's soul, the art historian Henry Tuckerman wrote in the broadside that accompanied the exhibition of the statue. Christian iconography clothed Palmer's nude, as it did *The Greek Slave,* in moral purity.[20]

Lander's sculpture reconceptualized the popular captivity narrative. *Virginia Dare* assumed the competing identities of a "high-born English girl," with her "refined and exquisite womanliness," and an "Indian maiden." Her beautifully coiffed hair and regal *contrapposto* suggested an elite and proper femininity; the beach crane at her side recalled her "barbaric" nature. Unlike the docile victims depicted by Powers and Palmer, the figure presented by Lander was a strong and acculturated woman who openly embraced an alternative life. If such a "refined and exquisite" woman as Virginia Dare had accepted membership in an Indian tribe, then it would appear that any woman had the potential to abandon "true womanhood" for a life uncontrolled by conventional domesticity.[21]

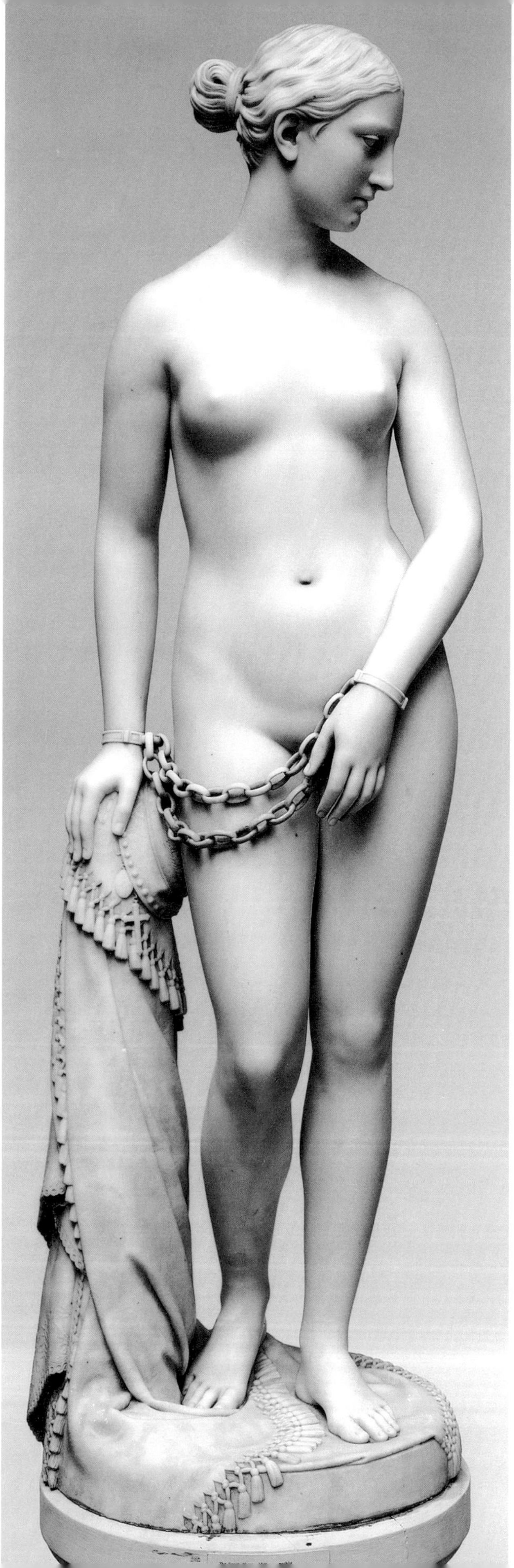

FIG. 26 *(opposite)*
Hiram Powers, *The Greek Slave,* modeled 1841–43, carved 1846, marble, 65 7/8 × 20 1/4 × 18 1/2 in. Corcoran Gallery of Art, Washington, D.C., gift of William Wilson Corcoran.

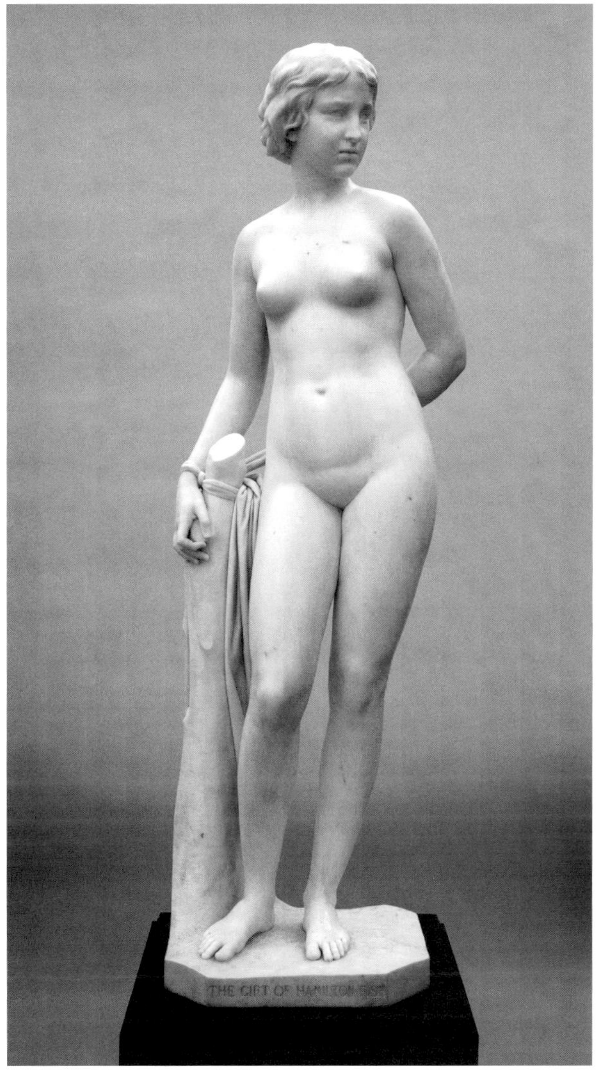

FIG. 27
Erastus Dow Palmer, *The White Captive,* 1857–58, carved 1858–59, marble, 65 × 20 1/4 × 17 in. The Metropolitan Museum of Art, New York, bequest of Hamilton Fish, 1894, 94.9.3.

With its partial nudity, competing identities, and implied sexual violence, *Virginia Dare* received a noticeably cool reception in Rome. In its distance from established models of victimhood, Lander's sculpture—like Hosmer's pendants *Daphne* (fig. 12) and *Medusa* (fig. 13)—represented the female as an active agent in the world, in control of her own destiny. Lander's *Virginia Dare,* it seemed, had embraced the "savage" life. Neither clothed in the purity of neoclassicism nor shrouded by Christianity's elevating morality, this standing female nude challenged the limits of feminine propriety in patriarchal Rome.[22]

## *The Hawthornes in Rome*

Only once did Nathaniel Hawthorne comment upon the sculptures in Lander's studio. "*Virginia Dare* is certainly very beautiful," he wrote upon one of his first visits to her studio, in February of 1858.[23] The Hawthorne family had arrived in Rome the previous month and was immediately welcomed by the community of Anglo-American artists and writers living in the city, most notably Charlotte Cushman, Emma Stebbins, and Harriet Hosmer. The Hawthornes took up residence at Palazzo Larazani 37 on the via Porta Pinciana, a lovely road that bordered the parks of the Pincian Hill and the Borghese Gardens, not far from Cushman's via Gregoriana home.

In Rome, Hawthorne traveled in a circle of American artists that included the painters Thomas Buchanon Read and Cephas Giovanni Thompson and the sculptors Randolph Rogers, Joseph Mozier, William Wetmore Story, and Paul Akers; he was also acquainted with the British sculptor John Gibson. Story introduced Hawthorne to Louisa Lander, as they both hailed from the same hometown of Salem, Massachusetts. In the first few months of his residence in the city, Hawthorne conceived the idea for his last novel, *The Marble Faun,* a romance with American artists as protagonists. Published in 1860, the book brought to the attention of a wide Anglo-American public the careers of talented artists working and living in Rome. In fact, he loosely based his characters upon the lives of Lander, Hosmer, Story, and Akers. Tourists wandered the streets of Rome with *The Marble Faun* under their arms and visited the studios of American sculptors, hoping to get a glance at the famous *Cleopatra* by Story (fig. 63) or the *Dead Pearl Diver* by Akers (fig. 38), which were described at length in the novel. Hawthorne also celebrated Hosmer's *Zenobia in Chains* (fig. 25), claiming that "were he capable of stealing from a lady, he would certainly have made free with Miss Hosmer's noble statue" for use in his novel.[24]

Hawthorne was quite taken by Lander, who, at the age of thirty-three, led an exceptional life in Rome. She shared dinners and evenings with the family at the Palazzo Larazani. He recorded seventeen tourist outings with Lander over a five-month period. At times the Hawthorne family—Sophia and the children—joined them; at other times the two scoured the sites of Rome alone. She had "genuine talent, . . . spirit and independence," living in Rome "quite alone, in delightful freedom," he reported. "She was a young woman, living in almost perfect independence, thousands of miles from her New England home, going fearlessly about these mysterious streets, by night as well as by day, with no household ties, no rule or law but that within her; yet acting with quietness and simplicity, and keeping, after all, within a homely line of right."[25] His choice of words was interesting: "delightful freedom" suggested a sensual, perhaps even quietly illicit life.[26] She traveled the streets of Rome with "no household ties, no rule or law but that within her." Unlike the domesticity so carefully cultivated in the Cushman household, Lander did not partake of this feminine convention; she seemed to have no "household" to keep her within "a homely line of right." This independence—the word is used twice—put her at risk in the Roman community.

Hawthorne consented to sit for his portrait, believing that Lander showed "great genius in her work."[27] She worked on the bust for several months, declaring the clay model finished on

March 31, 1858. By April 7, she was putting the finishing touches on the plaster bust.[28] For Hawthorne, the portrait process had been very intimate. "During the sitting, I talked a good deal with Miss Lander, being a little inclined to take a similar freedom with her moral likeness to that which she was taking with my physical one."[29] Lander, by necessity, pursued the activity of looking; Hawthorne, by choice, became the object of her gaze. This reversal of gendered power relations was unnerving to him, so much so that he felt compelled to examine her "moral likeness" in response to her scrutiny of his physical bearing. In so doing, he repositioned the artist as spectacle within his own imagination, disempowering Lander's visual mastery over him.[30]

In spending so much time with Hawthorne, Lander put her moral character in jeopardy. Between February 6 and April 10, 1858, the author visited her fourteen times. Her large dreary studio became a site of dangerous transactions—both emotional and financial. The intimacy that developed between them was complicated by a commercial exchange. With the completion of the plaster bust in April 1858, he made partial payment to the artist for her services.[31] As was traditional in Roman studios, skilled workmen later put Hawthorne's bust into marble (fig. 28).

Sophia and Nathaniel Hawthorne were thrilled with the plaster version of the portrait, a lively representation of the handsome author. "Miss Lander . . . has made an excellent bust of me," Hawthorne raved in a letter to his publisher, William Ticknor. "Even Mrs. Hawthorne is delighted with it, and, as a work of art, it has received the highest praise from all the sculptors here, including Gibson." Hawthorne openly supported Lander's career, urging Ticknor to "do what may be in your power to bring Miss Lander's name favorably before the public. . . . She is a very nice person, and I like her exceedingly."[32]

Sophia Hawthorne would, at times, accompany her husband to Lander's studio. She was very much at home in Rome—in its artists' studios, museums, and churches, despite the fact that she had given up her artistic career ten years earlier. As an unmarried woman, she had had the freedom to pursue her professional career in Boston.[33] As wife and mother, she was expected to make a voluntary choice amounting to self-abnegation when her husband asked that she surrender her career as a painter.[34] In Rome, everything changed. After years of suffering from debilitating headaches, she spent her months in Italy pain-free. "There can be no doubt that the Roman atmosphere will prove beneficial to Mrs. Hawthorne's complaints," her husband admitted, "and most probably effect a perfect cure."[35]

Shortly after her arrival in the city, Sophia exclaimed, "I am in Rome, Rome, *Rome!*" She noted in her journal that she could now "understand the irresistible attraction [the city] has." Like Hosmer and Lander, she experienced "a sort of necessity of the soul to live here."[36] Making regular excursions to museums, the family rarely needed a guidebook, for her knowledge of art was enough to satiate them all. In fact, it was Sophia who introduced her husband to the great artworks in Rome. It was often her confident voice that appeared in *The Marble Faun* when art was the subject. In her journal, she authored articulate entries that examined and interpreted works of art in a sophisticated manner.[37] "The act of writing about art and gallery visits," literary critic Mary S. Schriber has explained, "liberate[d] . . .

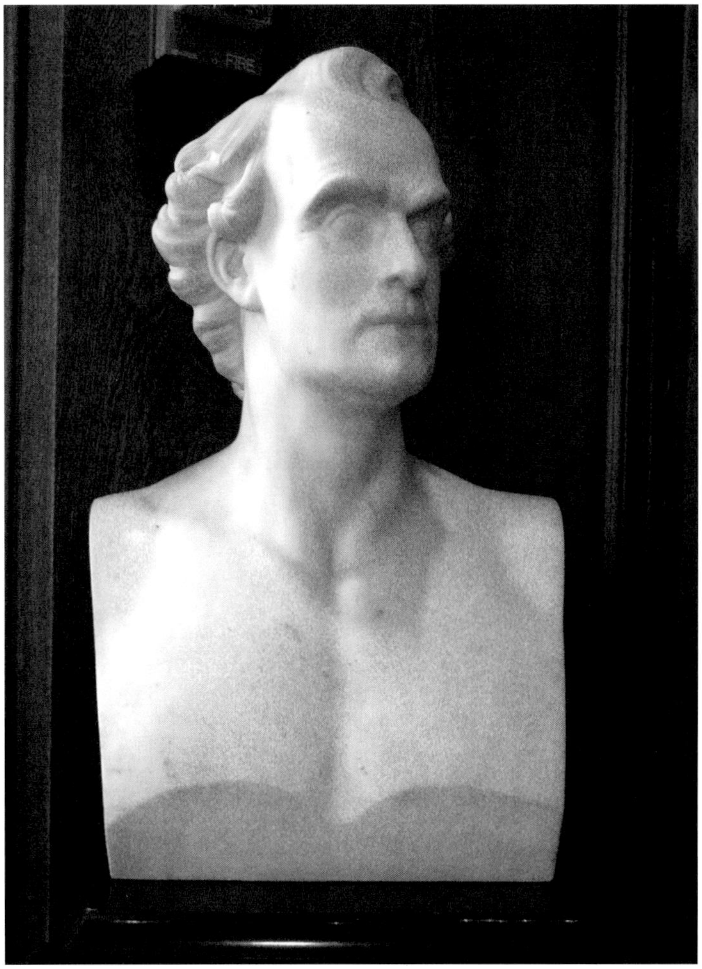

FIG. 28
Louisa Lander, *Nathaniel Hawthorne,* 1859, marble. Courtesy of the Concord Free Public Library, Concord, Mass.

an energy and enthusiasm" in Sophia that allowed her, at times, to break out of "the straitjacket" of true womanhood that had constricted her creativity after marriage.[38]

Together with her oldest daughter, Una, she visited Lander's and Hosmer's studios, where she studied their artwork with much admiration. Sophia was the first to visit Hosmer's studio on via Margutta, a full month before her husband. The artist "came forward with the most animated gesture to greet us," she wrote on March 11, 1858. Sophia noted with great detail Hosmer's appearance and apparel: "Her action was as bright, sprightly, and vivid as that of a bird: a small figure, round face, and tiny features, except large eyes; hair short, and curling up round a black velvet cap, planted directly upon the middle of her head, instead of jauntily on one side, as is usual with artists; her hands thrust into the pockets of a close-fitting cloth jacket—a collar and cravat like a young man's—and a snowy plaited chemisette, like a shirt-bosom." Unlike her husband, Sophia seemed comfortable with Hosmer's "emancipated life" and confided, "I liked her at once." She "was so frank and cheerful, independent, honest, and sincere—wide awake, energetic, yet not ungentle."[39] Though diminutive and birdlike in appearance, Hosmer's "large eyes," Sophia noticed, ensured her status as artist.[40]

Sophia and Una were entranced by the Roman atmosphere. Since their arrival in Rome in January of 1858, mother and daughter had spent many a day sketching in the city and countryside. They traversed the city with freedom, apprehending without restriction the beauty around them. In fact, Una wished to follow in the footsteps of her role models, Lander and Hosmer.[41] "My ideal of existence would be to live in Italy," she confessed, "often paying long visits to England, and sometimes to America, [to] pursue my studies and other occupations unmolested by mankind in general."[42] Una's wish to become an artist was anathema to her father, who worried, "Una spoke with somewhat alarming fervor of her love for Rome." Only reluctantly did he admit that his daughter's life would "be the better" for her stay in the Eternal City.[43]

The summer of 1858 saw many of Rome's Anglo-American inhabitants travel to cooler parts. In June, Lander departed for Boston, where she set up a temporary studio on Tremont Street.[44] Photographs of her work could be seen at Cotton's Gallery in July; the sculptures, the small-scale statuette of *Virginia Dare* and *Evangeline,* would arrive later. The artist was well received in Boston: "Miss Lander has many warm friends here who rejoice in her success," one critic noted.[45] Indeed, her career appeared very much on track.

The Hawthornes also left in June to spend the summer and early fall in Tuscany. As it turned out, Nathaniel Hawthorne preferred Florence to Rome; he even toyed with the idea of buying the villa in Siena where the Story family had been staying. In Florence, they joined a lively expatriate community. Initially, they lived in a thirteen-room house, the Casa Bello, whose backyard was filled with terraces of roses, jasmine, and groves of lemon and orange trees. Later they moved to the countryside, occupying the villa at Montaulto, with its picturesque tower. Figuring prominently in *The Marble Faun,* the domicile was where the romance took shape in the author's imagination. Hosmer, who was staying with the Storys, visited them often. The family spent many an evening at the Casa Guidi with Robert and Elizabeth Barrett Browning.[46] Hiram Powers's large studio was located across the street from the Casa Bello. Hawthorne visited on several occasions, engaging the sculptor in discussions about art, which would eventually find their way into his romance.[47]

### *Louisa Lander's Impropriety: "She Snaps Her Fingers at All Rome"*

The Roman expatriate community began to reassemble in the fall of 1858. The Hawthornes returned to Rome in mid-October and moved into 68 Piazza Poli, "the snuggest little set of apartments in Rome," located around the corner from the Trevi Fountain; from these lodgings Hawthorne could "hear the plash in the evening, when other sounds [were] hushed."[48] The day after their return, on October 17, 1858, a problem in the American expatriate community surfaced. The painter Cephas Thompson, a longtime friend of Hawthorne's, visited the family and relayed a damaging story about Lander.[49] With customary reserve, Hawthorne's only written response at the time was "What a pity!"[50] Rumor had it that Lander had ventured beyond the pale of appropriate feminine behavior by having an illicit relationship with a man in Rome.

The only written record of Lander's alleged malfeasance was a letter from the sculptor John Rogers, Lander's first cousin. He arrived in Rome in December and recorded what he knew of the situation, writing several letters home until his departure in February of 1859. "I don't know the whole story but there have been stories in circulation affecting Louisa's moral character," he wrote confidentially to his father. "Some of her friends have turned the cold shoulder to her and cut her in the street. . . . Coming out here alone as she did, she could not have been too careful of her conduct."[51] Indeed, Lander's independent lifestyle in Rome proved highly suspect to Rogers and his bourgeois family in Boston. He continued: "She has the reputation of having lived on uncommonly good terms with some man here. She is really vain of her figure, and a number of respectable people offer that she has [engaged?] herself as a model before them in a way that would astonish all modest Yankees. I suppose there is not much doubt of the [heart?] of the stories and it probably forms the foundation of the rest. . . . People don't come to her studio as they used to."[52]

In October, when the rumors began circulating, Lander had not yet returned from Boston. Hosmer and Cushman were made aware of the accusations and arrived at the Palazzo Poli the following day ostensibly to discuss the slanderous stories.[53] We have no record of the conversation that took place; however, we do know that two prominent women from the Roman community were concerned enough about the situation to visit Hawthorne immediately.

Ten days later, Una Hawthorne fell ill. After sketching on the Palatine Hill, a lovely area that overlooked the Forum, she contracted "Roman fever" and remained gravely ill with malaria for many months.[54] She suffered from high fevers and delirium; her parents feared for her life. Not until May 1859 did she fully recover, shortly before the family vacated Rome. Sophia, like all travelers to the city, had feared the dreaded contagion. "What a strange and mysterious retribution upon the Empress of the World is the malaria!" she wrote. "It is said to be increasing and encroaching, so that Rome will finally be left desolate, a sign and portent to the nations."[55]

Considered a deadly plague endemic to Rome and its environs, "Roman fever" regularly took the lives of travelers to the city. The atmosphere of the city and its surrounding area was believed to be infected with the mysterious contagion, now understood as contracted from mosquitoes that bred in the swampy lands outside the ancient city walls. In the cultural imagination of nineteenth-century travelers, the illness held associations with moral dis-ease. To Anglo-American women, in particular, "Roman fever" was synonymous with the moral dangers attributed to an ambitious or independent life.[56] To Nathaniel Hawthorne, the illness may have represented retribution for Una's illicit desire to live an emancipated life like that of the women artists in Rome.

Lander returned to Rome in November and was eager to see her friends. Together with her sister Elizabeth, she called upon the Hawthornes on the evening of November 9; but to their surprise they were not admitted. The following day, she left her card at the Piazza Poli. Again, no response. The following week, she sent more letters to the Hawthornes; December 5 marked her last attempt to communicate with those whom she had once considered friends.[57]

Hawthorne, distraught by his daughter's illness, felt compelled to explain his reasons for turning Lander away. In a missive, he used the formal third person to ensure an emotional detachment from his former friend: "Mr. Hawthorne is glad to be informed that some (he hopes many) of Miss Louisa Lander's friends are convinced of the purity of her life and character. He is himself open to conviction on that subject; but as guardian of the sanctity of his domestic circle, he is compelled to be more cautious than if he were acting merely for himself." Hosmer and Cushman were, most likely, among Lander's friends who had testified to the "purity of her life and character." Hawthorne himself appeared "open to [this] conviction" but was bewildered by the accusation of moral turpitude. Lander's impropriety not only stung him but threatened to disturb the "sanctity of his domestic circle." Her presence at the Palazzo Poli was no longer welcomed; it was as if her moral deficit were a contagion—like the "Roman fever"—that had already infected his family. He continued,

> *Before calling at Mr. Hawthorne's residence, Miss Louisa Lander had been made fully aware that reports were in circulation, most detrimental to her character; and he cannot but think that any attempt at social intercourse with her former friends . . . should have been preceded by a full explanation and refutation of these reports. . . . If Mr. Hawthorne were one of those friends who have faith in Miss Lander's innocence, his first and last advice to her would be to sift those charges thoroughly, to meet them fully, and to throw her life open to the world. This should be done at once . . . to retain her position. Should Miss Lander decide to take this course, no one will be more rejoiced at the triumphant vindication of her character than the present writer.*[58]

There is a possibility that Hawthorne had developed a romantic interest in Lander during the previous spring. When confronted with the rumor of her supposed improprieties, he may have been seized with a guilty fear that the modeling sessions in her studio would implicate him as being on "uncommonly good terms" with the artist. He could not afford to take such a risk, as his own reputation and that of his family were at stake.[59] On November 13, 1858, he closed the book on the relationship, sadly writing: "In any case Miss Lander may be assured of Mr. Hawthorne's silence on this painful subject. He has no wish to say a word that may injure her, and would most gladly be enabled again to think and speak as highly of her as he has done hitherto."[60]

In early December, the author met again with Lander's supporters—Cushman, Hosmer, Stebbins, and Barrett Browning—to try to resolve the situation.[61] Unfortunately, the meeting came to naught. Hawthorne was true to his pledge and remained forever silent on the issue. Sophia stood steadfastly with her husband. Despite her admiration for the women artists in Rome, she discontinued any association with Lander, whose improprieties she viewed as toxic to her family.[62]

No firm proof of wrongdoing by Lander ever came to light—only the rumors circulated by Thompson and transcribed by Rogers, who had, after all, begun his narrative with "I don't know the whole story but . . ." For several months, the Anglo-American community in Rome wrestled with this dilemma. Rogers reported that Story headed up a tribunal, of sorts, to get to the bottom of the allegations. A number of meetings took place, the last of which occurred the day after Christmas, December 26, to hear testimony for and against Lander in the hopes of clearing her name.[63] Although urged by Hawthorne "to throw her life open to the world," Lander kept her silence. She refused to dignify the accusations with testimony before the tribunal, led by Lewis Cass, the American consul in Rome.[64]

Lander had hoped to diffuse the situation with her silence; instead, it implicated her more deeply. "If I had been in her place," Rogers wrote, "such a loss of reputation would have killed me. . . . She snaps her fingers at all Rome and has not the least desire to leave."[65] What was absolutely clear to the feminist community in Rome was that the mere semblance of impropriety would be enough to destroy a woman's personal and professional reputation. This was an important lesson that expatriate women took to heart.

Lander's independence and resilience, nonetheless, outpaced her cousin's. "If I had a quarter of the pluck that our artistic cousin has," he admitted in a letter to his family, "I should be all right."[66] By Rogers's own account, he was quite unhappy in Rome. He did not feel welcomed by the community of Anglo-American artists; nor did he feel equipped to pursue the study of neoclassical sculpture. The women's colony was particularly troubling to him. "[Cushman] is one of those . . . Cyclops that I am afraid of," he explained to his brother. "I didn't pursue the acquaintance very far. She and Miss Hosmer and Miss Stebbins . . . smoke cigars together and are quite intimate."[67] This group of independent (phallic) women challenged him to his core. By March of 1859, he had departed for Paris; by June, he was back in the United States.[68]

Lander remained in Rome for more than a year following the outbreak of the scandal. In February 1859, she began work on a small-scale statue *Undine* (now lost), commissioned by an American patron, Mary Warren. The sculpture would be situated within a fountain of Lander's design for Warren's Beacon Street home.[69] An interesting subject for a sculptor under such professional pressure, the sea spirit Undine was transformed from a headstrong, willful water sprite into a loving, patient, dutiful wife. Mistreated and cast away by her husband, she later returned vengefully to kill him. In the end, she took her own life and dissolved into a spring at the foot of his tomb. In Lander's treatment of the myth, *Undine* was a "light, airy figure, rising as a water-jet," the central element of a fountain, the base of which was surrounded by shells.[70] As one of her last works produced in Rome, this sculpture may be a clue to her state of mind. To the artist, Undine may have served as an alter ego, representing an imaginary avenger who retaliated against the sins of the patriarchal order.

In Rome, Lander was engaged in daring and challenging work, focusing upon the female nude in sculpture. Her *Virginia Dare* was remarkably sensual. The fishnet both concealed and partially revealed the hips and buttocks of the figure (fig. 29). It certainly is not surprising that Hawthorne would have felt uncomfortable in Lander's studio with this figure.[71] Like the American public in general, Hawthorne was ambivalent in his attitude toward the nude. He loved the modest

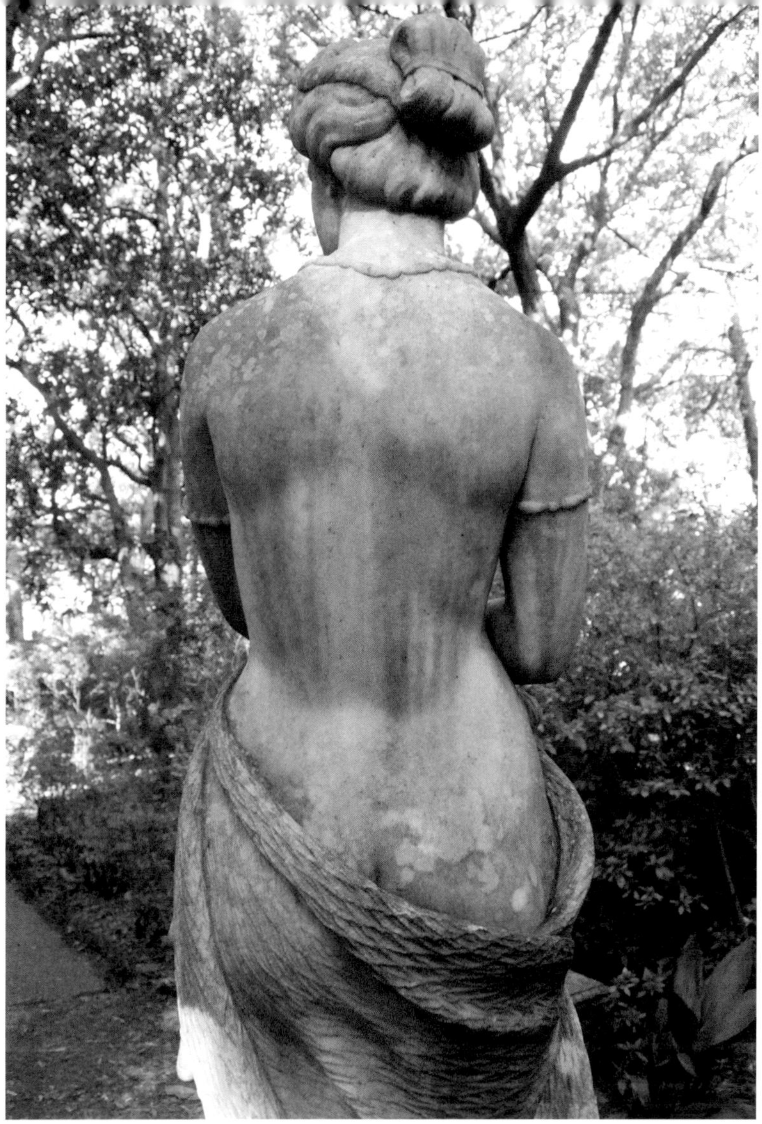

FIG. 29
Louisa Lander, *Virginia Dare* (fig. 24), view of the back.

*Venus de Medici,* which he saw in the Uffizi Gallery in Florence, believing that contact with the Greek aesthetic ideal exerted a "refining" influence upon him.[72] "Nude statues of antiquity are as modest as violets, and sufficiently draped in their own beauty," he wrote in *The Marble Faun.*[73] But he was less accepting of the contemporary nude—that is, the neoclassical nude produced by his peers in Rome. "Every young sculptor seems to think that he must give the world some specimen of indecorous womanhood, . . . call it Eve, Venus, a Nymph, or any name that may apologize for a lack of decent clothing. . . . An artist . . . cannot sculpture nudity with a pure heart, if only because he is compelled to steal guilty glimpses at hired models. The marble inevitably loses its chastity under such circumstances."[74] In this soliloquy from *The Marble Faun,* Hawthorne posits a sinful guilt that inheres in both the artist and the sculpture. The artist cannot have "a pure heart" if "he" sculpts the nude. Nor can the sculpture (and those who view it) remain "chaste" under these conditions. Such guilt is doubly true for a woman artist.

Lander, perhaps more than any other woman in Rome at the time, evoked a range of anxieties in Hawthorne and other male sculptors. He questioned Lander's "pure heart," as she stole "guilty glimpses" of the female body, for he admitted feeling ashamed when looking "at naked limbs in the company of women."[75] Lander's transgressions—her undomesticated personal life and daring professional career—posed a threat to the social order of Rome.

Through rumor and innuendo, Lander was repositioned as a sexualized spectacle—defined as an object of male desire, having "lived on uncommonly good terms with some man." Rogers had described her as "really vain of her figure"; in other words, she had been accused of exposing herself as a model and was thus identified with the sensuous sculpture that she had created. This psychic process, termed the Pygmalion effect, posits a woman sculptor as "coincident with the objects she creates," art historian Nancy Proctor explains, and associates her "inherent moral nature with her work's narrative figures."[76] Aligning Lander's moral temperament with her controversial nudes, Hawthorne and others created a scenario in which the artist was judged guilty, if only by association, and thus was considered unchaste and impure in character.

In Rome, Lander's punishment assumed yet another form. Some "American and a person of culture," Julian Hawthorne reported, had taken it upon himself to improve upon her portrait of Hawthorne. While she was away in Boston, "this mysterious person" directed Roman workmen to make changes to the marble bust. This event—whether real or imagined—reasserted artistic creativity as masculine. This superimposition of masculine authority by an "American and person of culture" reinstated traditional gendered power relations.[77] The female artist was once again assumed to be the student and/or amateur in need of masculine supervision.

On April 1, 1860, Lander returned to Boston, where she was well received by critics, patrons, and the general public. Never losing her pluck, she immediately set to work in her Tremont Street studio. In 1861, she exhibited the statuettes *Undine* and *Evangeline* at the Williams and Everetts Gallery; at the Boston Athenaeum she displayed a new work, *America Defending Her Children.*[78] One critic praised the artist for her "vast industry," which served as "proof of the progress made . . . as regards 'woman's sphere' and woman's capabilities." Addressing the Roman scandal, the critic claimed that Lander was "endowed with genius," a fact "conceded even by those hypercritics who cavil at 'women-artists.'" To be sure, the Boston art world allowed Lander to recuperate her badly damaged career, asserting that she would "add lustre to the American name should her life be spared and she be permitted to pursue her profession."[79]

In March of 1861, she exhibited a large-scale marble version of *Virginia Dare* in Boston. The sculpture had been roughly cut into marble by Italian workmen under her careful direction; in Rome, she had remained directly involved in every aspect of the carving process. When the sculpture was near completion, she "assumed [the figure's] entire finish," one writer reported, "not permitting even the most experienced workman to touch it."[80] Distrusting the time-worn Roman tradition of hiring skilled carvers to polish and clean the marble with a pumice stone, Lander assumed full responsibility for the completion of the work, demonstrating her own virtuoso carving skills. Sadly, after the sculpture was shipped to Boston in December of 1860, it was temporarily lost at sea in a shipwreck. Two months later, the sculpture washed ashore at Palos, Spain. After much logistical wrangling, Lander reclaimed her sculpture, shipped it to Boston, and restored it to its original state.[81] "[N]o unloving hand has been allowed to prune away a muscle . . . or wander over the sweet lines of the face. No," one critic emphasized when the sculpture was exhibited in Boston. "Miss Lander holds to the old belief, that it is absolutely necessary that the artist's hand should leave upon the marble the stamp that marks the individuality of the work and the sculptor. No ordinary workman . . . has been allowed . . . to destroy the vitality that comes and only comes from the hand of genius."[82]

Despite her professional success in Boston, she volunteered for the war effort in May of 1861. Along with other reformist women, like the author Louisa May Alcott and the sculptor Sarah Fisher Ames, she moved to Washington, D.C., where she administered to wounded soldiers in local hospitals.[83] In Hosmer's view, as she confided to Wayman Crow, Lander's transformation into a "Florence Nightingale" was a "more appropriate occupation for her than sculpture."[84] Clearly relieved that the troubled sculptor had quit Rome, Hosmer became suspicious of malicious rumors that began to circulate around her. Were women becoming open targets in Rome's patriarchal society? Hosmer continued to follow Lander's career in the United States, where she would open her own studio in Washington, D.C., and pursue a sculptural career until the early 1870s, when historical documentation of her life comes to an end.[85]

## The *Zenobia* Scandal

In 1857, Hosmer began work on her *Zenobia in Chains* (fig. 25), creating a small-scale version of the sculpture for which the British historian Anna Jameson provided advice and guidance. Jameson had long fought for women's rights, especially the right of women artists to enter the Royal Academy School in London. Her support for the young sculptor bolstered Hosmer's reputation while stimulating the market for her work in Britain.[86]

By February of 1858, Hosmer had created her four-foot-high clay model of the Palmyrene queen who, in antiquity, had been conquered by the emperor Aurelian and paraded through the streets of Rome.[87] Workmen from John Gibson's studio prepared the clay and armature for the full-sized model. Upon her return from Tuscany in October 1858, she encountered not only the crisis surrounding Lander's career but also malevolent rumors about her own work, "the malignant sarcasm of some of [her] rivals," Jameson explained, who were suspicious of her professional association with Gibson.[88]

Jameson counseled the young artist to ignore the comments heard at the Caffè Greco, the eatery near the Spanish Steps where Anglo-American artists took their meals, engaged in conversation and gossip, and at times learned of commissions. "The originality of a conception remains your own, with the stamp of your mind upon it," she wrote to Hosmer. "Impertinent and malicious insinuations die away, [but] your work and your fame [will] remain, as I hope, for a long, long future."[89]

By March of 1859, Hosmer was sufficiently advanced on the full-sized clay figure to invite

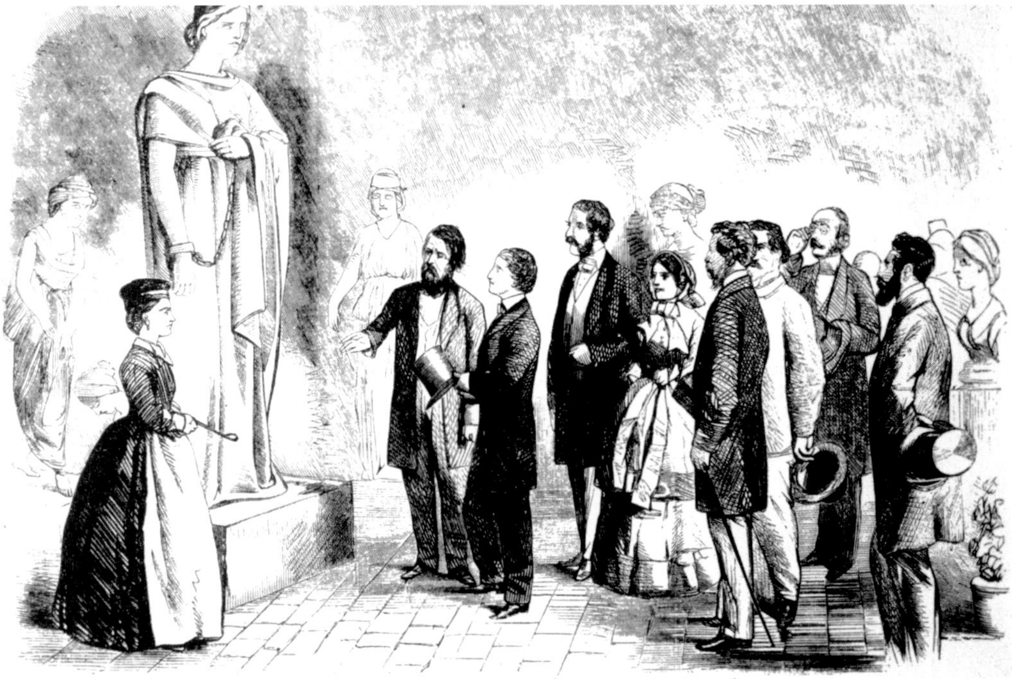

FIG. 30
*The Prince of Wales at Miss Hosmer's Studio,* from *Harper's Weekly,* May 1859.

visitors to her studio. Together with his wife, Hawthorne viewed the *Zenobia.* The sculpture "stood in the centre of the room," he declared, "as yet unfinished in the clay, but a very noble and remarkable statue indeed, full of dignity and beauty." He claimed that he had "seldom or never been more impressed by a piece of modern sculpture."[90] By the summer, Hosmer was prepared to put her *Zenobia* into marble, after having selected the stone block herself.[91]

In May, the Prince of Wales visited Rome. Gibson, as the leading British sculptor in the city, had the privilege of escorting him to forty artists' studios, the Vatican and Capitoline Museums, and the Villa Albani. Naturally, he led the prince to Hosmer's studio on via Margutta. *Harper's Weekly* recorded this visit in an engraving, *The Prince of Wales at Miss Hosmer's Studio* (fig. 30).[92] The image is telling. Gibson, the prince, and his entourage stand before the monumental sculpture of Zenobia. The artist, diminutive in comparison with her towering work, stands to the side with arms folded and modeling tool in hand. She wears her signature beret but no pantaloons; an apron covers her skirt. She stands silently by—as much the object of the viewers' gaze as her sculpture. Scattered around the studio are several female sculptures and busts. It is the bearded Gibson who discusses the *Zenobia* with the prince; he is the authority, not the young artist. The image reinforced the notion that Gibson held mastery over his young charge.[93]

*Zenobia* sailed for Britain in 1862 for display in the International Exposition in London's

Crystal Palace. In May, Cushman, Stebbins, Gibson, and Hosmer traveled to England to view the exhibition.[94] Hosmer was pleased with her sculpture's placement in the center of the exhibition hall "in a small octagonal temple . . . with niches on four sides . . . lined with Pompeiian red." Three niches contained Gibson's tinted *Venus*es (fig. 11); the fourth niche, to the rear of the temple, held the monumental *Zenobia.* More than six hundred thousand people visited the exhibition during its six-month run.[95] As Hosmer was the only woman to exhibit work at the London Exposition, her career began to surge. "The majestic *Zenobia,*" the Irish feminist Frances Power Cobbe explained, attracted attention by speaking to the burgeoning women's rights movement in Britain.[96] She also showed the *Medusa* bust (fig. 13) owned by Lady Marian Alford and the *Puck,* purchased by the Prince of Wales (fig. 22).

The American astronomer Maria Mitchell visited Hosmer's Roman studio in 1858 and described the technical process by which her fancy piece *Puck* came into existence.

> *The hard-handed men of Italy worked in marble from the designs put before them; one copied the leaves . . . ; another turned with his tool the folds of the drapery; another wrought up the delicate tissues of the flesh; none of them dreamed of ideas: they were copyists. . . .*
>
> *. . . [Hosmer] thinks in clay. . . . [When] the model [is] finished[,] cast in dull, hard, inexpressive plaster, she stands by the workmen while they put it into the marble. She must watch them, for a touch of the tool in the wrong place might alter the whole expression of the face, as a wrong accent in the reader will spoil a line of poetry.*[97]

Indeed, Hosmer was the artist who "[thought] in clay," her studio workmen the technicians who carefully carved the work in marble. Like her male colleagues in Rome, she, while occupied with the details of a busy international career, relied on skilled workmen to put her sculptures into marble.

Allegations that Hosmer did not do her own work had circulated throughout the Roman community since 1858. Even Cushman had criticized the young sculptor for doing too little work in her studio and enjoying herself too much in Roman society. Writing to Emma Crow, she complained that Hosmer "really does very little of her own work. . . . She can afford to employ other people to do it for her—and she takes the credit and the profit."[98] Almost a year later, in 1863, she reiterated: Hosmer "does less of [her own work] every day of her life. . . . And [with] this getting about—all other female artists suffer from the same imputation."[99] Cushman was aware that the creative authority of women artists in Rome was regularly challenged. She feared that Hosmer's reliance on studio assistants would damage not only her own career but also the professional reputations of other women. Eventually, Cushman relented and lent her support to Hosmer's studio procedures. Although the sculptor had more work "done for her than anyone else," Cushman conceded that Hosmer was ultimately "right" in her choices. For Cushman was concerned about her partner, Stebbins, who "assume[ed] labours [in the studio] for which she ha[d] neither physical nor mental strength."[100] In the wake of the scandals concerning Lander—and now Hosmer—that occupied the Roman community, it was not surprising that both Stebbins and Margaret Foley would insist upon authorial authenticity by carving their own marbles in Rome, despite adverse effects on their health.

Libelous comments against Hosmer first found their way into print in the obituary of the

British sculptor Alfred Gatley, published in the *Queen: The Lady's Newspaper and Pictorial Times* in July 1863. Envious of the attention that *Zenobia* had garnered in London, Gatley was "a disappointed man," wrote a friend and supporter of the recently deceased sculptor. The obituary leveled a direct salvo at Hosmer: "the 'Zenobia'—said to be by Miss Hosmer"—was "really executed by an Italian workman at Rome."[101] With these public remarks, Hosmer was portrayed as a fraud, "a trader in mass-produced goods," the art historian Deborah Cherry explained, "not fit for the category of artist." The *Queen,* a relatively lowbrow publication, probably wanted to increase its circulation with a little juicy slander.[102] Six weeks later the story found its way into the *Art-Journal,* the most distinguished British art periodical of the time.

Hosmer was furious at the accusations. Having heard these innuendos for too long, she hired a London lawyer to defend her reputation.[103] Her friends came to her defense. In December, Gibson avowed, "If Miss Hosmer's works were the productions of other artists, and not her own, there would be in my studio two imposters—Miss Hosmer and myself."[104] Story published a defense in the *Athenaeum,* a distinguished English journal of arts and letters with a large circulation, claiming the "utter falsity" of the accusations.[105] "Those who know this amiable lady and accomplished artist," he wrote, "will treat [this accusation] with the contempt it deserves. . . . The 'Zenobia' was the product of Miss Hosmer's own mind and her own hands." He explained that the workman, Signor Nucci, assisted her "in the first manual labour of putting up the irons and clay from her original sketch . . . [then] the statue passed into the hands of Miss Hosmer, by whom solely it was carried forward and completed."[106]

Unlike Lander, who had remained silent throughout her ordeal, Hosmer went on the attack. In several venues and with different strategies she confronted her accusers. She first wrote a letter to the *Art-Journal:* "Silence on my part would be equivalent to an admission of [the] truth [of this slander]. . . . We all know that few artists who have been in any degree successful enjoy the truly friendly regard of their professional brethren; but a *woman* artist, who has been honoured by frequent commissions, is an object of peculiar odium. I am not particularly popular with any of my brethren."[107] In January 1864 both journals offered their apologies to the artist; retractions were also printed in the *London Times* and the *Galignani Messenger* in Rome.[108]

Hosmer did not stop there. She wrote a sardonic poem about the male artists in Rome and published it in the *New York Evening Post* in the fall of 1864. Furthermore, in December 1864 she submitted to the *Atlantic Monthly* a detailed article that "raise[d] the veil upon the mysteries of the studio."[109] Using both playful humor and a serious approach to the profession of sculpture, she insisted her voice be heard.

In her "Doleful Ditty of the Roman Caffè Greco," she parodied the male sculptors' anguish over female accomplishments in Rome:

*'Tis time, my friends, we cogitate,*
*And make some desperate stand,*
*Or else our sister artists here*
*Will drive us from the land.*

*It does seem hard that we at last*
*Have rivals in the clay,*
*When for so many happy years*
*We had it all our way.*

Ultimately, the narrator, a painter, offers advice to the disgruntled sculptors:

> *Suppose you try another plan,*
> *More worthy [of] art and you;*
> *Suppose you give them for their works*
> *The credit which is due.*
>
> *An honest and a kindly word,*
> *If spoken now and then,*
> *Would prove what seems a doubtful point*
> *You could, at least, be* men.[110]

On a more serious note, she reiterated in the *Atlantic Monthly* the sculptural process inaugurated by Canova and taught to her by Gibson, the standard practice used by most sculptors in Rome. The artist began with a small clay model "in which he carefully studie[d] the composition of his statue, the proportions, and the general arrangement of the drapery," without regard to finish. This small model was cast in plaster to preserve it. Then skilled workmen enlarged the work in clay, building an iron-and-wood armature. The artist gave the statue "the last refinement of beauty," then he passed it on to the workmen to be cast into plaster before working it up into marble. "The sculptor merely direct[ed] and correct[ed] the work as it proceed[ed]. . . . In some cases, the finishing touches [were] introduced by the artist himself . . . [but most preferred] to occupy themselves with some new creation." She hastened to distinguish the artist, who "conceive[d], compose[d], and complete[d] the design," from the workman, who "translate[d] the original thought of the sculptor, written in clay, into the language of marble." Hosmer was a forceful feminist, arguing that "we women-artists have no objection to its being known that we employ assistants; we merely object to its being supposed that it is a system peculiar to *ourselves*." She concluded, "It is high time . . . that the public should understand in what the sculptor's work properly consists, and thus render less pernicious the representations of those who . . . [would] deprive [artists], and more particularly women-artists, of the credit to which, by talent or conscientious labor, they are justly entitled."[111]

In her last volley, she named the perpetrator of this scandal: the American sculptor Joseph Mozier, who, although appearing to be a friend, had "never lost an opportunity of defaming [her] artistic reputation."[112] Artists regularly perpetuated "petty jealousies" in Rome, Hawthorne explained. For example, Lander accused Mozier of plagiarism when producing his *Prodigal Son* group of 1858. She mentioned to Hawthorne that he had "stolen—adopted, we will rather say—the attitude and general idea of this groupe" from a student at the French Academy.[113] Artists in Rome, Hawthorne wrote, "are not generous or gracious critics of one another; and I hardly remember any full-breathed and whole-souled praise from sculptor to sculptor, or from painter to painter. They dread one another's ill-word, and scrupulously exchange little attentions for fear of giving offence; they pine, I suspect, at the sight of another's success, and would willingly keep a rich stranger from the door of any studio save their own."[114]

Hosmer ultimately profited from the *Zenobia* scandal. Her reputation soared, transforming her career in Rome, Britain, and the United States. Before the sculpture was shown in Boston in 1865, for example, the authorial scandal only "enhanced its European reputation, and awakened [a] universal desire . . . for its exhibition" in the United States.[115] Hosmer took no chances with its viewing conditions, distributing the *Atlantic Monthly* article as an exhibition broadside in all its venues (New York, Boston, and Chicago). The artist was on the defensive, explaining her sculptural process and proclaiming the work her own.[116]

Boston gave Hosmer a rousing hometown welcome. According to one source, thirty thousand people crowded the Childs and Jenks Gallery.[117] "No single work of art," Anna Ticknor wrote from Boston, "ever attracted so much attention here. . . . It has made a strong impression on the New England mind."[118] The *Boston Evening Transcript* reprinted her humorous tirade about male artists in Rome, "The Doleful Ditty of the Roman Caffè Greco." Julia Ward Howe, editor of the *Boatswain's Whistle*—the daily paper of the Boston Sanitary Commission—profiled the artist's life and baldly defended her reputation against calumny.[119] Because of *Zenobia*'s popularity, the gallery extended the length of the show to four months and added extra viewing hours each day. The show finally closed the first week of May 1865.[120]

With the success of the *Zenobia,* Hosmer began plans for a new luxurious studio in Rome at via delle Quattro Fontane 26. She jokingly called it the Palazzetto Barberini (the small Barberini palace) because it was situated just down the street from the grand Palazzo Barberini, where the Story family resided.[121] This was one of the choicest neighborhoods in Rome. "When [the studio] is done," she claimed "without exaggeration, there will be no studio in Rome which can hold a candle to it."[122] After years of struggle, she had become financially independent through the sale of her sculpture. She had more work than she could handle, even with a studio full of workmen. "Croesus has smiled on me this year," she wrote happily. "I have nothing to complain of in the way of work."[123] In 1865, her new expanded workplace became one of the most famous studios in the city. "Miss Hosmer has one of the most beautiful studios in Rome," one visitor opined, with "plants and flowers and a fountain setting [for] her statues and busts."[124]

In her "palace-like studio," Hosmer presented a new public persona to the art world.[125] No longer the "little impish boy" of earlier years; she now regularly dressed in full Victorian wear—flouncy skirts and lacy cuffs—and sported longer, more carefully coiffed hair, a feminized image in keeping with her mature, professional stature (fig. 31). Her weekly reception days at the new studio were highly celebrated, as she received all her visitors in person. "It was pleasant to find a bright, piquant, woman," one visitor noted, "instead of the Amazon . . . which our fancy had conjured from the shadowy realm of gossip."[126] Like Cushman and Stebbins, Hosmer adopted the identity of a proper bourgeois matron, no longer assuming the guise of a "tomboy" or "Amazon." Her life as a professional sculptor and her embrace of true womanhood seemed in harmony rather than in conflict.

No matter how "ladylike" she had become, however, Hosmer never lost her sense of humor. Shortly after moving into the new studio, she had a series of photographs taken with her workmen. Posing for these images, she stood with either crossed arms or clasped hands among her large force of workmen around a replica of *The Fountain of the Siren,* commissioned by her friend and patron Lady Marian Alford (fig. 32). These images were quite popular, Hosmer admitted. So many

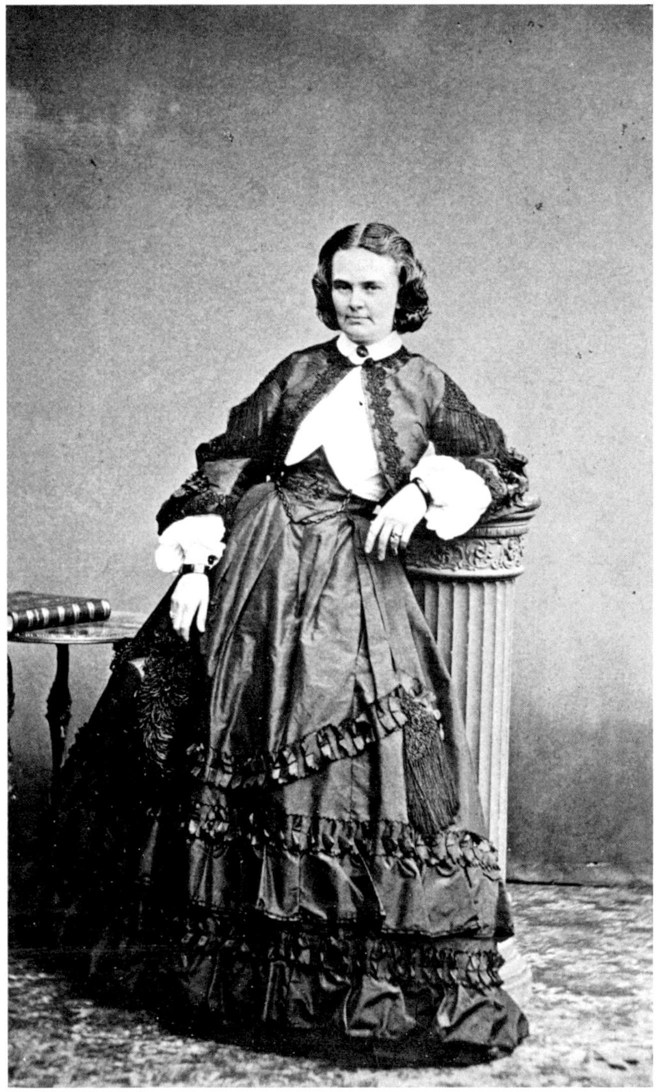

FIG. 31
Harriet Hosmer, ca. 1867, photograph. Harriet Goodhue Hosmer Papers, The Schlesinger Library, Radcliffe Institute, Harvard University, A162-72-7.

friends wanted copies, she could not keep track of them: "I don't know how many photographs I might have given away."[127] Posing for the photograph "by way of a joke," she called the image *Hosmer and Her Men,* creating a parody of the gender dynamics of the Roman art world. With her success, she felt free to mock the very real obstacles that stood in the way of feminine artistic production in Rome.

## *Margaret Foley's Studio in Rome*

Margaret Foley had dreamed of living in Rome since 1857, but ill health and meager finances kept her in Boston until 1861, when she accompanied Cushman and Stebbins on their return trip to Italy. A pale, slender woman with a mass of brown hair that "when loosened" swept "the floor when she sat," Foley initially joined the Cushman

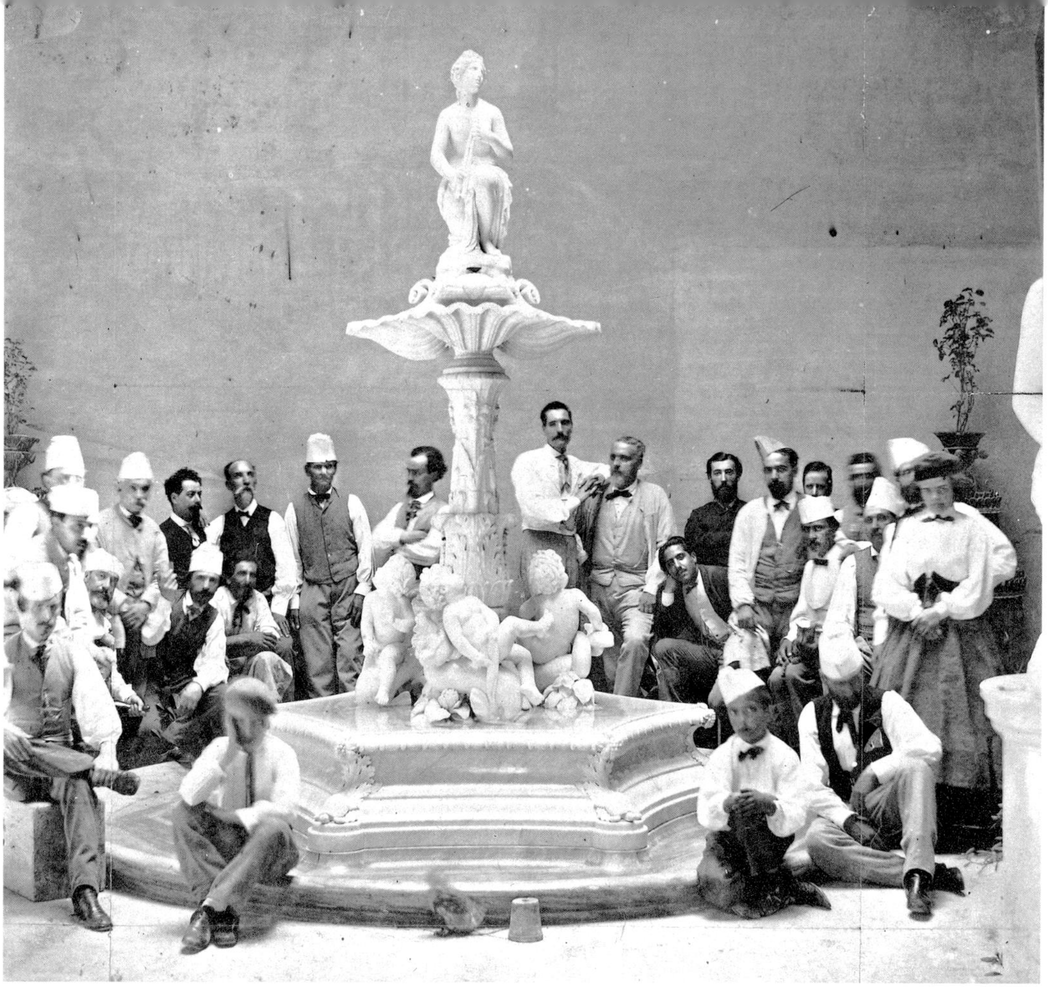

FIG. 32
*Hosmer and Her Men,* 1864, photograph. Harriet Goodhue Hosmer Papers, The Schlesinger Library, Radcliffe Institute, Harvard University, A162-74-2.

household in Rome. Warmly greeted by Hosmer, she temporarily shared Stebbins's studio on via Sistina. Although she managed to save $400 for the voyage, her financial situation in Rome proved difficult because of the unfavorable exchange rate.[128] As was her way, Cushman procured commissions for the struggling artist, securing medallion portraits of Wayman Crow and his daughter Emma. To supplement her income, Foley also wrote about art for the *Boston Evening Transcript* and the *Crayon*.[129] She personified the "American dream" as a self-made woman. Despite humble origins and having worked as an operative in a textile mill in her youth, she now found herself in Rome. "Without prestige, influence, or money, with no friends but those of her own making," one critic wrote, she succeeded with "absolutely no advantages but those she created by the way."[130]

After studying with John Gibson, Foley opened her own studio on via Due Macelli. There is little doubt that the art market drove her aesthetic choices. For the most part, she produced relief medallions and fancy pieces, while continuing to work as a cameo carver. Relief medallions were less expensive for patrons than sculpture in the round—less costly both in materials and in shipping.[131] One critic lamented that the artist was "forced to confine herself too closely to portrait medallions to allow the freest development of her genius."[132] Simultaneously, she was commended for her "great taste, purity and tenderness," particularly as manifested in these medallions.[133]

American and British tourists visited her studio with regularity; British women, in fact, made up the majority of her patrons.

Foley carved her own marbles until failing health prevented this endeavor. Like Lander and Stebbins, she was inclined to do her own carving, not just for financial reasons, but to assure authorial control over her works. In the wake of the scandal that surrounded Hosmer's *Zenobia*, she went to great lengths to "practice . . . openness regarding her work" and invited visitors to "watch and criticize her . . . method of handling" the marble.[134] Of the women sculptors at work in Rome, Hosmer was the only one to employ studio assistants. She did so as a matter of principle, of course. But it was also true that Hosmer had the most flourishing career, with commissions that required constant assistance.

By the second half of the 1860s, Foley had developed a thriving professional career. "We all rejoice in Miss Foley's success," a Boston friend wrote from Rome. "She is so earnest and has striven so hard to overcome difficulties." Within a ten-day period in January of 1868, the writer explained, Foley received four orders for sculptures, totaling $3,000 in commissions.[135] Moreover, she showed her medallions, portraits, and ideal heads in Rome, New York, and Philadelphia, at international expositions in Dublin and Paris, and in the Exhibition of the Society of Female Artists in London.[136]

Foley was praised for her technical skills; she executed her marble medallions in relatively low relief, giving them qualities of lightness, precision, and grace.[137] Among her most well-known pieces was *Pascuccia* (1866; fig. 33), a marble relief medallion of the famous Neapolitan model, "whose rich and splendid beauty," one writer noted, was also seen in many other contemporary images. The relief presents the head, neck, and shoulders in strict profile. The model is bejeweled with earrings and necklace, sporting a shawl that covers the back of her head. She wears a Renaissance-style garment with a bodice revealing delicate textures. The hair displays deeply carved curls and ringlets, a technique learned, no doubt, from studying ancient Roman portraiture in the Capitoline Museum. The carving is precise and detailed.

The facial features are highly specific—recalling a historical personage rather than an ideal rendering. In an interesting way, the portrait recalls the polyglot of cultures that constituted Rome and the South of Italy in the nineteenth century. Referencing the centrality of Christianity to Roman identity, the model wears a cross attached to a double string of shells around her neck. Yet the face recalls an Eastern exoticism, displaying Semitic rather than classicizing facial features. As one writer opined, the artist "is gifted with a rapid insight into character, which is as important an element in depicting the human face divine as the deft fingers of the draughtsman." In this work, Foley captured a distant and exotic Roman world that appealed to patrons (she sold at least four versions of this sculpture), tourists, and artists alike.[138]

In 1869, she opened a studio on via Margutta, in the Palazzo Patrizi. "The walls of Miss Foley's room are well lined with medallion portraits, in which she has been so successful, and which have gained for her so wide a reputation."[139] By 1872, she owned her own house in Rome and managed two studios—one for work and one for exhibition purposes.[140]

Foley never suffered from the opprobrium that haunted the careers of Lander and Hosmer, as she was securely ensconced in a tightly knit

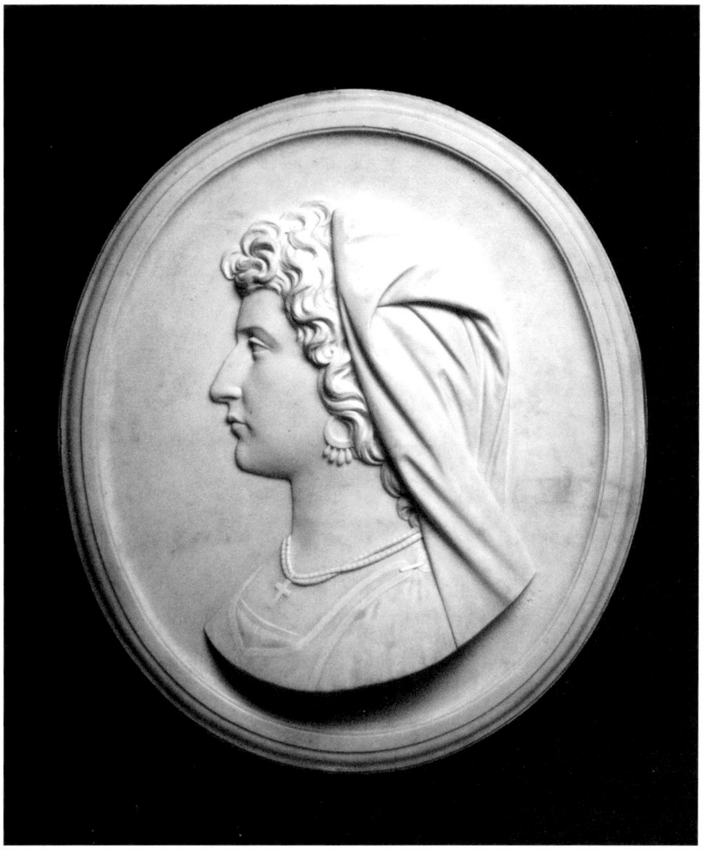

FIG. 33
Margaret Foley, *Pascuccia,* 1866, stone, 23 × 21 in. Museum of Fine Arts, Boston, gift of The Prince Company, Inc., 1987.472. Photograph © 2014 Museum of Fine Arts, Boston.

expatriate feminine world. Known for her sympathy, tenderness, and warmheartedness by those who visited her studio or house, she showered her "deepest affections on her little domestic circle," which included the British painter Lizzie Hadwen, with whom she shared her home, the reformer Mary Howitt, and other English friends with whom she "lived in the most intimate relationship."[141] Among all the women artists in Rome, Foley may have been the most successful in creating a safe haven of same-sex domesticity.

By the early 1870s, her health began to fail. In 1874, she spent much of the year recovering from a "long and serious illness" that had "hindered her from all exertion," including her artwork.[142] On December 7, 1877, the artist succumbed to a stroke in Meran, Austria. She became a martyr in death, the only American woman sculptor to die at a young age in Europe. Her legacy was that of a saintly figure—fragile, loving, and selfless—the perfect embodiment of true womanhood in Rome.[143]

# *Part Two*

## *Women Sculptors and the Politics of Rome*

# Four

## *Rome in the Colonial Imagination*

"Italy, for America, functioned as the perfect other," literary critic Leonardo Buonomo has explained. In the nineteenth century, it was not considered a place of historical and material consequence, but a "gigantic picture, or a stage where a performance [was] continually held for the sake of a foreign audience."[1] In the timeless Campagna (the open landscape outside the ancient city walls), for example, dotted with Roman aqueducts and other picturesque ruins, American visitors imagined the pleasures and beauties of a distant arcadian past in which antique fauns and quaint *contadini* (peasants) idly rambled. In the city of Rome, however, these expectations were frustrated. American travelers were surprised, even taken aback, by the desperately poor Romans, the squalid conditions in which they lived, and the political tyranny to which they had been subjected for centuries.

Throughout the nineteenth century, tourists and expatriates enacted the role of "cultural colonizers" in Italy, maintaining an air of innate superiority over its vulnerable population. For Anglo-Americans in particular, this social positioning had its roots in a specifically ethnocentric worldview as neither Great Britain nor the United States held material interest or wielded imperial power on the Italian peninsula.[2] Since the late eighteenth century, Enlightenment thinking had posited that the territory north of the Alps had become the epicenter of Western civilization, that modern progressive nations—including Great Britain and the United States—had become the true heirs to the legacy of the classical tradition.[3]

The novelist Nathaniel Hawthorne captured this paradoxical sentiment perfectly when describing the Pincian Hill, the park nearest to the area where the foreigners lived in Rome. He ironically explained that this famous locale "belongs less to the native inhabitants [of Rome] than to the barbarians from Gaul, Great Britain, and beyond the sea, who have established a peaceful usurpation over whatever is enjoyable or memorable in the Eternal City."[4] This assertion remapped the status of northern Europe and the United States in relation to the Mediterranean. What was once considered the territory of the barbarian Huns and Gauls had now come to represent enlightened civilization; conversely, Italy—the once great center of a classical empire—had, in modern times, fallen into decrepitude, its people the helpless victims of tyrannical political regimes.

A perceived racial supremacy informed the encounter with the modern Italian population, whose difference from northern Europeans and Americans was apparent. The South of Italy, in particular, whose boundaries were flexible enough to include Rome, was characterized by sloth and squalor, rustic traditions, and Catholic superstition, in opposition to the industrious, civilized, and freedom-loving virtues typified by northern Europe and America. Indeed, the South of Italy was often referred to as Africa.[5]

To the nineteenth-century mind, the Italian peninsula lay on the margins of modern civilization, bordering upon the primitivism of Africa and the exoticism of the Middle East and Turkey. Between 1886 and 1887, the African-American activist and writer Frederick Douglass traveled to Europe to lay claim to the world of Western culture. Committed to the idea that Western civilization had its source in Africa, he considered Rome and Egypt important destinations on his own Grand Tour. In his journals, he described his travels from Paris to Rome as a journey toward "blackness." He explained, "As the traveler moves eastward and southward between these two great cities, he will observe an increase of black hair, black eyes, full lips, and dark complexions. He will observe a southern and eastern style of dress, gay colors, startling jewelry, and an outdoor free-and-easy movement of the people."[6] For Douglass, all roads led to Africa. The mixed-race peoples he saw in southern Italy—particularly in Rome—made evident to him the multiracial origins of modern culture.

For the most part, northern Europeans and Americans saw this racial hybridity differently. We need not look further than a genre painting by the German-American painter Albert Bierstadt to illustrate the sense of racial superiority held by American tourists in Rome. His only urban scene, *Roman Fish Market, Arch of Octavius* (1858; fig. 34), was inspired by the artist's visit to Italy in 1856–57.[7] The painting depicts a fish market in the Jewish Ghetto of Rome, near the Theatre of Marcellus, a center for local commerce rather than touristic display since the twelfth century. In all, the image contains close to three dozen figures and an accumulation of picturesque and exotic details.[8] The women in the foreground are dressed in the garb of the *contadina.* One holds a sleeping child on her lap; the other, a distaff and spindle as she spins her wool. The men gamble, tout their wares, or lazily snooze, illustrating the striking absence of work in what appears to be an arrested society. A large marble slab, supported by ancient capitals, reveals the remnants of gutted fish and demonstrates how the modern Romans had let their own cultural treasures sink into decay. The shabbiness of the scene—with its disheveled cobblestone piazza, crumbling plaster, strewn garbage, and half-torn posters—reinforced the belief of northern Europeans and Anglo-Americans that Rome was in a state of dereliction.

Toward the far right of the painting, an American couple stumbles unexpectedly upon this scene. The man—dressed in red, white, and blue—holds his easily identifiable red *Murray's* guide prominently under his arm.[9] The diminutive woman clutches her husband in fear, turning back as if to locate an exit from this frightful terrain. Guidebooks paid little attention to the ghetto, calling it "one of the dirtiest quarters" of the city.[10] An Italian beggar doffs his hat and extends his hand for alms, an especially notorious Roman vice as begging was linked to the tyranny of the Catholic Church. To American travelers, "Romanist, or papist, Italy" appeared as a backward and primitive society in which the pope and his despotic cardinals, who lived in unimaginable wealth in the walled city of the Vatican,

FIG. 34 *(opposite)* Albert Bierstadt, *Roman Fish Market, Arch of Octavius,* 1858, oil on canvas, 27 5/8 × 37 3/8 in. Fine Arts Museums of San Francisco, gift of Mr. and Mrs. John D. Rockefeller 3rd, 1979.7.12.

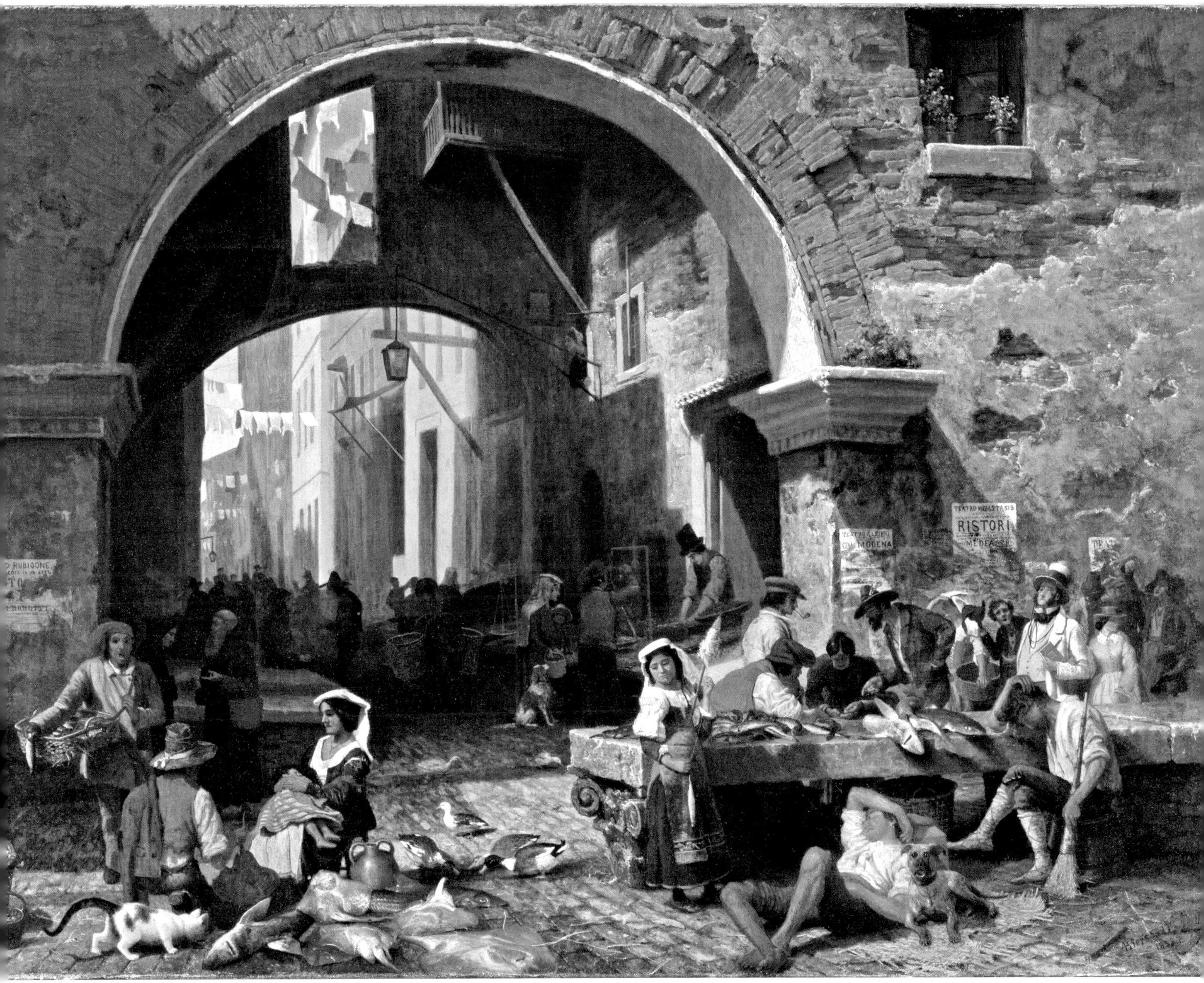
MODENA
RISTORI
MEDEA
RUBIGONE

imposed unspeakable poverty upon the city and its inhabitants.[11]

Bierstadt's choice of Roman locale suggests a doubling of difference—the foreign nature of Mediterranean life suffused with the influence of a local and ancient Judaism, whose population had been confined to the ghetto since 1556.[12] In the shadows under the ancient arch, an exotic bearded rabbi converses with a woman draped in black. In contrast to this backward culture, with its squalid conditions, the American tourists represent an enlightened, modern, and civilized world, far superior to the local population, who, lazy, ignorant, and unclean, appear unfit for modern democratic institutions. The painting reinforced a racist attitude that divided the world of degraded Italians from that of the American self-reliant individual.[13]

Hawthorne certainly agreed with this perception of Italy, writing immediately upon his arrival in the city, "Old Rome lies like a dead and mostly decayed corpse, retaining here and there a trace of the noble shape it was." Rome had "a sort of fungous growth upon it, and no life but of the worms that creep in and out."[14] In his *Notebooks,* the author regularly grumbled about the physical condition of the city—its dampness, dirt, decrepitude, and dust. Moreover, he saw the city as an inherently dangerous place, "so cold, so alley-like, into which the sun never falls, and where a chill wind forces its deadly breath into our lungs."[15] Malaria was Rome's "deadly breath," conceived of as a physical and metaphoric malady, a "contagious element rising foglike from the ancient depravity of Rome."[16]

In his last novel, *The Marble Faun; or, The Romance of Monte Beni,* Hawthorne envisioned a colonial encounter with Italy.[17] "Rome, as it now exists," he wrote, "has grown up under the Popes, and seems like nothing but a heap of broken rubbish, thrown into the great chasm between our own days and the Empire."[18] He described the dire economic, political, and cultural conditions of Rome. The Vatican controlled the city and its environs and had only its own material interests in mind. Hawthorne was rabidly antipapal, as were most Protestant visitors to the city, but at the same time he remained intrigued, even seduced, by the pomp and circumstance of Catholic ritual as performed in St. Peter's and throughout the city.

With his wife, Sophia, he visited many churches in Rome: the medieval Ara Coeli on the Capitoline Hill; the Lateran, the bishop's seat in Rome; and the Pantheon, the famed structure from antiquity that became a Catholic church dedicated to the Virgin Mary in the nineteenth century. But no church impressed like St. Peter's: "A magnificent, comprehensive, majestic symbol of religious faith," he wrote in the *Marble Faun.* "In this vast and hospitable Cathedral, worthy to be the religious heart of the whole world, there was room for all nations."[19] The relationship between religion and art both fascinated and disturbed Hawthorne and other Protestant visitors to the city. The privileging of aesthetic beauty, though sinfully attractive, represented a sensuality and decadence with which Americans were uncomfortable.[20]

*The Marble Faun* informed most American tourists' understanding of Rome in the mid–nineteenth century. It functioned as a literary travel guide, directing its readers from one site to another across the city. Virtually every American traveler to Rome had read it. Moreover, the illustrated edition, like a portable museum, served as a cultural reference for the reader. The novel opens in the gallery of the Capitoline Museum that housed (as it still does today) the *Faun of Praxiteles* (now called the *Resting Satyr*, fig. 35), the *Dying Gaul* (today entitled the *Dying Gallic Trumpeteer*), and other famous antique statuary. Three of the four main characters in the novel are American artists. Hilda, the New England Yankee, is a painter-turned-copyist of grand-master paintings. The exotic dark-haired Miriam, a sensual and mysterious woman—possibly the heiress of a Jewish banker or mulatto daughter of a Southern American plantation owner—is a talented oil painter.[21] Kenyon is a neoclassical sculptor whose character is loosely based upon the American expatriate sculptors William Wetmore Story and Paul Akers. Donatello—the only Italian character among the protagonists—is a young and handsome count whom the Americans liken to the *Faun of Praxiteles*.

Hawthorne constructs his novel as an encounter with otherness. Donatello, having descended from an ancient family of fauns, is identified by the pointed ears that lie hidden under his thick black hair. "The animal nature, indeed, is a most essential part of the Faun's composition," Hawthorne notes, "for the characteristics of the brute creation meet and combine with those of humanity, in this strange, yet true and natural conception of antique poetry and art."[22] In the doubling of the character Donatello/the Faun, Hawthorne envisions the perfect mélange of stereotypes that haunted the American imagination in Rome. As a descendant of an Arcadian family, Donatello references a distant mythical past, an imaginary and ahistorical Italy to which American tourists were attracted. Simultaneously, as a foreign being of the "lower orders of creation," the Faun/Donatello represents a racialized other, whose animalistic characteristics mark his subordination to the American protagonists.[23] Indeed, Hawthorne imagined his character as a type of "Noble Savage," exhibiting the nobility of antique statuary and, at the same time, the savagery of the bestial order. "Neither man nor animal and yet no monster," Hawthorne declares, "but a being in whom both races meet on friendly ground."[24] In his popular novel, Hawthorne conjures two Italys: the imaginary Italy of touristic desire—a mythic Arcadia—and the historical Italy loathed as a land inhabited by "the lower orders of creation."

In the opening chapter, Donatello playfully assumes the pose of the *Faun of Praxiteles*. All eyes focus on him: Kenyon examines the marble and the man "with the accuracy of a sculptor's eye"; Hilda and Miriam exercise a similar privilege, as they gaze freely upon the nude statue and the body of the exotic Italian.[25] Art authorized an empowered way of seeing in Rome and allowed women visual access to the male body—both sculptural and "in the flesh." Displaying a "most concentrated form of American independence," American women artists embodied the freedom and possibilities that the New World had to offer.[26] In Rome, these freedoms depended explicitly upon their unequal relations with the Italian people.

With *The Marble Faun* in hand, most Americans arrived in Rome ideologically inclined to enact the role of the "cultural colonizer." Predisposed toward such a racialized worldview in their assumed superiority to African-American slaves and Native American peoples, many Americans perceived the Italians as a subordinate race.[27] "No Faun in Arcadia was ever a greater simpleton than Donatello," Miriam whispered. "He has hardly a man's share of wit."[28] The journalist

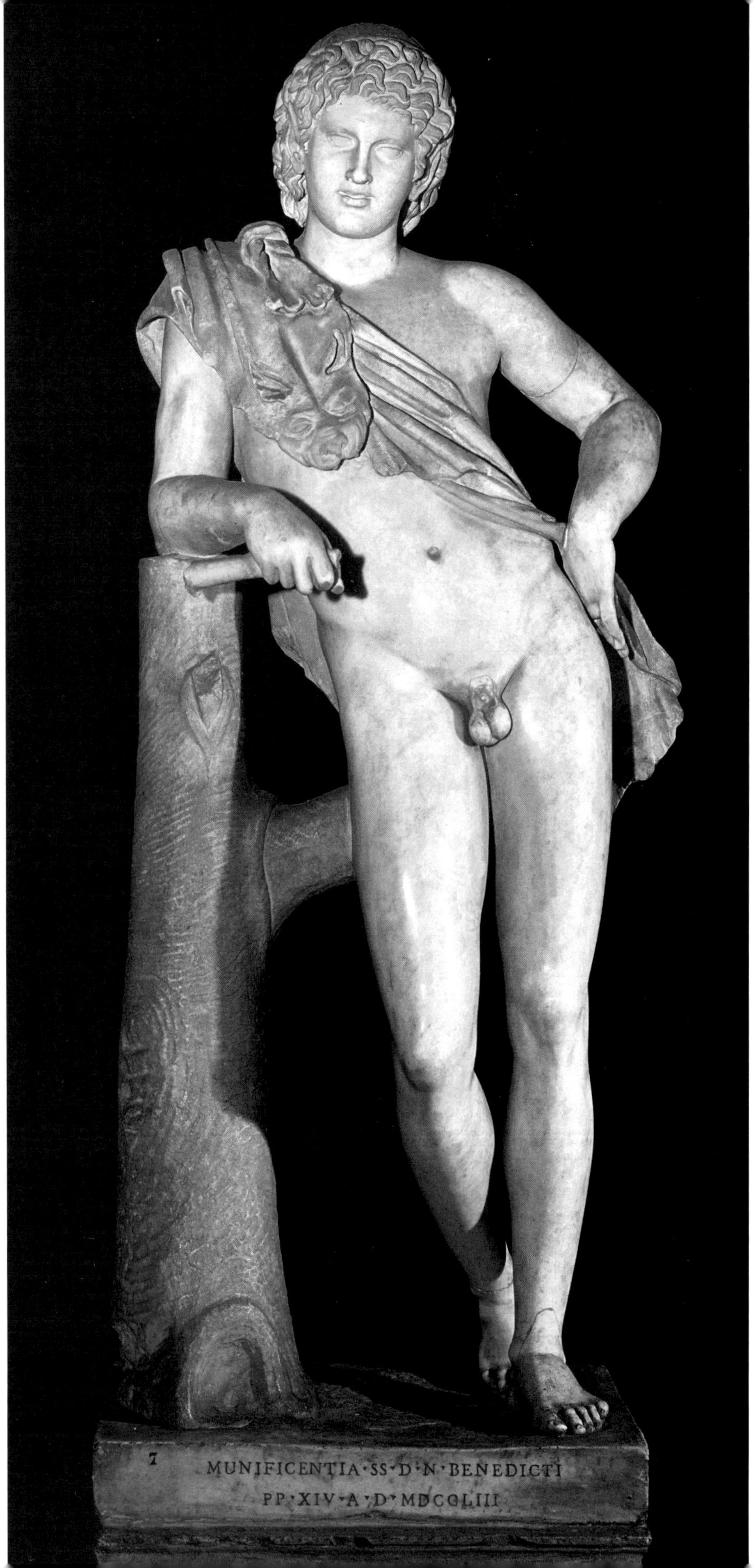


FIG. 35
*Resting Satyr,* copy of a fifth-century B.C.E. Greek statue by Praxiteles, formerly at the Villa D'Este, Tivoli, now in the Hall of the Galatian, Palazzo Nuovo, Musei Capitolini, Rome.

Margaret Fuller railed against such prejudice. The "shallow" or "ignorant" travelers, she insisted, "talk about the corrupt and degenerate state of Italy as they do about the slaves at home." They come to Rome "ready trained to that mode of reasoning which affirms that because men are degraded by bad institutions, they are not fit for better."[29]

American public sculpture—much of which was produced in Rome—was complicit in conveying this racialist message to the nation. In 1850, the U.S. Congress, for example, legislated the expansion of the Capitol building in Washington, D.C., and commissioned a decorative program that illustrated the ideology of Manifest Destiny while simultaneously addressing the "Indian Question."[30] In the mid–nineteenth century, the belief in a divinely ordained Manifest Destiny masked imperial motives. That is to say, cultural, intellectual, economic, and political processes worked together in the formation and perpetuation of the ideologies of both racial supremacy and westward expansion.[31]

While in Rome, the American expatriate sculptor Thomas Crawford submitted a design for the Senate pediment, entitled the *Progress of Civilization,* which narrated the history of the nation's settlement across the continent. The pediment included a variety of figural types: soldier, merchant, youth, teacher, mechanic, pioneer, and an Indian group. His more-than-life-sized sculpture *The Indian: The Dying Chief Contemplating the Progress of Civilization* (fig. 36) was a heroic nude figure inspired by the antique *Belvedere Torso,* which he knew from the Vatican collection. To some critics, the *Indian Chief* was Crawford's most impressive work, as he adroitly fused a national symbol with the classical ideal. "Emblematic of the extinction of the Indian race," the sculptor explained, this despondent figure wore a feathered headdress to signify his race while pondering the inevitable destiny of his people.[32] On the ground before him was an ax, whose handle an animal pelt partially covered, a not-so-subtle reference to the activity of the pioneer who tamed the wilderness for Euro-American habitation. The "Vanishing Indian," the image of a vulnerable and subjugated people, which appeared many times in the decoration of the Capitol, articulated an ideology that rendered progress inevitable and internal colonial control of Native peoples invisible.

Continental expansion in the United States was integrally related to the phenomenon of nineteenth-century European imperialism on the Italian peninsula. Comparing the treatment of the Romans by the papal regime to that of the Indians by the American government, the feminist writer and progressive reformer Catharine Maria Sedgwick explicitly aligned intra-European colonialism with governmental control over Native peoples in the United States. Whether the imperialist mission consisted in the external subjugation of colonies, as in Italy, or the internal consolidation of power within a sovereign nation, as in the United States, the effects were the same.[33] In fact, one could argue that a citizen of the United States was defined by such an imperialist worldview in the nineteenth century; put another way, imperialism was part and parcel of what it meant to be an American in the nineteenth century.

## *The Yankee Girl*

Women travelers and expatriates in Rome were emblematic of the expansiveness and vigor of

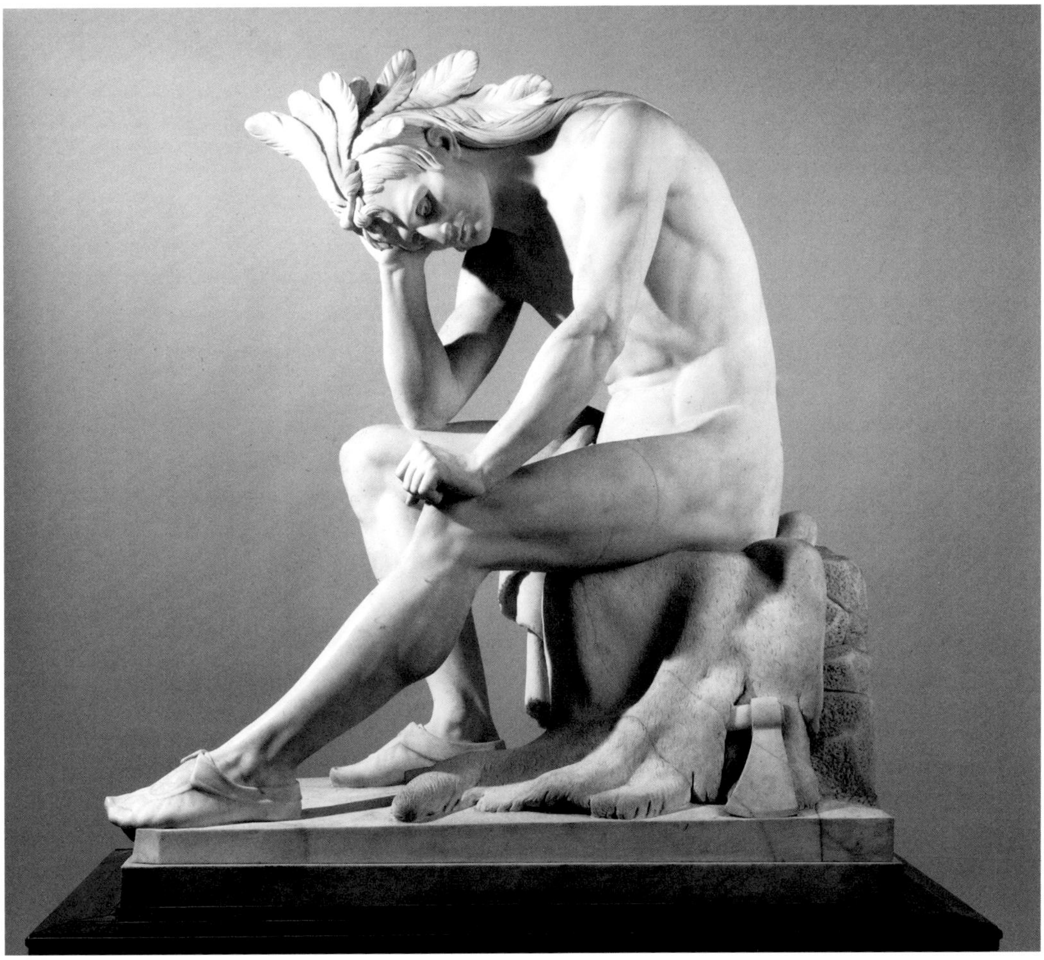

FIG. 36
Thomas Crawford, *The Indian: The Dying Chief Contemplating the Progress of Civilization,* 1856, white marble and wood, overall: 60 × 55 ½ × 28 in. Collection of The New-York Historical Society, negative #8035; object #1875.4.

American culture. Serving as emissaries of the American republic abroad, they symbolized the nation's progressive destiny and its millennial promise in contrast to the old world history and traditions of Europe. Harriet Hosmer, in particular, was regularly celebrated in the American press as "the Yankee Girl" and "one of our representative women" abroad.[34] The term "Yankee" conveyed a specific political meaning in mid-nineteenth-century Rome, referring to the Anglo-Saxon Protestant New Englander who assumed a position of racial privilege within the colonized territories of the Italian peninsula.[35]

In Rome, racial and class hierarchies shifted traditional gendered power relations and granted American women artists, writers, and reformers unparalleled freedoms within Italian culture. Embodying the tenets of republicanism, women sculptors experienced a sense of independence usually reserved for men in the Roman art world.[36] The poet Julia Ward Howe expressed her sense of personal elation in a series of poems she wrote after a visit to Rome in 1850 *without* the companionship (and guardianship) of her famous husband, the abolitionist Dr. Samuel Gridley Howe. According to her observations, she experienced the city without social constraints, indulging in privileges guaranteed her by her Anglo-Saxon heritage, American nationality, and elite social status. Enjoying the innocence and curiosity of a child, the poet reveled in the city as her playground: "I knew a day of glad surprise in Rome / Free to the childish joy of wandering." In her daily sojourns, she explored Rome, "without a 'wherefore' or 'to what end'?"[37] When she eventually departed Rome, she did so "with infinite reluctance." For Howe, "America seemed the place of exile," where the requirements of proper bourgeois femininity limited her dreams and aspirations. "Rome," however, was "the home of sympathy and comfort," where the fulfillment of her feminist desires was possible.[38] Indeed, for the community of creative women who settled in the Eternal City, the privileges of nationality and race trumped the limitations of gender.

Hawthorne acknowledged these extraordinary liberties in *The Marble Faun*. Hosmer identified with the characters in the novel, which she knew were based in part upon her own Roman experiences. Writing to her patron Wayman Crow in 1860, she expressed her pleasure in reading the romance: "I suppose you have read Hawthorne's new book. What a delicious . . . picture of Italy and Italian life!"[39] One of the novel's protagonists, Hilda, is described variously as the "fair-haired Saxon girl," a "Yankee" from New England, and the "daughter of the Puritans. . . . This young American girl was an example of the freedom of life which it is possible for a female artist to enjoy at Rome." She lived and traveled "all alone, perfectly independent, under her own sole guardianship . . . doing what she liked, without a suspicion or a shadow upon the snowy whiteness of her fame."[40] In projecting this sense of feminine liberty upon the urban spaces of Rome, Hawthorne underscores Hilda's Yankee heritage and her "snowy white" racial privilege. "The customs of artist life bestow such liberty upon the sex, which is elsewhere restricted within so much narrower limits." He continues disingenuously, "The system seems to work unexceptionally in Rome," unless, of course, one considers the career of Louisa Lander.[41]

Anglo-American women enacted a contested freedom that was both disarming and troubling to the expatriate community in Rome. They were free to traverse the streets of Rome unescorted and ride their horses across the Campagna. Hosmer, in particular, challenged the codes of proper feminine conduct. Known as a particularly good horsewoman, she was notorious for her daily rides. "Hatty takes a high hand here with Rome," the sculptor William Wetmore Story wrote in 1853, "and would have the Romans know that a Yankee girl can do anything she pleases, walk alone, ride her horse alone, and laugh at their rules." Like Hawthorne, Story recognized "the freedom of life . . . possible for a female artist to enjoy at Rome," but he did so begrudgingly. "The police interfered and countermanded the riding alone on account of the row it made in the streets," Story continued. "I believe *that* is over, but I cannot affirm."[42]

In a small undated and unattributed sketch, *The Sister Sculptresses Taking a Ride* (fig. 37), Hosmer and her older, more conventional

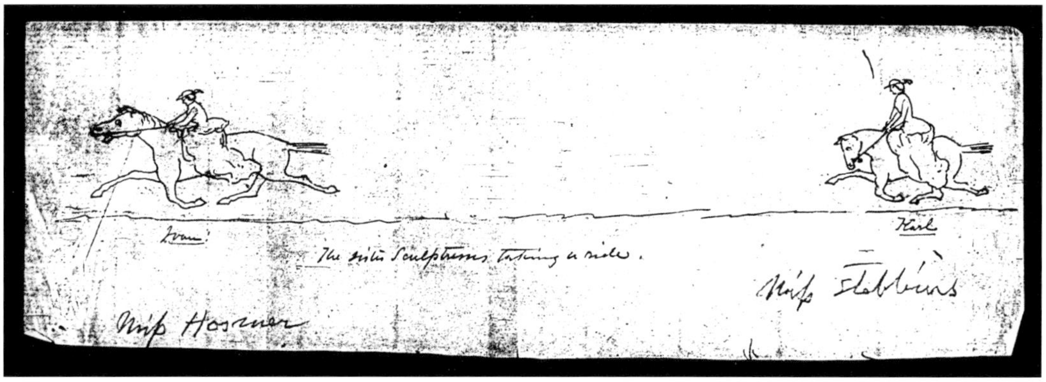


FIG. 37
*The Sister Sculptresses Taking a Ride*, early to mid-1850s, pen and ink on paper. Harriet Goodhue Hosmer Papers, The Schlesinger Library, Radcliffe Institute, Harvard University, A-162-82.

"sister sculptress" Emma Stebbins gallop with abandon across the Campagna. Both riders and horses are named: "Miss Hosmer" rides "Joan"; "Miss Stebbins," "Karl." Decked in their riding habits—feathered and brimmed hats, and full-length dresses—they fly over the Roman ground. To augment the sensation of unbridled speed, none of the horses' hooves touches the earth. Positioned toward the margins of the drawing, the two women bracket, and thus occupy, the large expanse of open land. The unusual spatial configuration visualizes the sense of freedom the women experienced in Rome.[43] As "Yankee girls," Hosmer and Stebbins had unfettered access to the Italian landscape, making it their own, and they did so within feminine convention—riding sidesaddle.[44]

Participation in Rome's urban life framed what women artists could see, experience, and represent in their art. They studied public and private art collections, visited artists' studios throughout the city, and enrolled in classes at various art academies. At the French Academy, on the Pincian Hill, where male models were available, they extended their legitimate field of vision to the male body in order to perfect their understanding of human anatomy.[45] Although officially condemned in papal Rome, life drawing was regularly taught at the academy. "No Roman is allowed to pose nude under penalty of excommunication from the Church," one writer explained. Nonetheless, nude models were readily available.[46] If women artists attended Gigi's Academy in Rome, they also had access to a model, who was either a "young [Italian] woman clothed only in a mask, or sometimes without it; [or] sometimes a naked Arab, or an [Italian] peasant boy."[47]

For the women sculptors in Rome, the ability to study from the live model was an opportunity rarely available to them elsewhere. In the United States, bourgeois women were socially conditioned to refrain from visual contact with men, as direct address was considered immodest. In general, the ability to survey their world remained highly regulated. In Rome, however, the artistic gaze—with its active knowing feminine subject—had the potential to reduce the Italian male model to a definitive object.[48] The power of the gaze positioned women sculptors in the superior role of cultural colonizers and thus reversed traditional gendered power relations.

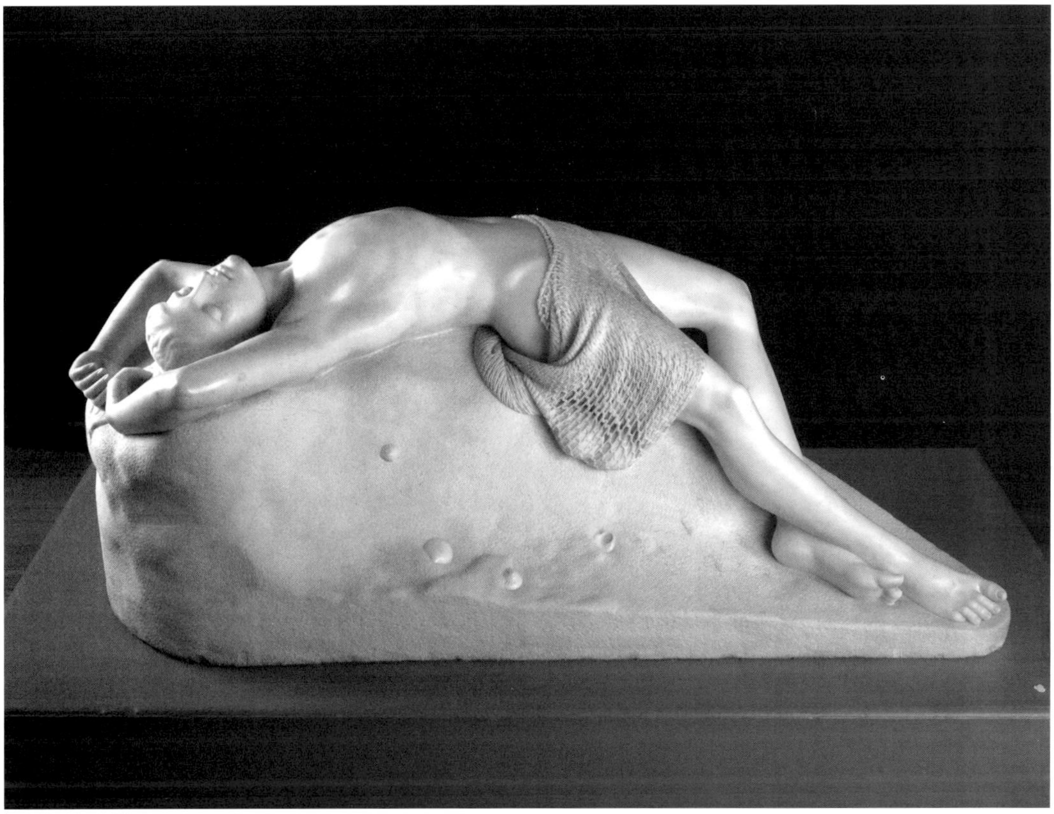

FIG. 38
Paul Akers, *Dead Pearl Diver,* 1858, marble, 27 × 67 × 28 in. Portland Museum of Art, Maine, museum purchase with support from Mrs. Elizabeth Akers Allen, John M. Adams, F. R. Barrett, John M. Brown, Philip H. Brown, Abba H. Burnham, A. W. H. Clapp, Nathan Cleaves, Francis Cushing, William G. Davis, Henry Deering, John E. DeWitt, Mark P. Emery, Francis Fessenden, S. C. Gordon, Charles M. Gore, J. H. Hamlin, George S. Hunt, James H. McMullan, W. F. Milliken, Edward A. Noyes, Lewis Pierce, William L. Putnam, Thomas B. Reed, H. W. Richardson, Henry St. John Smith, A. A. Strout, D. M. Sweat, W. W. Thomas, Payson Tucker, George P. Wescott, 1888.

## *Claiming the Male Nude*

Through the British neoclassical sculptor John Gibson, Emma Stebbins met Paul Akers, with whom she would study in Rome.[49] After sailing for Italy in 1852, Akers settled in Florence for one year before returning to the United States. In 1855, he moved permanently to Rome and opened a seven-room studio on via Antonio Canova. Akers became an integral part of the expatriate community; his close friends included Robert and Elizabeth Barrett Browning and Nathaniel and Sophia Hawthorne, as well as Charlotte Cushman and Harriet Hosmer. He regularly visited the sculpture galleries of the Capitoline and Vatican Museums, where he gained inspiration for many of his works. By 1858 his health forced him to return to the United States, where he maintained his career for a few more years. He died in Philadelphia in May of 1861.[50]

In 1857, when Stebbins studied with Akers, he was one of the most famous of the expatriate artists in Rome.[51] He was at work on his *Dead Pearl Diver* (fig. 38), completed in 1858, a sculpture of an Italian youth whose life had been lost in pursuit of pearls for the tourist economy.[52] Akers places the adolescent nude on full display: his body draped over a rock, with arms raised over his head, after having been pulled from the sea. In so doing, he aestheticizes the youthful dead body. An intricate netting, which holds two oyster shells, conceals his pelvic area. This virtuoso carving calls attention to itself, as the netting slips tantalizingly low upon the boy's hips. His extended legs are delicately crossed at the ankles. The immature—almost feminized—body conveys a safe, tame, and domesticated sexuality that did not threaten the mores of Victorian viewers. Refusing the intense carnality of the mature male body, the languorous youth, with its softly modeled limbs and torso, gently titillated viewers with its erotic display. In death the body remained forever passive, unable to return the pleasurable gaze.[53]

Akers's sculpture was the stellar attraction of his studio. Hawthorne paid homage to it in the preface to *The Marble Faun:* "The Author laid felonious hands upon . . . a statue of a Pearl-Diver, which he found in the studio of Mr. PAUL AKERS, and secretly conveyed [it] to the premises of his imaginary friend, in the Via Frezza."[54] After Hawthorne showcased this neoclassical work in his novel, it became one of the most visited sculptures in Rome.[55] Highlighting the figure's pubescent sexuality and low-class status, the sculpture trafficked in exotic spectacle and thus appealed to the American vision of Italy as a touristic playground whose vulnerable inhabitants were available for their scopic pleasure.

Stebbins was well aware of the popularity of such exotic sculptural subjects. Under the direction of Akers, she created *The Lotus Eater (Ganymede),* a small-scale male nude, between 1857 and 1860 (fig. 39). She was the first American woman artist to undertake the male nude in sculpture, modeling her thirty-inch-high marble statuette for a private patron. In this work, she alluded to Tennyson's poem "The Lotos-Eaters," which conveyed the sensuous yet dangerous pleasures that lured Odysseus's men from their ship to a paradise, where "the languid air did swoon." Tennyson created a world without time, or at least where time stood still—"In the afternoon they came unto a land / In which it seemed always afternoon."[56] Representing a "mild-eyed melancholy," "The Lotos-Eaters" suggest a withdrawal from the modern world to an exotic and illicit paradise not unlike the fabled *dolce far niente* of nineteenth-century Italian life.[57] The poem is redolent with the exotic pleasures, sensuality, and beauty associated with an imagined arcadian Italy.

Stebbins's *Lotus Eater,* with its bent head and closed eyes, appeared as if in an opium-induced state, "breathing like one that hath a weary dream."[58] Moreover, the figure's quiet languor, apparent in its exaggerated *contrapposto* pose, suggested the "idyllic lassitude" of the poem's exotic locale. In the nineteenth century, the Lotos-Eaters, the inhabitants of a faraway and remote land, were often understood within an imperialist paradigm.[59] Stebbins's *Lotus Eater* evoked the exoticism of an imagined ahistorical past while simultaneously conveying the idle passivity associated with the modern Italian subject.

In conceiving *The Lotus Eater,* Stebbins looked for inspiration to the *Faun of Praxiteles* (fig. 35), which she studied upon her many visits to the Capitoline Museum. In the nineteenth century, guidebooks attributed this work to the Greek sculptor Praxiteles, who was known for his soft and sensual style, which magically transformed the hard cold marble into a semblance of

FIG. 39
Emma Stebbins, *The Lotus Eater,* 1857–60, now lost. Photograph, Emma Stebbins Scrapbook, 1858–82, Archives of American Art, Smithsonian Institution, Washington, D.C.

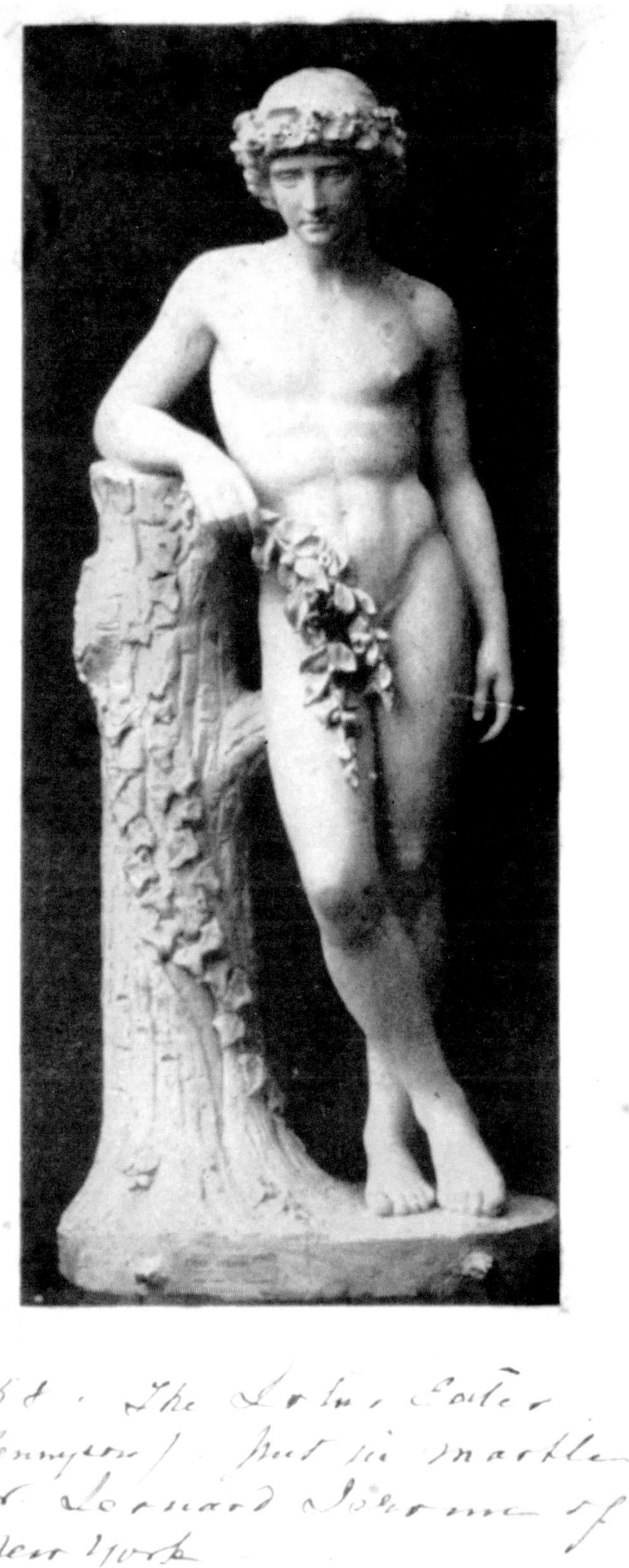

warm flesh.[60] Like the *Faun of Praxiteles,* Stebbins's *Lotus Eater* leaned rather languorously against a tree trunk, with his legs gently crossed at the ankles. Her figure wore a wreath of lotus flowers around his head and held a lotus branch in his hand, which showcased the virtuosity of her sculpting technique.[61] The beautifully rendered lotus branch, in its shape and downward positioning, highlighted the figure's eroticism by at once calling attention to the genitalia yet concealing them behind the foliage.

In 1861, Stebbins exhibited her sculpture in New York and Boston, at the moment that Hawthorne's novel achieved international acclaim. Contemporary critical writings focused upon the sensuality of the nude sculpture. A New York critic expressed relief that Stebbins had not created the "wild-eyed, melancholy lotus eater" that, he believed, Tennyson had imagined in his poem. In fact, the critic misquoted the verse, which actually noted "mild-eyed melancholy" Lotos-Eaters. Such an inaccuracy was telling, as it referenced a latent fear of the sculpture's eroticism.[62]

Hawthorne admired Stebbins's sculpture and sent her a greeting in which he encouraged her to create other works "as beautiful (if possible) as the *Lotus Eater.*"[63] He was drawn to the male nude in Rome and made numerous visits to see the *Faun of Praxiteles* in the Capitoline, closely examining every aspect of the sculpture.[64] As he writes in *The Marble Faun,* "The whole statue—unlike anything else that ever was wrought in that severe material of marble—conveys the idea of an amiable and sensual creature." The stone appears "warm to the touch," Hawthorne continues, and "comes very close to some of our pleasantest sympathies."[65] The *Faun of Praxiteles* and Stebbins's *Lotus Eater*—in their conflation of arcadian and modern stereotypes—depict passive nudes available to the male and female gaze. Within the Roman setting, the nude—an often controversial subject—became aesthetically palatable to American audiences.

Stebbins's refined character, grounded in the purity of her Anglo-Saxon bourgeois femininity, imbued the male nude with respectability. As one Boston writer stated, "God bless and keep [the women sculptors in Rome] true to their highest ideal, for the character of the artist shines out from his [*sic*] marble, and it is only the pure and noble who can do pure and noble works."[66] In depicting a "pure and noble work," Stebbins had kept her moral purity and personal nobility intact. This melding of creativity and morality proved necessary for the success of women artists in Rome; when this balancing act failed, as it did with Louisa Lander, the results were disastrous. Unlike Lander and Hosmer, who provoked a series of crises in Rome with their female nudes, Stebbins's male nude, a "beautiful showing of Youth as it look[ed] to woman," generated no controversy in Rome or in the United States.[67]

Hosmer was also taken with the character of Donatello/the Faun in Hawthorne's novel. "For me . . . Donatello's creation is one of the most exquisite poems penned," she wrote to Wayman Crow. "I don't know anything half so ideal and artistic as it is."[68] Five years later, she created her own sculptural version of this "exquisite" creature. The *London Times* wrote glowingly that "Hawthorne's description . . . of the Faun of Praxiteles has been quoted in a great measure" in Hosmer's *Sleeping Faun* (fig. 40).[69]

Remarkable in her marketing skills, Hosmer put her *Sleeping Faun* into marble in 1865, in response to the popularity of Hawthorne's

FIG. 40 *(opposite)* Harriet Hosmer, *Sleeping Faun,* after 1865, marble, 43 ½ × 41 × 16 ½ in. Museum of Fine Arts, Boston, gift of Mrs. Lucien Carr, 12.709. Photograph © 2014 Museum of Fine Arts, Boston.

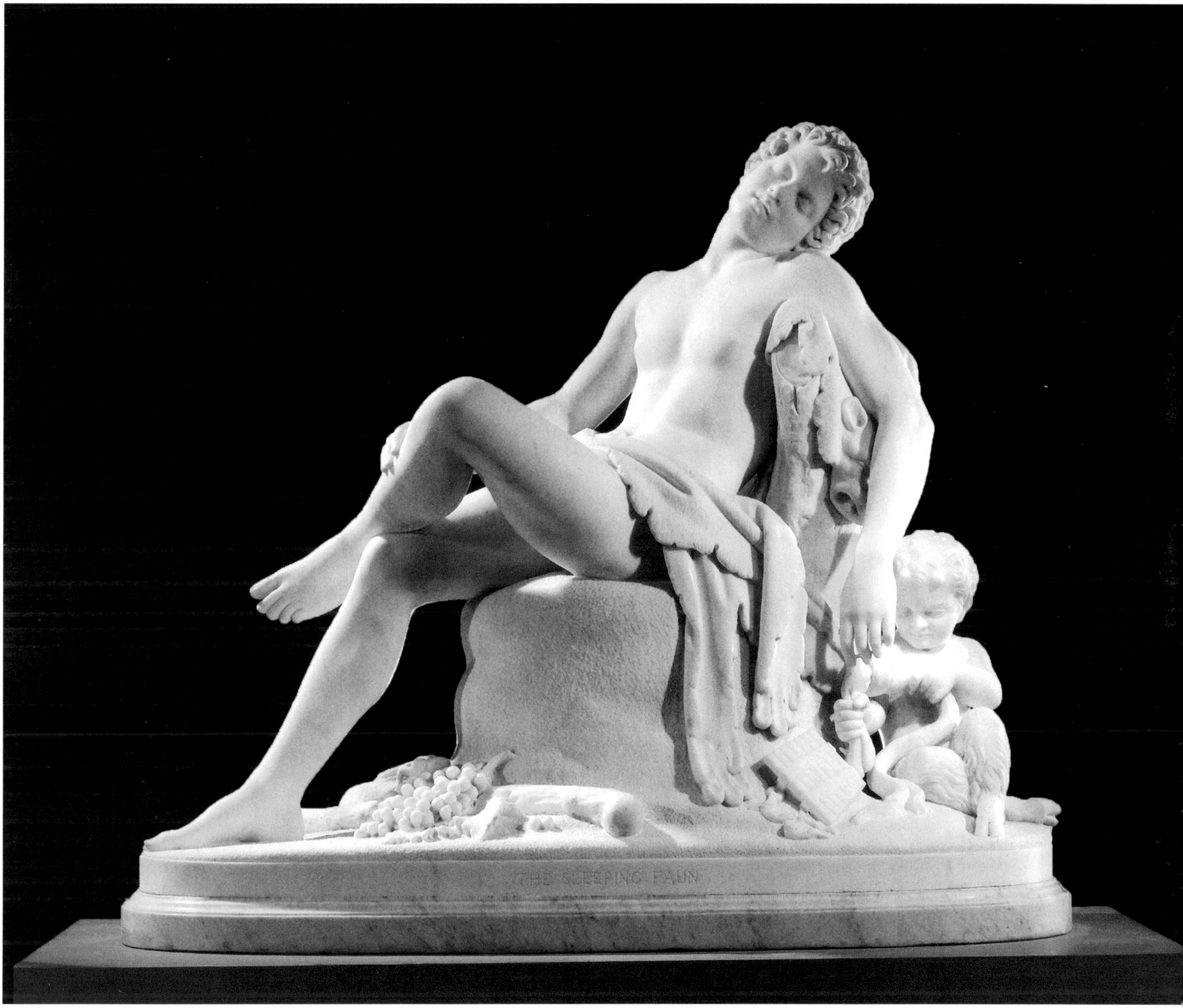
THE SLEEPING FAUN

novel. She presented her faun as an adolescent boy whose pointy ears are hidden under dense curly hair. Having dropped his reed pipe on the ground, he sleeps while leaning against a tree stump. His head leans against his left shoulder, with mouth slightly open and eyes closed. His listless left arm, draped over the tree trunk, leads the viewer's eye to the baby satyr, who, with cloven hooves, curly hair, and horns, mischievously secures the sleeping faun to the tree stump with an animal pelt. The faun crosses his left lower leg onto his right knee; his right arm stretches the length of his torso and rests gracefully on the calf of the crossed leg. His idealized features and immature anatomy signal his youth. His body is fully on display except where an animal skin modestly covers his groin. The anatomical details of the torso—the figure's ribs, sternum, pectorals, and abdomen—are clearly visible and suggest that Hosmer worked from a live model. When the statue is viewed from the back, the buttocks and upper thigh are also available to the gaze. A small lizard, a bunch of grapes, and a walking staff inhabit the base of the sculpture (fig. 41).

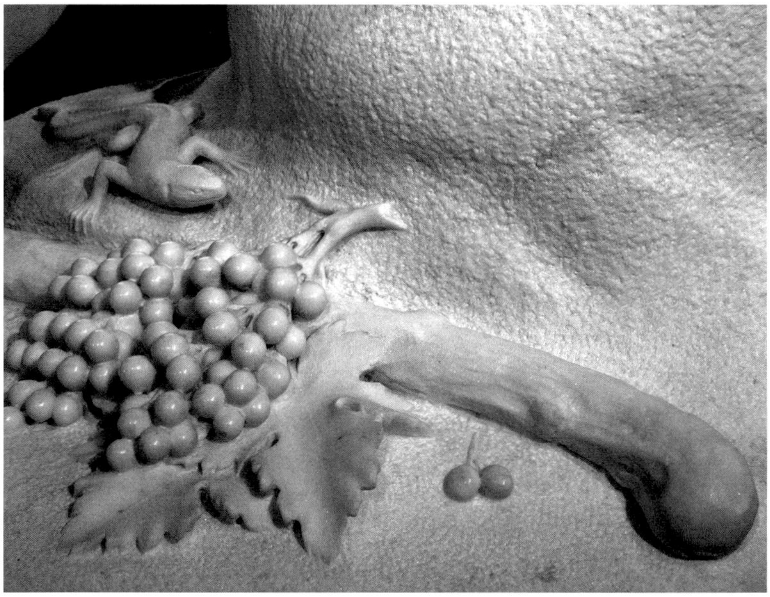

FIG. 41
Harriet Hosmer, *Sleeping Faun* (fig. 40), detail of the base.

FIG. 42 *(opposite)*
*Barberini Faun,* Roman copy after Hellenistic original, ca. 220 B.C.E., marble. Glyptotek, Staatliche Antikensammlung, Munich.

Hosmer's faun occupies a world balanced between refinement and vulgarity, the arcadian and the exotic.[70] With its highly polished surface, the sculpture imitates the sensual style of Praxiteles and his school. The delicacy of the limbs, feet, toes, and fingers suggests a feminized sensuality, reminiscent of a hermaphrodite or androgyne. The faun's carnality is visually displaced onto the accoutrements of the base—the languorous lizard, the grapes of merrymaking, and the phallic staff with twin grapes suggesting the masculine sexuality repressed in the figure itself.[71]

An American critic at the Dublin Exhibition of 1865, where Hosmer first showed the work, described the sculpture as "less coarse . . . and less inebriate" than the *Barberini Faun,* a Hellenistic sculpture that presents an image of uninhibited sexuality (fig. 42). The powerful male body reclines in a drunken state, with legs splayed and genitals in full view. Bierstadt alludes to this bawdy sculpture in his *Roman Fish Market* (fig. 34), in which he poses one of the sleeping Italian men in this indecent pose, clearly referencing the bestial nature of the Italian male. In contrast to the *Barberini Faun,* Hosmer's faun, the critic continued, is "not a savage, but a comparatively graceful and refined impersonation of sylvan nature; one of the fauns of Arcady."[72] The Irish feminist Frances Power Cobbe wrote at length about the sculpture and described it as "an image of ease and joy, and pure, sensuous, delight-brimming *existence.*"[73] Sensual yet chaste, nude but modest, youthful rather than carnal,

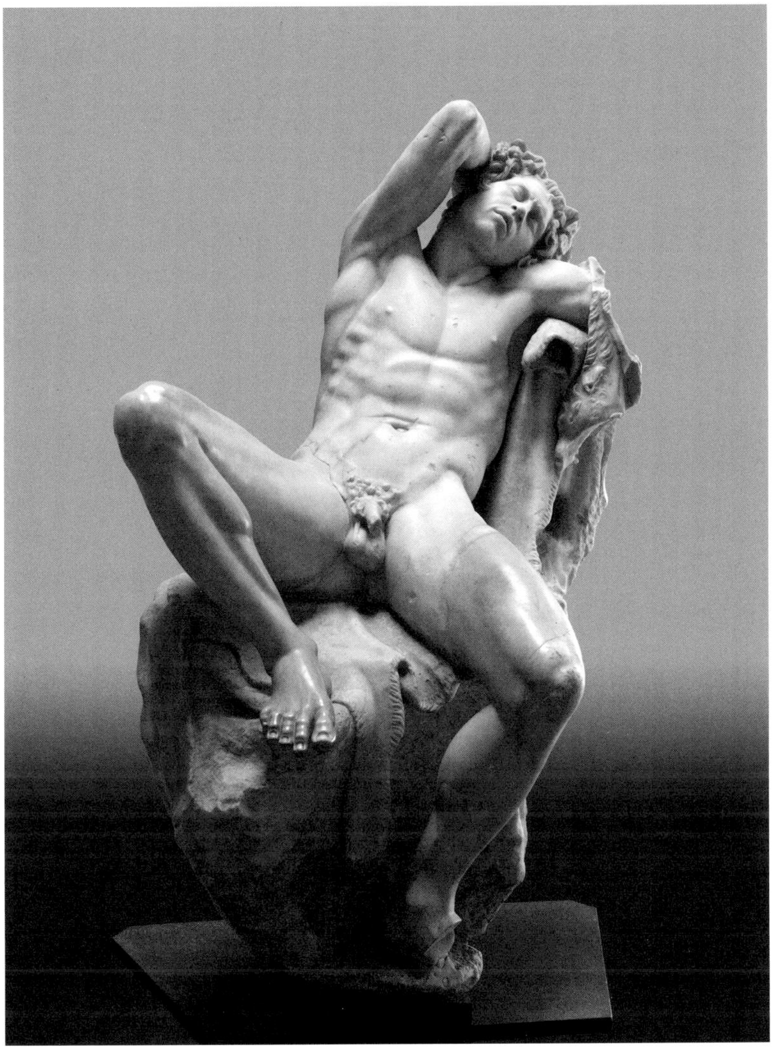

Hosmer's innocent faun sleeps, unaware of the male or female gaze.

The sculpture revealed its racialized exoticism below a veneer of ideality. John Gibson observed that, in its reinstatement of classical ideals, Hosmer's *Sleeping Faun* was "worthy to be an Antique," and compared it favorably to the famous bronze *Sleeping Faun* from Herculaneum.[74] The British press was equally ebullient about the piece: "Were it dug out of the ruins of the *Forum Romanum,* [it] might be held in public estimation as a fit companion for the *Apollo Belvedere.*"[75] It is quite possible that Hosmer had given her sculpture a "flesh tint," which, marring its pearly white finish, aligned her technique with that of Canova and Gibson. To at least some viewers, the faun's bestial nature remained evident in the slightly tinted marble, which "expresse[d] the dark skin of the satyr races," as the exhibition catalogue explained.[76]

Hosmer produced a pendant to her famous sculpture. In *The Waking Faun* (fig. 43), which she completed in 1867, the young faun awakened to catch the baby satyr at its mischief. Although posed similarly to the *Sleeping Faun,* the figure appeared more active and engaged: the feet were animated and pointed, instead of relaxed and passive; both hands grasped the baby satyr, instead of resting languidly. The sculpture did not receive the same acclaim as its predecessor. Hosmer had hoped to exhibit both in Paris in 1867 but was unable to resolve *The Waking Faun* to her satisfaction, explaining that it "fell too far short of the other."[77] In its active response to the immediate environment, *The Waking Faun* short-circuited the gaze. The figure engaged in activity that energized the spectatorial field and thus challenged the viewer's scopic experience.

The previously controversial male nude achieved legitimacy in mid-nineteenth-century Rome. Hawthorne's *Marble Faun* (or *Resting Satyr,* fig. 35), Akers's *Dead Pearl Diver* (fig. 38), Stebbins's *Lotus Eater* (fig. 39), and Hosmer's *Sleeping Faun* (fig. 40) offered themselves up for visual consumption by allowing the pleasurable gaze to go unchallenged. Flourishing as an aesthetic and erotic free zone, the mythic Italy liberated American tourists to construct and explore alternative identities. Simultaneously, colonized Rome functioned like a "relatively accessible and not too disquieting Orient," as Leonardo Buonomo explained.[78] In displacing the exotic and erotic content of the nude onto the arcadian faun and the vulnerable Italian body, American artists and writers tamed the racialized other into subservience and created a morally and aesthetically safe zone for the contemporary spectator.

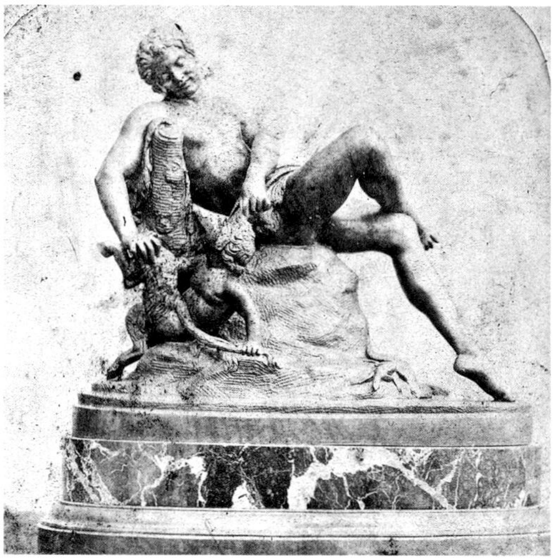

FIG. 43
Harriet Hosmer, *The Waking Faun*, 1866–67, now lost. Photograph, Harriet Goodhue Hosmer Papers, The Schlesinger Library, Radcliffe Institute, Harvard University, A162-175f-6b.

### *Anne Whitney: From Boston to Rome*

Much had transpired in Boston in the many years since Harriet Hosmer had left her hometown in 1852. The successful poet-turned-sculptor Anne Whitney had the opportunity to visit the *Dying Slave* of Michelangelo as well as a growing number of other plaster casts on display in the Boston Athenaeum. She no doubt saw the illustrations of the *Faun of Praxiteles* that accompanied Hawthorne's novel. And she looked closely at Emma Stebbins's *Lotus Eater* when it was displayed in Boston in 1861 (fig. 39). Born into a prominent Watertown, Massachusetts, family, Whitney turned her attention to sculpture in 1859, at the age of thirty-eight. She studied anatomy at a Brooklyn hospital and took her first art courses at the Pennsylvania Academy of the Fine Arts in 1860. Between 1862 and 1864, she studied with the eccentric doctor-turned-sculptor William Rimmer, who taught anatomy and modeling in Boston.[79]

Encouraged by the successful careers of the women sculptors in Rome, Whitney pushed the boundaries of artistic production in the United States, producing two extraordinary male nudes between 1862 and 1867. Rimmer was an important resource for Whitney and other women artists in Boston as he offered his students the opportunity to draw and/or sculpt from the live model. By the 1850s, he had a developed a reputation as an expert in art anatomy, and in 1864 and 1877 he published books on the subject.[80] Like Thomas Eakins a generation later, Rimmer generated much controversy when he offered women art students the same artistic training that was available to men, arguing that "art intellectually is as independent of sex as thought itself. . . . I [see] no reason why the same knowledge should not be conferred upon [women] as on [men]."[81] One outraged Boston critic demanded that female pupils remain veiled during lessons to prevent any embarrassment should student and model encounter one another in public. The veil, he argued, ensured that women's modesty would be protected. Not surprisingly, Rimmer's students,

Whitney among them, did not take well to this "Mohammedan solution."[82]

One of Whitney's male nudes, a life-size marble figure, was originally entitled *The Youth* (also known as *Dream of Love* and *Boy with a Palm*) (fig. 44).[83] Reminiscent of both the *Faun of Praxiteles* (fig. 35) and Stebbins's *Lotus Eater* (fig. 39), Whitney's figure stood in an exaggerated *contrapposto,* leaning one elbow against the trunk of a palm tree. The other arm was placed behind the figure's back. The pose allowed the body to be on full display. Whitney later confided to her friend the abolitionist Maria Weston Chapman that she and her friends jokingly referred to the sculpture as "The Boy and the Palm."[84]

She employed workmen to carve the sculpture, after importing five blocks of marble in 1863. As it turned out, she was not satisfied with the work of the marble carvers, conceding that their inadequate carving skills "will only give me the more to do."[85] Like many of the women sculptors in Rome, she probably took on the difficult task of recarving the marble figure herself. In 1867, she showed the work at the De Vries Gallery in Boston. Most likely experiencing some trepidation about the public's response to the male nude, she added a fig leaf to the figure as a so-called modesty shield.[86]

In Boston, she also modeled a statuette of the *Chaldean Shepherd* in 1862 (fig. 45), an ancient figure who practiced an early form of astronomy while tending his flocks at night.[87] The shepherd, with a sleeping dog by his side, gazes upward into the sky. Actively engaging the world, he measures the heavens with two extended fingers serving as a sextant. Unlike her teacher Rimmer, whose sculptural style emphasized a detailed realism, Whitney worked within a neoclassical paradigm, rendering the ideal body in terms of mathematical proportions and visual harmony. In its maturity and idealization, her figure recalled Thomas Crawford's *Orpheus and Cerberus* (fig. 9), which had been on permanent display in the Boston Athenaeum since 1844.[88] Rather than depict a listless (and more modest) nude as she had with her life-size *Youth,* she sculpted an active male body whose frontal nudity flaunted its virility. Struggling, no doubt, with the propriety of the male nude in Boston, she abandoned work on this small-scale model until her arrival in Rome.

In March of 1867, Charlotte Cushman's circle of women artists, writers, and reformers welcomed Whitney and her partner, the painter Adeline Manning, to Rome. The expatriate women's community was well established by this time. Cushman and Stebbins had secured the entire four-story house at via Gregoriana 38 for themselves in 1864; Harriet Hosmer, previously occupying the third floor, had moved into her own apartment next door. With her ebullient warmth, Hosmer referred to Whitney as "Sister Anne" and when addressing Whitney called herself "your twin," as both hailed from the Boston suburb of Watertown. Stebbins and Whitney, similar in age and social background, formed a life-long friendship.[89]

This community of women sculptors—together with their companions and friends—all lived and worked within a few blocks of each other. Whitney found a studio on via San Nicola da Tolentino in May 1868. The following month, Whitney, Manning, and the painter Fidelia Bridges secured a lovely five-room house, which they called Il Tempietto, on the Piazza San Trinità dei Monti, a luxurious address atop the Spanish Steps. Margaret Foley was their upstairs neighbor.

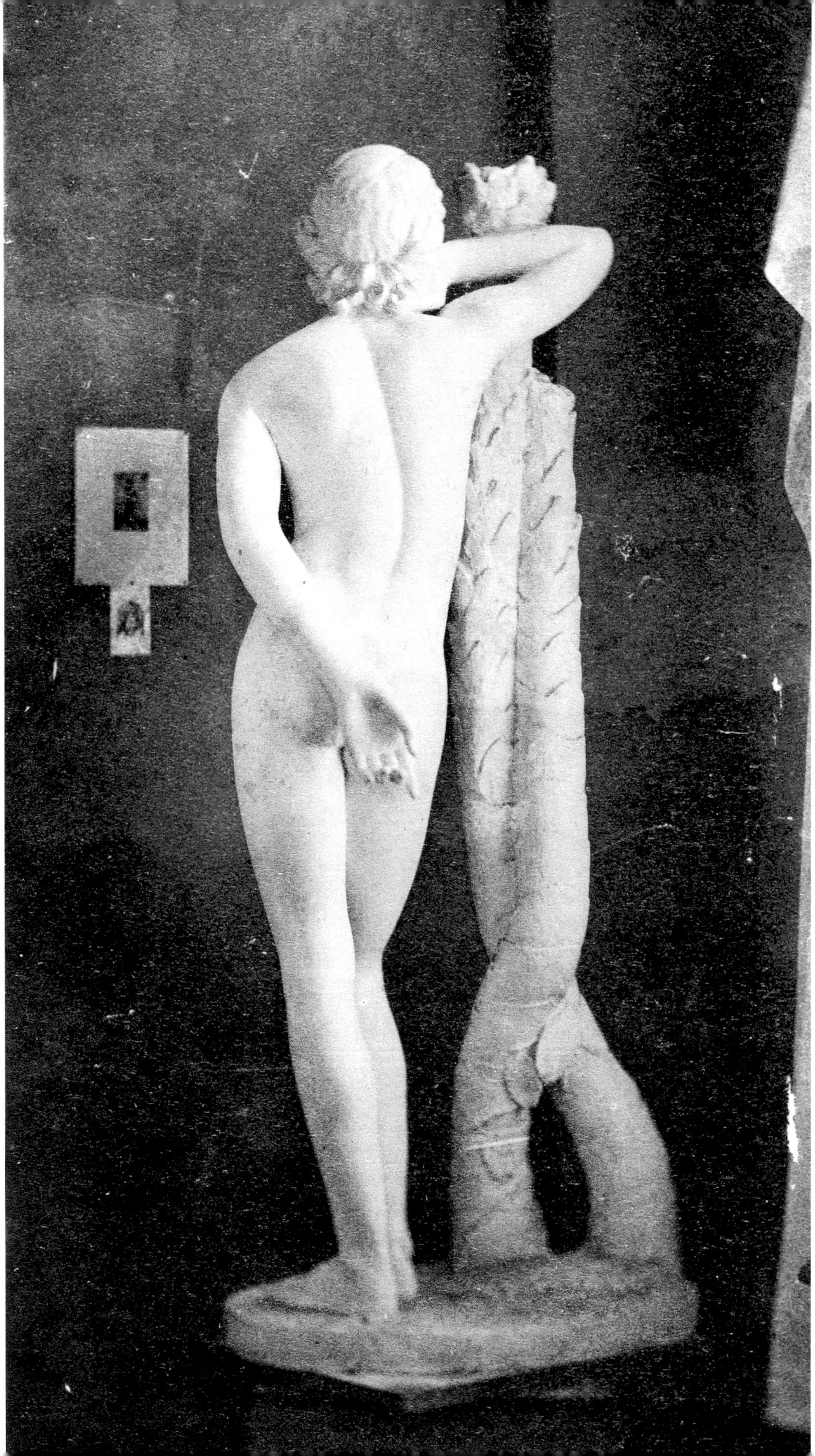

FIG. 44 *(opposite)*
Anne Whitney, *The Youth* (*Dream of Love* or *Boy with a Palm*), ca. 1862–63, now lost. Photograph dated ca. 1862–67, courtesy of the Wellesley College Archives, Papers of Anne Whitney.

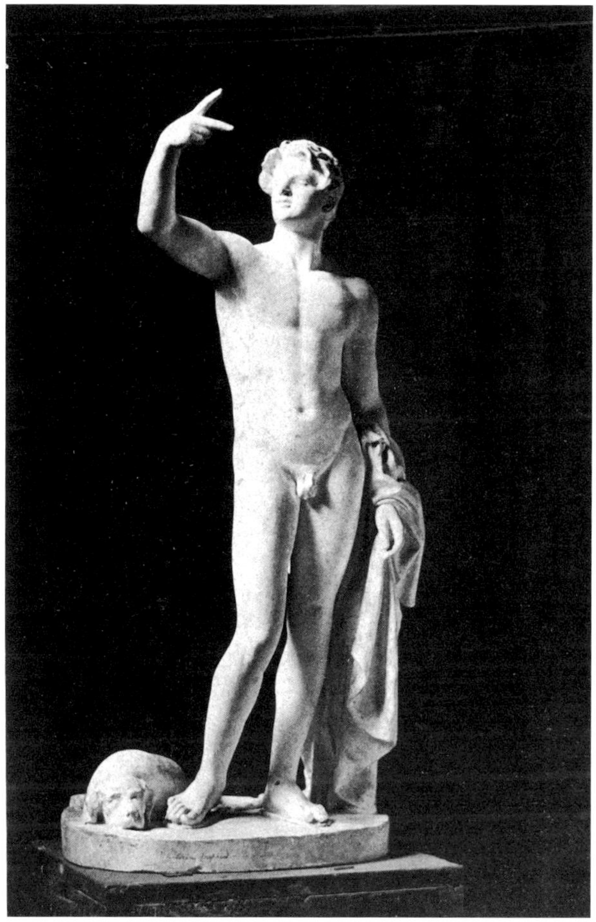

FIG. 45
Anne Whitney, *Chaldean Shepherd,* 1862, first version now lost. Photograph courtesy of the Wellesley College Archives, Papers of Anne Whitney.

In October, Whitney moved to a new three-room studio with excellent light, just across the Piazza di Spagna from their new home.[90] Writing to her family, Whitney was elated: "I am more satisfied than I was before coming that Rome is the best place for work we are likely to find anywhere abroad."[91]

Whitney studied antique statuary available throughout Rome. Like Stebbins and Hawthorne, she was enamored with the famous *Faun of Praxiteles* in the Capitoline Museum, which she was now able to study in person rather than in reproduction. Once again she viewed Stebbins's *Lotus Eater,* now in her large new studio on via San Basilio. She certainly visited Hosmer's *Sleeping Faun,* which had been highly praised in the international press, and saw her *Waking Faun,* which the sculptor was still developing.[92] In October of 1868, she attended art classes at the French Academy, located in the Medici Palace atop the Pincian Hill, just a few blocks from her home. Whitney studied plaster casts taken

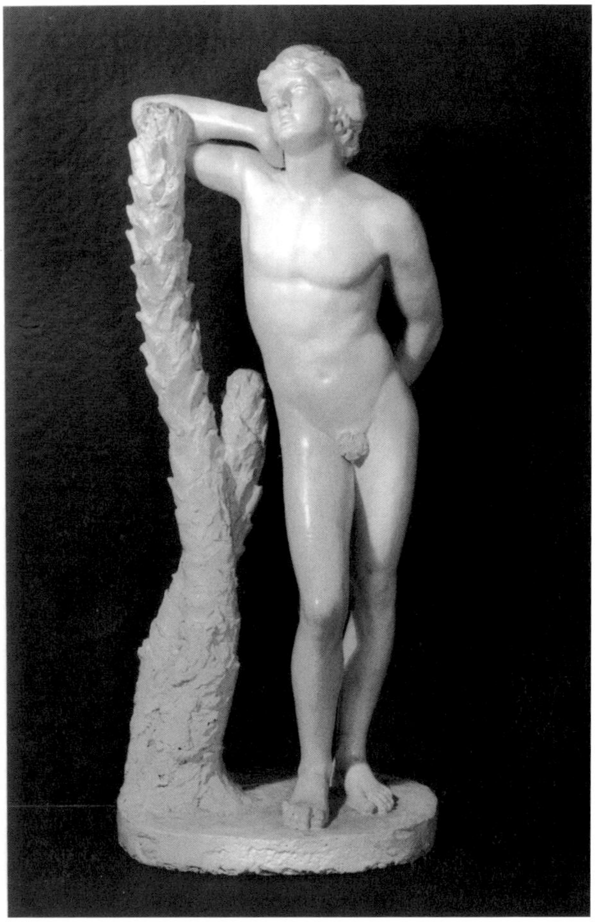

FIG. 46
Anne Whitney, *Lotus Eater,* 1868, plaster, 35 1/4 × 15 1/4 × 12 1/4 in. Collection of The Newark Art Museum, gift of Mr. and Mrs. Hugh S. Hince, 1963, 63.75.

from life and used live models "unsparingly," especially the young peasants who congregated on the Spanish Steps to seek employment with foreign artists. She fully adopted the "art life" in Rome.[93] In a letter home, she wrote, "It has been a very satisfactory two months of study and gives me a feeling of confidence in the step I have taken in coming abroad."[94]

Receiving a commission for a statuette from a patron in Buffalo, New York, Whitney reconfigured the life-sized sculpture that she had begun in Boston (fig. 46).[95] In the version of the sculpture that exists today, she reduced the scale, modified the figural form, and retitled the sculpture *Lotus Eater,* an allusion to Tennyson's poem "The Lotos-Eaters" and, probably, to Stebbins's sculpture of the same name.[96] The anatomical details of the statuette, such as the belly button, pectorals, and musculature of the arms and neck, reveal close attention to nature, evidence that she worked from the live model. The feet and hands are delicately carved, down to the individual

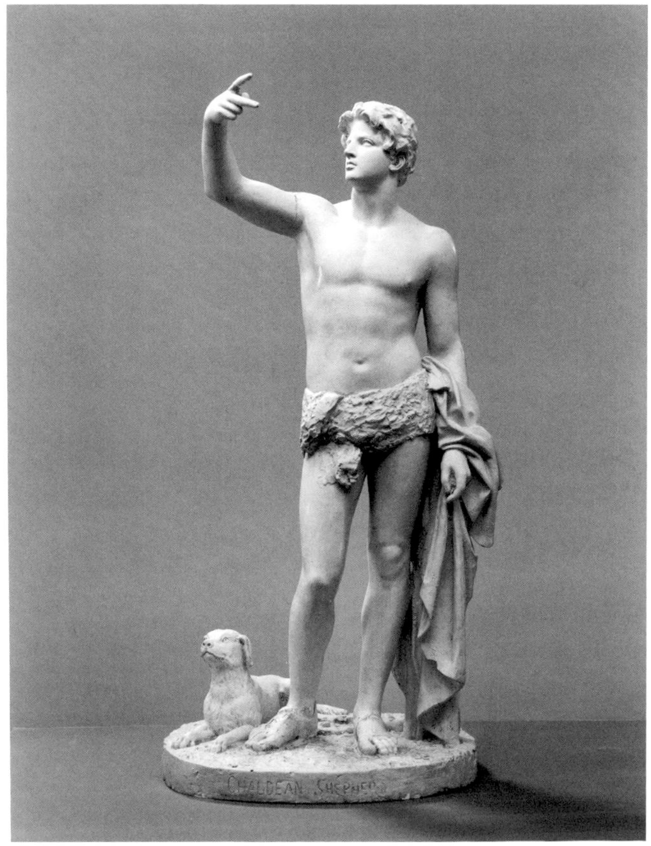

FIG. 47
Anne Whitney, *The Chaldean Shepherd*, ca. 1868, plaster, 34 × 15 1/2 × 14 5/8 in. Smith College Museum of Art, Northampton, Mass., gift of Mrs. Hugh Stratton Hince (Marion L. Stone, class of 1913), SC1967:50.

toenails. The left arm is placed behind the figure, with the back of the hand visibly resting against the buttocks, as in the original work. With his sleepy head tilted upward and supported by his bent right arm, his dreamy expression and deep-set eyes with heavy lids, the figure is suffused with a passive torpor. Transformed into one of Tennyson's Lotos-Eaters, the sculpted figure, like that of Stebbins, conflates arcadian and modern stereotypes in the passive Italian male body.

In 1868, Whitney also resumed work on her *Chaldean Shepherd*.[97] In reconceptualizing the sculpture, she aroused the dog, who now gazed attentively with his master at the sky (fig. 47). She revised the proportions of the nude, adding some heft to the lean body, which had previously displayed ideal Praxitelean proportions. Most likely, this more fully articulated body type mirrored that of the live Roman model with whom she worked. Importantly, she hastily added a sketchy plaster loincloth to the figure, which had never before sported even a fig leaf. One can only speculate about the addition of the sheepskin loincloth. Without fig leaf or drapery, this highly detailed nude proved too daring. Nonetheless, she playfully added a vertical flap of sheepskin below the loincloth both to signal and to conceal the phallic form. In so doing, she may have jokingly called attention to the prudery of her audience.

*The Chaldean Shepherd* did not conform to the dictates of the arcadian male nude. The figure sported a well-developed and mature body that telegraphed a powerful virility, despite the application of the sheepskin loincloth. His demeanor was active rather than passive as he gazed with rapt attention at the night sky. Even the dog's alertness activated the space around the sculpture. This interactivity with the viewer's world pushed the limits of what was acceptable in Rome.

Writing to a friend years later, Whitney confessed, "I am extremely partial to [nudes] when they are made not to know it. And as I am sure there is no consciousness in my mind, there should not be in the work."[98] In this strangely worded passage, Whitney grapples with the circuit of gazes in which the viewer (along with the sculptor herself) is implicated. First, she insists that the nude itself be "made not to know" that it is the object of the gaze. In other words, the nude must not actively return the look. Second, the viewer should have "no consciousness" of his or her viewing pleasure. An innocent gaze was essential. Never resolving the boldness of this work, she considered *The Chaldean Shepherd* an unfinished study.[99]

American women sculptors' relationship with the colonialist discourse in Italy was fraught with such contradictions. Nonetheless, Frances Power Cobbe, who lived at the Cushman domicile in the early 1860s, promoted the notion of Rome as a utopia. Italy seemed "the favorite land of gifted Americans," she exclaimed. "American women, in particular, seem to find it a congenial sphere for the development of the more marked individuality which characterizes them."[100] For Anglo-American women in Rome, the city promised to fulfill their feminist desires for creative liberty. But what did this creative liberty comprise?

Whitney and Hosmer, in particular, were curious actors upon this imperial stage. Although they exhibited a wide range of progressive political beliefs, their privileged position in Rome was ultimately premised upon an idea of racial hierarchy and the superiority of their white Anglo-Saxon heritage. Most American citizens saw themselves as inherently anti-imperialist, conditioned by their own country's struggle for independence from British rule.[101] Hosmer and Whitney were no different in this belief. Nonetheless, they did not demur to the advantages that their American nationality, Anglo-Saxon heritage, and elite social status conferred upon them in Italy. Indeed, their professional successes were possible exactly because they leveraged these privileges in a colonized Rome.

# Five

## *Reimagining Italy*

Martin Johnson Heade's *Roman Newsboys* (1848; fig. 48), candidly chronicles Roman politics at midcentury. In one of his few genre paintings, Heade brings to light recently realized freedoms available to the Roman people under the short-lived Republic.[1] He depicts two street urchins who openly distribute copies of the satirical publication *Il Don Pirlone: Giornale di caricature politiche* (a newspaper of political satire, or "the Punch of Rome," as the American journalist Margaret Fuller described it).[2] In this image, Heade illustrates the tenets of the two political parties associated with the *Risorgimento,* the movement to liberate the Italian peninsula from foreign control and to unify the land as a sovereign nation-state.[3] One newsboy wears a papal cap with "Pio IX" (Pope Pius IX) embroidered upon it, a reference to those who supported Vincenzo Gioberti and the Neo-Guelph party and advocated for an Italian confederation with a liberal pope at its helm. Gioberti was an admirer of Pope Pius IX, who, immediately upon coming to power in 1846, allowed freedom of the press in the Papal States and granted amnesty to the nearly twenty thousand persons jailed under the previous regime of Pope Gregory XVI. By the following year, however, it was clear to many revolutionaries—including progressive Americans in Rome—that Pius was reconsidering his liberal policies.

As if upon a pedestal, the other newsboy, wearing the Republican tricolors of white, blue, and red, sits upon a post designed to protect the *palazzo* walls. He dons a Greek cap with a red ribbon, a reference to the recent Greek War of Independence and a symbol of the radical Mazzinian republic installed in Rome. His newspaper assails the pope as a *pirlone,* or hypocrite.[4] Giuseppe Mazzini, a charismatic leader of the *Risorgimento,* was revered by progressive Americans at home and abroad. Unlike Gioberti's, his was a secular vision for Italy in which he promised individual liberties without mediation from the pope. On February 8, 1849, a Proclamation of the Republic was issued throughout the Papal States; Mazzini returned from exile to lead the government. After electing a Constitutional Assembly, the Romans decreed that the pope no longer held temporal rule but remained free to exercise his spiritual powers. In place of papal authority, this peaceful revolution created a Republican state that offered full citizenship to the Romans. From his exile in Gaeta, the pope issued a Manifesto of Excommunication aimed at all Republican revolutionaries.[5]

The presence of the newsboys in the painting stands in striking opposition to the graffiti that litters the palace wall behind them, an age-old expression of Roman resistance to

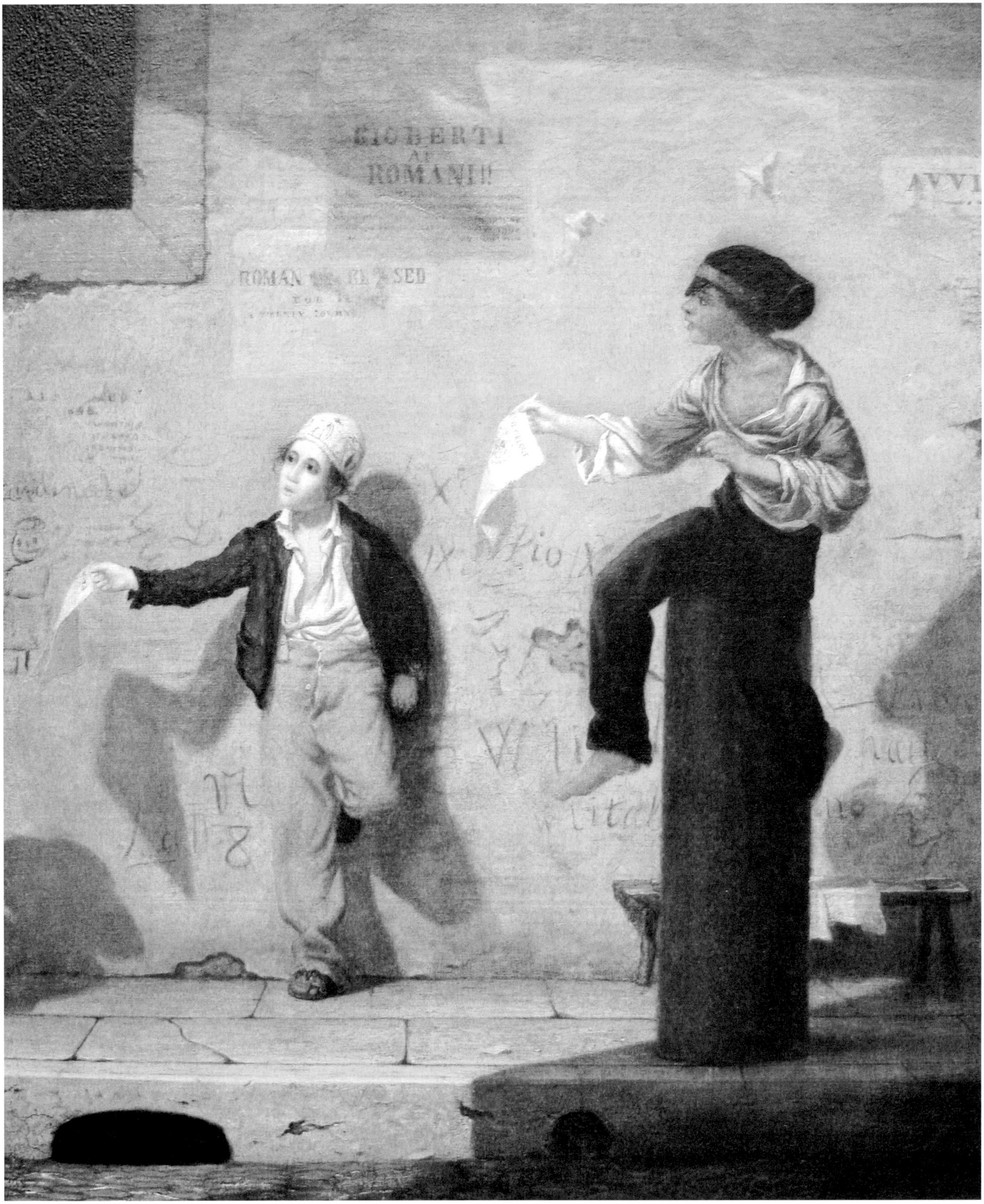
GIOBERTI
AI
ROMANI!!
AVVI

censorship. Pasted above the head of the boy with the papal cap are two posters: one with the headline "Gioberti ai Romani!!" (Gioberti for the Romans!!) and a clipping from an English newspaper that may have alluded to Pius's prisoner amnesty, "Roman[s] [R]el[ea]sed." "Pio IX" and "Viva Italia" are also scrawled upon the wall. To the far left of the painting appears a caricature of a cardinal (*cardinale*), at whom the newsboy seems to thrust his caustic broadside. In the lower right corner is a shadowed profile of the dreaded Cardinal Giacomo Antonelli, secretary of state in the Vatican.[6] Roman politics were quite intricate, indeed perplexing, to the foreigner. On the one hand, many Romans felt an allegiance and actual love for their pontiff, with whom they sympathized in these trying times; on the other hand, they loathed the political tyranny of the papacy and blamed their political misfortunes upon the sinister Antonelli, who, many believed, wielded the actual power in the Vatican. This painting succinctly captures the complex issues of the day and demonstrates the degree to which Americans, like Heade, were familiar with the events and actors of the Roman political stage.[7]

FIG. 48 *(opposite)* Martin Johnson Heade, *Roman Newsboys*, 1848, oil on canvas, 28 1/2 × 24 5/16 in. Toledo Museum of Art, purchased with funds from the Florence Scott Libbey Bequest in memory of her father, Maurice A. Scott, 1953.68.

The Roman Republic was in existence for five months, from February to July of 1849. Progressive Americans at home were keenly aware of these revolutionary events, as chronicled with great sympathy by Margaret Fuller in the *New York Daily Tribune* and elsewhere. Nonetheless, the United States remained officially neutral in the internal affairs of the peninsula. In Rome, expatriates urged their government to use its moral influence on behalf of the popularly elected Republican government. After all, the Italians looked to the United States for inspiration in their political struggle and claimed that "the Americans are indeed our brothers."[8] On July 4, papal troops with the aid of the French army routed the Italian military leader Giuseppi Garibaldi and the Republican forces. A few weeks later, the *Daily Tribune* ran a memorial to the Roman Republic: "In Memory of the Martyrs of Human Liberty Who Fell During the Siege, May and June, 1849, as Defenders of Rome."[9]

Pope Pius IX returned to Rome in April 1850 and immediately instituted repressive measures that denied all civil rights to Romans. French troops, in the service of the Vatican, patrolled the city, refusing to allow even small groups of people to congregate in public. "In the streets, where two or three [were] gathered together," the American journalist Grace Greenwood reported, "there [was] presently a soldier in their midst, or a policeman . . . with a polite admonition to move on."[10] Censorship of the press was severely imposed. The military presence in the city had grown to twenty thousand French troops, which functioned as an occupying force. No criticism of the papal regime was tolerated. Romans were forced to remain silent on political issues, unjustly accused by foreign visitors of passivity and resignation. Civil society functioned by fear and coercion.[11]

Mazzini went into exile in London. As a member of the British Negro Emancipation League, he maintained contact with radical American abolitionists, such as William Lloyd Garrison and Theodore Dwight Weld. Garrison had reported the events of the Roman Republic and defended Mazzini's political principles in his antislavery journal the *Liberator.* Just as Mazzini equated the Italian struggle for sovereignty with the emancipation of the American slaves, Garrison believed that the Italians and

Americans shared fundamental political values. In Mazzini's radical political vision, he imagined an Italy free of class, gender, and racial distinctions and claimed that the Italian people were "fighting the same sacred battle for freedom and emancipation of the oppressed" as the Americans. In an 1859 letter to Weld, the founder of the American Anti-Slavery Society, he professed a belief in God, before whom there was "no Master, no Slave, no Man, no Woman, but only Human Nature, which must be everywhere responsible, therefore free." To his supporters in the United States, he proclaimed: "May God bless your efforts and ours!"[12] In turn, the American antislavery press expressed great sympathy for the Italian cause.[13]

Since 1848, almost all progressive Americans had agreed that the Italian people were enslaved by tyrannical imperial regimes. They supported the liberation of the peninsula from foreign dominance and the establishment of civil rights for the Italian people. International sympathy for Italy was generated, in part, by the artists, poets, and academics who traveled to Italy, studied its past, and wrote of its turbulent present. Rome, in particular, was regularly described in Whig and Republican "free-labor" rhetoric as a corrupt slave power.[14]

At the same time, Americans perceived similarities, both historical and ideological/racial, between Italians and black slaves. Nineteenth-century Americans were predisposed to view black slaves and Italians as racial inferiors. Both had for centuries been subjected to brutal repression, which denied them the ability to govern themselves and assume the duties of citizenship. Moreover, scientific writers established a racial typing system that positioned modern Italians as inferior to, and hence legitimately subordinated by, Anglo-Saxons. For example, in their book *Types of Mankind* (1854), Josiah C. Nott, a Southern physician, and George R. Giddon, a British Egyptologist, compared the "blond" Germanic races, which held superior moral and intellectual capacities, with the less developed "brown" southern Mediterranean peoples and posited a racial hierarchy between the two populations. At root, Americans were predisposed to a type of paternalism that insisted the black slave and the Italian patriot were helpless victims in need of benevolent intervention.[15]

Anglo-American women artists, writers, and reformers in Rome exhibited a complicated and at times contradictory response to contemporary Italian politics. On the one hand, they imposed upon the *Risorgimento* a sense of republican promise coincident with their own desire for radical egalitarianism between the sexes.[16] On the other hand, they benefited from a privileged racial and class status in Rome. Thus a colonialist worldview haunted their support for Italian emancipation and sovereignty. These paradoxical convictions informed their sculptural production. Harriet Hosmer and Anne Whitney, while equating female emancipation with Italian independence, addressed contemporary Roman politics in gendered and racialized terms.

## *American Response to the* Risorgimento

Most Americans in the United States assumed a rather moderate approach to "the Italian Question": that is, in what way and by what means should Italian nationalism come to fruition? A *New York Times* editorial, for example, argued

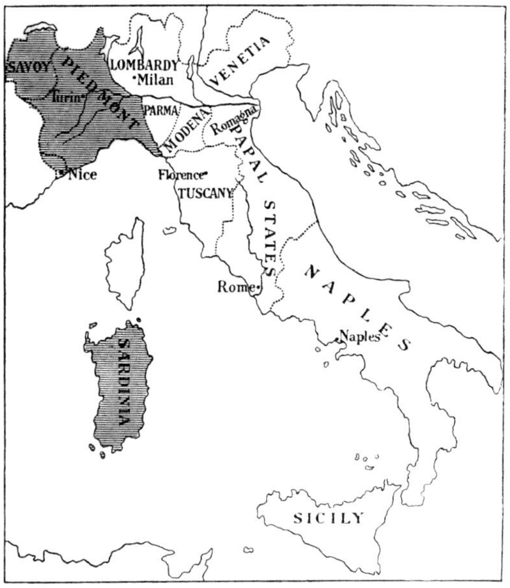


MAP 2
Map of the Italian peninsula, April 1859, from Bolton King, *A History of Italian Unity: Being a Political History of Italy from 1814 to 1871* (New York: Charles Scribner's Sons, 1899), vol. 2, frontispiece. Photo: Daniel P. Younger.

that the dream of Italian republicanism was not only unrealistic but also utopian, given that the peninsula had not achieved its most basic ends: independence from foreign rule or unity as a nation-state.[17]

By the late 1850s, Mazzini's radical Republican movement was in crisis, replaced by a more pragmatic and strategic nationalism led by Count Camille Cavour and Garibaldi. Under Cavour, the *Risorgimento* became less revolutionary and more respectable in the eyes of most Anglo-Americans in its association with material progress and modernity, rather than with a radical egalitarianism. The international press helped spread the new political idea of Italy. The narrative of Italian nationalism was explained by a simple but powerful moral choice: papal corruption and Austrian repression versus political freedom and national independence.[18]

In 1859, the Piedmont (the northern territory of Italy) was emancipated from Hapsburg control (map 2). With the ensuing Treaty of Villafranca, Venice remained part of the Hapsburg Empire until its liberation in 1866. "Romans are daily joining the army of liberty," the German historian Ferdinand Gregorovius wrote from Rome. By June 1859, nearly five thousand Romans alone had enlisted in the war against the Austrians.[19] By March 1860, an independent Kingdom of Italy was declared. Within the new Italian constitutional monarchy, Cavour held the post of prime minister; Victor Emmanuel II became king. In the United States, progressive reformers celebrated the new sovereign nation. "The new birth of Italy is already the grandest event of the modern period," the Harvard professor of art history Charles Eliot Norton exclaimed in 1860. "It gives one fresh hope for the future."[20]

Events cascaded at record speed. In May 1860, Garibaldi famously led the "Expedition of the Thousand" to Sicily and Naples, freeing the South of Italy from Spanish Bourbon control (map 3). In a dramatic gesture, Garibaldi, the powerful and popular military leader, handed over these territories to King Victor Emmanuel II and returned to peacetime life on his island of Caprera for a short time. In so doing, he earned a reputation for selflessness and magnanimity that remained with him throughout his life. In refusing absolute political power, he was often referred to as "the Washington of Italy" in the American and Italian press, as both leaders recalled the legendary Roman general Cincinnatus, who returned to a civilian life of farming after leading his army to victory.[21]

Garibaldi was a hero to many Americans, who followed his every move between 1859 and

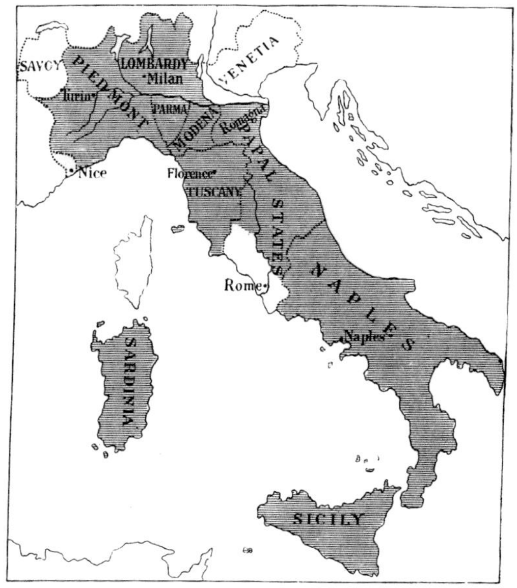


MAP 3
Map of the Italian peninsula, November 1860, from Bolton King, *A History of Italian Unity: Being a Political History of Italy from 1814 to 1871* (New York: Charles Scribner's Sons, 1899), vol. 2, frontispiece. Photo: Daniel P. Younger.

1860. In November of 1859, the New York Garibaldi Fund Committee supplied the "Expedition of the Thousand" with $100,000 (around $2.3 million in today's terms) and one million muskets. The following year, American artists donated sketches, drawings, and paintings to benefit his army. American volunteers fought with Garibaldi in Sicily and the South of Italy, part of a wave of international enthusiasm that surged in support of the Italian cause.[22]

Some of the most distinguished mid-nineteenth-century American writers and reformers published glowing reports of Garibaldi's military feats. With the invention of the telegraph, correspondents were able to send daily dispatches from Italy to their news organizations at home.[23] Henry Adams, for example, joined Garibaldi in Sicily, where he interviewed him for the *Boston Courier.* "We were in the presence of a hero," Adams wrote in May of 1860. "Here I was at last, then, face to face with one of the great events of our day."[24] The illustrator Thomas Nast, while working for the *New York Illustrated News,* traveled to Sicily and Naples to cover Garibaldi's military campaigns between June and November 1860.[25] While traveling with the troops, he sketched Garibaldi, who cut a dashing and charismatic figure with full beard and flaming red shirt and neck scarf, the uniform for which the *Garibaldini* were known. In November, the *New York Illustrated News* published an image of Nast, "*Thos. Nast, Esq., Our Special Artist, Now Attached to Garibaldi's Staff, in His Calabrian Costume*" (fig. 49).[26] In Washington, D.C., red shirts became the fashion of the day.[27] On the international stage, Garibaldi was the incarnation of the *Risorgimento;* simultaneously, his fiery temperament personified an ideal of American liberalism. "The progress of Garibaldi is just now even of greater interest to us than that of our own election campaign [of 1860]," Norton claimed. "It is a fine thing to be living in times which can produce such a man."[28]

Garibaldi's fame was such that President Abraham Lincoln offered him a command in the Union Army in the summer after the North's defeat at Bull Run. Garibaldi considered the opportunity but insisted upon the right to abolish slavery in every territory that he conquered. The Union leaders declined his political mandate; Garibaldi refused the appointment. Nonetheless, he remained associated with the Union cause in the American imagination throughout the war years. Black abolitionists, in particular, viewed the Italian military leader as a hero. Frederick Douglass, the famous abolitionist and journalist, compared his liberation of Sicily with John Brown's leadership of the 1859 slave insurrection

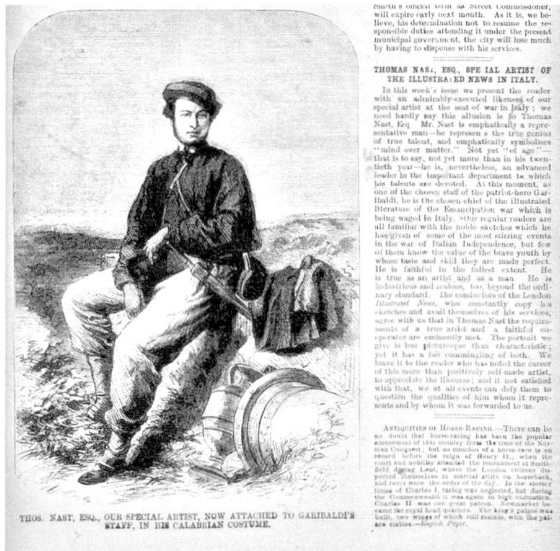

THOS. NAST, ESQ., OUR SPECIAL ARTIST, NOW ATTACHED TO GARIBALDI'S STAFF, IN HIS CALABRIAN COSTUME.

Smith's official term as Street Commissioner, will expire early next month. As it is, we believe, his determination not to resume the responsible duties attending it under the present municipal government, the city will lose much by having to dispense with his services.

THOMAS NAST, ESQ., SPECIAL ARTIST OF THE ILLUSTRATED NEWS IN ITALY.

In this week's issue we present the reader with an admirably-executed likeness of our special artist at the seat of war in Italy; we need hardly say this allusion is to Thomas Nast, Esq. Mr. Nast is emphatically a representative man—he represents the true genius of true talent, and emphatically symbolises "mind over matter." Not yet "of age"—that is to say, not yet more than in his twentieth year—he is, nevertheless, an advanced leader in the important department to which his talents are devoted. At this moment, as one of the chosen staff of the patriot-hero Garibaldi, he is the chosen chief of the illustrated literature of the Emancipation war which is being waged in Italy. Our regular readers are all familiar with the noble sketches which he has given of some of the most stirring events in the war of Italian Independence, but few of them know the value of the brave youth by whose taste and skill they are made perfect. He is faithful in the fullest extent. He is true as an artist and as a man. He is industrious and zealous, too, beyond the ordinary standard. The conductors of the London *Illustrated News*, who constantly copy his sketches and avail themselves of his services, agree with us that in Thomas Nast the requirements of a true artist and a faithful cooperator are eminently met. The portrait we give is less picturesque than characteristic; yet it has a fair commingling of both. We leave it to the reader who has noted the career of this more than positively self-made artist, to appreciate the likeness; and if not satisfied with that, we at all events can defy them to question the qualities of him whom it represents and by whom it was forwarded to us.

ANTIQUITIES OF HORSE RACING.—There can be no doubt that horse-racing has been the popular amusement of this country from the time of the Norman Conquest; but no mention of a horse-race is on record before the reign of Henry II., when the court and nobility attended the tournament at Smithfield during Lent, where the London citizens disported themselves in martial attire on horseback, and races were the order of the day. In the stormy times of Charles I, racing was neglected, but during the Commonwealth it was again in high estimation. Charles II was our great patron. Newmarket became the royal head quarters. The king's palace was built, two wings of which still remain, with the palace stables.—*English Paper.*

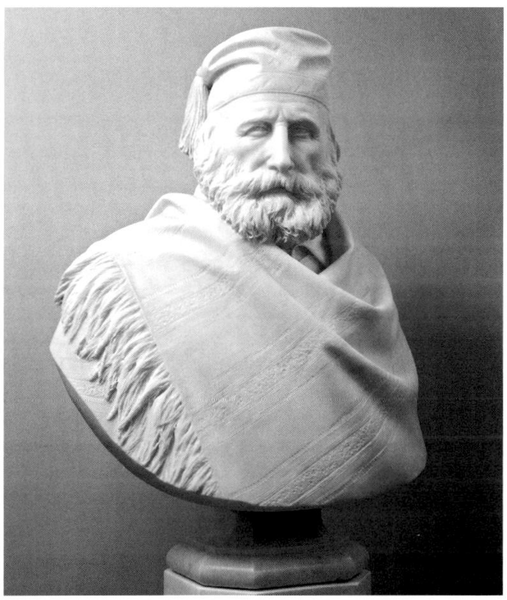

FIG. 49
*"Thos. Nast, Esq., Our Special Artist, Now Attached to Garibaldi's Staff, in His Calabrian Costume,"* from the *New York Illustrated News*, November 3, 1860, 405.

FIG. 50
Giuseppe Martegana, *Giuseppe Garibaldi*, 1882–ca. 1887, marble, height 32 in. U.S. Senate Collection, U.S. Capitol, gift of members of the Italian Society of Washington, Citizens of Italian Descent, 1888.

in Harper's Ferry, Virginia. Douglass saw modern Italians and black slaves not as passive victims of slavery but as militant rebels who courageously fought against social and political injustice.[29] Garibaldi's bust was installed in the U.S. Capitol in 1888 as a gift of the Italian Society of Washington, Citizens of Italian Descent (fig. 50).

The nation-state of Italy came into being in 1860; the United States recognized the sovereign country in 1861. Rome now became the locus of struggle for liberation from papal control. The cosmopolitan city would remain outside the new unified Italy until 1870. "The condition of Rome grows more and more curious," Gregorovius chronicled in 1859. "A spark would suffice to blow up the mine and sweep away the clergy. . . . The city is divided into two great parties, the clerical and the national."[30] Regular skirmishes between the papal troops and nationalist sympathizers occurred. In March of 1860, papal Zouaves violently dispelled public gatherings in honor of the establishment of the new Kingdom of Italy. From the Piazza Colonna to via Condotti, the locale where the foreigners lived, soldiers assaulted Americans who joined the celebrations.[31] Political demonstrations continued on a regular basis as the Romans marched throughout the city—often beginning at the Capitoline and the Forum and winding their way to St. John the Lateran, just outside the city walls.[32]

International attention was centered upon Rome. "The Papacy [is] now at war with the nation and with the freedom of Italy," Gregorovius wrote.[33] The Roman National Committee—the revolutionary movement to liberate Rome—worked in total secrecy; no one knew their membership or their meeting places. "The Roman question," Charlotte Cushman averred, "can only be solved by making Rome a free city."[34] To progressive Americans at home and abroad, a permanently degraded Rome stood as the political anathema to their cherished ideals of nationhood.[35]

## La Bella Libertà

Discussing the "great questions of the day," the British expatriate poet Elizabeth Barrett Browning hosted winter salons in Rome from 1858 to 1860. Her household overflowed with international visitors conversant with the "Italian Question." Writing from Rome in 1858, she exclaimed, "We think of little but politics."[36] Over the years, Barrett Browning had witnessed the fluid state of events in Italy, from the short-lived Republic installed in Florence in 1848 and 1849 to the current struggle for independence under way throughout the peninsula. When the Florentine population rebelled against Austrian rule in 1848, she watched the mass political meetings from her apartment window across the street from the Pitti Palace. Responding to the fleeting moments of the Florentine Republic, she wrote part 1 of her epic poem, *Casa Guidi Windows.* In "A Hope for Italy," she recounted the popular excitement and optimism after Grand Duke Leopold had fled Tuscany and a Republican government was installed in Florence.[37] In 1849, after the Austrians had defeated the Italians and marched back into Florence, she completed part 2 of her poem, describing the process of recolonization that she witnessed once again from her window. With her husband, the poet Robert Browning, she had intended "to write on the Italian question" and "to publish jointly," but the project never came to fruition.[38]

In Rome, Robert Browning engaged in secret political meetings, met with Sicilian patriots at night, and searched for current news accounts in cafés by day. Such dangerous activities were not open to Barrett Browning.[39] Instead, she welcomed conversations with politically engaged women, like Jesse White Mario, the first British woman journalist to be assigned a foreign post. Mario had covered events in Italy for the London *Daily News* since 1849. Like Margaret Fuller, she had reported on the short-lived Roman Republic and commended the leadership of Mazzini. She lectured to American and British audiences about the complicated chess game that was Italian politics at the time.[40] On behalf of nationalism for the Italian people, she appealed to her audiences to "assist and defend the principles of individual liberty."[41]

Barrett Browning responded to the exciting events transpiring around her in Italy by revising the role of the woman poet. In her writing, she developed a "public female rhetorical voice" that circumvented the private lyrical style usually associated with feminine creativity. She forged a "new political poetics" when she wrote openly about *la bella libertà*—a concept that first appeared in the opening stanza of her poem *Casa Guidi Windows* of 1851—and became synonymous with the liberation of women and Italy. A decade later in Rome, she returned to "civic poetry" in a collection of eight political verses, all but one relating to the "Italian Question."[42] In her *Poems Before Congress,* she reimagined a new identity for Italy. Rather than portray the peninsula as a collection of abject colonies, she gave voice to a new sovereign nation-state. "But Italy, my Italy / Can it last—this gleam? / Can she live and be strong / Or is it another dream?" Reluctant at first to believe that the independent nation would last, the poet eventually embraced the new liberal Kingdom of Italy wholeheartedly. "Can it be true, be true, / That she lives anew?" Barrett Browning pictured Italy as entering modernity; the new nation was a strong, albeit weary, historical agent. "Italy, Italy—loosed at length from the tyrant's thrall, / Pale and calm in her strength." Through the doubling of "Italy, Italy" in these verses, she evoked the historical presence of the new nation. "But this is Italy / Who rises up to her place!"[43] With these words, she replaced the familiar colonialist trope of a passive and vulnerable "Italy-as-woman" with her concept of *la bella libertà,* Italy as a triumphant, active, feminine revolutionary archetype. Until her death in 1861, she chronicled Italian politics with passion and commitment, refusing to impose the mythos of a timeless arcadia upon this politically awakened land.[44]

Barrett Browning saw herself in a feminine tradition ranging from Sappho and Corinne to Margaret Fuller and Jesse White Mario. Her words encouraged Anglo-American women to participate in the public sphere of Italian politics. Italy had freed her to write poetry that addressed the nature of citizenship, and in particular an imagined feminine citizen. With *Corinne, or Italy,* Madame de Staël provided a cultural and political legacy for Barrett Browning, who described the novel as "an immortal book [that] deserves to be read three score and ten times—that is, once every year in the age of man."[45]

De Staël was a champion of women's rights and condemned "domestic slavery" in her political writing. In 1803, Napoleon exiled her from France because of her staunch criticism of his regime; for the following ten years, she traveled abroad to Italy and Germany, during which time she wrote *Corinne, or Italy.* Imagining the possibility of a utopian feminist republic, de Staël created a heroine who represented the "embodiment of a reformist enlightenment spirit," an ideal traditionally associated with the male sphere. Using only one name, Corinne denied her patriarchal lineage and re-created herself as a sovereign agent. In her public performances, she critiqued the masculine public sphere and gestured toward an alternative future—a truly democratic and culturally enlightened nation. Captivated by de Staël's artistry, insight, and achievement, Barrett Browning was animated by her personal and political vision for women.[46]

## Beatrice Cenci

Harriet Hosmer grew cognizant of contemporary Italian politics under the tutelage of Elizabeth Barrett Browning, whose influence—both personal and political—was apparent in the sculptor's recent works, *Beatrice Cenci* (fig. 51) and *Zenobia in Chains* (fig. 25). Both sculptures heralded historical heroines, whose imagery resonated with the chords of Barrett Browning's *la bella libertà.* Hosmer seemed to be searching for a visual language that would articulate a modern emancipated womanhood at the same that it would assent, by necessity in quiet terms, to the liberation of Rome.

The young sculptor had finished her *Beatrice Cenci* in 1856, in the midst of what could only be called "Cenci-mania" in Rome. Artists and tourists flocked to the ground-level gallery of the Palazzo Barberini to see what was then considered the most beautiful portrait by Guido Reni, his *Beatrice Cenci* (fig. 52).[47] After arriving in Rome in 1859, Sophia Hawthorne was also thrilled to see the painting in the flesh, located just downstairs from the lovely apartments occupied by William Wetmore Story and his family. She noted that painted and engraved reproductions

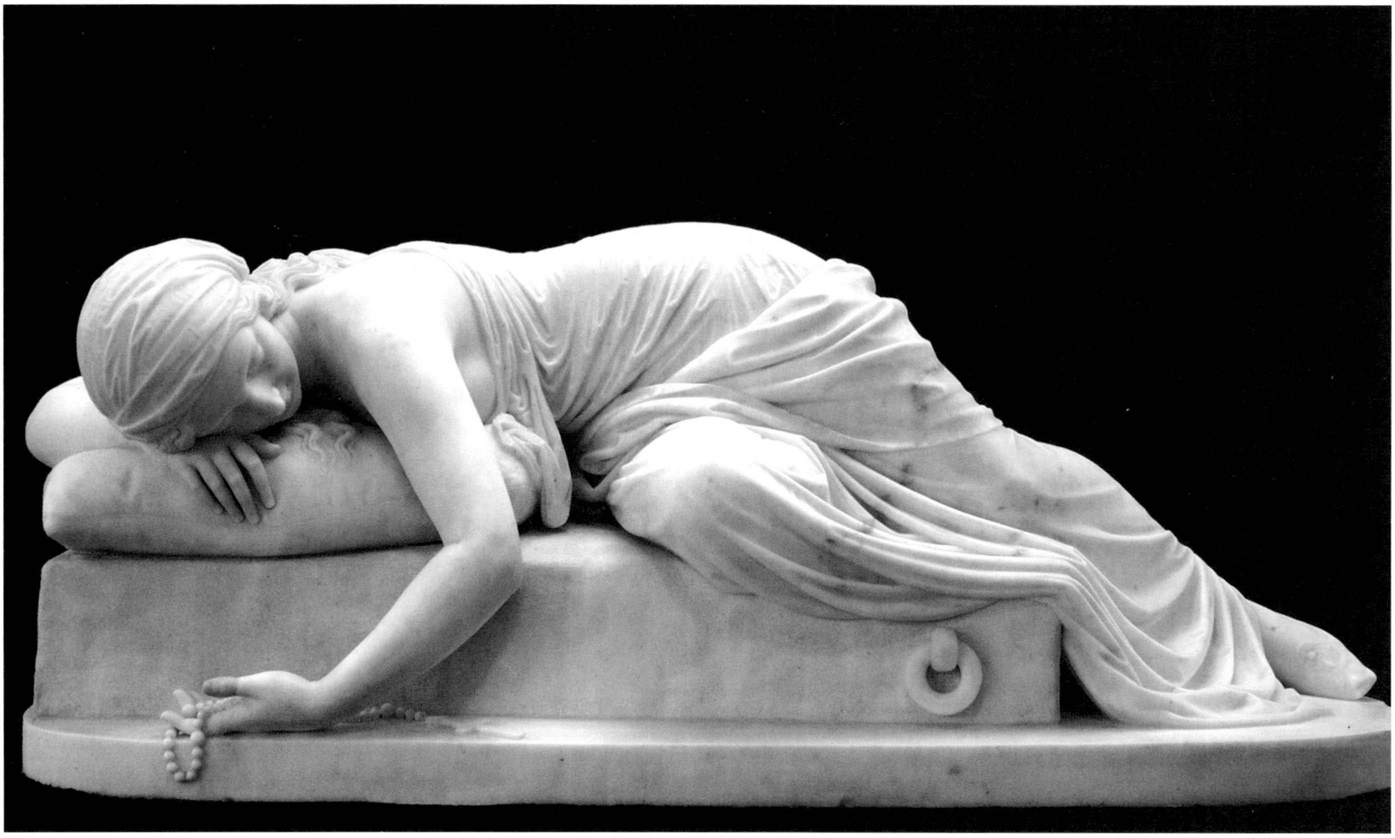

FIG. 51 *(opposite)*
Harriet Hosmer, *Beatrice Cenci*, 1856, marble. From the collections of the St. Louis Mercantile Library at the University of Missouri–St. Louis.

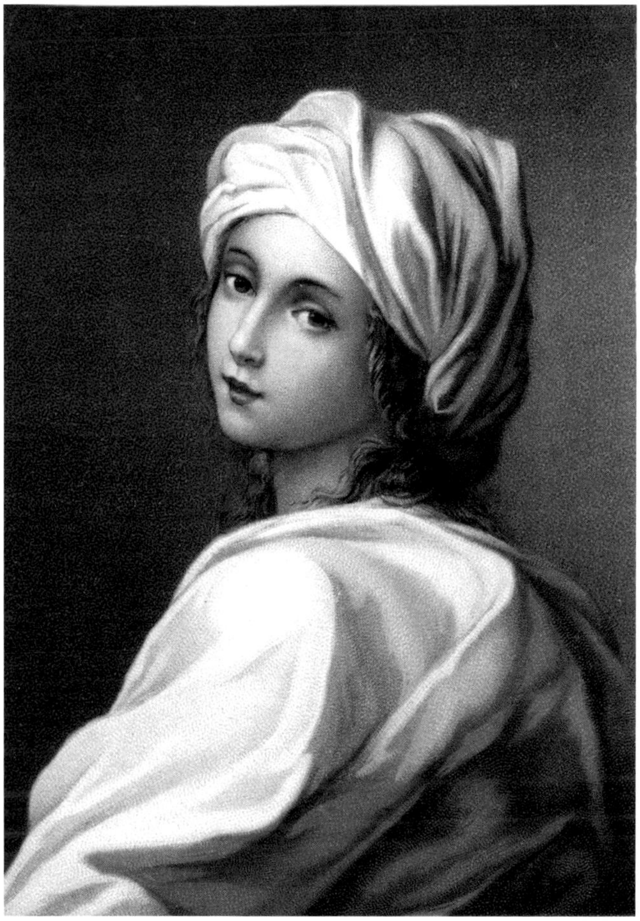

FIG. 52
*Beatrice Cenci*, postcard printed in Italy. Courtesy of the author. Photo: Daniel P. Younger.

were available all over Rome, in "every picture dealer's shop, of every size." Since the sixteenth century, Cenci's martyrdom had generated such interest that it required an icon, art historian Barbara Groseclose has explained, and this supposed "portrait" attributed to Reni served the purpose well.[48]

The historical figure of Beatrice Cenci fascinated the Victorian mind. Physically and sexually abused by her father, Beatrice, together with her stepmother and brother, conspired to kill the dangerous patriarch, Francesco Cenci. Accused and convicted of patricide in a spectacular trial, she was imprisoned in Rome and publicly executed by beheading. Afterward her head and body were carried through the streets of Rome like venerated relics. From the moment of her death, in 1598, her martyrdom has been enshrined.[49] The nineteenth-century narrative, replete with sexuality and violence, presumed the spiritual innocence of the young woman. "There was, in her suffering countenance, an expression of resignation and fortitude," the British art historian Anna Jameson wrote in her *Lives of Celebrated Female Sovereigns and Illustrious Women,* "a calmness of religious hope that drew tears from the spectators." The figure of Beatrice was able to reconcile contradictory notions. She was both resigned to her impending death and strong in her convictions and actions. In her feminist history of great women, Jameson characterized Cenci as heroic.[50]

In her sculpture, Hosmer envisioned a similar complexity in the heroine's character. Beatrice is depicted in her jail cell the night before her execution, silent, at peace, with cross and rosary in her hand. In its three-quarter scale, Hosmer's figure appears petite and fragile as she sleeps on a hard rectangular block that the sculptor left deliberately unfinished in its rough, coarse surface. Beatrice's body is draped over the stone bed, her head and shoulders resting upon a pillow and her left leg and arm falling onto the sculptural base. Her left hand holds the rosary and cross; the rosary beads encircle her index finger and rest across her upturned palm. The holy beads fall into the viewer's space—the only sculptural element not contained by the oval base (fig. 53). This detail assumes a coded political meaning in nineteenth-century Rome, alluding to the strong moral beliefs that propelled her crime and to the oppressive power of the church that martyred her for these convictions.

Guilty of murder yet morally pure, Beatrice Cenci posed a conundrum that haunted the writings of Romantic authors in Italy, England, and the United States. Her story saw several incarnations in the nineteenth century. Percy Bysshe Shelley, the British expatriate poet living in Rome, in 1819 wrote his only play, *The Cenci,* which introduced the historical character of Beatrice to English-speaking audiences. Originally a warning against violent revolution, the play reenvisioned for a contemporary readership the actions of Beatrice as Italian resistance to political oppression.[51] Margaret Fuller saw her as a woman who revolted against tyranny—a subversive figure whose life and image recalled the internal contradictions of patriarchy. "Thou wert not so happy to die for thy country or thy brethren, but thou wert worthy of such an occasion," Fuller wrote in her feminist history, *Woman in the Nineteenth Century.*[52]

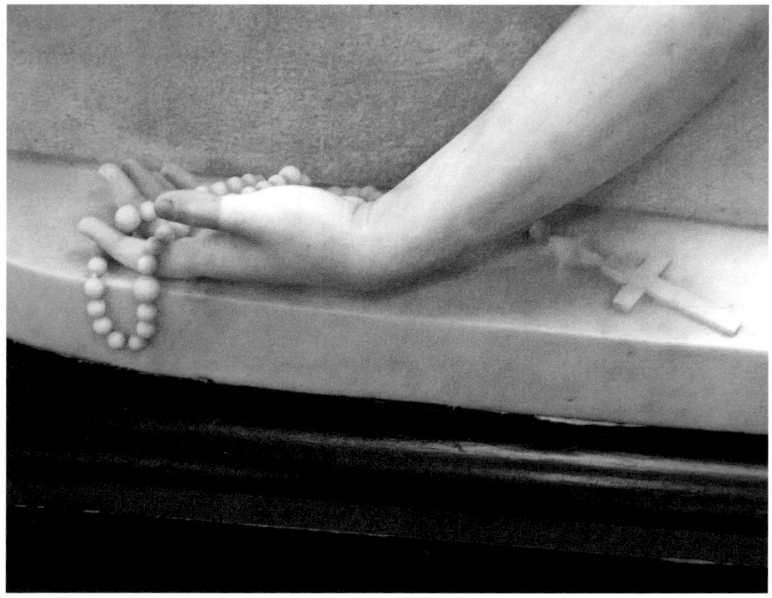

FIG. 53
Harriet Hosmer, *Beatrice Cenci* (fig. 51), detail of hand with rosary.

The Italian patriot and novelist F. D. Guerrazzi originally published his *Beatrice Cenci* in 1851, appealing to a young generation of readers "always to believe in the beautiful and the good."[53] In the novel, he posited the "beautiful and good" Beatrice as a symbol of the *Risorgimento,* an emblem of feminine resistance to political tyranny. The book had a powerful effect upon "impassionate and vehement readers" in Italy, one American writer noted. Posing a threat to social order, the book was censored in Rome and throughout the peninsula. "Certain of the governments have interdicted its publication," the American writer continued, "and it is now rarely seen in Italy." An English translation appeared in 1857,[54] the same year Hosmer exhibited her sculpture in the United States.

Hosmer began her sculpture *Beatrice Cenci* in the fall of 1854, three years after Guerrazzi had published his novel in Italy. She had been offered a commission for a full-length figure from a colleague of Wayman Crow's in St. Louis—and she decided upon a statue of Beatrice Cenci.[55] In the mid–nineteenth century, a narrative surfaced that situated Reni in the heroine's cell, in the act of painting her, on the eve of her death.[56] Not surprisingly, those holding nationalist sympathies read this newly conceived depiction of her incarceration in terms of contemporary papal absolutism and the thousands of political prisoners detained in the Vatican. In the sculpture, two small details on the work's frontal plane suggest the tyranny to which Beatrice had been subjected. The prominence of the rosary beads represents the power of the Catholic Church. As they bring her comfort in prayer, they simultaneously signify the agent of her oppression—the papal decree of execution. Held within her delicately carved fingers, the beads drape off the base and provide a visual balance to the ring bolt attached further to the right of the frontal plane. Though lacking chains, the bolt offers a direct reference to her imprisonment. The proximity of the rosary beads to the ring bolt reinforces Beatrice's plight and serves as a visual metaphor for the absolute power that the papal regime held over women and Rome in the nineteenth century; the beads themselves serve as a sign for the chain that binds her. To Anglo-American artists and reformers, Beatrice most likely embodied an ideal of individual dignity and womanly autonomy when viewed within the politicized space of Rome. She acted decisively against injustice and was punished for her agency. A martyr to a patriarchal system, she was doubly victimized by a brutal father and despotic pope.[57]

The plight of Beatrice Cenci brings to mind the mythological figure Medusa, an important signifier in Hosmer's early career. The artist had completed her bust of Medusa in 1854 (fig. 13), the same year that she began her sculpture of Beatrice Cenci. Both figures had been beheaded in a redoubling of punishments. Ravished by Neptune, betrayed by Minerva, and ultimately beheaded by Perseus, the beautiful Medusa in nineteenth-century narratives fell victim to cruelty beyond her control. Appealing to Romantic writers and artists, Medusa, like Beatrice, appeared simultaneously as accountable for evil yet innocent of the horror she had generated. In his verse fragment "On the Medusa of Leonardo da Vinci in the Florentine Gallery," Shelley wrote: "Yet it is less the horror than the grace / Which turns the gazer's spirit into stone." The poet imagined Medusa as lovely and humanized, a vulnerable victim rather than a hideous monster.[58]

The image of Medusa has often stood as a symbol of cultural and, sometimes, revolutionary change. As I indicated in chapter 2, women and men have historically understood the Medusa narrative in different terms. To the male viewer, her decapitated head—a symbol of castration—references the "manly woman" and signifies an anxiety about an unleashed feminine power that poses a threat to the autonomy and independence of the privileged male sphere. To the female viewer, Medusa represents an allegory of feminine empowerment. For example, nineteenth-century scholars located the Medusa myth in Africa, where Libyan Amazons worshipped the Gorgon as their serpent goddess.[59] In the progressive women's community in Rome, the figure of Medusa—as represented by Hosmer—served as a sign of women's emancipation. So expressive was this image that the sculptor displayed the popular feminist symbol on her front door to identify her home on via Gregoriana (fig. 17).

When the *Beatrice Cenci* was viewed in the artist's studio, Hosmer doubtless cashed in on "Cenci-mania." Nonetheless, its reception was grounded in contemporary Roman history—that is, in Italian resistance to political tyranny—its narrative association with *Medusa* evident to Rome's Anglo-American feminists. The two sculptures together offered a visual correlate to Barrett Browning's poetic trope *la bella libertà.* A young woman who acted decisively against personal dishonor, the figure signified by Hosmer's *Beatrice Cenci* embodied feminine resistance to sexual subjugation. In concert with the Medusa image, she became an emblem of revolt against patriarchal authority. Within the context of the *Risorgimento,* the sculpture represented not only the horrors of papal power as exercised over women but also the political tyranny imposed upon the vulnerable inhabitants of Rome.

When shown in the United States in 1857, the sculpture elicited a different response from its viewers, one grounded, for the most part, in contemporary antipapist rhetoric. Hosmer, a shrewd businesswoman at the age of twenty-six, exhibited her *Beatrice Cenci* in London, Boston, New York, Philadelphia, and New Orleans. She accompanied the sculpture to the United States, where large crowds viewed the piece. When shown at Cotton's Gallery in Boston, the figure appealed to a wide audience and generated diverse responses, including a uniquely American political reading.

Protestant and Catholic viewers associated the *Beatrice Cenci* with Italy, but in radically different ways. Catholic bishops and priests were in political agreement with the Vatican. Boston's large population of Irish Catholics, for example, insisted that the pope maintain temporal rule over Rome in order to assure his spiritual independence, a position that alienated Catholics from Protestants, Jews, and freethinkers, who embraced the Italian struggle for sovereignty. American Catholics sponsored anti-*Risorgimento* rallies and raised funds for the pope. Many others petitioned the Roman consul to serve in the papal army.[60]

By contrast, Protestant support for a liberal Italy went hand in hand with hatred of the pope. The secretive Know Nothing Party, with its popular "No-Popery" campaign, had captured the political imagination of many Americans in the 1850s, a decade that saw the publication of anti–Roman Catholic texts such as Charles Frothingham's *Convent's Dream* (1854) and Edward Beecher's *Papal Conspiracy Exposed* (1855). With its anti-immigrant platform, the Know Nothing Party fueled nativist sentiment throughout the country, especially in the Northeast, where many immigrants had settled. Boston, where the *Beartice Cenci* was exhibited, was an epicenter of virulent anti-Catholicism. In the minds of most Protestants, blind allegiance to papal absolutism on the part of millions of Catholic immigrants posed a clear threat to American democracy.[61]

Americans were both drawn to and repulsed by Catholic traditions, as art historian John Davis and others have discussed. However, when it came to the power of the papacy, there was little disagreement. American Protestants of all political stripes—from radical abolitionists to Southern slave owners—agreed that "Romanism," with its papal oppression, was a growing menace to American liberty. From the painter and inventor Samuel F. B. Morse to the critic James Jackson Jarves, Protestant cultural elites combined support for the "No-Popery" campaign and its religious prejudice against Catholics with a sympathy for the Italian state and its struggle for independence.[62]

Responsive to the young female Italian martyr, American Protestants viewed Hosmer's *Beatrice Cenci* through this nativist lens. Her rumpled drapery, exposed breast, and long flowing tresses suggested a sexual vulnerability reminiscent of the horrors of convent narratives that regularly appeared in the popular press. "Her name is a synonym for suffering innocence, the type of sorrowing beauty, which, appealing to our sympathies, wins our unconscious homage," one critic wrote. To Protestant audiences, her alleged guilt was predicated upon "the judgment of tribunals [and] the verdicts of executioners," a not-so-subtle reference to papal tyranny and injustice.[63] Shown to equal acclaim in Boston and New Orleans, the sculpture reinforced the nativist rhetoric of the Know Nothing Party, whose allure briefly substituted the polarizing specter of sectionalism for a unifying anti-Catholic zeal.[64] The reception of this sculpture revealed the strength of anti-Catholic prejudice as it informed attitudes toward the "Italian Question" in the United States.

## Zenobia in Chains

Like the *Beatrice Cenci, Zenobia in Chains* evoked a range of contemporary responses, which depended upon the geographical site of its exhibition and the sexual positionings of its viewers (fig. 25).[65] To the Anglo-American feminist community in Rome, *Zenobia in Chains* embodied the utopian dreams given poetic form in Barrett Browning's phrase *la bella libertà*. The sculpture later traveled to various venues in New York, Boston, and Chicago between 1864 and 1865, where slavery and abolition framed the sculpture's reading.

When producing the initial models for the Palmyrene queen, Hosmer turned to Anna Jameson for guidance.[66] An intimate of Charlotte Cushman's inner circle, Jameson was at home in Italy, making Florence her primary residence. From March until May 1857, she resided briefly in Rome when Hosmer was planning her sculpture. Jameson had originally met the young sculptor at the Brownings' residence in Florence the year before. An increasingly vocal advocate of women's rights, she supported feminine endeavors in medicine, publishing, and the arts. Writing essays on the historical figures of Beatrice Cenci and Zenobia in her well-known book *Lives of Celebrated Female Sovereigns and Illustrious Women,* she pioneered a form of feminist criticism that brought her international recognition as an authority on female artists. A friend, colleague, and mentor to many young American and

British women, she asserted, "It is for women I write." Particularly savvy about the difficulties that female artists faced, she supported Hosmer when rumors circulated that challenged the authenticity of *Zenobia* and thus threatened to taint the artist's professional reputation. Until her death in 1860, Jameson led an independent and public professional life that served as a model for ambitious Anglo-American women in Rome.[67]

In her *Lives,* Jameson reconceptualized the historical figure of Zenobia as both a warrior queen and learned intellectual. In this baldly feminist narrative, she professed that Zenobia and her husband reigned Palmyra jointly, that the queen was both a student of Neoplatonism and a scholar of Greek and Latin, and that she was a great patron of architecture. Claiming Cleopatra, with her Ptolemaic heritage, among her progenitors, Zenobia adopted Greek and Roman manners, distancing herself from the Arab tribes she ruled. Jameson thus positioned this Eastern queen firmly within the privileged history of the West. Other writers emphasized Zenobia's exoticism, bringing attention to her "dark" and "swarthy hue" and powerful black eyes; some identified her as Jewish.[68] Mirroring the multiple identities often assigned to nineteenth-century Italy, Zenobia straddled two worlds, melding attributes of the exotic East with those of the classical West. Addressing this blending of cultures, Lydia Maria Child wrote that Hosmer "spared no pains to ascertain the probable admixture of Grecian and Oriental in the costume of Zenobia and her court." As Child expanded: "Cleopatra and Zenobia descended from the same line of Macedonian kings, and both received a wonderful inheritance of beauty; but neither in the character [n]or the person of Zenobia was there any trace of the voluptuousness and coquetry which distinguished her royal relative of Egypt. It was her womanly modesty, her manly courage, and her intellectual tastes, which first attracted Miss Hosmer toward her."[69]

Hosmer imagined a powerful, beautiful, and exotic monarch in her sculpture. In October of 1859, she put the *Zenobia in Chains* into marble; the imposing sculpture stands eighty-two inches high. She also produced a smaller-scaled marble version, a roughly four-foot-high copy of the original clay model (the *bozzetto*). The monumental *Zenobia* appears to walk with a regal bearing, demonstrating an uprightness that signals both strength and confidence. Her powerful physical authority emanates from her large body, thick muscled arms, and layers of vestments—a cloak, part of which is bundled under her left arm, hangs over a chiton-like garment, which, in turn, reveals an underslip. The drapery clings to her right thigh, revealing an otherwise invisible body below. Indeed, her monumental stature and intricate drapery allude to the materiality of a fluted column. *Zenobia*'s face, depicted with Severe-style classicism, wears a gentle expression with downcast eyes. Her forelocks flow over her shoulders; a chignon contains the remainder of her hair. Upon her head is a large crown. Heavy iron manacles around her wrists support the decorative chain that loops before her. The figure seems to walk slowly and deliberately, with the left foot raised as if poised to move forward off the pedestal. Her royal costume is highly detailed, replete with decorative buttons on her pleated right sleeve. She displays a Medusa's head, with curving snakes serving as clasps, on her belt. The placid face of the Gorgon is highly visible, only partially concealed by the cloak and chains (figs. 54 and 55).

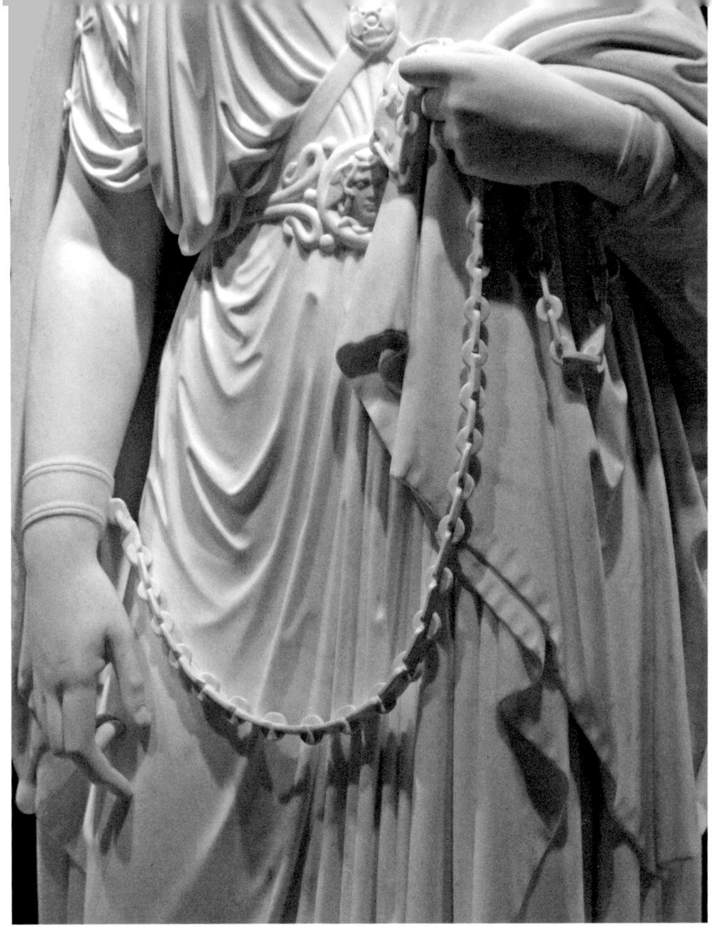

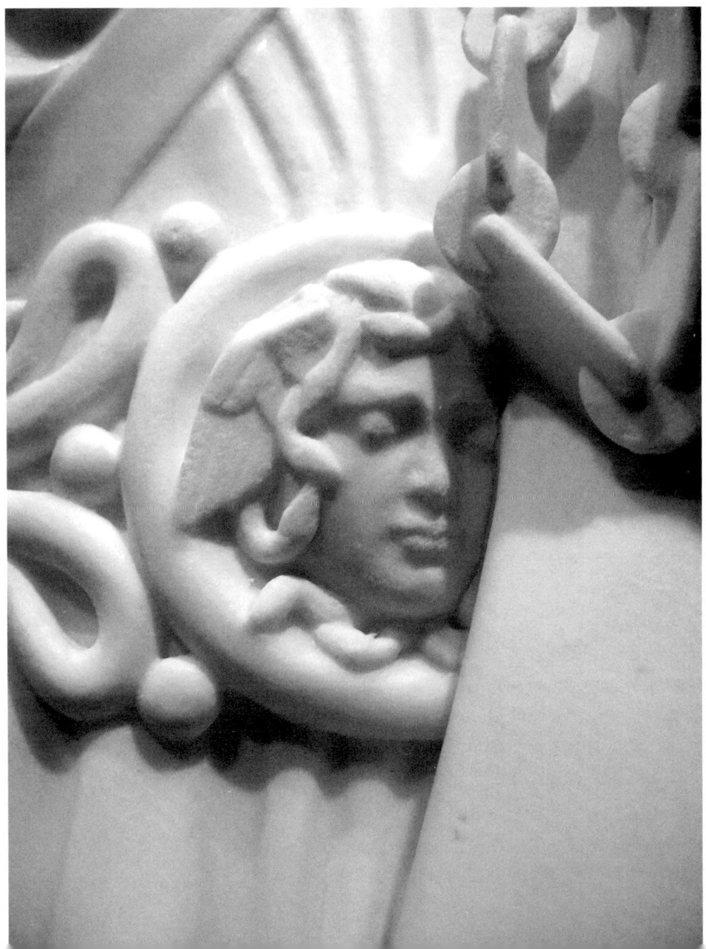

FIG. 54
Harriet Hosmer, *Zenobia in Chains* (fig. 25), detail of the bodice. © Courtesy of the Huntington Art Collections, San Marino, Calif.

FIG. 55
Harriet Hosmer, *Zenobia in Chains* (fig. 25), detail of Medusa head. © Courtesy of the Huntington Art Collections, San Marino, Calif.

Informed, at least in part, by political events swirling around her in Rome, Hosmer conceived of her heroine in unique terms. Together with Louisa Lander's *Virginia Dare* (fig. 24), *Zenobia in Chains* offered an alternative model to the traditional captivity-narrative protagonist, upending the feminine colonial stereotype of the passive, languishing victim. Both figures stand tall and alert, revealing neither a pathetic victimization, like Hiram Powers's *Greek Slave* of 1843 (fig. 26), nor fear and consternation, like Erastus Dow Palmer's *White Captive* of 1859 (fig. 27). In contrast to the potentially scandalous female nude, *Zenobia* embodies a proper femininity, fully covered from head to foot.[70] "I have tried to make [*Zenobia*] too proud to exhibit passion or emotion of any kind," Hosmer wrote to Child. A stoic heroine, the queen was "not subdued, though a prisoner[;] calm, grand, and strong within herself."[71] With her words, Hosmer echoed the moral and political fortitude that Barrett Browning had envisioned for Italy in her *Poems Before Congress:* "Italy, Italy—loosed at length from the tyrant's thrall, / Pale and calm in her strength." With this sculpture, she gave visual form to Barrett Browning's poetic conceit.

In 1859, Hosmer exhibited *Zenobia in Chains* at the Accademia de' Quiriti, an archaeological institute in Rome in which the artist held membership. Located in the Villa Torlonia, the academy supported women's participation in the arts—from sponsoring exhibitions to highlighting "old and young poetess[es] recit[ing] sonnets."[72] No record of the critical response to Hosmer's work has come to light. However, the sculpture appeared in Rome when the process of national unification was well under way. Writing to her friend Cornelia Carr, Hosmer advised, "Don't be frightened at the rumors of war and bloodshed here."[73]

When viewed in Rome under such conditions, *Zenobia in Chains* surreptitiously referenced contemporary Roman politics through its formal and iconographical associations with the mythological figures Minerva and Medusa. Such subterfuge was necessary to circumvent the severe censorship imposed upon the city by the papal regime. The goddess Minerva, worshipped in the Capitoline Temple with Jupiter and Juno, had been associated with the city of Rome since antiquity. The goddess was a popular figure among Rome's expatriate women's community. Charlotte Cushman had owned a large plaster bust of Minerva, which she donated to the Boston Athenaeum in 1857. Hosmer had a plaster cast of Minerva in her studio in 1859, according to reports from Nathaniel Hawthorne.[74] An antique marble version of the sculpture was (and still is) on display in the Capitoline Museum (fig. 56). Hosmer turned to this monumental and austere sculpture for inspiration. *Zenobia*'s posture and arm gesture—one bent, the other at her side—mirror that of the *Minerva.* Both sculptures' demeanors suggest agency, as they appear to walk commandingly off their pedestals. With its formal allegiance to the Capitoline sculpture, Hosmer's *Zenobia in Chains* referenced a proud, yet still enchained, Rome.

Like the goddess Minerva, who wore the Medusan image upon her breastplate (fig. 57), *Zenobia* also brandished this protective emblem on her regal costume. Medusa was a key image in Hosmer's iconography, serving as a subversive emblem of feminine endurance.[75] Traditionally feared by men because her gaze would turn them to stone, Medusa signaled an opposition to patriarchal domination. Hosmer's *Zenobia* conjoined

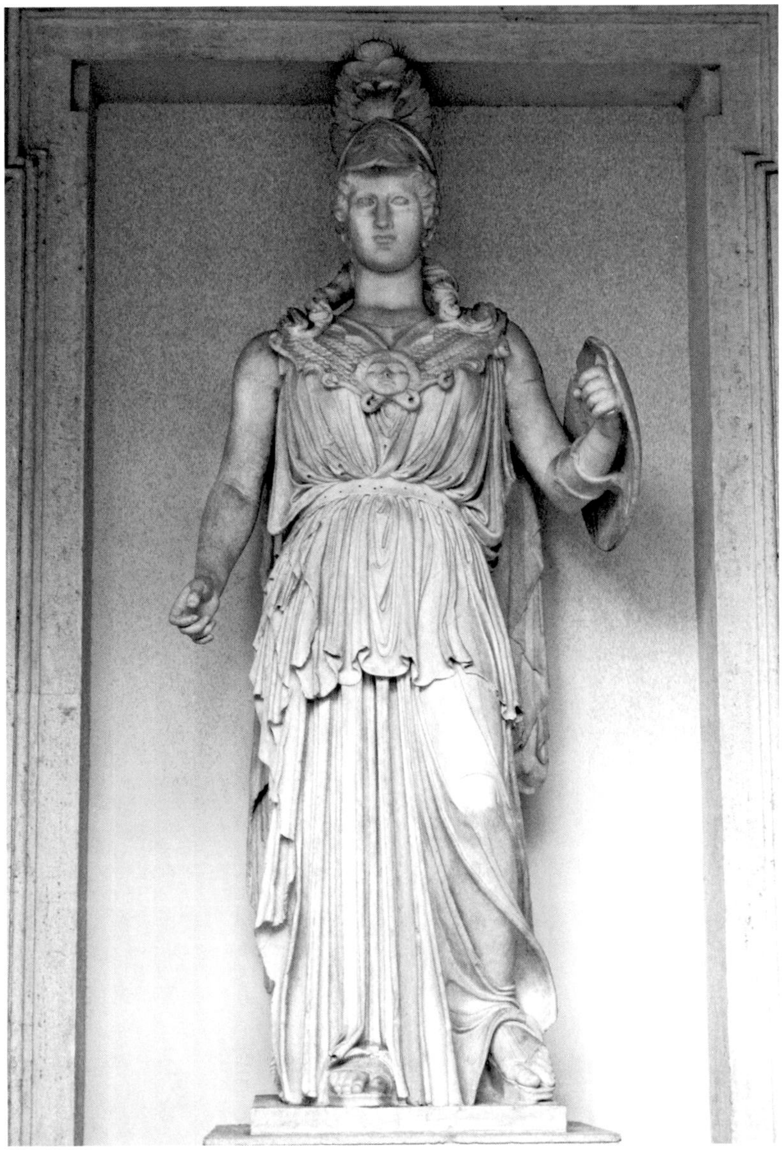

FIG. 56
*Minerva*, second century B.C.E., marble. Palazzo Nuovo, Capitoline Museums, Rome.

feminist resistance in the emblem of the Medusa with the idea of a once powerful Rome in the image of Minerva. In this way, the sculpture stood as a paean to Barrett Browning's *la bella libertà*—her devotion to Italian revolutionary politics and women's emancipation—while simultaneously visualizing a new iconography of sovereign power and feminine resistance.

Within a few years, both Jameson and Barrett Browning were dead. Jameson died in 1860; Barrett Browning in 1861.[76] After the loss of these powerful mentors, Hosmer's life in Rome took an astounding turn. She entered into a friendship with Maria Sophia, the queen of Naples. When Garibaldi and his famous "Expedition of the Thousand" liberated Naples and the Kingdom of the Two Sicilies from Bourbon control in 1861, Pope Pius IX offered the young king and queen asylum in Rome. Italian nationalists staged counterdemonstrations to denounce their presence. Hosmer, however, openly welcomed the queen, who became a frequent visitor to her studio.

Maria Sophia had garnered a reputation as a modern warrior queen. She was known as a strong monarch who reigned briefly with her husband, King Francesco.[77] During the Siege of Gaeta from 1860 to 1861, the young queen was praised for her bravery after she joined her husband on the ramparts. Dressed in a legendary cloak, she took command of the Neapolitan military when her husband was too weak to lead. "The Queen [of Naples at Gaeta] looks calm and energetic" in photographs, Gregorovius wrote in January of 1861. "She is not devoid of charm, but is coquettish; wears a jacket with gold trimming and a Calabrian hat. The young King stands in thought, looks unimpressive and melancholy, just like a man gazing into an abyss."[78] In exile, the queen was heralded as a courageous heroine among European royalty and developed a cultlike following.[79]

There is little doubt that Hosmer fell prey to this cult of celebrity. In 1868, she began work on a full-length sculptural portrait of the queen. "She came to me the other day dressed exactly as she was" in Gaeta, Hosmer explained. "It will make an interesting statue, for the subject is invested with so much that is historic."[80] No images of the sculpture exist; whether it was ever translated into marble or just remained in clay is unclear to this day. However, a description of the sculpture from 1872 survives: "The Queen is erect and slightly defiant. . . . While the right hand rests upon the fold of the cloak where it is thrown across the breast and over the shoulder, the other points downward to the cannonballs that lie close to her feet. The head, surrounded by a splendid coronet of hair, is slightly thrown back. . . . It is an extremely handsome head, somewhat disdainful and breathing the utmost firmness and resolution."[81]

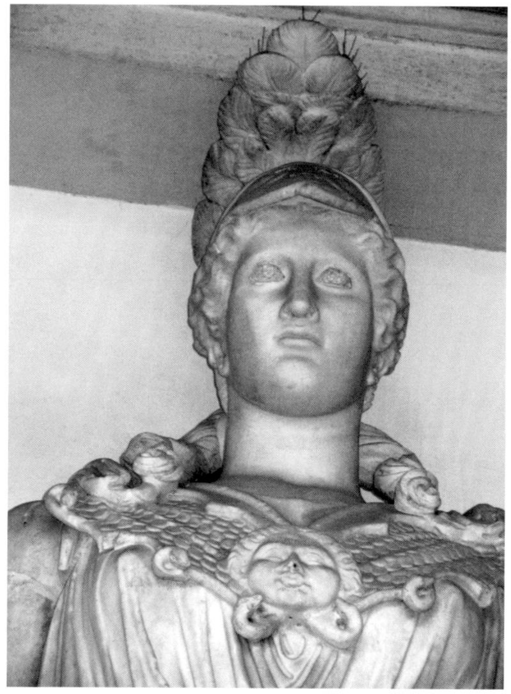

FIG. 57
*Minerva* (fig. 56), detail of Medusa head.

In the Neapolitan queen, Hosmer had found a contemporary heroine to commemorate. Demonstrating a "firmness and resolution" in her "slightly defiant" posture, the queen embodied an emancipated woman. As an active, powerful, historical agent, rather than a passive victim of circumstances, she was a living, breathing incarnation of Zenobia, the ancient queen with whom Hosmer had been so obsessed. The queen, like the historical Zenobia, had been forced from her throne. Unlike *Zenobia in Chains,* who stood as a personification of an oppressed Rome, Queen Maria Sophia embodied the power of the colonial forces aligned with the Austrian Empire.

Struck by the "romance" surrounding the queen, Hosmer never voiced second thoughts about commemorating an enemy of the new Italian state. Was her flirtation with Maria Sophia an affront to the memory of Barrett Browning, who had recently been memorialized as the "Poet of the *Risorgimento*"? By 1868, Austria—the colonial power against whom Barrett Browning railed in her epic book of poems *Casa Guidi Windows*—had been vanquished, no longer wielding power on the Italian peninsula. The poet's influence upon the sculptor's life and work was indisputable; *Zenobia in Chains* stood as a testament to their friendship.[82]

Yet Hosmer remained mesmerized by the Neapolitan queen. Her identification with the privileges of the Bourbon monarchy seemed equal, at times, to her sympathy for Italy and the Italian people. At the same time, she would celebrate when the Italian nationalists took Rome from the papal forces in 1870. "Rome belongs no more to the dear old gentleman with the Tiara!" she crowed.[83] Caught between her Republican desires and colonial privileges, Hosmer enacted the contradictions of expatriate life in mid-nineteenth-century Italy.

## Roma

The sculptor Anne Whitney remained in Boston until the Civil War ended. While Italy was undergoing its struggle for unification, the United States was torn apart by its own internal conflict. For the most part, travel to Italy was difficult during the war, and American numbers diminished in the Eternal City. With "anxious suspense and doubt," those American travelers and expatriates in Rome followed the war at home as best they could.[84] "We Americans read and talk little else than Harper's Ferry and sublime old John Brown," one Bostonian noted in early 1860.[85] Charlotte Cushman helped quell anxiety among those abroad by serving as an important conduit for war news in Rome. She had connections in high political circles in Washington and traveled frequently to the United States, acting in Sanitary Commission benefits for the Union Cause. She performed in Philadelphia, Boston, New York, Baltimore, and Washington, D.C., in 1863, donating her proceeds—more than $8,000—to the Union cause.[86]

In Rome, the Italian nationalists sympathized with the Union effort. In 1862, King Victor Emmanuel II sent a letter of support to President Lincoln from the Italian people. In return, the U.S. government asked that the sale of all guns and munitions to the South be halted and that the Italians desist from officially recognizing the Confederacy.[87] The Romans, in particular, who struggled against economic and political exploitation by the Vatican, empathized with the struggle to abolish chattel slavery in the plantation South. By contrast, the Papal States extended their political support to the Confederacy, whose sympathizers found their way to Rome as a seemingly safe political zone. Whenever possible, however, the Italian national government, in an alliance with President Lincoln, hunted them down. Until 1866, the Italian nationalists continued to extradite Confederates to the United States.[88]

In 1867, the year that Whitney arrived in Rome, the city was in political turmoil. Explosions occurred without warning throughout its precincts, killing innocent passersby. On October 27, a bomb fell on the Piazza di Spagna, in the heart of the expatriate neighborhood. Hosmer had fled Rome briefly due to the violence. Writing from England, she explained: "One of my men was going up the via Tritone [near the Piazza Barberini] when a bomb exploded and injured his right hand. He was obliged to have the middle finger cut off."[89]

American tourists began flocking to Rome again following the Civil War, oblivious to the dangers and ignorant of the political situation in Italy. Their numbers grew exponentially as travel restrictions were lifted, transatlantic journeys became easier, and postwar industrial wealth filtered down to the middle classes. Despite the turbulence, they continued to treat the Eternal City as a touristic spectacle, concerned only with its picturesque *contadini* (peasants) and exotic Catholic rituals. Meanwhile, Italian nationalists continued their efforts to liberate Rome.

In 1867, Garibaldi broke his alliance with King Victor Emmanuel II and staged an attack upon the Papal Guards. The mission failed when the French army routed his troops at Mentana, about thirty miles outside the city.[90] Garibaldi's bold attempt to capture Rome was praised in the international press. The progressive Americans at home saw this tactic as proof of the "resolute power of republicanism." Hosmer, upon her return from London, considered riding to Mentana "to see where the Garibaldians were gobbled up." To her credit, she decided against this ill-considered adventure.[91]

Together with Edmonia Lewis, another Boston sculptor recently arrived in the city, Whitney witnessed the French troops reentering Rome after their victory in Mentana. They numbered close to four thousand.[92] As a supporter of the Roman cause, she wrote to her sister, "I wish that a peaceful revolution might be brought about by a combined moral influence—an idea which would raise a guffaw in the Italian revolutionary party, for whoever heard of the papal govt being acted on by moral means. But one may wish for anything."[93] Lewis also railed against the troops and insisted, quite indelicately, that they were going "to the devil."[94] Both artists remained sensitive to the political and historical circumstances that shaped the environment of Rome; both learned Italian and engaged directly with the Roman people.[95]

Whitney was caught off guard by the striking poverty of the city and its large number of beggars, who, she reported, were "an interesting feature of society" there. They were a "a badly-governed people [who] find it almost impossible to earn" a fair living.[96] The poet Julia Ward Howe, in Rome for the third time in 1868, concurred: "Look at these rough people, unwashed, uncombed, untaught. . . . They are kept like human cattle, and have been so kept for centuries."[97] Beggary, to Whitney and Howe, was a political ill, not a character flaw of the modern Italian people.

In 1869, Whitney opened her Roman studio to the public to show a plaster version of *Roma*, an image of an Italian beggar woman (fig. 58). She based her sculpture on women she saw on Roman streets: "Old beggar women (and men) come around you and plead, with eighty or more winters . . . in their wrinkles . . . I for one cannot refuse." Writing to her sister, she decried the horrible living conditions of these women, who "sit in the chill mornings in the sun with their hands

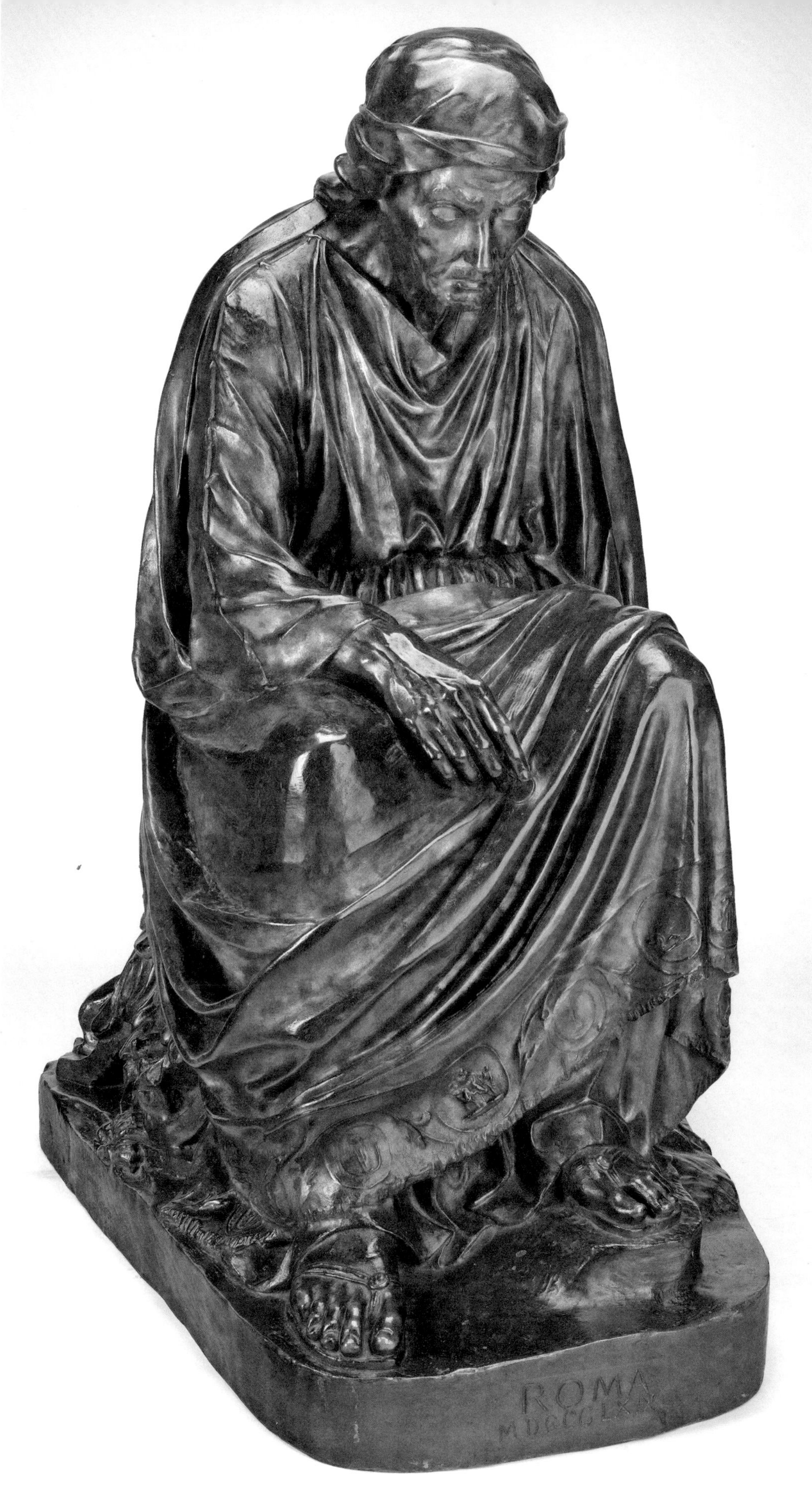


FIG. 58
Anne Whitney, *Roma*, 1869, bronze, 27 × 15 ½ in. Davis Museum and Cultural Center, Wellesley College, Wellesley, Mass., gift to the college by the class of 1886.

folded round the friendly scaldino [footwarmer] under their rags."[98] In her sculpture, Whitney acknowledged in no uncertain terms the social and political plight of the Roman people.

In the original version of *Roma,* Whitney modeled the figure of an elderly, exhausted woman seated upon a Corinthian capital. Dressed in a long robe, the *signora* leans forward with shoulders drooping and eyes downcast. Her face shows signs of aging. The figure holds in one hand a small oval disk on a chain—a license to beg—upon which Whitney has etched a cynical inscription, "Questevante in Roma" (This is what comes to you in Rome).[99] The other hand grasps a few small coins (fig. 59).[100] Her richly embroidered robe contrasts with her physical destitution. In the medallions on the garment's hem, some of Rome's most famous monuments appear, such as the *Apollo Belvedere,* the *Laocoön,* the *Farnese Hercules,* the *Dying Gaul,* and the Tempietto, making explicit the riches of the Vatican in contrast to the poverty of the Roman people. In this work, Whitney moved away from the idealized neoclassical style that she had perfected in her male nudes. By contrast, *Roma* exhibits a harsh naturalism, a visual language that she believed commensurate with the difficult lives of the Roman people.

Whitney, like most Americans, was virulently anti-Catholic, a conviction that fueled her hatred of papal tyranny. She had originally included the face of Cardinal Antonelli, the notorious secretary of state to the Vatican, in one of the medallions. This contemporary portrait made explicit the political commentary of the work by disrupting any potential nostalgic reading by viewers. This beggar woman was not a picturesque *contadina* but rather a historical subject

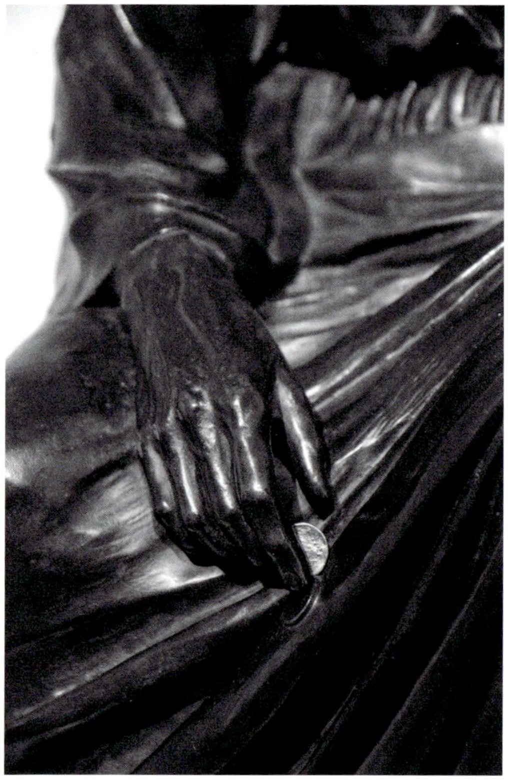

FIG. 59
Anne Whitney, *Roma* (fig. 58), detail of hand with coins.

who suffered from the repressive political policies of the pope.

When shown to the Roman public in June of 1869, the plaster sculpture caused quite a sensation among those who understood its open criticism of papal power. All the inhabitants of the city—native-born and foreign—were subject to censorship; any criticism of the pope was a punishable offense. Under these circumstances, the public display of *Roma* was quite a daring act. The following month, Whitney dispatched the sculpture to the home of George Marsh, the American consul in Florence, for safekeeping. She feared that the Vatican police would confiscate the work or, worse yet, destroy it. By October, she bowed to political pressure and removed the image of Antonelli, replacing it with a triple miter, a symbol of the papacy. In a letter to her sister, she explained that the sculpture was displayed in the front room of her studio in the Piazza di Spagna without its caustic image of Antonelli. "If people understand it—well—if not—I do not explain."[101]

The sculpture brought Whitney international fame; she showed the work to favorable reviews in London and in Boston.[102] An antiheroic figure, *Roma* referenced the poverty and decay of the city. She did not picture Rome as a mythical or arcadian site. In contrast, she depicted Rome as a participant in an emerging modern world. Originally titling the work *18 ROMA 69,* Whitney emphatically placed the sculpture within a context of current political events, making clear her support for the Italian nationalist cause.[103]

## Toussaint L'Ouverture in Prison

Between 1869 and 1871, Whitney produced another daring sculpture that referenced the Italian political struggle. Her small-scale sculpture *Toussaint L'Overture in Prison* (now lost) represented the Haitian leader who had led a successful slave revolt in 1791 and liberated the island from colonial rule (fig. 60). Later captured by Napoleon's forces, he was imprisoned within the Fortress of Joux in the Jura region of France and died of starvation in 1803. In her poem "The Prisoner of St. Joux," Whitney described the young heroic Toussaint as filled with "the great breath of liberty."[104]

The black leader to whom Whitney paid homage had shaped, albeit temporarily, the first multiracial republic in the Western Hemisphere. Whitney portrayed Toussaint, although sixty years old at the time of his death, as young and virile, his partially nude body strong and powerful despite the starvation that would eventually kill him. His shoulders and arms swelled with energy, a departure from conventional depictions of Toussaint in military uniform. His face revealed handsome African features—short, cropped hair, wide nose, and thick lips; his ears were adorned with hoop earrings. Leaning forward, he engaged the viewer's gaze directly, and pointed to the inscription, "Dieu se charge" (God is in charge), which he had etched upon his cell floor. With his dynamic posture and direct address, he appeared to spring into action and reveal a consciousness that belied his current state of abjection. Whitney figured Toussaint at the end of his life, imprisoned and awaiting death. Like Hosmer's *Beatrice Cenci,* he was both a historical actor on the political stage and a martyr for the larger cause of freedom.

This powerful black leader stood as an important model of political action for many progressive Americans. The influential abolitionist leader Wendell Phillips celebrated him as "one of the most remarkable men of the last generation." As an "unmixed negro, with no drop of white blood in his veins," Toussaint exemplified the potential of "the negro race, instead of being [an] object of pity or contempt." Phillips concluded, "[J]udged by the facts of history," heroic black leaders like Toussaint had earned "a place close by the side of the Saxon."[105] To radical abolitionists like Phillips and Whitney, the revolution in Haiti, with Toussaint at its helm, represented the achievement of an oppressed people while serving as a vindication of the black slave's capacity to enact his own freedom.[106]

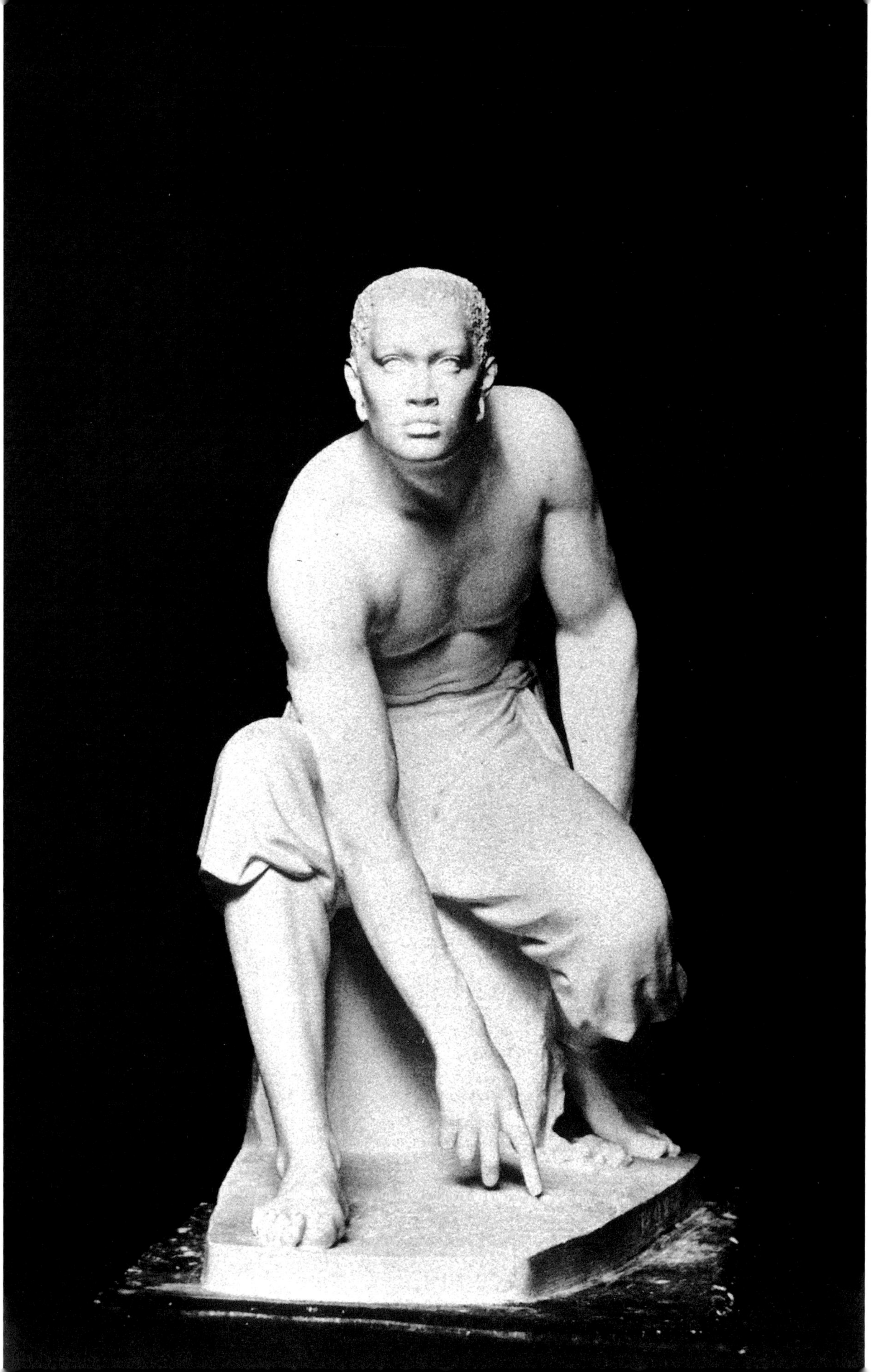

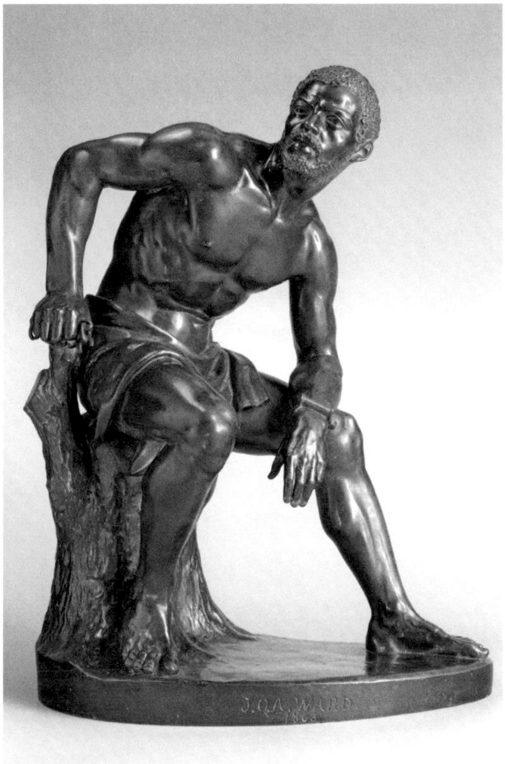

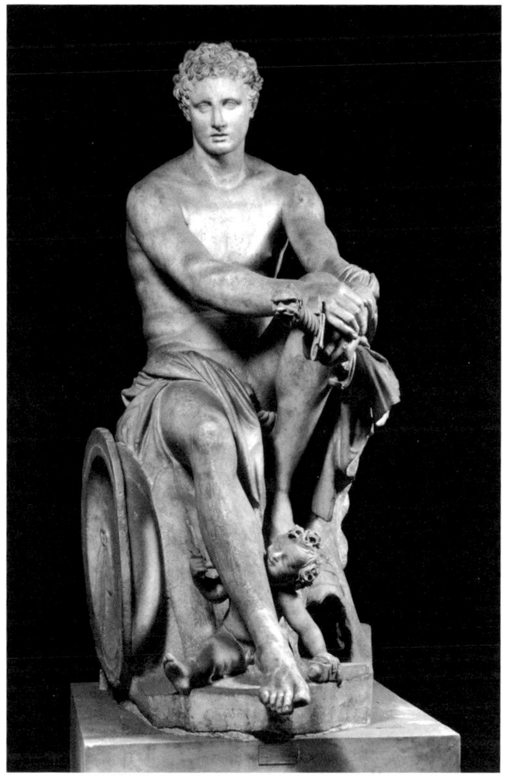

FIG. 60 *(opposite)* Anne Whitney, *Toussaint L'Ouverture in Prison,* 1869–71, now lost. Photograph courtesy of the Wellesley College Archives, Papers of Anne Whitney.

FIG. 61 John Quincy Adams Ward, *The Freedman,* 1863, this cast 1891, bronze, 19 1/2 × 14 3/4 × 9 3/4 in. The Metropolitan Museum of Art, New York, gift of Charles Anthony Lamb and Barea Lamb Seeley, in memory of their grandfather, Charles Rollinson Lamb, 1979, 1979.394.

FIG. 62 *Mars (Ares) Ludovisi,* Hellenistic sculpture. Museo Nazionale Romano (Palazzo Altemps), Rome.

Whitney blended aspects of the real and the ideal in her sculpture, probably working from the live model in Rome.[107] She also looked for inspiration to John Quincy Adams Ward's *Freedman* (fig. 61), which had been exhibited at the National Academy of Design in 1863, as well as the *Mars Ludovisi* (fig. 62), which she knew as a plaster cast in the Boston Athenaeum and in its marble original in Rome. *The Freedman* exhibits a combination of ethnographic realism and classical ideality. The figure is both black and heroic; his active and agile posture rejects the language of subjection to reveal an agent who shapes his own destiny.[108] In loosely basing the pose of Toussaint upon the *Ludovisi Mars,* the god of war, Whitney deployed a classical source that indexed military might, thus highlighting Toussaint's role as general and statesman.[109]

When viewed in Rome, the sculpture was understood within the frame of Italian politics. The heroic Toussaint was captured and jailed by the French, the very power that occupied Rome in the service of the pope. As is well known, Italian nationalists and American abolitionists regarded the antislavery struggle and the "Roman question" in tandem. Within the frame of *Risorgimento* politics, Toussaint L'Ouverture's political victories were proof that a revolution could succeed and that an oppressed population could demonstrate resilience and self-reliance.

By the time of its exhibition in a solo show at Doll's Gallery in Boston in 1873, the work had lost its historical specificity. Listed in the catalogue as "The Liberator, an African Slave, who is free and aspires to Greatness," it was read by an American public as an image of an anonymous freed black man. Serving as a sign of racial otherness, the nearly nude male body signified vulnerability and powerlessness.[110] The political agency of the heroic leader vanished, eradicated by the spectacle of the black body on display.

## *Liberated Rome*

Anne Whitney departed Rome in June of 1870, only to arrive back in the city a few months later to find a newly unified Kingdom of Italy with Rome as its capital. The French troops, called home to fight in the Franco-Prussian War and later to defend Paris during the bloody Commune, had withdrawn permanently from Rome. On September 20, 1870, General Raffaele Cadorna and his army breached the ancient walls of the city at the Porta Pia. Living nearby, Harriet Hosmer witnessed firsthand the liberation of the city. "After just five and a half hours, the cannonading ceased and Rome became *Italian*," she wrote. "We can scarcely believe it, and such rejoicings. . . . How many times I have thanked my stars that I was here!"[111]

After the fighting had stopped, Hosmer ventured to Napoleon's villa just inside the Porta Pia to examine the scene. What she witnessed was shocking. "I . . . saw a sight I shall never forget," she wrote to Wayman Crow. She described "a dead Zouave all covered with dust, his hands and face like marble, and a most frightful gunshot wound in the lower part of his face, which must have killed him on the spot." The momentousness of the event did not escape her. Apologizing to Crow for writing in such "a disjointed manner," she explained: "my head is entirely dazed with what I have seen and heard."[112]

Throughout the city, nationalist sympathizers celebrated the newly liberated Rome.[113] The Papal States disappeared from the map of Europe. Refusing to recognize the new secular state of Italy, Pope Pius IX declared himself a "Prisoner of the Vatican," where he remained in seclusion for the next seven years.[114] "The dear old Pope won't perform any of his parts in the theatre of St. Peter's or anywhere else," Hosmer declared in 1871. He "stays behind the scenes in the Vatican, a prisoner under his own frescoes."[115]

For artists, modern Rome offered new challenges. In order to visit museum collections, entrance tickets from the American consul were now required. For sculptors it was especially difficult, as they could only enter the Vatican collection with a permit and for a maximum of two hours. "The good health of the city and the cheap apartments are more than counterbalanced by the closing of the finest galleries [at the Vatican] and the withdrawal of church festivities and papistical splendors generally," Whitney noted.[116] By 1871, Hosmer predicted that "the place will be spoiled" for artists.[117]

Rome was losing its allure for Americans, an allure grounded in its colonial status, as the spectacular side of Catholicism was no longer visible on its city streets. Indeed, the Vatican implemented a strategy that would impose a stranglehold on Rome's tourist economy. "Antonelli . . .

counsels general mourning, no ceremonies in the churches, not a whisk of a candle towards an illumination, nothing to attract *forestieri* [the foreigners]," Hosmer reported.[118] Many visitors to Rome, like the author Henry James, who first arrived in October of 1869, bemoaned the loss of the older cosmopolitan city, which, he believed, had belonged to all nations and all ages. He was unsympathetic toward Italian politics, which he thought had punched "a hole" in the "vast, rich canvas" of preunification Italy.[119]

As the modern capital of a new sovereign state, the city offered fewer privileges to expatriate American artists. "Rome is slicking up a little," Hosmer grumbled. "In time it will become like every other city in the universe, clean, tidy, and hatefully *progressive*. We want it just as it was—with all its dirt and all its charms."[120] Mary Howitt, the British reformer, described the modernization of the city: "Rome was indeed becoming a busy and populous city. . . . New streets were being laid out, and new houses have been built."[121] Disappointed, James felt robbed of the exotic, intriguing, and arcadian character of "Old Rome." "The Italy of the old order was so amply enjoyable," he wrote. Modern Italy made him feel "shut out from a paradise."[122]

The modernization of Rome evoked the divided loyalties of American artists. As avid Republicans and feminists, Hosmer and Whitney celebrated the liberation of Rome and the autonomy of the Italian nation-state. As artists, however, they found themselves at a loss, without the freedoms of colonial privilege to which they had become quite accustomed. In the end, there seems to have been an implicit conflict between women artists' support of Italian liberation and their own needs as professional sculptors. As the freedoms of the Italian people surged, the circumstances that allowed expatriate women to flourish in Rome changed. Their professional successes were premised upon the political struggles of others. As Hosmer had predicted, it was "hateful" progress that had transformed the city forever.

# Part Three

## The Civil War, Reconstruction, and the Suffrage Debates

# *Six*

## *Antislavery Sermons in Stone*

### *Emancipation in a Transatlantic Context*

While in Rome, many American expatriate artists remained engaged with the politics of race in the United States. Informed by the political struggles they witnessed on the Italian peninsula, Anne Whitney, Edmonia Lewis, and Harriet Hosmer addressed issues of emancipation (freedom, citizenship, and suffrage) and Reconstruction (the potential for a new multiracial society) in their sculptural imagery. They looked to the work of William Wetmore Story, who, although a permanent resident of Rome, was quite vocal about his progressive politics. Throughout the 1850s, he maintained close friendships with a host of famous abolitionists, such as the writer and activist Lydia Maria Child; the Massachusetts senator Charles Sumner, who, in 1856, had been caned on the Senate floor because of his antislavery beliefs;[1] and Harriet Beecher Stowe, the author of the internationally acclaimed novel *Uncle Tom's Cabin.* Stowe's novel was translated into Italian almost immediately after its publication in 1852. Upon the author's arrival in Rome in 1857, she was fêted as a true heroine by cosmopolitan abolitionists as well as Italian nationalists.[2]

As dean of the Anglo-American expatriate community, Story aligned himself with an international cadre of abolitionists who resided in or visited Rome. In particular, his wife, Emelyn, and he were close to the British expatriate poets Robert and Elizabeth Barrett Browning. While concerned with contemporary events in Italy, Barrett Browning also followed the sectional politics unfolding in the United States. In 1854, she boldly confronted the issue of slavery in her poem "A Curse for a Nation." The opening stanza reads: "I heard an angel speak last night, / And he said, Write! / Write a nation's curse for me, / And send it over the Western Sea."[3] She repeated the imperative "Write!" with great urgency, as if issuing a divine command. Together with Barrett Browning, Story published abolitionist poems in Maria Weston Chapman's *Liberty Bell,* the literary magazine of the Boston Female Anti-Slavery Society.[4]

It was not until meeting Barrett Browning in Rome that Hosmer reconsidered her position on slavery. Upon her visit to St. Louis in 1850, she had not been troubled by the fact that her friend and future patron Wayman Crow owned three slaves as household servants. An adherent of the moderate Whig policy of gradual voluntary manumission, he eventually freed his slaves in 1853, much to Hosmer's approval. Child later mocked the young sculptor in a friendly manner: "If you had had your will, little 'Missouri Ruffian' . . . [a]nd had exterminated the abolitionists, you would have destroyed the *wheat* of the country and left nothing but the *chaff*."[5]

Anne Whitney and Edmonia Lewis were both members of the Boston abolitionist community. The city attracted Lewis because of its population of prominent African-Americans, such as the doctor, writer, lecturer, and former slave William Wells Brown and the political activist Rev. Leonard A. Grimes. Before arriving in Boston, Lewis had attended Oberlin College, in Ohio, where she began her study of art. A scandal forced her to abandon her education. In Boston, she was introduced to the abolitionist sculptor Edward Brackett, with whom she studied briefly. His patrons were among the most famous antislavery leaders of the time: William Cullen Bryant, editor of the progressive *New York Evening Post;* the poet Henry Wadsworth Longfellow; the minister Wendell Phillips; Senator Sumner; and the abolitionist leader William Lloyd Garrison, many of whom followed Lewis's professional career in Boston and in Rome.[6]

Whitney was an active participant in reform activities in Boston, complaining that attendance at "emancipation leagues and Anti-slavery conventions" kept her too busy to devote time to her sculpture.[7] She had a particular interest in the African-American subject in sculpture, producing a number of models of black figures throughout her career, such as *Toussaint L'Ouverture in Prison* (fig. 60). None was put into permanent form; all are lost to us, except in photographs. One commentator noted, "I know no artist who has dared to treat the negro as a proper subject for art; but Miss Whitney has done it over and over again."[8]

## *The Antislavery Sculpture of William Wetmore Story*

In Rome, Story produced two sculptures, *Cleopatra* (1858–60; fig. 63) and *The Libyan Sibyl* (1861; fig. 64), in which he developed an iconography that progressive Anglo-American audiences associated with the abolitionist cause. *Cleopatra* is seated upon her throne, resting her head against her bent and raised right arm. Her left arm is relaxed, positioned upon her left thigh. An asp curls around her forearm as the queen meditates upon her imminent death. Adding authenticity to the Egyptian imagery, the details of the headdress display archaeological accuracy.[9]

In the nineteenth century, the image of Cleopatra represented a complicated melding of Egyptian (North African) otherness and Western (European) whiteness. Cleopatra was of Greek origin, part of the Ptolemaic line descended from Alexander the Great, and thus a representative of the Western classical heritage. Within Roman culture, however, she was consistently depicted as foreign and exotic. Marrying the general Mark Antony, who betrayed his Roman allegiances by investing her with imperial power and privilege, Cleopatra became the archenemy of the Roman state. In 31 B.C.E., the Roman general Octavian (Augustus) vanquished the Egyptian army in the Battle of Actium. Cleopatra chose suicide rather than surrender to Roman might.[10]

Story's *Cleopatra*—her power safely contained by imminent death—signified racial difference. As a personification of Egypt, she symbolized black Africa to a wide spectrum of American abolitionists.[11] Indeed, the writer and journalist Henry Adams noted that Story's *Cleopatra,* which he saw in Rome in 1860, was "an Egyptian woman,

FIG. 63 *(opposite)* William Wetmore Story, *Cleopatra,* modeled 1858, carved 1860, marble on polychrome wood platform, 55 × 24 × 48 in. Los Angeles County Museum of Art, Los Angeles, Calif., gift of Mr. and Mrs. Henry M. Bateman, 78.3.

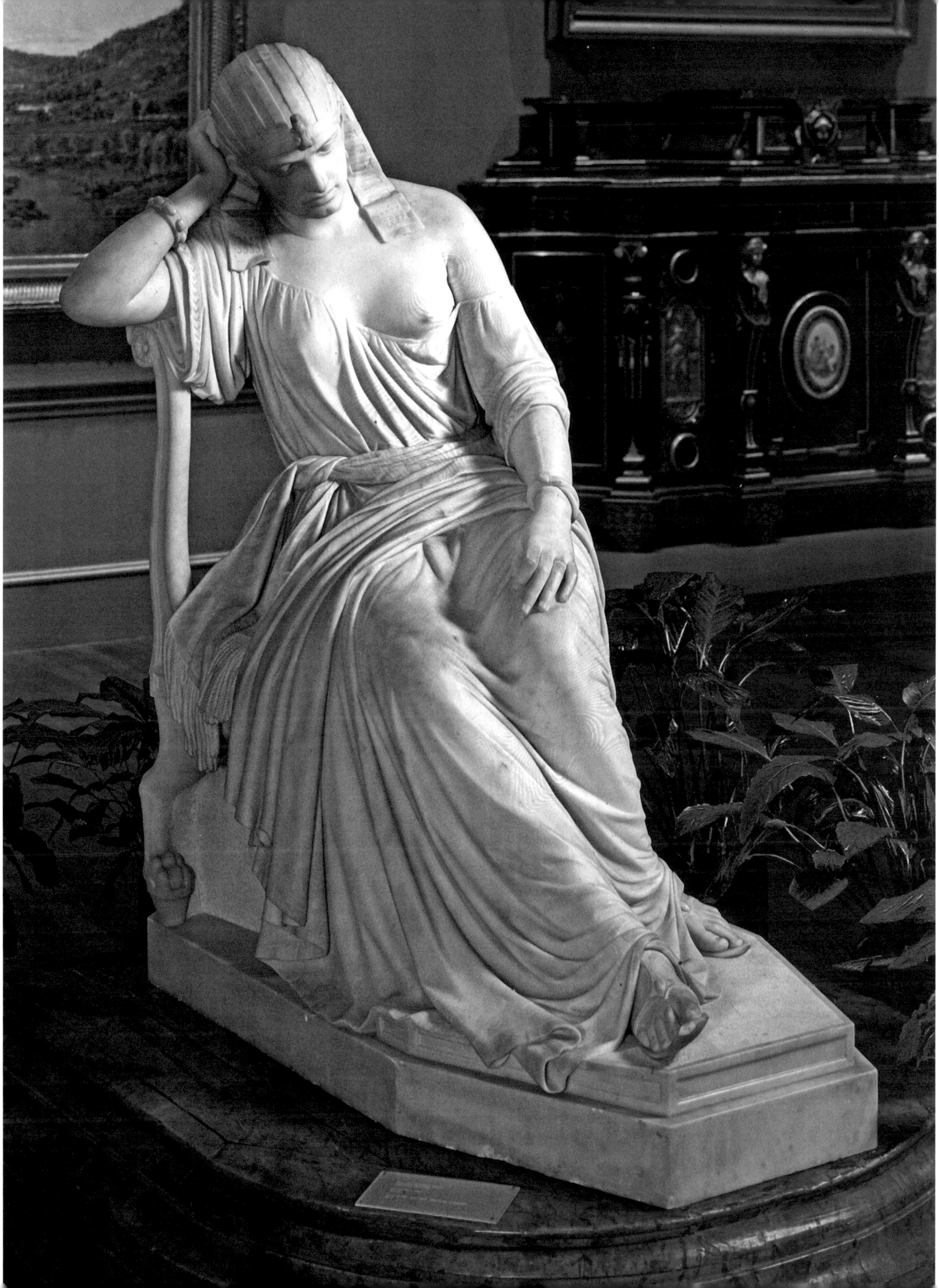

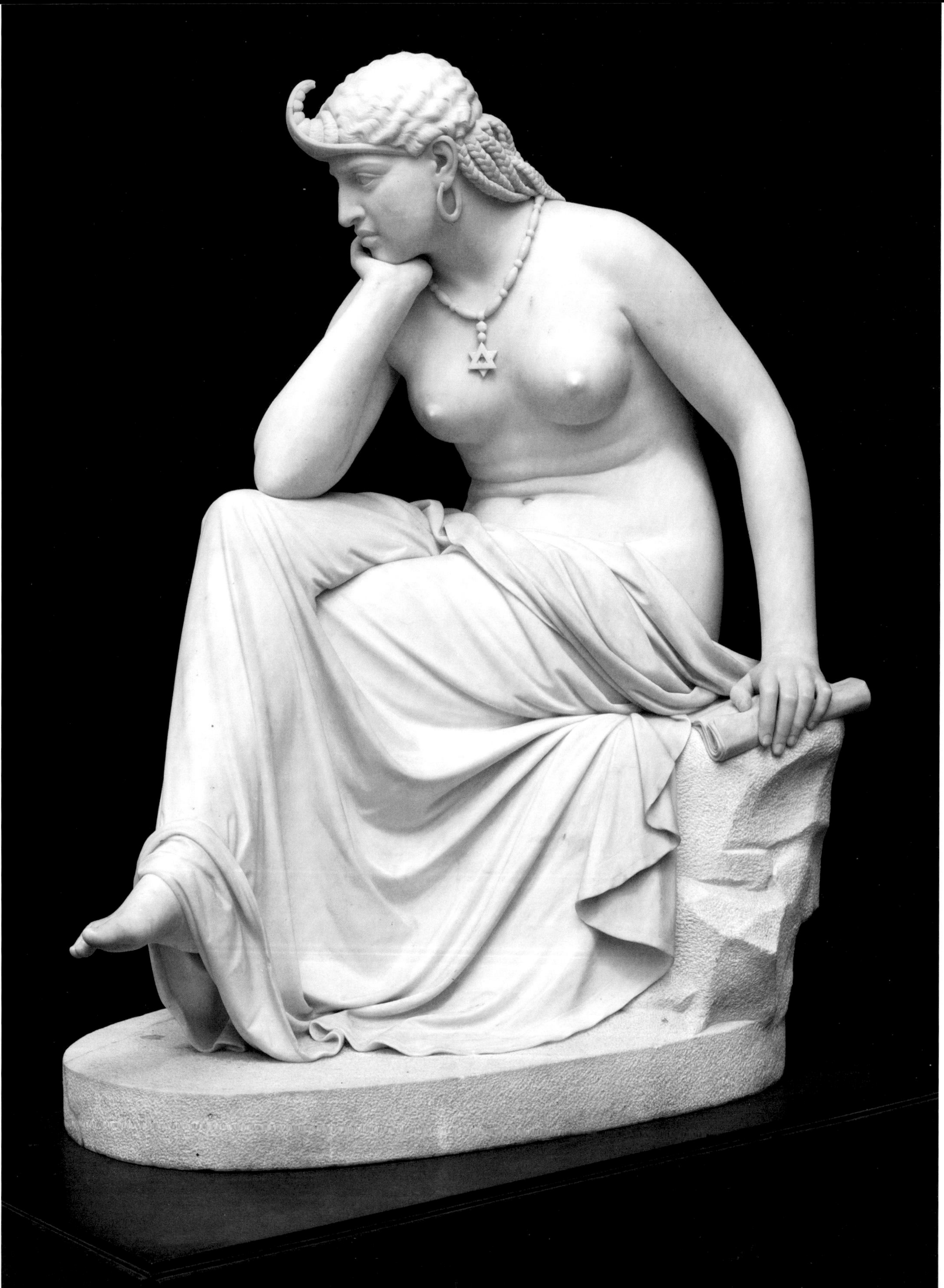

not a Grecian or Italian girl."[12] Similarly, the novelist Nathaniel Hawthorne, after visiting Story's Roman studio, understood the work in "Africanized" terms. Appropriating the sculpture for his novel *The Marble Faun,* he says of the work, "The face was a miraculous success. . . . The sculptor had not shunned to give the full Nubian lips, and other characteristics of the Egyptian physiognomy."[13] To nineteenth-century viewers, Story's *Cleopatra* served as an exoticized spectacle.

For Story, however, his *Libyan Sibyl* more directly addressed the abolitionist cause. He considered this sculpture his best work; in an 1861 letter to Sumner, he described it as his "Anti-Slavery Sermon in Stone."[14] The sculptor revised the Greek facial type common to neoclassical sculpture and depicted his sibyl with features more deliberately racialized than those appearing in the *Cleopatra:* full lips, a wide nose, flared nostrils, and broad flat cheekbones. Describing *The Libyan Sibyl* to Charles Elliot Norton, the first professor of art history at Harvard and noted abolitionist, he wrote: "I have taken the pure Coptic head and figure, the great massive sphinx face, full-lipped, long-eyed, low-browed and lowering, and the largely-developed limbs of the African." Story explained, "She is looking out of her black eyes into futurity and sees the terrible fate of her race. This is the theme of the figure—Slavery on the horizon." The Star of David on her beaded necklace marks her ancient mystical powers.[15] Story's pre-Christian prophetess looks to the future and foresees the inevitability of slavery and its devastating effect on the American nation.

FIG. 64
William Wetmore Story, *The Libyan Sibyl,* 1860, this version 1861, marble, 53 × 27 3/4 × 45 1/2 in. The Metropolitan Museum of Art, New York, gift of Erving Wolf Foundation, in memory of Diane R. Wolf, 1979, 1979.266.

Story represented Africa with all the dignity that Western artistic conventions could muster at the time. Neoclassical sculpture strove to embody the "ideal"—that which expresses universal and eternal values. This obsession with the classical ideal complicated the notion of race as it developed in Enlightenment thought. Nineteenth-century scientific studies of natural history involved the observation, comparison, and measurement of human bodies' visible characteristics. Certain differences, such as skin color, facial structure, and body type, came to be correlated with moral and intellectual capacity and thus indicative of a hierarchy of racial categories. Scientists (and artists) looked to antique sculpture as a way of documenting a superior white race, thus linking the classical canon with the authority of knowledge. In so doing, they produced what philosopher Cornel West called a "normative gaze," in which classical ideals of beauty served as the standard in Western culture and occluded all other depictions of humanity.[16]

Struggling with the aesthetic dilemma of depicting African features within a classicizing high-art tradition, Story explained, "I made her head as melancholy and severe as possible, not at all shirking the real African type. On the contrary, it is thoroughly African—Libyan African of course, not Congo." In the end, he insisted on a "Libyan," or North African/Mediterranean, identity for his figure and thus appealed to an Africa that was safely within the sphere of European/classical influence. For it was west central Africa that was most closely associated with the American slave whose reputed "grotesque" features were carefully avoided in the work. Departing from the more canonical proportions of his *Cleopatra,* he fashioned *The Libyan Sibyl* as a "massive figure, big-shouldered, large-bosomed, with nothing of the Venus in it, but, as far as I could make it, luxuriant and heroic."[17] He no doubt looked to the art of Michelangelo, whose *Libyan Sibyl* on the Sistine

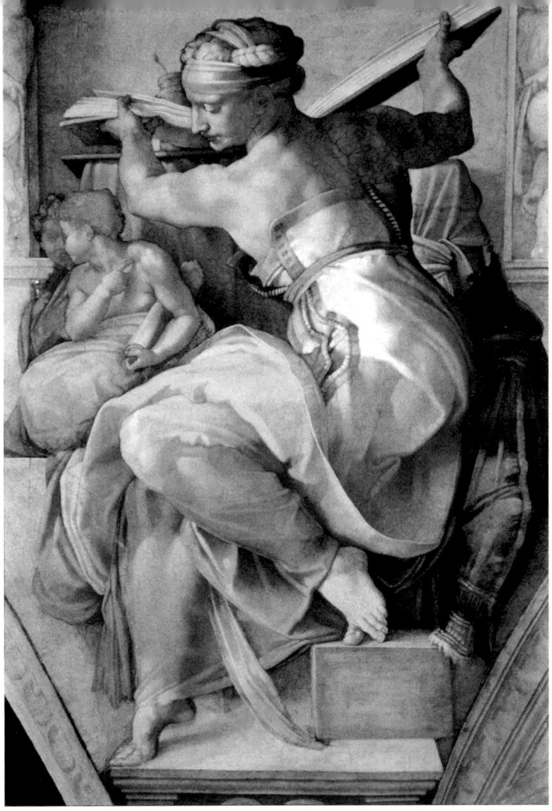

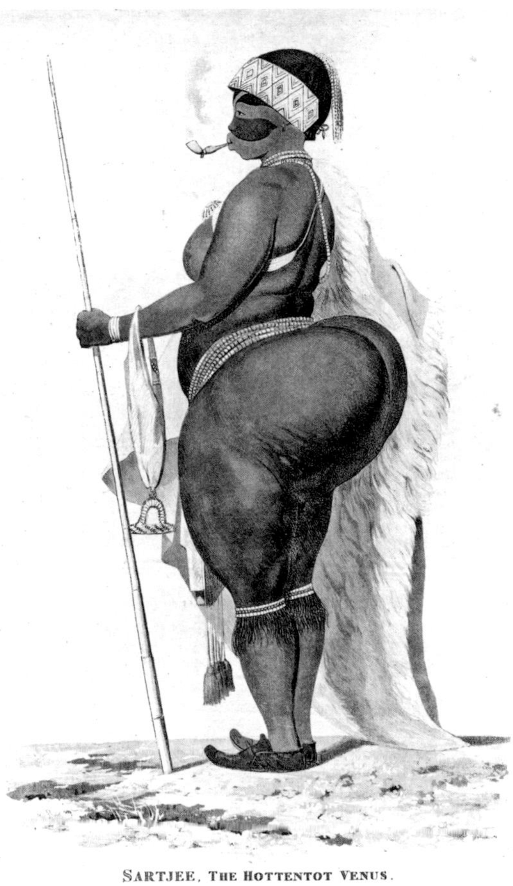


FIG. 65
Michelangelo Buonarroti, *The Libyan Sibyl,* detail of the Sistine Chapel ceiling, fresco, after restoration. Sistine Chapel, Vatican Palace, Vatican City.

FIG. 66
Attributed to Frederick Christian Lewis, *Sartjee, the Hottentot Venus,* 1810, etching and aquatint.

ceiling (fig. 65) and powerful sculptural Madonnas he had seen in Rome.[18] These famous masterpieces both inspired and legitimated his sculptural vocabulary of the (North) African female form.

Story's image stood in opposition to common stereotypes of the African woman, such as the "Hottentot Venus" (fig. 66). The nineteenth-century fascination with the Hottentot as a type was based primarily on the observation of one woman, Saartje Baartman (Sarah Bartmann), who was put on display in Paris for more than five years. She died in 1815 at an early age, but pseudoscientific studies of her continued throughout the century in both Europe and the United States, with her image circulating in many popular magazines and newspapers. With her steatopygia, or protruding buttocks, this black African woman looked different. Functioning as a colonial stereotype, she signified a black female sexuality that was both primitive and pathological.[19]

Unlike the Hottentot Venus, Story's *Libyan Sibyl* was tempered by Western artistic conventions. Modestly draped, the sculpture reveals a partial nudity that signifies the realm of the universal. Her physical appearance—the relatively large scale of her body ("the largely-developed limbs of the African")—signals the imagined black female as laborer and breeder.[20] Incorporating visual elements of blackness within a neoclassical paradigm of the ideal, Story attempted to make the sculpture readable as an antislavery statement.

In an 1863 article in the *Atlantic Monthly*, Harriet Beecher Stowe wrongly claimed that Sojourner Truth, an inspired orator and former slave, had served as the inspiration for Story's sculpture.[21] Although false, this association was telling. Truth was an imposing figure, standing six feet tall. The force of her physical presence was apparent in her legendary performance at the 1851 Akron Women's Rights Convention, when she held up her muscled arm and is reported to have claimed, "A'n't I a woman? Look at me! Look at my arm!" Most likely inserting this phrase twelve years later in her "Sketch of Sojourner Truth," the feminist abolitionist Frances Dana Gage described the speaker as "this almost Amazon form."[22] In her article, Stowe equated Truth's identity with that of Africa—exoticized yet connected with the destiny of her race: "Sojourner . . . seemed to impersonate the fervor of Ethiopia, wild, savage, hunted of all nations, but burning after God in her tropic heart, and stretching her scarred hands towards the glory to be revealed."[23] Racialized readings of classical and neoclassical sculpture—as demonstrated by the blending of Truth's identity with that of Story's exoticized *Libyan Sibyl*—dictated the ways in which the black subject was represented in American art.

Contemporary viewers saw in Story's sculpture a metaphor for Africans in bondage. *The Libyan Sibyl*'s bodily and facial features served as codes for the seismic changes the country was undergoing. Its subtle message was clearly understood despite the lack of manacles, chains, and other overt symbols of servitude. In fact, Stowe, after seeing these works in Story's studio, urged that both sculptures—*Cleopatra* and *The Libyan Sibyl*—should adorn the Capitol grounds as companions to Horatio Greenough's *George Washington*.[24]

## *Edmonia Lewis and the Abolitionist Circle in Boston*

While Story's sculptures were being hailed as antislavery masterpieces on the international stage,

William Lloyd Garrison and Lydia Maria Child welcomed the young sculptor Edmonia Lewis to Boston. Garrison was at the helm of an organization that was dedicated to the immediate abolition of slavery and establishment of the rights of women, as neither slaves nor women held legal or political standing in American society. Garrison and his followers argued that in marriage, as in chattel slavery, women were owned, restrained, and deprived of civil rights within patriarchal governing structures.[25]

At the center of radical reformist circles that endorsed interracial marriage, Child championed Lewis, whom she sought out shortly after the sculptor moved to Boston in 1864. She was immediately intrigued by Lewis's mixed-race heritage, as the sculptor proudly proclaimed that her mother was full-blooded Chippewa and her father African-American. It now appears, however, that her heritage was a bit more complicated. Her maternal grandfather was an escaped slave, and her maternal grandmother was of mixed ancestry—black and Ojibwa.[26] Nonetheless, Lewis constructed a public persona that traded upon an authentic black or Indian identity throughout her professional career.

Child served as mentor, tutor, and patron to the young black artist, but not without demonstrating strain. She described her first meeting with Lewis in the antislavery journal the *Liberator:* "One of the most interesting individuals I met . . . was Edmonia Lewis, a colored girl about twenty years old, who is devoting herself to sculpture. Her frank, intelligent countenance and modest manners prepossessed me in her favor." Together with the reformer Elizabeth Peabody, the poet Anna Quinsy Waterston, and Maria Weston Chapman, Child lent emotional and financial support to the young artist. For the most part, as art historian Kirsten Buick explains, these prominent white women shaped, even manufactured, Lewis's public persona in their writings, an act in which Lewis was certainly complicit.[27]

Lewis showed *Bust of Colonel Robert Gould Shaw* at the Boston Soldier's Relief Fair in 1864 (fig. 67).[28] Among her first sculptures of abolitionist heroes and heroines, the bust was well received by the Shaw family, as they believed it an excellent likeness. The young Shaw had led the 54th African-American regiment, dying with many of his troops near Fort Wagner, Morris Island, South Carolina, in July of 1863. On the base of the sculpture Lewis inscribed the words "Martyr for Freedom." Child viewed the bust in the artist's studio and was clearly moved when she saw Lewis sprinkle the clay model with water. "The sight of that little brown hand . . . tenderly baptizing the 'fair-haired Saxon hero' affected me deeply," she wrote. "There was something inexpressibly beautiful and touching in the efforts of a long-oppressed race to sanctify the memory of their martyr. Indeed, I think the deep feeling of admiration and gratitude, which the artist felt for the young hero . . . was one great reason why she succeeded so well."[29] Implicit in this statement is a condescending paternalism, as demonstrated by Child's characterization of Shaw as a "fair-haired Saxon hero" compared with her observation of Lewis's "little brown hands"—a diminutive that challenged the artist's creative integrity. Expressing "admiration and gratitude" for the "long-oppressed race," Lewis was expected to speak for all freed blacks. Throughout her early career, the artist was caught in an untenable position: She looked to the Boston abolitionist community for genuine and meaningful support but was often

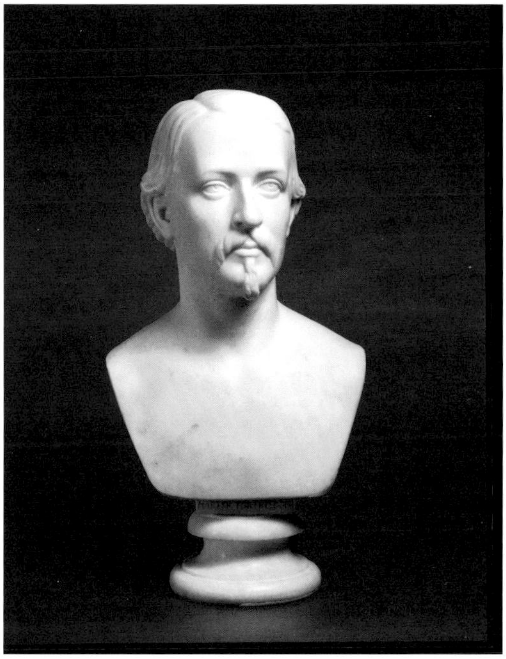

FIG. 67
Edmonia Lewis, *The Bust of Robert Gould Shaw*, 1867, marble. Museum of African American History, Boston and Nantucket, Mass.

subject to patronizing flattery and worse. Confirming this conundrum in an interview with Child, she explained: "Some praise me because I am a colored girl, and I don't want that kind of praise. I had rather you point out my defects, for that will teach me something."[30]

Lewis met Anne Whitney in 1864, when they both worked in Boston's Studio Building on Tremont Street. Like Child, Whitney publicly supported Lewis's sculptural career. But in private, her patronizing and at times belittling tone was quite evident. Whitney seemed genuinely puzzled by this young woman by her mixed Native American and black identity. "Edmonia is very much of an aboriginal," she wrote to her partner, Adeline Manning, "grateful, vengeful, a little cunning, and not altogether scrupulous about the truth when dealing with those she doesn't love[;] open, kind and liberal as day with those she does. I like her in spite of her faults, and will help her all I can."[31] Elite white antislavery women demonstrated conflicting attitudes toward freed black women. Like Harriet Beecher Stowe, who had characterized Sojourner Truth as a "savage," Whitney judged Lewis an "aboriginal." In the end, however, Whitney felt a spiritual kinship with Lewis, "in spite of her faults," and offered her guidance and support in Boston and Rome.[32]

## Ethiopia Shall Soon Stretch Out Her Hands to God, or Africa

In Boston, Whitney self-consciously struggled with the creation of a new sculptural vocabulary for black womanhood. Between 1862 and 1864, she produced her life-sized allegorical work, *Ethiopia Shall Soon Stretch Out Her Hands to God, or Africa* (fig. 68), in response to the Emancipation Proclamation, which President Lincoln had first drafted in the summer of 1862. In this work, she depicted a gargantuan reclining female figure who raised herself up on one arm and turned her head toward the future, shielding her eyes from the blinding light of history. This female image personified the continent of Africa, with its people awakened by the American Civil War. After modeling the life-sized sculpture in clay, she cast it in plaster in 1863 but never produced a finished marble. Although in retrospect she considered the sculpture "one of the best things" she had ever produced, she destroyed it sometime after 1874.[33]

The somewhat ambiguous wording of Psalm 68:31, a narrative through which black Americans often read their future, served as the inspiration for Whitney's sculpture: "Princes shall come out

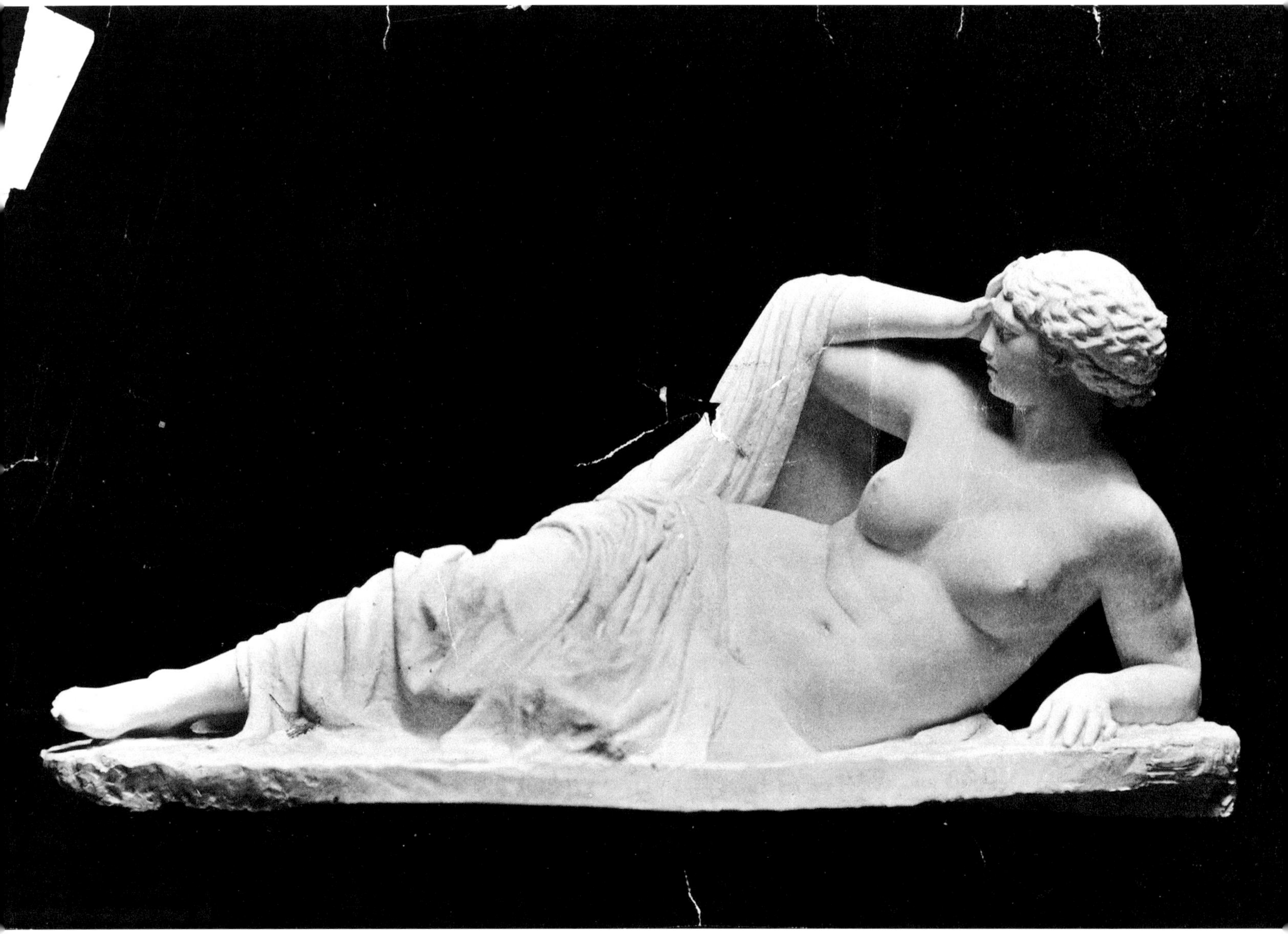

FIG. 68 *(opposite)* Anne Whitney, *Ethiopia Shall Soon Stretch Out Her Hands to God, or Africa,* 1862–64, plaster, destroyed. Photograph courtesy of the Wellesley College Archives, Papers of Anne Whitney.

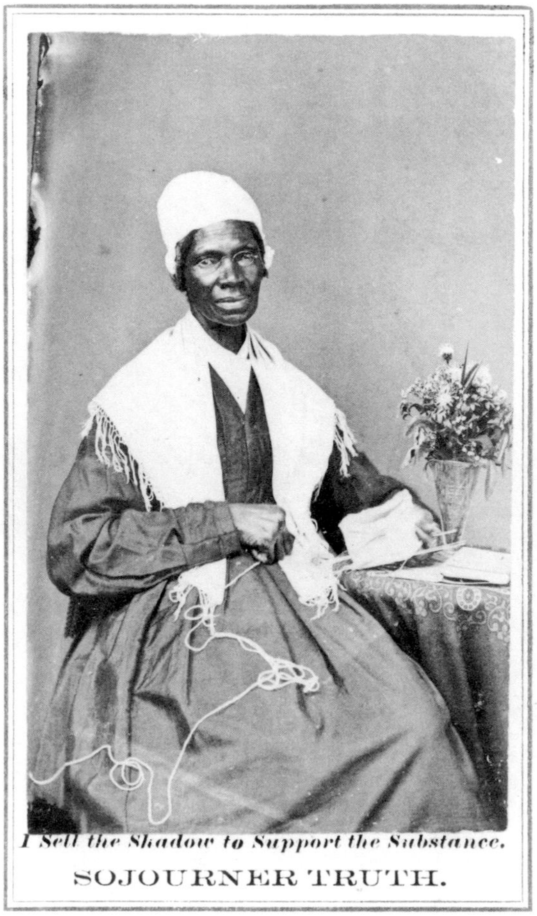


FIG. 69 Sojourner Truth, carte de visite. Courtesy of the Wellesley College Archives, Papers of Anne Whitney.

of Egypt and Ethiopia shall soon stretch forth her hands unto God."[34] When Whitney was at work on her sculpture, the psalm was understood to refer to the black race—identified as both Ethiopian and Egyptian—and to herald the glories of the African past. Redeeming the continent as a flourishing center of ancient civilizations, white and black abolitionists refuted the charge that the culture of modern Africans and African-Americans was inherently inferior to that of white Anglo-Saxons.

Whitney looked to several sources for her revolutionary new image of emancipation. She used her nineteen-year-old friend, the painter Elizabeth Howard Bartol, as a model.[35] She may have discussed this artistic project with the legendary abolitionist Harriet Tubman and likely used her appearance as inspiration for *Ethiopia*'s stylized hair.[36] And she no doubt had read Stowe's famous words about Sojourner Truth in the *Atlantic Monthly.* Moreover, she owned a carte de visite of the famous orator (fig. 69), whose public performances revealed her multiple and complex identities—former slave, worker, feminist, and proper bourgeois woman.[37] Redefining black femininity in broader and more inclusive terms, Truth gave visibility to the contemporary freed black woman in American culture. Truth's outspokenness, however, at times shocked elite white antislavery women, as certain of her behaviors were considered inappropriate. In response to this criticism, she refashioned her public image and typically depicted herself within the framework of middle-class femininity. In the carte de visite, for example, Truth is dressed modestly with shawl and cap and brandishes her knitting. To augment her association with true womanhood, she pictured herself with the feminine symbol of flowers and a Bible lying open on the table. Not surprisingly, her mythic dimension in the feminist-abolitionist community—combined with her domesticated self-portraiture—positioned her as an intriguing visual model for white antislavery women like Whitney.

*Ethiopia* received only guarded praise when shown in Boston, New York, and Chicago in late 1864 and early 1865. In Boston, the monumental plaster was on view at the Childs and Jenks Gallery. For one week in November, the exhibition formed part of the National Sailor's Fair to support the Union effort.[38] The abolitionist press, however, gave *Ethiopia* much attention. In the *Anti-Slavery Standard,* Child wrote glowingly about the sculpture and likened the work to William Wetmore Story's *Libyan Sibyl* (fig. 64):

> *At the present epoch, Africa is everywhere uppermost in the thoughts and feelings of mankind. . . . So pervasive is the atmosphere, that artists are breathing it also. Passing through the soul of Story, it came forth in the shape of an African Sibyl; and so strangely fascinating was the subject, that [*Ethiopia*] attracted more attention than any other in the grand exhibition [at the National Academy of Design]. From Miss Whitney's poetic mind it comes out in the shape of Africa Waking from Sleep.*[39]

Among commentators not aligned with the abolitionist press, Whitney's iconography of black womanhood evoked confusion. In response to *Ethiopia*'s showing in New York, one critic cited the figure's "bold magnificence, a wild abandonment, and at the same time a yearning aspiration in the expression of the face that both astonishes and excites a deeper sentiment of admiration." *Ethiopia,* the writer continued, "positively offends by a voluptuousness amounting almost to a coarseness, so that at first you scarcely know whether to praise or to blame it . . . until, as you gaze upon it . . . its external blemishes pass away, and the only sentiment remaining in your heart is that you are gazing upon the great embodiment of a great idea." The writer's attitude transformed over the course of a single sentence, at first observing in the work a "voluptuousness" and "coarseness" that "positively offends" and later "the great embodiment of a great idea." The writer concluded, "For the artist has sought to express in her statue a nation's life, and she has nobly succeeded in a high attempt."[40] These comments reflected an understanding of African-American womanhood that vacillated between the exotic and sexualized *and* the virtuous and ideal.

In its blending of realism and idealism, *Ethiopia* demonstrated an ideological tension. Contemporary audiences associated the black female body—as epitomized in the Hottentot Venus—with rampant eroticism, based upon nineteenth-century medical knowledge on sexuality.[41]

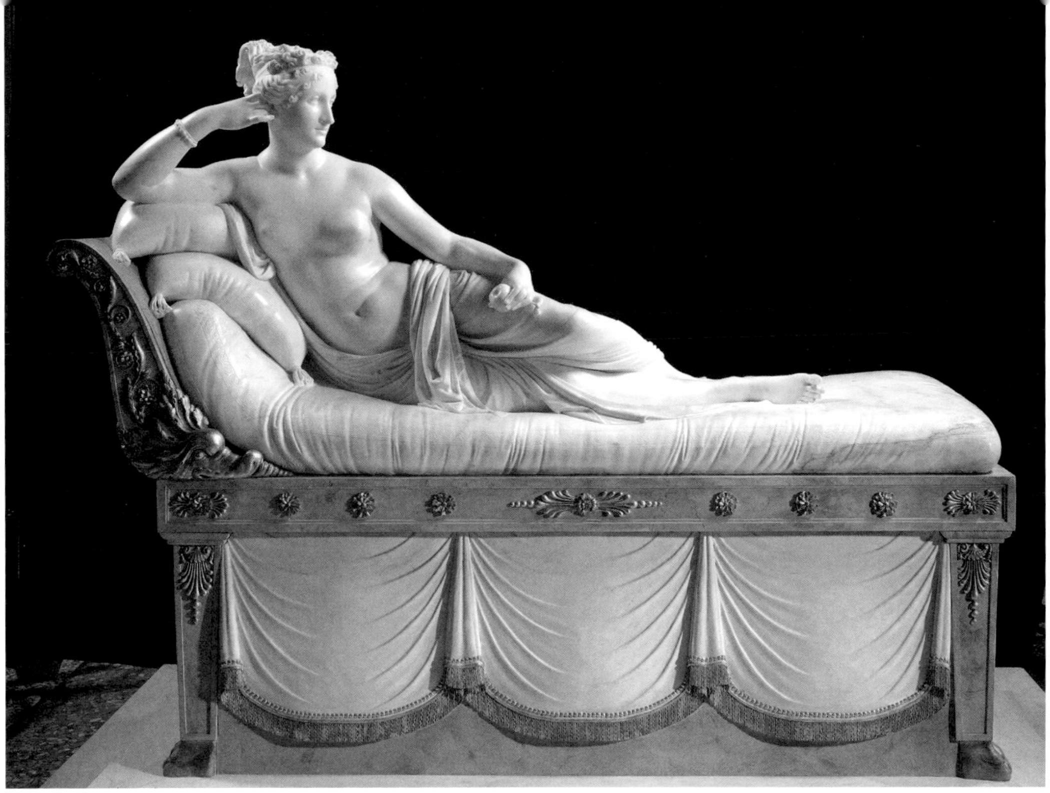

FIG. 70
Antonio Canova, *Paolina Borghese as Venus Victorious*, 1803–6, marble. Galleria Borghese, Rome.

*Ethiopia*'s substantial body and erotic features—large hips, fulsome breasts, and erect nipples—attracted many viewers' attention. Moreover, with its swelling arm muscles, wrinkled midsection, and detailed navel, the specificity of the body referenced the excessive sexuality, mandatory childbearing, and overbearing toil that constituted the lives of female slaves.[42] Simultaneously, *Ethiopia* struck a pose similar to Antonio Canova's *Paolina Borghese as Venus Victorius* (fig. 70), a neoclassical sculpture in Rome's Borghese Gallery that Whitney probably knew in reproduction. Canova's sculpture revealed an aesthetic ambivalence that pitted the ideal forms of the classicizing body of the goddess Venus against the detailed specificity of the historical figure of Paolina Borghese. In referencing both the colonialist stereotype of the Hottentot Venus and the neoclassical imagery of *Paolina Borghese as Venus Victorius, Ethiopia* not only signified blackness through the eroticized female body but also claimed allegorical status as "the great embodiment of a great idea," that is, a symbol of the progressive ideals of a multiracial nation.

*Ethiopia*'s massive figural form differed from the more conventionally proportioned neoclassical nudes, such as Hiram Powers's *Greek Slave* (fig. 26). When *The Greek Slave* was first exhibited in the United States, between 1847 and 1851, it elicited a variety of readings; but all viewers agreed upon the figure's Christian piety and moral innocence. Although referencing a young Christian girl sold into bondage by Turks, abolitionists understood the manacles as a symbol of enslavement and thus claimed the figure as their own; Frederick Douglass argued in the *North Star* that the sculpture stood for every slave. Feminist abolitionists, such as Lucy Stone, saw her as emblematic of womanhood. Outside abolitionist circles, *The Greek Slave* represented an ideal of whiteness, as popular among patrons in New Orleans as in Boston. Her aquiline features—easily read in profile—distanced her from the problematic facial type of the black slave; her pathetic, victimized demeanor positioned her within the bounds of proper femininity.[43] Whitney refused the frailty and vulnerability apparent in Powers's work and created for *Ethiopia* a new allegorical language that highlighted her "Africanized features" and insisted upon the strength of her ample body.

As it turns out, Whitney was never fully satisfied with the sculpture. In fact, there were disagreements about the "Africanized features" of *Ethiopia* in the critical press. One writer argued, "The African and Egyptian type of features are most wonderfully fused, the former sufficiently prominent to indicate its meaning, without bordering on the more vulgar and broader developments of the African peculiarity."[44] Typically, the critic read the "Egyptian features" as a way to mediate African influence and thus keep the sculpture within the realm of Western conventions. By contrast, a review of the National Academy of Design exhibition chastised the artist for a lack of boldness: "Miss Whitney has only half dared, and between realism and idealism has made a woeful fall."[45]

Thomas Wentworth Higginson, the white abolitionist commander of the First South Carolina Volunteers, the earliest black regiment to be recruited in the South, privately challenged the artist to envision "the added triumph of Africanized features":

> *The aesthetic effect of your statue would thus not be marred, and its symbolism greatly enhanced—because precisely that which has held Africa down has been the prejudice of the nations against this physical type. It is nothing for her to rise and abnegate her own features in rising; she must rise as God made her or not at all. To my eyes, all that your statue asserts, the features of the face deny; and I believe that every one . . . would appreciate the added triumph of Africanized features. . . . Even Story has (it is said) gone out of his way to give such features to* Cleopatra.

In a postscript, Higginson went so far as to recommend a new model to Whitney: "A young colored girl at Pigeon Cove [Gloucester, Mass.] who would be an admirable model of feature for you. A face and figure large and statuesque, broad, placid, intelligent, . . . great size without coarseness, very dignified and refined manners, and strong, calm nature."[46]

Whitney took these criticisms to heart. In the following months, she reworked the face, hands, and feet of her sculpture (fig. 71). She seemed to be satisfied with the powerful body of *Ethiopia*—having developed its "great size without coarseness." However, the "Africanized" facial features so desired by Higginson seemed to defeat her. She privately admitted, "It is impossible, I think in art, thus to generalize, or to make an abstract of all possible African types. I should simply have sought to do the best with what I know of the negro."[47] In the later version of the sculpture, she subtly revised the facial features to include fuller lips, wider nose, and broader cheekbones (figs. 72 and 73)—perhaps in the manner of Story's *Libyan Sibyl*—but she remained ever unhappy with the work. In 1866, she wrote to Adeline Manning, "I am not satisfied with the face of the woman. What it has gained in strength of feature, it has lost in feeling and expression."[48]

Like Story before her, Whitney had reached the ideological limits of the high-art tradition. The demand for "Africanized features"—visual codes for the compelling racial politics of the day—impinged upon the neoclassical world,

FIG. 71 *(opposite)* Anne Whitney, *Ethiopia Shall Soon Stretch Out Her Hands to God, or Africa,* reworked 1865–66, plaster, destroyed. Photograph courtesy of the Wellesley College Archives, Papers of Anne Whitney.

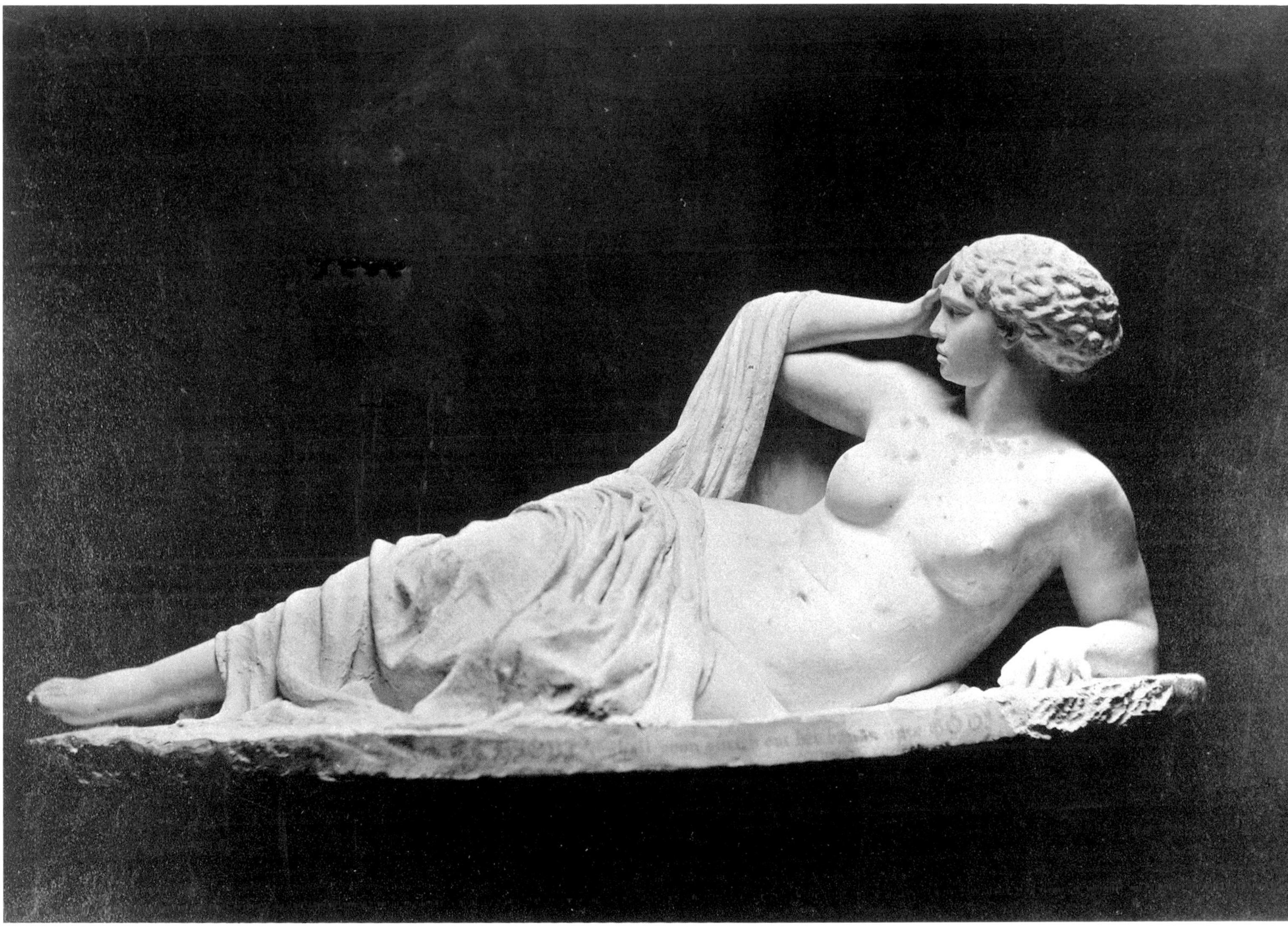

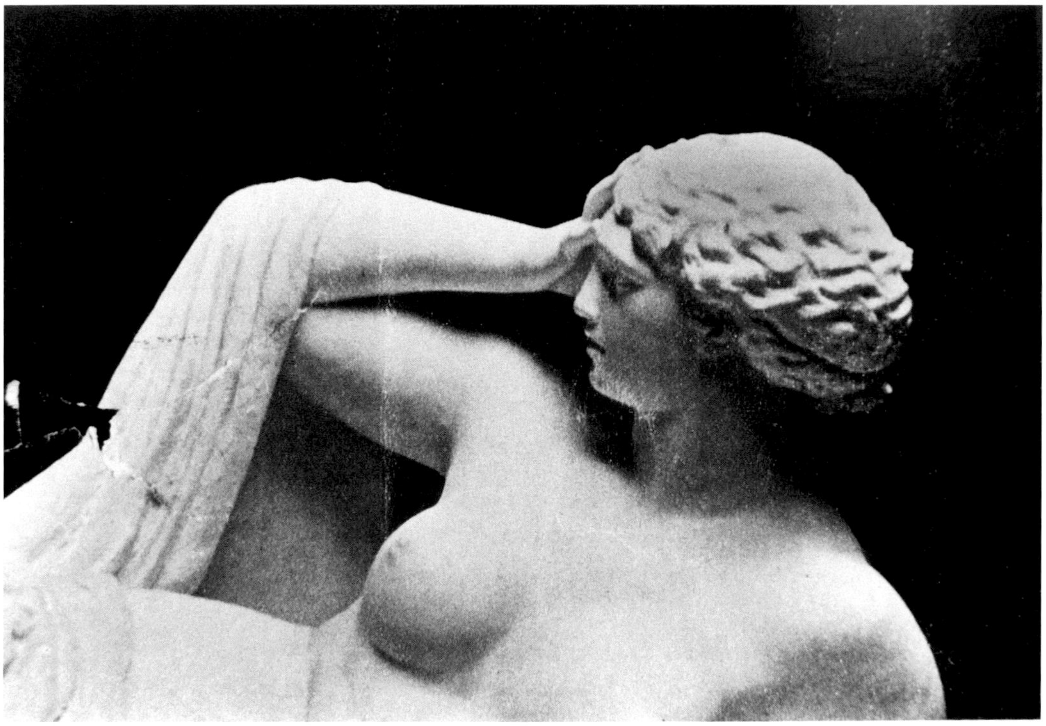

FIG. 72
Anne Whitney, *Ethiopia Shall Soon Stretch Out Her Hands to God, or Africa,* 1862–64 (fig. 68), detail of the head.

where the category of whiteness, as evident in *The Greek Slave,* found its expression in the nineteenth century. Contemporary audiences understood classical and neoclassical sculpture within this racial paradigm. The *Apollo Belvedere* (fig. 7), for example, came to serve as a benchmark of the human despite its idealized proportions and features. To the nineteenth-century mind, such sculptures held dual status—as ideal representations of the Enlightenment individual and as canonical measures of (white) mankind. They served not just as hallmarks of an antique past but also as universal signifiers of the Anglo-Saxon body. Neoclassical sculptures, in their association with high culture and classical civilization, were themselves transformed by participation in this racialized theory. Indeed, the whiteness of the marble itself insisted upon the hierarchies of race and the privileges of Anglo-Saxon identity.[49]

In her attempt to produce a neoclassical allegory of emancipation, Whitney confronted this aesthetic conundrum. Her dissatisfaction with *Ethiopia* made her fear that the sculpture lacked artistic merit. This lack of confidence derived in part from her inexperience as a sculptor. Not until her sojourn to Rome in 1867 was she convinced of her native ability and secure in her artistic training. But her dissatisfaction with *Ethiopia* also derived in part from its originality. She dared to imagine a sculptural vocabulary that expressed the new and expanded possibilities of black citizenship in the United States. Her constant disappointment with the sculpture stemmed, at least in part, from the inability of contemporary aesthetic

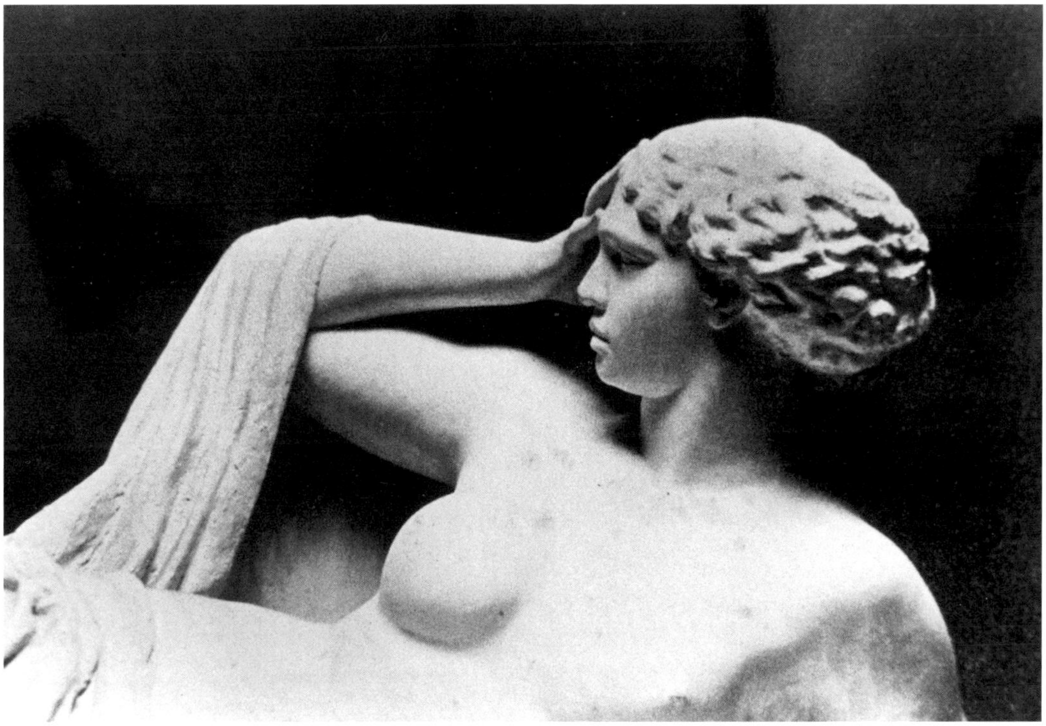

FIG. 73
Anne Whitney, *Ethiopia Shall Soon Stretch Out Her Hands to God, or Africa,* reworked 1865–66 (fig. 71), detail of the head.

conventions to visualize or communicate such a radical new social concept.

Like others before her, she worked within the limited vocabulary of neoclassicism and produced a sculptural vision that mediated between the formal qualities derived from African features and those of classical (white) beauty. Whitney may have gravitated toward a "romantic racialism" by assigning a mixed-race identity to her *Ethiopia.*[50] Although couching their beliefs in paternalist language, radical abolitionists like Child and Theodore Parker, an abolitionist Unitarian minister, professed the inherent goodness of the black race, whose childlike innocence and docility were attributable to pious Christian virtue. Parker argued that Anglo-Saxon blood would be improved by mixing with that of Negroes and Indians "to furnish a new composite tribe, far better . . . than the old," and that intermarriage between the races would simultaneously challenge notions of white supremacy.[51]

In the antebellum imagination, the idealized black woman was of mixed racial heritage. Women's sentimental literature on abolition focused upon the mulatta—a female figure with one black parent and one white. Depicted as pious, pure, domestic, and frail, the light-skinned woman was a veritable model of bourgeois true womanhood.[52] Child, in her 1867 novel, *The Romance of the Republic,* was among the first to fictionalize mixed-race marriage, using it as her chief metaphor for an egalitarian partnership of the races. Despite the radical nature of the proposition, interracial marriage did not fundamentally challenge the social order that subordinated women to men and blacks to whites. Instead, it provided a means of gradually absorbing blacks into white middle-class society and in so doing homogenizing black culture into a white bourgeois ideal. Moreover, this fictional account did not reflect the historical realities of black women's lives. In many cases, miscegenation was the effect of a forceful act of violence rather than a matter of personal choice, an arrangement in which a woman's survival depended upon her endurance of horrific physical abuse.[53] Nonetheless, for white middle-class reformers, a mixed-race identity permitted black women to assimilate more easily into the social category of bourgeois womanhood. Within this racialist context, Story's *Libyan Sibyl* and Whitney's *Ethiopia*—with their carefully blended African and Western conventions—gave visual form to a contemporary image of black womanhood.

## *Edmonia Lewis: From Boston to Rome*

On public view in Boston in late 1864 and early 1865, Anne Whitney's *Ethiopia,* Harriet Hosmer's *Zenobia in Chains* (fig. 25), and Louisa Lander's *Virginia Dare* (fig. 24) contributed to a racial ideology popular among progressive audiences. Each of the sculptures made reference to a mixed-race identity: *Ethiopia* represented the mulatta; *Zenobia* blended an Eastern exoticism with a Western classical identity; and *Virginia Dare* stood as a hybrid of Anglo-American and Native American cultural characteristics. Lewis probably saw *Ethiopia* and *Zenobia* at the Childs and Jenks Gallery and visited the *Virginia Dare* in Lander's Tremont Street studio, where Lander staged a lavish showing of the work.

Like the *Ethiopia,* Hosmer's *Zenobia* and Lander's *Virginia Dare* were well received in progressive circles in Boston. Both sculptures were interpreted within a nationalist frame. The poet and abolitionist John Greenleaf Whittier opined that Hosmer, "like the soldiers in the field and the public officers in their departments," was "truly serving her country" with such works.[54] With Zenobia's mixed-race ancestry—melding dark-skinned Arab with Western Greek blood—the sculptural figure allegorized racial difference and the struggle against slavery being fought in the United States.[55]

Both Lander and her sculpture were lavishly praised as "essentially and entirely American."[56] *Virginia Dare,* one critic noted, revealed the "blended characteristics of both races [Anglo-Saxon and Indian] . . . into one harmonious physique."[57] The sculpture seemed to stand apart from the works by Whitney, Hosmer, and Story. "'Virginia Dare' is not 'Zenobia' and was not intended to be; neither is she [Whitney's] 'Africa,' [nor Story's] 'Cleopatra,'" one critic declared. *Virginia Dare* represented a "fresh example" of a new type of American art.[58] The image of the Indian princess, it appeared, would always remain as a nationalist symbol.

Lewis was no doubt influenced by the Bostonian cultural environment that privileged and embraced such mixed-race identities. She met Hosmer when the sculptor stopped by her studio in 1865 to see her *Bust of Colonel Robert Gould Shaw.* Suitably impressed with the work, Hosmer encouraged Lewis to visit her in Rome.[59] After selling one hundred plaster copies of the Shaw bust at fifteen dollars apiece, Lewis earned enough money to fund her sojourn to Italy.

After arriving in Italy in November of 1865, she first visited Florence, where she met the

FIG. 74
Henry Rocher, *Edmonia Lewis*, ca. 1870, photograph, albumen silver print. National Portrait Gallery, Smithsonian Institution, Washington, D.C.

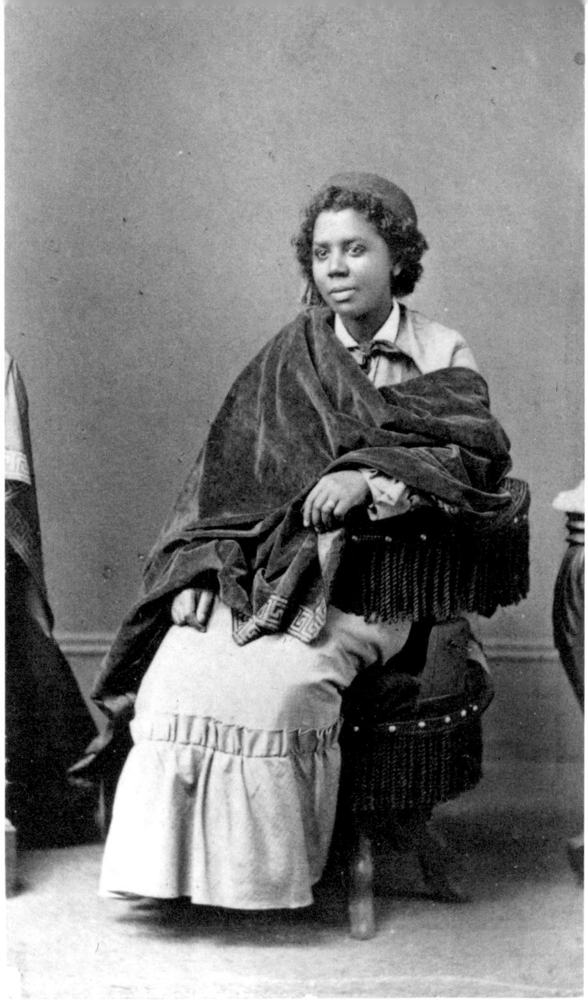

American sculptors Thomas Ball and Hiram Powers. In Rome, she was immediately greeted by Charlotte Cushman and Hosmer. She rented a studio once inhabited by the neoclassical sculptor Antonio Canova, the very studio that Lander had used during her abbreviated stay in Rome. She was in regular touch with Hosmer, visiting her new and luxurious studio on via delle Quattro Fontane. By 1867, she was living on via Gregoriana, in close proximity to Cushman, Hosmer, Whitney, and others in Rome's Anglo-American women's community. As a lifelong devout Catholic, however, she was certainly in the minority in an expatriate community composed almost entirely of Protestants.[60]

Although little is known of Lewis's life in Rome, she seemed to adapt well as an expatriate. Despite her initial poverty, she took music lessons, visited museums and artists' studios, and generally led what was called the "Art-Life." She was welcomed into the women's community, joining Hosmer and Cushman for their usual rides on the Compagna. As a professional sculptor, she appears to have comported herself in a manner consistent with those in Cushman's circle, adopting a type of dress that signaled feminine independence from social convention. In a carte de visite by Henry Rocher commissioned by the artist in ca. 1870, Lewis is seated in an elaborately fringed chair and wears a beret, jacket, and ruffled skirt, with a large velvet shawl around her shoulders (fig. 74). The signature beret, jacket, and cravat align the artist with the practical dress of the young Hosmer and others (fig. 1). To various

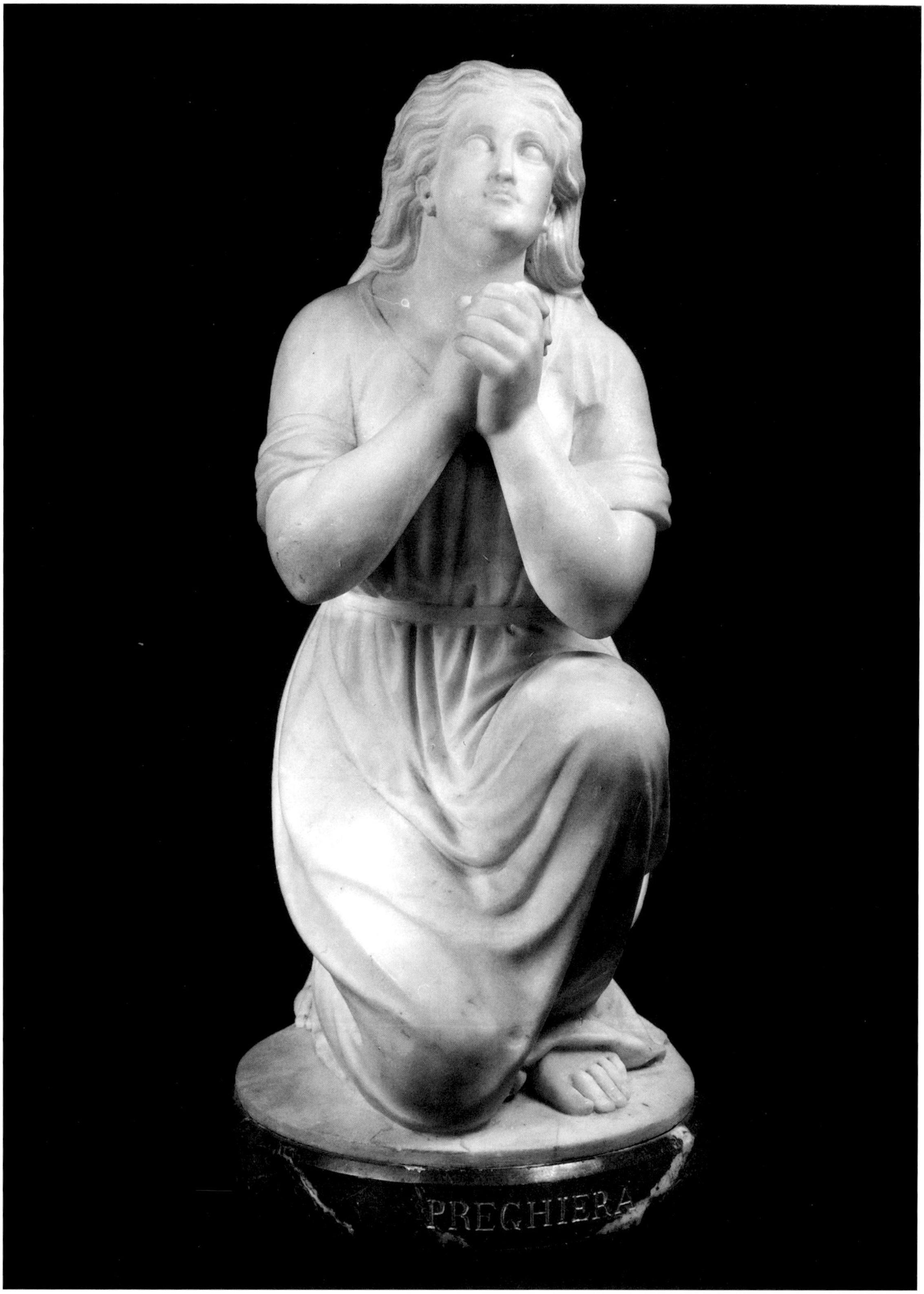


FIG. 75
Edmonia Lewis, *Preghiera,* 1866, marble. Collection of Kathryn Chenault, courtesy of Conner-Rosenkranz, New York, and Peg Alston Fine Arts.

commentators, she appeared either “masculine” or “childish and boyish.”[61] The ruffled full-length skirt, elaborate shawl, and ringed hand suggest a connection to bourgeois femininity. In her public performance as artist, Lewis balanced an independent manly identity with that of traditional womanhood. Like others in the Cushman circle in Rome, she masked the audacity of her professional life within a cloak of feminine propriety.

## *Forever Free*

Among the first works that Lewis produced in Rome were three neoclassical sculptures that brought attention to the contemporary freedwoman: *Preghiera* (*Prayer*) of 1866 (fig. 75), *Freedwoman and Child* of 1866 (now lost), and *Forever Free* of 1867 (fig. 76).[62] *Preghiera,* related in stance to the two other works, depicts a young woman on bended knee with hands raised in prayer and eyes in supplication. Her facial features are nearly identical to those of the female figure in *Forever Free.* This pious figure of Christian womanhood reveals a sturdy body with stocky proportions—thick neck, muscular arms, strong hands, and large feet. Lewis represented the body of a black woman—indeed, a classed body that exhibited the brawny arms of a former slave and worker.

The composition of *Preghiera* reveals a formal allegiance to the feminist antislavery emblem *Am I Not a Woman and a Sister?* (fig. 77), designed in Britain in 1828 in response to the emblem *Am I Not a Man and a Brother?* of 1787 (fig. 78). William Lloyd Garrison adopted this imagery in 1832 for the Ladies Department of the *Liberator,* his influential antislavery publication. By 1845, American antislavery women, both black and white, had adopted the symbol as their own. In keeping with the radical abolitionist view that collapsed the oppression of slaves with that of women, the female figure in the antislavery emblem, unlike her male companion, is fettered to the ground and cannot rise, her shackled arms and pleading eyes raised upward. Her vulnerable and enchained stance appears immutable. By contrast, the masculine emblem reveals a muscular body that holds the possibility of action. Although his wrists and ankles bear heavy shackles, the toes on his right foot are curled under like a runner ready to rise.[63] While indebted to the popular imagery of the antislavery movement, the female figure *Preghiera* conveyed contradictory meanings. On the one hand, she signified empowerment through the strong classed body; on the other hand, she expressed piety and subjection through her submissive kneeling pose.

Lewis borrowed many formal elements from *Preghiera* when creating *Forever Free.* Originally calling the sculpture *The Morning of Liberty,* she later decided on a phrase from the Emancipation Proclamation: “all persons held as slaves . . . shall be then, thenceforward, and forever free.”[64] The sculpture is a study in contrasts. A black man stands with raised fist and broken shackle in hand. To his side kneels a young woman who is tethered at the ankle (fig. 79). The chain links that emerge from her manacle, instead of lying free, appear embedded in the ground and provide a visual connection to the iron ball—not unlike the imagery depicted in the feminist antislavery emblem. Her male partner steps on the iron ball and places his large hand protectively on her shoulder. These are triumphal gestures for the black man but secure the young woman firmly in her place—kneeling (rather than standing),

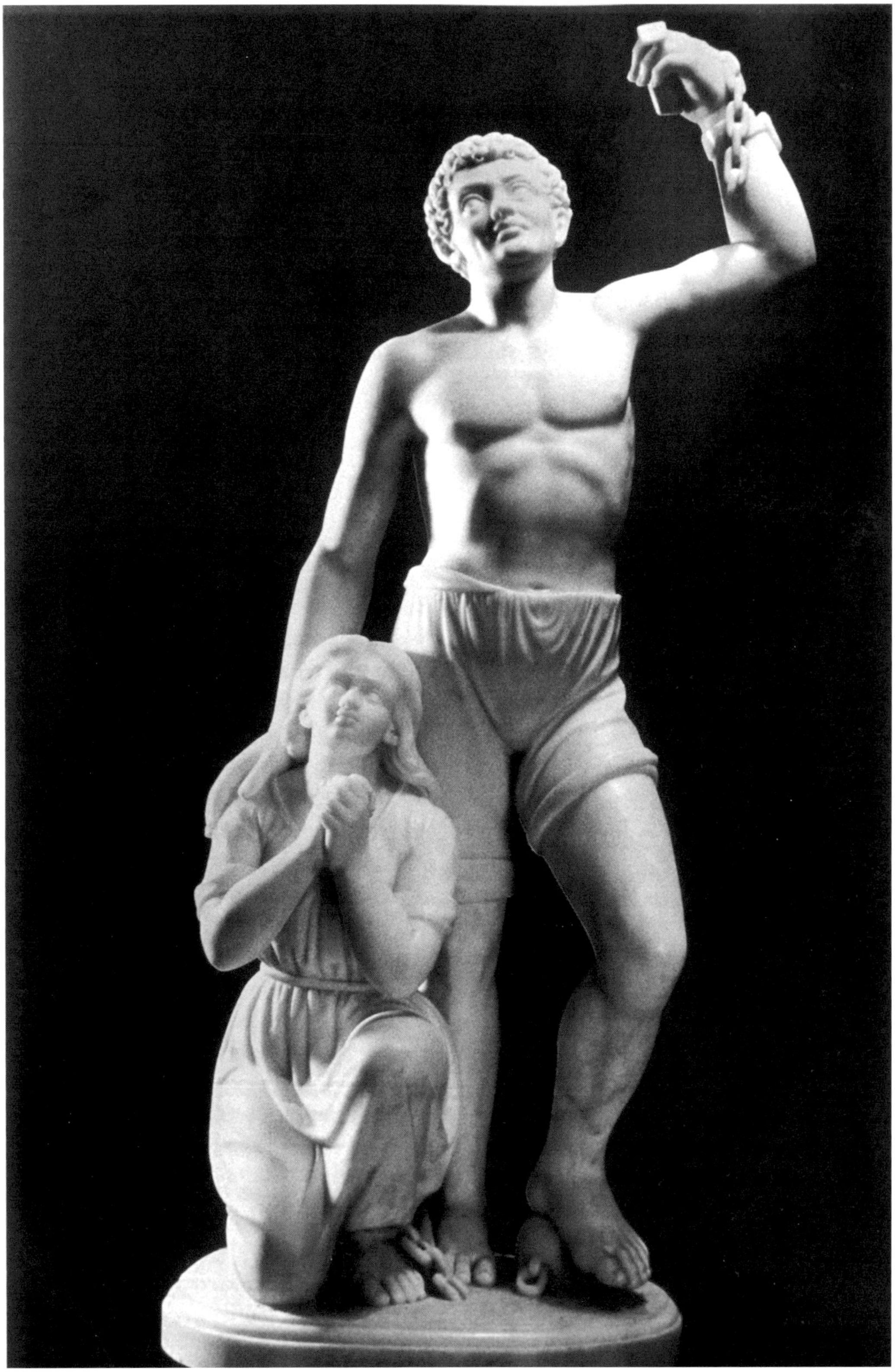

FIG. 76 *(opposite)* Edmonia Lewis, *Forever Free,* 1867, marble. Howard University Gallery of Art, Washington, D.C.

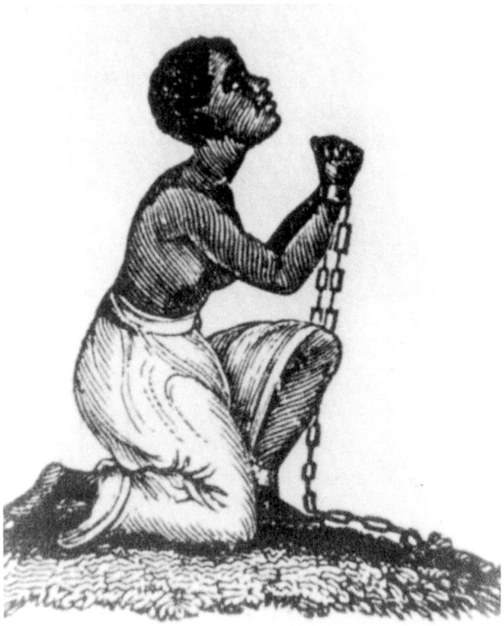

FIG. 77 *Am I Not a Woman and a Sister?,* 1845, from *Specimen of Modern Printing Types, Cast at the Letter Foundry of the Boston Type and Stereotype Company* (Boston: White, Lewis & Potter, 1845).

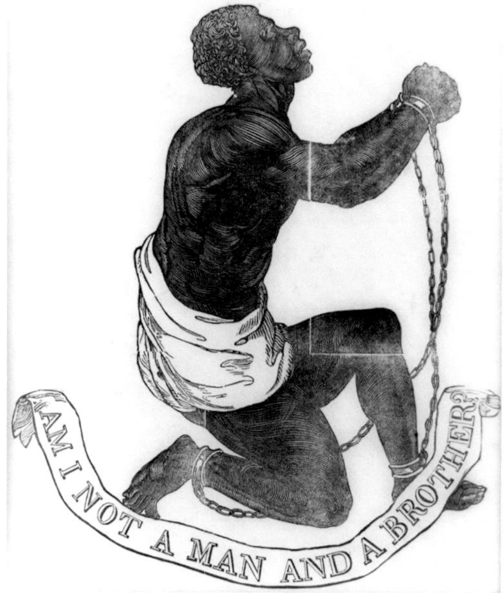


FIG. 78 *Am I Not a Man and a Brother?,* 1837, woodcut. Library of Congress Rare Book and Special Collections Division, Washington, D.C.

subservient (rather than triumphant), and shackled to the ground (rather than free). Her disproportionately dainty head and mixed-race features signal an alliance with white middle-class femininity. However, with her sturdy body, massive arms, and large feet, she signifies racial and class difference—a strength and determination specific to the freed black woman.[65]

Lewis sought and followed advice about her sculptures from her abolitionist patrons, particularly Lydia Maria Child and Maria Weston Chapman, mailing to them photographs of the works in process. Child had privately critiqued an earlier sculpture: "The group of *The Freedwoman and Her Child* strikes me disagreeably. The face is pretty good, but the figure is shockingly disproportionate. The feet are monstrous."[66] Just the previous year, Child had praised Whitney's *Ethiopia*—a figure that demonstrated similar proportions in its small head, strong body, and large feet—when displayed at the National Academy of Design. But when these same characteristics appeared in the female figure of *Forever Free,* she suggested that Lewis was not sufficiently skilled to depict the female anatomy. The lack of classical proportionality served as a deliberate visual strategy for Lewis, as it also had for Whitney. Both artists sought a unique visual language that would characterize the newly freed black woman.

Lewis suspected a problem when she wrote to Chapman in 1868. "It seems almost . . . impossible that not one of my many kind friends have . . . written to me some word about the group *Forever Free.* Will you be so kind as to let me know what has become of it?" It seemed that the sculpture had arrived in Boston without its $200 shipping

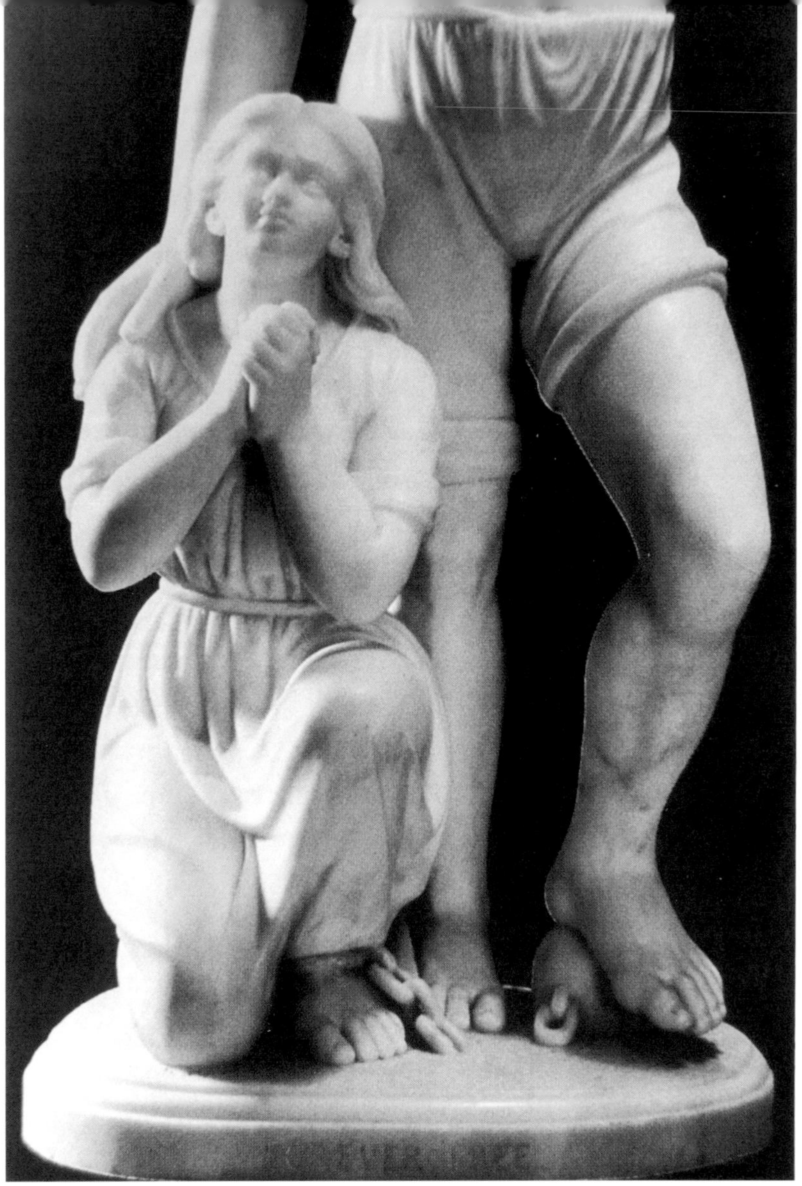

FIG. 79
Edmonia Lewis, *Forever Free* (fig. 76), detail of the kneeling woman.

costs paid. This extra expense infuriated many of her patrons, especially Child, who took it upon herself to reproach Lewis about her seemingly irresponsible spending habits. Intended as a gift to William Lloyd Garrison, it was exhibited at the Childs Gallery (formerly Childs and Jenks Gallery) in 1869 and presented instead to Rev. Leonard Grimes, the prominent African-American minister of Boston's Twelfth Baptist Church. The artist attended the dedication ceremony in Boston. The twenty-five-cent admission helped to defray the cost of the marble, which Lewis had purchased without a ready commission.[67] In discussing the statue privately, Child later admitted, "[Lewis] wanted me to write it up, but I could not do it conscientiously, for it seemed to me a poor thing." When Elizabeth Peabody wrote a glowing review of the piece, she offered this patronizing defense: "It's the work of a colored girl, it ought to be praised."[68]

Lewis was sensitive to the racial politics of her white patrons—both their condescending beneficence, as illustrated by Peabody's remarks, and their romantic racialism, which coded the artist herself as an exemplar of the mixed-race ideology. To Child, Lewis represented nothing less than the racial blending that would characterize the future of the American republic.[69] Lewis most likely responded to these romantic racialist views when she imagined the female figure in *Forever Free* with mulatta facial features, a strategy that allowed the freed slave to be read as "woman" and blackness to be legible within the tenets of neoclassical statuary.

The sculptor was not alone in such imaginings. Harriet Jacobs, for example, in her *Incidents in the Life of a Slave Girl: Written by Herself* (1861), produced literary characters who adhered to the tenets of true womanhood while becoming the shapers of their own identities and destinies.[70] Like Jacobs and Sojourner Truth, Lewis may have tried to redefine proper femininity in terms that would embody the tenets of freedom and make visually evident a new identity for the black female.

Gender roles were under negotiation in the reconstructed family, as evident in Lewis's *Forever Free.* For the freed black man, the nineteenth-century domestic ideal offered power and status as head of household. Stripped of his manhood during slavery, the freedman confirmed his masculine identity through this protective familial role. As historian James Oliver Horton has explained, "For black men the ability to support and protect their women became synonymous with manhood and manhood became synonymous with freedom. Often slaves demanding their freedom used the term 'manhood rights.'"[71]

By depicting her male figure with a sense of self-determination and empowerment, Lewis presented a radical new conception of the freed black man within the domestic sphere; his role as family provider was secured. The black man stands in *contrapposto* pose, poised for movement rather than enchained; his arms are unencumbered—one elevated in triumph, and the other protective of his female charge; and his head and eyes are raised heavenward in anticipation of a free future. In purifying the slave body of the telltale markings of bondage, she evoked the classical ideal and provided a visual antithesis to the antislavery emblem *Am I Not a Man and a Brother?* an image that delimited the character of black masculinity. The black man assumed full civic responsibility for himself and his family.[72]

Lewis's imagery evoked Christological overtones. The Christian tradition provided a useful framework for abolitionists to conceptualize their political mission. The biblical cycles of suffering, sacrifice, death, and resurrection commonly underpinned both the rhetoric and the visual culture of their publicity campaigns. Most significantly, abolitionists frequently associated emancipation with aspects of the risen Christ—linking the theme of freedom with that of resurrection. The third and final masthead of the *Liberator,* designed by Boston illustrator Hammatt Billings in 1850, used such imagery (fig. 80). A standing Christ with one arm raised in triumphant ascendance stands at the center of the masthead. To Christ's right, the symbolic location of saved souls, is a kneeling male slave who offers prayer in the exact posture of the figure in the antislavery emblem. To Christ's left—signifying the damned—a white slave owner turns and flees Christ's judgment.[73]

Lewis's sculptural composition offers striking similarities to this imagery. In *Forever Free,*

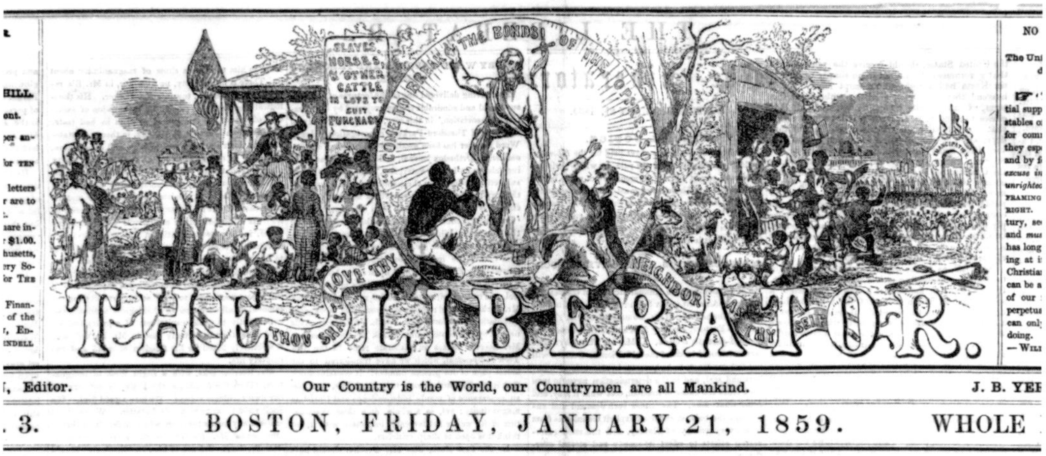


FIG. 80
Final masthead of the *Liberator,* by Alonzo Hartwell after Hammett Billings. First used May 31, 1850. Boston Athenaeum.

the freed black man resembles the risen Christ in Billing's design, as both stand in *contrapposto* with one arm raised in triumph. Lewis's kneeling freedwoman replaces the supplicant slave, evoking an image of one of the three Marys who piously worshipped at Christ's tomb. Lewis transforms the conventional image of the black male from that of abject slave, as defined by the antislavery emblem, to that of empowered man, as envisioned in the form of the triumphant Christ.

Despite these Christological overtones, the powerful black male body caused consternation even among the abolitionist public. When Elizabeth Peabody wrote about the sculpture for the *Christian Register* in 1869, she described the male figure in great detail: "The noble figure of the man, his very muscles seeming to swell with gratitude; the expression of the right now to protect, with which he throws his arm around his kneeling wife; the 'Praise de Lord'—hovering on their lips; the broken chain,—all so instinct with life, telling in the very poetry of stone the story of the last ten years." In discussing the figure's strong muscles, she suggested that they "swelled with gratitude" rather than rancor, and assured her audience of the figure's docility. She read this sculpture as testimony to the reunited black family in which the black male finally had "the right to protect" his wife.[74] At the same time, she employed the "Praise de Lord" stereotype that aligned the black man with the lackey. Peabody's comments simultaneously empowered and disempowered the newly freed black man.

Domesticity signaled a different set of experiences for the freed black woman. Lewis no doubt understood that self-sacrifice and submission were traditional values associated with true womanhood and that they crossed class, racial, and sectional lines in the United States. These qualities provided an incomparable moral authority to women in the domestic sphere. The female figure in *Forever Free* served as just such an exemplar of piety, a central tenet of true womanhood that underscored her role as purveyor of Christian virtue within the family.[75] However, her kneeling pose and the shackled ankle simultaneously suggested both the pious subservience of the domestic ideal *and* the political oppression of patriarchal power.

Although claiming that patriarchy was the central institution in the oppression of slaves and women, feminist abolitionists held contradictory views about domesticity. White middle-class women believed that it remained the source of their power and virtue while also serving as the rationale for their "enslavement." In the case of black women, however, abolitionists argued that the cult of domesticity was the only means of entry into true womanhood, since slavery had undermined the institution of the family.[76] For freed black women, patriarchal family structures remained in place by necessity.

Lewis may have questioned these contradictory claims regarding domesticity in her sculpture. She was well aware of feminist critiques of patriarchy from her days in Boston. She had eschewed, or at least reconfigured, the culture of domesticity in Rome by living unchaperoned in Cushman's feminist circle and seeking the identity of a professional artist. Is it possible to imagine that Lewis, in the company of her Roman sisters, imagined a different type of domesticity for the freed black woman? She envisioned the advantages *and* the limitations of a patriarchal family structure in her sculpture by simultaneously bringing attention to the pious virtue of her freed black woman and to her subservient status.[77]

Lewis brought a unique perspective to her sculptural production in Rome. She had become part of the international art world, where her identity as an American woman sculptor was as important as her African or Native American heritage. In Rome, she investigated social and political issues—like slavery and freedom—that were relevant not only to the progressive Anglo-American expatriate community but also to Italian nationalists.[78] Within this progressive cosmopolitan community, she encountered new visual strategies by which to forge an ideological and historical presence for freed black women.

## *The Freedman's Memorial to Abraham Lincoln*

In April 1865, the news of President Lincoln's assassination reached the American colony in Rome "like a thunderbolt," as Emma Stebbins put it. Expatriates and tourists alike met on the streets, "look[ed] at each other, and burst into tears."[79] On the morning of April 28, at 11:00 A.M., Americans convened in rooms draped in black at the U.S. Legation in the Palazzo Zuccari on via Sistina. Rev. J. Lyman, chaplain to the legation, performed a memorial service in honor of the slain president. All Americans in Rome wore black crepe on their left sleeves for thirty days as a sign of respect for the departed president.[80]

The entire spectrum of Italian politics from the Vatican to the Italian national government and the Roman National Committee sent their condolences to the people of the United States. The Roman National Committee, which was leading the movement to liberate Rome, honored Lincoln with a stone tablet taken from the tomb of Servius Tullius, the sixth king of Rome, which they hoped to contribute to the yet unfinished Washington Monument.[81] The Roman nationalists drew parallels between the two leaders, both struck down by assassins—Lincoln, who liberated the slaves, and Servius Tullius, who granted the plebs Roman citizenship. "The Romans still hope for that liberty which the Americans so largely enjoy," their document read. "May this antique stone be the augury of the perpetuity of your freedom and the advent of ours."[82]

In the United States, plans for a memorial for the beloved president were immediately entertained. The idea for a "freedman's memorial to Abraham Lincoln" originated with the donation of five dollars by freedwoman Charlotte Scott to a Lincoln memorial fund. This money represented her first earnings as a freedwoman. The plan gained currency among the freed-slave community as a means of showing gratitude to the late president. The Western Sanitary Commission managed the project, headed by James Yeatman, a friend of Wayman Crow's. The monument charter urged that "the circumstances attending the act of emancipation should form . . . the principle features of the design."[83]

In Rome, Hosmer began work on her design in October of 1865 and completed her model by the summer of 1866 (fig. 81). In January 1867, her design was selected by the commission and exhibited at the Boston Athenaeum to much acclaim. For support of this design, the Western Sanitary Commission appealed to the "women of America" by targeting a population that had been active in pursuing the goal of emancipation. In so doing, it traded upon the popularity of a female sculptor—Hosmer—and a female patron—Scott.

The monument presented an elaborate formal and iconographic program. Hosmer described the project as her "Temple of Fame," in which the two great acts of Lincoln's administration would be featured: emancipation of the slaves and preservation of the Union. A recumbent effigy of the late president crowned the monument. Upon the base of the templelike structure, she inscribed bas-reliefs of thirty-six female figures, representing the states of the Union. Adorning the temple's foundation were four bas-relief scenes from the life of the president. Mourning victories inhabited the outside corners of the monument. Four black male figures stood toward the conceptual center of the monument.[84]

She imagined the requirements of the monument's charter with daring and imagination, envisioning the journey from slavery to freedom as that from disempowerment to manhood.[85] The black male figures represented "the progressive stages of Liberation," she explained. Each figure embodied a different stage in the "act of emancipation": one slave was "exposed in chains for sale," a slave with a hoe was "laboring on a plantation," a scout was "guiding and assisting the loyal [Union] troops," and the freedman was "serving as a soldier of the Union."[86] In her bold design, black male citizenship culminated in an image of the African-American soldier.

Critics responded favorably to her model; the African-American community in Boston gave it a ringing endorsement. "The finest portion of the work, as it now stands, is the series of four negro figures, representing various stages of development from slavery to freedom and self-defense," an editorial in the *Freedman's Record* noted. "These [figures] are strikingly characteristic, yet graceful and pleasing."[87] In visualizing the various stages of emancipation, Hosmer positioned the two poles of black manhood to the front of the monument: the seminude slave and the uniformed soldier with a gun. In so doing,

FIG. 81 *(opposite)* Harriet Hosmer, *Freedman's Memorial to Abraham Lincoln,* 1866, plaster, now lost. Watertown Free Public Library, Watertown, Mass.

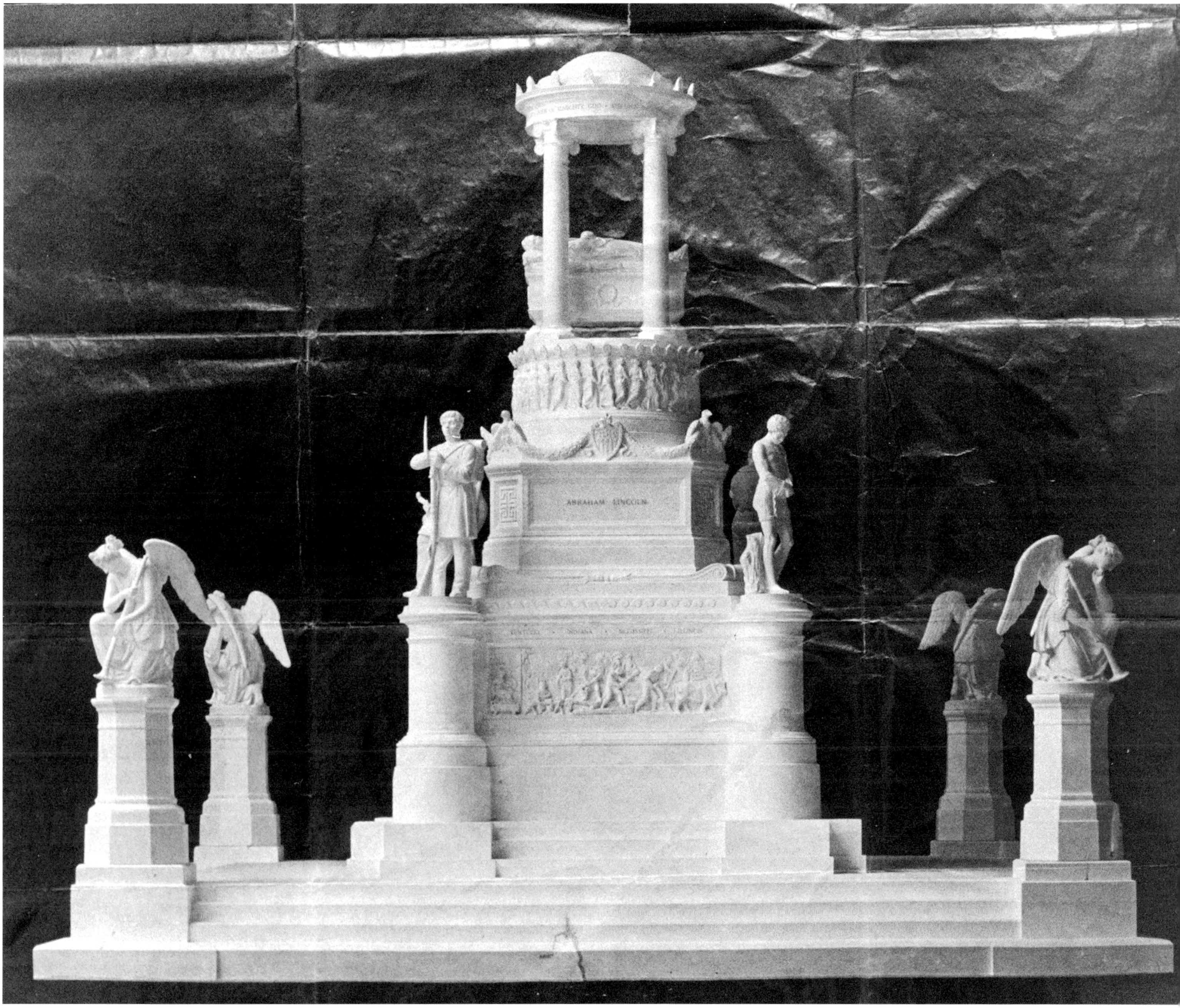
ABRAHAM LINCOLN

she brought attention to the visual convention of depicting the slave in terms of the nude racialized body.

In the image of the contemporary armed black soldier, Hosmer produced a radical new visualization of black manhood. Within the social consciousness of whites and blacks alike, military service acknowledged the capacity of freed slaves to adopt characteristics of white bourgeois masculinity—determination, endurance, self-reliance, and self-discipline. In her monumental design, Hosmer gave the black soldier a clear social identity, "the citizen-soldier keeping vigil," an image that would appear in hundreds of Union monuments of white soldiers across the north.[88] This representation of black manliness directly confronted the anxieties of a nation in social and political flux. In the era of Reconstruction, the image of the black soldier with a gun openly challenged white citizenry as it invoked an ideal of equality that black men were actually able to defend.

Hosmer remained the favored candidate for the commission until 1868. However, her bold design would never be implemented. With the cost of the project soaring to $100,000, the monument committee found itself in financial trouble. After several failed attempts to merge with other national commissions for Lincoln monuments, it dropped Hosmer's complex project in favor of a simpler and less costly one. Through a series of financial dealings, the committee reassigned the commission to Thomas Ball.[89]

By the early 1870s, the commemoration of emancipation and the black freed subject revealed a radical shift in ideological content. Ball's *Emancipation Monument* of 1876 serves as a case in point (fig. 82). In depicting Lincoln bestowing freedom upon a kneeling slave, Ball changed the meaning of emancipation to manumission and upheld the traditional power relations between the races. The pose of the newly freed slave, Archer Alexander, resembles that of the figure in the antislavery emblem *Am I Not Man and a Brother?* Giving visual form to contemporary racial politics, this hierarchical composition positions a powerful white leader dominating the vulnerable yet freed black slave. In its new incarnation, the *Emancipation Monument* allows political agency to President Lincoln alone. Although depicting the black man in public statuary for the first time, the monument commemorates an image of slavery, not freedom, as the design freezes the figure of the slave within a posture of perpetual subservience.[90] Ball's monument fails to imagine the full meaning of emancipation despite the commission's promising charter and its original choice of Hosmer's daring design.

### *Reconstruction and the "Woman Question"*

After the collapse of the Lincoln commission, Hosmer pursued a more conventional project. In the early 1870s, she began a study for an *African Sibyl* but never brought it to completion. In the only remaining drawing for the project, she envisioned an enormous sibyl, seated with an open tome in her arms (fig. 83). Inscribed upon its pages is Lincoln's famous maxim "If slavery is not wrong, nothing is wrong," a phrase mandated by the 1865 commission for the *Freedman's Memorial to Abraham Lincoln*.[91] At the sibyl's feet crawls a black baby, whose hands reach upward in adoration. Described alternately as her great

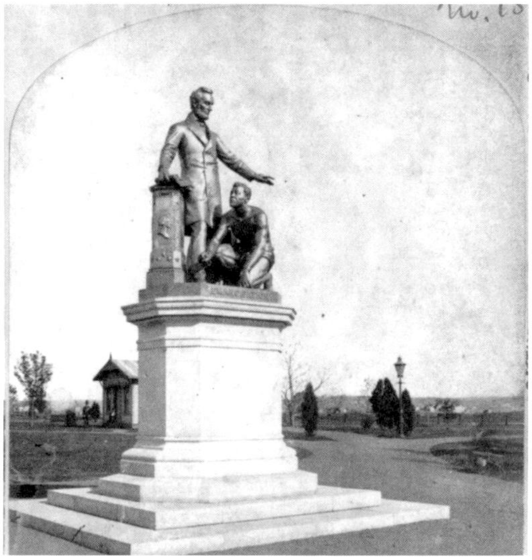

FIG. 82
Thomas Ball, *Emancipation Monument,* 1876, Lincoln Park, Washington, D.C. Photographic print on stereo card, Library of Congress Prints and Photographs Division, Washington, D.C.

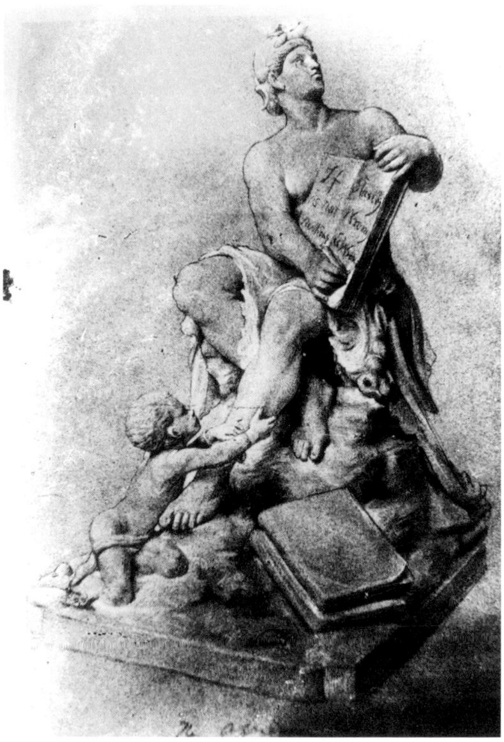

FIG. 83
Harriet Hosmer, *African Sibyl,* design for a portion of the Lincoln Monument, ca. 1890, now lost. Watertown Free Public Library, Watertown, Mass.

figure of "Emancipation" and the "African Sibyl Foreshadowing the Freedom of her Race," this sculpture was to be unveiled in the Women's Pavilion of the 1876 Centennial Exposition in Philadelphia.[92]

Like William Wetmore Story and Anne Whitney before her, Hosmer conceived of her sibyl in powerful terms. However, in place of a calm and stable composition, she created a gigantic body whose force was released within a dynamic diagonal. Moreover, the face exhibited aquiline rather than "Africanized" features. Hosmer, like Story, looked to traditional models for inspiration, most likely to Michelangelo's *Libyan Sibyl* from the Sistine ceiling—a figure she knew well in Rome—with its androgynous body and twisted posture (fig. 65). In her allegorical imagery, she attempted to reconcile the artistic traditions of the High Renaissance with the radically new politics of Reconstruction, but this traditional vocabulary was insufficient to the task. Her figure of "Emancipation" did not address the politics of racial representation. Blackness was relegated to the figure of the baby, whose small and vulnerable image remained subservient to the ideals of Western high culture.[93]

There is no doubt that black women made gains after emancipation: they could own property, marry, and move about more freely. However, only men won the right to vote. As early as 1866, the provisional wording of the Fifteenth Amendment limited suffrage to male citizens, the first time gender had been inserted into the Constitution. Whitney was quite troubled by this political development, writing to Adeline Manning in 1866: "Have you seen what Mr. Sumner proposes, in his amendment to the Constitution, so as to insert the word male, which interposes a barrier immediate and complete against any action on the woman question?"[94] Sojourner Truth, having defended political rights for both black men and women throughout her life, bitterly denounced manhood suffrage in 1867: "There is a great stir about colored men getting their rights, but not a word about the colored women; and if colored men get their rights, and not colored women theirs, you see the colored men will be masters over the women, and it will be just as bad as it was before." With the ratification of the Fifteenth Amendment in 1870, all women—but especially black women—were relegated to political invisibility.[95]

In the end, Whitney, Lewis, and Hosmer did not fully succeed in their task of depicting freed black womanhood in a post-emancipation society. Lewis's Boston patrons were less than enthusiastic about her work. Whitney destroyed her sculpture sometime after 1874. Hosmer never produced the female figure of "Emancipation" for the centennial celebration, though she returned to the project again in the 1890s.[96] As engaged participants in the changing social, political, and aesthetic practices of the mid–nineteenth century, these women suffered both successes and failures as they worked to create new representational strategies. Their experience illuminated how the constraints of high-art theory—in particular the mandate of neoclassicism as articulated in Rome and in Boston—coupled with the tensions of contemporary racial and gender politics, shaped the ways in which emancipation was envisioned in their sculpture. Their unique visions stood as testaments to the struggle, promise, and ultimately dashed hopes of this significant historical moment.

# Seven

## Women Sculptors, Suffrage, and the Public Stage

With great fanfare, Vinnie Ream's life-size sculpture of Abraham Lincoln was unveiled on January 25, 1871, in the U.S. Capitol Rotunda (fig. 84). In attendance were all manner of dignitaries, from President Ulysses S. Grant and General William Tecumseh Sherman to senators, congressmen, judges, and the general public. The large crowd assembled in the Rotunda to hear the many speeches and to see the young twenty-four-year-old sculptor, who appeared on the podium with her mother. "Could it be," a reporter for the *Washington Evening Star* wrote, "that the fragile youthful figure standing there, pale and anxious, and rendered more child-like in appearance by her petite form and wealth of Dora-like curls, had made a success where so many older sculptors—[Henry Kirke] Brown notably and recently—had failed?"[1]

In her public role as sculptor, Ream was compared to the fictive character Corinne in Madame de Staël's popular novel *Corinne, or Italy* (1807). "Never since the crowning of Corinne at the capital of Italy," wrote one journalist, "has a woman's genius and work been so publicly and worthily honored." Another writer declared, "What was the crowning of Corinne at Rome compared with this triumph of an American girl in the capital of the country? And yet it was vastly more than the triumph of one woman—it was a national recognition of American womanhood." The *Revolution,* a suffrage journal founded in 1868 by Susan B. Anthony and Elizabeth Cady Stanton, reported upon Ream's professional career: "It was a supreme moment for the courageous little girl, when she was 'crowned at the Capitol.' We sincerely hope her unprecedented success, so early in life, may not stultify her genius . . . but only stimulate her to strive for more complete excellence in her glorious art."[2]

Within the turbulent world of post–Civil War America, Ream represented a new kind of public woman, who was both self-made and commercially successful. She participated openly in the realms of politics and finance, acting as an equal to men in the public sphere. In her unconcealed ambition, she launched an active campaign of self-promotion to market her sculpture. For these seeming transgressions, she attracted much criticism, often from feminist women, like the sculptor Anne Whitney, who quipped, "One can't help wondering if the girl has any discernment to note the difference between notoriety and fame."[3] For Whitney and other reform-minded women, Ream refused to negotiate the tenets of true womanhood appropriately by conforming to an ideal of selfless, nurturing, and pious virtue,

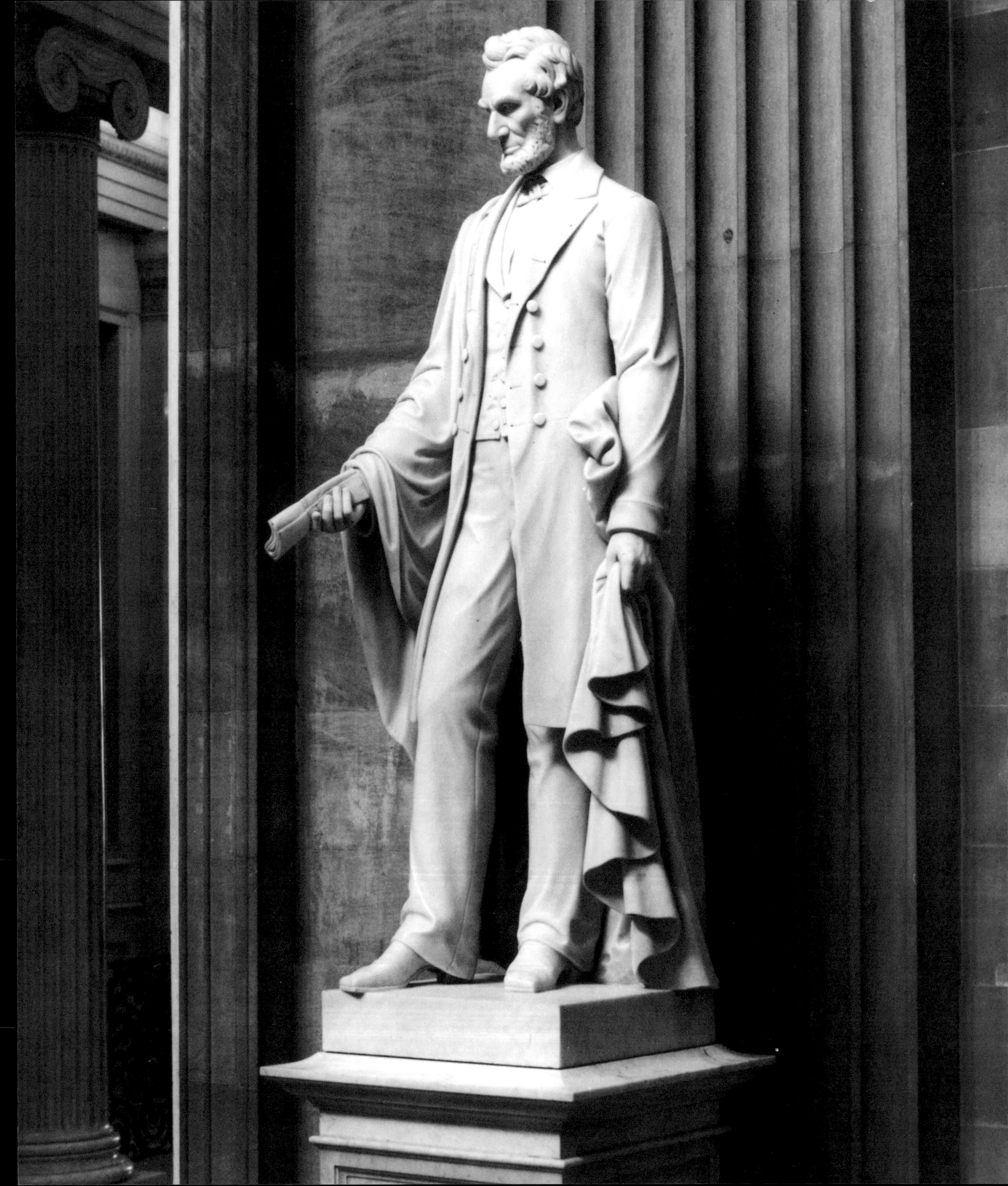

FIG. 84 *(opposite)*
Vinnie Ream, *Abraham Lincoln,* 1870, marble. U.S. Capitol Rotunda.

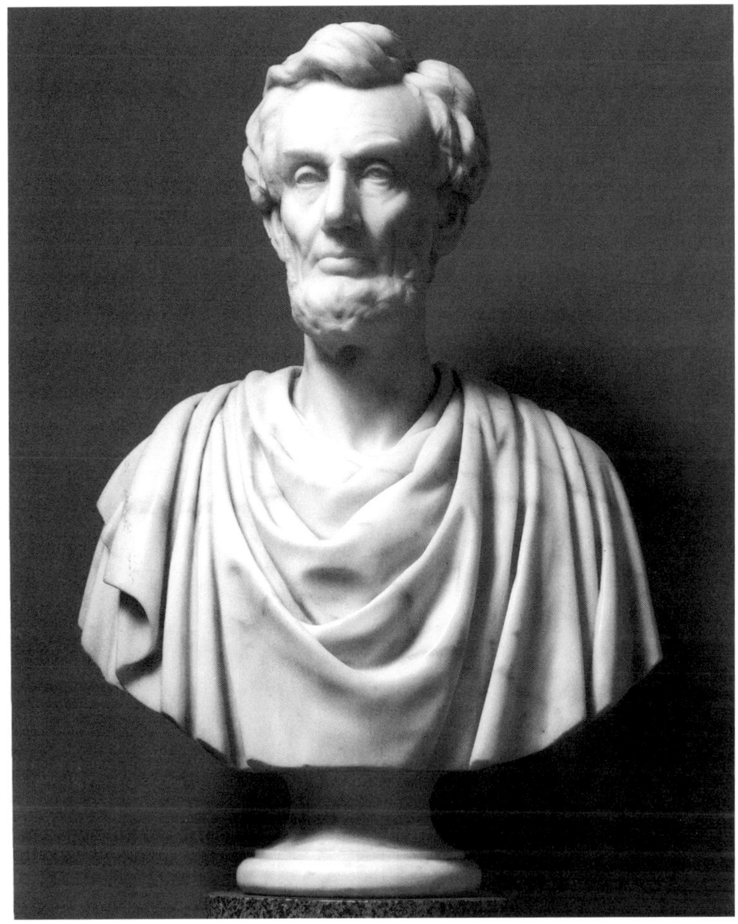

FIG. 85
Sarah Fisher Clampitt Ames, *Abraham Lincoln,* 1868, marble. U.S. Senate Collection, Washington, D.C.

thereby revealing a higher moral and spiritual standard than that of men. Not surprisingly, with her flamboyant career, she attracted a number of powerful supporters and, in turn, inspired many vociferous detractors.

The sculptor Sarah Fisher Ames and Ream were the first artists commissioned to produce monuments of the deceased president; both sculptures adorned the halls of the U.S. Capitol. Ames sculpted a marble bust of Lincoln that the Senate purchased in 1866 (fig. 85). Hailing from a prominent New England family, Ames, like Whitney, was a feminist reformer of an older generation. By inhabiting a proper bourgeois world, she maintained an unblemished professional persona, despite her participation in the cosmopolitan world of monument making. Because of her elite social status and embrace of true womanhood, she managed a public career that was inoculated against moral taint.

Ames, Whitney, and Ream inhabited complicated positions in both the public and the private spheres. Like many females involved in reform movements, Ames and Whitney expanded the social spaces that proper women of their status occupied at midcentury. Their performance of femininity lent them the legitimacy to act without recrimination in the realms of art, politics, and commerce, a legitimacy that many denied to their much younger and insistently self-promotional colleague Ream.

## *Sarah Fisher Ames*

Sarah Fisher Ames's powerful image of Abraham Lincoln—with his creviced face, angular features, and drooping eyelids—was the first work of art that the U.S. government commissioned from a woman artist. She depicted the president with broad shoulders and clad in classicizing drapery that not only added heft to his lean physique but also introduced a quiet dignity to his character. When juxtaposed with the naturalism of his visage, the classicizing style ennobled the president's character, imbuing him with wisdom and fortitude. Idealized portrait busts of public figures, like that of Lincoln, performed an important civic task in the nineteenth century. Rather than simply serve as mirror likenesses, they referenced the *exemplum virtutis* (example of virtue) and thus represented heroic models of high-minded morality for emulation by the American citizenry.[4]

Ames was a member of elite artistic and social circles in Boston, Rome, and Washington, D.C. Born Sarah Fisher Clampitt, she married the portrait painter Joseph Alexander Ames in 1845 and soon traveled with him to Rome for a lengthy stay during which she had ample opportunity to study ancient and Renaissance masterworks. She most likely lent her support to the unification movement in Italy.[5] Although little is known of her life, she was probably the first of the American women sculptors to travel to Rome, sometime between 1845 and 1852, the year Harriet Hosmer arrived in the city.

In 1862, Ames volunteered to serve the Union cause in Washington as a Sanitary Commission nurse, working in several field hospitals, including the U.S. Capitol, which housed thousands of wounded Union soldiers during the war. In this charitable endeavor, she joined many other reform-minded women from the North, including Louisa Lander, who had recently returned from Rome; the author Louisa May Alcott, who in her semiautobiographical narrative *Hospital Sketches* wrote about her wartime experiences; and the feminist-abolitionist editor Jane Grey Swisshelm.[6]

While working for the Sanitary Commission in Washington, Ames developed a personal acquaintance with President Lincoln and apparently persuaded him to sit for a portrait bust. Lincoln was hesitant to pose, ostensibly because of the time involved for such a project. He did consent, however, to a series of photographic portraits taken at the studio of Alexander Gardner on November 8, 1863 (just days before the Gettysburg Address), in a sitting that Ames attended and probably arranged.[7] With the aid of Gardner's pictures, Ames created a half-life-sized plaster cabinet bust of the president sometime between 1863 and November 1865 (fig. 86). The small-scale bust (less than a foot high) was crudely modeled, intended for purchase by middle-class collectors. According to newspaper accounts, she hoped that the modest cost (between five and ten dollars)

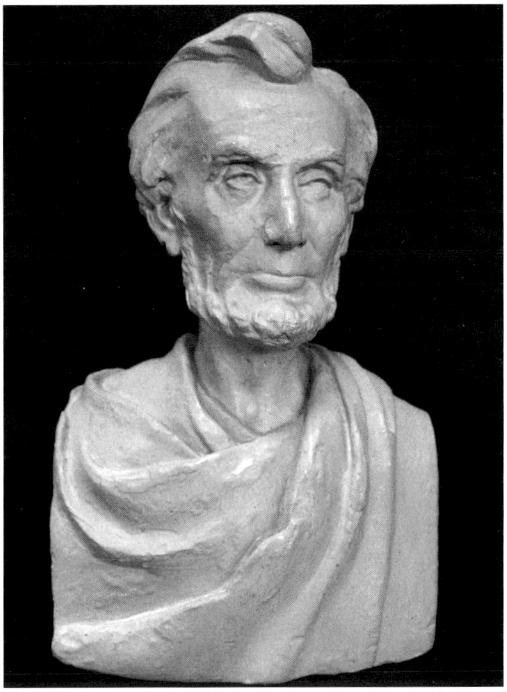

FIG. 86
Sarah Fisher Clampitt Ames, *Abraham Lincoln*, 1865, plaster cabinet bust, height 10 ½ in. The Lynn Museum and Historical Society, Lynn, Mass.

would allow many American citizens to own an affordable plaster bust of the departed president. In 1866, she patented the design and exhibited the bust in Boston and New York, advertising that all proceeds from the sales would go toward the establishment of a home in New York for the care and instruction of orphans of soldiers and sailors.[8] With her philanthropic mission, she deflected any sharp criticism that may have been leveled against this commercial venture. Critics considered Ames an "amateur artist" when she patented the design for her plaster bust of Lincoln. Yet the following year, after having received the Senate commission, she was lauded as an "artist of genius." The popularity of the small plaster portrait led to a number of requests for marble and bronze busts of Lincoln, all of which were produced in Europe.[9] Within this two-year period, her reputation advanced considerably, and she assumed a respected role in the domain of national commemoration.

With its origins in plaster, the portrait of Lincoln suggested a commingling of elite and popular audiences. His visage and demeanor were well known to most Americans, as he had been the first president to put photography to political service, using tintype campaign buttons and distributing cartes de visite with his image as president. His plaster portrait bust thus demanded a high level of realism to satisfy middle-class patrons.[10] When the Senate commissioned the marble bust, some members feared that the president's lanky physique and strong features did not lend themselves to the type of idealization that would embody the founding principles of the weary and war-torn nation. One need only look at the photographic portrait of the president taken by Gardner shortly before his assassination, on April 14, 1865, which revealed his chiseled features, sunken eyes, graying beard and hair, and disheveled collar and bowtie, to see the emotional and physical toll that the war had deeply etched upon his appearance (fig. 87). In her portrait of the deceased president, Ames successfully blended the naturalism of the photographic image with an idealization of the high-art tradition. Critics praised her for capturing an expression of "firmness . . . mirthfulness, and tenderness," rather than the "coarse exaggerations of his features often displayed in other portraits."[11] When the bust was exhibited at the Pennsylvania Academy of the Fine Arts in 1868, one reviewer noted that it was "one of the best portraits of Lincoln we have ever seen." Moreover, many critics read the Lincoln portrait through the prism of gender. One writer argued that only a woman such as Ames, with her "pliant sympathy," could represent "the tender spirit" of the president.[12]

From all available evidence, Ames cultivated a public persona replete with the feminine virtues of sensitivity, humanitarianism, and charity while pursuing a livelihood in the professional arena of art making. In her roles as wife, mother, and volunteer nurse, she exemplified the benevolent nature of proper bourgeois femininity and demonstrated the purity of spirit necessary to depict the "tender" and noble character of Lincoln. Ream, by contrast, was a working woman, charged from an early age with the financial responsibility of supporting herself and her parents. Engaging in a much more overt relationship with the financial world, she pioneered a more daring—and scandalous—professional life than did Ames and Whitney.

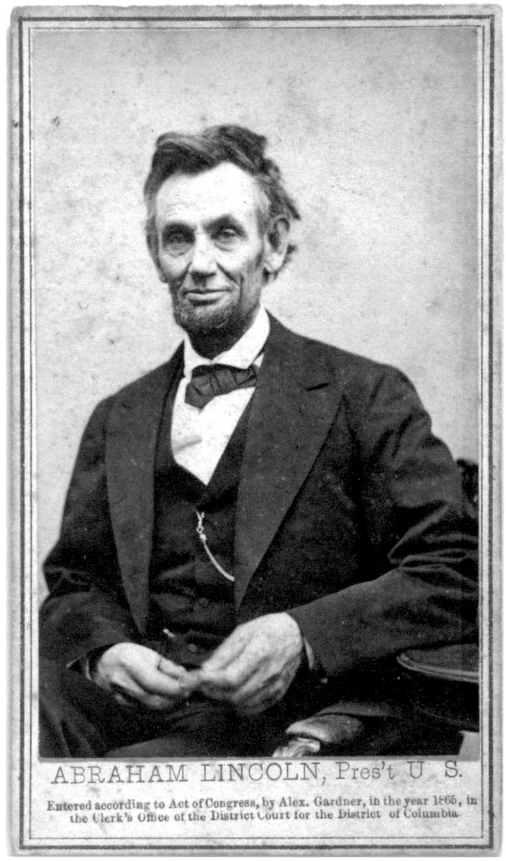


FIG. 87
Alexander Gardner,
*Abraham Lincoln,*
1865, albumen silver print, 3 7/16 × 2 1/8 in.
National Portrait Gallery, Smithsonian Institution, Washington, D.C.

### *Vinnie Ream*

Raised on the Wisconsin frontier, Vinnie Ream occupied a social class quite different from that of her more comfortable colleague Sarah Fisher Ames. Having lived in several western and southern states, she finally settled in Washington with her family at the start of the Civil War. When her father's health failed, she took advantage of wartime employment opportunities in the post office and served as a clerk in Representative James Rollins's office. For the most part, she labored outside the home with little time for philanthropic activities, as her primary commitment was support of her family. She could not afford to give her earnings to charity as had Ames. In 1864, however, she aided the war effort by volunteering to sew straps and epaulets on uniforms and to work for the Ladies Great National Sanitary Fair in Washington.[13]

In 1864, at the age of seventeen, Ream became an apprentice in the Washington studio of the sculptor Clark Mills. Between December of that year and April of the next, she made visits to the White House to model a bust of Lincoln from life. The exact circumstances of these sittings are not known. However, despite his earlier reluctance to pose, the president did permit her, most likely after the personal intercession of two senators, to sculpt his visage while he worked in his office.[14] Later accused of copying the 1866 portrait bust of Lincoln by Fisk Mills (her teacher's

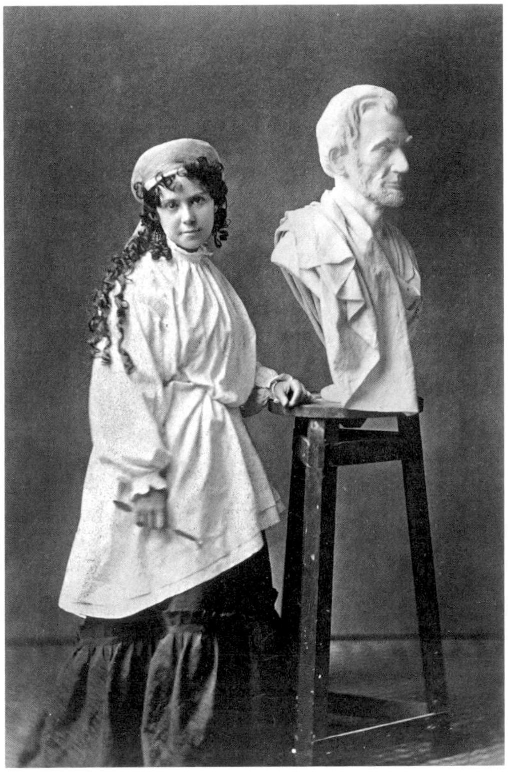

FIG. 88
Vinnie Ream at work on her Lincoln bust, ca. 1865, photograph, 8 × 10 in. Library of Congress Prints and Photographs Division, Washington, D.C.

son), Ream (together with Mills) fiercely denied the allegations.[15] This would be the first of many controversies that clouded her personal life and professional career.

In beret and smock and with chisel in hand, Ream was photographed with her plaster bust of Lincoln (fig. 88). The young artist looks directly at the viewer in an address that confirms her artistic legitimacy. Her youth and beauty stand in sharp contrast to the grave countenance of the president. This image was the first of many in which the artist presented herself as a female prodigy. Bursting upon the professional art world in a daring manner, she actively marketed herself and her sculpture by staging events in her studio and courting newspaper attention. Catering to a public taste for flamboyant figures, she copyrighted and sold many such photographic images as a public-relations strategy. Unlike Ames, who was older, married to a successful artist, and associated with the "proper" social circles, Ream embodied a new model of feminine creativity that emerged from the women's rights movement in the postwar years.[16]

When Congress commissioned the life-size standing sculpture of the deceased president in 1866, Ream showed her recently completed bust of Lincoln, which she had publicized through the distribution of cartes de visite (fig. 89). Nineteen other sculptors submitted models, among them Ream's teacher Clark Mills, Harriet Hosmer, William Wetmore Story, and (probably) Sarah Fisher Ames. The young artist clearly knew how to manipulate the political system, having frequented the Capitol building during her apprenticeship in Mills's studio. Ream was acquainted with many lawmakers from both parties, from whom she solicited signatures for a petition in support of her sculptural entry. Forgoing all proper legislative channels, Republican Congressman Thaddeus Stevens from Pennsylvania proposed that the commission be awarded directly to Ream; the House of Representatives promptly passed this measure.[17] In the Senate, however, Senator Charles Sumner opposed Ream on rather reasonable grounds: her inexperience. After all, she had never produced a standing marble figure. Instead, he supported his friend William Wetmore Story.[18]

But the Senate debate turned on other issues. Senator James Willis Nesmith of Oregon argued that Ream was a "young scion of the West, the same land from which Lincoln came." With her "intuitive genius" and ability "to copy the works of nature" faithfully, he argued, she was exceptionally qualified for the commission. In contrast to Nesmith's nativism, Sumner supposedly represented what was considered an elite East Coast constituency with an effete interest in European rather than homegrown art. The discussion deteriorated on the Senate floor when Senator Jacob Howard of Vermont accused Ream of being a "lobbyist"—a term denoting a public woman of dubious reputation—a slanderous indictment that would dog her for years.[19] Senator Howard most likely thought that because she worked in Mills's studio in the Capitol and was a well-known curiosity to many senators and congressmen—and hence a public figure—he was free to attack her personal reputation. Indeed, the charge of "jugglery or perversion of justice" remained a persistent refrain over the next several years.[20] But in the end, those who spoke of her "native genius" won the battle. Congress awarded Ream the commission in August of 1866.

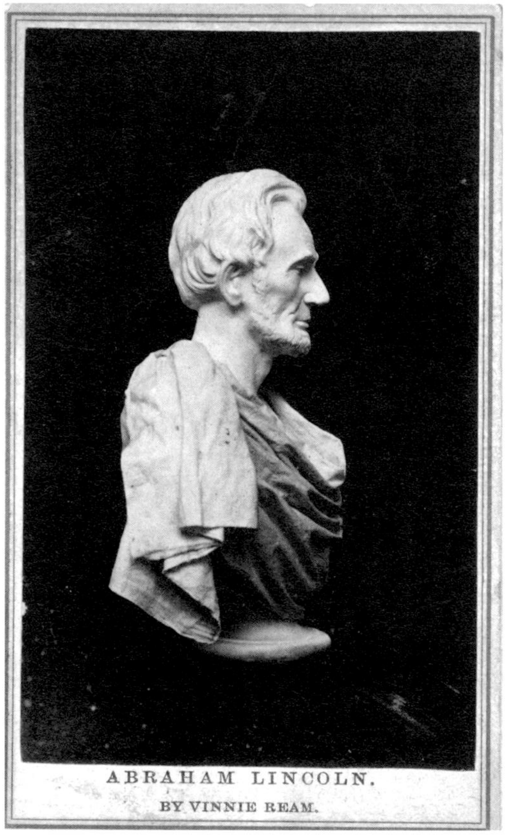


FIG. 89
Vinnie Ream, *Abraham Lincoln,* ca. 1865–66, carte de visite. Research Division of the Oklahoma Historical Society.

Every step of this tumultuous commission became a battleground for this (now) twenty-one-year-old sculptor. On the one hand, Ream was a controversial choice because of her youth and inexperience. On the other hand, she was vilified as a fraud, charlatan, and a harlot because she had transgressed the boundaries of the public arena of self-marketing, an enterprise that both encouraged her celebrity status and boosted her studio sales. The criticism did not all come from men, however. Rather than defend Ream, the newspaper editor Jane Grey Swisshelm, an often outspoken advocate for women's rights, launched a fierce attack upon the young sculptor's character after learning of her selection. Opinionated and domineering, Swisshelm tended to work in relative isolation, never part of an inner circle of women reformers. An artist in her own right, she had given up a career to pursue her marital responsibilities and caustically conceded: "I put away my brushes; resolutely crucified my divine gift; and while it hung writhing on the cross, spent my best years and powers cooking cabbage."[21]

Perhaps in this case Swisshelm's friendship with the sculptor Ames and her own frustrations as an artist manqué motivated her blistering remarks about Ream, which were reprinted in several newspapers in 1867:

*She is a young girl, about twenty, has only been studying her art a few months, never made a statue, has some plaster busts on exhibition in the Capitol, including her own, minus clothing to the waist, has a pretty face, with a turn-up nose, bright black eyes, long dark curls, and plenty of them, wears a jockey hat and a good deal of jewelry, sees all the members [of Congress] at their lodgings or the reception-room of the Capitol, urges her claims fluently and confidently, sits in the [Senate and House] galleries in a conspicuous position and in her most bewitching dress, while those claims are discussed on the floor, nods and smiles as a member rises and delivers his opinion on the merits of the case, with the air of a man sitting for his picture; and so she carries the day over [Hiram] Powers and [Thomas] Crawford, and Hosmer and who not?*[22]

The attack echoed the salvos launched against Ream in the Senate chamber: lack of professional experience and improper decorum. Swisshelm's comments also condensed into one statement a wide range of criticisms leveled against the young artist in the popular press.

Ream's beauty and erudition became notorious, often framed within a gendered context of narcissistic self-absorption and display.[23] In her unyielding visual inspection, Swisshelm perpetrated this narcissistic fantasy—as did the press in general—by obsessively recalling every detail of Ream's personal appearance: from "her long dark curls" to her "bewitching dress" and jewelry. A supporter of the artist called Swisshelm to task for this relentless attention to the young sculptor's appearance. Moreover, the writer queried Swisshelm as to why Ream's "virtue" and "chastity" were also the subject of scrutiny. "Scrutiny means, in this case, to suspect and accuse," the writer noted. "Men are subject to no such Swisshelm 'scrutiny.'"[24]

Swisshelm offered yet another charge in her 1867 diatribe: she asserted that the half-nude neoclassical bust on display in Ream's Capitol studio was actually a self-portrayal by the artist ("plaster busts on exhibition . . . including her own, minus clothing to the waist"). In the popular press, Ream's sculpture often seemed of secondary importance to critics, unless, of course, it was read through the body of the artist. In this case, Swisshelm conflated the female sculptor with her artwork, through what has been called the Pygmalion complex, an association of artist and artwork also witnessed in Louisa Lander's studio in Rome. As the woman artist was stripped of her moral purity by the relentless scrutiny of her detractors, the neoclassical bust, in Ream's case, was also divested of its ideal status when the eroticized body of the artist was projected upon it.

For the young artist, being a "woman in public" was fraught with all kinds of dangers. As a Washington insider, she became embroiled in the impeachment proceedings against President Andrew Johnson. When Senator Edmund G. Ross of Kansas, a family friend who lodged at the Ream residence on Capitol Hill, cast the decisive vote against removing Johnson from office, she was spuriously accused of influencing his decision. Radical Republicans were furious that the impeachment vote had failed. Representative Stevens, who had earlier supported her bid for the Lincoln commission, targeted Ream with an order to evacuate her Capitol studio with the unfinished Lincoln statue in tow. Only when Henry Kirk Brown and John Quincy Adams Ward, powerful New York sculptors, intervened on her behalf was she allowed to remain in her workplace.[25]

Considered impudent in their challenge to the prevailing norms of comportment, nineteenth-century public women like Ream seemed, at times, to violate the culture's deepest instincts about sex and gender. In an attempt to avoid such slanderous treatment, Hosmer and other women sculptors deliberately rejected such performances of femininity, choosing instead to present themselves publicly in an androgynous fashion. Regularly criticized by male and female guardians of the separate spheres, public women—no matter what their public personas might have been—seemed to offer an affront to femininity itself.[26]

As an artist in the public eye, Ream actively flaunted her femininity by fashioning herself as a beauty. In adopting what is understood today as the feminine "masquerade," she performed an exaggerated womanliness in part to draw attention away from her creative talents and public ambitions.[27] With this strategy, Ream exposed herself to a controlling gaze in which her physical beauty tendered a reassuring presence rather than a dangerous feminine challenge within the public arena. Given her penchant for public performance, it was not surprising, perhaps even inevitable, that Ream actively sought and embodied the feminine role as spectacle—the object of the look.

Alternatively, she adopted other guises. In highlighting her diminutive stature and youthful appearance, Ream—like the young Hosmer in Rome—appropriated a childlike demeanor. As one reporter stated, Ream was "about twenty-three years old but look[ed] like a child."[28] In Rome, she pursued an identity described as "childlike in the frankness and simplicity of her manners."[29] At the unveiling of her Lincoln sculpture in the Capitol Rotunda, she sat "child-like in appearance" on the podium with her mother. If hyperfemininity proved a successful marketing scheme in the public sphere, the enactment of girlishness associated her professionalism with the chaste domestic realm and thus mitigated any threat that she posed to masculine artistic dominance.

In her role as artist, however, Ream was an active agent of the look. Tellingly, the press responded by focusing relentlessly on her eyes, fetishizing their appeal. Just to take one example: "Her eyes are dark, lustrous, and very impressive—to use a metaphor, 'she talks with her eyes.'"[30] Such language attempted to contain the anxiety provoked by a woman who appropriated the gaze and insisted upon the action of looking. As a woman and as an artist, Ream inhabited two subject positions, flaunting her transgressive behavior as both subject and object of desire.[31]

## *A Roman Sojourn*

In June 1869, the Committee on Public Buildings and Grounds, the government agency charged with oversight of the Lincoln sculpture, approved Ream's completed plaster model and appropriated the sum of $10,000 to the artist. With funding securely in hand, she traveled to Europe, accompanied by her parents, for sixteen months. As was common for American sculptors of the time, she would have the plaster model of Lincoln carved in marble in Italy.

She arrived in Paris on June 13, 1869. During her four-month stay, she engaged a studio on the Place Clichy, studied drawing with the French painter Leon Bonnat, and, for the first time, worked from the live model. Painfully aware of the charges of artistic immaturity leveled against her, she worked diligently to gain expertise in the fundamentals of art, on one occasion working in her studio until four in the morning. In preparation for her Roman sojourn, she began her study of the Italian language. "My thoughts were filled with great designs," she recorded in her journal as she departed Paris.[32]

Rome was her ultimate destination, after a one-week stay in Florence. Arriving in the Eternal City on October 18, 1869, she was filled with awe. "Rome!" she gasped, as she passed through the northernmost gate, at the Piazza del Popolo. The magisterial St. Peter's—visible across the Tiber River—was among the first views to confront the young artist. "I shall never forget the impression [the dome] made on me," she exclaimed. Among her first acts in the city, she engaged a studio next door to the sculptor Emma Stebbins at via San Basilio 45.[33]

The American expatriate community—among them William Wetmore Story, Charlotte Cushman, Harriet Hosmer, Edmonia Lewis, Margaret Foley, Anne Whitney, and Stebbins—extended a hearty welcome to Ream and her family.[34] She immediately became an active member of the "American art circle in Rome." While attending a reception, one writer scrutinized Ream, and later described her thus: "A little girl with bright eyes, long black hair floating down her back, and [an] extremely simple, childlike appearance. . . . She looks like a clever, good little school girl, [and] is very natural and artless." With the possibility of gaining publicity in Rome, Ream immediately invited that correspondent to her studio. Maintaining her childlike identity, she promised, as if to a teacher, that she would "study just as hard" as she could while in Rome. Quite taken with the presence of her parents, who were "kind, quiet-looking, respectable persons," the journalist concluded that they made Rome seem "quite like home" to the young artist.[35] Ream's enactment of youthful innocence and her domestication of the Roman environment were obviously quite charming to her admirers. This careful pose formed an imaginative screen behind which Ream could conceal her professional ambition.

The young sculptor regularly visited with Hosmer, who was seventeen years her senior. It was clear that Ream was quite curious about this successful artist's life and surveyed Hosmer's appearance and abode with the same ferocity with which others regularly examined her. When invited to tea with her parents, she assessed Hosmer's dress: "She wore a black skirt [with] white tucked thick waist, locket [with] black velvet ribbon[,] and blue ribbon in her hair, diamond ring." Ream, no doubt, sought to emulate Hosmer's public persona and professional success. After visiting Hosmer's home, she itemized the furnishings as if producing an inventory: "No carpet on saloon [floor]. Furniture covered for summer. Empty jardinières, rich lamps. Two book cases, small fireplace, globe lamps, copy of 'Aurora' [*Aurora Leigh,* by Elizabeth Barrett Browning], crimson and gilt chairs, 3 lounging sofas, one little bouquet not fresh. Carpet on dining room floor, fine sideboards, plates hung down the walls, antique ware. . . . In the hall, many plaster sketches by [Hosmer's teacher, the neoclassical sculptor John] Gibson."[36] Ream looked at Hosmer with a critical eye, but seemed suitably impressed with her dress, noting the diamond ring, and her furnishings, with the exception of the "little bouquet, not fresh." Throughout her stay in Rome, she maintained a cordial relationship with Hosmer, who seemed to have taken the young artist under her wing.

While working on the Lincoln sculpture, Ream sought the counsel of many other American sculptors in Rome, including Joseph Mozier, Randolph Rogers, William Henry Rinehart, Chauncey Ives, and Story.[37] Rumors immediately surfaced that it was the Italian workmen in her studio, not the artist, who were responsible for the success of the statue. Even Whitney, after seeing the plaster sculpture in Ream's studio, considered it "a dreary performance," which, in her opinion, the Italian workmen would need to improve.[38] Of course, almost all American male sculptors used Italian assistants to aid them in sculptural projects. However, whenever a female sculptor did the same, it was not unusual for her artistic authority to be challenged.

There is little doubt that professional jealousy lay at the core of the charges leveled against Ream in Rome, as the Lincoln sculpture was one of the most highly prized commissions of the day. Even the Italian press was interested in her statue. Recall that Roman nationalists looked to the United States—and especially to the leadership of Lincoln—for inspiration. Lincoln was as much a hero in Rome as he was in the United States. Heaping praise upon the young sculptor, an Italian correspondent predicted that her name would always be associated with that of Lincoln and his "great act of abolition."[39]

Ream had a productive year in Rome, completing at least four major works in addition to the Lincoln sculpture and several commissioned portrait busts and medallions. Story helped the young artist select the workmen to put the Lincoln statue into marble. In Rome, she visited the Marmorata marble yard early in the morning and late in the evening, in the rain, "the best time," she explained, "to see the defects and discolorations as they appear much more plainly when the marble is wet." At Carrara, where she ultimately purchased the marble for the Lincoln sculpture, she sought the advice of expert Italian sculptors and carefully noted their selection process in her journals.[40]

When the plaster model of Lincoln was first finished, she held a grand reception in her studio. She "worked hard arranging" the space, she admitted, bedecking it with a large American flag and a photograph of Lincoln surrounded by a cypress wreath.[41] An array of baskets and bouquets of flowers decorated the room; in the corner was "a pile of stones, mossed and ivied over, upon which a pair of ring doves coo[ed]."[42] Many people attended the reception; it was a "fine day," Ream crowed. "Everything went off well."[43]

The studio served as an important means by which the artist presented a respectable form of femininity to the Roman art world. She domesticated the space with flowers, ivy, and cooing doves. At the same time, Ream advertised her nationalism—with the American flag and portrait of Lincoln. Filled with visitors and patrons on a daily basis, her studio became a cosmopolitan cultural center that attracted nearly five hundred guests over the course of the year.[44] Holding Wednesday-evening salons in her studio, Ream entertained her visitors with witty conversation, music (she was said to have a lovely voice and to play several instruments), and her personal beauty. She became known for her exotic dress, often wearing "a blue veil folded like a turban around her head, with the ends hanging loosely behind, from beneath which a few rich brown curls drop[ped] out."[45] Upon visiting the young sculptor, Whitney concurred that the artist was "a little thing, dark complexioned, black eyes, long curls, and somewhat pressing manners, warm in her invitations, urgent. . . . [She wore] a veil turbanwise in her studio." Perhaps anticipating her own crowning ceremonies in Washington, Ream, as a talented and ambitious public woman, emulated the guise of an ancient sibyl often associated with the famous fictional character Corinne, who, after all, had been heralded as the most beautiful and erudite woman in Rome.[46]

With a certain amount of bitterness, Whitney criticized the public careers of artists in Rome—including those of Ream and Hosmer—which focused too much upon spectacle, sales, and the market rather than the rarefied world of high art. She condemned the commercialism she witnessed around her, perhaps signaling envy of her more successful colleagues. "If I should turn my attention to selling with the vigor of some of my brethren here," she noted acidly, "I should have little life left for the study." Unlike Ream's studio, which was filled with visitors on a daily basis, Whitney's new studio in the Piazza di Spagna was a location to which "people ha[d] not yet found their way," she complained in a letter home.[47] Her critique was a bit disingenuous, to be sure. Envy certainly played a role in her remarks. Moreover, like the sculptors Ames and Stebbins, Whitney had the financial means to ignore market forces. Not all sculptors in Rome were so lucky. Ream and Hosmer depended upon sales for their livelihood and understood how to market themselves in international circles.

Ream's most notorious acquaintance in Rome was Cardinal Giacomo Antonelli, the secretary of state and right-hand man to Pope Pius IX. She met Antonelli in the summer of 1870. Befriending the influential papal emissary was anathema to the politically engaged Whitney, who had publicly shown her *Roma* the previous summer—with its denunciatory image of Antonelli clearly apparent on the figure's hem (fig. 58). Known as quite the lady's man, Antonelli had been appointed cardinal without being ordained a priest and was often seen around town accompanied by different women.[48] "Cardinal Antonelli paid a long visit to my studio of two hours," Ream noted. "His carriage and servants in gorgeous livery attracted the attention of all persons around the studio. He drank wine with us. He wore a short suit, stockings and knee buckles—Red watered silk Cardinal's cap on his head. . . . Fine eyes—hair tinged with gray." Ream was certainly taken with the pomp, splendor, and power of the papacy. "[Antonelli] seems like a man who is conscious of his great abilities—the first intellect of the Roman Church and government. Rich and powerful, with artistic taste and superior intelligence, he sees from his window at the Vatican a world which he sways. He looks upon the map and sees no country which does not feel the influence and power of the church of Rome."[49] The young artist was unaware of the political peril that the papacy was facing. Antonelli was at the end of his powerful career; it would be a few short months before the Papal States became Italian and Antonelli saw only the walled Vatican as his world of influence.

The cardinal invited Ream to his offices in the Quirinale Palace on three separate occasions. Most likely to impress the young sculptor, he shared with her the details of a recent assassination attempt on his life. "[He] live[s] in fear and splendor always," was her response.[50] Overwhelmed with the vast wealth before her, she detailed the treasures that she observed and, no doubt, coveted: "Long robe, embroidered chairs and sofas by his sister, crystal case, vases, . . . copies of Raphael, Chinese ivory carvings . . . Etruscan ornaments, antique rings and gems, mosaic tablets . . . collections of marbles, of gems of turquois, emeralds."[51]

Ream identified with the old Rome, the colonial Rome under the rule of Antonelli and Pope Pius. In fact, when photographed by Della Valle, she wore the dress and hairpiece of a *contadina,* a picturesque peasant girl who embodied the Italy of touristic spectacle (fig. 90). In a painting by the American expatriate George Peter Alexander Healy, most likely adapted from the photograph by Della Valle, Ream dons a necklace encrusted with a large cameo of Christ, one of several such gifts from Antonelli (fig. 91).[52] Her hand rests on a lute to signify her musical skills; she looks directly out at the viewer, with large brown eyes and dark ringlets encircling her face. Ream had little interest in or knowledge of the "Roman question" at this crucial time in history. Like most American tourists, she remained enthralled with Italy's timeless arcadian past, rather than cognizant of the historical changes about to take place. Although she resided in the city on September 20, 1870, when Rome was won by the nationalists, nowhere in her writings does she mention this momentous event. Her mission in Rome consisted solely of advancing her professional career in any way she could.

## *The Statue of Lincoln in the Capitol Rotunda*

In October of 1870 Ream returned to Washington, where she continued to enact an exoticism learned in Rome. "She wears in her studio a short dress, a blue blouse, and a small turban on her head, not unlike in the portrait of Raphael," one journalist reported.[53] The public lavished as much attention upon this colorful young sculptor as it

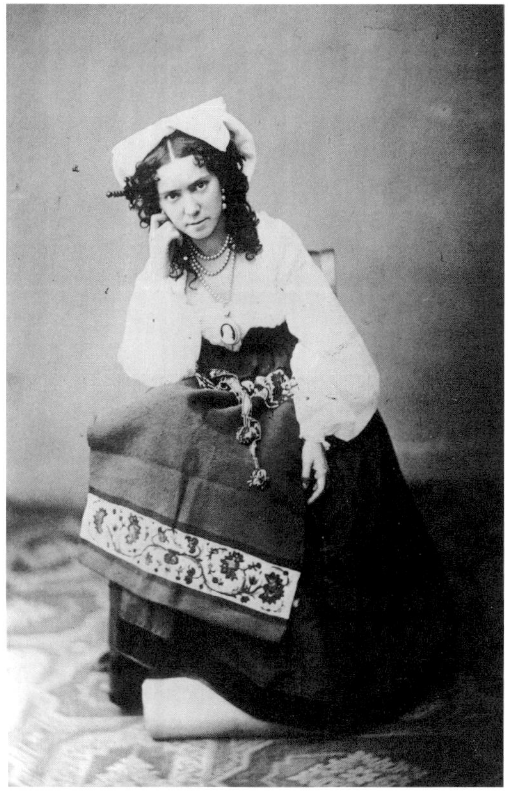

FIG. 90
Della Valle, Vinnie Ream as a *contadina* (Italian peasant girl), ca. 1869–70, photograph, 8 × 10 in. Library of Congress Prints and Photographs Division, Washington, D.C.

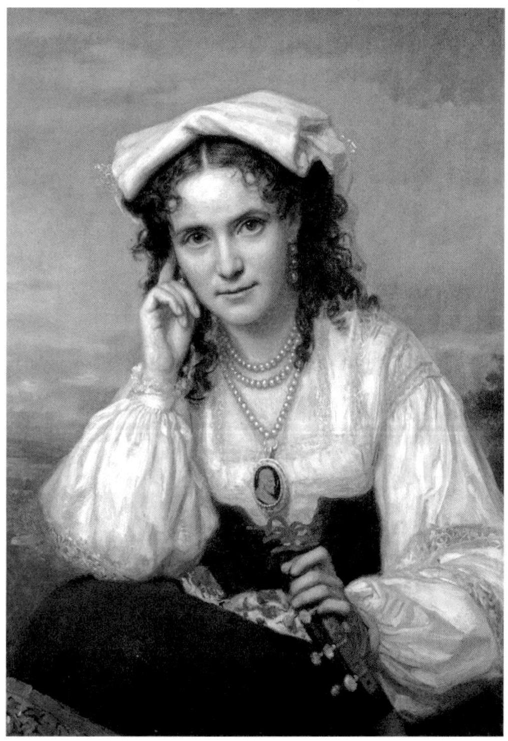

FIG. 91
George Peter Alexander Healy, *Vinnie Ream,* ca. 1870, oil on canvas, 31 3/8 × 22 1/2 in. Smithsonian American Art Museum, Washington, D.C., gift of Brigadier General Richard L. Hoxie.

did upon the Lincoln statue. Ream envisioned the standing figure of Lincoln dressed in contemporary garb, his frock coat open to reveal a buttoned waistcoat, neatly pressed shirt, and carefully tied cravat.[54] In the finished work, the president stands in *contrapposto*, with his right leg forward, slightly inching off the pedestal. His chiseled facial features, taken directly from a clay bust that Ream had earlier modeled from life, bear the marks of consternation, especially in the darkly shadowed deep-set eyes and somber expression. The realistic details of his appearance are counterbalanced by a cloak-like drapery that embraces the figure. The cloak wraps around Lincoln's right arm and shoulder, referencing the costume and stance of a Roman orator. The president's other hand holds a voluminous fold of drapery that gracefully cascades down his left leg. As a formal element, the drapery lends bulk to Lincoln's tall and bony frame and energizes the stately composition. Read symbolically, it represents "the protecting mantle of the Government," according to art critic Minor Kellogg. Through the conjoining of neoclassical drapery and modern garb, Ream produced a striking image of Lincoln as both historical figure and benevolent personification of the newly united nation.[55]

In this remarkable work, the image of the president stands as a testament to the progressive goals of Reconstruction, the building of a renewed American society that welcomed the free and equal participation of all citizens. The president's head inclines slightly downward as he extends a scroll-like document—the Emancipation Proclamation—to the implied viewers before him. Ream surely knew of Henry Kirke Brown's *Lincoln Monument*, which had recently been dedicated in Prospect Park, Brooklyn, in October 1869 (fig. 92). In that sculpture, Brown had represented the historical process of abolition with a simple sculptural device—the scroll in Lincoln's left hand that carries the words "shall be forever free." In a model for an "Emancipation Monument" (perhaps the sculptural failure disparaged in the *Washington Evening Star* article quoted above),[56] Brown intended to add a kneeling black man—bare chested, wearing trousers, boots, and a kepi cap marking him as a Union soldier (fig. 93). With his military garb—conspicuously lacking the accoutrements of enslavement—this young man appears already freed; however, his diminutive stature compared to Lincoln's towering presence reinstates racial hierarchies. Brown never put this model into permanent form.[57]

Ream offered an inventive alternative to Brown's emancipation motif. Her *Lincoln* stands with downward gaze, handing the Proclamation directly to an implied viewer, whom Kellogg had identified as "the defenseless beings who are to receive the inestimable boon of freedom."[58] However, the statue's location in the heart of the Capitol invited all Americans—white and black, male and female—to stand before it. Its open composition—with active hand gesture and attentive gaze—urged every viewer to assume the position of a "defenseless" slave about to be freed. This image of Lincoln encouraged American citizens to embrace a new progressive consciousness that was necessary to the political aims of Reconstruction. The sculpture embodied a daring call for egalitarianism, important to women and blacks alike in this postwar moment.

Ream's sculpture placed at the center of the national stage an affirmation of universal suffrage and citizenship at a critical moment in the history of the civil rights and women's rights

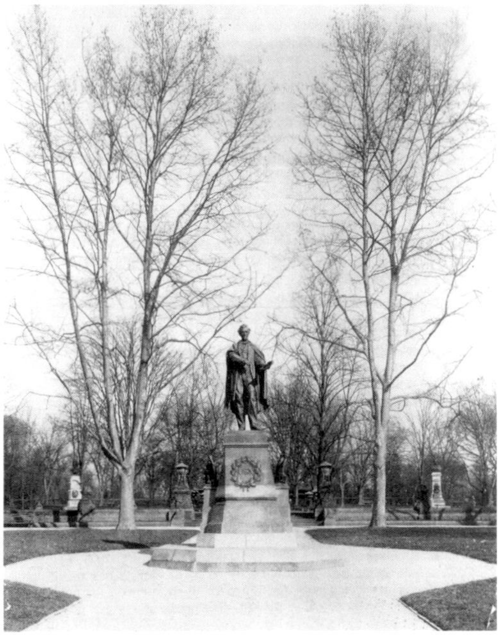

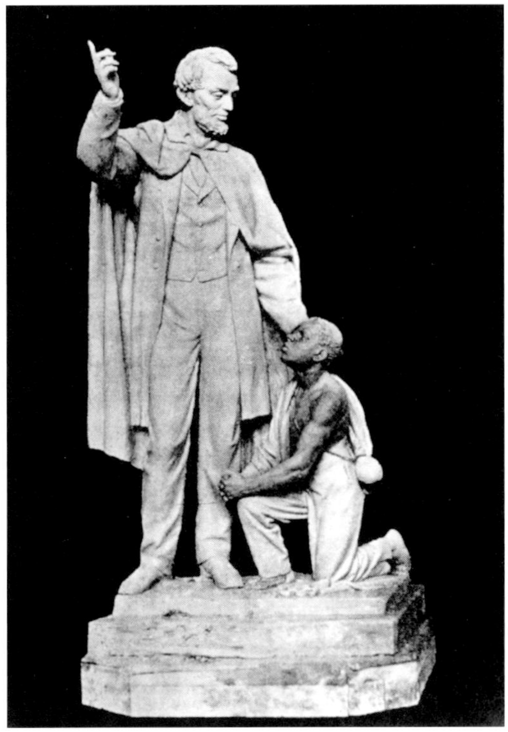

FIG. 92
Henry Kirke Brown, *Lincoln Monument,* 1869, bronze. Prospect Park, Brooklyn, N.Y. Library of Congress Prints and Photographs Division, Washington, D.C.

FIG. 93
Henry Kirke Brown, *Model for a Monument to Lincoln,* 1866–67, plaster, now lost. Library of Congress Prints and Photographs Division, Washington, D.C.

movements. She imagined a Lincoln who would extend the promise of citizenship to all, a goal that many women abolitionists had carried with them throughout the war years. With her sculpture, Ream participated in a public debate about nationalism, equal rights, and the new multiracial American society. In so doing, she attracted the attention of women's rights activists who linked the public sphere of monument making to the contemporary battle for women's suffrage.

## *Vinnie Ream and the Woman Question*

When the life-size sculpture of Lincoln was unveiled in the Capitol Rotunda, the obsessive public interest in the young artist dominated the popular press and eclipsed the potentially radical reading of her sculpture—its endorsement of equal rights for all Americans. *Woodhull and Claflin's Weekly* boldly stated: "The woman is of as much . . . perhaps of more importance than her works."[59]

Hiram Powers weighed in from Florence, attacking the young female sculptor rather than the sculpture: He was "disgust[ed]" with the statue "of our glorious old Lincoln . . . [by] a female lobby member, who has no more talent for art than the carver of weeping-willow tombstones."[60] In his remarks, Powers had reduced Ream to an anonymous, naïve, and most certainly unimportant carver who made her way in the world by carving the weeping-willow emblem on gravestones. A supporter of the young artist came immediately to her defense: "What does Mr. Powers mean by 'lobby member'? This phrase was evidently used as a term of detraction as applied to Miss Ream. . . . He too had a studio in the Capitol . . . and it was there that he first drew attention to his abilities and received assistance from representatives which carried him to Italy to study his profession. . . . [Powers] is disgusted with the success of the statue of our glorious old Lincoln, which he has never seen."[61]

Powers's early career was remarkably similar to Ream's: in 1834, his patron Nicholas Longworth had funded his move from Cincinnati to Washington, D.C., where he modeled the bust of President Andrew Jackson. Shortly thereafter he expatriated to Florence to advance his professional career. Ironically, Powers criticized Ream as a female "lobby member" for doing exactly as he had done many years earlier.[62] As a so-called public woman, she risked tainting her personal reputation by pursuing these professional activities. Indeed, Ream's participation in the public realm of monument making on an equal footing with her male colleagues provoked "disgust" in Powers and other champions of separate spheres. In response to Powers's diatribe, the *Revolution* wrote pointedly: "All we ask is that as sharp a line of demarcation be drawn between woman and artist, as between man and artist. Let the work receive all merited abuse; but spare the woman. . . . What she is as a woman is nobody's business; what she has done as an artist is the business of all the world."[63]

Supporters of Sarah Fisher Ames continued their assault on Ream. Grace Greenwood openly challenged Ream's successes by reporting that workmen in Rome had executed the *Lincoln* sculpture.[64] Not surprisingly, Hosmer rushed to the young sculptor's aid, writing from Rome: "I am remarkably familiar with that form of accusation, having heard it myself for years. . . . Vinnie Ream is as much entitled to the credit of her work as any artist I know."[65] The *Revolution* lauded Hosmer's letter, "We, for our part, consider [it] unexceptionable and admirably well timed, and are rejoiced at the generosity with which a distinguished woman has come to the defense of a sister artist."[66]

Mary Clemmer Ames, a champion of woman suffrage and a supporter of the newly emancipated black population, was the highest-paid newspaperwoman of her day. She first defended Ream in her struggle for equal treatment with men and then reneged upon these initial comments two years later, returning to the comfort of separate spheres. "The world never forgets the woman in the artist," she wrote in 1871. "It is slower to forgive her errors (even of judgment) as a woman, than it is to acknowledge her triumph as a genius." Clemmer Ames conceded that Ream could be "a little theatrical, and not at all to your taste." Nevertheless, she was quick to defend the young sculptor: "[H]er manners, whatever they may be, give you no just excuse for berating her work."[67]

A few years later, Clemmer Ames criticized women who dared invade the halls of Congress, maintaining that the true woman belongs at home. At this point, she probably saw Ream as an interloper into the chaotic world of politics. Positing Ream as a lobbyist who in no way embodied true womanhood with her public performances of celebrity, she disparaged her sculpture as "unilluminated by one mental or spiritual characteristic." By contrast, Sarah Fisher Ames's bust of the president, she argued, "transfixed more of the soul of Lincoln in the brow and eyes of his face than Miss Ream has in all the weary outline of her many feet of marble."[68]

Ream was caught in the crossfire between those suffragists who subscribed to the tenets of true womanhood and those in favor of equal rights. Supporters of equal rights saw Ream's successes as a sculptor of public monuments in a different light than, say, Greenwood and Clemmer Ames. Feminist leaders, including Victoria Woodhull, Pauline Wright Davis, Elizabeth Cady Stanton, and Susan B. Anthony followed her career with great interest.[69] Hoping to enlist her as an ally in their cause, they saw in Ream a skilled and independent woman whose autonomy, creativity, and professional competence were characteristics to be emulated. She represented "a national recognition of American womanhood" at a decisive moment in the suffrage battle.

The sculpture of Lincoln in the Capitol Rotunda took on a fresh significance for supporters of equal rights. Anthony, Stanton, and others had organized the Equal Rights Association in 1866, which uncompromisingly supported the civil rights of women and African-Americans during Reconstruction. After Congress proposed the Fifteenth Amendment for ratification in 1869, they disbanded the association and founded the National Women's Suffrage Association (NWSA). Seeking a constitutional amendment to guarantee woman's suffrage, they labored under the motto "Men their rights and nothing more; women their rights and nothing less." The American Women's Suffrage Association (AWSA), founded by Lucy Stone, supported the Fifteenth Amendment and sought woman's suffrage on a state-by-state basis.[70]

In 1870, Woodhull moved to Washington to lobby on behalf of women's suffrage. A member of the radical Equal Rights Party, she sought to educate the nation on the merits of universal rights.[71] In January 1871, the same month that Ream's *Lincoln* was installed in the Capitol, Woodhull spoke before the House Judiciary Committee and argued that a sixteenth amendment to the Constitution was not necessary for women to gain the vote. She reminded committee members that the recently ratified Fifteenth Amendment had already guaranteed "that the right of citizens of the United States to vote shall not be denied." At stake was the definition of the word "citizen." Woodhull argued that women were, in fact, citizens because they paid taxes, were charged with raising moral citizens, and contributed in innumerable ways to the welfare of the republic. She offered an eloquent defense of universal citizenship. In the end, the Judiciary Committee did not adopt her position, but leaders of the suffrage movement roundly praised her as an idealist and visionary.[72]

While in Washington, Woodhull was certainly aware of the installation of Ream's *Lincoln* and the ceremonies that took place at its unveiling. She was also cognizant of the criticisms hurled at Ream, slander that Woodhull herself bore regularly as a public figure. Not surprisingly, the *Woodhull and Claflin's Weekly* offered the young sculptor support in its "Art and Drama" column, arguing that "in the face of competition and detraction," Ream had "won an honorable position and it is to the credit of her Congressional friends that they should have supported her against much invidious and ungenerous opposition."[73] Representing a new kind of public woman, Ream and Woodhull had much in common. Both were raised in the American heartland (Wisconsin and Ohio, respectively), with modest economic means. Financial necessity determined both women's participation in the public sphere. At stake were class and social position; both had been savaged by feminists who policed the borders of bourgeois womanhood.

In the end, Ream could not bring herself to support the suffrage movement publicly. Stung by the criticism of women like Swisshelm and Clemmer Ames, and fearful of losing commissions if she appeared too political, she remained neutral in the suffrage debates. In January 1869, when the National Woman's Suffrage Convention was held in Washington, Stanton visited Ream's studio and asked for her signature on a petition. With this passionate (and somewhat disingenuous) statement, Ream refused: "Mrs. Stanton, no help has any woman given me here. From Grace Greenwood to Mrs. Swisshelm, they have all sought to strike me down. . . . Mrs. Clemmer Ames—All of them find no larger occupation than attacking a poor little girl, and their venom . . . has extended to personally canvassing against me."[74]

Nonetheless, Ream followed the suffrage debates and contributed in important, albeit indirect, ways to its mission. Her standing *Lincoln* in the U.S. Capitol was a public testament to the battle for equal rights, as the sculpture invited all American viewers to participate in the aim of Reconstruction. There is evidence that she modeled medallion portraits of the suffrage leaders Davis (an artist in her own right) and Anthony; she considered producing a portrait bust of Douglass.[75] Although working at a distance from the women's rights movements, she stood as a new model of the independent, successful woman—an equal to any man in the public sphere.

## *A Woman Cannot Model the Figure of a Man*

Anne Whitney, an ardent suffragist, followed the events of the women's rights movement. In Rome, she read the *Revolution* and its coverage of Ream and her Lincoln statue.[76] In 1872, she met and became an admirer of Lucy Stone, the founder of the AWSA. Advocating a radical feminist position, Whitney claimed, "What a shame that such noble women [as Stone] should [go] every year as humble petitioners before the conglomerate of self will[ed] and ignorant blockheadedness, asking them for what they should have no right either to give or refuse!"[77] Among the various tactics that women were employing to gain the vote was that of the AWSA, which petitioned individual state assemblies in hopes of passing suffrage legislation. Whitney believed that universal citizenship was an inalienable right for which one ought not need to petition. Nevertheless, the 1870s witnessed suffrage battles in the courts, in state legislatures, and at the polls. In 1871, Victoria Woodhull dared to cast her ballot in New York City. Susan B. Anthony and fifteen others voted in Rochester in 1872, only to be later arrested.[78]

The 1872 election signaled the defeat of the Radical Republicans in national politics and foreshadowed the death knell of the Reconstruction effort in 1877. Frederick Douglass rejected his nomination as the vice-presidential candidate on the Equal Rights Party ticket with Woodhull and supported, as did the African-American press, the reelection of President Ulysses S. Grant. Leadership in both the NWSA and the AWSA increasingly endorsed a conservative position—maintaining the ideology of gender difference within the separate spheres while privileging the interests of white middle-class women.[79]

Whitney competed for and won important artistic commissions during these years. In June of 1873, the Commonwealth of Massachusetts selected Whitney to model the patriot Sam Adams for the first national "Gallery of Art," to be housed in the old Hall of Representatives in the U.S. Capitol. Whitney began work on her clay model of *Samuel Adams* for this new statuary hall two years after Ream's *Lincoln* was installed in the Capitol Rotunda (fig. 94).[80] The *Commonwealth,* a progressive newspaper, was proud that their "native daughter" would represent the state in the nation's Capitol. The winning model, the paper declared, "represents a man of dignity and character, with a fine bearing and a good face; yet it will give no idea of Miss Whitney's genius." Proof of such genius rested upon the expressive power of her other sculptures, most notably, *Ethiopia Shall Soon Stretch Out Her Hands to God, or Africa* (1862–64; fig. 68) and *Toussaint L'Ouverture in Prison* (1869–71; fig. 60). Based on her previous successes, the paper hoped that Whitney would secure the commission for a national emancipation monument, then under consideration in Washington circles.[81]

In her model for the *Samuel Adams* sculpture, she depicted the patriot's involvement in the "Boston Massacre," a street fight that broke out between several dozen residents of the city and a squad of British soldiers. Five men died and six were wounded in the melee. On the following day, Adams demanded that the royal governor, Thomas Hutchinson, expel the British troops from the city. Whitney carved Adams's famous words upon the sculpture's pedestal: "Night is approaching; an immediate answer is expected. Both regiments or none! March 6, 1770."[82]

In comparison with Ream's *Lincoln,* the *Samuel Adams* is carved in a more pronounced realist style. Whitney depicted a tall defiant Adams, staring straight ahead with arms folded across his chest and holding a petition prepared by the aggrieved citizens of Boston. In keeping with popular taste, she modeled a highly detailed rendering of the patriot in contemporary costume, every button and wrinkle carefully articulated. Nods to neoclassicism, such as the drapery that enshrouds the figure of *Lincoln,* were kept to a minimum. Instead, only a hint of drapery floats gracefully behind the figure of *Adams,* serving to conceal the support for the marble statue.[83]

Before the artist returned to Italy to have the *Adams* sculpture carved in marble, a competition for the *Charles Sumner Memorial* was announced in Boston. Sumner had died in March of 1874, and supporters had set up a fund for a memorial to this senator who had accomplished so much for the antislavery movement through legislation. By the 1870s, Whitney had become one of the leading sculptors in Boston and was invited to submit an entry for this blind competition. She completed her plaster model in March of 1875 (fig. 95). In total, twenty-six models were submitted to the competition, including those by Harriet Hosmer and Emma Stebbins. Whitney was selected as one of the three finalists; Thomas Ball and Martin Milmore were also under consideration.[84] In her winning submission, Whitney represents Sumner in a casual manner, seated with one foot extended beyond the pedestal.

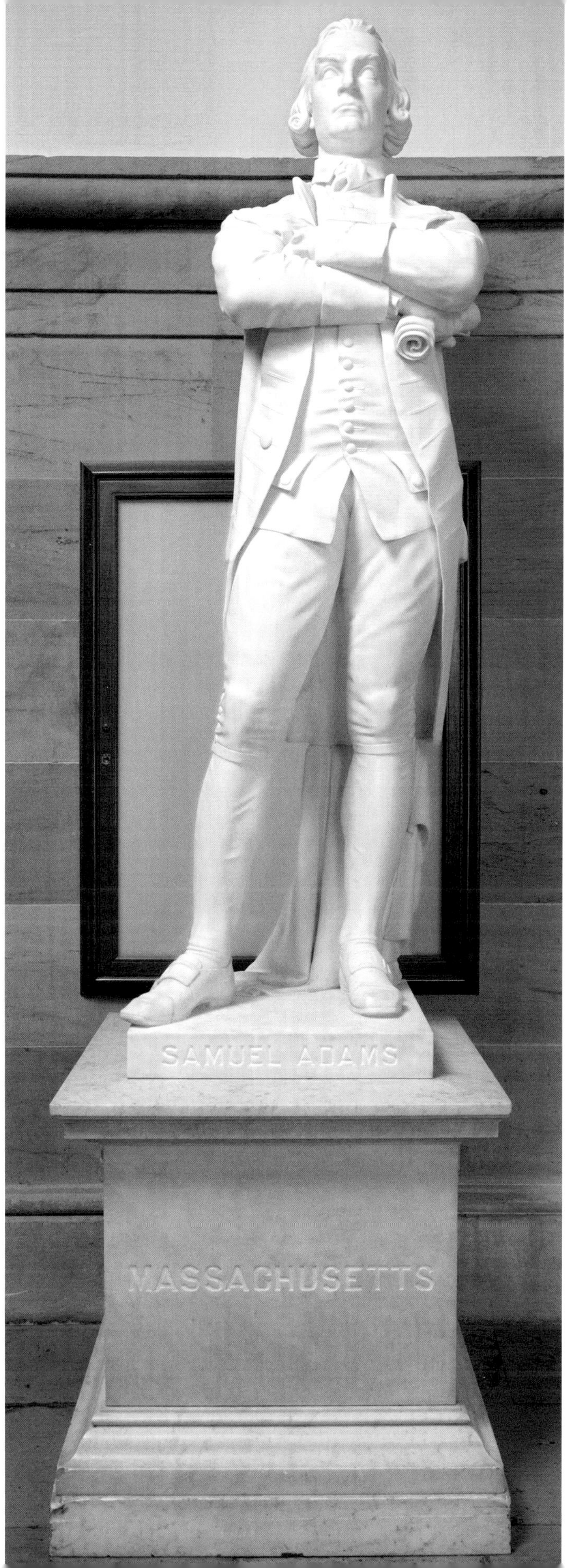


FIG. 94
Anne Whitney, *Samuel Adams*, 1876, marble, height 7 ft. 8 in. U.S. Capitol.

She presents a carefully rendered image of the younger Sumner listening attentively to speeches within the Senate chamber, alert to the social injustices against which he fought. No idealization is apparent in the sculpture. In fact, Sumner appears as most remembered him: intense in his political commitments, healthy and vigorous before his dreadful caning on the Senate floor in 1856, and a bit disheveled with his wrinkled and only partially buttoned waistcoat.

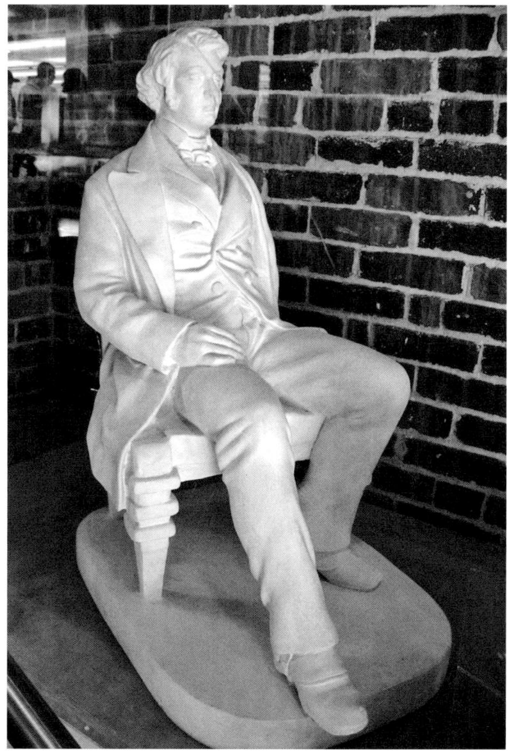

FIG. 95
Anne Whitney, *Charles Sumner Memorial,* 1876, plaster model. Watertown Free Public Library, Watertown, Mass.

In April 1875, Whitney and Adeline Manning traveled to Europe. Manning settled in France, while Whitney shuttled between Ball's studio in Florence, where she worked on the *Adams* sculpture, and studios in Écouen and Paris, where she created some exciting new sculptural pieces. Writing home to her sister, the sculptor reported: "*Sam Adams* is in a little building (apart from the studio) where marble is blocked out. . . . I much prefer it should not be generally known to be there [because] the sharp-nosed correspondents . . . will be informing you before long that I am a pupil of T[homas] B[all]."[85] Whitney was referring to the accusations regularly hurled at women sculptors—in particular, Ream and Hosmer—that others were responsible for executing their marble sculptures. Ironically, Whitney had participated in this dangerous discourse a few years earlier when she impugned Ream for using Italian workmen to refashion the *Lincoln* statue in Rome.

Although indebted to the Italian experience for all that it had taught her, Whitney appreciated the time she spent in France. Earlier in her career, she had begun experimentation with a more naturalist style, which she most fully articulated in the figure of *Toussaint L'Ouverture,* produced in Rome between 1869 and 1871. Pioneered first by Henry Kirke Brown and John Quincy Adams Ward, this realist tendency in American sculpture vied with the neoclassical conventions employed by expatriate artists in Italy. A younger generation of American sculptors based in Paris and trained at the École des Beaux-Arts in the 1870s adopted an expressive naturalism that became a hallmark of the Gilded Age monument tradition.

At the center of this new realist style, Paris had now preempted Rome as Whitney's most favored location. She viewed contemporary sculpture at the 1875 Salon and was especially taken with Emmanuel Frémiet's monumental *Joan of Arc,* which had recently been installed in the Place des Pyramides. Frémiet was best known

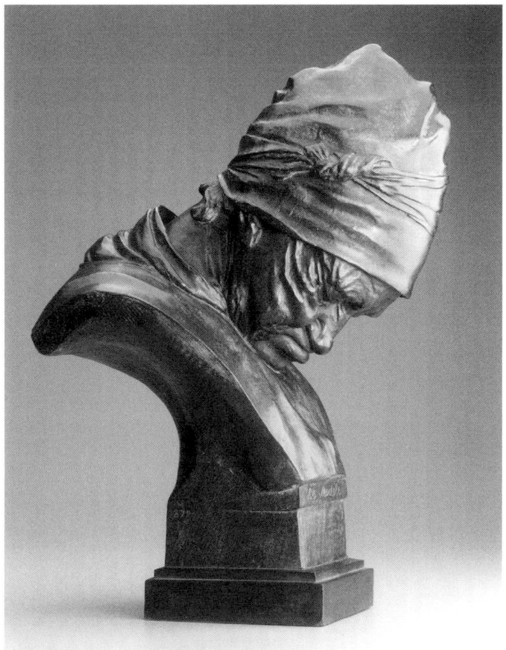

FIG. 96
Anne Whitney, *Le Modèle,* 1875, bronze, 18 1/2 × 9 3/4 × 12 1/2 in. Museum of Fine Arts, Boston, gift of Mrs. Maria Weston Chapman, 85.423. Photograph © 2014 Museum of Fine Arts, Boston.

as an *animalier* and was a pioneer in the field of life-size animal sculpture.[86] Whitney was probably attracted to the monument for several reasons. She certainly supported the valorization of historic women like Joan of Arc, the seventeen-year-old who had fought to liberate Paris from English invaders. Moreover, she appreciated the exacting naturalism, exquisite detail, and skillful modeling apparent in the horse's anatomy.

Armed with a new sculptural vocabulary, Whitney adopted a manner of working that allowed a more dynamic surface expression and an adherence to naturalist detail. In *Le Modèle* of 1875, for example, she modeled the bust of a French peasant woman in clay, deliberately exaggerating the wrinkles of her worn face. Cast in bronze, the agitated surface created a dynamic play of light and shadow while capturing the likeness of this popular model from Écouen (fig. 96). Inspired by the laboring peasants of Jean-François Millet, she created an image of a weary worker. Such imagery would later reach a wide audience in both the United States and Europe in works by Jules Dalou and Constantin Meunier. In terms of both subject matter and style, this piece represented a new sculptural experiment for Whitney. Before sailing home in March of 1876, she wrote to Manning: "If I were to make it [the *Adams* sculpture] over, I should make it better, for I have grown, I am sure, since I came to Paris."[87]

Whitney returned to Florence in December of 1875. Upon her arrival, she learned that she had lost the commission for the *Sumner Memorial.* Originally awarded to Whitney, it was instead given to her colleague Thomas Ball. She was furious over this turn of events. In response to the injustice, Sarah Whitney wrote to her sister in Florence, "Women are so earnestly fighting the universal suffrage battle [in Boston] just now that they haven't time to attend to the details of particular grievances" (like the *Sumner Memorial* debacle).[88] Suspicion hung over the decision to select Ball. From Boston, Whitney's well-connected brother Edward had written that the twelve commissioners believed her work to be the best submitted. In correspondence with the artist, Charles Slack, secretary of the Sumner Monument Committee and close friend of her brother's, seemed to admit this. He explained that her sculpture had "won universal encomium for its free, easy, open and 'breezy' pose so characteristic of Mr. Sumner in his healthier days. . . . Then came the question of experience, familiarity with the male figure, etc. On this basis the selection

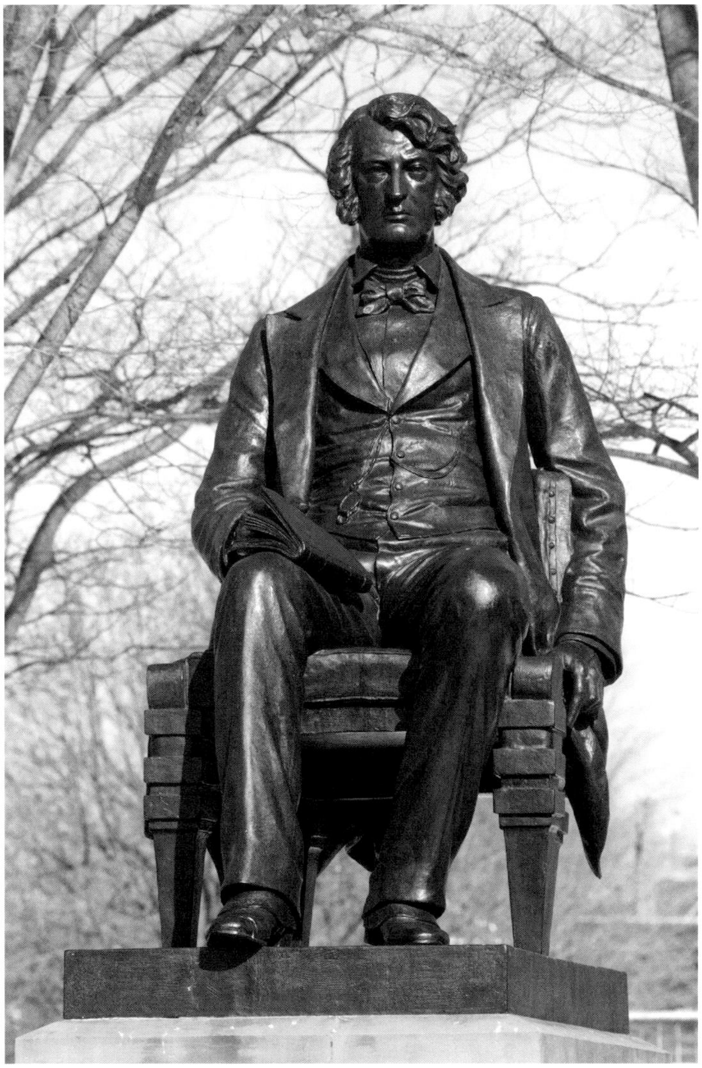

FIG. 97
Anne Whitney, *Charles Sumner Memorial,* 1900, bronze. Cambridge Commons, Cambridge, Mass.

fell." The commission had initially awarded Whitney a monetary prize of $500. But after much debate, some of the judges felt that it would be improper for a woman to sculpt the figure of a man; and they rescinded the award. Slack concluded his letter by declaring, "You must judge [from these events] whether the *woman question* came in or not. I think it did. . . . I am sorry you did not get the commission."[89]

The reasoning of the commission could not have been more flimsy. Whitney had spent several years in Boston and in Rome perfecting her knowledge of the male nude and honing her skills as a sculptor. Moreover, she had received critical praise for her *Samuel Adams,* which would soon stand proudly in the nation's Capitol. When Slack highlighted the "woman question," the issue of equal rights spilled over into the public sphere of monument making once again. This was particularly galling to Whitney as a longtime supporter of woman's suffrage. "Believe me," she wrote, "wherever I go, I uphold [the suffrage] standard."[90] To be sure, Whitney saw this event in broader terms than simply her own professional loss. The Sumner debacle represented another arena in which the political struggle for equality was being fought. To her credit, she held no animosity toward her friend and colleague Ball. However, if the motive for choosing Ball's model had been prejudice against women, "it becomes my duty," she wrote, "not to let it pass without protest. . . . It is a matter involving a far wider question than just whether I shall make the statue or not. It is a question of whether Boston is to be ruled by two or three bigoted men in affairs of this kind."[91] In the end, she was allowed to keep the $500 prize if the Sumner model remained in the possession of the committee. Not until 1900 would she see the erection of her *Sumner Memorial* on the Cambridge (Massachusetts) Common (fig. 97).

In the meantime, Whitney's *Samuel Adams* was exhibited at the Boston Athenaeum before proceeding in July to its permanent home in Washington, D.C. The sculpture was well received in Boston. A writer from the *Commonwealth* quipped, "Those who have said 'a woman [cannot] model that figure of a man' may well review their dictum."[92] As only the second full-size sculpture produced by a woman for the Capitol, *Samuel Adams* was praised at the official unveiling ceremonies, which took place on December 19, 1876.[93] Throughout her life, Whitney continued to fight for equal rights, even as the political tide turned away from such progressive positions.

# *Postscript*

As interest in the equal rights struggle waned and the ideology of separate spheres became more pronounced in the last quarter of the nineteenth century, women's access to the public sphere of monument making changed dramatically. In fact, Vinnie Ream's career offered a stunning parallel to the fate of the women's rights movement, which fractured after the passage of the Fifteenth Amendment, in 1870. Ream domesticated her public image by transforming herself into a *salonnière* and hosting weekly receptions on Wednesday evenings from nine to midnight in her Washington home. At times, up to twenty or thirty people crowded into her rooms, many from the ranks of politics, the military, and business.[1] Not surprisingly, the American press remained fascinated with her new elegant persona and covered her weekly salons with great interest: "She is famous for her fine attractions, socially as well as artistically, and her reception rooms are crowded weekly by the most refined and elegant people in Washington, who find a double pleasure in her beautiful statuary and her own sweet self. . . . She is a genius worthy of patronage, and deserves it, as she uses her income in the laudable way of supporting her aged father and mother, as well as a widowed sister."[2] Ream adopted the model of feminine professionalism put forward by Elizabeth Ellet in 1859.[3] This model of feminine artistic practice informed the lives of Emma Stebbins, Charlotte Cushman, and Harriet Hosmer in Rome. Like these artists, Ream adopted the characteristics of bourgeois womanhood as a guise that shielded her overtly ambitious professional agenda from criticism.

In the manner of the genteel sculptor Sarah Fisher Ames, Ream maintained her sculptural career while reinventing herself as a proper bourgeois woman. She associated with "refined and elegant people" in her salons. Her feminine "sweetness" infused her "beautiful statuary"; her selfless charity transformed her into a "laudable angel of mercy." This public reception was a far cry from the immodest accusation of "lobbyist" hurled at the artist earlier in her career. After the installation of her Lincoln sculpture in the Rotunda of the Capitol, Ream nurtured her career within a domesticated environment in which the notions of genius and true womanhood cohabitated with ease.

In 1875, Ream received the commission for a Civil War memorial honoring Admiral David Farragut, probably the last public monument produced by a woman sculptor in this generation.[4] Plans for a monument to Farragut, the distinguished Union naval commander during the Civil

War and the first admiral of the U.S. Navy, began immediately after his death in 1870. As is typical of government commissions, the process took several years to finalize, with Ream as an active competitor for the prize. Despite her personal transformation, Ream continued to lobby her supporters relentlessly. She received some friendly ribbing about her ambition from a Kansas patron: "Vinnie, you are, as I have often told you, the biggest and most delightful fraud I ever met. Your methods are a most amusing study, and I have laughed a thousand times to see your ingenious tactics and maneuvers, your wiles and stratagems to achieve your ends."[5] The use of the term "delightful fraud" is telling. Although cultivating a gracious and genteel demeanor, Ream remained a ferocious competitor in the professional arena. She sought petitions from influential friends and gained the support of both General William Tecumseh Sherman and Virginia Farragut, the admiral's widow.[6] With such powerful supporters in her corner, her winning of the commission was almost assured. The government awarded her the contract for the *Farragut Memorial* in January of 1875.[7]

In a publicity photograph, Ream put the finishing touches on the full-scale plaster model (fig. 98). As in her Roman studio, huge American flags adorn her workplace. Perched on scaffolding, Ream is shown hard at work on her monumental sculpture. She retains her exotic persona by means of a colorful scarf worn over her head, like that she had donned in Rome to recall the inspirational figure of Corinne. Moreover, she proudly wears the prized cameo of Christ around her neck, a memento of her engagement with Vatican officials in Rome.

Dwarfed by the more-than-life-size figure of the admiral, Ream aligns herself in this image with Harriet Hosmer, one of the first women sculptors to be awarded a major public commission. Ream had admired Hosmer since her days in Rome and certainly appreciated her kind words during the Lincoln-sculpture controversies. In 1860, the Missouri legislature had commissioned Hosmer to produce a bronze statue of Senator Thomas Hart Benton. Both Wayman Crow and Charlotte Cushman lobbied on her behalf.[8] In an 1862 photograph, she is at work on the monumental figure (fig. 99). Standing atop a tall staircase in her via Margutta 40 studio in Rome, she holds tools in one hand and wears her legendary beret, as well as pantaloons under her skirt. Deeply appreciative of the commission, Hosmer wrote, "I have . . . reason to be grateful to [the Missouri legislature], because I am a woman, and [know] what barriers must in the outset oppose all womanly efforts." She concluded that the "kindness" of the legislature "will now afford me an ample opportunity of proving to what rank I am really entitled as an artist; for this work must be, as we understand the term, a 'manly work.'"[9] In the completed work, the figure of Benton unfurls a scroll-like map and faces westward toward the Pacific shore. This important commission served as a triumph in the face of recent allegations that her *Zenobia* was not her own work (fig. 25). Hosmer cautiously positioned herself within the public sphere of monument making by assuring the Missouri legislature that she was capable of producing a "manly work."

Ream completed the model for the *Farragut Memorial* in 1878. That same year she married Lieutenant Richard Leveridge Hoxie, a career military officer who was well connected in Washington's elite social circles.[10] With characteristic aplomb, she deliberately inserted a reproduction

FIG. 98 *(opposite)* Vinnie Ream at work on the *Farragut Memorial*, ca. 1879, photograph, 8 × 10 in. Library of Congress Prints and Photographs Division, Washington, D.C.

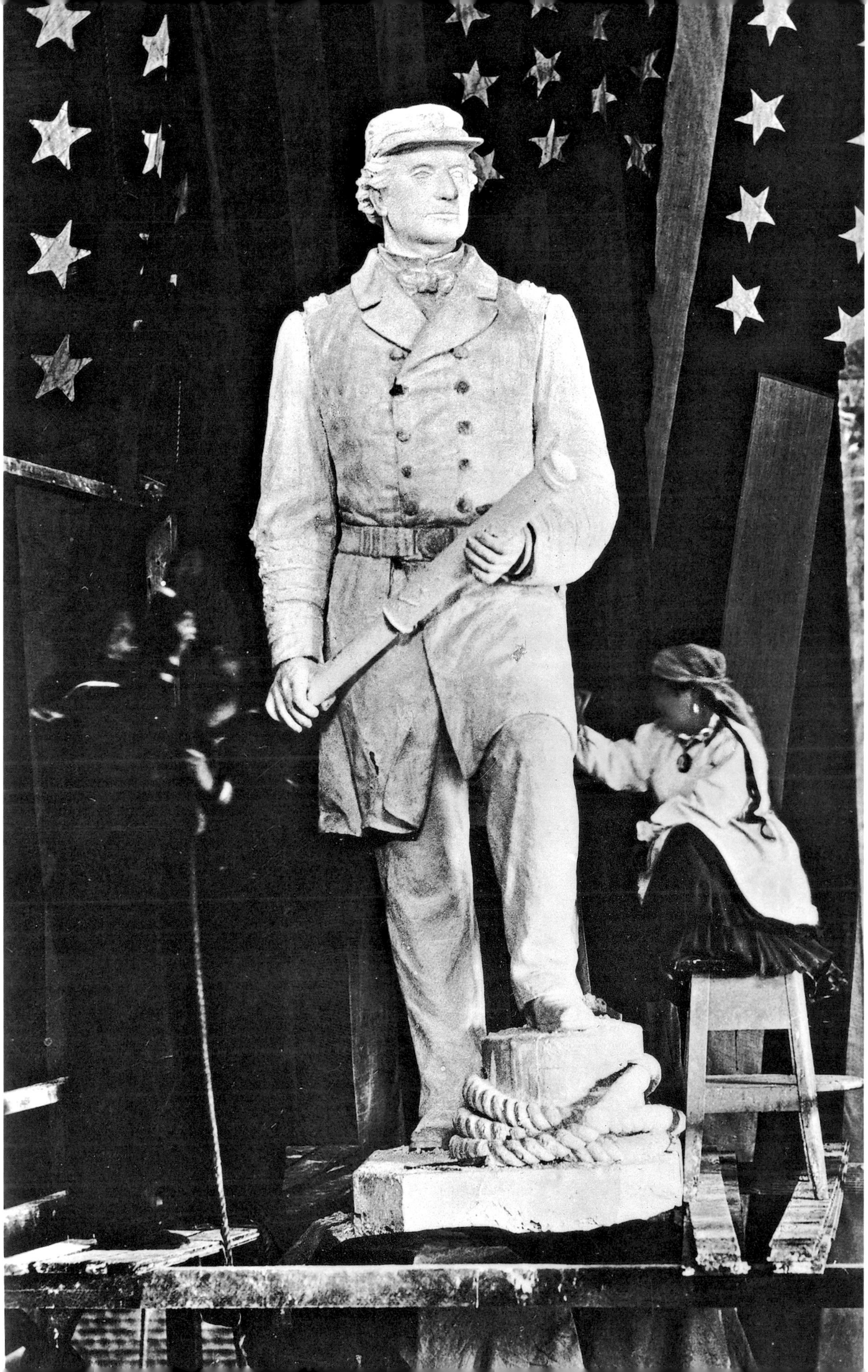

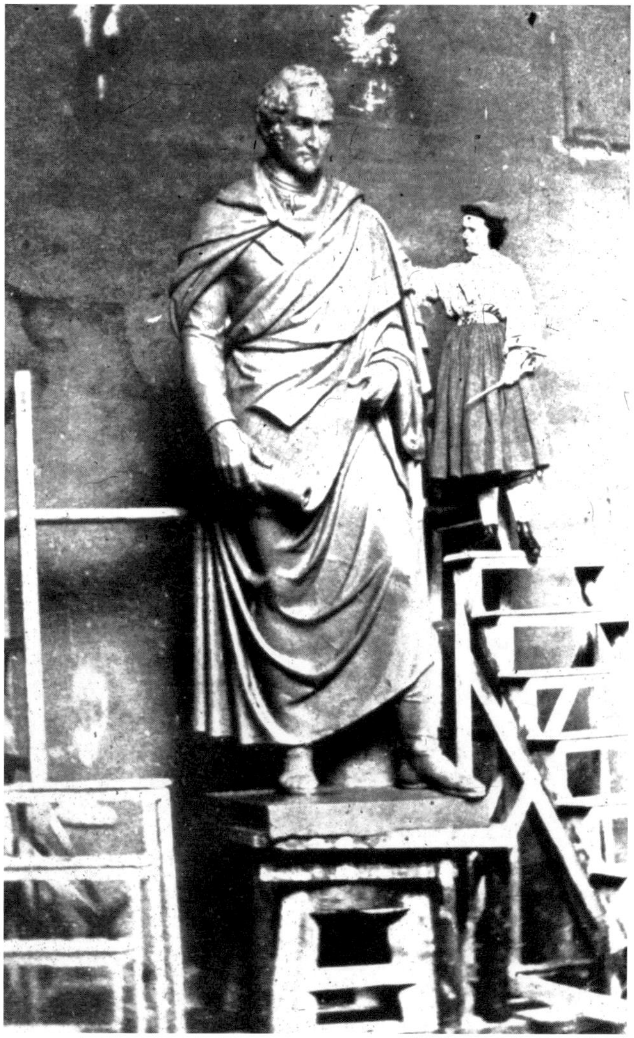

FIG. 99
Harriet Hosmer at work on the clay model of Thomas Hart Benton, ca. 1862. Harriet Goodhue Hosmer Collection, The Schlesinger Library, Radcliffe Institute, Harvard University, A162-72-11.

of the Farragut monument in the background of her marriage portrait, taken in her well-appointed Dupont Circle home (fig. 100). Ream is dressed in her luxurious bridal gown with long train and veil. Gazing out of the picture, she is seated with hand to chin, as if deep in thought. Behind her, an image of the *Farragut Memorial* hovers in space, as if a figment of her rich imagination. For Ream, this photograph asserted that marriage and a professional career were compatible.

Hoxie was initially sympathetic to his wife's career and supported her work on the monumental commission. Installed in Farragut Square in 1880, the sculpture stood in one of the most fashionable districts of the city. The figure faced southeast toward Lafayette Park and the White House, just two blocks away. Alert with a marine glass in hand and his foot resting on a block and tackle, the figure of Farragut stood thirty feet high upon its base. The monument was unveiled

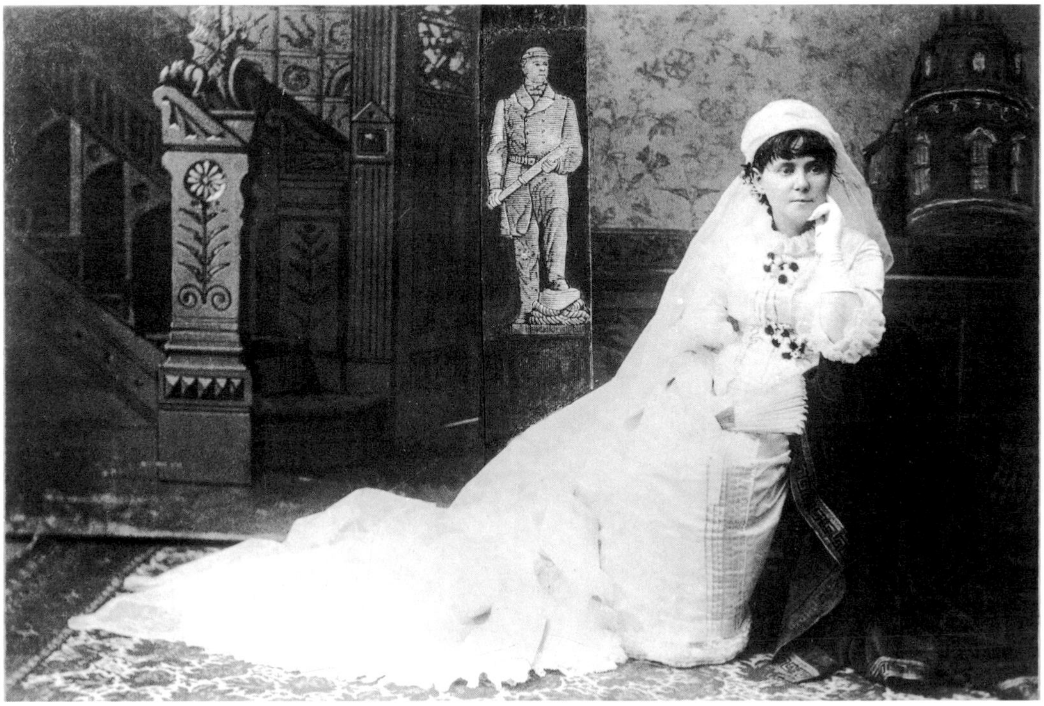

FIG. 100
Vinnie Ream in wedding dress, ca. 1878, photograph. Library of Congress Prints and Photographs Division, Washington, D.C.

on April 25, 1881, in front of a large celebratory crowd.

Ream's career as a sculptor and her identity as wife and (soon-to-be) mother were intermingled as she juggled the demands of professionalism with her personal duties in the domestic sphere. She found it harder and harder to balance these responsibilities, particularly after the birth of her son, in 1884. In fact, her husband and friends, such as General Sherman, encouraged her to devote her life to her family. As it turned out, the Farragut monument was her last major sculptural work.[11]

There is no doubt that Ream's life and career mirrored the political currents of the day. As the country entered an era of "monument mania" in the years following the Civil War, women were nearly eliminated from public memorial projects. Participation in the public arena had been intimately related to the progressive reform politics of the day, and especially to suffrage. With citizenship now limited by law to men, the nation enjoyed a complacency engendered by a growing industrial economy, while eschewing efforts at further social and political change. With her new lifestyle, Ream anticipated the backlash against women who dared succeed in the domain of official memory and public commemoration.

With the close of Reconstruction and the loss of the suffrage battle, the heady moment of women's sculptural practice came to an end. In Rome, the women's community began to disperse. Cushman, diagnosed with breast cancer in 1869, returned to the United States with Stebbins the following year. By 1876, the famous thespian was dead.[12] Hosmer entered into a lifelong partnership with Lady Louisa Ashburton and spent more and more time in England, where she conceived of herself as much an inventor as a sculptor.[13] Edmonia Lewis's career flourished in Rome throughout the 1870s. She eventually made her way to Brook Green, Hammersmith, on the outskirts of London, most likely to join its colony of Catholics.[14] Finally, Whitney, after the *Sumner Memorial* debacle, declined to enter further public competitions, although she maintained a lively sculptural career in Boston.[15]

After the Civil War, a younger generation of women artists had come to prominence, adopting professional strategies appropriate to Gilded Age America. A new artistic movement was taking hold in Paris, to which women traveled in the 1870s and 1880s in search of professional training and personal freedoms, much as they had to Rome a quarter of a century earlier. In December 1875, Grace Greenwood joined Whitney and Adeline Manning in Paris, where she began writing her travel letters for the *New York Times*. Whitney wrote to friends that "opportunities for study [seem] to me more favorable here [in Paris] than elsewhere."[16] Most women artists were now engaged in painting rather than sculpture and studied in the ateliers of academic painters.[17] Within the private world of the studio, middle-class and elite women maintained the moral high ground of separate spheres while engaging in respectable and lucrative professional careers. Not until the Progressive Era would women reemerge in the public arena as muralists and sculptors of the City Beautiful Movement. With their help, the suffrage battle would finally be won in 1920.

# Notes

## Introduction

1. Madame de Staël, *Corinne, or Italy,* trans. Sylvia Raphael (New York: Oxford University Press, 1998), 23, 28.

2. Kirsten Swinth analyzes the development of the professional woman artist in her *Painting Professionals: Women Artists and the Development of Modern American Art, 1870–1930* (Chapel Hill: University of North Carolina Press, 2001).

3. Contemporary women artists are particularly interested in the lives of these nineteenth-century women. See, for example, Patricia Cronin's multimedia installation and publication *Harriet Hosmer: Lost and Found; A Catalogue Raisonné* (Milan: Edizioni Charta, 2009).

4. Henry James, *William Wetmore Story and His Friends: From Letters, Diaries, and Recollections* (New York: Houghton, Mifflin, 1903), 1:257.

5. Jane Mayo Roos, "Another Look at Henry James and the 'White Marmorean Flock,'" *Woman's Art Journal* 4, no. 1 (Spring–Summer 1983): 32.

6. Nancy Elizabeth Proctor, "American Women Sculptors in Rome in the Mid-Nineteenth Century: Feminist and Psychoanalytical Readings of a Displaced Canon" (Ph.D. diss., University of Leeds, 1998). See also Charmaine A. Nelson, *The Color of Stone: Sculpting the Black Female Subject in Nineteenth-Century America* (Minneapolis: University of Minnesota Press, 2007). I would like to thank my friend and editor Judy Sacks, a sheep farmer in Gambier, Ohio, for her observations on James's metaphor. There is no doubt that James witnessed flocks of sheep grazing atop the hills of Rome. The type of sheep that was raised in Rome in the nineteenth century was Merino; the Maremma is an Italian sheepdog. Both terms reference "marmorean" alliteratively.

7. Three previous scholars have also addressed the phenomenon of a women's community in Rome. William H. Gerdts Jr. first brought scholarly attention to this group of American women sculptors in his introduction to the Vassar College Art Gallery exhibition catalogue of 1972, *The White, Marmorean Flock: Nineteenth Century American Women Neoclassical Sculptors.* Two unpublished feminist dissertations take these women artists as their focus. Sarah Foose Parrott, in "Expatriates and Professionals: The Careers in Italy of Nineteenth-Century American Women Writers and Artists" (George Washington University, 1988), follows the lives of visual artists and writers working in Rome and argues for the importance of de Staël's *Corinne* to their self-identities. More recently, Nancy Elizabeth Proctor, under the directorship of Griselda Pollock, wrote "American Women Sculptors in Rome in the Mid-Nineteenth Century: Feminist and Psychoanalytic Readings of a Displaced Canon."

8. Among the most useful recent studies are Deborah Cherry, *Beyond the Frame: Feminism and Visual Culture, Britain, 1850–1900* (New York: Routledge, 2000); Swinth, *Painting Professionals;* Laura R. Prieto, *At Home in the Studio: The Professionalization of Women Artists in America* (Cambridge: Harvard University Press, 2001); Erica E. Hirshler, *A Studio of Her Own: Women Artists in Boston, 1870–1940* (Boston: MFA Publications, 2001); Nelson, *Color of Stone;* April F. Masten, *Art Work: Woman Artists and Democracy in Mid-Nineteenth-Century New York* (Philadelphia: University of Pennsylvania Press, 2008); Kirsten Pai Buick, *Child of the Fire: Mary Edmonia Lewis and the Problem of Art History's Black and Indian Subject* (Durham: Duke University Press, 2010); and Kate Culkin, *Harriet Hosmer: A Cultural Biography* (Amherst: University of Massachusetts Press, 2010).

9. William W. Stowe, *Going Abroad: European Travel in Nineteenth-Century American Culture* (Princeton: Princeton University Press, 1994), 7.

10. D., "Artists in Rome," *Evening Post* (New York), March 5, 1851, 1.

11. "American Artists in Rome—Crawford's Condition," *Daily Evening Bulletin* (Philadelphia), February 24, 1857, 1.

12. Cole continued, "This exaltation of sculpture above painting, which in [Italy] has prevailed, is unjust, and has never been acknowledged in the past. There is no necessity for insisting upon the superior claims of either, and particularly upon those of sculpture, for they are the least tenable." As quoted in Louis L. Noble, *Course of Empire, Voyage of Life, and Other Pictures of Thomas Cole, N.A.* (New York: Cornish, Lamport, 1853), 377.

13. Albert TenEyck Gardner, *Yankee Stonecutters: The First American School of Sculpture, 1800–1850*

(New York: Columbia University Press for the Metropolitan Museum of Art, 1945), 45–46.

14. Nathaniel Hawthorne, *The Marble Faun; or, The Romance of Monte Beni* (1860; repr., New York: Penguin Books, 1990).

15. E. D. W., "A Woman's Experience in Europe," *Daily Evening Bulletin* (Philadelphia), April 9, 1868, 1.

16. As quoted in Otto Wittman Jr., "The Italian Experience (American Artists in Italy, 1830–1875)," *American Quarterly* 4, no. 1 (Spring 1952): 6. See William Cullen Bryant, *Letters of a Traveller; or, Notes of Things Seen in Europe and America* (New York: D. Appleton, 1859), 260.

17. Henry James, *Daisy Miller* (1878; repr., New York: Penguin Books, 1986).

18. W. Stowe, *Going Abroad,* 29.

19. Erwin Panofsky, *Idea: A Concept in Art Theory* (published originally in German 1924), trans. Joseph J. S. Peake (Columbia: University of South Carolina Press, 1968).

20. My discussion of neoclassical practice is indebted to Satish Padiyar, *Chains: David, Canova, and the Fall of the Public Hero in Postrevolutionary France* (University Park: Pennsylvania State University Press, 2007), 89–116.

21. Herman Melville, "Statues in Rome" (1857), in Merton M. Sealts Jr., *Melville as Lecturer* (Cambridge: Harvard University Press, 1957), 150.

22. Caroline Winterer, *The Culture of Classicism: Ancient Greece and Rome in American Intellectual Life, 1780–1910* (Baltimore: Johns Hopkins University Press, 2002), 1 (quote), 29; Wendy Cooper, *Classical Taste in America, 1800–1840,* exh. cat. (Baltimore: Baltimore Museum of Art; New York: Abbeville Press, 1993), 8–13, 191–94.

23. Caroline Winterer, "Victorian Antigone: Classicism and Women's Education in America, 1840–1900," *American Quarterly* 53, no. 1 (March 2001): 75.

24. Margaret Fuller reported that Greenough did so with an understanding of "the real mind [and] the vital blood of Italy." Dispatch 17, Rome, October 18, 1847, in Margaret Fuller, *"These Sad but Glorious Days": Dispatches from Europe, 1846–1850,* ed. Larry J. Reynolds and Susan Belasco Smith (New Haven: Yale University Press, 1991), 159. See also Albert Boime, *The Art of the Macchia and the Risorgimento: Representing Culture and Nationalism in Nineteenth-Century Italy* (Chicago: University of Chicago Press, 1993), 22–23; Norma Broude, *The Macchiaioli: Italian Painters of the Nineteenth Century* (New Haven: Yale University Press, 1987), 2–5; Lucy Riall, *The Italian Risorgimento: State, Society, and National Unification* (New York: Routledge, 1994), xi; and Larry J. Reynolds, *European Revolutions and the American Literary Renaissance* (New Haven: Yale University Press, 1988).

25. Hiram Powers to Nicholas Longworth, September 22, 1847 (Florence), as quoted in Vivien Green Fryd, "Hiram Powers's *America:* 'Triumphant as Liberty and in Unity,'" *American Art Journal* 18, no. 2 (Spring 1986): 57. See also Sylvia E. Crane, *White Silence: Greenough, Powers, and Crawford, American Sculptors in the Nineteenth Century* (Coral Gables: University of Miami Press, 1972), 117–19.

26. Barbara Novak, "Arcady Revisited," in Charles C. Eldredge, *The Arcadian Landscape: Nineteenth-Century American Painters in Italy,* exh. cat. (Lawrence: University of Kansas Museum of Art, 1972), xix–xx.

27. Jenny Franchot, *Roads to Rome: The Antebellum Protestant Encounter with Catholicism* (Berkeley: University of California Press, 1994), 17.

28. Mary Louise Pratt, *Imperial Eyes: Travel Writing and Transculturation* (New York: Routledge, 1992), 10.

29. Matthew Craske, *Art in Europe, 1700–1830* (New York: Oxford University Press, 1997), 254.

30. As quoted in Leonardo Buonomo, *Backward Glances: Exploring Italy, Reinterpreting America (1831–1866)* (London: Associated University Presses, 1996), 12.

31. John Agnew, "The Myth of Backward Italy in Modern Europe," in *Revisioning Italy: National Identity and Global Culture,* ed. Beverly Allen and Mary Russo (Minneapolis: University of Minnesota Press, 1997), 34.

32. Duke Litta-Visconti-Arese, ed., *The Birth of Modern Italy: Posthumous Papers of Jesse White Mario* (London: T. Fischer Unwin, 1909), 251.

33. Elizabeth Cady Stanton, "'Declaration of Sentiments' from *The History of Women's Suffrage*" (1848), reprinted in *Feminist Theory: A Reader,* ed. Wendy K. Komar and Frances Bartkowski, 2nd ed. (New York: McGraw-Hill, 2005), 71.

34. Barbara Welter, "The Cult of True Womanhood: 1820–1860," *American Quarterly* 18, no. 2, pt. 1 (Summer 1966): 151–74. For a historiography of the separate-spheres ideology, see Linda K. Kerber, "Separate Spheres, Female Worlds, Woman's Place: The Rhetoric of Women's History" (1988), reprinted in *Toward an Intellectual History of Women* (Chapel Hill: University of North Carolina Press, 1997), 159–200.

35. Stanton, "'Declaration of Sentiments,'" 73.

36. Ellen Carol DuBois et al., "Politics and Culture in Women's History: A Symposium," *Feminist Studies* 6, no. 1 (Spring 1980): 29.

37. Cathy N. Davidson, "Preface: No More Separate Spheres!" *American Literature* 70, no. 3 (September 1998): 443–63. Davidson edited this special issue in an attempt to complicate the separate-spheres interpretive model.

38. Michael Warner, *Publics and Counterpublics* (New York: Zone Books, 2002), 21–63. The bibliography addressing public-sphere theory is large. Scholarly publications relevant to my arguments in this book include Nancy Fraser, "Rethinking the Public Sphere: A Contribution to the Critique of Actually Existing Democracy," in *Habermas and the Public Sphere,* ed. Craig Calhoun (Cambridge: MIT Press, 1992), 109–43; Mary P. Ryan, "Gender and Public Access: Women's Politics in Nineteenth-Century America," in ibid., 259–89; Joan B. Landes, "The Public and Private Sphere: A Feminist Reconsideration," in *Feminism, the Public and the Private,* ed. Joan B. Landes (New York: Oxford University Press, 1998), 135–64; Leonore Davidoff, "Regarding Some 'Old Husbands' Tales': Public and Private in Feminist History," in ibid., 164–95; and Mary P. Ryan, *Women in Public: Between Banners and Ballots, 1825–1880* (Baltimore: Johns Hopkins University Press, 1990).

39. Martha Vicinus, *Intimate Friends: Women Who Loved Women, 1778–1928* (Chicago: University of Chicago Press, 2004), xviii. See also Vicinus, *Independent Women: Work and Community for Single Women, 1850–1920* (Chicago: University of Chicago Press, 1985), 34–35.

40. Carnal sexuality was linked with working-class women—both white and black. Leila J. Rupp, *A Desired Past: A Short History of Same-Sex Love in America* (Chicago: University of Chicago Press, 1999), 41, 43, 50; Nancy F. Cott, *The Bonds of Womanhood: "Woman's Sphere" in New England, 1780–1835* (New Haven: Yale University Press, 1977), 161; Linda K. Kerber, "The Republican Mother: Woman and the Enlightenment—An American Perspective" (1976), reprinted in *Toward an Intellectual History of Women,* 58.

41. Rupp, *Desired Past,* 1–12, 37–73. The bibliography that attempts to untangle the fragmentary strands of nineteenth-century female sexuality is large. In addition to the sources listed above, the following texts have been useful to my thinking: Martha Vicinus, "Lesbian History: All Theory and No Facts or All Facts and No Theory?" *Radical History Review* 60 (1994): 57–75; Vicinus, "'They Wonder to Which Sex I Belong': The Historical Roots of the Modern Lesbian Identity," in *Lesbian Subjects: A Feminist Studies Reader,* ed. Martha Vicinus (Bloomington: Indiana University Press, 1996), 233–61; Carroll Smith-Rosenberg, "The Female World of Love and Ritual: Relations Between Women in Nineteenth-Century America," in *Disorderly Conduct: Visions of Gender in Victorian America* (New York: Oxford University Press, 1985): 53–77; Terry Castle, *The Apparitional Lesbian: Female Homosexuality and Modern Culture* (New York: Columbia University Press, 1993); and, most recently, Emma Donoghue, *Inseparable: Desire Between Women in Literature* (New York: Alfred A. Knopf, 2010).

42. In general, we must be careful not to saturate the female subject with homosexual or heterosexual desire and thus erase other aspects of her identity. Since the eighteenth century, sexuality has been conterminous with female identity, invading her rational and spiritual faculties. In *Vindication of the Rights of Women* (1797), Mary Wollstonecraft argued that "the sexual should not destroy the human character" within feminine experience. As quoted in Denise Riley, *"Am I That Name?": Feminism and the Category of "Women" in History* (Minneapolis: University of Minnesota Press, 1988), 13.

43. Lisa Merrill, *When Romeo Was a Woman: Charlotte Cushman and Her Circle of Female Spectators* (Ann Arbor: University of Michigan Press, 1999), 8.

44. Later in the century, Westphal's students Havelock Ellis and Richard von Krafft-Ebing would successfully medicalize the behaviors of the "inverted woman." Lillian Faderman, *Surpassing the Love of Men: Romantic Friendship and Love Between Women from the Renaissance to the Present* (New York: Morrow, 1981), 239–41; Cheshire Calhoun, "The Gender Closet: Lesbian Disappearance Under the Sign 'Woman,'" in Vicinus, *Lesbian Subjects,* 223. See also Michel Foucault, *The History of Sexuality: An Introduction,* trans. Robert Hurley (New York: Vintage Books, 1990), though he deals primarily with male sexuality.

45. As Teresa de Lauretis has explained, a feminist concept of subjectivity contains multiple, shifting, and often self-contradictory identities and "is a political-personal strategy for survival." De Lauretis, "Feminist Studies / Critical Studies: Issues, Terms, and Contexts," in *Feminist Studies / Critical Studies,* ed. de Lauretis (Bloomington: Indiana University Press, 1986), 9. See also Vicinus, *Intimate Friends,* xxi; Merrill, *When Romeo Was a Woman,* xvii; Judith Butler, "Performative Acts and Gender Constitution: An Essay in Phenomenology and Feminist Theory," in *Performing Feminisms: Feminist Critical Theory and Theatre,* ed. Sue-Ellen Case (Baltimore: Johns Hopkins University Press, 1990), 270–82.

*Chapter 1*

1. Debra Gold Hansen, *Strained Sisterhood: Gender and Class in the Boston Female Anti-Slavery Society* (Amherst: University of Massachusetts Press, 1993), 6; Katharine Wolff, *Culture Club: The Curious History of the Boston Athenaeum* (Amherst: University of Massachusetts Press, 2009), 120.

2. Debra Gold Hansen, "The Boston Female Anti-Slavery Society and the Limits of Gender Politics," in *The Abolitionist Sisterhood: Women's Political Culture in Antebellum America*, ed. Jean Fagan Yellin and John C. Van Horne (Ithaca: Cornell University Press, 1994), 46–49; Dolly Sherwood, *Harriet Hosmer: American Sculptor, 1830–1908* (Columbia: University of Missouri Press, 1991), 10, 36; Carolyn L. Karcher, *The First Woman in the Republic: A Cultural Biography of Lydia Maria Child* (Durham: Duke University Press, 1994), 267–95; Wolff, *Culture Club*, 115–16.

3. D. Sherwood, *Harriet Hosmer*, 10–16; Susan Van Rensselaer, "Harriet Hosmer," *Antiques*, October 1963, 424.

4. Lydia Maria Child, "Miss Harriet Hosmer," *Littell's Living Age* 56 (March 13, 1858): 697.

5. Emma Stebbins, *Charlotte Cushman: Her Letters and Memories of Her Life* (1879; repr., New York: Blom, 1972), 12. Cushman wrote: "I was born a tomboy. My earliest recollections are of dolls' heads ruthlessly cracked open to see what they were thinking about; I was possessed with the idea that dolls could and did think." Quoted in ibid., 13.

6. Carolyn Heilbrun, "Jo March: Male Model—Female Person," in *Critical Essays on Louisa May Alcott*, ed. Madeleine B. Stern (Boston: G. K. Hall, 1984), 144.

7. Judith Halberstam, *Female Masculinity* (Durham: Duke University Press, 1998), 51.

8. E. F. Ellet, *Women Artists in All Ages and Countries* (New York: Harper & Brothers, 1859), 354. See also Joseph Leach, "Harriet Hosmer: Feminist in Bronze and Marble," *Feminist Art Journal* 5 (Summer 1976): 10; Ann Blainey, *Fanny and Adelaide: The Lives of the Remarkable Kemble Sisters* (Chicago: Ivan R. Dee, 2001), 148; John Townes, "225 Years: The Lenox of Today Is a Product of Its Colorful History," http://www.townoflenox.com/Public_Documents/LenoxMA_WebDocs/about, accessed October 10, 2006; D. Sherwood, *Harriet Hosmer*, 18–20; Culkin, *Harriet Hosmer*, 10.

9. Brigitte Bailey, "Tourism and Visual Subjection in *Letters from Abroad* and 'An Incident at Rome,'" in *Catharine Maria Sedgwick: Critical Perspectives*, ed. Lucinda L. Damon-Bach and Victoria Clements (Boston: Northeastern University Press, 2003), 212–28. See also Catharine Sedgwick, *Letters from Abroad to Kindred at Home*, vol. 2 (New York: Harper & Brothers, 1841).

10. As quoted in Mary Kelley, *Private Woman, Public Stage: Literary Domesticity in Nineteenth-Century America* (New York: Oxford University Press, 1984), 239. See also Catharine Sedgwick, *Married or Single?* 2 vols. (New York: Harper, 1857), and Deborah Gussman, "'Equal to Either Fortune': Sedgwick's *Married or Single?* and Feminism," in Damon-Bach and Clements, *Catharine Maria Sedgwick*, 252–67.

11. Kemble wrote a series of letters to Elizabeth Sedgwick that became the basis for her *Journal of a Residence on a Georgian Plantation*, a vivid account of the horrors of slavery, with a particular focus on the plight of slave women. In her *Journal*, she recorded the events that she had witnessed firsthand while living on her husband's plantation between 1838 and 1839. Eventually published in 1863, the *Journal* propelled Kemble to the center of the Massachusetts abolitionist community. Lyde Cullen Sizer, *The Political Work of Northern Women Writers and the Civil War, 1850–1872* (Chapel Hill: University of North Carolina Press, 2000), 144–47. See also Blainey, *Fanny and Adelaide*, 147.

12. Cott, *Bonds of Womanhood*, 160, 177, and 185 (quote from Catharine Maria Sedgwick diary entry, May 16, 1834).

13. Ellet, *Women Artists in All Ages*, 328; D. Sherwood, *Harriet Hosmer*, 32.

14. Elizabeth Reitz Mullenix, "'So Unfemininely Masculine': Discourse, True/False Womanhood, and the American Career of Fanny Kemble," *Theatre Survey* 40, no. 2 (November 1999): 27–42; [Amelia Bloomer], "Men's Sensitivity to Women's Dress," *The Lily* 1, no. 12 (December 1, 1849): 94, reprinted in *The Radical Women's Press of the 1850s*, ed. Ann Russo and Cheris Kramarae (New York: Routledge, 1991), 257–58; Blainey, *Fanny and Adelaide*, 149, 246. See also Nancy Isenberg, *Sex and Citizenship in Antebellum America* (Chapel Hill: University of North Carolina Press, 1998), 53.

15. Rupp, *Desired Past*, 43; Martha Vicinus, "Distance and Desire: English Boarding School Friendships, 1870–1920," in *Hidden from History: Reclaiming the Gay and Lesbian Past*, ed. Martin Duberman, Martha Vicinus,

and George Chauncey Jr. (New York: Meridian, 1990), 212–29; Prieto, *At Home in the Studio,* 34; Ellet, *Women Artists in All Ages.*

16. Perry Miller, ed., *Margaret Fuller, American Romantic: A Selection from Her Writings and Correspondence* (Ithaca: Cornell University Press, 1963), x; Carolyn L. Karcher, "Margaret Fuller and Lydia Maria Child: Intersecting Careers, Reciprocal Influences," in *Margaret Fuller's Cultural Critique: Her Age and Legacy,* ed. Fritz Fleischmann (New York: Peter Lang, 2000), 78–79. See also Margaret Fuller, *Woman in the Nineteenth Century* (New York: Greeley & McElrath, 1845).

17. Acknowledging friendships between men and between women was central to the Transcendentalist worldview. Fuller explained that "a woman may be in love with a woman, and a man with a man . . . only it is purely intellectual and spiritual." Margaret Fuller Ossoli, *Woman in the Nineteenth Century and Kindred Papers Relating to the Sphere, Condition, and Duties of Woman* (Boston: J. P. Jewett, 1855), 342–43, as quoted in Faderman, *Surpassing the Love of Men,* 160.

18. Caroline Healy Dall, *Margaret and Her Friends; or, Ten Conversations with Margaret Fuller upon the Mythology of the Greeks and Its Expression in Art, Held at the House of Rev. George Ripley, Bedford Place, Boston, Beginning March 1, 1841* (Boston: Roberts, 1895), 8.

19. Phebe A. Hanaford, *Daughters of America; or, Women of the Century* (Augusta, Maine: True, 1882), 221. Ames was described as a friend of Margaret Fuller. *The Revolution* 7, no. 2 (January 12, 1871).

20. Ednah Dow Cheney, *Reminiscences of Ednah Dow Cheney* (Boston: Lee & Shepard, 1902), 205.

21. For Fuller, Greek mythology and its incarnation in Greek art "expressed immortality as much as Christian art." As quoted in Charles Capper, "Margaret Fuller as Cultural Reformer: The Conversations in Boston," *American Quarterly* 39, no. 4 (Winter 1987): 516; see also 513, 523. Fuller held one "mixed class," with both men and women, in 1841. The twenty-five-year-old sculptor William Wetmore Story attended this conversation. Dall, *Margaret and Her Friends,* 13. See also Thomas Wentworth Higginson, *Margaret Fuller Ossoli* (1884; repr., Boston: Houghton, Mifflin, 1912), 113–16.

22. Comments on Margaret Fuller's Conversations, Fall 1840(?), Peabody Sisters Letters, Horace Mann Papers, p. 1313, Antioch College, Yellow Springs, Ohio.

23. Kathleen Lawrence, "Aesthetic Transcendentalism and Its Legacy: Margaret Fuller, William Wetmore Story, and Henry James" (Ph.D. diss., Boston University, 2003), 3; Gregory Staley, "'Beyond Glorious Ocean': Feminism, Myth, and America," in *Laughing with Medusa: Classical Myth and Feminist Thought,* ed. Vanda Zajko and Miriam Leonard (New York: Oxford University Press, 2006), 224.

24. Dispatch 14, Rome, May 1847, in Fuller, *"These Sad but Glorious Days,"* 131–39; Van Wyck Brooks, *The Dream of Arcadia: American Writers and Artists in Italy, 1760–1915* (New York: E. P. Dutton, 1958), 114–17; Brigitte Bailey, "Fuller, Hawthorne, and Imagining Urban Spaces in Rome," in *Roman Holidays: American Writers and Artists in Nineteenth-Century Italy,* ed. Robert K. Martin and Leland S. Person (Iowa City: University of Iowa Press, 2002), 180.

25. Responding favorably to the new pope, major American newspapers expressed an "earnest sympathy" with his "enlightened polic[ies] and liberal measures" and supported "the efforts of the Italian People for National Independence and Constitutional Freedom." As quoted in Howard R. Marraro, *American Opinion on the Unification of Italy, 1846–1861* (New York: Columbia University Press, 1932), 5. See also William L. Vance, *America's Rome,* vol. 2, *Catholic and Contemporary Rome* (New Haven: Yale University Press, 1989), 113.

26. Dispatch 17, Rome, October 18, 1847, in Fuller, *"These Sad but Glorious Days,"* 160.

27. Dispatch 19, Rome, December 17, 1847, in Fuller, *"These Sad but Glorious Days,"* 176; also quoted in Vance, *America's Rome,* 2:131.

28. Marraro, *American Opinion on the Unification of Italy,* 74; Madeleine B. Stern, "New England Artists in Italy, 1835–1855," *New England Quarterly* 14, no. 2 (June 1941): 255, 259.

29. Dispatch 30, Rome, May 6, 1849, in Fuller, *"These Sad but Glorious Days,"* 274.

30. Because of the danger, the Storys left Rome in May 1849, returning again to the city in 1852. Vance, *America's Rome,* 2:188. To this day, one can find bullets lodged in ancient trees and canon balls embedded in house foundations as memorials to these battles on the Janiculum Hill.

31. Dispatch 31, Rome, May 27, 1849, in Fuller, *"These Sad but Glorious Days,"* 280. In Rome, the newspaper *Le Donne Romane* (Roman Women), solicited the help of women of all classes. Litta-Visconti-Arese, *Birth of Modern Italy,* xxii. Mazzini appointed Princess Cristina di Belgioioso, a noted journalist, writer, and Republican sympathizer from Milan, director general of the military

ambulance squad. Upon her arrival in Rome, she was hailed by the Italian press as a "paragon of Italian women" and "venerated for her lofty ideals . . . the noble integrity of her principles, and . . . the devotion and sacrifices sustained by her at every moment *pro patria.*" *La Speranza,* December 23, 1847, as quoted in Beth Archer Brombert, *Cristina: Portraits of a Princess* (New York: Alfred A. Knopf, 1977), 177–79. In turn, the princess chose Fuller as *regolatrice* (coordinator) of the infirmary services for the Fatebenefratelli Hospital, the medieval complex located on Tiber Island, where she led a large cadre of Italian women in making bandages and tending to the wounded. Cristina Giorcelli, "La Repubblica romana di Margaret Fuller: Tra visione politica e impegno etico," in *Gli americani e la Repubblica romana del 1849,* ed. Sara Antonelli, Daniele Fiorentino, and Giuseppe Monsagrati (Rome: Gangemi Editore, 2000), 53–89.

32. Buonomo, *Backward Glances,* 27, 40. Garibaldi attained an American passport with the help of the American consul in Rome and traveled to the United States under the name of George Gray. Nelson Gay, "Le relazioni fra l'Italia e gli Stati Uniti (1847–1871)," *Nuova antologia,* 5th ser., 127 (January–February 1907): 657–71.

33. Emelyn Eldredge Story, a close friend of Fuller's in Rome, is the source of this personal information. See Giorcelli, "La Repubblicca romana di Margaret Fuller," 61, and Higginson, *Margaret Fuller Ossoli,* 238–45. See also Helen Barolini, *Their Other Side: Six American Women and the Lure of Italy* (New York: Fordham University Press, 2006), 27, and Vance, *America's Rome,* 2:105–6.

34. There are differing accounts of Fuller's marital status when she left Italy. Ann Douglas, *The Feminization of American Culture* (1977; repr., New York: Farrar, Straus & Giroux, 1998), 270–73; W. Stowe, *Going Abroad,* 103; Buonomo, *Backward Glances,* 27–28; Theodore E. Stebbins Jr., *The Lure of Italy: American Artists and the Italian Experience, 1760–1914,* exh. cat. (Boston: Museum of Fine Arts; New York: Harry N. Abrams, 1992), 198; Isenberg, *Sex and Citizenship,* 56; Barolini, *Their Other Side,* 44.

35. R[alph] W[aldo] Emerson, W[illiam] H[enry] Channing, and J[ames] F[reeman] Clarke, *Memoirs of Margaret Fuller Ossoli* (Boston: Roberts Brothers, 1875).

36. Dall, *Margaret and Her Friends,* 18.

37. James, *William Wetmore Story and His Friends,* 1:130–31.

38. Tamar Garb, "The Forbidden Gaze: Women Artists and the Male Nude in Late Nineteenth-Century France," in *The Body Imaged: The Human Form and Visual Culture Since the Renaissance,* ed. Kathleen Adler and Marcia Pointon (New York: Cambridge University Press, 1993), 35–36. On Foley and Lander, see "Editor's Department," *Arthur's Home Magazine* 1 (January 1853): 318; Ellet, *Women Artists,* 354; "Editor's Table," *Godey's Lady's Book* 45 (April 1852): 293.

39. D. Sherwood, *Harriet Hosmer,* 23–25. Wayman Crow was an important business leader, state senator, and patron of the arts in St. Louis. He also became the financial adviser to Hosmer, Cushman, and Kemble. Julia Markus, *Across an Untried Sea: Discovering Lives Hidden in the Shadow of Convention and Time* (New York: Alfred A. Knopf, 2000), 72.

40. William H. Gerdts Jr., "The *Medusa* of Harriet Hosmer," *Bulletin of the Detroit Institute of Arts* 56 (1978): 97; D. Sherwood, *Harriet Hosmer,* 44–47; Alfred, Lord Tennyson, "In Memoriam A. H. H." (1849), in *Tennyson: Poems and Plays* (New York: Oxford University Press, 1973), 230–66, quoted stanza on 262.

41. "Miss Foley the Artist," *Boston Evening Transcript,* July 29, 1857, 2.

42. Thomas Dublin, ed., *Farm to Factory: Women's Letters, 1830–1860,* 2nd ed. (New York: Columbia University Press, 1993), 3–17; Eleanor Tufts, "Margaret Foley's Metamorphosis: A Merrimack 'Female Operative' in Neoclassical Rome," *Arts Magazine* 56 (January 1982): 89–90; Eva Wood, "Prominent Woman Resident of Vergennes: Margaret F. Foley" (1935, unpublished manuscript), Smithsonian American Art Museum.

43. Harriet H. Robinson, *Loom and Spindle; or, Life Among the Early Mill Girls* (New York: Thomas Y. Crowell, 1898), 115–16. These "ideal mill-girls [were] full of hopes, desires, aspirations; poets of the loom, spinners of verse, artists of factory-life" (117).

44. Elsie B. Chatterton, "A Vermont Sculptor," *Vermont Historical Society News and Notes* 7 (1955): 11; Prieto, *At Home in the Studio,* 27–28; Tufts, "Margaret Foley's Metamorphosis," 90; Jean Gordon, "Early American Women Artists and the Social Context in Which They Worked," *American Quarterly* 30, no. 1 (Spring 1978): 56; Cheney, *Reminiscences,* 73–76. The Boston School of Design for Women was short-lived, according to its founder, because of the difficulties in finding a teacher who "had practical knowledge of designing for manufacturers." Ibid., 75.

45. Virginia Penny, *How Women Can Make Money* (1863; repr., New York: Arno and New York Times, 1971), 53; C. H. D., "Bust of Theodore Parker," *Boston Evening Transcript,* September 27, 1858, 2; Prieto, *At Home in the Studio,* 12–13, 38–39.

46. Monica Beth Fowler, "In Praise of Cameos," *Antiques and Art Around Florida,* Winter/Spring 1998, http://aarf.com/fecame98.htm, accessed October 12, 2006; Gertrude S. Cole, "Some American Cameo Portraitists," *Antiques* 50 (September 1946): 170. A cameo is "a small carving in relief on stone, glass, shell, lava, or other hard substance. Usually, but by no means invariably, this carving is executed on a material, like agate or shell, which occurs in layers of different colors, so that the cutting away of parts of one layer may leave the remaining surface strikingly set off against a contrasting background." Ibid., 171, citing Homer Eaton Keyes from *Antiques,* September 1929.

47. "Art Intelligence," *Boston Evening Transcript,* July 29, 1857, 2.

48. "Our Female Artist," *Boston Evening Transcript,* May 12, 1860, supplement, 2.

49. Unidentified article, *St. Louis Globe,* Harriet Goodhue Hosmer Papers, M-60, Reel 3, Folder 82, Schlesinger Library, Radcliffe Institute, Harvard University, Cambridge, Mass.

50. Dean Grodzins, "Theodore Parker," http://www.uua.org/uuhs/duub/articles/theodoreparker.html, accessed October 12, 2006.

51. C. H. D., "Bust of Theodore Parker," 2.

52. Charlotte Streifer Rubenstein, *American Women Sculptors: A History of Women Working in Three Dimensions* (Boston: G. K. Hall, 1990), 54–56; "Louisa Lander," *Cosmopolitan Art Journal,* March 1861, 26–27; quote from Ellet, *Women Artists in All Ages,* 328.

53. Frederic A. Sharf, "'A More Bracing Morning Atmosphere': Artistic Life in Salem, 1850–1859," *Essex Institute Historical Collection* 95 (1959): 149, 152; Ellet, *Women Artists in All Ages,* 302–3. Two of Lander's cameo vignettes survive in the Peabody Essex Museum: a figural group of *Romeo and Juliet* and *Cupid and Psyche.*

54. In 1848, the Athenaeum included in its annual exhibition the first sculpture by a woman, an 1841 bust of the reformer Robert Rantoul by Joanna Quiner. Pamela Hoyle, Jonathon P. Harding, and Rosemary Booth, *A Climate for Art: The History of the Boston Athenaeum Gallery, 1827–1873,* exh. cat. (Boston: Boston Athenaeum, 1980), 5, 30. Quiner began her sculpting career at the age of forty; she received critical acclaim for her work in the *North American Review.* Born in Beverly, Massachusetts, "she was a woman worthy of this century; a friend of temperance . . . and ever ready for any benevolent work." Hanaford, *Daughters of America,* 300.

55. Amateur, "Another Female Sculptor," *Boston Evening Transcript,* March 14, 1855, 1.

56. Hoyle, Harding, and Booth, *Climate for Art,* 1–9.

57. Ibid., 1–9, 32–33; Cornelia Carr, ed., *Harriet Hosmer: Letters and Memories* (New York: Moffat, Yard, 1912), 14.

58. A "cast" referred to a plaster cast of a marble or plaster original; a marble copy was a marble imitation of a famous work; an original was called a bust, statue, or head. Little scholarship exists on the phenomenon of plaster-cast collections in the United States except for Alan Wallach, "The American Cast Museum: An Episode in the History of the Institutional Definition of Art," in *Exhibiting Contradiction: Essays on the Art Museum in the United States* (Amherst: University of Massachusetts Press, 1998), 38–57. See also Betsy Fahlman, "A Plaster of Paris Antiquity: Nineteenth-Century Cast Collections," *Southeastern College Art Conference Review* 12, no. 1 (1991): 1–9, and Francis Haskell and Nicholas Penny, *Taste and the Antique: The Lure of Classical Sculpture, 1500–1900* (New Haven: Yale University Press, 1981).

59. Throughout the antebellum period, the Athenaeum's collection of classical casts grew with donations from George Cabot Ward, Charlotte Cushman, and William Wetmore Story, all of whom had spent significant time in Italy. Thomas G. Appleton donated the last cast to the museum in 1869, the famed *Mars Ludovisi* (fig. 62). Mabel Munson Swan, *The Athenaeum Gallery, 1827–1873: The Boston Athenaeum as an Early Patron of Art* (Boston: Boston Athenaeum, 1940), 139–58.

In keeping with its didactic mission, the Boston Athenaeum inaugurated the first sculpture galleries in the United States with its collection of over fifty statues. Approximately one-third of the pieces on exhibit were classical or neoclassical—either copies of ancient statues or contemporary figures with mythological themes. Portrait busts of patriots constituted the remainder of works exhibited. The museum hoped to lay a foundation for a school of sculpture that would make Boston the "Athens of America." Quite conscious of its cultural rivalry with New York and Philadelphia, the Athenaeum sponsored annual statuary exhibitions between 1839 and 1867 in hopes of educating its citizenry and instilling in them a sense refinement, taste, and civic pride. Hoyle, Harding, and Booth, *Climate for Art,* 23–27, 35.

60. Hoyle, Harding, and Booth, *Climate for Art,* 6. The Boston Athenaeum transferred most of its sculptural collection to the newly opened Boston Museum of Fine of Arts in 1876.

61. Harriet Goodhue Hosmer, *Boston and Boston People, in 1850* (Boston, 1850), 24.

62. Christopher M. S. Johns, "The Entrepôt of Europe: Rome in the Eighteenth Century," in *Art in Rome in the Eighteenth Century,* ed. Edgar P. Bowron and Joseph J. Rishel (Philadelphia: Philadelphia Museum of Art, 2000), 37.

63. For an extended discussion of the Arcadian Academy in Rome, see Melissa Dabakis, "Angelika Kauffmann, Goethe, and the Arcadian Academy in Rome," in *The Enlightened Eye: Goethe and Visual Culture,* ed. Evelyn K. Moore and Patricia Anne Simpson (Amsterdam: Rodopi Press, 2007), 25–41.

64. For information on Kauffmann, see Wendy Wassyng Roworth, "Kauffman and the Art of Painting in England," in *Angelika Kauffman: A Continental Artist in Georgian England,* ed. Wendy Wassyng Roworth (London: Reaktion Books, 1992), 11–95; Liliana Barroero and Stefano Susinno, "Arcadian Rome, Universal Capital of the Arts," in Bowron and Rishel, *Art in Rome in the Eighteenth Century,* 47; Angelica Goodden, *Miss Angel: The Art and World of Angelika Kauffman* (London: Pimlico, 2005).

65. Dabakis, "Angelika Kauffmann," 32–34. Within the academy, Corilla Olimpica was viewed as an enemy of the pope and a usurper of power.

66. The Arcadian Academy had moved to the Protomoteca of the Palazzo dei Conservatori atop the Capitoline Hill. It comprised a suite of eight rooms in which weekly meetings took place every Friday. Octavian Blewitt, *A Handbook for Travellers in Central Italy* (London: John Murray, 1850), 485, 526.

67. Raffaele De Cesare, *The Last Days of Papal Rome, 1850–1870,* trans. Helen Zimmern (London: Archibald Constable, 1909), 148–57; Madelyn Gutwirth, *Madame de Staël, Novelist: The Emergence of the Artist as Woman* (Urbana: University of Illinois Press, 1978), 173 n. 38; Paola Giuli, "Tracing a Sisterhood: Corilla Olimpica as Corinne's Unacknowledged Alter Ego," in *The Novel's Seductions: Staël's "Corinne" in Critical Inquiry,* ed. Karyna Szmurlo (London: Associated University Presses, 1999), 165.

68. Julia Ward Howe, *Reminiscences, 1819–1899* (Boston: Houghton, Mifflin, 1906), 130.

69. Angelica Goodden, *Madame de Staël: The Dangerous Exile* (New York: Oxford University Press, 2008), 156.

70. In one of the opening scenes of the novel, Corinne is ceremoniously crowned on the steps of the capitol, commemorating, no doubt, the famous episode from Corilla Olimpica's life. The Englishman Oswald, Lord Nelvil, soon to become Corinne's lover, muses that this "was the first time he had witnessed honour done to a woman, to a woman renowned only for the gifts of genius." Madame de Staël, *Corinne, or Italy,* 23.

The novel was translated into English in the year of its publication in French. Goodden, *Madame de Staël,* 175. The bibliography regarding this novel is large. For a useful discussion of Corinne within the American/Roman context, see Ellen Moers, *Literary Women* (Garden City, N.Y.: Doubleday, 1976), and English Showalter Jr., "Corinne as an Autonomous Heroine," in *Germaine de Staël: Crossing the Borders,* ed. Madelyn Gutwirth, Avriel Goldberger, and Karyna Szmurlo (New Brunswick: Rutgers University Press, 1991), 188–93.

71. Because of her erudition and skills as a conversationalist, Emerson famously dubbed Margaret Fuller "a new Corinne." Perry Miller, foreword to *Margaret Fuller, American Romantic,* xix. The sculptor Vinnie Ream (fig. 98) self-consciously donned a turban and was regularly identified by the press as an "American Corinne." Sophia Peabody Hawthorne and her sister Elizabeth Peabody had read *Corinne, or Italy* and aspired to emulate this new model of feminine creativity.

72. Maura O'Connor, *The Romance of Italy and the English Political Imagination* (New York: St. Martin's Press, 1998), 27–34. See also Lord Byron, *Childe Harold's Pilgrimage* (Philadelphia: George S. Appleton, 1847).

73. Hosmer to Carr, January 1852 (Watertown, Mass.), in Carr, *Harriet Hosmer,* 17; D. Sherwood, *Harriet Hosmer,* 42; Merrill, *When Romeo Was a Woman,* 169–71.

74. Hosmer to Crow, December 1, 1852 (Rome), in Carr, *Harriet Hosmer,* 22–23; Merrill, *When Romeo Was a Woman,* 171, 175, 181; D. Sherwood, *Harriet Hosmer,* 87. As far as I can tell, Grace Greenwood arrived in Rome in November of 1852, remained for three months at the via del Corso residence, and then left Italy in April 1853. Grace Greenwood, *Haps and Mishaps of a Tour in Europe* (Boston: Ticknor, Reed & Fields, 1854), 217.

75. D. Sherwood, *Harriet Hosmer,* 78 and 87.

76. See Merrill, *When Romeo Was a Woman,* 168–59; for a discussion of Meg Merrilies, see 101–3.

77. Martha Vicinus, "The Historical Roots of the Modern Lesbian Identity," in *Identity and Diversity: Gender and the Experience of Education,* ed. Maud Blair and Janet Holland, with Sue Sheldon (Philadelphia: Multilingual Matters, 1995), 232; Isenberg, *Sex and Citizenship,* 54; and Christine Battersby, *Gender and Genius: Towards a Feminist Aesthetics* (Bloomington: Indiana University Press, 1989), 3.

78. Barrett Browning described Matilda Hays as one of the "emancipated women" who dressed "like a

man down to the waist. . . . Certainly there's the waistcoat which I like—and the collar, neckcloth, and jacket made with a sort of wag-tail behind, which I don't like." Quoted in D. Sherwood, *Harriet Hosmer,* 90.

79. Halberstam, *Female Masculinity,* 46; Vicinus, "Lesbian History," 64; Martha Vicinus, "Laocoöning in Rome: Harriet Hosmer and Romantic Friendship," *Women's Writing* 10, no. 2 (2003): 357; Vicinus, *Intimate Friends,* 31; Merrill, *When Romeo Was a Woman,* 16, 22, 168, quote on 160.

80. Barrett Browning to Henrietta Cook (the poet's sister), December 30, 1853, as quoted in D. Sherwood, *Harriet Hosmer,* 90.

81. D. Sherwood, *Harriet Hosmer,* 89, 95; Elizabeth Barrett Browning, *Casa Guidi Windows,* ed. Julia Markus (New York: Browning Institute, 1977), xxxi, 72; Sandra M. Gilbert, "From *Patria* to *Matria:* Elizabeth Barrett Browning's Risorgimento," *PMLA* 99, no. 2 (March 1984): 196, 199.

82. Elizabeth Barrett Browning, *Aurora Leigh* (1856), ed. Margaret Reynolds (Athens: Ohio University Press, 1992). See also Elizabeth K. Helsinger, Robin Lauterbach Sheets, and William Veeder, *The Woman Question: Society and Literature in Britain and America, 1837–1883,* vol. 3, *Literary Issues* (Manchester: Manchester University Press, 1983), 33–47, 101–5; Linda Lewis, "The Artist's Quest in Elizabeth Barrett Browning's *Aurora Leigh,*" in *Images of the Self as Female: The Achievement of Women Artists in Re-envisioning Feminine Identity,* ed. Kathryn N. Benzel and Lauren Pringle de la Vars (Lewiston, N.Y.: Edwin Mellen Press, 1992), 77–91.

83. Barrett Browning to Mary Russell Mitford, May 10, 1854, in *The Letters of Elizabeth Barrett Browning,* ed. Frederick G. Kenyon (New York: Macmillan, 1898), 2:166.

84. Grace Greenwood [Sarah Jane Clarke Lippincott], "Miss Hosmer's Progress," *Boston Evening Transcript,* March 18, 1853, 1. See also Greenwood, *Haps and Mishaps,* 217.

85. Vicinus, "Laocoöning in Rome," 355.

86. D. Sherwood, *Harriet Hosmer,* 67–69, quote on 68; Culkin, *Harriet Hosmer,* 34; Blainey, *Fanny and Adelaide,* 255–56.

87. Merrill, *When Romeo Was a Woman,* xvi, 195; Vicinus, *Intimate Friends,* xxvii–xxix.

88. William Wetmore Story to James Russell Lowell, February 11, 1853, as quoted in James, *William Wetmore Story and His Friends,* 1:254.

89. Ibid., 1:256–57.

90. Merrill, *When Romeo Was a Woman,* 187; Joseph Leach, *Bright Particular Star: The Life and Times of Charlotte Cushman* (New Haven: Yale University Press, 1970), 287; D. Sherwood, *Harriet Hosmer,* 168.

91. E. Stebbins, *Charlotte Cushman,* 112.

92. D. Sherwood, *Harriet Hosmer,* 168–69; Merrill, *When Romeo Was a Woman,* 190, 299–300 n. 67.

93. Frances Power Cobbe, *Life of Frances Power Cobbe: As Told by Herself* (London: Swan Sonnenschein, 1904), 392.

94. At these events one could find everyone "from Roman Cardinals, to the poorest young artist, penniless and alone in a foreign city." Emma Crow Cushman, "Charlotte Cushman: A Memory" (unpublished manuscript), Charlotte Cushman Papers, Container 15, Library of Congress, Washington, D.C.

In the summer of 1858, Cushman traveled to the United States with Stebbins to oversee her finances. It was during this visit that she met Wayman Crow, whom Hosmer had recommended as a trusted financial adviser. In St. Louis, Cushman met Emma Crow, the younger sister of Hosmer's dear friend Cornelia, with whom she would maintain a lifelong infatuation. Unaware of the love triangle that was blossoming in St. Louis, Stebbins visited her family in New York. In July the party returned to Rome. Markus, *Across an Untried Sea,* 35–36; Merrill, *When Romeo Was a Woman,* 206.

95. Quotes from E. Stebbins, *Charlotte Cushman,* 114–15; Leach, *Bright Particular Star,* 288.

96. E. Stebbins, *Charlotte Cushman,* 115.

97. Ellet, *Women Artists in All Ages,* vi.

98. Prieto, *At Home in the Studio,* 32–37. Ellet was very much influenced by the writings in *The English Women's Journal.* Cherry, *Beyond the Frame,* 55. See also Sandra Langer, review of *Women Artists in All Ages and Countries,* by Elizabeth Fries Lummis Ellet, *Woman's Art Journal* 1, no. 2 (Autumn 1980–Winter 1981): 55–58.

99. Ellet, *Women Artists in All Ages,* 319–20.

100. Merrill, *When Romeo Was a Woman,* 189. Merrill does not insinuate an erotic relationship between Stebbins and Hosmer; Markus, in *Across an Untried Sea,* 31–32, claims that Stebbins and Hosmer were lovers. The use of the term "wife" in this circumstance is ambiguous.

101. Markus, *Across an Untried Sea,* 32–33; Merrill, *When Romeo Was a Woman,* 186; Parrott, "Expatriates and Professionals," 414.

102. Stebbins produced several sculptures of family members under Brackett, who, according to Ellet, had

also trained Hosmer and Edmonia Lewis in Boston. Ellet, *Women Artists in All Ages,* 320; Elizabeth Milroy, "The Public Career of Emma Stebbins: Work in Marble," *Archives of American Art Journal* 33, no. 3 (1993): 11 n. 7.

103. Karen J. Blair, *The Torchbearers: Women and Their Amateur Arts Associations in America, 1890–1930* (Bloomington: Indiana University Press, 1994), 22; Milroy, "Public Career of Emma Stebbins: Work in Marble," 4. A few years later, Stebbins's membership at the National Academy of Design was mysteriously terminated (along with the memberships of five other artists). See Milroy, "Public Career of Emma Stebbins," 11 n. 9.

104. Her sister Caroline Stebbins met the painter John Rollin Tilten in Rome; they married in 1858. D. Sherwood, *Harriet Hosmer,* 166.

105. H. M., "American Art," *Boston Evening Transcript,* December 7, 1860, 2.

106. In 1858, Stebbins modeled the figures of *Industry,* represented by a coal miner, and *Commerce,* an image of a sailor, both in the Heckscher Museum. The following year, she modeled the *Machinist* and *Machinist's Apprentice,* currently located in the Art Institute of Chicago. Also included in this sculptural series was a study of a California gold miner (now missing). Photographs of these works are located in the Emma Stebbins Papers, Scrapbook, Archives of American Art, roll 2082. During a short trip to New York in the summer of 1858, Stebbins met Richard Heckscher, a New York businessman who had made his fortune in coal mining. He ordered two allegorical figures of laborers, *Industry* and *Commerce.* Richard Heckscher was the cousin of August Heckscher, founder of the Heckscher Museum of Art. H. Nichols B. Clark, *A Marble Quarry: The James H. Ricau Collection of Sculpture at the Chrysler Museum of Art* (New York: Hudson Hills Press, 1997), 156. For a study of labor imagery in sculpture from the end of the nineteenth century to the Great Depression, see Melissa Dabakis, *Visualizing Labor in American Sculpture: Monuments, Manliness, and the Work Ethic, 1880–1935* (New York: Cambridge University Press, 1999).

107. Markus, *Across an Untried Sea,* 37, 203. Stebbins also produced a monument to Christopher Columbus, in 1867, originally intended for Central Park and now located on the grounds of the Brooklyn Civic Center.

108. Hays returned to London, where she joined a thriving community of feminist artists, writers, and intellectuals. She helped found the *English Woman's Journal,* a monthly reformist magazine that advocated, among other things, the fine arts as a woman's occupation, while publishing women artists' profiles, reviewing exhibitions of work by women, and discussing the standards by which women's art should be judged. This journal carefully followed the careers of American and British women in Rome. See Cherry, *Beyond the Frame,* for a lively chronicle of this important feminist community, who traveled regularly to Rome. For the *English Women's Journal* (1858–64), see 47–67.

109. Merrill, *When Romeo Was a Woman,* 184–85, 189.

110. E. Stebbins, *Charlotte Cushman,* 100. According to Elizabeth Milroy, Stebbins had supplanted Hosmer in Cushman's affections, asserting a rivalry between the two sculptors. The insinuation was that Cushman and Hosmer were romantically involved. Milroy, "Public Career of Emma Stebbins: Work in Marble," 4.

111. Merrill, *When Romeo Was a Woman,* 22, 209, 212; Markus, *Across an Untried Sea,* 4, 75.

112. Charlotte Cushman to Wayman Crow, 1858, as quoted in Milroy, "Public Career of Emma Stebbins: Work in Marble," 4.

113. Merrill, *When Romeo Was a Woman,* 190; Elizabeth Milroy, "The Public Career of Emma Stebbins: Work in Bronze," *Archives of American Art Journal* 34, no. 1 (1994): 9.

114. It was "the greatest privilege in my life to have known and lived in . . . association" with Stebbins, Cushman wrote. Charlotte Cushman to Emma Crow Cushman, March 11, 1865, as quoted in Milroy, "Public Career of Emma Stebbins: Work in Marble," 4.

115. Writing to Wayman Crow, Hosmer described Cushman as "a noble woman and as much of a mother to me as you are a Father." Quoted in D. Sherwood, *Harriet Hosmer,* 167.

116. Harriet Hosmer to Cornelia Carr, April 23, 1854, quoted in Carr, *Harriet Hosmer,* 26–27.

## *Chapter 2*

1. David Irwin, *Neoclassicism* (London: Phaidon Press, 1997), 24.

2. Howe, *Reminiscences,* 129.

3. Claudia Mattos, "The Torchlight Visit: Guiding the Eye Through Late Eighteenth- and Early Nineteenth-Century Antique Sculpture Galleries," *RES: Anthropology and Aesthetics,* nos. 49/50 (Spring–Autumn, 2006): 140. I wish to thank Roxanne Smith, an honors student of mine at Kenyon College, for bringing this article to my attention.

4. Jacob Abbott, *Rollo in Rome,* Rollo's Tour in Europe, vol. 10 (Boston: Brown, Taggard & Chase, 1858), 199; Mattos, "Torchlight Visit," 148.

5. The first major work that Crawford produced in Rome was his *Orpheus and Cerberus,* completing the plaster model in 1839 and the marble statue in 1843. Charles Sumner and George Washington Green, the American consul in Rome from 1837 to 1845, viewed the plaster model in Crawford's studio. So taken with this sculpture, Sumner raised $25,000 by subscription to purchase the work for the Boston Athenaeum. Thomas Crawford, *Orpheus* curatorial file, Museum of Fine Arts, Boston.

6. This practice of working by torchlight had come into popular use in European academies in the late eighteenth century. For the history of the use of such lighting in ateliers and academies, see Mattos, "Torchlight Visit," 145–49.

7. Charles Sumner most likely paid for the interior design of the gallery. Lauretta Dimmick, "Thomas Crawford's *Orpheus:* The American *Apollo Belvedere,*" *American Art Journal* 19, no. 4 (Autumn 1987): 84 n. 98.

8. William L. Vance, *America's Rome,* vol. 1, *Classical Rome* (New Haven: Yale University Press, 1989), 345.

9. Thomas Bulfinch, *The Age of Fable; or, Beauties of Mythology* (Boston: S. W. Tilton, 1855), 254–57.

10. Sumner published the article in the *United States Magazine and Democratic Review* in May of 1843. Thomas Crawford, *Orpheus* curatorial file, Museum of Fine Arts, Boston.

11. Quoted in Vance, *America's Rome,* 1:348.

12. Dimmick, "Thomas Crawford's *Orpheus,*" 68; Vance, *America's Rome,* 1:348.

13. Crawford quoted in Robert L. Gale, *Thomas Crawford, American Sculptor* (Pittsburgh: University of Pittsburgh Press, 1964), 15.

14. Thomas Crawford to Charles Sumner, June 12, 1842 (Rome), in Dimmick, "Thomas Crawford's *Orpheus,*" 65–68, quotes on 65. On Greenough's *Chanting Cherubs,* see Wayne Craven, *Sculpture in America* (New York: Thomas Y. Crowell, 1968), 103–4; Margaret Farrand Thorp, *The Literary Sculptors* (Durham: Duke University Press, 1965), 114. For an illustration of Greenough's *Angel and Child* of 1832, a work similar to the lost *Chanting Cherubs,* see Craven, *Sculpture in America,* 136.

15. Thomas Crawford, *Orpheus* curatorial file, Museum of Fine Arts, Boston; Hicks quoted in Dimmick, "Thomas Crawford's *Orpheus,*" 78. See also Lauretta Dimmick, "Veiled Memories, or, Thomas Crawford in Rome," in *The Italian Presence in American Art, 1760–1860,* ed. Irma B. Jaffe (New York: Fordham University Press; Rome: Istituto della Enciclopedia Italiana, 1989), 176–94.

16. Thomas Crawford to his sister, Jenny, 1839, as quoted in Gale, *Thomas Crawford,* 15.

17. As quoted in Jonah Siegel, *Desire and Excess: The Nineteenth-Century Culture of Art* (Princeton: Princeton University Press, 2000), 41.

18. Christina Ferando, "Staging Neoclassicism: Antonio Canova's Exhibition Strategies for *Triumphant Perseus,*" in *Das Originale der Kopie: Kopien als Produkte und Medien der Transformation von Antike,* ed. Tatjana Bartsch et al. (New York: Walter de Gruyter, 2010), 139. I wish to thank Christina Ferando for providing me with a copy of her article. See also Hugh Honour, *Neo-classicism* (1968; repr., New York: Penguin Books, 1979), 14.

19. Siegel, *Desire and Excess,* 43–47, 55–56.

20. Bulfinch explained that the language of myth was essential to everyday life in order "to comprehend the allusions so frequently made by public speakers . . . essayists and polite conversations." Bulfinch, *Age of Fable,* 6. See also Burton Feldman and Robert D. Richardson, *The Rise of Modern Mythology, 1680–1860* (Bloomington: Indiana University Press, 1972), 512.

21. Chris Weedon has argued that "the feminine discourses of mysticism, magic, poetry, and art" resisted patriarchal structures in their "rejection of . . . rationalist norms." Chris Weedon, *Feminist Practice and Poststructuralist Theory* (New York: Basil Blackwell, 1987), 72. See also Staley, "'Beyond Glorious Ocean,'" in Zajko and Leonard, *Laughing with Medusa,* 229.

22. In the writings on Praxiteles from Pliny to Winckelmann, the sculptor was recognized for two important developments: the introduction of naturalism, or worldly pleasure, into the austere ideal form and the invention of the female nude, the *Aphrodite of Knidos.* Caroline Arscott and Katie Scott, "Introducing Venus," in *Manifestations of Venus: Art and Sexuality,* ed. Caroline Arscott and Katie Scott (New York: Manchester University Press, 2000), 5.

23. Alex Potts, *The Sculptural Imagination: Figurative, Modernist, Minimalist* (New Haven: Yale University Press, 2000), 45.

24. Hugh Honour, "Canova's Studio Practice—I: The Early Years," *Burlington Magazine* 114, no. 828 (March 1972): 146–59. Canova's work was well known in the United States, having been exhibited in Boston and New York as early as 1818. Thomas Jefferson admired his oeuvre and recommended him for the important sculpture of George

Washington for the newly remodeled North Carolina State House. Because of the lack of native-born American sculptors in the early nineteenth century, most public commissions went to European artists. Canova accepted the commission in 1815; the sculpture was installed in 1821. As one of the most famous works of art at the time, it helped establish a monumental sculptural tradition in the United States.

Although destroyed in a fire in 1830, this sculpture introduced an American audience to the language of neoclassicism. Canova depicted Washington seated as a Roman general with toga, bare legs, and sandaled feet, his countenance taking on a quasi-classical appearance. He held a tablet and pen, about to compose his farewell address to the nation. Upon the tablet was inscribed "Georgio Washington ai Popolo degli Stati Uniti 1796 Amici e Concittidini" (George Washington to the People of the United States 1796 Friends and Fellow Citizens). Craven, *Sculpture in America,* 61–64; Fred Licht and David Finn, *Canova* (New York: Abbeville Press, 1983), 103–7, 181–87.

25. Honour, "Canova's Studio Practice—I," 147; Honour, "Canova's Studio Practice—II: 1792–1822," *Burlington Magazine* 114, no. 829 (April 1972): 217.

26. J. J. L. Whiteley, "Light and Shade in French Neoclassicism," *Burlington Magazine* 117, no. 873 (December 1975): 772.

27. Madame de Staël, *Corinne, or Italy,* 142–43.

28. Napoleon invaded Italy in April 1796; he entered and took control of the Papal States on June 18, 1796. One hundred works of art were surrendered to the French in the Treaty of Tolentino, among them the *Apollo Belvedere, Laocoön, Belvedere Torso,* and *Dying Gaul.* In February of 1797 the first cargo of objects was transported to France, where they remained on view in the Louvre for fifteen years. In 1815, Canova arrived in Paris and supervised the dismantling of the Musée Napoléon, restoring the collection to the papacy. The works arrived in Rome on January 4, 1816. Haskell and Penny, *Taste and the Antique,* 108–13. Canova's *Triumphant Perseus* was placed on the very same pedestal that had once held the *Apollo Belvedere.* Ferando, "Staging Neoclassicism," 150 n. 29.

29. Honour, "Canova's Studio Practice—I," 148, 156.

30. Thorwaldsen explained "that the clay model may be called creation, the plaster cast death, and the marble resurrection." As quoted in Ellet, *Women Artists in All Ages,* 324.

31. William H. Gerdts Jr., "Celebrities of the Grand Tour: The American Sculptors in Florence and Rome," in T. Stebbins, *Lure of Italy,* 71.

32. Paul Duro, "The Lure of Rome: The Academic Copy and the *Academie de France* in the Nineteenth Century," in *Art and the Academy in the Nineteenth Century,* ed. Rafael Cardoso Denis and Colin Trodd (New Brunswick: Rutgers University Press, 2000), 134.

33. Honour, "Canova's Studio Practice—II," 220. These treatments have faded with time; thus modern viewers are unable to replicate the original viewing conditions of his sculpture. Ferando, "Staging Neoclassicism," 147.

34. David J. Getsy, *Body Doubles: Sculpture in Britain, 1877–1905* (New Haven: Yale University Press, 2004), 10; Gerdts, "Celebrities of the Grand Tour," 66–67; Potts, *Sculptural Imagination,* 42–45.

35. Craske, *Art in Europe,* 51–53; George Washington Greene, "Personal Reminiscences of Thorwaldsen," *Putnam's Magazine* 1 (January 1853): 97.

36. Potts, *Sculptural Imagination,* 57.

37. As quoted in Dimmick, "Veiled Memories," 176.

38. Crane, *White Silence,* 280, quote on 283.

39. Gale, *Thomas Crawford,* 10–13; T. Stebbins, *Lure of Italy,* 166; Brooks, *Dream of Arcadia,* 89.

40. In 1829, Gibson achieved international recognition when elected to Rome's Academy of Saint Luke. Andreas Blühm, "In Living History: A Short History of Colour in Sculpture in the 19th Century," in Andreas Blühm et al., *The Colour of Sculpture, 1840–1910,* exh. cat. (Zwolle: Waanders, 1996), 25.

41. Gibson concluded, "The sculptor, duly imbued with the principles of his art, struggles on, and feels delight in his labours—for the study of the beautiful is his profession." Lady Eastlake, ed., *Life of John Gibson, R. A.* (London: Longmans, Green, 1870), 184–85.

42. For discussions of tinted statuary, see Benedict Read, *Victorian Sculpture* (New Haven: Yale University Press, 1982), 32–33, and Thayer Tolles, "'In a Class by Themselves': Polychrome Portraits by Herbert Adams," in *Perspectives on American Sculpture Before 1925,* ed. Thayer Tolles (New York: Metropolitan Museum of Art; New Haven: Yale University Press, 2003), 70–71.

43. Elisabeth S. Darby, "John Gibson, Queen Victoria, and the Idea of Sculptural Polychromy," *Art History* 4, no. 1 (March 1981): 40.

44. The sculpture was first commissioned by Robert Preston of Liverpool. Gibson kept a version of the *Tinted Venus* in his studio in Rome for four years before delivering it to his patron. Caroline Arscott, "Venus as Dominatrix: Nineteenth-Century Artists and Their Creations,"

in Arscott and Scott, *Manifestations of Venus,* 122; Andreas Blühm, "In Living Colour: A Short History of Colour in Sculpture in the Nineteenth Century," in Blühm et al., *Colour of Sculpture,* 25.

45. Maitland Armstrong, *Day Before Yesterday: Reminiscences of a Varied Life* (New York: Charles Scribner's Sons, 1920), 194.

46. Elizabeth Barrett Browning to Mrs. Anna Jameson, December 31, 1853 (Rome), in *Letters of Elizabeth Barrett Browning,* 2:148.

47. Carr, *Harriet Hosmer,* 217.

48. Greenwood, *Haps and Mishaps,* 217.

49. Harriet Hosmer to Wayman Crow, November 1857 (Rome), in Carr, *Harriet Hosmer,* 116. Hosmer paid tribute to Gibson in a marble medallion portrait of 1866, presenting her teacher in profile and portraying him according to his reputation—as young, dashing, and handsome, certainly nowhere near his seventy-six years. Included in this idealized image were naturalistic details, such as a furrowed brow, deep-set eyes, and dimpled chin. She carved his hair and beard in a soft sensuous manner that enlivened the marble surface. The portrait is now located in the Watertown Free Public Library, Watertown, Massachusetts.

50. Quoted in Eastlake, *Life of John Gibson,* 226. See also Arscott, "Venus as Dominatrix," 119–21.

51. Quoted in Carr, *Harriet Hosmer,* 24.

52. Nancy Proctor also discusses the theme of transformation as it relates to Edmonia Lewis's *Hagar,* Hosmer's *Zenobia in Chains,* and Elizabeth Ney's *Lady Macbeth.* Nancy Proctor, "Traveling Between the Borders of Gender and Nationality: Nineteenth-Century American Women Artists in Rome," *Prospero* 2 (1995): 46–55.

53. With the loss of the nymph, Apollo claimed the laurel tree as his arboreal emblem. Thorp, *Literary Sculptors,* 87; James Hall, *Dictionary of Subjects and Symbols in Art* (New York: Harper & Row, 1974), 28–29; Thayer Tolles, ed., *American Sculpture in the Metropolitan Museum of Art,* vol. 1, *A Catalogue of Works by Artists Born Before 1865* (New York: Metropolitan Museum of Art, 1999), 130; Robert Eisner, *The Road to Daulis: Psychoanalysis, Psychology, and Classical Mythology* (Syracuse: Syracuse University Press, 1987), 143. For the quotes, see Bulfinch, *Age of Fable,* 36, 37.

54. Linda C. Hunt, *A Woman's Portion: Ideology, Culture, and the British Female Novel Tradition* (New York: Garland Publishing, 1988), 76–77. My thanks to Cécile Whiting for bringing Brontë's novels to my attention.

55. Thanks to Eugene Dwyer, my colleague at Kenyon College, for bringing to my attention the Severe-style figures at the Temple of Zeus at Olympia and their possible influence on Hosmer's work. Hosmer may have viewed the plaster casts of these pedimental figures in Rome; or she may have looked to other Severe-style figures in Roman museums, such as the *Hestia Giustiniani* or the *Head of Perseus,* both located in the Capitoline Museum. See Brunilde Sismondo Ridgway, *The Severe Style in Greek Sculpture* (Princeton: Princeton University Press, 1970), plates 103 and 121.

56. Alex Potts, *Flesh and the Ideal: Winckelmann and the Origins of Art History* (New Haven: Yale University Press, 1994), 145–50.

57. As quoted in D. Sherwood, *Harriet Hosmer,* 87.

58. Marjorie Garber and Nancy J. Vicker, introduction to *The Medusa Reader* (New York: Routledge, 2003), 1–5, Shelley quote on 4.

59. As quoted in Bulfinch, *Age of Fable,* 161.

60. Ferando, "Staging Neoclassicism," 155. This version of the sculpture is located in the Metropolitan Museum of Art in New York.

61. Gerdts, "The *Medusa* of Harriet Hosmer," 100–102. The recent cleaning of the bust in the Capitoline Museum has spurred renewed debate about the sculpture's attribution. Nonetheless, it was exhibited in the 1850s with an attribution to Bernini.

62. Potts, *Sculptural Imagination,* 39, 51; Garber and Vicker, introduction to *Medusa Reader,* 2. Indeed, Canova scholar Christina Ferando has noted that "the introduction of the feminine form of Medusa into the conception of Perseus" was an important new development. "Staging Neoclassicism," 141 n. 7.

63. As quoted in Countess Albrizzi and Count Cicognara, *The Works of Antonio Canova,* vol. 1 (London: Septimus Prowett, Strand, 1826), n.p.

64. Sarah Burns, *Painting on the Dark Side: Art and the Gothic Imagination in Nineteenth-Century America* (Berkeley: University of California Press, 2004), 173–87. Nathaniel Hawthorne wrote a children's story about the Medusa myth, "The Gorgon's Head," in *A Wonder-Book for Girls and Boys* (1851; repr., Boston: James R. Osgood, 1874), 7–54.

65. Marcel Detienne, *The Creation of Mythology,* trans. Margaret Cook (Chicago: University of Chicago Press, 1986), ix. As Freud argued, "pure masculinity and pure femininity remain theoretical constructs of uncertain content." Weedon, *Feminist Practice and Poststructuralist Theory,* 42–51, quote on 49.

66. Garber and Vicker, introduction to *Medusa Reader,* 4.

67. Castration is a fantasy produced in response to the male child's puzzlement over the anatomical difference between the sexes (the presence or absence of the penis). According to Freud, the young boy assumes that everyone has a penis. A traumatic moment occurs when he first recognizes that his mother has no penis; he is horrified by her lack and fearful of his own castration. When the primal moment of recognition is repressed, the rational self struggles to keep these psychic fears at bay. Sexual difference is thus constantly reproduced and its anxiety never resolved.

68. Neil Hertz, "Medusa's Head: Male Hysteria Under Political Pressure," in *The End of the Line: Essays on Psychoanalysis and the Sublime* (New York: Columbia University Press, 1985), 166–67.

69. As quoted in Sigmund Freud, "Medusa's Head," reprinted in Garber and Vicker, *Medusa Reader,* 84–85.

70. Garber and Vicker, introduction to *Medusa Reader,* 1. See also Hertz, "Medusa's Head," 250–51 n. 9, and John Freccero, "'Medusa': The Letter and the Spirit," *Yearbook of Italian Studies* (1972): 7.

71. Garber and Vicker, introduction to *Medusa Reader,* 1. On Medusa's beauty, see Christine de Pizan, *The Book of the City of Ladies* (1405), reprinted in Garber and Vicker, *Medusa Reader,* 57. See also Hélène Cixous, "The Laugh of the Medusa" and "Sorties: Out and Out: Attacks / Ways Out / Forays," in *The Newly Born Woman,* trans. Betsy Wing (Minneapolis: University of Minnesota Press, 1986), 63–135. Not all feminist writers have embraced myth as a liberating force. Luce Irigaray rejected the utopianism of Cixous and saw myth as fossilizing existing hierarchies. She argued that oppressive myths of the past structure women's experience in the present. Zajko and Leonard, introduction to *Laughing with Medusa,* 4.

72. Thanks to Erin Sutherland of Washington University, who brought the imagery on this doorway to my attention. The image of Medusa on the door knocker resembles the *Medusa Rondanini* (Glyptothek, Munich), among the first ancient depictions of the humanized Gorgon.

73. Harriet Hosmer to Wayman Crow, October 12, 1854 (Rome), in Carr, *Harriet Hosmer,* 37.

74. Harriet Hosmer to Wayman Crow, August 1854 (Rome), in Carr, *Harriet Hosmer,* 36.

75. Harriet Hosmer to Wayman Crow, October 15, 1854 (Rome), in Carr, *Harriet Hosmer,* 41.

76. Harriet Hosmer to Wayman Crow, October 12, 1854 (Rome), in Carr, *Harriet Hosmer,* 37.

77. Harriet Hosmer to Wayman Crow, August 1854 and October 12, 1854 (Rome), in Carr, *Harriet Hosmer,* 36, 38.

78. Read, *Victorian Sculpture,* 53, 201; Greenwood, *Haps and Mishaps,* 217.

79. Janet Headley first noticed this resemblance in her dissertation, "English Literary and Aesthetic Influences on American Sculptors in Italy, 1825–1875" (University of Maryland, 1988).

80. D. Sherwood, *Harriet Hosmer,* 80; Tennyson, "Oenone," in *Poems and Plays,* 38–41.

81. "Do you draw from Teresa or any new model?" Robert Browning asked in a letter to Hosmer dated November 16, 1854, in Carr, *Harriet Hosmer,* 46.

82. Thomas Crawford to Louisa Crawford, July 5, 1854, Thomas Crawford Papers, Archives of American Art, Smithsonian Institution, Washington, D.C., microfilm reel D181, frame 783.

83. Barrett Browning to Ilsa Blagdon, May 8, 1854, quoted in D. Sherwood, *Harriet Hosmer,* 91.

84. Markus, *Across an Untried Sea,* 25.

85. Margaret Thorp, "Harriet Hosmer: Leader of the White Marmorean Flock," *Smith Alumni Quarterly,* Spring 1975, 150; D. Sherwood, *Harriet Hosmer,* 81; Lilian Whiting, *Women Who Have Ennobled Life* (Philadelphia: Union Press, 1915), 218.

86. Harriet Hosmer to Cornelia Crow, October 30, 18[54], as quoted in Merrill, *When Romeo Was a Woman,* 176.

87. Rupp, *Desired Past,* 10; Carroll Smith-Rosenberg, "The Female World of Love and Ritual: Relations Between Women in Nineteenth-Century America," in *Disorderly Conduct,* 53–77.

88. The romantic friendship sentimentalized strong female bonds into a spiritualized love, "the love of angels," as Catharine Sedgwick wrote in her diary regarding her intimate connection with Fanny Kemble. As quoted in Cott, *Bonds of Womanhood,* 185.

89. Harriet Hosmer to Cornelia Carr, April 22, 1854 (Rome), in Carr, *Harriet Hosmer,* 33.

90. Harriet Hosmer to Cornelia Carr, April 22, 1854 (Rome), in Carr, *Harriet Hosmer,* 32.

91. Matilda Hays to Cornelia Carr, April 1856 (Rome), in Carr, *Harriet Hosmer,* 70.

92. Greenwood, *Haps and Mishaps,* 222; Vance, *America's Rome,* 1:211.

93. Gerdts, "The *Medusa* of Harriet Hosmer," 99; "Samuel Appleton," in *Appletons' Cyclopædia of American Biography* (1900), http://en.wikisource.org/wiki/Appletons%27_Cyclop%C3%A6dia_of_American_Biography/Appleton,_Samuel, accessed August 13, 2010. See also Cronin, *Harriet Hosmer: Lost and Found,* 34.

94. Contributing to the Arts and Crafts movement in England, Lady Marian supported artisans in needlework and established a school of art needlework in South Kensington. She also wrote and published a book on the subject. D. Sherwood, *Harriet Hosmer,* 204–8, 212.

95. Alicia Faxon, "Images of Women in the Sculpture of Harriet Hosmer," *Woman's Art Journal* 2, no. 1 (Spring–Summer 1981): 27; D. Sherwood, *Harriet Hosmer,* 119, 347 n. 11. For a discussion of *Puck* as a self-portrait of the artist, see Culkin, *Harriet Hosmer,* 44–46.

96. For a full discussion of this commission, see Barbara S. Groseclose, "Harriet Hosmer's Tomb to Judith Falconnet: Death and the Maiden," *American Art Journal* 12, no. 2 (Spring 1980): 78–89.

97. Hosmer to Crow, August 1854 (Rome), Harriet Goodhue Hosmer Papers, Schlesinger Library, Radcliffe Institute, Harvard University, Cambridge, Mass. See also Carr, *Harriet Hosmer,* 35.

## *Chapter 3*

1. Prieto, *At Home in the Studio,* 47.

2. Kirk Savage, "Vinnie Ream's *Lincoln* (1871): The Sexual Politics of a Sculptor's Studio," in *American Pantheon: Sculptural and Artistic Decoration of the United States Capitol,* ed. Donald R. Kennon and Thomas P. Somma (Athens: Ohio University Press, 2004), 170–71.

3. Entry dated March 15, 1859, Rome, in Nathaniel Hawthorne, *The French and Italian Notebooks,* the Centenary Edition of the Works of Nathaniel Hawthorne, vol. 14, ed. Thomas Woodson (Columbus: Ohio State University Press, 1980), 508.

4. Ellet, *Women Artists in All Ages,* 326. Ellet had quoted at length from Matilda Hays's article in the *English Woman's Journal,* 1858.

5. In looking more closely at her, he noted that her face "looked, in one aspect, youthful, and yet there was something worn in it, too, as if it had faced a good deal . . . either morally or physically." Again, trepidation entered his writing. Entry dated April 3, 1858, in N. Hawthorne, *French and Italian Notebooks,* 158–59. The following month, he pursued, once again, this obsessive interest in the artist's appearance: "Miss Hosmer, to-day, had on a neat little jacket, a man's shirt-bosom, and a cravat with a brooch in it; her hair is cut short, and curls jauntily round her bright and smart physiognomy; . . . I never should have imagined that she terminated in a petticoat, any more than in a fish's tail. However, I do not mean to speak disrespectfully of Miss Hosmer, of whom I think very favorably; but, it seems to me, her reform of the female dress commences with its least objectionable part, and is no real improvement." Entry dated Sunday, May 23, 1858, in ibid., 230.

6. Entry dated February 15, 1858, in N. Hawthorne, *French and Italian Notebooks,* 76.

7. Ibid.

8. Sc****, "Art in Boston," *Boston Evening Transcript,* December 3, 1859, 4.

9. Cherry, *Beyond the Frame,* 122.

10. Crane, *White Silence,* 372.

11. Ellet, *Women Artists in All Ages,* 303; "Louisa Lander," *Cosmopolitan Art Journal,* March 1861, 27.

12. "American Artists in Rome—Crawford's Condition," *Daily Evening Bulletin* (Philadelphia), February 24, 1857, 1.

13. "Art Gossip," *Cosmopolitan Art Journal* 2 (December 1857): 38, courtesy of the Boston Athenaeum Curatorial Files; *Home Journal* (New York), February 27, 1858, 3; N., "Domestic Art Gossip," *The Crayon* 4, no. 8 (August 1857): 252. See also Henry Wadsworth Longfellow, *Evangeline: A Tale of Acadie* (Boston: William D. Ticknor, 1847).

14. *Home Journal* (New York), February 27, 1858, 3.

15. Sc****, "Art in Boston," 4.

16. "The National Statue, *Virginia Dare* by Louisa Lander," four-page pamphlet, 1865, courtesy of the Boston Athenaeum Curatorial Files.

17. Rubenstein, *American Women Sculptors,* 57; N., "Domestic Art Gossip," *The Crayon* 4, no. 8 (August 1857): 252; Vivien Green Fryd, *Art and Empire: The Politics of Ethnicity in the United States Capitol, 1815–1860* (New Haven: Yale University Press, 1992), 169–70.

18. Joy S. Kasson, *Marble Queens and Captives: Women in Nineteenth-Century American Sculpture* (New Haven: Yale University Press, 1990), 87. Quote from "The National Statue, *Virginia Dare* by Louisa Lander," four-page pamphlet, 1865, courtesy of the Boston Athenaeum Curatorial Files.

19. Kasson, *Marble Queens and Captives,* 73, 78–79; Annette Kolodny, "Turning the Lens on 'The Panther Captivity': A Feminist Exercise in Practical Criticism," *Critical Inquiry* 8, no. 2 (Winter 1981): 329–45. "The Indian

captivity narrative [may] function as *the* archetype of American culture in which initial contact between Europeans and Native Americans inevitably evolved into conflict and finally colonial conquest." Kathryn Zabelle Derounian-Stodola, ed., *Women's Indian Captivity Narratives* (New York: Penguin Books, 1998), xi.

20. Palmer's images appeared widely in high-quality photographs; reproductions of his works were sold in Italy. Tolles, *American Sculpture in the Metropolitan Museum of Art,* 1:60, quotes on 64. See also Clark, *Marble Quarry,* 164. For an alternative reading of the *Greek Slave* and the *White Captive,* see Nelson, *Color of Stone,* 75–113.

21. As quoted in "Miss Lander's 'Virginia Dare,'" *Evening Post* (New York), November 27, 1868, 2; Kasson, *Marble Queens and Captives,* 88.

22. "Miss Lander's 'Virginia Dare,'" *Boston Evening Transcript,* February 20, 1865, 2; Kasson, *Marble Queens and Captives,* 169–73.

23. Entry dated February 15, 1858, in N. Hawthorne, *French and Italian Notebooks,* 78; "Personal," *Home Journal* (New York), February 27, 1858, 3.

24. Julian Hawthorne, *Nathaniel Hawthorne and His Wife* (Boston: Houghton, Mifflin, 1884), 2:182; Nathaniel Hawthorne, preface to *The Marble Faun,* 4.

25. Entry dated February 15, 1858, in N. Hawthorne, *French and Italian Notebooks,* 78.

26. Prieto, *At Home in the Studio,* 78, 80.

27. Ada Shepard (the Hawthornes' governess in Rome) to H. C. Badger, February 7, 1858 (Rome), courtesy of the Robert L. Straker Collection of Horace Mann Papers, Antioch College, Yellow Springs, Ohio.

28. Entries dated March 31, 1858, and April 7, 1858, in N. Hawthorne, *French and Italian Notebooks,* 589, 590. A plaster bust of Hawthorne, by P. P. Caproni and Brother after the marble bust by Lander, is located in the Peabody Essex Museum. The original plaster is presumed lost.

29. Entry dated February 15, 1858, in N. Hawthorne, *French and Italian Notebooks,* 78.

30. In my thinking about the gendered gaze, I am influenced by Mary Ann Doane, "Film and the Masquerade: Theorizing the Female Spectator," in *The Feminism and Visual Culture Reader,* ed. Amelia Jones (New York: Routledge, 2003), 67.

31. T. Walter Herbert, *Dearest Beloved: The Hawthornes and the Making of the Middle-Class Family* (Berkeley: University of California Press, 1993), 230.

32. Nathaniel Hawthorne to William Ticknor, April 14, 1858 (Rome), in Nathaniel Hawthorne, *The Letters,* vol. 4, *1857–1864,* the Centenary Edition of the Works of Nathaniel Hawthorne, vol. 18, ed. Thomas Woodson, L. Neal Smith, and Norman Holmes Pearson (Columbus: Ohio State University Press, 1987), 140.

33. Herbert, *Dearest Beloved,* 229. Before her marriage to Hawthorne, Sophia Peabody took art lessons and supported herself as an artist. She produced several original landscapes and copied for resale to local patrons famous paintings she saw on exhibit in the Boston Athenaeum. At the height of her painting career, in the 1830s, she fetched as much as one hundred dollars per canvas for her romantic landscapes. In a letter to her sister Elizabeth in 1832, she proclaimed: "Oh why not live in Rome . . . the eternal, imperial 'mother of the dead emperors,' the city of the soul, the retreat of the arts and graces, the garden of nature—for three or four years!" As quoted in Algerina Neri, "Forbidden Rooms with a View: American Women Travellers in Europe in the Nineteenth Century," *Rivista di studi anglo-americani* 7, no. 9 (1993): 596–97.

For Sophia Peabody's career as an artist, see Mary Suzanne Schriber, *Writing Home: American Women Abroad, 1830–1920* (Charlottesville: University Press of Virginia, 1997), 91–132; Josephine Withers, "Artistic Women and Women Artists," *Art Journal* 35, no. 4 (Summer 1976): 330–36; Megan Marshall, *The Peabody Sisters: Three Women Who Ignited American Romanticism* (New York: Houghton Mifflin, 2005); Patricia Dunlavy Valenti, *Sophia Peabody Hawthorne: A Life,* vol. 1, *1809–1847* (Columbia: University of Missouri Press, 2004); and Patricia Dunlavy Valenti, "Sophia Peabody Hawthorne: A Study of Artistic Influence," in *Studies in the American Renaissance,* ed. Joel Myerson (Charlottesville: University Press of Virginia, 1990), 1–19.

34. "I am so happy that I require nothing more," Sophia Hawthorne wrote in 1848. Neither "art nor beauty can excel my daily life," she explained, for her husband and children had become her "exponents of all art and beauty." She continued, "I really have not even the temptation to go out of my house to find anything better." As quoted in Schriber, *Writing Home,* 122.

35. Nathaniel Hawthorne to Francis Bennoch, March 16, 1858 (Rome), in N. Hawthorne, *Letters,* 4:138.

36. "Rome, Rome, *Rome!*" as quoted in Rose Hawthorne Lathrop, *Memories of Hawthorne* (New York: Houghton, Mifflin, 1898), 354. "Irresistible attraction" as quoted in Mrs. Nathaniel (Sophia) Hawthorne, *Notes in England and Italy* (New York: G. P. Putnam's Sons, 1878), 541–42. See also Corsetta Fornasiero, "Mrs. Hawthorne's

Notes in Italy" (tesi di laurea, Università degli Studi Ca'Foscari, Venice, 1991–92), courtesy of the Centro Studi Americani, Rome.

37. Katharine Burton, *Sorrow Built a Bridge: A Daughter of Hawthorne* (New York: Longmans, Green, 1937), 3; J. Hawthorne, *Nathaniel Hawthorne and His Wife,* 2:194.

38. Schriber, *Writing Home,* 118.

39. Entry dated March 11, [1858], in S. Hawthorne, *Notes in England and Italy,* 265.

40. Nathaniel Hawthorne described Hosmer much as his wife did: "She is a small, brisk, wide-awake figure, of queer and funny aspect, yet not ungraceful . . . frank, simple, straight-forward, and downright." Entry dated April 3, 1858, in N. Hawthorne, *French and Italian Notebooks,* 158–59. Their impressions of the young artist were quite similar. In fact, it seemed that Nathaniel had relied upon his wife's responses to substantiate his own judgments. Both writers used the same terms to describe the artist's demeanor: "frank" and "wide-awake"; similar adjectives: "honest and sincere" and "straight-forward and downright"; and comparable syntax: "yet not ungentle" and "yet not ungraceful." This was clearly no coincidence.

41. Ada Shepard, together with Sophia's daughters, Una and Rose, visited Hosmer's studio. Like Una, Shepard was quite taken with Hosmer, whom she described as "a very bewitching little person, I think, in spite of her short hair combed like a gentleman's, her linen collar and shirt-bosoms, her gentleman's velvet cap which she wears in her studio, and her boyish manners. . . . She certainly is a great genius." Ada Shepard to Kate Shepard, April 9, 1858 (Rome), courtesy of the Robert L. Straker Collection of Horace Mann Papers, p. 4046, Antioch College, Yellow Springs, Ohio. Rose described Hosmer as "wittily gay [with] plenty of brain power" behind her clever words. Lathrop, *Memories of Hawthorne,* 366.

42. Una Hawthorne to Richard and Rebecca Manning, November 13, 1858, as quoted in Herbert, *Dearest Beloved,* 235. After Hawthorne's death, in 1865, Sophia Hawthorne brought her children to Dresden, where her son, Julian, attended engineering school, and the girls (Una and Rose) studied art and music. Schriber, *Writing Home,* 123. Later in life, Rose converted to Catholicism. Lathrop, *Memories of Hawthorne,* 352–53.

43. Entry dated May 23, 1858, in N. Hawthorne, *French and Italian Notebooks,* 230.

44. F., "Dear Crayon," *The Crayon* 5 (July 1858): 206. Lander sculpted a bust of Governor Gore for the Harvard Library. "Art Items," *Boston Evening Transcript,* September 20, 1858, 2.

45. "Extract of a Letter from Rome," *Boston Evening Transcript,* April 3, 1858, 4; F., "Dear *Crayon,*" *The Crayon* 5 (June 1858): 179–80, quote on 180.

46. Burton, *Sorrow Built a Bridge,* 43–48; Anna Jameson to Hosmer, October 10, 1859 (Brighton), in Carr, *Harriet Hosmer,* 149–50; J. Hawthorne, *Nathaniel Hawthorne and His Wife,* 2:191–92, 196.

47. "Hawthorne's Florentine Diary, June 2–July 2, 1858," Nathaniel Hawthorne Papers, Huntington Library, Art Collection, and Botanical Gardens, San Mareno, Calif. See also Nathalia Wright, *American Novelists in Italy; The Discoverers: Allston to James* (Philadelphia: University of Pennsylvania Press, 1965), 141. Hawthorne notes that he "began to write a Romance" on Monday, October 25, 1858. "The 1858 Pocket Diary," in N. Hawthorne, *French and Italian Notebooks,* 616.

48. "Snuggest little . . . apartments" as quoted in J. Hawthorne, *Nathaniel Hawthorne and His Wife,* 2:202; "hear the plash" from the entry dated October 21, 1858, in N. Hawthorne, *French and Italian Notebooks,* 491.

49. As it turned out, Lander knew Thompson, presumably from their hometown of Salem. She had earlier confided to Hawthorne that the painter was feeling disheartened because his work was so little appreciated. John L. Idol Jr. and Sterling Eisiminger, "Hawthorne Sits for a Bust by Maria Louisa Lander," *Essex Institute Historical Collections* 114, no. 4 (October 1978): 208. Hawthorne's biographer, T. Walter Herbert, suggested that Thompson was jealous of Lander's friendship with Hawthorne. "If Lander's success with Hawthorne had aroused animosity among the male artists at Rome, this occasion certainly gave them a chance to make things difficult for her," he ruminated. Herbert, *Dearest Beloved,* 231.

50. As quoted in Herbert, *Dearest Beloved,* 230.

51. John Rogers Jr. to John Rogers Sr., December 14, 1858 (Rome), John Rogers Papers, Box 2, New York Historical Society, New York, N.Y. (hereafter Rogers Papers).

52. John Rogers Jr. to Henry Rogers, February 13, 1859 (Rome), Rogers Papers.

53. N. Hawthorne, *French and Italian Notebooks,* 619, 620, 623; Ada Shepard Letters, Robert L. Straker Collection of Horace Mann Papers, p. 4032 (October 18, 1858), Antioch College, Yellow Springs, Ohio.

54. J. Hawthorne, *Nathaniel Hawthorne and His Wife,* 2:206–9. "Una decidedly has Roman fever," Hawthorne wrote on November 1, 1858. She had fallen ill

about a week earlier, on October 26, 1858. N. Hawthorne, "The 1858 Pocket Diary," in *French and Italian Notebooks,* 616, 617.

55. Entry dated March 31, [1858], in S. Hawthorne, *Notes in England and Italy,* 281.

56. Annamaria Formichella Elsden, *Roman Fever: Domesticity and Nationalism in Nineteenth-Century American Women's Writing* (Columbus: Ohio State University Press, 2004), xiii.

57. N. Hawthorne, *French and Italian Notebooks,* 619, 620, 623.

58. Nathaniel Hawthorne to Louisa Lander, November 13, 1858 (Rome), in Joel Myerson, *Selected Letters of Nathaniel Hawthorne* (Columbus: Ohio State University Press, 2002), 158–59.

59. Herbert, *Dearest Beloved,* 230–34. Hawthorne's biographer posits that the author may actually have had an affair with Lander; however, the historical record is very insubstantial.

60. Hawthorne to Lander, November 13, 1858 (Rome), in Myerson, *Selected Letters of Nathaniel Hawthorne,* 158–59.

61. Entry dated December 7, 1858, in N. Hawthorne, *French and Italian Notebooks,* 623.

62. Herbert, *Dearest Beloved,* 232–34; Rubenstein, *American Women Sculptors,* 60. When editing her husband's journals, Sophia eradicated Lander's name. It did not reappear until the recent 1980 edition of the journals, published by the Ohio State University Press. Sophia most likely edited Lander's name out of her own published journals, since we know that she did visit Lander's studio but have no written record of it.

63. John Rogers Jr. to Ellen Rogers, December 26, 1858 (Rome), Rogers Papers.

64. It was claimed that a Dr. Greene, physician to the gravely ill abolitionist minister Theodore Parker, knew facts that could exonerate Lander. Because she refused to testify, Dr. Greene held his silence. Lawrence, "Aesthetic Transcendentalism and Its Legacy," 144.

65. By February, Rogers concluded that "now [the scandal] all seems to have died away." John Rogers Jr. to Henry Rogers, February 13, 1859 (Rome), Rogers Papers.

66. Ibid.

67. John Rogers Jr. to Henry Rogers, January 9, 1859 (Rome), Rogers Papers.

68. Rogers began his artistic career as a genre sculptor, producing small-scale plasters of everyday scenes. In Rome, he immediately felt insecure about his talents, believing that the aesthetic standards of neoclassicism were too stringent for him. "I don't think I shall ever get into the classic style," he wrote immediately upon his arrival in the city. "I think my best course is to pursue the path I have begun . . . and make small figures in a bronze or very nice plaster . . . and not attempt any high art for I shall certainly step out of my depth if I do." He felt out of place in Rome and was eager to return to the States, confiding to his father: "If I still adhere to this plan . . . I shall return home in the summer." John Rogers Jr. to John Rogers Sr., December 14, 1858 (Rome), Rogers Papers. See also Kimberly Orcutt, "Neoclassicism and the Artist's Ideal," in *John Rogers: American Stories,* ed. Kimberly Orcutt (New York: New-York Historical Society, 2010), 41–59.

69. Rogers reported in February that Lander was "modeling a large *Virginia Dare* which she is having put into marble—but it is not ordered. And she has another little figure two or three feet high in marble and she is going to model an *Undine* on an uncertain order from Mary Warren. So you see her business . . . it is all money out of pocket." John Rogers Jr. to Henry Rogers, February 13, 1859 (Rome), Rogers Papers.

70. "Louisa Lander," 27; *Boston Evening Transcript,* June 24, 1861, 4.

71. As one of the most important icons of Western culture, the female nude represented the pinnacle of beauty, serving as the essence of the high-art tradition. As such, it was considered the sole preserve of the male artist. Tamar Garb, "The Forbidden Gaze: Women Artists and the Male Nude in Late Nineteenth-Century France," in Adler and Pointon, *The Body Imaged,* 33–35; Lynda Nead, "Getting Down to Basics: Art, Obscenity, and the Female Nude," in *New Feminist Discourses: Critical Essays on Theories and Texts,* ed. Isobel Armstrong (New York: Routledge, 1992), 199; Marcia Pointon, *Naked Authority: The Body in Western Painting, 1830–1908* (New York: Cambridge University Press, 1990), 14.

72. Wright, *American Novelists in Italy,* 146. With Story, he visited the farm where the ancient prototype of the Medicean *Venus* had been excavated. J. Hawthorne, *Nathaniel Hawthorne and His Wife,* 2:213.

73. N. Hawthorne, *Marble Faun,* 123.

74. The painter Miriam, for whom Lander may have been the inspiration, speaks this soliloquy in the novel. N. Hawthorne, *Marble Faun,* 123.

75. We know, for example, that Hawthorne was both drawn to and repulsed by Gibson's *Tinted Venus* (fig. 11).

He saw the work as "fascinating and delectable in [its] warm, yet delicate tint"; but at the same time he preferred "the snowy whiteness" of the marble. "For this lascivious warmth of hue," he continued, "quite demoralizes the chastity of the marble, and makes one feel ashamed to look at the naked limbs in the company of women." Entry dated April 3, 1858, in N. Hawthorne, *French and Italian Notebooks,* 156.

76. Nancy Proctor, "The Purloined Studio: The Woman Sculptor as Phallic Ghost in Hawthorne's *The Marble Faun,*" in Martin and Person, *Roman Holidays,* 65; and Proctor, "American Women Sculptors in Rome," 177.

77. According to Julian Hawthorne, his parents viewed the marble bust in Lander's studio while she was away. Herbert, *Dearest Beloved,* 231, 233. Hawthorne does not document this visit in his Roman journals.

78. "Statuary by Miss Lander," *Boston Evening Transcript,* June 18, 1861, 2; "The Statuette of Undine," *Boston Evening Transcript,* June 24, 1861, 2; "A New Work by Miss Lander," *Boston Evening Transcript,* June 25, 1861, 3. In 1863, she donated the original cast of *Captive Pioneer Mother and Daughters* (originally known as *America Defending Her Children*) to the East Indian Marine Society of Salem. The sculpture is no longer in this collection and presumed lost. "Valuable Donation," *Boston Evening Transcript,* August 13, 1863, 2.

79. "Louisa Lander," 28.

80. Ibid.

81. "Miss Lander," *Boston Evening Transcript,* December 5, 1860, 2; "Art Items," *Boston Evening Transcript,* February 26, 1861, 2.

82. W., "Virginia Dare," *Boston Evening Transcript,* March 16, 1865, 2.

83. "Personal Items," *Boston Evening Transcript,* May 3, 1861, 2.

84. As quoted in D. Sherwood, *Harriet Hosmer,* 215.

85. Lander was still living in Washington, D.C., in 1871. See *The Revolution* 8, no. 26 (June 29, 1871).

86. Cherry, *Beyond the Frame,* 109. The bibliography regarding Hosmer's *Zenobia* is large. Among the most important sources are the following (as well as those cited below): Gabrielle Gopinath, "Harriet Hosmer and the Feminine Sublime," *Oxford Art Journal* 28, no. 1 (2005): 61–81; Susan Waller, "The Artist, the Writer, and the Queen: Hosmer, Jameson, and *Zenobia,*" *Woman's Art Journal* 4, no. 1 (Spring–Summer 1983): 21–28; Allison Yarrington, "'Made in Italy': Sculpture and the Staging of National Identities at the International Exhibition of 1862," in *Performing National Identity: Anglo-Italian Cultural Transactions,* ed. Manfred Pfister and Ralf Hertel (New York: Rodopi, 2008), 75–103; Culkin, *Harriet Hosmer,* 55–83.

87. She had been working on the model for more than eight months. D. Sherwood, *Harriet Hosmer,* 219.

88. Anna Jameson to Hosmer, October 10, 1858 (Brighton), in Carr, *Harriet Hosmer,* 150–51.

89. Ibid.

90. Entry dated March 15, 1859, in N. Hawthorne, *French and Italian Notebooks,* 509–10.

91. Cherry, *Beyond the Frame,* 109, 234 n. 21. Although disputed, certain sources argue that Hosmer followed in her teacher's footsteps and colored the sculpture with a subtle rose tint. "She gave the beautiful marble a rose tint . . . and, much as I dislike colored statues, I cannot object to the delicate tinting." "Miss Hosmer in Rome," *Boston Evening Transcript,* April 18, 1862, 2.

92. *Harper's Weekly* 3 (May 7, 1859): 293. The same image, captioned "The Prince of Wales Visiting Miss Hosmer's Studio," was also reproduced in *Frank Leslie's Illustrated Newspaper* on May 7, 1859.

93. Requesting only a photograph of the *Zenobia,* the prince purchased her popular fancy piece, *Puck* (fig. 22), for his rooms at Oxford. T. Matthews, *The Biography of John Gibson, R. A., Sculpture, Rome* (London: William Heinemann, 1911), 224; D. Sherwood, *Harriet Hosmer,* 119–20, 217–18. For a different reading of this illustration, see Culkin, *Harriet Hosmer,* 62.

94. Harriet Hosmer to Wayman Crow, May 15, 1862 (Rome), in Carr, *Harriet Hosmer,* 187. Hosmer's father, Hiram Hosmer, died on April 15, 1862, casting a pall over her successes in London. Culkin, *Harriet Hosmer,* 67.

95. Harriet Hosmer to Wayman Crow, March 1862 (Rome), in Carr, *Harriet Hosmer,* 184–85; Culkin, *Harriet Hosmer,* 68.

96. Frances Power Cobbe, *Italics: Brief Notes on Politics, People, and Places in Italy, in 1864* (London: Trübner, 1864), 413. Cobbe lived with Cushman and Hosmer at the via Gregoriana residence in 1861 and 1862. Kate Culkin suggests that Cobbe "had a short flirtation" with Hosmer. Culkin, *Harriet Hosmer,* 66.

Art historian Deborah Cherry discovered that the sculpture elicited an anxious response from the British public in the wake of Queen Victoria's disappearance from public view after the death of Prince Albert. Cherry, *Beyond the Frame,* 131.

97. Phebe Mitchell Kendall, ed., *Maria Mitchell: Life, Letters, and Journals* (Boston: Lee & Shepard, 1896), 150.

98. Charlotte Cushman to Emma Crow, April 5, 1862 (Rome), Charlotte Cushman Papers, Library of Congress, Washington, D.C. (hereafter Cushman Papers).

99. Charlotte Cushman to Emma Crow, February 19 (Rome), 1863, Cushman Papers.

100. Charlotte Cushman to Emma Crow, February 4, 1864 (Rome), Cushman Papers.

101. "Obituary, Mr. Alfred Gatley," *Art-Journal* (London), n.s., 2 (September 1863): 181.

102. Cherry, *Beyond the Frame,* 105.

103. D. Sherwood, *Harriet Hosmer,* 218–19.

104. *The Queen,* December 1863, as quoted in Cherry, *Beyond the Frame,* 106–7. See also "The Art Journal on Miss Hosmer," *Boston Evening Transcript,* December 22, 1863, 2.

105. Culkin, *Harriet Hosmer,* 73.

106. W. W. Story, "Our Weekly Gossip," *Athenaeum* 34, no. 1886 (December 19, 1863): 840. See also the *Boston Evening Transcript,* January 5, 1864, 2.

107. Originally dated November 14, 1863, and cosigned by John Gibson. Harriet G. Hosmer (countersigned by John Gibson), "To the Editor of the *Art-Journal,*" *Art-Journal* (London), n.s., 3 (January 1, 1864): 27.

108. D. Sherwood, *Harriet Hosmer,* 220; Carol Zastoupil, "Creativity, Inspiration, and Scandal: Harriet Hosmer and *Zenobia,*" in Jaffe, *Italian Presence in American Art, 1760–1860,* 206 n. 30.

109. Harriet Hosmer, "The Process of Sculpture," *Atlantic Monthly* 14 (December 1864): 734–37. The *Atlantic Monthly* catered to an intellectual and relatively highbrow audience. Culkin, *Harriet Hosmer,* 189 n. 81.

110. Carr, *Harriet Hosmer,* 194–97, and *Boston Evening Transcript,* November 17, 1864, 1.

111. Hosmer, "The Process of Sculpture," 735–37.

112. Harriet G. Hosmer (countersigned by John Gibson), "To the Editor of the *Art-Journal,*" 27.

113. Entry dated April 3, 1858, in N. Hawthorne, *French and Italian Notebooks,* 154. To many in Rome, Mozier, a wealthy New York merchant turned sculptor, had a reputation as a malicious gossip. He slandered Hiram Powers and belittled the deceased journalist Margaret Fuller, claiming that she had never written her now lost *History of the Roman Revolution.*

114. Hawthorne concluded, "Their public is so much more limited than that of the literary men, that they have the better excuse for these petty jealousies." Entry dated May 21, 1858, in N. Hawthorne, *French and Italian Notebooks,* 220.

115. "The Statue of 'Lady Godiva,'" *Boston Evening Transcript,* October 7, 1864, 2.

116. Miss Anna Elliot Ticknor to Harriet Hosmer, February 27, 1865 (Boston), in Carr, *Harriet Hosmer,* 202.

117. Lydia Maria Child announced that fifteen thousand people had seen the *Zenobia* in its first three weeks of exhibition. Carr, *Harriet Hosmer,* 191.

118. As quoted in Carr, *Harriet Hosmer,* 201–2.

119. Harriet Hosmer, "The Doleful Ditty of the Roman Caffe Greco," *Boston Evening Transcript,* November 17, 1864, 1; S. C., "Harriet Hosmer," *Boatswain's Whistle,* November 18, 1864, 1.

120. Zastoupil, "Creativity, Inspiration, and Scandal," 205 n. 14; "The Exhibition of the Statue of Zenobia," *Boston Evening Transcript,* April 27, 1865, 2.

121. D. Sherwood, *Harriet Hosmer,* 238.

122. Harriet Hosmer to Wayman Crow, December 30, 1864 (Rome), in Carr, *Harriet Hosmer,* 205.

123. Harriet Hosmer to Wayman Crow, January 1865 (Rome), in Carr, *Harriet Hosmer,* 206.

124. "Gossip from Rome," *Evening Post* (New York), February 21, 1870, 1.

125. Dr. Samuel Osgood, "American Artists in Italy," *Harper's New Monthly Magazine* 41 (August 1870): 422.

126. Katharine C. Walker, "American Studios in Rome and Florence," *Harper's New Monthly Magazine* 33 (June 1866): 102.

127. Kasson, *Marble Queens and Captives,* 156; quotes from Harriet Hosmer to Wayman Crow, November 1867 (Ashridge, England), in Carr, *Harriet Hosmer,* 249–50.

128. Quote from "Art Notes," *Boston Evening Transcript,* December 18, 1880, 10. Before Cushman persuaded her to make the journey to Rome, Foley had considered working as a nurse with the Sanitary Commission to support the Northern troops in the war effort. Merrill, *When Romeo Was a Woman,* 199; Margaret Howitt, "A Memoir of the Sculptor Margaret F. Foley," *Art-Journal* (London), n.s., 17 (April 1, 1878): 101; D. Sherwood, *Harriet Hosmer,* 213; Tufts, "Margaret Foley's Metamorphosis," 91; Cheney, *Reminiscences,* 145.

129. Several articles were signed "M.F.F." and "F." See F., "Dear *Crayon,*" *The Crayon* 6 (1859): 256; 7 (May 1860): 176, (June 1860): 205, and (August 1860): 264. Parrott, "Expatriates and Professionals," 482.

130. "Art Notes," *Boston Evening Transcript,* December 18, 1880, 10.

131. Hosmer reported that she was "pegging away cutting cameos" in Rome. As quoted in D. Sherwood, *Harriet Hosmer,* 213; "Americans Artists Abroad," *Daily Evening Bulletin* (Philadelphia), March 23, 1865, 4. Foley did produce some ideal works, such as *Cleopatra* of 1872 (Smithsonian American Art Museum), which she exhibited at the 1876 Centennial Exposition in Philadelphia. William H. Gerdts Jr., "The Neoclassic Relief," in Tolles, *Perspectives on American Sculpture Before 1925,* 7.

132. "American Artists Abroad," *Daily Evening Bulletin* (Philadelphia), March 23, 1865, 4. See also Walker, "American Studios in Rome and Florence," 101–5.

133. "Visits to the Studios of Rome," *Art-Journal* (London), n.s., 10 (1871): 164, as quoted in Prieto, *At Home in the Studio,* 72.

134. Howitt, "A Memoir of the Sculptor Margaret F. Foley," 103.

135. Mary C. Shannon to Sarah Whitney, January 16, 1868 (Rome), Anne Whitney Papers, Wellesley College Archives, Wellesley, Mass. (hereafter Anne Whitney Papers). Anne Whitney concurred, "Miss Foley has more work than she can find time to do—time and strength." Anne Whitney to her family, April 3, 1868 (Rome), as quoted in Elizabeth Payne, "Anne Whitney: Nineteenth Century Sculptor and Liberal" (unpublished manuscript), Wellesley College Archives, Wellesley, Mass.

136. "Exhibition of the Society of Female Artists," *Art-Journal* (London), n.s., 10 (March 1871): 90; "The National Academy of Design," *Evening Post* (New York), June 19, 1971, 4. Formed in 1856, the organization changed its name to the Society of Lady Artists in 1872. See Whitney Chadwick, *Women, Art, and Society* (New York: Thames & Hudson, 1990), 168.

137. Howitt, "A Memoir of the Sculptor Margaret F. Foley," 102.

138. *The Revolution,* May 4, 1871, as quoted in Clara Erskine Clement, *Artists of the Nineteenth Century and Their Works,* rev. ed. (Cambridge, Mass.: Houghton, Mifflin, 1884), 260.

139. The German American painter Albert Bierstadt said he knew "of no artist who, in the same length of time, [had] made so many portraits as Miss Foley." *The Revolution,* May 4, 1871, as quoted in Clement, *Artists of the Nineteenth Century and Their Works,* 260.

140. "Art Items," *Daily Evening Bulletin* (Philadelphia), December 10, 1869, 2; Tufts, "Margaret Foley's Metamorphosis," 93.

141. Howitt, "A Memoir of the Sculptor Margaret F. Foley," 103.

142. "An American Lady-Sculptor," *Boston Evening Transcript,* November 19, 1874, 5.

143. In death, Foley was memorialized "as a womanly icon of purity" and as an exemplary model of feminine professionalism in Rome. Prieto, *At Home in the Studio,* 73.

## *Chapter 4*

1. Buonomo, *Backward Glances,* 14–15.

2. The "cultural colonizer" is different from the political and economic colonizer. For Anglo-Americans, this subject position was discursively constructed. My thanks to both Ivonne M. Garcia and David O'Brien for their extremely helpful thoughts regarding both colonialism and imperialism when applied to the American experience in Italy.

3. Pratt, *Imperial Eyes,* 10.

4. Hawthorne estimated that about 1,500 Americans were in Rome during the roughly two years of his stay, from 1858 to 1859. Quote from N. Hawthorne, *Marble Faun,* 99.

5. Vasiliki Galani-Moutafi, "The Self and Other: Traveler, Ethnographer, Tourist," *Annals of Tourism Research* 27, no. 1 (January 2000): 207–9; Brigitte Bailey, "Gender, Nation, and the Tourist Gaze in the European 'Year of Revolutions': Kirkland's *Holidays Abroad,*" *American Literary History* 14, no. 1 (March 2002): 61; Nelson Moe, *The View from Vesuvius: Italian Culture and the Southern Question* (Berkeley: University of California Press, 2002), 3; John Dickie, *Darkest Italy: The Nation and Stereotypes of the Mezzogiorno, 1860–1900* (New York: St. Martin's Press, 1999), 3, 20–22.

6. *Life and Times of Frederick Douglass* (1892), as quoted in Robert S. Levine, "Road to Africa: Frederick Douglass's Rome," in Martin and Person, *Roman Holidays,* 232.

7. T. Stebbins, *Lure of Italy,* 213. The scene is mislabeled; what it actually shows is the Portico of Octavia. This beautiful arch still stands today in the Jewish quarter of Rome. The painting was originally exhibited under the title *Arch of Octavius, Jews' Quarter, Rome.* When the painting was exhibited in Boston that same year, the Athenaeum quickly purchased it for its collection. Vance, *America's Rome,* 2:154.

8. This effect of the real, with its plethora of particularities, suggests "a visual document of nineteenth-century colonialist ideology," the art historian Linda Nochlin explains, "in the language of a would-be transparent naturalism." Linda Nochlin, "The Imaginary Orient" (1983), reprinted in *The Politics of Vision: Essays on Nineteenth-Century Art and Society* (New York: Harper & Row, 1989), 35.

9. Paul A. Manoguerra, "Anti-Catholicism in Albert Bierstadt's *Roman Fish Market, Arch of Octavius,*" *Nineteenth-Century Art Worldwide* (Winter 2003): 2, http://www.19thc-artworldwide.org/winter_03/articles/mano_print.html, accessed June 2007.

10. *[Murray's] Handbook to Central Italy: Rome* (1853 ed.), 14, 86, as quoted in Vance, *America's Rome,* 2:154. The concept of filth is central to the imperialist mission. As Sara Mills explains, "This assigning of dirtiness to the other nation is a common way of separating the colonized nation from the colonizer." Sara Mills, *Discourses of Differences: An Analysis of Women's Travel Writing and Colonialism* (New York: Routledge, 1991), 90. Mills references Mary Douglas, *Purity and Danger: An Analysis of Concepts of Pollution and Taboo* (London: Routledge & Kegan Paul, 1966).

11. "Begging in Rome," the sculptor William Wetmore Story explained, "was as much a profession as praying and shop keeping." William Wetmore Story, *Roba di Roma,* 4th ed. (New York: D. Appleton, 1864), 46.

12. Rome claims one of the oldest Jewish communities in the world, in existence before the burning of the Temple of Solomon, thus predating the Diaspora. As such, it became part of the Roman Empire. Before confinement to the ghetto in the sixteenth century, Roman Jews lived in Trastevere, across the Tiber River. Not until after 1870 would the walls of the Jewish ghetto be toppled and a magnificent new synagogue be built upon the site. See Joan Goodnick Westenholz, ed., *The Jewish Presence in Ancient Rome* (Jerusalem: Bible Lands Museum, 1995).

13. Vance, *America's Rome,* 2:153; Manoguerra, "Anti-Catholicism," 3; John Carlos Rowe, "Nathaniel Hawthorne and Transnationality," in *Hawthorne and the Real: Bicentennial Essays,* ed. Millicent Bell (Columbus: Ohio State University Press, 2005), 91.

14. As quoted in J. Hawthorne, *Nathaniel Hawthorne and His Wife,* 2:176.

15. N. Hawthorne, *Marble Faun,* 325.

16. Ibid., 412.

17. Historian Joseph Ruane defines colonialism in broad terms and describes an environment in which American tourists and expatriates were seemingly comfortable. He not only alludes to the circumstances under which Native peoples in the United States lived but also indexes the conditions to which the Italian people were subjected while occupied by foreign powers. "Colonialism as a process refers to the intrusion into and conquest of an inhabited territory by representatives . . . of an external power; the displacements of the native inhabitants . . . from resources and positions of power; the subsequent exercise of economic, political, and cultural control over the territory and native population by the intruders and their descendents in their own interests." As quoted in Terrence McDonough, introduction to *Was Ireland a Colony? Economics, Politics, and Culture in Nineteenth-Century Ireland,* ed. Terrence McDonough (Portland, Ore.: Irish Academic Press, 2005), xiv n. 4.

18. N. Hawthorne, *Marble Faun,* 110.

19. Ibid., 346, quotes on 350 and 356.

20. Buonomo, *Backward Glances,* 23.

21. Richard H. Brodhead, introduction to N. Hawthorne, *Marble Faun,* xxvii; N. Hawthorne, *Marble Faun,* 22–23.

22. N. Hawthorne, *Marble Faun,* 9. In his diaries, Hawthorne wrote that the faun was "a natural and delightful link betwixt human and brute life, and with something of a divine character intermingled." Entry of April 18, 1858, in N. Hawthorne, *French and Italian Notebooks,* 173–74.

23. Mark A. R. Kemp, "*The Marble Faun* and American Postcolonial Ambivalence," *Modern Fiction Studies* 43, no. 1 (Summer 1997): 230; N. Hawthorne, *Marble Faun,* 10.

24. Entry of April 18, 1858, in N. Hawthorne, *French and Italian Notebooks,* 173–74.

25. N. Hawthorne, *Marble Faun,* 8.

26. H., "The Lotus Eater," *Boston Evening Transcript,* March 22, 1861, 2.

27. Robert S. Levine, "'Antebellum Rome' in *The Marble Faun,*" *American Literary History* 2, no. 1 (Spring 1990): 20.

28. N. Hawthorne, *Marble Faun,* 7.

29. Dispatch 17, Rome, October 18, 1847, in Fuller, *"These Sad but Glorious Days,"* 159.

30. For a detailed discussion of this project, see Fryd, *Art and Empire,* 109–25.

31. Amy Kaplan, "'Left Alone with America': The Absence of Empire in the Study of American Culture," in *Cultures of United States Imperialism,* ed. Amy Kaplan and Donald E. Pease (Durham: Duke University Press, 1993), 14, quote on 12.

32. As quoted in Fryd, *Art and Empire,* 116.

33. For Sedgwick's comparison of Italians with Native Americans, see Vance, *America's Rome,* 2:117; A. Kaplan, "'Left Alone with America,'" 12.

34. "Atelier," *Cosmopolitan Art Journal* 1 (March 1857): 90; "Atelier," *Cosmopolitan Art Journal* 1 (June 1857): 122.

35. Schriber, *Writing Home,* 34; Rowe, "Nathaniel Hawthorne and Transnationality," 91.

36. Cherry, *Beyond the Frame,* 45, 82. Moreover, the "true" American woman participated in a civilizing mission in foreign lands, having "the exalted privilege of extending over the world those blessed influences, that are to renovate degraded man, and 'clothe all climes with beauty,'" Catherine Beecher argued. As quoted in Schriber, *Writing Home,* 34.

37. Julia Ward Howe, "Rome," in *Passion-Flowers* (Boston: Ticknor, Reed & Fields, 1854). See also Buonomo, *Backward Glances,* 28–30.

38. After observing urban life during the day, she returned home at night to care for her children. Indeed, the requirements of domesticity and the freedoms of the city did not seem at odds. See Julia Ward Howe, *From the Oak to the Olive: A Plain Record of a Pleasant Journey* (Boston: Lee & Shepard, 1868), 45.

39. Harriet Hosmer to Wayman Crow, May 20, 1860 (Watertown, Mass.), in Carr, *Harriet Hosmer,* 156.

40. N. Hawthorne, *Marble Faun,* 54, 56. Hawthorne used similar language in his journal to describe Louisa Lander, who lived "in almost perfect independence" and "delightful freedom" in Rome. Entry dated February 15, 1858, in N. Hawthorne, *French and Italian Notebooks,* 78.

41. N. Hawthorne, *Marble Faun,* 47.

42. William Wetmore Story to James R. Lowell, February 11, 1853 (Rome), as quoted in James, *William Wetmore Story and His Friends,* 1:255.

43. I wish to thank Ellen Todd for this interesting observation regarding the spatial configuration of the drawing.

44. Women's horseback riding signified many things in the nineteenth-century bourgeois imagination, among them the terrors of an unbridled femininity, that is, women beyond masculine control. Moreover, horse riding held symbolic force as a sexually charged activity. Not surprisingly, a rider sitting sidesaddle had less control of her steed than when she grasped the horse between her legs. Cherry, *Beyond the Frame,* 82.

45. Susan P. Casteras, "With Palettes, Pencils, and Parasols: Victorian Women Artists Traverse the Empire," in *Intrepid Women: Victorian Artists Travel,* ed. Jordana Pomeroy (Burlington, Vt.: Ashgate, 2005), 22.

46. As quoted in E. D. W., "A Woman's Experience in Europe," *Daily Evening Bulletin* (Philadelphia), April 9, 1868, 1; William H. Gerdts Jr., *American Neo-classic Sculpture: The Marble Resurrection* (New York: Viking Press, 1973), 62.

47. As quoted in Armstrong, *Day Before Yesterday,* 196–97. See also Mary K. McGuigan, "'This Market of Physiognomy': American Artists and Rome's Art Academies, Life Schools, and Models, 1825–1870," in William L. Vance, Mary K. McGuigan, and John F. McGuigan Jr., *America's Rome: Artists in the Eternal City, 1800–1900,* exh. cat. (Cooperstown, N.Y.: Fenimore Art Museum, 2009), 39–73.

48. Deborah Cherry, *Painting Women: Victorian Women Artists* (New York: Routledge, 1993), 114–15; E. Ann Kaplan, *Looking for the Other: Feminism, Film, and the Imperial Gaze* (New York: Routledge, 1997), xvi–xviii, 4–6. Kaplan argues that the male gaze and the imperial gaze are inseparable in the nineteenth-century colonial spaces. In response to this contention, recent lesbian/queer theorists label this elision the "heterocentric bias in feminist thought." In their view, Stebbins, Whitney, and Hosmer did not necessarily lay claim to male social privilege as active bearers of the gaze but asserted a homosocial identity that refused the heterosexual contract and functioned in a world of gender difference. Renée C. Hoogland, *Lesbian Configurations* (New York: Columbia University Press, 1997), 2. See also Biddy Martin, "Sexual Practice and Changing Lesbian Identities," in *Destabilizing Theory: Contemporary Feminist Debates,* ed. Michèle Barrett and Anne Phillips (Stanford: Stanford University Press, 1992), 93–120.

49. Rubinstein, *American Women Sculptors,* 63.

50. Akers had hoped to produce marble copies of all the chief works of ancient sculpture and place them in a free gallery in New York where "students might have all the benefits . . . of Europe." In 1858, for example, he was working on a copy of the *Dying Gladiator* in the Capitoline collection for Edward King of Newport, Rhode Island. I. E. C., "Benjamin Paul Akers, Sculptor" (obituary), *Evening Post* (New York), August 2, 1861, 1. To one critic, this project would provide "a valuable service to his country." "American Artists Abroad," *Home Journal* (New York), July 18, 1857, 3. See also Craven, *Sculpture in America,* 282–83; "American Artists in Rome," *Evening Post* (New York), March 19, 1858, 1.

51. Craven, *Sculpture in America,* 281; Milroy, "Public Career of Emma Stebbins: Work in Marble," 4.

52. "Personal," *Home Journal* (New York), September 18, 1858, 3; "Worth Telling to You," *Home Journal* (New York), March 2, 1861, 2.

53. Alison Smith, *The Victorian Nude: Sexuality, Morality, and Art* (New York: Manchester University Press, 1996); Leland S. Person, "Falling into Heterosexuality: Sculpting Male Bodies in *The Marble Faun* and *Roderick Hudson*," in Martin and Person, *Roman Holidays*, 116.

Literary theorist John Carlos Rowe has argued that the *Dead Pearl Diver* appealed to viewers in its combining of death and sexual desire, "the conjunction of *thanatos* and *eros*." Rowe suggests that viewing this sculpture caused discomfort and that this conjunction was "troubling." John Carlos Rowe, "Hawthorne's Ghost in James's Italy: Sculptural Form, Romantic Narrative, and the Function of Sexuality in *The Marble Faun*, 'Adina,' and *William Wetmore Story and His Friends*," in Martin and Person, *Roman Holidays*, 87.

54. N. Hawthorne, *Marble Faun*, 4.

55. Craven, *Sculpture in America*, 284.

56. Tennyson, "The Lotos-Eaters," in *Poems and Plays*, 51.

57. David G. Riede, *Allegories of One's Own Mind: Melancholy in Victorian Poetry* (Columbus: Ohio State University Press, 2005), 54–55.

58. Tennyson, "The Lotos-Eaters," in *Poems and Plays*, 51.

59. The Lotos-Eaters enacted only a passive reaction to external powers, which Isobel Armstrong describes as "the idyllic lassitude of a colonialist dream." Isobel Armstrong, *Victorian Poetry: Poetry, Poetics, Politics* (New York: Routledge, 1993), 87–88.

60. The sculpture is probably a Hadrianic copy of the Greek statue. Haskell and Penny, *Taste and the Antique*, 210.

61. Stebbins did not use studio workmen but carved her own marbles. Charlotte Cushman said of her, "She cannot be contented with anything she does and ever sighs for her ideal." Charlotte Cushman to Emma Crow, March 26, 1860 (Rome), as quoted in Milroy, "Public Career of Emma Stebbins: Work in Marble," 6.

62. "Art Items," *New York Daily Tribune*, January 31, 1861, 7. In Boston, another writer noted that the sculpture was "beautifully modeled," especially the "soft and fleshy" body. At the same time, "the whole figure [was] in beautiful harmony." "The Lotus Eater," *Boston Evening Transcript*, March 22, 1861, 2.

63. Quoted in Milroy, "Public Career of Emma Stebbins: Work in Marble," 12 n. 19.

64. He admitted in his journal, "I like these strange, sweet, playful rustic creatures." Entry of April 18, 1858, in N. Hawthorne, *French and Italian Notebooks*, 173–74.

65. N. Hawthorne, *Marble Faun*, 8–9.

66. "The Lotus Eater," *Boston Evening Transcript*, March 22, 1861, 2.

67. "Worth Telling to You," *Home Journal* (New York), March 2, 1861, 2.

68. Harriet Hosmer to Wayman Crow, May 20, 1860 (Watertown, Mass.), in Carr, *Harriet Hosmer*, 156.

69. As quoted in Carr, *Harriet Hosmer*, 210.

70. Andrea Mariani, "Sleeping and Waking Fauns: Harriet Goodhue Hosmer's Experience of Italy, 1852–1870," in Jaffe, *Italian Presence in American Art, 1760–1860*, 66. Mariani has suggested that Hosmer infused Christian piety into the work when she modeled the hanging left arm of the faun after Christ's arm in Michelangelo's *Pietà*, on public view in St. Peter's. Ibid., 77–78.

71. These sculptural details were variously positioned in the different replicas of the sculpture. The representation of the faun remained the same in all versions. Cronin, *Harriet Hosmer: Lost and Found*, 70.

72. "Miss Hosmer's Faun and Satyr," *Boston Evening Transcript*, September 4, 1865, 1.

73. Cobbe continued, "It needed to be born in a New World and to drink in Roman sunshine for a whole joyous youth to conceive this figure. The 'Faun' is pure Life—life defecated of all its pains and troubles; life in its flush and spring-tide; life as life might be unworn by a single care, unburdened by a single sin." Frances P. Cobbe, "Ireland and Her Exhibition in 1865," *Fraser's Magazine* 72 (July–December 1865): 422.

74. Carr, *Harriet Hosmer*, 210. Hosmer probably saw either the original bronze in the Naples Museum or a plaster cast in Rome.

75. *Art-Journal* (London) 4 (1865): 346, from the *Sleeping Faun* curatorial file, Museum of Fine Arts, Boston.

76. Harry Parkman and Peter L. Simmonds, eds., *The Illustrated Record and Descriptive Catalogue of the Dublin International Exhibition of 1865* (London: E. & F. N. Spon, 1866), 479, photocopy in Harriet Goodhue Hosmer Collection, Watertown Free Public Library, Watertown, Mass. According to another source, she gave this sculpture a "flesh tint" when shown at the 1867 Paris exhibition. See "The Exposition and Its Visitors," *Boston Evening Transcript*, May 14, 1867, 4.

Sir Benjamin Guinness purchased the sculpture on the first day of the exhibition for one thousand pounds ($5,000). D. Sherwood, *Harriet Hosmer*, 240. Four known versions of the sculpture exist. The copy owned by Guinness is now in the Department of Foreign Affairs and Trade, Iveagh House, Dublin; the replica owned by the

Prince of Wales is located in the Cleveland Museum of Art. Charlotte Cushman, Lady Ashburton, and John Shortall, a Chicago realtor, also purchased replicas. Shortall gave his sculpture to Radcliffe College, which put it up for auction; it is now lost. Lady Ashburton's sculpture was most likely sold upon her death, in 1903. Cornelia Carr gave a replica of the sculpture to the Museum of Fine Arts, Boston. *Sleeping Faun* curatorial file, Museum of Fine Arts, Boston; for a detailed provenance of this piece, see Cronin, *Harriet Hosmer: Lost and Found,* 70.

77. Lady Louisa Ashburton, an intimate friend, eventually purchased the sculpture. D. Sherwood, *Harriet Hosmer,* 262–63, 267, quote on 262.

78. Buonomo, *Backward Glances,* 15.

79. Gordon, "Early American Women Artists," 59; Elizabeth Rogers Payne, "Anne Whitney: Art and Social Justice," *Massachusetts Review* 12, no. 2 (Spring 1971): n.p.; Hirshler, *A Studio of Her Own,* 15.

80. Burns, *Painting on the Dark Side,* 130.

81. Quoted in Hirshler, *A Studio of Her Own,* 10.

82. Ibid., 12. It is quite possible that Whitney hired male models while at work in her Boston studio. "This is the day our model comes;" Elizabeth Bartol (Whitney's friend and studio mate) "had done the negotiating with him, proffered him the pay, which he utterly declined taking." Anne Whitney to Adeline Manning, February 1866 (Belmont, Mass.), as quoted in Elizabeth Payne, "Anne Whitney: Nineteenth Century Sculptor and Liberal" (unpublished manuscript), 603, Wellesley College Archives, Wellesley, Mass.

83. Payne, "Anne Whitney: Nineteenth Century Sculptor and Liberal," 603; Anne Whitney, *Lotus Eater* curatorial file, Newark Museum of Art, Newark, N.J.

84. Anne Whitney to Maria Weston Chapman, January 5, 1879, as quoted in Mrs. Wilson F. Payne to William Gerdts, March 4, 1965 (Needham, Mass.) (photocopy), in Anne Whitney, *Lotus Eater* curatorial file, Newark Museum of Art, Newark, N.J.

85. Whitney wrote that a Mr. Carew from Cambridge "had had experience and will be accurate—only he grooves out hair like a carpenter." Letter from Anne Whitney dated July 1863, as quoted in Mrs. Wilson F. Payne to William Gerdts, January 3, 1964 (Needham, Mass.) (photocopy), in Anne Whitney, *Lotus Eater* curatorial file, Newark Museum of Art, Newark, N.J. The Milmore Brothers of Boston may also have been involved in the carving of this sculpture. Payne, "Anne Whitney: Nineteenth Century Sculptor and Liberal," 485.

86. The price of the sculpture was $1,500. Payne, "Anne Whitney: Nineteenth Sculptor and Liberal," 443, 486–87, 556, 679. The fig leaf "is only a conventional method by which the artist may help himself to bridge the chasm between the world and him." Anne Whitney to Maria Weston Chapman, January 5, 1879, as quoted in Mrs. Wilson F. Payne to William Gerdts, March 4, 1965 (Needham, Mass.) (photocopy), in Anne Whitney, *Lotus Eater* curatorial file, Newark Museum of Art, Newark, N.J.

87. Rimmer had recently completed a *Chaldean Shepherd* (now lost) and *Falling Gladiator* of 1861, an expressive nude to which Whitney had been attracted when it was exhibited in Boston. Payne, "Anne Whitney: Nineteenth Century Sculptor and Liberal," 441, 724A.

88. Ibid., 711A, 724A. Whitney consulted the sculptors Henry Kirk Brown, Thomas Ball, and Edward A. Brackett for advice on this sculpture. Parrott, "Expatriates and Professionals," 431.

89. Harriet Hosmer to Anne Whitney, 1869 and 1870(?) (Rome), Anne Whitney Papers; Payne, "Anne Whitney: Nineteenth Century Sculpture and Liberal," 829.

90. Whitney paid thirteen-dollars-a-month rent to live in Rome. Payne, "Anne Whitney: Nineteenth Century Sculptor and Liberal," 4–6, 9.

91. Anne Whitney to her family, August 8, 1868 (Munich), as quoted in ibid., 703.

92. Markus, *Across an Untried Sea,* 193; Mary C. Shannon to Sarah Whitney, January 16, 1868 (Rome), Anne Whitney Papers; Anne Whitney to her family, June 26, 1868 (Rome), as quoted in Payne, "Anne Whitney: Nineteenth Century Sculptor and Liberal," 722.

93. In Whitney's own words: "The vast difference between working here and at home is at once manifest in the abundance with which the necessities of study present themselves to you without any wearisome search." Anne Whitney to her family, November 18, 1867 (Rome), as quoted in Payne, "Anne Whitney: Nineteenth Century Sculptor and Liberal," 691.

94. Anne Whitney to her family, March 22, 1868 (Rome), as quoted in ibid., 771A.

95. Ibid., 603; Anne Whitney to Maria Weston Chapman, January 5, 1879, as quoted in Mrs. Wilson F. Payne to William Gerdts, March 4, 1965 (Needham, Mass.) in Anne Whitney, *Lotus Eater* curatorial file, Newark Museum of Art, Newark, N.J.

96. This sculpture served as the plaster studio model from which other replicas were created. The mold marks have not been removed from the statuette. Anne Whitney,

*Lotus Eater* curatorial file, Newark Museum of Art, Newark, N.J. See also Payne, "Anne Whitney: Nineteenth Century Artist and Liberal," 716, as well as 705, 711A, 724A.

97. Payne, "Anne Whitney: Nineteenth Century Sculptor and Liberal," 724A.

98. Anne Whitney to Maria Weston Chapman, January 5, 1879, as quoted in Mrs. Wilson F. Payne to William Gerdts, March 4, 1965 (Needham, Mass.) (photocopy), in Anne Whitney, *Lotus Eater* curatorial file, Newark Museum of Art, Newark, N.J.

99. Hirshler, *A Studio of Her Own*, 15.

100. Cobbe, *Italics*, 375.

101. A. Kaplan, "'Left Alone with America,'" 14.

*Chapter 5*

1. Heade possibly produced three other, now unlocated, paintings while in Italy: *Street Scene in Rome, The Roman Goat Herd,* and *Beatrice Cenci (After Guido).* Paul A. Manoguerra, "This Cause Is Ours: Martin Johnson Heade's *Roman Newsboys* and American Reaction to the Roman Republic of 1848–1849," in *Classic Ground: Mid-Nineteenth-Century American Painting and the Italian Encounter,* exh. cat., ed. Paul A. Manoguerra (Athens: Georgia Museum of Art, 2004), 48 n. 4. See Manoguerra for an alternate reading of this painting.

2. *Il Don Pirlone* was published between September 1848 and July 1849. It began publication under the liberal government of Pius IX, criticized his growing conservatism, and finally became the organ of the Roman Republic. Historian Paola Gemme reads this painting as an image of "political disorder, over which . . . preside children as figures of irrationality, capriciousness, and impulsiveness." Paola Gemme, *Domesticating Foreign Struggles: The Italian Risorgimento and Antebellum American Identity* (Athens: University of Georgia Press, 2005), 47. An abridged version of the publication's political cartoons was published in New Orleans in about 1850. Manoguerra, "This Cause Is Ours," 44.

3. For an overview of the history of the *Risorgimento,* see Riall, *Italian Risorgimento.*

4. Manoguerra, "This Cause Is Ours," 36; Gail E. Husch, *Something Coming: Apocalypic Expectation and Mid-Nineteenth-Century American Painting* (Hanover: University Press of New England, 2000), 54.

5. Brigitte Bailey, "Fuller, Hawthorne, and Imagining Urban Spaces in Rome," in Martin and Person, *Roman Holidays,* 181–83; Dispatch 27, Rome, February 1849, in Margaret Fuller, *"These Sad but Glorious Days,"* 248.

6. The seated newsboy with Greek cap may have indicated the political leaning of the artist himself. Vance, *America's Rome,* 2:126, and Theodore Stebbins, "Martin Johnson Heade," in *Lure of Italy,* 201–3. Paul Manoguerra suggests that the dark shadow in the lower right of the painting may represent a "shadowy Jesuit . . . plotting against the Roman Republic and Italian unification." Manoguerra, "This Cause Is Ours," 46.

7. Among the other American painters who resided in Rome during the Republic were Luther Terry, Jasper Francis Cropsey, and Thomas Hicks, who painted a stunning portrait of Margaret Fuller in 1848 (fig. 2). For American support of the Roman Republic, see *Proceedings of a Public Meeting of the Citizens of the City and County of Philadelphia, Held January 6, 1848, to Express Their Cordial Approval of the Liberal Policy of Pope Pius IX, in His Administration of the Temporal Government of Italy* (Philadelphia: Jos. Severns, 1848) as quoted in Manoguerra, "This Cause Is Ours," 40.

8. As quoted in Dispatch 21, Rome, December 31, 1847, in Fuller, *"These Sad but Glorious Days,"* 199. Lewis Cass Jr., the American consul in Rome, angered many progressives with this official policy of neutrality; however, he unofficially aided the Republic in any way he could. He helped open the first Constitutional Assembly in 1849 and accorded Mazzini diplomatic immunity after the failure of the Republic. Gay, *Le relazioni,* 5.

9. Marraro, *American Opinion on the Unification of Italy,* 80–92, quote on 82.

10. Greenwood, *Haps and Mishaps,* 260.

11. Between 1852 and 1854, for example, Vatican forces took 58,523 political prisoners into custody. Marraro, *American Opinion on the Unification of Italy,* 119–21; Vance, *America's Rome,* 2:118, 139, 195. Heade created a second version of *Roman Newsboys* (private collection), in which he depicted "the military and political defeat of the Roman Republic." Manoguerra, "This Cause Is Ours," 46–47.

12. As quoted in Paola Gemme, "Domesticating Foreign Struggles: American Narratives of Italian Revolutions and the Debate on Slavery in the Antebellum Era," *Prospects* 27 (2002): 84, 98 n. 20. In espousing an egalitarian vision of society, Mazzini earned the support of the feminist antislavery movement. Esther Schor, "Acts of Union: Theodosia Garrow Trollope and Frances Power

Cobbe on the Kingdom of Italy," in *Unfolding the South: Nineteenth-Century British Women Writers and Artists in Italy,* ed. Alison Chapman and Jane Stabler (New York: Manchester University Press, 2003), 91. Moreover, suffrage leaders, like Lucretia Mott, also supported Mazzini's radical agenda for Italy as he welcomed women into the revolutionary struggle. Rosanna De Longis, "Patriote ed infermiere," in *Fondare la nazione: I repubblicani del 1849 e la difesa del Gianicolo,* ed. Lauro Rossi (Rome: Palombi, 2001), 99–107. Thanks to Cathy Geffen, who brought this citation to my attention when I was in residence at the American Academy in Rome.

13. Buick, *Child of the Fire,* 23.

14. Vance, *America's Rome,* 2:200; Lucy Riall, *Garibaldi: Invention of a Hero* (New Haven: Yale University Press, 2007), 142; Levine, "'Antebellum Rome' in *The Marble Faun,*" 23.

15. Gemme, "Domesticating Foreign Struggles," 77, 81, 89.

16. O'Connor, *Romance of Italy,* 109.

17. Marraro, *American Opinion on the Unification of Italy,* 220–21.

18. O'Connor, *Romance of Italy,* 104; Riall, *Garibaldi,* 140, 146.

19. Ferdinand Gregorovius, *The Roman Journals of Ferdinand Gregorovius, 1852–1874,* ed. Friedrich Althaus, trans. Mrs. Gustavus W. Hamilton (London: G. Bell & Sons, 1911), 59 (June 24, 1859), quote on 60 (July 2, 1859).

20. Quoted in A. William Salomone, "The Nineteenth-Century Discovery of Italy: An Essay in American Cultural History; Prolegomena to a Historiographical Problem," *American Historical Review* 73, no. 5 (June 1968): 1384.

21. Dennis Berthold, "Melville, Garibaldi, and the Medusa Revolution," *American Literary History* 9, no. 3 (Autumn 1997): 433. "Though he has all the power of an Emperor," Henry Adams wrote, "he will not even adopt the state of a General. Europeans are fond of calling him the Washington of Italy, principally because they know nothing about Washington." Henry Adams, "Documents: Henry Adams and Garibaldi, 1860," *American Historical Review* 25, no. 2 (January 1920): 247.

Theodore Dwight, author of *The Roman Republic of 1849* (New York: R. Van Dien, 1851), translated into English the autobiography of Garibaldi, whom he called "Italy's Washington." See Giuseppe Garibaldi, *The Life of General Garibaldi,* trans. Theodore Dwight (New York: A. S. Barnes & Burr, 1859).

22. Marraro, *American Opinion on the Unification of Italy,* 287–88; Riall, *Garibaldi,* 296, 300.

23. Riall, *Garibaldi,* 185.

24. The dispatches were published on July 10 and 13, 1860. Adams, "Documents: Henry Adams and Garibaldi, 1860," 247. Cultural critic and Italophile Henry Tuckerman also wrote a laudatory article about Garibaldi. See Henry T. Tuckerman, "Giuseppe Garibaldi," *North American Review* 92 (1861).

25. Patricia Hills, "Cultural Racism: Resistance and Accommodation in the Civil War Art of Eastman Johnson and Thomas Nast," in *Seeing High and Low: Representing Social Conflict in American Visual Culture,* ed. Patricia Johnston (Berkeley: University of California Press, 2006), 107 n. 16, 121.

26. *New York Illustrated News,* November 3, 1860, 405. See also Albert Bigelow Paine, *Thomas Nast: His Period and His Pictures* (1904; repr., Broomall, Pa.: Chelsea House Press, 1997), 47–62.

27. Michael Bacarella, *Lincoln's Foreign Legion: The 39th New York Infantry, the Garibaldi Guard* (Shippensburg, Pa.: White Mane Publishing, 1996), 34.

28. Quoted in Salomone, "Nineteenth-Century Discovery of Italy," 1384. See also Peter R. D'Agostino, *Rome in America: Transnational Catholic Ideology from the Risorgimento to Fascism* (Chapel Hill: University of North Carolina Press, 2004), 41.

29. Gemme, "Domesticating Foreign Struggles," 87, 90, 95.

30. Gregorovius, *Roman Journals,* 60–61.

31. Gay, *Le relazioni,* 10. From 1864 to 1870, Florence temporarily served as the capital of the new nation.

32. French troops wounded one hundred Romans and arrested many more. In October, Napoleon III reinforced his garrison with ten thousand more men. "The city is alive with French soldiers," Gregorovius reported. Gregorovius, *Roman Journals,* 81 (March 29, 1860), 116 (December 31, 1860–January 1, 1861), 128–29 (March 16, 1861), quote on 106 (October 16, 1860).

33. Ibid., 127 (March 15, 1861).

34. As quoted in E. Stebbins, *Charlotte Cushman,* 191.

35. Vance, *America's Rome,* 2:114.

36. Elizabeth Barrett Browning to Miss E. F. Haworth, December 1858 (Rome), in *Letters of Elizabeth Barrett Browning,* 2:357.

37. Boime, *Art of the Macchia,* 22–23; Riall, *Italian Risorgimento,* xi–xii. For the first time, Tuscans enjoyed

freedom of the press and establishment of a national guard, "the first step toward truly national institutions and a representation of the people," Fuller reported in the *New York Daily Tribune*. Dispatch 17, Rome, October 18, 1847, in Fuller, *"These Sad but Glorious Days,"* 158.

38. Elizabeth Barrett Browning to Sarianna Browning, March 1860, in *Letters of Elizabeth Barrett Browning*, 2:368.

39. Flavia Alaya, "The Ring, the Rescue, and the Risorgimento: Reunifying the Brownings' Italy," *Browning Institute Studies* 6 (1978): 1. "It was only in the cafés people knew what went on in the world; there they saw the newspapers." The city of Rome was regularly under a news blackout. Gregorovius, *Roman Journals*, 63 (July 14, 1859).

40. Litta-Visconti-Arese, *Birth of Modern Italy*, xxii, xxiv, 276.

41. O'Connor, *Romance of Italy*, 6, 103. Elizabeth Adams Daniels, *Jessie White Mario: Risorgimento Revolutionary* (Athens: Ohio University Press, 1972), 78–83, quote on 78. In 1865, White became a lifelong analyst for the *Nation* magazine in the United States and covered the development of the emerging Italian nation for its readers.

42. Alaya, "The Ring, the Rescue, and the Risorgimento," 1; Alison Chapman, "'In Our Own Blood Drenched the Pen': Italy and Sensibility in Elizabeth Barrett Browning's *Last Poems* (1862)," *Women's Writing* 10, no. 2 (2003): 269, 271; O'Connor, *Romance of Italy*, 97; for the "public female rhetorical voice," see Isobel Armstrong, "*Casa Guidi Windows:* Spectacle and Politics in 1851," in Chapman and Stabler, *Unfolding the South*, 51–69. Browning, *Casa Guidi Windows*, xv–xvii, xxxii, 72; Glenda Sluga, "Gender and the Nation: Madame de Staël or Italy," *Women's Writing* 10, no. 2 (2003): 241. For a discussion of "civic poetry," see Richard Cronin, "*Casa Guidi Windows:* Elizabeth Barrett Browning, Italy, and the Poetry of Citizenship," in Chapman and Stabler, *Unfolding the South*, 35–50.

43. Elizabeth Barrett Browning, *Poems Before Congress*, in *Poems of Elizabeth Barrett Browning* (New York: A. L. Burt, 1887), 426–30.

44. Alaya, "The Ring, the Rescue, and the Risorgimento," 15, 23, quote on 15; Edward Y. Hincks, "Elizabeth Barrett Browning," in *Eminent Women of the Age: Being Narratives of the Lives and Deeds of the Most Prominent Women of the Present Generation*, ed. James Parton et al. (Hartford, Conn.: S. M. Betts, 1869), 237. British critics denounced her poetry as mere pamphleteering. Incredulous that "any critic should consider the occasions of great tragic movements (such as a war for the life of a nation) unfit occasions for poetry," Barrett Browning wrote, it "fills me with an astonishment which I can scarcely express." Elizabeth Barrett Browning to Mr. Chorley, May 2, 1860 (Rome), in *Letters of Elizabeth Barrett Browning*, 2:382. See also Cronin, "*Casa Guidi Windows*," 35–38.

45. Sandra Gilbert imagined this poetic tradition as a *Risorgimento* "of the lost community of women." Gilbert, "From *Patria* to *Matria*," 194–95, quote on 195; Elizabeth Barrett-Browning to Anna Jameson, early 1860 (Rome), in *Letters of Elizabeth Barrett Browning*, 2:364.

46. John Isbell, introduction de Madame de Staël, *Corinne, or Italy*, viii; Lori Jo Marso, *(Un)Manly Citizens: Jean-Jacques Rousseau's and Germaine de Staël's Subversive Women* (Baltimore: Johns Hopkins University Press, 1999), 109, 114, 126. De Staël's verses alluded to an Italy "free, spontaneous, and governed by native rhythms," historian Angelica Goodden has explained. Goodden, *Madame de Staël*, 158. See also Katharine Rodier, "Nathaniel Hawthorne and *The Marble Faun:* Textual and Contextual Reflections of *Corinne, or Italy*," in Szmurlo, *Novel's Seductions*, 230.

47. Art-historical scholarship has determined that this portrait is neither by Guido Reni nor of Beatrice Cenci. The original portrait came into the possession of the Barberini family at the end of the eighteenth century. It is first mentioned in 1783; by 1794, it was attributed to Guido Reni. When the figure became "Beatrice" is unknown. The Galleria Nazionale d'Arte Antica purchased the work in 1934; it hangs today in the Palazzo Barberini, Rome. Belinda Jack, *Beatrice's Spell: The Enduring Legend of Beatrice Cenci* (London: Pimlico/Random House, 2005), 5–6.

48. S. Hawthorne, *Notes in England and Italy*, 212; Barbara Groseclose, "A Portrait Not by Guido Reni of a Girl Who Is Not Beatrice Cenci," *Studies in Eighteenth-Century Culture* 11 (1982): 111.

49. To this day, a Mass is said in her honor on September 11 in the church of San Pietro in Montorio on the Janiculum Hill, where she is buried in an unmarked grave. Jack, *Beatrice's Spell*, 2.

50. Anna Jameson, *Lives of Celebrated Female Sovereigns and Illustrious Women* (1831; repr., ed. Mary E. Howitt, Philadelphia: Porter & Coates, 1870), 155–77, quote on 170 (originally published under the title *Memoirs of Celebrated Female Sovereigns*, 2 vols.).

51. "Everyone has read Shelley's tragedy, founded upon the painful history of the Cenci family." "Miss Hosmer's *Beatrice Cenci*," *Home Journal* (New York),

October 31, 1857, 3. The play was not performed on stage in Rome until 1886 due to the strict censorship laws. See also John Carlos Rowe, "Swept Away: Henry James, Margaret Fuller, and 'The Last of the Valerii,'" in *Readers in History: Nineteenth-Century American Literature and the Contexts of Response,* ed. James L. Machor (Baltimore: Johns Hopkins University Press, 1993), 37–38.

52. Margaret Fuller, *Woman in the Nineteenth Century* (1845; repr., Mineola, N.Y: Dover Publications, 1999), 124.

53. F. D. Guerrazzi, *Beatrice Cenci: A Historical Novel of the Sixteenth Century,* trans. Luigi Monti (New York: Rudd & Carleton, 1858), 1:xiv.

54. "There will, undoubtedly, be a great desire to see this volume," which, the writer averred, will finally present "the correct exposition of this sad history. "Miss Hosmer's *Beatrice Cenci,*" 3.

55. Harriet Hosmer to Wayman Crow, October 12, 1854 (Rome), in Carr, *Harriet Hosmer,* 40.

56. Groseclose, "A Portrait Not by Guido Reni of a Girl Who Is Not Beatrice Cenci," 125; for two illustrations showing Beatrice in her cell on the night of her execution, see ibid., 124 and 125.

57. Herbert, *Dearest Beloved,* 220–22. With this sculpture, Vivien Green Fryd has explored the crime of incest, arguing that Hosmer's "nonnormative sexuality gave her a vantage point from which to consider another type of nonnormative sexuality: incest." In her resistance to such abuse, Beatrice Cenci offered a critique of patriarchal culture. Vivien Green Fryd, "The 'Ghosting' of Incest and Female Relations in Harriet Hosmer's *Beatrice Cenci,*" *Art Bulletin* 88, no. 2 (June 2006): 292–310, quote on 292.

58. Literary theorist Jerome J. McGann has argued that "Shelley would not have been able to see [Medusa] as anything but a victim of the tyranny and cowardice of established power." Jerome J. McGann, "The Beauty of Medusa: A Study in Romantic Literary Iconology," *Studies in Romanticism* 11, no. 1 (Winter 1972): 4, 7, verse quoted on 5; Bertholdi, "Melville, Garibaldi, and the Medusa Revolution," 449.

59. See Lucan, *Pharsalia: Dramatic Episodes of the Civil Wars,* trans. Henry Thomas Riley (London: Henry G. Bohn, 1853), as cited in Maria Cristina Nisco, "The Languages of the Black Medusa: Dorothea Smartt and Ingrid Mwangi," in *From Word to Canvas: Appropriations of Myth in Women's Aesthetic Production,* ed. V. G. Julie Rajan and Sanja Bahun-Radunović (Newcastle upon Tyne: Cambridge Scholars, 2009), 144.

60. John Davis, "Catholic Envy: The Visual Culture of Protestant Desire," in *The Visual Culture of American Religions,* ed. David Morgan and Sally M. Promey (Berkeley: University of California Press, 2001), 109; D'Agostino, *Rome in America,* 3, 11, 32, 37–43; Marraro, *American Opinion on the Unification of Italy,* 168; Leo Francis Stock, ed., *United States Ministers to the Papal States: Instructions and Dispatches, 1848–1868* (Washington, D.C.: Catholic University Press, 1933), 323.

61. Levine, "'Antebellum Rome' in *The Marble Faun,*" 23; D'Agostino, *Rome in America,* 20.

62. For more on the "No-Popery campaign," see Davis, "Catholic Envy," 109, and Patricia Johnston, "Samuel F. B. Morse's *Gallery of the Louvre:* Social Tensions in an Ideal World," in Johnston, *Seeing High and Low,* 42–66.

63. "Art Gossip," *Cosmopolitan Art Journal* 2 (December 1857): 38, as quoted in Joy S. Kasson, *Marble Queens and Captives: Women in Nineteenth-Century American Sculpture* (New Haven: Yale University Press, 1990), 120.

64. For the notion of anti-Catholic zeal unifying the nation, see Franchot, *Roads to Rome,* 103–4.

65. Zenobia was the inspiration for many literary works, most notably William Ware's *Zenobia, or the Fall of Palmyra* of 1836, which was originally published under the title *The Letters of Lucius Piso.* Carol Zastoupil, "Creativity, Inspiration, and Scandal: Harriet Hosmer and *Zenobia,*" in Jaffe, *Italian Presence in American Art, 1760–1860,* 197.

66. In 1857, Hosmer grew increasingly obsessed with creating her larger-than-life-size sculpture of the Palmyrene queen. "Her whole soul was filled with Zenobia," her friend Lydia Maria Child later explained. L[ydia] M[aria] C[hild], "Miss Hosmer's Zenobia," *Boston Evening Transcript,* February 2, 1865, 2.

67. Waller, "The Artist, the Writer, and the Queen," 22–23; Judith Johnston, *Anna Jameson: Victorian, Feminist, Woman of Letters* (Brookfield, Vt.: Scolar Press, 1997), 7, 224; D. Sherwood, *Harriet Hosmer,* 157; Alison Booth, "The Lessons of the Medusa: Anna Jameson and the Collective Biographies of Women," *Victorian Studies* 42, no. 2 (January 1, 1999): 257, 259, 282 n. 5, quote on 268; Merrill, *When Romeo Was a Woman,* 139.

68. Jameson, *Lives of Celebrated Female Sovereigns and Illustrious Women,* 25. See also Waller, "The Artist, the Writer, and the Queen," 23; Cherry, *Beyond the Frame,* 133.

69. Hosmer copied the dress and ornaments of a mosaic Madonna in the monastery of San Marco in Florence and fashioned a regal costume. C[hild], "Miss Hosmer's Zenobia," 2. See also Carr, *Harriet Hosmer,* 192.

70. For an important feminist analysis of this sculpture, see Kasson, *Marble Queens and Captives,* 141–66. Draped in a modest and armorial manner, the sculpture telegraphs a "civic propriety." Gopinath, "Harriet Hosmer and the Feminine Sublime," 67.

71. As quoted in Lydia Maria Child, "Miss Hosmer's *Zenobia,*" *Home Journal,* October 8, 1859, 2. See also C[hild], "Miss Hosmer's Zenobia," 2.

72. As quoted in Gregorovius, *Roman Journals,* 28 (April 30, 1856). In the same year, Hosmer became a member of this academy, which "numbered the most distinguished of the artists, sculptors, and scientific men [*sic*] in the world," according to Australian painter Adelaide Ironside. D. Sherwood, *Harriet Hosmer,* 177. Her diploma, dated February 24, 1859, is located in the Harriet Goodhue Hosmer Collection, Watertown Free Public Library, Watertown, Mass. The Villa Torlonia, located on via Saleria, was built for Cardinal Alessandro Albani, whose collection of classical sculpture was organized by Johann Winckelmann in 1765. It served as the home of the academy between 1852 and 1866, when Princess Alessandra Torlonia purchased it. Alta Macadam, *Blue Guide: Rome* (New York: W. W. Norton, 2006), 548.

Adelaide Ironside lived in Rome from 1855 until her death of consumption, in 1867. She studied with John Gibson, was a member of the Accademia de' Quiriti, and most certainly knew Hosmer. For more on Ironside, see Ros Pesman, "In Search of Professional Identity: Adelaide Ironside and Italy," *Women's Writing* 10, no. 2 (2003): 307–29; for the Accademia de' Quiriti, see 317–18. I would like to thank my colleague Eugene Dwyer for this citation and his useful thoughts on the Accademia de' Quiriti.

73. Harriet Hosmer to Cornelia Carr, November 12, 1859 (Rome), in Carr, *Harriet Hosmer,* 152.

74. Entry dated March 15, 1859, in N. Hawthorne, *French and Italian Notebooks,* 509–10.

75. Jameson also extolled the majesty of Medusa in her description of Greek gems and bas-reliefs. "With a supernatural grace," the Medusa evoked "a presence, a power, and an enchantment." As quoted in Booth, "Lessons of the Medusa," 279.

76. To Hosmer, Barrett Browning was "the most perfect human being" that she had ever known, their friendship "one of the happiest events" of her life. D. Sherwood, *Harriet Hosmer,* 294, quote on 209. See also Carr, *Harriet Hosmer,* 271.

77. The Bavarian princess was eighteen when she was married by proxy to Francesco, Crown Prince of the Kingdom of the Two Sicilies. She joined him in Naples in February 1859. In May, with the death of his father, King Ferdinand II, Francesco became king of Naples for a short time. The same month, Garibaldi began his invasion of the Kingdom of the Two Sicilies. D. Sherwood, *Harriet Hosmer,* 294. The couple vacated Rome in 1870, when the city joined the Kingdom of Italy. Culkin, *Harriet Hosmer,* 113.

78. Gregorovius, *Roman Journals,* 122 (January 26, 1861).

79. Culkin, *Harriet Hosmer,* 113; Cronin, *Harriet Hosmer: Lost and Found,* 80.

80. Harriet Hosmer to Wayman Crow, January 4, 1869 (Rome), in Carr, *Harriet Hosmer,* 270.

81. "Italy," *Times of London,* May 24, 1872, as quoted in Kasson, *Marble Queens and Captives,* 163.

82. Markus, *Across an Untried Sea,* 230. Barrett Browning died the same year and month as the Italian patriot Count Camillo Cavour, whom she strongly admired. Writing from Rome, Hosmer was saddened by Cavour's death, which, she explained, "certainly was a frightful blow. This country has lost a good champion in him." Harriet Hosmer to Wayman Crow, June 1861 (Rome), in Carr, *Harriet Hosmer,* 178.

83. Harriet Hosmer to Wayman Crow, September 21, 1870 (Rome), in Carr, *Harriet Hosmer,* 283.

84. Gay, *Le relazioni,* 10–12; E. Stebbins, *Charlotte Cushman,* 185–87, quote on 162.

85. A Bostonian, "Foreign Correspondence of the *Transcript,*" *Boston Evening Transcript,* January 17, 1860, 2.

86. Emma Crow Cushman, "Charlotte Cushman: A Memory" (unpublished manuscript), Cushman Papers, Container 15.

87. Livio Chersi, *Italia e Stati Uniti: Relazioni diplomatiche 1861–1935* (Trieste: Edizioni Alabarda, 1937), 18, 23; H. Nelson Gay, "Le relazioni fra l'Italia e gli Stati Uniti (1847–1871)" (typescript), Nelson Gay Papers, Museo Centrale del Risorgimento, Vittoriano, Rome; Gregorovius, *Roman Journals,* 137.

88. Chersi, *Italia e Stati Uniti,* 24. The most interesting case was that of John H. Surratt, who was wanted in connection with the assassination of President Lincoln. Escaping to Rome, he joined the Papal Zouaves for a short time until his arrest in October of 1866. Stock, *United States Ministers to the Papal States,* 392–95, 405; Howard R. Marraro, "Canadian and American Zouaves in the Papal Army, 1868–1870" (unpublished paper), courtesy of the Huntington Library, Art Collection, and Botanical Gardens, San Mareno, Calif. When Rufus King, minister

to Rome, brought up the Surratt matter with Antonelli, the Vatican cooperated with the Americans. Osborn H. Oldroyd, *The Assassination of Abraham Lincoln: Flight, Pursuit, Capture, and Punishment of the Conspirators* (Washington, D.C.: O. H. Oldroyd, 1901), 229.

89. Gregorovius, *Roman Journals,* 297 (October 25, 1867) and 300 (October 27, 1867); Harriet Hosmer to Wayman Crow, November 1867 (Ashridge, England), in Carr, *Harriet Hosmer,* 250.

90. D'Agostino, *Rome in America,* 45. In a severe breach of American diplomatic neutrality, Ned Cushman, the American consul to Rome and Cushman's adopted nephew, rode with papal mercenaries against Garibaldi, thereby aligning U.S. interests with the suppression of the Italians. He was so little prepared for his duties as consul that he had no understanding of the implications of his actions and thus drew severe reprimand from the U.S. State Department. Markus, *Across an Untried Sea,* 231. His consular reports, laced with a colonial paternalism, documented his ignorance of Roman affairs. "From my observation of the Roman people," he declared, "I do not think they desire any change, particularly if that change is to increase their taxation or to interfere in any way with their habits of indolence." Defending his "first-hand" accounts of the Roman situation, he disavowed the reporting of Italian affairs in American journals and newspapers, claiming it inaccurate. Consular report by Edwin C. Cushman to William H. Seward, November 15, 1867, in *Consular Relations Between the United States and the Papal States; Instructions and Despatches,* ed. Leo F. Stock (Washington, D.C.: American Catholic Historical Association, 1945), 323; William H. Seward to Edwin C. Cushman, January 21, 1868, in ibid., 327–28; Edwin C. Cushman to William H. Seward, April 20, 1868, in ibid., 330–31.

91. Riall, *Garibaldi,* 367; Harriet Hosmer to Wayman Crow, December 5, 1867, in Carr, *Harriet Hosmer,* 256.

92. Gregorovius, *Roman Journals,* 303 (November 6, 1867).

93. As quoted in Lisa B. Reitzes, "The Political Voice of the Artist: Anne Whitney's *Roma* and *Harriet Martineau,*" *American Art* 8, no. 2 (Spring 1994): 47.

94. Buick, *Child of the Fire,* 25.

95. As soon as Whitney arrived in the city, she engaged a teacher to learn Italian. Anne Whitney to her family, May 13, 1867 (Rome), in Elizabeth Payne, "Anne Whitney: Nineteenth Century Sculptor and Liberal" (unpublished manuscript), 661, Wellesley College Archives, Wellesley, Mass. Lewis was fluent in Italian, according to Frederick Douglass, who was in Rome in 1887. Buick, *Child of the Fire,* 28.

96. As quoted in Reitzes, "Political Voice of the Artist," 48.

97. Howe, *From the Oak to the Olive,* 47.

98. As quoted in Reitzes, "Political Voice of the Artist," 48.

99. J. Falino, "Anne Whitney," in T. Stebbins, *Lure of Italy,* 238.

100. Payne, "Anne Whitney: Art and Social Justice."

101. Reitzes, "Political Voice of the Artist," 52; Anne Whitney to Sarah Whitney, January 2, 1870 (Rome), as quoted in Payne, "Anne Whitney: Nineteenth Century Sculptor and Liberal," 12.

102. Whitney felt that it was her best work to date and thus had it carved in marble by a stonecutter recommended by Emma Stebbins before she had a patron. Her friend Charles How bought the small-scale marble in 1871. She may have also exhibited it at the Philadelphia Centennial Exposition in 1876. A monumental plaster, dated 1882, was displayed in the Fine Arts Section of the World's Columbian Exposition in Chicago in 1893. Adeline Manning presented the work to Washington University in St. Louis; it was on display at the Saint Louis Art Museum. The sculpture was deaccessioned and destroyed in 1940. The extant bronze *Roma* was produced in 1890 for Wellesley College. Payne, "Anne Whitney: Nineteenth Century Sculptor and Liberal," 11–12, 251; Reitzes, "Political Voice of the Artist," 45, 53.

103. Proctor, "American Women Sculptors in Rome," 295. Proctor suggests that *Roma* may have been designed for mass consumption when shown as a small-scale plaster sculpture in Rome. Ibid., 296.

104. Payne, "Anne Whitney: Nineteenth Century Sculptor and Liberal," 251; Eric Foner, *Nothing but Freedom: Emancipation and Its Legacy* (Baton Rouge: Louisiana State University Press, 1983), 10–11; Anne Whitney, *Poems by Anne Whitney* (Boston, 1906), 127, courtesy of the Anne Whitney Papers. I would like to thank Paul Kaplan for his astute comments on this sculpture.

105. Wendell Phillips, *Speeches, Lectures, and Letters* (Boston: Lee & Shepard, 1884), 468–94, quote on 468. Because Toussaint left no writings, Phillips looked to other secondary sources for inspiration, most notably the 1841 novel by the English reformer Harriet Martineau, *The Hour and the Man: A Historical Romance,* which sympathetically chronicled the achievements of this black

revolutionary. Payne, "Anne Whitney: Nineteenth Century Sculptor and Liberal," 413, 808, and Harriet Martineau, *The Hour and the Man: A Historical Romance* (1841; repr., New York: AMS Press, 1974).

106. On the other hand, the Haitian Revolution—with all its brutality—shocked America's slaveholding society. Foner, *Nothing but Freedom*, 11, 41.

107. Payne, "Anne Whitney: Nineteenth Century Sculptor and Liberal," 807.

108. For the most comprehensive analysis of Ward's *Freedman* and other sculptural representations of the nude slave/black man, see Kirk Savage, *Standing Soldiers, Kneeling Slaves: Race, War, and Monument in Nineteenth-Century America* (Princeton: Princeton University Press, 1997), 52–88. See also Michael Hatt, "'Making a Man of Him': Masculinity and the Black Body in Mid-Nineteenth-Century American Sculpture," *Oxford Art Journal* 15, no. 1 (1992): 21–35. Neither Savage nor Hatt discusses Whitney's *Toussaint L'Ouverture in Prison.*

109. The *Mars* was located in a newly created public museum on the Ludovisi estate on the Pincian Hill, not far from Whitney's home. The cupid that currently appears at the foot of the god was an addition by Bernini. Haskell and Penny, *Taste and the Antique*, 260.

110. Payne, "Anne Whitney: Nineteenth Century Sculptor and Liberal," 955–58. As art historian Michael Hatt has explained, "The male nude . . . is not a simple sign of power, but can be used and contextualised in ways that separate physical and political power." He continues, "It can both endorse masculine identity, but keep this distinct from the social implications of what masculinity permits." Hatt, "'Making a Man of Him,'" 28.

111. Payne, "Anne Whitney: Nineteenth Century Sculptor and Liberal," 13; Harriet Hosmer to Wayman Crow, September 21, 1870 (Rome), in Carr, *Harriet Hosmer*, 284.

112. Hosmer to Crow, September 21, 1870 (Rome), in Carr, *Harriet Hosmer*, 284–85.

113. Following the success of her "Battle Hymn of the Republic," Julia Ward Howe composed a "Hymn for the Celebration of Italian Unity" to be sung to the same tune. D'Agostino, *Rome in America*, 43–48; Vance, *America's Rome*, 2:210.

114. The papacy was cloistered in the Vatican for sixty years, as an internal colony of Italy. In 1929 the Fascists signed the Lateran Pact with the Holy See, an agreement that allowed the papal territories, including the Vatican, the Lateran palaces in Rome, and the papal villa at Castel Gandolfo, to become an independent political entity, as it remains today. Vance, *America's Rome*, 2:39.

115. As quoted in Carr, *Harriet Hosmer*, 292.

116. Vance, *America's Rome*, 2:223; Anne Whitney to her family, December 5, 1870 (Rome), as quoted in Payne, "Anne Whitney: Nineteenth Century Sculptor and Liberal," 13. On May 7, 1871, Whitney departed Rome for London; she arrived in Boston in August.

117. As quoted in Carr, *Harriet Hosmer*, 292.

118. Harriet Hosmer to Wayman Crow, December 24, 1870 (Rome), in Carr, *Harriet Hosmer*, 287.

119. As quoted in Alaya, "The Ring, the Rescue, and the Risorgimento," 37.

120. As quoted in D. Sherwood, *Harriet Hosmer*, 319.

121. Entry of November 3, 1871, in Mary B. Howitt, *Mary Howitt, an Autobiography* (London: W. Isbister, 1889), 2:234.

122. James, *William Wetmore Story and His Friends*, 1:97.

*Chapter 6*

1. On May 22, 1856, South Carolina representative Preston Brooks severely beat Sumner with his cane. Sumner did not attend the Senate for the next three years while recuperating from a head trauma. He spent part of that time with Story in Rome. James, *William Wetmore Story and His Friends*, 2:3–75.

2. Buick, *Child of the Fire*, 19–20.

3. Elizabeth Barrett Browning, "A Curse of a Nation," in *Poems of Elizabeth Barrett Browning*, 438.

4. Jean Fagan Yellin, *Women and Sisters: The Antislavery Feminists in American Culture* (New Haven: Yale University Press, 1989), 85; Jan M. Seidler, "A Critical Reappraisal of the Career of William Wetmore Story (1819–1895), American Sculptor and Man of Letters" (Ph.D. diss., Boston University, 1985), 512.

5. Lydia Maria Child to Harriet Hosmer, September 16, 1860, A-162, Reel 1, Folder 3, Harriet Goodhue Hosmer Papers, Schlesinger Library, Radcliffe Institute, Harvard University, Cambridge, Mass. Also cited in Carr, *Harriet Hosmer*, 161–62. "Missouri ruffian" refers to the Kansas-Nebraska Act of 1854, which allowed states to choose "free soil" or slave status. "Border ruffians" from Missouri invaded Kansas and attacked settlers with abolitionist leanings.

6. Lewis was accused of poisoning her two white female roommates while a student at Oberlin College.

After being beaten by townspeople and left for dead in a field, she stood trial and was cleared of all charges. She left school the following year. Buick, *Child of the Fire*, 4–12; Buick, "The Sentimental Education of Mary Edmonia Lewis: Identity, Culture, and Ideal Works" (Ph.D. diss., University of Michigan, 1999), 42–44.

The bibliography on Lewis is large and growing. The sources most useful for my study (in addition to those cited above) have been Kirsten Pai Buick, "The Ideal Works of Edmonia Lewis: Invoking and Inventing Autobiography," *American Art* 9 (Summer 1995): 5–19; Juanita Marie Holland, "Mary Edmonia Lewis's *Minnehaha:* Gender, Race, and the 'Indian Maid,'" *Bulletin of the Detroit Institute of Arts* 69, nos. 1–2 (1995): 26–36; Nelson, *Color of Stone;* and Proctor, "American Women Sculptors in Rome."

7. Elizabeth Payne, "Anne Whitney: Nineteenth Century Sculptor and Liberal" (unpublished manuscript), 461, 518, Wellesley College Archives, Wellesley, Mass.

8. Ibid., 453, 446–47; quote from unidentified clipping, *The Commonwealth*, July 26, 1873, Anne Whitney Scrapbook, vol. 1, Anne Whitney Papers.

9. Lauretta Dimmick, "*Cleopatra*, 1858," in Tolles, *American Sculpture in the Metropolitan Museum of Art*, 1:87–88.

10. Mary Hamer, *Signs of Cleopatra: History, Politics, Representation* (New York: Routledge, 1993), xix. See also Griselda Pollock, "Feminist Mythologies and Missing Mothers: Virginia Woolf, Charlotte Brontë, Artemisia Gentileschi, and *Cleopatra*," in *Differencing the Canon: Feminist Desire and the Writing of Art's Histories* (New York: Routledge, 1999), 129–69; Buick, *Child of the Fire*, 133–209; and Susan Walker and Sally-Ann Ashton, eds., *Cleopatra Reassessed* (London: Trustees of the British Museum, 2003). For Story's *Cleopatra*, see Seidler, "Critical Reappraisal"; Kasson, *Marble Queens and Captives*, 208–17; and Nelson, *Color of Stone*, 143–57.

11. Kirsten Pai Buick, "Edmonia Lewis in Art History: The Paradox of the Exotic Subject," in Leslie King-Hammond and Tritobia Hayes Benjamin, *Three Generations of African-American Women Sculptors: A Study in Paradox*, exh. cat. (Philadelphia: Afro-American Historical and Cultural Museum, 1996), 14.

12. Henry Adams to Charles Francis Adams Jr., May 17, 1860, as quoted in Dimmick, "*Cleopatra*, 1858," 87.

13. N. Hawthorne, *Marble Faun*, 126.

14. Critics often confused *Cleopatra* and *The Libyan Sibyl* in their remarks. William Wetmore Story to Charles Sumner, May 13, 1861 (Rome), as quoted in Seidler, "Critical Reappraisal," 511.

15. William Wetmore Story to Charles Elliot Norton, August 16, 1861 (Rome), as quoted in Seidler, "Critical Reappraisal," 504. Although the Star of David appeared in the medieval mystical teachings of Judaism, ancient astronomers used it as a mathematical emblem of magical powers to represent the interrelationships of the natural and spiritual worlds. It was an appropriate symbol for a sibyl who divined signs in the everyday world. Ibid., 508–9. Thanks to Miriam Dean-Otting for her insights on the meaning of the Star of David.

16. West asserted, "The role of classical aesthetics and cultural norms in the emergence of the idea of white supremacy as object of modern discourse cannot be underestimated." Cornel West, "A Genealogy of Modern Racism" (1982), reprinted in *Knowledge and Postmodernism in Historical Perspective*, ed. Joyce Appelby et al. (New York: Routledge, 1996), 476–86, quote on 479.

17. Story to Norton, August 16, 1861 (Rome), as quoted in Seidler, "Critical Reappraisal," 504, and James, *William Wetmore Story and His Friends*, 2:70–71. Freeman Henry Morris Murray, in his commentary on the representation of the freed black in American sculpture, has claimed that "most people will find [*The Libyan Sibyl*] less African than Story's description would lead them to expect." Freeman Henry Morris Murray, *Emancipation and the Freed in American Sculpture: A Study in Interpretation* (1916; repr., Freeport, N.Y.: Books for Libraries Press, 1972), 8. Murray cites Story's letters on 5–6.

18. My thanks to Kristen van Ausdall for her suggestions regarding stylistic influences from Rome.

19. Sander L. Gilman, "The Hottentot and the Prostitute: Toward an Iconography of Female Sexuality," in *Difference and Pathology: Stereotypes of Sexuality, Race, and Madness* (Ithaca: Cornell University Press, 1985), 85–92. See also Charmaine Nelson, *Representing the Black Female Subject in Western Art* (New York: Routledge, 2010), 126; Rachel Holmes, *African Queen: The Real Life of the Hottentot Venus* (New York: Random House, 2007); Janell Hobson, *Venus in the Dark: Blackness and Beauty in Popular Culture* (New York: Routledge, 2005); Deborah Willis, ed., *Black Venus, 2010: They Called her "Hottentot"* (Philadelphia: Temple University Press, 2010).

20. Nelson, *Color of Stone*, 117.

21. For different narratives concerning the relationship between Stowe, Story, and Truth, see Harriet Beecher Stowe, "Sojourner Truth, the Libyan Sibyl," *Atlantic*

*Monthly* 11 (April 1863): 481; Seidler, "Critical Reappraisal," 514–18; Nell Irvin Painter, "Difference, Slavery, and Memory: Sojourner Truth in Feminist Abolitionism," in Yellin and Van Horne, *Abolitionist Sisterhood,* 153–54; and Painter, *Sojourner Truth: A Life, a Symbol* (New York: W. W. Norton, 1996), 151–64.

22. Painter, "Difference, Slavery, and Memory," 143, 152, 155, 158; Painter, *Sojourner Truth,* 164–78; "Reminiscences by Frances D. Gage: Sojourner Truth," in *History of Woman Suffrage,* ed. Elizabeth Cady Stanton, Susan B. Anthony, and Matilda Joslyn Gage (New York, 1881), 1:116, as quoted in Karen Sánchez-Eppler, "Bodily Bonds: The Intersecting Rhetorics of Feminism and Abolition," *Representations* 24 (Fall 1988): 53 n. 16. Painter cites Gage's entire account of the event in *Sojourner Truth,* 164–69.

23. H. B. Stowe, "Sojourner Truth," 477.

24. Ibid., 481.

25. Sánchez-Eppler, "Bodily Bonds," 29, 31; Sánchez-Eppler, *Touching Liberty: Abolition, Feminism, and the Politics of the Body* (Berkeley: University of California Press, 1993), 14–50; Debra Gold Hansen, "The Boston Female Anti-Slavery Society and the Limits of Gender Politics," in Yellin and Van Horne, *Abolitionist Sisterhood,* 54; Ellen DuBois, "Women's Rights and Abolition: The Nature of the Connection," in Lewis Perry and Michael Fellman, eds., *Antislavery Reconsidered: New Perspectives on the Abolitionists* (Baton Rouge: Louisiana State University Press, 1979), 238–52; Isenberg, *Sex and Citizenship,* 103–19.

26. Buick, *Child of the Fire,* 4.

27. "A Letter from L. Maria Child," *The Liberator,* February 19, 1864 (photocopy), courtesy of the Edmonia Lewis Curatorial Files, Smithsonian American Art Museum; Buick, *Child of the Fire,* 4, 13.

28. Child referred to this event as the Fair for Colored Soldiers. Lewis carved many subjects who struggled for racial equality in the United States: Wendell Phillips (1865), William Lloyd Garrison (1865), Anna Quincy Waterston (1866), Maria Weston Chapman (1867), Sgt. William Carney (1867, a soldier in the 54th Regiment who was wounded in battle), Abraham Lincoln (1870), John Brown (1872), Charles Sumner (1876), and Frederick Douglass (1887). Buick, "Sentimental Education of Mary Edmonia Lewis," 50–51.

29. As quoted in Payne, "Anne Whitney: Nineteenth Century Sculptor and Liberal," 509–10; for a more detailed discussion of Lewis's bust of Shaw, see Buick, "Sentimental Education of Mary Edmonia Lewis," 49–53, and Buick, *Child of the Fire,* 13–16.

30. *The Liberator,* February 19, 1864, n.p., as quoted in Buick, *Child of the Fire,* 13; for a discussion of Child's ambivalent attitude toward Lewis, see ibid., 17.

31. Anne Whitney to Adeline Manning, August 9, 1864 (Watertown, Mass.), in Payne, "Anne Whitney: Nineteenth Century Liberal and Sculptor," 512. See also Nelson, *Color of Stone,* 27, for a discussion of this quote.

32. Whitney did not meet Child until 1877, when she offered to sculpt the aging reformer's portrait bust. Child graciously declined but nurtured an intimate friendship with Whitney that lasted until Child's death, in 1880. Lydia Maria Child to Anne Whitney, April 8, 1877 (Boston), Anne Whitney Papers; Karcher, *First Woman in the Republic,* 596–98, 604.

33. An 1874 photograph of the work exists; therefore it must have been destroyed after this date. Misc. file, Anne Whitney Papers. See also Elizabeth Payne, "Anne Whitney, Sculptor," *Art Quarterly* 25 (Autumn 1962): 249.

34. Albert J. Raboteau, *A Fire in the Bones: Reflections on African-American Religious History* (Boston: Beacon Press, 1995), especially chap. 2, "'Ethiopia Shall Soon Stretch Forth Her Hands': Black Destiny in Nineteenth-Century America," 37–56. Thanks to Judi Fagan for bringing this chapter to my attention.

35. Bartol was the daughter of Rev. Cyrus A. Bartol, the Unitarian minister of the West Church in Boston. Between 1864 and 1865, she shared a studio with Whitney at 60 Mount Vernon Street. Payne, "Anne Whitney: Nineteenth Century Sculptor and Liberal," 462.

36. The abolitionist Thomas Wentworth Higginson wrote that Whitney had an "interview with Harriet Tubman" and because of it "modified the features of [her] sculpture," in this case, "the hair" of *Ethiopia.* Thomas Wentworth Higginson to Anne Whitney, November 27, 1864 (Newport, R.I.), Anne Whitney Papers.

37. Anne Whitney to Adeline Manning, May 2, 1866 (Belmont, Mass.), Anne Whitney Papers.

38. "National Sailor's Fair," *Boston Evening Transcript,* November 9, 1864, 2. See also "Art Items," *Boston Evening Transcript,* December 2, 1864, 2.

39. L[ydia] M[aria] C[hild], "A Chat with the Editor of the Standard," *Anti-Slavery Standard,* January 14, 1865, courtesy of the Edmonia Lewis Curatorial Files, Smithsonian American Art Museum.

40. Esperance [pseud.], "Academy of Design, Sculpture," *New York Leader* [1865], as quoted in Payne, "Anne Whitney: Nineteenth Century Sculptor and Liberal," 567–68. Another anonymous critic described *Ethiopia* in

terms of the "luxuriance of the tropics" yet called for the sculpture to be erected as a monument to Lincoln in Central Park or elsewhere. Unidentified newspaper clipping [1865], as quoted in ibid., 569–70.

41. Gilman cites a *Dictionary of Medical Sciences* (1819): Black women's "voluptuousness [is] developed to a degree of lascivity unknown in our climate, for their sexual organs are much more developed than those of whites." Gilman, "The Hottentot and the Prostitute," 85.

42. Nelson, *Color of Stone,* 118.

43. For *The Greek Slave*'s complicated relationship to abolitionism, see Vivien M. Green, "Hiram Powers's *Greek Slave:* Emblem of Freedom," *American Art Journal* 14, no. 4 (Autumn 1982): 31–39; Yellin, *Women and Sisters,* 99–125; Savage, *Standing Soldiers, Kneeling Slaves,* 28–31; Kasson, *Marble Queens and Captives,* 65–68; Nelson, *Color of Stone,* 75–113; and Nelson, *Representing the Black Female Subject,* 147–49.

44. "Statues of *Lady Godiva* and *Africa* at the Gallery of Messers. Childs and Jenks" (unidentified clipping [1864]), Anne Whitney Scrapbook, vol. 1, Anne Whitney Papers.

45. "A Word About Statues," *New Path,* June 1865, 104, as quoted in Payne, "Anne Whitney: Nineteenth Century Sculptor and Liberal," 570–71.

46. Higginson to Whitney, November 27, 1864 (Newport, R.I.), Anne Whitney Papers. Higginson is probably referring to Story's *Libyan Sibyl* in this letter.

47. Anne Whitney to Liver Ingraham Lay, July 3, 1865, as quoted in Payne, "Anne Whitney: Nineteenth Century Sculptor and Liberal," 574.

48. Anne Whitney to Adeline Manning, February 28, 1866, as quoted in ibid., 607.

49. For a detailed discussion of neoclassicism's participation in racial theories of the day, see Savage, *Standing Soldiers, Kneeling Slaves,* 9–15. See also Nelson, *Color of Stone,* 58–69, and Nelson, *Representing the Black Female Subject,* 147.

50. Charmaine Nelson refers to a mixed-race identity as "the miscegenated white-Negro body." Nelson, *Representing the Black Female Subject,* 141.

51. In its radical advocacy of racial mixing, this position was repugnant to most contemporary Americans, including moderate abolitionists. George M. Fredrickson, *The Black Image in the White Mind: The Debate on Afro-American Character and Destiny, 1817–1914* (New York: Harper & Row, 1971), 101–26, quote on 120; Karcher, *First Woman in the Republic,* 513.

52. Art historian Charmaine Nelson explains, "The representational impossibility of the black female body, specifically its antithetical constitution within the Eurocentric conception of beauty, was such that the figure of the . . . interracial black woman became almost synonymous with *the black woman* within American neoclassical sculpture and arguably within other forms of western art." Nelson, *The Color of Stone,* 126–27. Jean Fagin Yellin has defined "the tragic mulatta" as "a slave woman of mixed race who wants to conform to patriarchal definitions of true womanhood but is prevented from doing so by the white patriarchy." Yellin, *Women and Sisters,* 71.

53. Lydia Maria Child, *A Romance of the Republic* (1867; repr., Lexington: University of Kentucky Press, 1997); Carolyn L. Karcher, "Lydia Maria Child's *A Romance of the Republic:* An Abolitionist Vision of America's Racial Destiny," in *Slavery and the Literary Imagination,* ed. Deborah E. McDowell and Arnold Rampersad (Baltimore: Johns Hopkins University Press, 1989), 83, 96; Beth Maclay Doriani, "Black Womanhood in Nineteenth-Century America: Subversion and Self-Construction in Two Women's Autobiographies," *American Quarterly* 43, no. 2 (June 1991): 205–6.

54. As quoted in Carr, *Harriet Hosmer,* 192–93. In May of 1865, Hosmer exhibited *Zenobia* (owned by Almond Griswald) at the Sanitary Commission Fair in Chicago. The *Chicago Evening Journal* paid her the highest of compliments, comparing her sculpture to that of Thorwaldsen. "Miss Hosmer is a Roman now; she has devoted her life to art; but her American heart beats as warmly as ever." As quoted in Carr, *Harriet Hosmer,* 367. My thanks to Beth Belanger for locating a letter from Hosmer to the Committee of the Chicago Sanitary Fair, May 30, 1865, Chicago Historical Society.

55. Jameson, *Lives of Celebrated Female Sovereigns and Illustrious Women,* 25. Hosmer showed *Zenobia in Chains* at the Derby Gallery in New York in November of 1864. At the opening reception, many in attendance, such as the art critic Henry Tuckerman, the poet William Cullen Bryant, the feminist writer Catharine Sedgwick, and Harriet Beecher Stowe, were public supporters of both the Italian struggle and the Union cause. Carr, *Harriet Hosmer,* 199; D. Sherwood, *Harriet Hosmer,* 228–29; "Harriet Hosmer's Statue of 'Zenobia,'" *Boston Evening Transcript,* November 14, 1864, 2. Zenobia, one critic noted, was a truly powerful and defiant woman, "proud in her captivity, scornful of her position, and heart broken at her fate." "An Evening Among the Artists of New York," *Boston Evening Transcript,* November 21, 1864, 1.

56. Referring to her work as "The National Statue," Lander published a four-page broadside that accompanied the exhibition. *The National Sculpture, Virginia Dare, by Louisa Lander,* exhibition brochure (Boston, 1865); "Miss Lander," *Boston Evening Transcript,* December 5, 1860, 2; "Art Items," *Boston Evening Transcript,* February 26, 1861, 2. *Virginia Dare* also appeared in Salem for the benefit of sick and wounded Union soldiers that same year.

57. "Miss Lander's 'Virginia Dare,'" *Boston Evening Transcript,* February 20, 1865, 2.

58. "Virginia Dare," *Boston Evening Transcript,* March 1, 1865, 2. A few weeks later, possibly the same critic wrote, "What have we [Americans] to do with Palmyra, Europe and Africa? Let us congratulate Miss Lander on having nobly written the first page of our nation's history in undying marble. 'Zenobia' and 'Africa' tell an old story." W. "'Virginia Dare,'" *Boston Evening Transcript,* March 16, 1865, 2.

59. Proctor, "American Women Sculptors in Rome," 178–81; Buick, "Sentimental Education of Mary Edmonia Lewis," 193 n. 117.

60. Nelson, *Color of Stone,* 32, 34; Buick, *Child of the Fire,* 14, 20, 25–26, 250 n. 130. As Lewis said when writing to Child of her new life in Rome in the spring of 1866: "Miss Hosmer has since called on me and we often meet." *Independent,* April 5, 1866, as quoted in Nelson, *Color of Stone,* 33; see also Buick, *Child of the Fire,* 64.

61. Nelson, *Color of Stone,* 22, as quoted in Buick, *Child of the Fire,* 51 and 73. Her passport listed her as four feet tall. Ibid., 141.

62. *The Freedwoman on the First Hearing of Her Liberty* (or the *Freedwoman and Child*) is first mentioned in the contemporary literature in 1866. Henry Wreford wrote, "She has thrown herself on her knees with clasped hands and uplifted eyes, she blesses God for her redemption. Her boy, ignorant of the cause of her agitation, hangs over her knees and clings to her waist. She wears the turban which was used when at work. Around her wrists are the half broken manacles, and the chain lies on the ground still attached to a large ball." H[enry] W[reford], *Athenaeum,* no. 2001 (March 3, 1866): 302. The *Freedman's Record* reported that Lewis proposed "to dedicate her work to Miss H. E. Stevenson and Mrs. E[dna] D[ow] Cheney, as an expression of gratitude for their labors on behalf of the education of her father's race." *Freedman's Record* 2, no. 4 (April 1866): 69. In 1916 Freeman Henry Morris Murray reported that he was unable to locate the sculpture. Murray, *Emancipation and the Freed in American Sculpture,* 21. Lewis's sculptures of freedmen and women and those of Native Americans were produced simultaneously in Rome between 1866 and 1875. This chapter addresses only those works that address slavery, the freedwoman, and the freedman.

63. The image first appeared in the United States in May 1830. Phillip Lapsansky, "Graphic Discord: Abolitionist and Antiabolitionist Images," in Yellin and Van Horne, *Abolitionist Sisterhood,* 205–6; Yellin, *Women and Sisters,* 8–9, 15, 23, 171.

64. As quoted in Buick, "Ideal Works of Edmonia Lewis," 18 n. 5.

65. Buick brings an alternate reading to this sculpture. "The figures read as a unit, rather than in opposition. Together they form a compact silhouette made up of a series of discrete triangles, beginning with the horizontal triangle formed by [the freedman's] upraised arm and his right shoulder." She concludes, "Within the composition itself, the bodies are in perfect harmony in spite of the fact that [the freedwoman] kneels and he stands, that she is chained and he is not." Buick, *Child of the Fire,* 52–53.

66. Lydia Maria Child to Sarah Blake Sturgis Shaw, April 8, 1866, New York Public Library Manuscript Division, Personal Miscellany.

67. Edmonia Lewis to Maria Weston Chapman, May 3, 1868 (Rome), Anti-Slavery Collection, Department of Rare Books and Manuscripts, Boston Public Library, courtesy of the Trustees of the Boston Public Library/Rare Books; *Boston Evening Transcript,* October 18, 1869, 2; Buick, "Ideal Works of Edmonia Lewis," 7, 9; James Oliver Horton and Lois E. Horton, "The Affirmation of Manhood: Black Garrisonians in Antebellum Boston," in *Courage and Conscience: Black and White Abolitionists in Boston,* ed. Donald M. Jacobs (Bloomington: Indiana University Press, 1993), 128.

68. As quoted by Lydia Maria Child in a letter to Sarah Blake Sturgis Shaw, August 1870, Houghton Library, Harvard University, bMS AM 1417 (105).

69. Child argued that Lewis exemplified the linking of the races and the way in which the "lines of demarcation between classes and races [were] melting away." Karcher, *First Woman in the Republic,* 475; C[hild], "A Chat with the Editor of the Standard," n.p.

70. Doriani, "Black Womanhood in Nineteenth-Century America," 201–2.

71. Buick, "Ideal Works of Edmonia Lewis," 6. James Oliver Horton, "Freedom's Yoke: Gender Conventions Among Antebellum Free Blacks," *Feminist Studies* 12, no. 1 (Spring 1986): 55. Horton concluded, "Manhood and freedom were tied to personal power."

72. Savage, *Standing Soldiers, Kneeling Slaves,* 58; Horton and Horton, "Affirmation of Manhood," 136; Buick, "Sentimental Education of Mary Edmonia Lewis," 155.

73. For a discussion of this masthead, see Bernard F. Reilly Jr., "The Art of the Antislavery Movement," in Jacobs, *Courage and Conscience,* 62–63.

74. Buick, *Child of the Fire,* 60.

75. For a fuller discussion of self-sacrifice, submission, and domesticity in the mid-nineteenth century, see Kathryn Kish Sklar, *Catherine Beecher: A Study in American Domesticity* (New Haven: Yale University Press, 1973).

76. Sánchez-Eppler, "Bodily Bonds," 46; Kristin Hoganson, "Garrisonian Abolitionists and the Rhetoric of Gender, 1850–1860," *American Quarterly* 45, no. 4 (December 1993): 558–96.

77. Buick arrives at a different interpretation of the work. "Contrary to the most current interpretations of the sculpture, I propose that the statue is not a feminist statement by Lewis about the dual burdens of sexism and racism that the black woman in America was forced to bear." She concludes that Lewis's work "facilitated the continuity of the dominant ideologies [of] sentimentalism [and] true womanhood." Buick, *Child of the Fire,* 55, 133.

78. Buick suggests that Lewis was a supporter of Italian nationalism and viewed Giuseppe Garibaldi, like Lincoln, as a hero. Buick, *Child of the Fire,* 3, 22, 24, 27.

79. Charlotte Cushman to Fanny Seward, as quoted in E. Stebbins, *Charlotte Cushman,* 200.

80. George G. Wynne, *Early Americans in Rome* (Rome: Daily American Printing, 1966), 34; Stock, *United States Ministers to the Papal States,* 337. Immediately upon receiving word of Lincoln's assassination, a Committee of Five, including General Rufus King, the minister to Rome from 1865 to 1867, Story, and Reverend Lyman, prepared an official response from the expatriate community, which they forwarded to the State Department, the family of the late president, the New York Associated Press, and the *Washington Chronicle.* It read in part:

> *Resolved: In common with every . . . American, at home and abroad, we regard the loss of Abraham Lincoln as a national bereavement of unsurpassed magnitude; recognizing in him an able, upright, zealous, and conscientious statesman whose valuable life was consecrated to the public service and whose tragic death has added the crown of martyrdom to the civic wreath which a grateful country had already placed upon his brow. . . .*
>
> *Resolved: That in token of our respect for the memory of the illustrious dead, we will wear the customary badge of mourning for a period of thirty days, and that the Chaplain of the Legation be requested to hold a special religious service at some convenient hour tomorrow.*

Edward S. Lacey to Charlotte Cushman, April 28, 1865 (Rome), Cushman Papers, Container 1.

81. William James Stillman, *The Autobiography of a Journalist* (Boston: Houghton, Mifflin, 1901), 1:346. Stillman was American consul in Rome from 1861 to 1865.

82. W. J. Stillman (acting U.S. consul) to William H. Seward, June 25, 1865 (Rome), in Stock, *Consular Relations Between the United States and the Papal States,* 302. Also quoted in Wynne, *Early Americans in Rome,* 34–35. The stone was eventually sent by an act of Congress in 1870 to Springfield, Illinois, where it was enshrined in the base of the Lincoln Monument.

83. "Freedman's Memorial," *National Freedman* 1 (August 15, 1865): 231; D. Sherwood, *Harriet Hosmer,* 244–45, as quoted in "The Freedman's Monument to Abraham Lincoln," *Art-Journal* (London) 1, no. 1 (January 1, 1868): 8.

84. My interpretation of Hosmer's model is indebted to Kirk Savage's detailed analysis of the project. See Savage, *Standing Soldiers, Kneeling Slaves,* 94–100, for a full discussion of Hosmer's monumental design.

85. Horton, "Freedom's Yoke," 53, 59.

86. "Harriet Hosmer, Description of Monument," Harriet Goodhue Hosmer Papers, M-60, Reel 3, Folder 67, Schlesinger Library, Radcliffe Institute, Harvard University, Cambridge, Mass.; this document is reproduced in Carr, *Harriet Hosmer,* 368–69.

87. "A Freedman's Monument to Abraham Lincoln," *Freedman's Record* 3 (January 1867): 2–3. Lewis viewed the monument model in Hosmer's studio in April of 1866, as she was working on her *Forever Free.* Kirsten Buick suggests that Lewis might have borrowed elements of the slave figure—the curly hair and cloth shorts—for her own male figure. Buick, "Sentimental Education of Mary Edmonia Lewis," 160–62, and Buick, *Child of the Fire,* 64–65.

88. Hatt, "'Making a Man of Him,'" 21–25; Savage, *Standing Soldiers, Kneeling Slaves,* 98.

89. *Boston Evening Transcript,* January 29, 1867, 2; Savage, *Standing Soldiers, Kneeling Slaves,* 94; D. Sherwood, *Harriet Hosmer,* 274.

90. Yellin, *Women and Sisters,* 8; Savage, *Standing Soldiers, Kneeling Slaves,* 114.

91. "Freedman's Memorial," *National Freedman* 1 (August 15, 1865): 231.

92. For information on Hosmer's *African Sibyl,* see *Boston Evening Transcript,* May 2, 1874, 4; "Art and Artists,"

*Boston Evening Transcript,* May 7, 1875, 4–5; the *Evening Post* (New York), September 10, 1875, 2; "Miss Hosmer's Golden Gates," *Boston Evening Transcript,* September 15, 1875, 6.; and D. Sherwood, *Harriet Hosmer,* 313.

93. Savage, *Standing Soldiers, Kneeling Slaves,* 125–28.

94. Whitney continued, "Mrs. [Caroline] Dall and her co-laborers in this field are willing to drop, for the present, their demand for suffrage in order not to break the other issue, but to see this rock in the Channel ahead is too much to bear." Anne Whitney to Adeline Manning, January 18, 1866 (Belmont), quoted in Payne, "Anne Whitney: Nineteenth Century Sculptor and Liberal," 595. Caroline Dall was a prominent feminist who wrote *Women's Right to Education* (1859), *Woman's Right to Labor* (1860), and *Woman's Right Under the Law* (1861).

95. Catherine Clinton, *The Other Civil War: American Women in the Nineteenth Century,* rev. ed. (New York: Hill & Wang, 1999), 87–93; Eleanor Flexner, *Century of Struggle: The Woman's Rights Movement in the United States* (1959; repr., New York: Atheneum, 1971), 143–47; quote from Painter, *Sojourner Truth,* 229.

96. She submitted a proposal for a Lincoln monument for Chicago. At the top of the structure was a seated figure of Lincoln, underneath which was an "African sibyl" and a black child. On the outside of the monument was a female allegory of a mourning Victory. For a fuller description and analysis of this proposed monument, see Savage, *Standing Soldiers, Kneeling Slaves,* 125–28.

## *Chapter 7*

1. "Vinnie Ream: The Lincoln Statue; The Official View To-day," *Washington Evening Star,* January 7, 1871, 1, Vinnie Ream Hoxie Papers, Container 4, Folder: Commissions: Lincoln, Library of Congress, Washington, D.C. (hereafter VRH Papers). "Dora-like" is a reference to a sweet but childish character in Charles Dickens's *David Copperfield.*

2. M. B. L., "Our Washington Letter," *Daily Advertiser* (Chicago), February 24, 1879; "A Woman's Letter from Washington" (unidentified clipping), February 1871; and "Miss Ream's Triumph," *The Revolution* 7, no. 5 (February 2, 1871). Another writer declared Ream "to be a handsome likeness of the picture of Mde. de Stael." "Vinnie Ream: An Interesting Page in Her History," *The Globe* (New York). All references found in VRH Papers, Container 8, Scrapbook 1871–1878.

3. Anne Whitney to her family, January 9, 1870 (Rome), as quoted in Elizabeth Payne, "Anne Whitney: Nineteenth Century Sculptor and Liberal" (unpublished manuscript), 813, Wellesley College Archives, Wellesley, Mass.

4. Rosemary Booth, "A Taste for Sculpture," in Hoyle, Harding, and Booth, *Climate for Art,* 25.

5. Sarah Fisher Clampitt's marriage to Joseph Ames was announced in the *Boston Evening Transcript* on September 12, 1845; "Notes About Women," *The Revolution* 7, no. 2 (January 12, 1871).

6. Louisa May Alcott, *Hospital Sketches* (Boston: J. Redpath, 1863).

7. For the Gardner photographs, see Harold Holzer, "Mrs. Ames and Mr. Lincoln," *Civil War Times Illustrated* 28, no. 2 (April 1989): 28–31, and Kirsten Pai Buick, "Sarah Fisher Ames (1817–1901): *Bust of Abraham Lincoln,* ca. 1864–1866," in *American Dreams: American Art to 1950 in the Williams College Museum of Art,* ed. Nancy Mowll Mathews (New York: Hudson Hills Press in association with the Williams College Museum of Art, 2001), 54–57, with one of the Gardner photos on 56. In his November 8, 1863, journal entry, John Hay wrote: "Went with Mrs. Ames to Gardner's Gallery & were soon joined by Nico [John G. Nicolay] and the Pres[ident]. We had a great many pictures taken. Some of the Pres[ident], the best I have seen. Nico & I immortalized ourselves by having ourselves done in group with the Pres[ident]." *Lincoln and the Civil War in the Diaries and Letters of John Hay* (New York: Dodd, Mead, 1939), 117.

8. "[The plaster cabinet bust] comes out at a most timely moment to be made a Christmas and New Year's gift. . . [its modest price makes it] convenient to become one of the Penates [household gods] of every home." *Boston Evening Transcript,* November 29, 1865. See also *Boston Evening Transcript,* February 6, 1866, 2, on the bust's philanthropic mission. The Lynn Museum and Historical Society in Lynn, Massachusetts, owns the only known surviving plaster cabinet bust.

9. For "amateur artist," see "Fine Arts," *Evening Post* (New York), February 1, 1866, 1; for "artist of genius," see "Mrs. Ames's Bust of Abraham Lincoln," *Boston Evening Transcript,* April 17, 1867, 2. Ames was paid $2,000 for the Senate bust, which is located in the east corridor, third floor, Senate wing of the U.S. Capitol. In 1867, Massachusetts purchased a bust for their statehouse, the first funded accession by the commonwealth. *Art in the Massachusetts State House,* Massachusetts Art Commission, courtesy of the Office of the Senate Curator, the United States Senate. Other marble busts are located in the Woodmere Art Museum, Philadelphia, and the Williams College Museum of Art, Williamstown, Mass. The Ohio Statehouse in

Columbus also ordered a marble bust; at present this bust has not been located.

10. For a discussion of the popular market for sculpture in the nineteenth century, see Michele Bogart, "The Development of a Popular Market for Sculpture in America, 1850–1880," *Journal of American Culture* 4 (Spring 1981): 3–28. Bogart surmises: "Critics and writers' comments seem to suggest that Americans bought sculpture for two main reasons: to refine themselves and to gain status. . . . Owning a portrait of a popular figure gave Americans opportunities to emulate heroes, remember friends, or simply to decorate their home" (18).

11. This writer criticized other portrait busts for their "emasculated and finical look." "Mrs. Ames's Bust of Abraham Lincoln," *Boston Evening Transcript,* April 17, 1867, 2.

12. "The Academy of Fine Arts—Second Article on Sculpture," *Daily Evening Bulletin* (Philadelphia), May 24, 1868, 1.

13. In Washington, Robert Ream, the sculptor's father, found work as a mapmaker for the War Department until rheumatism forced his early retirement. He was decidedly pro-Union, but her brother fought for the Confederacy. When she was young, Ream sympathized with the South, but after the war began, she aligned herself with the Union cause. Edward S. Cooper, *Vinnie Ream: An American Sculptor* (Chicago: Academy Chicago Publishers, 2004), 2–5; "The Vinnie Ream Wedding," *Newark Daily Advertiser,* May 31, 1878, 1; and "Personal Recollections of Lincoln—Vinnie Ream Tells of a Girl's Impressions of the Great Emancipator," *Sunday Star* (Washington, D.C.), February 9, 1913, 7, Vinnie Ream Hoxie Folder, Office of the Architect of the Capitol, Washington, D.C.

14. The suffragist Pauline Wright Davis claimed that she had seen Vinnie Ream in 1856, when the artist was nine years old, "elbow-deep in the clay" in the Washington studio of Paul Akers. No other source has confirmed that Ream studied with Akers, who was in Rome in 1856. "What a Girl Has Done," *The Revolution* 8, no. 9 (March 2, 1871).

For Ream's apprenticeship with Mills, see Rep. James Rollins of Missouri to Mrs. Crittenden, April 22, 1864, VRH Papers, General Correspondence, Folder 1864. It is difficult to separate fact from fiction in the accounts of Ream's life. Some scholars have dismissed as false Ream's claim of visiting the White House and modeling Lincoln's bust from life. However, Ream's critics never questioned her access to the president after she was awarded the Lincoln commission, even though they scrutinized most other facets of her life and criticized her character with impunity. E. Cooper, *Vinnie Ream,* 22, and Carmine A. Prioli, "'Wonder Girl from the West': Vinnie Ream and the Congressional Statue of Abraham Lincoln," *Journal of American Culture* 12, no. 4 (Winter 1989): 2.

15. Stephen W. Stathis and Lee Roderick, "Mallet, Chisel, and Curls," *American Heritage* 27, no. 2 (February 1976): 95.

16. For a discussion of this new model of public woman, see Amanda Frisken, *Victoria Woodhull's Sexual Revolution: Political Theater and the Popular Press in Nineteenth-Century America* (Philadelphia: University of Pennsylvania Press, 2004), and Helen Lefkowitz Horowitz, *Rereading Sex: Battles over Sexual Knowledge and Suppression in Nineteenth-Century America* (New York: Alfred A. Knopf, 2002), 342–58. For a divergent picture of the artist, see Kirk Savage, "Vinnie Ream's *Lincoln* (1871): The Sexual Politics of a Sculptor's Studio," in Kennon and Somma, *American Pantheon,* 163.

17. Glenn V. Sherwood, *A Labor of Love: The Life and Art of Vinnie Ream* (Hygiene, Colo.: SunShine Press Publications, 1997), 117; Vinnie Ream to John Rice, chairman of the Committee on Public Buildings and Grounds, May 31, 1866, VRH Papers, Container 1, General Correspondence, 1854–1873, Folder 1870. For a more detailed discussion of the House bill, see Prioli, "'Wonder Girl from the West'"; Harold E. Miner, "Vinnie and Her Friends," Archives of American Art, roll 297, Smithsonian Institution, Washington, D.C.; E. Cooper, *Vinnie Ream,* 27.

18. "I wish you might make a statue of Lincoln. He is a historic character, worthy of bronze and marble." Charles Sumner to William Wetmore Story, December 16, 1866, Charles Sumner Papers, Huntington Library, Art Collection, and Gardens, San Marino, Calif.

19. Cong. Globe, 39th Cong., 1st Sess. (Senate, July 27, 1866), 4225, 4231–33, 4235–36, quote on 4233.

20. "Fine Art: The Sculpture in America," *The Albion,* February 27, 1869, 109–10.

21. As quoted in Margaret Farrand Thorp, *Female Persuasion: Six Strong-Minded Women* (New Haven: Yale University Press, 1949), 65.

22. Jane Grey Swisshelm, "Miss Vinnie Ream," January 16, 1867, unidentified source, VRH Papers, Scrapbook, Container 8. For more on Swisshelm, see Sylvia D. Hoffert, *Jane Grey Swisshelm: An Unconventional Life, 1815–1884* (Chapel Hill: University of North Carolina Press, 2004).

23. Freud had argued that this condition was particularly apparent in beautiful women who called attention to their physical beauty in order to secure the adoration of others. Elisabeth Young-Bruehl, ed., *Freud on Women: A Reader* (New York: W. W. Norton, 1990), see especially

"Selections from 'On Narcissism: An Introduction,'" 190–96; Rosemarie Tong, *Feminist Thought: A Comprehensive Introduction* (Boulder, Colo.: Westview Press, 1989), 142.

24. "The Feminine Regime" (unidentified clipping), VRH Papers, Container 9, Scrapbook 1864–1876.

25. Vinnie Ream to John Quincy Adams Ward, June 1868 (photocopy), Lincoln File, Office of the Architect of the Capitol, Washington, D.C.; original letter in J. Q. A. Ward Papers, Albany Institute of History and Art, Albany, N.Y. On the impeachment debacle, see G. Sherwood, *Labor of Love,* 85–103.

26. Warner, *Publics and Counterpublics,* 22–31.

27. In 1929, the psychiatrist Joan Riviere investigated the concept of the feminine masquerade. "Womanliness," she explained in 1929, "could be assumed and worn as a mask, both to hide the possession of masculinity and to avert reprisals expected if [a talented woman] was found to possess it." She continued, "The reader may now ask how I define womanliness or where I draw the line between genuine womanliness and the 'masquerade.' My suggestion is not . . . that there is any such difference; . . . they are the same thing." Riviere also explained that talented and competent women "resented any assumption" that they were not equal to men, "and, in private, would reject the idea of being subject to their judgment or criticism." Joan Riviere, "Womanliness as a Masquerade," *International Journal of Psychoanalysis* 10 (1929): 305–6; Mary Ann Doane, "Film and the Masquerade: Theorizing the Female Spectator," in Jones, *Feminism and Visual Culture Reader,* 60–72; Mary Kelly, "Desiring Images / Imaging Desire," in ibid., 72–76; Judith Butler, "Performative Acts and Gender Constitution: An Essay in Phenomenology and Feminist Theory," in ibid., 392–402; and in Case, *Performing Feminisms,* 270–82.

28. Undated newspaper clipping, quoted in E. Cooper, *Vinnie Ream,* 142.

29. "Female Sculptors in Rome," *Evening Post* (New York), April 12, 1870, 1.

30. "Vinnie Ream: An Interesting Page in Her History," *The Globe* (New York), undated clipping, VRH Papers, Container 8, Scrapbook 1871–1878.

31. Laura Mulvey was among the first to theorize the gaze in her now classic text "Visual Pleasure and Narrative Cinema" (1975), reprinted in Jones, *Feminism and Visual Culture Reader,* 44–53. See also Kelly, "Desiring Images / Imaging Desire," 72–73, and Doane, "Film and Masquerade," 67.

32. Ream purchased her own sculptural tools in Paris at a hefty cost of thirty dollars. Journals from Abroad, June 13–October 13, 1869, VRH Papers, Container 5.

33. Journals from Abroad, October 19–24, 1869, VRH Papers, Container 5, quote dated October 18, 1869.

34. Miner, "Vinnie and Her Friends," 144–45, AAA, role 297; G. Sherwood, *Labor of Love,* 125.

35. "Foreign Correspondence, Letter from Rome (Dated October 29, 1869)," *Daily Evening Bulletin* (Philadelphia) November 19, 1869, 2.

36. Journals from Abroad, June 7, 1870, VRH Papers, Container 5.

37. Journals from Abroad, December 15, 1869, VRH Papers, Container 5; G. Sherwood, *Labor of Love,* 125.

38. Anne Whitney to Sarah Whitney, December 25, 1869 (Rome), as quoted in Payne, "Anne Whitney: Nineteenth Century Sculptor and Liberal," 804–5.

39. "Cose d'arte," *Buonarroti* 5 (February 1870): 54. A second article, written in June, discussed the remainder of the works that she produced in Rome. "Una visita allo studio di M. Vinnie Ream," *Buonarroti* 5 (July 1870): 200–202.

40. Ream visited Carrara between May 21 and 25, 1870. Journals from Abroad, May 27, 1870, VRH Papers, Container 5; receipt for purchase of Carrara marble, VRH Papers, Container 1, General Correspondence, 1854–1873, Folder 1870; Miner, "Vinnie and Her Friends," 148, AAA, roll 297.

41. Journals from Abroad, March 7–10, 1870, VRH Papers; Miner, "Vinnie and Her Friends," 147, AAA, roll 297.

42. "Female Sculptors in Rome," *Evening Post* (New York), April 12, 1870, 3.

43. Journals from Abroad, March 9, 1870, VRH Papers, Container 5.

44. Miner, "Vinnie and Her Friends," 149, AAA, roll 297; G. Sherwood, *Labor of Love,* 151.

45. "Female Sculptors in Rome," 3.

46. Anne Whitney to Sarah Whitney, December 25, 1869 (Rome), as quoted in Payne, "Anne Whitney: Nineteenth Century Sculptor and Liberal," 804–5; Madame de Staël, *Corinne, or Italy.* In the novel, Corinne often dons a turban, an exotic headpiece worn by sibyls in many Renaissance and Baroque paintings. See also Parrott, "Expatriates and Professionals."

47. Anne Whitney to her family, January 17, 1869 (Rome), as quoted in Payne, "Anne Whitney: Nineteenth Century Sculptor and Liberal," 9.

48. David I. Kertzer, *Prisoner of the Vatican: The Popes, the Kings, and Garibaldi's Rebels in the Struggle to Rule Modern Italy* (New York: Houghton Mifflin, 2004), 5, 15.

49. Journals from Abroad, July 5, 1870, VRH Papers, Container 5.

50. Journals from Abroad, July 1 and 5, 1870, VRH Papers, Container 5. According to one source, Ream, dressed in a white gown, requested an audience with Antonelli; he was so taken with her beauty that he consented to sit for his portrait bust. Gordon Langley Hall, *Vinnie Ream: The Story of the Girl Who Sculptured Lincoln* (New York: Holt, Rinehart & Winston, 1963), 71.

51. Journals from Abroad, July 7, 1870, VRH Papers, Container 5.

52. On the cameo of Christ, see Journals from Abroad, July 12, 1870, VRH Papers. Antonelli also gave Ream a "medallion with the head of the Virgin Mary on it in stone." Ibid., July 14, 1870.

53. Undated newspaper clipping, quoted in E. Cooper, *Vinnie Ream,* 142.

54. Ream had borrowed the actual clothing that the president had worn at the time of his death. See the letter from James S. Rollins to Mary Todd Lincoln, August 22, 1866, and Mrs. Lincoln's response to Ream, September 10, 1866, VRH Papers, Container 1, General Correspondence, 1854–1873, Folder 1866. Mrs. Lincoln did not favor Ream's receiving the sculptural commission.

55. Minor Kellogg, "Vinnie Ream," *Washington Evening Star,* January 7, 1871, 1, VRH Papers, Container 4, Folder: Commissions: Lincoln.

56. The referenced quote bears note number 1 at the beginning of this chapter.

57. Karen Lemmey, "Reconstructing Lincoln: New York City's Monuments to a Slain President," 2001 (unpublished paper). My thanks to Dr. Lemmey for sending me a copy of this paper. See also Savage, *Standing Soldiers, Kneeling Slaves,* 66–69, 73–76, 81–83. Ream had contacted Brown a few years earlier for advice regarding the life-size plaster model of *Lincoln.* Savage explains that the Emancipation Proclamation scroll would become a well-known trope in sculptural images of Lincoln.

58. Kellogg, "Vinnie Ream."

59. "Art and Drama," *Woodhull and Claflin's Weekly* [1871], VRH Papers, Container 5, unmarked folder.

60. "Letter from Mr. Hiram Powers," *Evening Post* (New York), June 19, 1871.

61. Argus, "The Petulant Powers," *Brooklyn Eagle,* June 1871, VRH Papers.

62. For an overview of Powers's years in Washington, D.C., see Craven, *Sculpture in America,* 112–13.

63. "Woman and Artist," *The Revolution* 7, no. 9 (March 2, 1871).

64. For more on Greenwood's attack, see Joan A. Lemp, "Vinnie Ream and *Abraham Lincoln,*" *Woman's Art Journal* 6, no. 2 (Autumn 1985–Winter 1986): 26. A few years later, Grace Greenwood snidely wrote: "I have not the slightest malevolence toward the young lady in question [Vinnie Ream]. I do not begrudge her her reputation or her recompense." [Grace Greenwood], "Grace Greenwood and Vinnie Ream," *Daily Evening Bulletin* (San Francisco), February 5, 1873, 4. Of course, "reputation" could mean several things in this context.

65. Harriet Hosmer, "Vinnie Vindicated—A Card from Miss Harriet G. Hosmer," [*New York Tribune*], April 1871, VRH Papers, Container 6, Folder: Misc.

66. "Notes About Women," *The Revolution* 7, no. 16 (May 4, 1871). The *Revolution* also came to Ream's rescue: "Why . . . should Miss Ream be deprived of the credit due to her when she faithfully accompanied her model [to Rome], selected the most perfect and spotless of blocks for the statue, and with her own hand put that finishing work to it which she would entrust to no mechanic, however skilled?" H. C. Ingersoll, "Miss Ream and *The Tribune*" (letter to the editor), *The Revolution* 7, no. 8 (February 23, 1871). In fact, Ream did hire Italian carvers, as was common among American sculptors in Rome.

67. [Mary Clemmer Ames], "The Independent and Miss Ream's Statue of Lincoln," *Art Review* 1 (March 1871): 13.

68. Mary Clemmer Ames, *Ten Years in Washington: Life and Scenes in the National Capital as a Woman Sees Them* (Hartford, Conn.: A. D. Worthington, 1874), 112; Schriber, *Writing Home,* 36. Sarah Fisher Ames and Mary Clemmer Ames were not related by blood or marriage.

69. The *Revolution* also celebrated the careers of Margaret Foley, Louisa Lander, and Edmonia Lewis. Moreover, they published articles on the status of women artists in the United States and the status of women in the new nation of Italy.

70. Ryan, *Women in Public,* 155; Paula Baker, "The Domestication of Politics: Women and American Political Society, 1780–1920," *American Historical Review* 89, no. 3 (June 1984): 634. Senator Charles Sumner and Frederick Douglass, formerly advocates for women's right to vote, supported the Radical Republicans' "Negro first" strategy. Stanton and Anthony refused to put the rights of African-American males ahead of women. Ryan, *Women in Public,* 153–65; Clinton, *Other Civil War,* 93–94; Flexner, *Century of Struggle,* 152. See also Ellen Carol DuBois, "Outgrowing the Compact of the Fathers: Equal Rights, Woman Suffrage, and the United States Constitution,

1820–1878," *Journal of American History* 74, no. 3 (December 1987): 853.

71. Horowitz, *Rereading Sex,* 343. Woodhull had come from social obscurity to political success in the suffrage movement and, with her sister, Tennessee Claflin, was the first woman to open a brokerage firm, Woodhull, Claflin & Company, Brokers, in New York City. Cornelius Vanderbilt helped finance the brokerage firm. Frisken, *Victoria Woodhull's Sexual Revolution,* 20.

72. Representative Benjamin Butler, a Massachusetts Republican who supported labor reform and woman suffrage, invited Woodhull to speak. Some Republicans supported this initiative and gave suffragists a room in the Capitol from which to lobby. Lois Beachy Underhill, *The Woman Who Ran for President: The Many Lives of Victoria Woodhull* (New York: Penguin Books, 1995), 94–106; DuBois, "Outgrowing the Compact of the Fathers," 853–55. When women offered a challenge to the Fifteenth Amendment in 1875 (*Minor v. Happersett*), the Supreme Court unanimously held that if the authors of the Constitution had intended a woman to vote, they would have explicitly said so. "Minor v. Happersett, 1875," in *Women's America: Refocusing the Past,* ed. Linda K. Kerber and Jane Sherron De Hart (New York: Oxford University Press, 2000), 245.

Woodhull is often remembered as a sexual radical who advocated free love. She argued that individuals had the inalienable right to participate in sexual relations as they desired. "Yes, I am a Free Lover," she claimed in a speech given in New York City in 1871. "I have an inalienable, constitutional and natural right to love whom I may, . . . and it is your duty not only to accord [my right], but, as a community, to see that I am protected in it." Quoted in DuBois, "Outgrowing the Compact of the Fathers," 856. Woodhull's open support of free love threatened the legitimacy of the NWSA, which rescinded its official support of the party in May of 1872. Horowitz, *Rereading Sex,* 349.

73. "Art and Drama," *Woodhull and Claflin's Weekly* [1871], VRH Papers, Container 5, unmarked folder.

74. Unidentified clipping, *Missouri Democrat,* VRH Papers, Scrapbook 1871–1878, as quoted in E. Cooper, *Vinnie Ream,* 93.

75. For reference to the Douglass bust, see "Art," *The Chronicle,* April 22, 1871; for the medallion of Davis, see an unidentified clipping, VRH Papers, Container 8, Scrapbook 1871–1878; a medallion study of Susan B. Anthony is located in the Oklahoma Historical Society.

76. Whitney's sister, Sarah Whitney, made reference to the article in the *Revolution,* "Woman and Artist," which Sarah "like[d] very much, in which [the author] deprecates all this personal twaddle about [Ream's] hair and eyes." Sarah Whitney to her family, March 27, 1871 (Rome), as quoted in Payne, "Anne Whitney: Nineteenth Century Sculptor and Liberal," 874.

77. Anne Whitney to Ednah Dow Cheney, February 21, 1875 (Belmont, Mass.), quoted in ibid., 999.

78. DuBois, "Outgrowing the Compact of the Fathers," 853.

79. Baker, "Domestication of Politics," 634.

80. Payne, "Anne Whitney: Nineteenth Century Sculptor and Liberal," 963, 967.

81. *The Commonwealth,* July 26, 1873, as quoted in ibid., 972–73.

82. The Massachusetts monument committee had requested that this quotation appear on the pedestal. The full context of Adams's words reads: "It is the unanimous opinion of the meeting that the reply to the vote of the inhabitants in the morning is by no means satisfactory; nothing less will satisfy them than a total and immediate removal of the troops. If you have power to remove one regiment, you have power to remove both. It is at your peril if you refuse. . . . Night is approaching; an immediate answer is expected. Both regiments or none!" 44 Cong. Rec. 282 (December 19, 1876).

83. Inevitably, Whitney's *Adams* was compared to Ream's *Lincoln:* "Among the many excellent pieces of statuary at the capitol, perhaps that of *Samuel Adams* is the best of all, because it is natural in every respect as well as in size. . . . Vinnie Ream's *Lincoln* is of the natural size, but the legs are much too large and the coat is badly cut. . . . the face, head and general appearance are good." "Art and Artists," *Boston Evening Transcript,* July 19, 1876, 6.

84. For a thorough examination of the Sumner memorial process, see Eleanor Tufts, "An American Victorian Dilemma, 1875: Should a Woman Be Allowed to Sculpt a Man?" *Art Journal* 51, no. 1 (Spring 1992): 51–57. See also "Models for the Sumner Statue," *Evening Post* (New York), August 3, 1875, 2; "The Sumner Statue," *Boston Evening Transcript,* November 6, 1875, 4.

85. Payne, "Anne Whitney: Nineteenth Century Sculptor and Liberal," 1105, 1008; Anne Whitney to Sarah Whitney, May 19, 1875 (Florence), as quoted in ibid., 1010.

86. Peter Fusco and H. W. Janson, *The Romantics to Rodin: French Nineteenth-Century Sculpture from North American Collections* (Los Angeles: Los Angeles County Museum of Art; New York: George Braziller, 1980), 272.

87. Anne Whitney to Adeline Manning, March 15, 1876, as quoted in Payne, "Anne Whitney: Nineteenth Century Sculptor and Liberal," 1107–8; Hirshler, *A Studio of Her Own,* 19–20.

88. Sarah Whitney to Anne Whitney, February 3, 1876 (Watertown, Mass.), as quoted in Payne, "Anne Whitney: Nineteenth Century Sculptor and Liberal," 1092.

89. Tufts, "American Victorian Dilemma," 51–52. In her correspondence with Adeline Manning, Whitney cited these passages from a letter she had received from Charles Slack, February 27, 1876 (Florence), as quoted in Payne, "Anne Whitney: Nineteenth Century Sculptor and Liberal," 1093–94.

90. Whitney continued, "In the month that I spent in Florence, I met several Englishwomen who were zealous in this matter as we could wish, & they told me of the constantly growing interest among Italian women." Anne Whitney to Marianne Dwight Orvis and Ednah Dow Cheney, July 25 [1875] (Écouen), as quoted in Payne, "Anne Whitney: Nineteenth Century Sculptor and Liberal," 1034.

91. Anne Whitney to Edward Whitney, December 22, 1875 (Paris), as quoted in ibid., 1068–69; Tufts, "American Victorian Dilemma," 51.

92. *The Commonwealth* (Boston), June 15, 1876, as quoted in Payne, "Anne Whitney: Nineteenth Century Sculptor and Liberal," 1130.

93. One spokesman proclaimed that Whitney's resolute figure captured "with marked success . . . the stately form and commanding features of the great popular leader." 44 Cong. Rec. 283 (December 19, 1876). Four years later, a bronze replica was placed on view in Boston. Hirshler, *A Studio of Her Own,* 16.

*Postscript*

1. E. Cooper, *Vinnie Ream,* 324.

2. Quoted in the *Washington Evening Star,* April 24, 1874, 1; "Personal," *Evening Post* (New York), January 8, 1975, 2.

3. Ellet, *Women Artists in All Ages.*

4. With the exception of Anne Whitney's *Sumner Memorial,* which was installed belatedly, in 1900, on the Cambridge (Mass.) Commons.

5. John J. Ingalls to Vinnie Ream, July 15, 1874 (Atchison, Kans.), VRH Papers, Container 2, Folder 1874.

6. See, for example, W. T. Sherman, General, to Vinnie Ream, February 20, 1873 (Washington, D.C.), VRH Papers, Container 1, General Correspondence, 1854–1873, Folder 1873. See also E. Cooper, *Vinnie Ream,* 161. Mrs. Farragut also supplied Ream with a photograph from which to work.

7. For a thorough discussion of the *Farragut Memorial* commission, see Ruth L. Bohan, "The Farragut Memorial: A Decade of Art and Politics, 1871–1881," in *Records of the Columbia Historical Society of Washington, D.C., 1973–1974,* ed. Francis C. Rosenberger (Washington, D.C.: Columbia Historical Society, 1976), 209–43.

8. In fact, Crow sat on the commission committee. D. Sherwood, *Harriet Hosmer,* 188.

9. Hosmer added, "I am indebted to the chivalry of the West." F., Sketchings," *The Crayon* 7 (New York), September 1860, 264.

10. "The Vinnie Ream Wedding," *Newark Daily Advertiser,* May 31, 1878, 1.

11. E. Cooper, *Vinnie Ream,* 240.

12. Milroy, "Public Career of Emma Stebbins: Work in Marble," 11.

13. For example, Hosmer invented "Petrified Marble," a plaster-like substance that mimicked the appearance of marble, and a perpetual-motion machine. Culkin, *Harriet Hosmer,* 116–35.

14. Marilyn Richardson has turned up Lewis's death certificate. She was diagnosed with chronic Bright's disease and died in 1907. See "Edmonia Lewis, First Internationally Acclaimed African-American Sculptor," www.edmonialewis.com/death_of_mary_edmonia_lewis.html; "Sculptor's Death Unearthed: Edmonia Lewis Died in London in 1907," http://222.cowanauctions.com/about-us/news.aspx?NewsID=367; and "Sculptor's Death Unearthed," Art and History, January 9, 2011, www.artandhistory.wordpress.com/2011/01/09/edmonia_lewis_died_in_1907.

15. "Anne Whitney," Anne Whitney Folder, Office of the Architect of the Capitol, Washington, D.C.

16. Anne Whitney to Marianne Dwight Orvis and Ednah Dow Cheney, July 25, 1875 (Paris), as quoted in Elizabeth Payne, "Anne Whitney: Nineteenth Century Sculptor and Liberal" (unpublished manuscript), 1030, Wellesley College Archives, Wellesley, Mass.

17. The artists Lizzie Boott, Elizabeth Bartol, Mary Cassatt, Maria Oakey, and Manning worked in Thomas Couture's studio, anxious to learn his more spontaneous painting techniques, which eschewed careful and deliberate underpainting. Nonetheless, Manning believed that Couture had no "high appreciation of woman's capacity and judge[d them] accordingly." Adeline Manning to Anne Whitney, March 19, 1876 (Paris), as quoted in Payne, "Anne Whitney: Nineteenth Century Sculptor and Liberal," 1109. For a thorough discussion of women artists' training in Paris, see Swinth, *Painting Professionals,* 37–63.

# Selected Bibliography


*Archives*

Americans in Italy. Centro Studi Americani, Rome, Italy.
Sarah Fisher Ames Folder. Office of the Architect of the Capitol, Washington, D.C.
Anti-Slavery Collection. Department of Rare Books and Manuscripts. Boston Public Library.
Thomas Crawford Papers. Archives of American Art. Smithsonian Institution, Washington, D.C.
Charlotte Cushman Papers. Library of Congress, Washington, D.C.
Nelson Gay Papers. Museo Centrale del Risorgimento. Vittoriano, Rome, Italy.
Nathaniel Hawthorne Papers. Huntington Library, Art Collection, and Botanical Gardens, San Mareno, Calif.
Harriet Goodhue Hosmer Collection. Watertown Free Public Library, Watertown, Mass.
Harriet Goodhue Hosmer Papers. Schlesinger Library. The Radcliffe Institute, Harvard University, Cambridge, Mass.
Vinnie Ream Hoxie Folder. Office of the Architect of the Capitol, Washington, D.C.
Vinnie Ream Hoxie Papers. Archives of American Art. Smithsonian Institution, Washington, D.C.
Vinnie Ream Hoxie Papers. Library of Congress, Washington, D.C.
Peabody Sisters Letters. Horace Mann Papers. Antioch College, Yellow Springs, Ohio.
John Rogers Papers. New York Historical Society, New York, N.Y.
Ada Shepard Letters. Robert L. Straker Collection of Horace Mann Papers. Antioch College, Yellow Springs, Ohio.
Emma Stebbins Papers. Archives of American Art. Smithsonian Institution, Washington, D.C.
Robert L. Straker Collection of Horace Mann Papers. Antioch College, Yellow Springs, Ohio.
Charles Sumner Papers. Huntington Library, Art Collection, and Botanical Gardens, San Mareno, Calif.
Anne Whitney Folder. Office of the Architect of the Capitol, Washington, D.C.
Anne Whitney Papers. Wellesley College Archives, Wellesley, Mass.

*Primary Sources*

Abbott, Jacob. *Rollo in Rome.* Rollo's Tour in Europe, vol. 10. Boston: Brown, Taggard & Chase, 1858.
Albrizzi, Countess, and Count Cicognara. *The Works of Antonio Canova.* Vol. 1. London: Septimus Prowett, Strand, 1826.
Adams, Henry. "Documents: Henry Adams and Garibaldi, 1860." *American Historical Review* 25, no. 2 (January 1920): 241–55.
Ames, Mary Clemmer. *Ten Years in Washington: Life and Scenes in the National Capital as a Woman Sees Them.* Hartford, Conn.: A. D. Worthington, 1874.
Armstrong, Maitland. *Day Before Yesterday: Reminiscences of a Varied Life.* New York: Charles Scribner's Sons, 1920.
Blewitt, Octavian. *A Handbook for Travellers in Central Italy.* London: John Murray, 1850.
Browning, Elizabeth Barrett. *Aurora Leigh.* 1857. Edited by Margaret Reynolds. Athens: Ohio University Press, 1992.
———. *Casa Guidi Windows.* Edited by Julia Markus. New York: Browning Institute, 1977.
———. *The Letters of Elizabeth Barrett Browning.* Edited by Frederick G. Kenyon. Vol. 2. New York: Macmillan, 1898.
———. *Poems of Elizabeth Barrett Browning.* New York: A. L. Burt, 1887.
Bryant, William Cullen. *Letters of a Traveller; or, Notes of Things Seen in Europe and America.* New York: D. Appleton, 1859.
Bulfinch, Thomas. *The Age of Fable; or, Beauties of Mythology.* Boston: S. W. Tilton, 1855.
Burton, Katharine. *Sorrow Built a Bridge: A Daughter of Hawthorne.* New York: Longmans, Green, 1937.
Byron, George Gordon (Lord). *Childe Harold's Pilgrimage.* Philadelphia: George S. Appleton, 1847.
Caesare, Raffaele De. *The Last Days of Papal Rome, 1850–1870.* Translated by Helen Zimmern. London: Archibald Constable, 1909.

Carr, Cornelia, ed. *Harriet Hosmer: Letters and Memories.* New York: Moffat, Yard, 1912.

Cheney, Ednah Dow. *Reminiscences of Ednah Dow Cheney.* Boston: Lee & Shepard, 1902.

Child, Lydia Maria. *A Romance of the Republic.* 1867. Reprint, Lexington: University of Kentucky Press, 1997.

Clement, Clara Erskine. *Artists of the Nineteenth Century and Their Works.* Rev. ed. Cambridge, Mass.: Houghton, Mifflin, 1884.

Cobbe, Frances Power. *Italics: Brief Notes on Politics, People, and Places in Italy, in 1864.* London: Trübner, 1864.

———. *Life of Frances Power Cobbe: As Told by Herself.* London: Swan Sonnenschein, 1904.

Dall, Caroline Healy. *Margaret and Her Friends; or, Ten Conversations with Margaret Fuller upon the Mythology of the Greeks and Its Expression in Art, Held at the House of Rev. George Ripley, Bedford Place, Boston, Beginning March 1, 1841.* Boston: Roberts, 1895.

———. *Transcendentalism in New England: A Lecture.* Boston: Roberts Brothers, 1897.

Dwight, Theodore. *The Roman Republic of 1849.* New York: R. Van Dien, 1851.

Eastlake, Elizabeth Rigby (Lady), ed. *Life of John Gibson, R. A.* London: Longmans, Green, 1870.

Ellet, E. F. *Women Artists in All Ages and Countries.* New York: Harper & Brothers, 1859.

Emerson, R[alph] W[aldo], W[illiam] H[enry] Channing, and J[ames] F[reeman] Clarke. *Memoirs of Margaret Fuller Ossoli.* 2 vols. Boston: Roberts Brothers, 1875.

Fuller (Ossoli), Margaret. *"These Sad but Glorious Days": Dispatches from Europe, 1846–1850.* Edited by Larry J. Reynolds and Susan Belasco Smith. New Haven: Yale University Press, 1991.

———. *Woman in the Nineteenth Century.* 1845. Reprint, Mineola, N.Y.: Dover Publications, 1999.

Garibaldi, Giuseppe. *The Life of General Garibaldi.* Translated by Theodore Dwight. New York: A. S. Barnes & Burr, 1859.

Gay, Nelson. "Le relazioni fra l'Italia e gli Stati Uniti (1847–1871)." *Nuova antologia,* 5th ser., 127 (January–February 1907): 657–71.

Greenwood, Grace [Sarah Jane Clarke Lippincott]. *Haps and Mishaps of a Tour in Europe.* Boston: Ticknor, Reed & Fields, 1854.

Gregorovius, Ferdinand. *The Roman Journals of Ferdinand Gregorovius, 1852–1874.* Edited by Friedrich Althaus, translated by Mrs. Gustavus W. Hamilton. London: G. Bell & Sons, 1911.

Guerrazzi, F. D. *Beatrice Cenci: A Historical Novel of the Sixteenth Century.* Translated by Luigi Monti. 2 vols. New York: Rudd & Carleton, 1858.

Hanaford, Phebe A. *Daughters of America; or, Women of the Century.* Augusta, Maine: True, 1882.

Hawthorne, Julian. *Nathaniel Hawthorne and His Wife.* Vol. 2. Boston: Houghton, Mifflin, 1884.

Hawthorne, Mrs. Nathaniel (Sophia Peabody). *Notes in England and Italy.* New York: G. P. Putnam's Sons, 1878.

Hawthorne, Nathaniel. *The French and Italian Notebooks.* The Centenary Edition of the Works of Nathaniel Hawthorne, vol. 14. Edited by Thomas Woodson. Columbus: Ohio State University Press, 1980.

———. *The Letters.* Vol. 4, *1857–1864.* The Centenary Edition of the Works of Nathaniel Hawthorne, vol. 18. Edited by Thomas Woodson, L. Neal Smith, and Norman Holmes Pearson. Columbus: Ohio University Press, 1987.

———. *The Marble Faun; or, The Romance of Monte Beni.* 1860. New York: Penguin Books, 1990.

Higginson, Thomas Wentworth. *Margaret Fuller Ossoli.* 1884. Reprint, Boston: Houghton, Mifflin, 1912.

Hosmer, Harriet Goodhue. *Boston and Boston People, in 1850.* Boston, 1850.

———. "The Doleful Ditty of the Roman Caffe Greco." *Evening Transcript* (Boston), November 17, 1864, 1.

———. Letter to the editor. *Art Journal* (London) 111 (January 1, 1864): 27.

———. "The Process of Sculpture." *Atlantic Monthly* 14 (December 1864): 734–37.

Howe, Julia Ward. *From the Oak to the Olive: A Plain Record of a Pleasant Journey.* Boston: Lee & Shepard, 1868.

———. *Passion-Flowers.* Boston: Ticknor, Reed & Fields, 1854.

———. *Reminiscences, 1819–1899.* Boston: Houghton, Mifflin, 1906.

Howitt, Margaret. "A Memoir of the Sculptor Margaret F. Foley." *Art Journal* (London), n.s., 17 (April 1, 1878).

Howitt, Mary B. *Mary Howitt, an Autobiography.* Vol. 2. London: W. Isbister, 1889.

James, Henry. *Daisy Miller.* 1878. New York: Penguin Books, 1986.

———. *William Wetmore Story and His Friends: From Letters, Diaries, and Recollections.* 2 vols. Boston: Houghton, Mifflin, 1903.

Jameson, Anna. *Lives of Celebrated Female Sovereigns and Illustrious Women.* 1831. Reprint, edited by Mary E. Howitt. Philadelphia: Porter & Coates, 1870.

Kendall, Phebe Mitchell, ed. *Maria Mitchell: Life, Letters, and Journals.* Boston: Lee & Shepard, 1896.

Lathrop, Rose Hawthorne. *Memories of Hawthorne.* Boston: Houghton, Mifflin, 1898.

Litta-Visconti-Arese, Pompeo (Duke), ed. *The Birth of Modern Italy: Posthumous Papers of Jesse White Mario.* London: T. Fischer Unwin, 1909.

Martineau, Harriet. *The Hour and the Man: A Historical Romance.* 1841. Reprint, New York: AMS Press, 1974.

Matthews, T. *The Biography of John Gibson, R. A., Sculptor, Rome.* London: William Heinemann, 1911.

Melville, Herman. "Statues in Rome." 1857. Reprinted in Merton M. Sealts Jr., *Melville as Lecturer,* 127–54. Cambridge: Harvard University Press, 1957.

Murray, Freeman Henry Morris. *Emancipation and the Freed in American Sculpture: A Study in Interpretation.* 1916. Reprint, Freeport, N.Y.: Books for Libraries Press, 1972.

Russo, Ann, and Cheris Kramarae, eds. *The Radical Women's Press of the 1850s.* New York: Routledge, 1991.

Sedgwick, Catharine. *Letters from Abroad to Kindred at Home.* Vol. 2. New York: Harper & Brothers, 1841.

———. *Married or Single?* 2 vols. New York: Harper, 1857.

Staël, Madame de [Germaine Necker]. *Corinne, or Italy.* Translated by Sylvia Raphael. New York: Oxford University Press, 1998. (Originally published in French as *Corinne ou l'Italie,* 1807.)

Stanton, Elizabeth Cady. "'Declaration of Sentiments' from *The History of Women's Suffrage.*" 1848. Reprinted in *Feminist Theory: A Reader,* edited by Wendy K. Komar and Frances Bartkowski, 2nd ed., 71–73. New York: McGraw-Hill, 2005.

Stebbins, Emma. *Charlotte Cushman: Her Letters and Memories of Her Life.* 1879. Reprint, New York: Blom, 1972.

Stillman, William James. *The Autobiography of a Journalist.* Vol 1. Boston: Houghton, Mifflin, 1901.

Stock, Leo Francis, ed. *Consular Relations Between the United States and the Papal States; Instructions and Dispatches.* Washington, D.C.: American Catholic Historical Association, 1945.

———, ed. *United States Ministers to the Papal States: Instructions and Dispatches, 1848–1868.* Washington, D.C: Catholic University Press, 1933.

Story, William Wetmore. *Roba di Roma.* 4th ed. New York: D. Appleton, 1864.

Stowe, Harriet Beecher. "Sojourner Truth, the Libyan Sibyl." *Atlantic Monthly* 11 (April 1863): 473–81.

Tennyson, Alfred (Lord). *Tennyson: Poems and Plays.* New York: Oxford University Press, 1973.

Tuckerman, Henry T. "Giuseppe Garibaldi." *North American Review* 92 (1861): 15–56.

Whiting, Lilian. *Women Who Have Ennobled Life.* Philadelphia: Union Press, 1915.

*Secondary Sources*

Adler, Kathleen, and Marcia Pointon, eds. *The Body Imaged: The Human Form and Visual Culture Since the Renaissance.* New York: Cambridge University Press, 1993.

Alaya, Flavia. "The Ring, the Rescue, and the Risorgimento: Reunifying the Brownings' Italy." *Browning Institute Studies* 6 (1978): 1–41.

Allen, Beverly, and Mary Russo, eds. *Revisioning Italy: National Identity and Global Culture.* Minneapolis: University of Minnesota Press, 1997.

Antonelli, Sara, Daniele Fiorentino, and Giuseppe Monsagrati, eds. *Gli americani e la Repubblica romana del 1849.* Rome: Gangemi Editore, 2000.

Armstrong, Isobel, ed. *New Feminist Discourses: Critical Essays on Theories and Texts.* New York: Routledge, 1992.

———. *Victorian Poetry: Poetry, Poetics, Politics.* New York: Routledge, 1993.

Arscott, Caroline, and Katie Scott, eds. *Manifestations of Venus: Art and Sexuality.* New York: Manchester University Press, 2000.

Bacarella, Michael. *Lincoln's Foreign Legion: The 39th New York Infantry, the Garibaldi Guard.* Shippensburg, Pa.: White Mane Publishing, 1996.

Bailey, Brigitte. "Gender, Nation, and the Tourist Gaze in the European 'Year of Revolutions': Kirkland's *Holidays Abroad.*" *American Literary History* 14, no. 1 (March 2002): 60–82.

Baker, Paula. "The Domestication of Politics: Women and American Political Society, 1780–1920." *American Historical Review* 89, no. 3 (June 1984): 620–47.

Barolini, Helen. *Their Other Side: Six American Women and the Lure of Italy.* New York: Fordham University Press, 2006.

Barrett, Michèle, and Anne Phillips, eds. *Destabilizing Theory: Contemporary Feminist Debates.* Stanford: Stanford University Press, 1992.

Battersby, Christine. *Gender and Genius: Towards a Feminist Aesthetics.* Bloomington: Indiana University Press, 1989.

Bell, Millicent, ed. *Hawthorne and the Real: Bicentennial Essays.* Columbus: Ohio State University Press, 2005.

Benzel, Kathryn N., and Lauren Pringle de la Vars, eds. *Images of the Self as Female: The Achievement of Women Artists in Re-envisioning Feminine Identity.* Lewiston, N.Y.: Edwin Mellen Press, 1992.

Berthold, Dennis. "Melville, Garibaldi, and the Medusa of Revolution." *American Literary Review* 9, no. 3 (Autumn 1997): 425–59.

Blainey, Ann. *Fanny and Adelaide: The Lives of the Remarkable Kemble Sisters.* Chicago: Ivan R. Dee, 2001.

Blühm, Andreas, et al. *The Colour of Sculpture, 1840–1910.* Exh. cat. Van Gogh Museum, Amsterdam, July 26–November 17, 1996; Henry Moore Institute, Leeds, December 13, 1996–April 6, 1997. Zwolle: Waanders, 1996.

Bogart, Michele. "The Development of a Popular Market for Sculpture in America, 1850–1880." *Journal of American Culture* 4 (Spring 1981): 3–28.

Bohan, Ruth L. "The Farragut Monument: A Decade of Art and Politics, 1871–1881." In *Records of the Columbia Historical Society of Washington, D.C., 1973–1974,* edited by Francis C. Rosenberger, 209–43. Washington, D.C.: Columbia Historical Society, 1976.

Boime, Albert. *The Art of the Macchia and the Risorgimento: Representing Culture and Nationalism in Nineteenth-Century Italy.* Chicago: University of Chicago Press, 1993.

Booth, Alison. "The Lessons of the Medusa: Anna Jameson and the Collective Biographies of Women." *Victorian Studies* 42, no. 2 (January 1, 1999): 257–88.

Bowron, Edgar P., and Joseph J. Rishel, eds. *Art in Rome in the Eighteenth Century.* Philadelphia: Philadelphia Museum of Art, 2000.

Brooks, Van Wyck. *The Dream of Arcadia: American Writers and Artists in Italy, 1760–1915.* New York: E. P. Dutton, 1958.

Broude, Norma. *The Macchiaioli: Italian Painters of the Nineteenth Century.* New Haven: Yale University Press, 1987.

Buick, Kirsten Pai. *Child of the Fire: Mary Edmonia Lewis and the Problem of Art History's Black and Indian Subject.* Durham: Duke University Press, 2010.

———. "The Ideal Works of Edmonia Lewis: Invoking and Inventing Autobiography." *American Art* 9 (Summer 1995): 5–19.

———. "The Sentimental Education of Mary Edmonia Lewis: Identity, Culture, and Ideal Works." Ph.D. diss., University of Michigan, 1999.

Buonomo, Leonardo. *Backward Glances: Exploring Italy, Reinterpreting America (1831–1866).* London: Associated University Presses, 1996.

Burns, Sarah. *Painting on the Dark Side: Art and the Gothic Imagination in Nineteenth-Century America.* Berkeley: University of California Press, 2004.

Calhoun, Craig, ed. *Habermas and the Public Sphere.* Cambridge: MIT Press, 1992.

Capper, Charles. "Margaret Fuller as Cultural Reformer: The Conversations in Boston." *American Quarterly* 39, no. 4 (Winter 1987): 509–28.

Case, Sue-Ellen, ed. *Performing Feminisms: Feminist Critical Theory and Theatre.* Baltimore: Johns Hopkins University Press, 1990.

Castle, Terry. *The Apparitional Lesbian: Female Homosexuality and Modern Culture.* New York: Columbia University Press, 1993.

Chadwick, Whitney. *Women, Art, and Society.* New York: Thames & Hudson, 1990.

Chapman, Alison. "'In Our Own Blood Drenched the Pen': Italy and Sensibility in Elizabeth Barrett Browning's *Last Poems* (1862)." *Women's Writing* 10, no. 2 (2003): 269–86.

Chapman, Alison, and Jane Stabler, eds. *Unfolding the South: Nineteenth-Century British Women Writers and Artists in Italy.* New York: Manchester University Press, 2003.

Cherry, Deborah. *Beyond the Frame: Feminism and Visual Culture, Britain, 1850–1900.* New York: Routledge, 2000.

———. *Painting Women: Victorian Women Artists.* Exh. cat. Rochdale Art Gallery, April 4–May 30, 1987, and at three other British galleries through February 1988. Rochdale: Rochdale Art Gallery, 1987.

———. *Painting Women: Victorian Women Artists.* New York: Routledge, 1993.

Chersi, Livio. *Italia e Stati Uniti: Relazioni diplomatiche 1861–1935.* Trieste: Edizioni Alabarda, 1937.

Cixous, Hélène. *The Newly Born Woman.* Translated by Betsy Wing. Minneapolis: University of Minnesota, Press, 1986. (Originally published in French as *La jeune née,* 1975.)

*Classic Ground: Mid-Nineteenth-Century American Painting and the Italian Encounter.* Exh. cat. Edited by Paul A. Manoguerra. Athens: Georgia Museum of Art, 2004.

Clinton, Catherine. *The Other Civil War: American Women in the Nineteenth Century.* Rev. ed. New York: Hill & Wang, 1999.

Cooper, Edward S. *Vinnie Ream: An American Sculptor.* Chicago: Academy Chicago Publishers, 2004.

Cooper, Wendy. *Classical Taste in America, 1800–1840.* Exh. cat. Baltimore Museum of Art, June 27–September 26, 1993; Mint Museum of Art, Charlotte, N.C., November 20, 1993–March 13, 1994; Museum of Fine Arts, Houston, May 1–July 24, 1994. Baltimore: Baltimore Museum of Art; New York: Abbeville Press, 1993.

Cott, Nancy F. *The Bonds of Womanhood: "Woman's Sphere" in New England, 1780–1835.* New Haven: Yale University Press, 1977.

Crane, Sylvia E. *White Silence: Greenough, Powers, and Crawford, American Sculptors in the Nineteenth Century.* Coral Gables: University of Miami Press, 1972.

Craske, Matthew. *Art in Europe, 1700–1830.* New York: Oxford University Press, 1997.

Craven, Wayne. *Sculpture in America.* New York: Thomas Y. Crowell, 1968.

Cronin, Patricia. *Harriet Hosmer: Lost and Found; A Catalogue Raisonné.* Milan: Edizioni Charta, 2009.

Culkin, Kate. *Harriet Hosmer: A Cultural Biography.* Amherst: University of Massachusetts Press, 2010.

Dabakis, Melissa. "Angelika Kauffmann, Goethe, and the Arcadian Academy in Rome." In *The Enlightened Eye: Goethe and Visual Culture,* edited by Evelyn K. Moore and Patricia Anne Simpson, 25–41. Amsterdam: Rodopi Press, 2007.

D'Agostino, Peter R. *Rome in America: Transnational Catholic Ideology from the Risorgimento to Fascism.* Chapel Hill: University of North Carolina Press, 2004.

Damon-Bach, Lucinda L., and Victoria Clements, eds. *Catharine Maria Sedgwick: Critical Perspectives.* Boston: Northeastern University Press, 2003.

Daniels, Elizabeth Adams. *Jessie White Mario: Risorgimento Revolutionary.* Athens: Ohio University Press, 1972.

Darby, Elisabeth S. "John Gibson, Queen Victoria, and the Idea of Sculptural Polychromy." *Art History* 4, no. 1 (March 1981): 37–53.

Davidson, Cathy N., and Jessamyn Hatcher, eds. *No More Separate Spheres.* Durham: Duke University Press, 2002.

Denis, Rafael Cardoso, and Colin Trodd, eds. *Art and the Academy in the Nineteenth Century.* New Brunswick: Rutgers University Press, 2000.

Derounian-Stodola, Kathryn Zabelle, ed. *Women's Indian Captivity Narratives.* New York: Penguin Books, 1998.

Dickie, John. *Darkest Italy: The Nation and Stereotypes of the Mezzogiorno, 1860–1900.* New York: St. Martin's Press, 1999.

Dimmick, Lauretta. "Thomas Crawford's *Orpheus:* The American *Apollo Belvedere.*" *American Art Journal* 19, no. 4 (Autumn 1987): 46–84.

Donoghue, Emily. *Inseparable: Desire Between Women in Literature.* New York: Alfred A. Knopf, 2010.

Doriani, Beth Maclay. "Black Womanhood in Nineteenth-Century America: Subversion and Self-Construction in Two Women's Autobiographies." *American Quarterly* 43, no. 2 (June 1991): 199–222.

Douglas, Ann. *The Feminization of American Culture.* 1977. Reprint, New York: Farrar, Straus & Giroux, 1998.

Douglas, Mary. *Purity and Danger: An Analysis of Concepts of Pollution and Taboo.* London: Routledge & Kegan Paul, 1966.

DuBois, Ellen Carol. "Outgrowing the Compact of the Fathers: Equal Rights, Woman Suffrage, and the United States Constitution, 1820–1878." *Journal of American History* 74, no. 3 (December 1987): 836–62.

DuBois, Ellen Carol, Mari Jo Buhle, Temma Kaplan, Gerda Lerner, and Carroll Smith-Rosenberg. "Politics and Culture in Women's History: A Symposium." *Feminist Studies* 6, no. 1 (Spring 1980): 26–64.

Eldredge, Charles C. *The Arcadian Landscape: Nineteenth-Century American Painters in Italy.* Exh. cat. University of Kansas Museum of Art, Lawrence, November 4–December 3, 1972. Lawrence: University of Kansas Museum of Art, 1972.

Faderman, Lillian. *Surpassing the Love of Men: Romantic Friendship and Love Between Women from the Renaissance to the Present.* New York: Morrow, 1981.

Fahlman, Betsy. "A Plaster of Paris Antiquity: Nineteenth-Century Cast Collections." *Southeastern College Art Conference Review* 12, no. 1 (1991): 1–9.

Faxon, Alicia. "Images of Women in the Sculpture of Harriet Hosmer." *Woman's Art Journal* 2, no. 1 (Spring–Summer 1981): 25–29.

Feldman, Burton, and Robert D. Richardson. *The Rise of Modern Mythology, 1680–1860.* Bloomington: Indiana University Press, 1972.

Ferando, Christina. "Staging Neoclassicism: Antonio Canova's Exhibition Strategies for *Triumphant Perseus.*" In *Das Originale der Kopie: Kopien als Produkte und Medien der Transformation von Antike,* edited by Tatjana Bartsch, Marcus Becker, Horst Bredekamp, and Charlotte Schreiter, 139–63. New York: Walter de Gruyter, 2010.

Fleischmann, Fritz, ed. *Margaret Fuller's Cultural Critique: Her Age and Legacy.* New York: Peter Lang, 2000.

Flexner, Eleanor. *Century of Struggle: The Woman's Rights Movement in the United States.* 1959. Reprint, New York: Atheneum, 1971.

Foner, Eric. *Nothing but Freedom: Emancipation and Its Legacy.* Baton Rouge: Louisana State University Press, 1983.

Formichella Elsden, Annamaria. *Roman Fever: Domesticity and Nationalism in Nineteenth-Century American Women's Writing.* Columbus: Ohio State University Press, 2004.

Franchot, Jenny. *Roads to Rome: The Antebellum Protestant Encounter with Catholicism.* Berkeley: University of California Press, 1994.

Fredrickson, George M. *The Black Image in the White Mind: The Debate on Afro-American Character and Destiny, 1817–1914.* New York: Harper & Row, 1971.

Frisken, Amanda. *Victoria Woodhull's Sexual Revolution: Political Theater and the Popular Press in Nineteenth-Century America.* Philadelphia: University of Pennsylvania Press, 2004.

Fryd, Vivien Green. *Art and Empire: The Politics of Ethnicity in the United States Capitol, 1815–1860.* New Haven: Yale University Press, 1992.

———. "The 'Ghosting' of Incest and Female Relations in Harriet Hosmer's *Beatrice Cenci.*" *Art Bulletin* 88, no. 2 (June 2006): 292–310.

———. "Hiram Powers's *America:* 'Triumphant as Liberty and in Unity.'" *American Art Journal* 18, no. 2 (Spring 1986): 54–75.

Galani-Moutafi, Vasiliki. "The Self and Other: Traveler, Ethnographer, Tourist." *Annals of Tourism Research* 27, no. 1 (January 2000): 203–24.

Gale, Robert L. *Thomas Crawford, American Sculptor.* Pittsburgh: University of Pittsburgh Press, 1964.

Garber, Marjorie, and Nancy J. Vicker, eds. *The Medusa Reader.* New York: Routledge, 2003.

Gardner, Albert TenEyck. *Yankee Stonecutters: The First American School of Sculpture, 1800–1850.* New York: Columbia University Press for the Metropolitan Museum of Art, 1945.

Gemme, Paola. "Domesticating Foreign Struggles: American Narratives of Italian Revolutions and the Debate on Slavery in the Antebellum Era." *Prospects* 27 (2002): 77–101.

———. *Domesticating Foreign Struggles: The Italian Risorgimento and Antebellum American Identity.* Athens: University of Georgia Press, 2005.

Gerdts, William H., Jr. *American Neo-classic Sculpture: The Marble Resurrection.* New York: Viking Press, 1973.

———. Introduction to *The White, Marmorean Flock: Nineteenth Century American Women Neoclassical Sculptors.* Exh. cat. Vassar College Art Gallery, Poughkeepsie, N.Y., April 4–30, 1972. Poughkeepsie: Vassar College Art Gallery, 1972.

———. "The *Medusa* of Harriet Hosmer." *Bulletin of the Detroit Institute of Arts* 56 (1978): 97–107.

Getsy, David J. *Body Doubles: Sculpture in Britain, 1877–1905.* New Haven: Yale University Press, 2004.

Gilbert, Sandra M. "From *Patria* to *Matria:* Elizabeth Barrett Browning's Risorgimento."*PMLA* 99, no. 2 (March 1984): 194–211.

Gilman, Sander L. *Difference and Pathology: Stereotypes of Sexuality, Race, and Madness.* Ithaca: Cornell University Press, 1985.

Goodden, Angelica. *Madame de Staël: The Dangerous Exile.* New York: Oxford University Press, 2008.

Gopinath, Gabrielle. "Harriet Hosmer and the Feminine Sublime." *Oxford Art Journal* 28, no. 1 (2005): 61–81.

Gordon, Jean. "Early American Women Artists and the Social Context in Which They Worked." *American Quarterly* 30, no. 1 (Spring 1978): 54–69.

Groseclose, Barbara. "Harriet Hosmer's Tomb to Judith Falconnet: Death and the Maiden." *American Art Journal* 12, no. 2 (Spring 1980): 78–89.

———. "A Portrait Not by Guido Reni of a Girl Who Is Not Beatrice Cenci." *Studies in Eighteenth-Century Culture* 11 (1982): 107–32.

Gutwirth, Madelyn. *Madame de Staël, Novelist: The Emergence of the Artist as Woman.* Urbana: University of Illinois Press, 1978.

Gutwirth, Madelyn, Avriel Goldberger, and Karyna Szmurlo, eds. *Germaine de Staël: Crossing the Borders.* New Brunswick: Rutgers University Press, 1991.

Halberstam, Judith. *Female Masculinity.* Durham: Duke University Press, 1998.

Hall, Gordon Langley. *Vinnie Ream: The Story of the Girl Who Sculptured Lincoln.* New York: Holt, Rinehart & Winston, 1963.

Hamer, Mary. *Signs of Cleopatra: History, Politics, Representation.* New York: Routledge, 1993.

Hansen, Debra Gold. *Strained Sisterhood: Gender and Class in the Boston Female Anti-Slavery Society.* Amherst: University of Massachusetts Press, 1993.

Haskell, Francis, and Nicholas Penny. *Taste and the Antique: The Lure of Classical Sculpture, 1500–1900.* New Haven: Yale University Press, 1981.

Hatt, Michael. "'Making a Man of Him': Masculinity and the Black Body in Mid-Nineteenth-Century American Sculpture." *Oxford Art Journal* 15, no. 1 (1992): 21–35.

Headley, Janet. "English Literary and Aesthetic Influences on American Sculptors in Italy, 1825–1875." Ph.D. diss., University of Maryland, 1988.

Heilbrun, Carolyn. "Jo March: Male Model—Female Person." In *Critical Essays on Louisa May Alcott,* edited by Madeleine B. Stern, 143–45. Boston: G. K. Hall, 1984.

Helsinger, Elizabeth K., Robin Lauterbach Sheets, and William Veeder. *The Woman Question: Society and Literature in Britain and America, 1837–1883.* Vol. 3, *Literary Issues.* Manchester: Manchester University Press, 1983.

Herbert, T. Walter. *Dearest Beloved: The Hawthornes and the Making of the Middle-Class Family.* Berkeley: University of California Press, 1993.

Hertz, Neil. *The End of the Line: Essays on Psychoanalysis and the Sublime.* New York: Columbia University Press, 1985.

Hirshler, Erica E. *A Studio of Her Own: Women Artists in Boston, 1870–1940.* Boston: MFA Publications, 2001.

Hobson, Janell. *Venus in the Dark: Blackness and Beauty in Popular Culture.* New York: Routledge, 2005.

Hoffert, Sylvia D. *Jane Grey Swisshelm: An Unconventional Life, 1815–1884.* Chapel Hill: University of North Carolina Press, 2004.

Hoganson, Kristin. "Garrisonian Abolitionists and the Rhetoric of Gender, 1850–1860." *American Quarterly* 45, no. 4 (December 1993): 558–96.

Holland, Juanita Marie. "Mary Edmonia Lewis's *Minnehaha:* Gender, Race, and the 'Indian Maid.'" *Bulletin of the Detroit Institute of Arts* 69, nos. 1–2 (1995): 26–36.

Holmes, Rachel. *African Queen: The Real Life of the Hottentot Venus.* New York: Random House, 2007.

Honour, Hugh. "Canova's Studio Practice—I: The Early Years." *Burlington Magazine* 114, no. 828 (March 1972): 146–59.

———. "Canova's Studio Practice—II: 1792–1822." *Burlington Magazine* 114, no. 829 (April 1972): 214–29.

———. *Neo-classicism.* 1968. Reprint, New York: Penguin Books, 1979.

Hoogland, Renée C. *Lesbian Configurations.* New York: Columbia University Press, 1997.

Horowitz, Helen Lefkowitz. *Rereading Sex: Battles over Sexual Knowledge and Suppression in Nineteenth-Century America.* New York: Alfred A. Knopf, 2002.

Horton, James Oliver. "Freedom's Yoke: Gender Conventions Among Antebellum Free Blacks." *Feminist Studies* 12, no. 1 (Spring 1986): 51–76.

Hoyle, Pamela, Jonathon P. Harding, and Rosemary Booth. *A Climate for Art: The History of the Boston Athenaeum Gallery, 1827–1873.* Exh. cat. Boston Athenaeum, October 3–29, 1980. Boston: Boston Athenaeum, 1980.

Hunt, Linda C. *A Woman's Portion: Ideology, Culture, and the British Female Novel Tradition.* New York: Garland Publishing, 1988.

Husch, Gail E. *Something Coming: Apocalyptic Expectation and Mid-Nineteenth-Century American Painting.* Hanover: University Press of New England, 2000.

Idol, John L., Jr., and Sterling Eisiminger. "Hawthorne Sits for a Bust by Maria Louisa Lander." *Essex Institute Historical Collections* 114, no. 4 (October 1978): 207–12.

Irwin, David. *Neoclassicism.* London: Phaidon Press, 1997.

Isenberg, Nancy. *Sex and Citizenship in Antebellum America.* Chapel Hill: University of North Carolina Press, 1998.

Jack, Belinda. *Beatrice's Spell: The Enduring Legend of Beatrice Cenci.* London: Pimlico/Random House, 2005.

Jacobs, Donald M., ed. *Courage and Conscience: Black and White Abolitionists in Boston.* Bloomington: Indiana University Press, 1993.

Jaffe, Irma B., ed. *The Italian Presence in American Art, 1760–1860.* New York: Fordham University Press; Rome: Istituto della Enciclopedia Italiana, 1989.

Johnston, Judith. *Anna Jameson: Victorian, Feminist, Woman of Letters.* Brookfield, Vt.: Scolar Press, 1997.

Johnston, Patricia, ed. *Seeing High and Low: Representing Social Conflict in American Visual Culture.* Berkeley: University of California Press, 2006.

Jones, Amelia, ed. *The Feminism and Visual Culture Reader.* New York: Routledge, 2003.

Kaplan, Amy, and Donald E. Pease, eds. *Cultures of United States Imperialism.* Durham: Duke University Press, 1993.

Kaplan, E. Ann. *Looking for the Other: Feminism, Film, and the Imperial Gaze.* New York: Routledge, 1997.

Karcher, Carolyn L. *The First Woman in the Republic: A Cultural Biography of Lydia Maria Child.* Durham: Duke University Press, 1994.

Kasson, Joy S. *Marble Queens and Captives: Women in Nineteenth-Century American Sculpture.* New Haven: Yale University Press, 1990.

Kelley, Mary. *Private Woman, Public Stage: Literary Domesticity in Nineteenth-Century America.* New York: Oxford University Press, 1984.

Kemp, Mark A. R. "*The Marble Faun* and American Postcolonial Ambivalence." *Modern Fiction Studies* 43, no. 1 (Spring 1997): 209–36.

Kennon, Donald R., and Thomas P. Somma, eds. *American Pantheon: Sculptural and Artistic Decoration of the United States Capitol.* Athens: Ohio University Press, 2004.

Kerber, Linda K. *Toward an Intellectual History of Women.* Chapel Hill: University of North Carolina Press, 1997.

Kerber, Linda K., and Jane Sherron De Hart, eds. *Women's America: Refocusing the Past.* 5th ed. New York: Oxford University Press, 2000.

Kertzer, David I. *Prisoner of the Vatican: The Popes, the Kings, and Garibaldi's Rebels in the Struggle to Rule Modern Italy.* New York: Houghton Mifflin, 2004.

King-Hammond, Leslie, and Tritobia Hayes Benjamin. *Three Generations of African-American Women Sculptors: A Study in Paradox.* Exh. cat. Afro-American Historical and Cultural Museum, Philadelphia, March–September 1996, and elsewhere November 1996–August 1998. Philadelphia: Afro-American Historical and Cultural Museum, 1996.

Kolodny, Annette. "Turning the Lens on 'The Panther Captivity': A Feminist Exercise in Practical Criticism." *Critical Inquiry* 8, no. 2 (Winter 1981): 329–45.

Landes, Joan B., ed. *Feminism, the Public and the Private.* New York: Oxford University Press, 1998.

Langer, Sandra L. Review of *Women Artists in All Ages and Countries,* by Elizabeth Fries Lummis Ellet. *Woman's Art Journal* 1, no. 2 (Autumn 1980–Winter 1981): 55–58.

Lawrence, Kathleen. "Aesthetic Transcendentalism and Its Legacy: Margaret Fuller, William Wetmore Story, and Henry James." Ph.D. diss., Boston University, 2003.

Leach, Joseph. *Bright Particular Star: The Life and Times of Charlotte Cushman.* New Haven: Yale University Press, 1970.

———. "Harriet Hosmer: Feminist in Bronze and Marble." *Feminist Art Journal* 5 (Summer 1976): 9–13, 44–45.

Lemp, Joan A. "Vinnie Ream and *Abraham Lincoln.*" *Woman's Art Journal* 6, no. 2 (Autumn 1985–Winter 1986): 24–29.

Levine, Robert S. "'Antebellum Rome' in *The Marble Faun.*" *American Literary History* 2, no. 1 (Spring 1990): 19–38.

Licht, Fred, and David Finn. *Canova.* New York: Abbeville Press, 1983.

Loomba, Ania. *Colonialism/Postcolonialism.* New York: Routledge, 1998.

Manoguerra, Paul A. "Anti-Catholicism in Albert Bierstadt's *Roman Fish Market, Arch of Octavius.*" *Nineteenth-Century Art Worldwide* (Winter 2003). http://www.19thc-artworldwide.org/index.php/component/content/article/79-winter03article/245-anti-catholicism-in-albert-bierstadts-roman-fish-market-arch-of-octavius.

Markus, Julia. *Across an Untried Sea: Discovering Lives Hidden in the Shadow of Convention and Time.* New York: Alfred A. Knopf, 2000.

Marraro, Howard R. *American Opinion on the Unification of Italy, 1846–1861.* New York: Columbia University Press, 1932.

Marshall, Megan. *The Peabody Sisters: Three Women Who Ignited American Romanticism.* New York: Houghton Mifflin, 2005.

Marso, Lori Jo. *(Un)Manly Citizens: Jean-Jacques Rousseau's and Germaine de Staël's Subversive Women.* Baltimore: Johns Hopkins University Press, 1999.

Martin, Robert K. and Leland S. Person, eds. *Roman Holidays: American Writers and Artists in Nineteenth-Century Italy.* Iowa City: University of Iowa Press, 2002.

Masten, April F. *Art Work: Woman Artists and Democracy in Mid-Nineteenth-Century New York.* Philadelphia: University of Pennsylvania Press, 2008.

Mattos, Claudia. "The Torchlight Visit: Guiding the Eye Through Late Eighteenth- and Early Nineteenth-Century Antique Sculpture Galleries." *RES: Anthropology and Aesthetics,* nos. 49/50 (Spring–Autumn 2006): 139–50.

McDonough, Terrence, ed. *Was Ireland a Colony? Economics, Politics, and Culture in Nineteenth-Century Ireland.* Portland, Ore.: Irish Academic Press, 2005.

McDowell, Deborah E., and Arnold Rampersad, eds. *Slavery and the Literary Imagination.* Baltimore: Johns Hopkins University Press, 1989.

McGann, Jerome J. "The Beauty of Medusa: A Study in Romantic Literary Iconology." *Studies in Romanticism* 11, no. 1 (Winter 1972): 3–25.

Merrill, Lisa. *When Romeo Was a Woman: Charlotte Cushman and Her Circle of Female Spectators.* Ann Arbor: University of Michigan Press, 1999.

Miller, Perry, ed. *Margaret Fuller, American Romantic: A Selection from Her Writings and Correspondence.* Ithaca: Cornell University Press, 1963.

Mills, Sara. *Discourses of Differences: An Analysis of Women's Travel Writing and Colonialism.* New York: Routledge, 1991.

Milroy, Elizabeth. "The Public Career of Emma Stebbins: Work in Bronze." *Archives of American Art Journal* 34, no. 1 (1994): 2–14.

———. "The Public Career of Emma Stebbins: Work in Marble." *Archives of American Art Journal* 33, no. 3 (1993): 2–12.

Moe, Nelson. *The View from Vesuvius: Italian Culture and the Southern Question.* Berkeley: University of California Press, 2002.

Moers, Ellen. *Literary Women.* Garden City, N.Y.: Doubleday, 1976.

Morgan, David, and Sally M. Promey, eds. *The Visual Culture of American Religions.* Berkeley: University of California Press, 2001.

Mullenix, Elizabeth Reitz. "'So Unfemininely Masculine': Discourse, True/False Womanhood, and the American Career of Fanny Kemble." *Theatre Survey* 40, no. 2 (November 1999): 27–42.

Nelson, Charmaine A. *The Color of Stone: Sculpting the Black Female Subject in Nineteenth-Century America.* Minneapolis: University of Minnesota Press, 2007.

———. *Representing the Black Female Subject in Western Art.* New York: Routledge, 2010.

Neri, Algerina. "Forbidden Rooms with a View: American Women Travellers in Europe in the Nineteenth Century." *Rivista di studi anglo-americani* 7, no. 9 (1993): 593–601.

Nochlin, Linda. *The Politics of Vision: Essays on Nineteenth-Century Art and Society.* New York: Harper & Row, 1989.

O'Connor, Maura. *The Romance of Italy and the English Political Imagination.* New York: St. Martin's Press, 1998.

Orcutt, Kimberly. "Neoclassicism and the Artist's Ideal." In *John Rogers: American Stories,* edited by Kimberly Orcutt, 41–59. New York: New-York Historical Society, 2010.

Padiyar, Satish. *Chains: David, Canova, and the Fall of the Public Hero in Postrevolutionary France.* University Park: Pennsylvania State University Press, 2007.

Paine, Albert Bigelow. *Thomas Nast: His Period and His Pictures.* 1904. Reprint, Broomall, Pa.: Chelsea House Press, 1997.

Painter, Nell Irvin. *Sojourner Truth: A Life, a Symbol.* New York: W. W. Norton, 1996.

Panofsky, Erwin. *Idea: A Concept in Art Theory.* Translated by Joseph J. S. Peake. Columbia: University of South Carolina Press, 1968. (Originally published in German as *Idea: Ein Beitrag zur Begriffsgeschichte der älteren Kunsttheorie,* 1924.)

Parrott, Sarah Foose. "Expatriates and Professionals: The Careers in Italy of Nineteenth-Century American Women Writers and Artists." Ph.D. diss., George Washington University, 1988.

Payne, Elizabeth Rogers. "Anne Whitney, Sculptor." *Art Quarterly* 25 (Autumn 1962): 244–61.

———. "Anne Whitney: Art and Social Justice." *Massachusetts Review* 12, no. 2 (Spring 1971): 245–60.

Perry, Lewis, and Michael Fellman, eds. *Antislavery Reconsidered: New Perspectives on the Abolitionists.* Baton Rouge: Louisiana State University Press, 1979.

Pesman, Ros. "In Search of Professional Identity: Adelaide Ironside and Italy." *Women's Writing* 10, no. 2 (2003): 307–29.

Pointon, Marcia. *Naked Authority: The Body in Western Painting, 1830–1908.* New York: Cambridge University Press, 1990.

Pollock, Griselda. *Differencing the Canon: Feminist Desire and the Writing of Art's Histories.* New York: Routledge, 1999.

Pomeroy, Jordana, ed. *Intrepid Women: Victorian Artists Travel.* Burlington, Vt.: Ashgate, 2005.

Potts, Alex. *Flesh and the Ideal: Winckelmann and the Origins of Art History.* New Haven: Yale University Press, 1994.

———. *The Sculptural Imagination: Figurative, Modernist, Minimalist.* New Haven: Yale University Press, 2000.

Pratt, Mary Louise. *Imperial Eyes: Travel Writing and Transculturation.* New York: Routledge, 1992.

Prieto, Laura R. *At Home in the Studio: The Professionalization of Women Artists in America.* Cambridge: Harvard University Press, 2001.

Prioli, Carmine A. "'Wonder Girl from the West': Vinnie Ream and the Congressional Statue of Abraham Lincoln." *Journal of American Culture* 12, no. 4 (Winter 1989): 1–20.

Proctor, Nancy Elizabeth. "American Women Sculptors in Rome in the Mid-Nineteenth Century: Feminist and Psychoanalytic Readings of a Displaced Canon." Ph.D. diss., University of Leeds, 1998.

———. "Traveling Between the Borders of Gender and Nationality: Nineteenth-Century American Women Artists in Rome." *Prospero* 2 (1995): 46–55.

Raboteau, Albert J. *A Fire in the Bones: Reflections on African-American Religious History.* Boston: Beacon Press, 1995.

Rajan, V. G. Julie, and Sanja Bahun-Radunović, eds. *From Word to Canvas: Appropriations of Myth in Women's Aesthetic Production.* Newcastle upon Tyne: Cambridge Scholars, 2009.

Read, Benedict. *Victorian Sculpture.* New Haven: Yale University Press, 1982.

Reitzes, Lisa B. "The Political Voice of the Artist: Anne Whitney's *Roma* and *Harriet Martineau.*" *American Art* 8, no. 2 (Spring 1994): 44–65.

Reynolds, Larry J. *European Revolutions and the American Literary Renaissance.* New Haven: Yale University Press, 1988.

Riall, Lucy. *Garibaldi: Invention of a Hero.* New Haven: Yale University Press, 2007.

———. *The Italian Risorgimento: State, Society, and National Unification.* New York: Routledge, 1994.

Riede, David G. *Allegories of One's Own Mind: Melancholy in Victorian Poetry.* Columbus: Ohio State University Press, 2005.

Riley, Denise. *"Am I That Name?": Feminism and the Category of "Women" in History.* Minneapolis: University of Minnesota Press, 1988.

Riviere, Joan. "Womanliness as a Masquerade." *International Journal of Psychoanalysis* 10 (1929): 303–13.

Roos, Jane Mayo. "Another Look at Henry James and the 'White Marmorean Flock.'" *Woman's Art Journal* 4, no. 1 (Spring–Summer 1983): 29–34.

Rossi, Lauro, ed. *Fondare la nazione: I repubblicani del 1849 e la difesa del Gianicolo.* Rome: Palombi, 2001.

Rowe, John Carlos. "Swept Away: Henry James, Margaret Fuller, and 'The Last of the Valerii.'" In *Readers in History: Nineteenth-Century American Literature and the Contexts of Response,* edited by James L. Machor, 32–54. Baltimore: Johns Hopkins University Press, 1993.

Roworth, Wendy Wassyng, ed. *Angelika Kauffman: A Continental Artist in Georgian England.* London: Reaktion Books, 1992.

Rubenstein, Charlotte Streifer. *American Women Sculptors: A History of Women Working in Three Dimensions.* Boston: G. K. Hall, 1990.

Rupp, Leila J. *A Desired Past: A Short History of Same-Sex Love in America.* Chicago: University of Chicago Press, 1999.

Ryan, Mary P. *Women in Public: Between Banners and Ballots, 1825–1880.* Baltimore: Johns Hopkins University Press, 1990.

Salomone, A. William. "The Nineteenth-Century Discovery of Italy: An Essay in American Cultural History; Prolegomena to a Historiographical Problem." *American Historical Review* 73, no. 5 (June 1968): 1359–91.

Sánchez-Eppler, Karen. "Bodily Bonds: The Intersecting Rhetorics of Feminism and Abolition." *Representations* 24 (Fall 1988): 28–59.

———. *Touching Liberty: Abolition, Feminism, and the Politics of the Body.* Berkeley: University of California Press, 1993.

Savage, Kirk. *Standing Soldiers, Kneeling Slaves: Race, War, and Monument in Nineteenth-Century America.* Princeton: Princeton University Press, 1997.

Schriber, Mary Suzanne. *Writing Home: American Women Abroad, 1830–1920.* Charlottesville: University Press of Virginia, 1997.

Seidler, Jan M. "A Critical Reappraisal of the Career of William Wetmore Story (1819–1895), American Sculptor and Man of Letters." Ph.D. diss., Boston University, 1985.

Sharf, Frederic A. "'A More Bracing Morning Atmosphere': Artistic Life in Salem, 1850–1859." *Essex Institute Historical Collection* 95 (1959): 149–64.

Sherwood, Dolly. *Harriet Hosmer: American Sculptor, 1830–1908.* Columbia: University of Missouri Press, 1991.

Sherwood, Glenn V. *A Labor of Love: The Life and Art of Vinnie Ream.* Hygiene, Colo.: SunShine Press Publications, 1997.

Siegel, Jonah. *Desire and Excess: The Nineteenth-Century Culture of Art.* Princeton: Princeton University Press, 2000.

Sizer, Lyde Cullen. *The Political Work of Northern Women Writers and the Civil War, 1850–1872.* Chapel Hill: University of North Carolina Press, 2000.

Sklar, Kathryn Kish. *Catherine Beecher: A Study in American Domesticity.* New Haven: Yale University Press, 1973.

Sluga, Glenda. "Gender and the Nation: Madame de Staël or Italy." *Women's Writing* 10, no. 2 (2003): 241–51.

Smith, Alison. *The Victorian Nude: Sexuality, Morality, and Art.* New York: Manchester University Press, 1996.

Smith-Rosenberg, Carroll. *Disorderly Conduct: Visions of Gender in Victorian America.* New York: Oxford University Press, 1985.

Stathis, Stephen W., and Lee Roderick. "Mallet, Chisel, and Curls." *American Heritage* 27, no. 2 (February 1976): 45–47, 94–96.

Stebbins, Theodore E., Jr. *The Lure of Italy: American Artists and the Italian Experience, 1760–1914.* Exh. cat. Museum of Fine Arts, Boston, September 16–December 13, 1992; Cleveland Museum of Art, February 3–April 11, 1993; and Museum of Fine Arts, Houston, May 23–August 8, 1993. Boston: Museum of Fine Arts; New York: Harry N. Abrams, 1992.

Stern, Madeleine B. "New England Artists in Italy, 1835–1855." *New England Quarterly* 14, no. 2 (June 1941): 243–71.

Stowe, William W. *Going Abroad: European Travel in Nineteenth-Century American Culture.* Princeton: Princeton University Press, 1994.

Swan, Mabel Munson. *The Athenaeum Gallery, 1827–1873: The Boston Athenaeum as an Early Patron of Art.* Boston: Boston Athenaeum, 1940.

Swinth, Kirsten. *Painting Professionals: Women Artists and the Development of Modern American Art, 1870–1930.* Chapel Hill: University of North Carolina Press, 2001.

Szmurlo, Karyna, ed. *The Novel's Seductions: Staël's "Corinne" in Critical Inquiry.* London: Associated University Presses, 1999.

Thorp, Margaret Farrand. *Female Persuasion: Six Strong-Minded Women.* New Haven: Yale University Press, 1949.

———. "Harriet Hosmer: Leader of the White Marmorean Flock." *Smith Alumni Quarterly,* Spring 1975.

———. *The Literary Sculptors.* Durham: Duke University Press, 1965.

Tolles, Thayer, ed. *American Sculpture in the Metropolitan Museum of Art.* Vol. 1, *A Catalogue of Works by Artists Born Before 1865.* New York: Metropolitan Museum of Art, 1999.

———. *Perspectives on American Sculpture Before 1925.* New York: Metropolitan Museum of Art; New Haven: Yale University Press, 2003.

Tong, Rosemarie. *Feminist Thought: A Comprehensive Introduction.* Boulder, Colo.: Westview Press, 1989.

Tufts, Eleanor. "An American Victorian Dilemma, 1875: Should a Woman Be Allowed to Sculpt a Man?" *Art Journal* 51, no. 1 (Spring 1992): 51–57.

———. "Margaret Foley's Metamorphosis: A Merrimack 'Female Operative' in Neo-classical Rome." *Arts Magazine* 56 (January 1982): 88–95.

Underhill, Lois Beachy. *The Woman Who Ran for President: The Many Lives of Victoria Woodhull.* New York: Penguin Books, 1995.

Valenti, Patricia Dunlavy. *Sophia Peabody Hawthorne: A Life.* Vol. 1, *1809–1847.* Columbia: University of Missouri Press, 2004.

———. "Sophia Peabody Hawthorne: A Study of Artistic Influence." In *Studies in the American Renaissance,* edited by Joel Myerson, 1–19. Charlottesville: University Press of Virginia, 1990.

Vance, William L. *America's Rome.* 2 vols. New Haven: Yale University Press, 1989.

Vance, William L., Mary K. McGuigan, and John F. McGuigan Jr. *America's Rome: Artists in the Eternal City, 1800–1900.* Exh. cat. Fenimore Art Museum, Cooperstown, N.Y., May 23–December 31, 2009. Cooperstown, N.Y.: Fenimore Art Museum, 2009.

Van Rensselaer, Susan. "Harriet Hosmer." *Antiques,* October 1963, 424–28.

Vicinus, Martha. "Distance and Desire: English Boarding School Friendships, 1870–1920." In *Hidden from History: Reclaiming the Gay and Lesbian Past,* edited by Martin Duberman, Martha Vicinus, and George Chauncey Jr., 212–29. New York: Meridian, 1990.

———. "The Historical Roots of the Modern Lesbian Identity." In *Identity and Diversity: Gender and the Experience of Education,* edited by Maud Blair and Janet Holland, with Sue Sheldon, 225–44. Philadelphia: Multilingual Matters, 1995.

———. *Intimate Friends: Women Who Loved Women, 1778–1928.* Chicago: University of Chicago Press, 2004.

———. "Laocoöning in Rome: Harriet Hosmer and Romantic Friendship." *Women's Writing* 10, no. 2 (2003): 353–66.

———. "Lesbian History: All Theory and No Facts or All Facts and No Theory?" *Radical History Review* 60 (1994): 57–75.

———, ed. *Lesbian Subjects: A Feminist Studies Reader.* Bloomington: Indiana University Press, 1996.

Walker, Susan, and Sally-Ann Ashton, eds. *Cleopatra Reassessed.* British Museum Occasional Paper, no. 103. London: Trustees of the British Museum, 2003.

Wallach, Alan. *Exhibiting Contradiction: Essays on the Art Museum in the United States.* Amherst: University of Massachusetts Press, 1998.

Waller, Susan. "The Artist, the Writer, and the Queen: Hosmer, Jameson, and *Zenobia.*" *Women's Art Journal* 4, no. 1 (Spring–Summer 1983): 21–28.

Warner, Michael. *Publics and Counterpublics.* New York: Zone Books, 2002.

Weedon, Chris. *Feminist Practice and Poststructuralist Theory.* New York: Basil Blackwell, 1987.

Welter, Barbara. "The Cult of True Womanhood: 1820–1860." *American Quarterly* 18, no. 2, pt. 1 (Summer 1966): 151–74.

West, Cornel. "A Genealogy of Modern Racism." 1982. In *Knowledge and Postmodernism in Historical Perspective,* edited by Joyce Appleby, Elizabeth Covington, David Hoyt, Michael Latham, and Allison Sneider, 476–86. New York: Routledge, 1996.

Whiteley, J. J. L. "Light and Shade in French Neoclassicism." *Burlington Magazine* 117, no. 873 (December 1975): 768–73.

Willis, Deborah, ed. *Black Venus, 2010: They Called Her "Hottentot."* Philadelphia: Temple University Press, 2010.

Winterer, Caroline. *The Culture of Classicism: Ancient Greece and Rome in American Intellectual Life, 1780–1910.* Baltimore: Johns Hopkins University Press, 2002.

———. "Victorian Antigone: Classicism and Women's Education in America, 1840–1900." *American Quarterly* 53, no. 1 (March 2001): 70–93.

Withers, Josephine. "Artistic Women and Women Artists." *Art Journal* 35, no. 4 (Summer 1976): 330–36.

Wittman, Otto, Jr. "The Italian Experience (American Artists in Italy, 1830–1875)." *American Quarterly* 4, no. 1 (Spring 1952): 2–15.

Wolff, Katharine. *Culture Club: The Curious History of the Boston Athenaeum.* Amherst: University of Massachusetts Press, 2009.

Woloch, Nancy. *Women and the American Experience.* New York: Alfred A. Knopf, 1984.

Wright, Nathalia. *American Novelists in Italy; The Discoverers: Allston to James.* Philadelphia: University of Pennsylvania Press, 1965.

Wynne, George G. *Early Americans in Rome.* Rome: Daily American Printing, 1966.

Yarrington, Allison. "'Made in Italy': Sculpture and the Staging of National Identities at the International Exhibition of 1862." In *Performing National Identity: Anglo-Italian Cultural Transactions,* edited by Manfred Pfister and Ralf Hertel, 75–103. New York: Rodopi, 2008.

Yellin, Jean Fagan. *Women and Sisters: The Antislavery Feminists in American Culture.* New Haven: Yale University Press, 1989.

Yellin, Jean Fagan, and John C. Van Horne, eds. *The Abolitionist Sisterhood: Women's Political Culture in Antebellum America.* Ithaca: Cornell University Press, 1994.

Young-Bruehl, Elisabeth, ed. *Freud on Women: A Reader.* New York: W. W. Norton, 1990.

Zajko, Vanda, and Miriam Leonard, eds. *Laughing with Medusa: Classical Myth and Feminist Thought.* New York: Oxford University Press, 2006.

# Index

Page numbers in *italics* refer to maps and figures.


Abbott, Jacob, 37, *39*
abolitionism
  Barrett Browning and, 149
  Boston and, 150, 155–57
  Brown, Henry K., and, 195
  Child and, 15, 156
  Christianity and, 173
  Fuller and, 19
  gender and, 161–62, 169–75
  Hosmer and, 131, 149–50, 166
  Lewis and, 149, 150, 155–57, 169–75
  race and, 149–50, 150–55, 156–57, 159–60, 161–62, 165–66, 195
  *Risorgimento* and, 119–20, 122–23
  Story and, 149, 150–55
  Whitney and, 141–44, *142*, 149, 150
  womanhood and, 161–62, 165–66, 169–75
*Abraham Lincoln* (Ames), 183, *183*, 184–86, *185*, 198
*Abraham Lincoln* (Gardner), 185, *186*
*Abraham Lincoln* (Ream), *182*, *187*, *188*
  generally, 181, 183, 186–90, 192, 194–99
  *Samuel Adams* (Whitney) compared with, 200
Academy of Saint Luke, 44, 67, 224n. 40
Accademia de' Quiriti, 134
Adams, Henry, 122, 150–53, 239n. 21
Adams, Samuel, 200, *201*, 202, 204, 205
Africa, 94, 130, 150–55, 157–66
*African Sibyl* (Hosmer), 178–80, *179*
*Age of Fable* (Bulfinch), 41
Akers, Benjamin Paul
  *Dead Pearl Diver*, 72, 103–4, *103*, 109–10
  in *The Marble Faun* (Hawthorne), 97
  Ream and, 251n. 14
  in Rome, generally, 4, 72
  Stebbins and, 103–4
  studios of, 65
Akron Women's Rights Convention, 155
Albani, Alessandro, 242n. 72
Albert (prince), 231n. 96
Alberti, Leon Battista, 42
Alcott, Louisa May, 17, 25, 81, 184
Alexander, Archer, 178, *179*
Alexander the Great, 150
Alford, Marian, 60, 83, 86
*America Defending Her Children* (Lander), 80
American Anti-Slavery Society, 15, 120
American Art Union, 33
American Civil War
  abolitionism and, 195
  artists during, 81, 137, 184, 186, 232n. 128
  *Ethiopia Shall Soon Stretch Out Her Hands to God, or Africa* (Whitney) and, 157
  Garibaldi during, 122
American Declaration of Independence, 8
American Women's Suffrage Association, 198, 199, 200
Ames, Joseph Alexander, 184
Ames, Sarah Fisher
  *Abraham Lincoln*, 183, *183*, 184–86, *185*, 198
  *Abraham Lincoln* (Ream) and, 187, 188, 197
  American Civil War and, 81
  Fuller and, 19
  professionalism and, 183–84, 186, 187, 193, 207
  in Rome, generally, 2
  womanhood and, 183–84, 186
*Am I Not a Man and a Brother?*, 169, *171*, *173*, *178*
*Am I Not a Woman and a Sister?*, 169, *171*
*Angel of the Waters* (Stebbins), 34, *34*
Anthony, Susan B., 181, 198, 199, 253n. 70
*Anti-Slavery Standard*, 160
Antonelli, Giacomo
  Lincoln assassination and, 243n. 88
  Ream and, 193–94
  *Roma* (Whitney) and, 140, 141
  *Roman Newsboys* (Heade) and, 119
  tourism and, 144–45
Antony, Mark, 150
*Apollo and Daphne* (Bernini), 49–50, *50*
*Apollo Belvedere*, *38*
  Boston Athenaeum and, 26
  *Ethiopia Shall Soon Stretch Out Her Hands to God, or Africa* (Whitney) and, 164
  Napoleon and, 42
  neoclassicism and, 6
  *Orpheus and Cerberus* (Crawford) and, 40
  *Roma* (Whitney) and, 140
  *Sleeping Faun* (Hosmer) and, 109
  torchlight viewings of, 37
  Treaty of Tolentino and, 224n. 28
*An Appeal in Favor of That Class of Americans Called Africans* (Child), 15
Appleton, Samuel, Mrs., 59
Appleton, Thomas G., 219n. 59
Ara Coeli, 96
Arcadian Academy, 1, 27–28
Arch of Octavius, 94–96, *95*
Armstrong, Isobel, 236n. 59
Art Institute of Chicago, 222n. 106
artisans. *See* workmen
artists. See also *individual artists and genres*; studios
  Boston and, 15
  gender and, 2–3, 26–27, 27–28, 32, 33, 61, 63, 80, 84–85, 131–32, 134, 203–5, 211–12
  marriage and, 61
  Rome and, generally, 1–5, 27–28, 116, 120, 144–45
  womanhood and, 2–3, 10, 18–19, 73–75

*Art-Journal*, 84
Ashburton, Louisa, 212, 237n. 76, 237n. 77
Athena, 51
*Athenaeum*, 84
*Atlantic Monthly*, 84, 85, 86, 155, 159, 232n. 109
Aurelian, 81
*Aurora Leigh* (Barrett Browning), 1, 30, 191
Austria, 121, 124, 137
authenticity
  Foley and, 89
  Hosmer and, 67, 81, 83–86, 132, 208
  Ream and, 186–87, 192, 197, 202
  Whitney and, 202
autonomy. *See also* emancipation; women's rights
  domesticity and, 72
  gender and, 53–55, 100–102, 129–30
  Hosmer and, 101–2
  nudes and, 109–10
  womanhood and, 49–51, 53–55

Baartman, Saartje, *154*, 155
Ball, Thomas
  *Emancipation Monument*, 178, *179*
  Lewis and, 167
  studios of, 202
  Sumner memorial and, 200, 203, 205
  Whitney and, 237n. 88
*Barberini Faun*, 108, *109*
Barrett Browning, Elizabeth
  abolitionism and, 149
  Akers and, 103
  *Aurora Leigh*, 1, 30, 191
  *Casa Guidi Windows*, 124, 137
  "A Curse for a Nation," 149
  death of, 135, 242n. 82
  Hawthorne and, 77
  on Hays, 220n. 78
  Hosmer and, 57, 59, 67, 125, 149, 242n. 76
  in Italy, generally, 28–31, 75
  *Poems Before Congress*, 124–25, 134
  *Risorgimento* and, 124–25, 130, 131, 134, 135, 137
  Story and, 149
  *Tinted Venus* (Gibson) and, 46, 57
Bartol, Cyrus A., 246n. 35
Bartol, Elizabeth Howard, 159, 237n. 82, 255n. 17
"Battle Hymn of the Republic" (Howe), 244n. 113
*Beatrice Cenci* (Guerrazzi), 128–29
*Beatrice Cenci* (Hosmer), 125–31, *126*, *128*, 141
*Beatrice Cenci* (Reni), 125–27, *127*, 129
*Beatrice Cenci (After Guido)* (Heade), 238n. 1
beauty
  gender and, 189–90
  morality and, 5, 128–29
  neoclassicism and, 40–41, 51–53
  professionalism and, 189–90, 192–93
  race and, 165
  womanhood and, 189–90
Beecher, Catherine, 235n. 36
Beecher, Edward, 130
Beecher, Henry Ward, 17
Belgioioso, Cristina di, 217n. 31
*la bella libertà*, 124–25, 130, 131, 135
*Belvedere Torso*, *100*, 224n. 28
Benton, Thomas Hart, 208, *210*
Bernini, Gian Lorenzo, 49–50, *50*, 51, 52, 244n. 109
Bible, 157–59, 160, 173
Bierstadt, Albert, 94–96, *95*, 108, 233n. 139
Billings, Hammatt, 173–74, *174*
Bloomer, Amelia, 18
Bogart, Michele, 251n. 10
Bonheur, Rosa, 29
Bonnat, Leon, 189
Boott, Lizzie, 255n. 17
Borghese, Paolina, 161, *161*
Borghese Gallery, 49, 161
Boston
  abolitionism and, 150, 155–57
  artists in, generally, 15
  neoclassicism and, 37–41
  professionalism and, 15, 18–19
  race and, 166
  sculpture and, 22–27, 37–41, 75, 80–81, 85–86, 110–11, 130–31, 144
"Boston and Boston People" (Hosmer), 26–27
Boston Athenaeum
  *America Defending Her Children* (Lander) at, 80
  Foley at, 25
  *Freedman's Memorial to Abraham Lincoln* (Hosmer) at, 176
  Hawthorne, Sophia Peabody, and, 228n. 33
  *Mars Ludovisi* at, 143
  Minerva and, 134
  *Orpheus and Cerberus* (Crawford) at, 26, 37, 40–41, 67, 111, 223n. 5
  Quiner at, 219n. 54
  role of, generally, 26–27
  *Roman Fish Market, Arch of Octavius* (Bierstadt) at, 233n. 7
  torchlight viewings at, 45
  Whitney at, 110, 205
*Boston Courier*, 122
*Boston Evening Transcript*, 86, 88
Boston Female Anti-Slavery Society, 15, 19, 149
Boston Massacre, 200
Boston Mechanics Association, 26
Boston Museum of Fine Arts. *See* Museum of Fine Arts, Boston
Boston Sanitary Commission, 86
Boston Soldier's Relief Fair, 156
*Boy with a Palm* (Whitney). *See* *The Youth* (Whitney)
Brackett, Edward A., 33, 150, 237n. 88
Bragdon, Ilsa, 57
Bremer, Frederika, 17
Bridges, Fidelia, 111
British Negro Emancipation League, 119
Brontë, Charlotte, 49
Brooklyn Civic Center, 222n. 107
Brooks, Preston, 244n. 1
Brown, Henry Kirke
  *Lincoln Monument*, 195, *196*
  *Model for a Monument to Lincoln*, 195, 196
  naturalism and, 202
  Ream and, 181, 189
  Whitney and, 237n. 88
Brown, John, 122–23, 137, 246n. 28
Brown, William Wells, 150
Browning, Robert
  Akers and, 103
  Hawthornes and, 75
  Hosmer and, 226n. 81
  marriage of, 30

*Risorgimento* and, 124
Story and, 149
Brumidi, Constantino, 69
Bryant, William Cullen, 4, 150, 247n. 55
Buick, Kirsten, 156, 248n. 65, 249n. 77, 249n. 78, 249n. 87
Bulfinch, Thomas, 41, 51
Buonomo, Leonardo, 93, 110
Burns, Sarah, 53
*Bust of Colonel Robert Gould Shaw* (Lewis), 156–57, *157*, 166
*Bust of Medusa* (Bernini), 51–53, *52*
Butler, Benjamin, 254n. 72
Butler, Pierce, 18
Byron, Lord, 28

Cadorna, Raffaele, 144
cameo carving, 24–25, 26, 88
Canova, Antonio
Boston Athenaeum and, 26
as mentor, 45
neoclassicism and, 41–44, 58
*Paolina Borghese as Venus Victorius*, 161, *161*
production process of, 85
studios of, 65, 167
*Triumphant Perseus*, 42, *43*, 51–53, *52*
Washington sculpture by, 223n. 24
Capitoline Museum
Akers at, 103
*Bust of Medusa* (Bernini) at, 51, 225n. 61
*Corinne, or Italy* (de Staël) and, 1, 27
Crawford at, 44
*Dying Gladiator* at, 235n. 50. See also *Dying Gaul*
*Faun of Praxiteles* at, 113
Foley and, 89
Gibson at, 82
Hosmer at, 225n. 55
in *The Marble Faun* (Hawthorne), 96–97
Minerva at, 134
Stebbins at, 104
Capitoline Temple, 134
*Capitoline Venus*, 26
captivity narrative, 69–71, 134
Carew, Mr., 237n. 85
Carney, William, 246n. 28
Carr, Cornelia (née Crow), 22, 28, 35, 59, 134, 237n. 76
Carr, Lucien, 59
*Casa Guidi Windows* (Barrett Browning), 124, 137
Cass, Lewis, 78, 238n. 8
Cassatt, Mary, 255n. 17
castration, 53
Catholic Church
American Civil War and, 137
Hosmer and, 128, 129, 130–31, 144–45
Lincoln assassination and, 175
nudes and, 102
Ream and, 193–94, 208
*Risorgimento* and, 99, 117–20, 123, 130–31, 134, 138, 140–41, 144, 193
*Roma* (Whitney) and, 140–41
*Roman Fish Market, Arch of Octavius* (Bierstadt) and, 94–96
tourism and, 144–45
Cavour, Camillo, 121, 242n. 82
Cellini, Benvenuto, 42
*The Cenci* (Shelley), 128
Cenci, Beatrice, 125–31, *126*, *127*, *128*, 141
Cenci, Francesco, 127
Centennial Exposition, 179, 243n. 102
Central Park, 222n. 107, 247n. 40
*Chaldean Shepherd* (Rimmer), 237n. 87
*Chaldean Shepherd* (Whitney), 111, *113*, 115–16, *115*
*Chanting Cherubs* (Greenough), 40
Chapman, Maria Weston, 111, 149, 156, 171, 246n. 28
*Charles Sumner Memorial* (Whitney), 200–202, *202*, 203–5, *204*
Cheney, Ednah Dow, 19, 24, 26, 248n. 62
Cherry, Deborah, 84, 231n. 96
*Chicago Evening Journal*, 247n. 54
Child, Lydia Maria
abolitionism and, 15, 149–50, 156, 165
*An Appeal in Favor of That Class of Americans Called Africans*, 15
Fuller and, 19
Hosmer and, 132, 134, 149–50, 232n. 117, 241n. 66
Lewis and, 156–57, 171, 172, 173
as mentor, generally, 15, 17, 24, 156
race and, 165–66
*The Romance of the Republic*, 165–66
Story and, 149
Whitney and, 160, 171, 246n. 32
*Childe Harold's Pilgrimmage* (Byron), 28
Childs and Jenks Gallery, 86, 160, 166
Childs Gallery, 172
Christ, 173–74, 194, 208
*Christian Register*, 174
Cincinnatus, 121
Civil War. *See* American Civil War
Cixous, Hélène, 53
Claflin, Tennessee, 254n. 71
class. *See also* poverty
emancipation and, 171
professionalism and, 207
race and, 160
womanhood and, 3, 171, 199
women's rights and, 199, 200
Clemmer Ames, Mary, 197, 199
Cleopatra, 132
*Cleopatra* (Foley), 233n. 131
*Cleopatra* (Story), 72, 150–53, *151*, 155, 162, 166
Cleveland Museum of Art, 237n. 76
clothing
in *Abraham Lincoln* (Ream), 194–95
of Cushman, 29
gender and, 18, 29, 31, 35, 65
of Hays, 29, 31
of Hosmer, 18, 31, 65, 74–75, 82, 86, 102, 167, 190, 191, 208
in Italy, 94
of Lander, 65
of Lewis, 167–69
in *Margaret Fuller* (Hicks), 21
professionalism and, 31
of Ream, 192–93, 194, 208, 210, 220n. 71
in *Roma* (Whitney), 140
in *Samuel Adams* (Whitney), 200
sexuality and, 29, 31, 65
womanhood and, 65, 86–87, 167–69
*Zenobia in Chains* (Hosmer) and, 132

Cobbe, Frances Power, 32, 83, 108, 116
Cole, Thomas, 4
colonialism. *See* imperialism
Columbus, Christopher, 222n. 107
*Commerce* (Stebbins), 222n. 106
*Commonwealth*, 200, 205
Conti Guoli, Elena dei, 27–28
*Convent's Dreams* (Frothingham), 130
*Corinne, or Italy* (de Staël)
  Barrett Browning and, 30, 125
  Canova in, 42
  generally, 1–2, 28
  Ream and, 181, 193, 208
Cotton's Gallery, 75, 130
Couture, Thomas, 255n. 17
Craske, Matthew, 7
Crawford, Thomas
  *Abraham Lincoln* (Ream) and, 189
  Hosmer and, 57, 67
  *The Indian*, 99, *100*
  Lander and, 67–69
  *Orpheus and Cerberus*, 26, 37–41, *39*, 67, 111
  *Progress of Civilization*, 99
  *Risorgimento* and, 5, 7, 20
  in Rome, generally, 4, 44
*Crayon*, 88
Cropsey, Jasper Francis, 238n. 7
Crow, Emma, 32, 83, 88
Crow, Wayman
  Cushman and, 34, 218n. 39
  Foley and, 88
  Hosmer and, 22, 28, 55, 61, 81, 101, 106, 129, 144, 149, 208
  Kemble and, 218n. 39
  slavery and, 149
  Yeatman and, 176
Culkin, Kate, 231n. 96
Cupid, 49
*Cupid* (Praxiteles), 46
"A Curse for a Nation" (Barrett Browning), 149
Cushman, Charlotte, *30*, *34*
  Akers and, 103
  American Civil War and, 137
  Boston Athenaeum and, 219n. 59
  clothing of, 29
  Cobbe and, 116
  Crow and, 218n. 39
  Foley and, 87–88
  Hawthorne and, 72, 76, 77
  Hays and, 28, 29, 34, 35
  horseback riding by, 167
  Hosmer and, 28–29, 31–32, 35, 83, 208, 222n. 110, 237n. 76
  Jameson and, 131
  Lander and, 65, 76, 77
  latter years of, 212
  Lewis and, 167, 175
  mannish woman stereotype and, 29, 31, 35, 55, 86
  as mentor, generally, 4, 15, 17, 28–29, 31–32, 35, 59
  Minerva and, 134
  professionalism and, 207
  Ream and, 190
  residences of, 28–29, 31–33, 35, 167, 231n. 96
  *Risorgimento* and, 123
  Rogers and, 78
  in Rome, generally, 28–29, 31–33, 34–35, 54, 59, 72
  Stebbins and, 34–35, 111, 221n. 94, 236n. 61
  tomboy stereotype and, 17
  Whitney and, 111
Cushman, Ned, 243n. 90

Dall, Caroline Healy, 22, 250n. 94
Dalou, Jules, 203
*Daphne* (Hosmer), 46–51, *47*, 59–60, 71
*David Copperfield* (Dickens), 250n. 1
Davidson, Cathy, 9
Davis, John, 131
Davis, Pauline Wright, 198, 199, 251n. 14
*Dead Pearl Diver* (Akers), 72, 103–4, *103*, 109–10
"Declaration of Sentiments," 8–9, 61
de Lauretis, Teresa, 215n. 45
Della Valle, 194, *194*
de Pizan, Christine, 53
Derby Gallery, 247n. 55
de Staël, Madame. *See Corinne, or Italy* (de Staël)
De Vries Gallery, 111
*Dial*, 19
Diana, 49
Dickens, Charles, 250n. 1
Diderot, Denis, 5
*Discourse VI* (Reynolds), 41
"Doleful Ditty of the Roman Caffè Greco" (Hosmer), 84–85, 86
Doll's Gallery, 144
domesticity
  autonomy and, 72
  captivity and, 69–71
  emancipation and, 173–75
  gender and, 173–75
  Lewis and, 173–75
  marriage and, 29, 31, 34–35, 59
  morality and, 8–9, 24, 77
  neoclassicism and, 69–71
  professionalism and, 18–19, 59, 61, 63–65, 80, 191, 192, 207
  race and, 173–75
  Ream and, 191, 192, 207
  salons and, 207
  sexuality and, 9, 29, 31, 34–35, 59, 69–71, 77
  studios and, 63–65
  womanhood and, 5, 8–9, 10, 29–33, 34–35, 69–71, 90, 174–75
  women's rights and, 8–9
*Il Don Pirlone: Giornale di caricature politiche*, 117
Douglass, Frederick
  on Garibaldi, 122–23
  on *Greek Slave* (Powers), 161
  Lewis and, 243n. 95, 246n. 28
  on race, 94
  women's rights and, 199, 253n. 70
*Dream of Love* (Whitney). *See The Youth* (Whitney)
dress. *See* clothing
Dress Reform Movement, 18
Dublin Exhibition, 108
*Dying Gaul*, 97, 140, 224n. 28
*Dying Gladiator*, 235n. 50. See also *Dying Gaul*
*Dying Slave* (Michelangelo), 110

Eakins, Thomas, 110
Eastlake, Lady, 46
École des Beaux-Arts, 202
*Edmonia Lewis* (Rocher), 167–68, *167*
education
  of Fuller, 19, 30
  of Hosmer, 15–19, 45, 46, 67–69

of Lander, 67–69
at Lennox Academy, 17, 18–19, 22
nudes and, 102
painting and, 212
for sculpture, 22, 24, 33, 41, 44, 45, 46, 67–69, 102, 103–4, 110–11, 113–14, 150, 186, 189–90, 202, 212, 219n. 59
womanhood and, 18–19
women's rights and, 81
*Edward Lander* (Lander), 26
Egypt, 150, 157–59, 162
Ellet, Elizabeth
on Brackett, 221n. 102
on Lander, 25
professionalism and, 18–19, 207
*Women Artists in All Ages and Countries*, 33, 65
Ellis, Havelock, 215n. 44
emancipation, 149–50, 157, 169–75, 176–80, 194–99
*Emancipation Monument* (Ball), 178, *179*
Emancipation Proclamation, 157, 169, 195
Emerson, Ralph Waldo, 20, 22, 220n. 71
emotionalism, 50
*English Woman's Journal*, 222n. 108
Enlightenment
gender and, 6–7, 27, 55
imperialism and, 93
neoclassicism and, 5–7, 7–8, 55
race and, 153, 164
Equal Rights Association, 198
Equal Rights Party, 198, 200
*Eros of Centocelle*, 21
Ethiopia, 155, 157–59
*Ethiopia Shall Soon Stretch Out Her Hands to God, or Africa* (Whitney), *158*, *163*, *164*, *165*
*African Sibyl* (Hosmer) and, 179
destruction of, 180
*Forever Free* (Lewis) and, 171
generally, 157–66
*Samuel Adams* (Whitney) and, 200
Eurydice, 40
*Evangeline* (Lander), 65–67, 69, 75, 80
expatriation. *See also* tourism
gender and, 3
Italy and, 93
neoclassicism and, 5–6
race and, 8
*Risorgimento* and, 5–6, 7–8
Rome and, 1–2, 3–5, 93, 137, 144–45

Fair for Colored Soldiers, 246n. 28
Falconnet, Judith, 60–61
*Falling Gladiator* (Rimmer), 237n. 87
*Farnese Hercules*, 140
Farragut, David, 207–8, *209*, *211*
Farragut, Virginia, 208
*Farragut Memorial* (Ream), 207–11, *209*, *211*
*Faun of Praxiteles*, *98*
in *The Marble Faun* (Hawthorne), 97, 109–10
Stebbins and, 104–6, 113
Whitney and, 110, 111, 113
Ferando, Christina, 225n. 62
Ferdinand II, 242n. 77
Fifteenth Amendment, 179–80, 198, 207
First Women's Rights Convention, 8–9
Florence, 7, 75, 124
Foley, Margaret
authenticity and, 83
in Boston, generally, 22, 23–25
class and, 3
*Cleopatra*, 233n. 131
*Pascuccia*, 89, *90*
Ream and, 190
*Revolution* celebrates, 253n. 69
in Rome, generally, 2, 4, 29, 61, 111
studios of, 63, 87–90
in *Women Artists in All Ages and Countries* (Ellet), 33
*Forever Free* (Lewis), 169–75, *170*, *172*, 249n. 87
*Forum Romanum*, 109
*The Fountain of the Siren* (Hosmer), 86
France, 20, 119, 138, 144, 202–3
Francesco, 136
Franco-Prussian War, 144
*Frank Leslie's Illustrated Newspaper*, 231n. 92
*The Freedman* (Ward), 143, *143*
*Freedman's Memorial to Abraham Lincoln* (Hosmer), 176–78, *177*
*Freedman's Record*, 176
freedom. *See* autonomy; emancipation
*Freedwoman and Child* (Lewis), 169, 171
Frémiet, Emmanuel, 202–3
French Academy, 44, 67, 85, 102, 113
Freud, Sigmund, 53, 225n. 65, 226n. 67, 251n. 23
friendship, 9–10, 59, 111. *See also* love; marriage
Frothingham, Charles, 130
Fryd, Vivien Green, 241n. 57
Fuller, Margaret
Barrett Browning and, 125
on Cenci, 128
*Corinne, or Italy* (Staël) and, 1, 220n. 71
education of, 19, 30
generally, 19–22
*History of the Roman Revolution*, 232n. 113
*Margaret Fuller* (Hicks), *21*, 24–25, 238n. 7
Mozier and, 232n. 113
on racism, 97–99
*Risorgimento* and, 19–20, 117, 119, 124, 239n. 37
on sexuality, 217n. 17
Ward sisters and, 67
*Woman in the Nineteenth Century*, 19, 128

Gage, Frances Dana, 155
Galatea, 37
*Galignani Messenger*, 84
Galleria Nazionale d'Arte Antica, 240n. 47
Gardner, Alexander, 184, 185, *186*
Garibaldi, Giuseppe
*Giuseppe Garibaldi* (Martegana), 123, *123*
*Risorgimento* and, 20, 119, 121–23, 135–36, 138
Garrison, William Lloyd
abolitionism and, 156, 169
Brackett and, 150
Lewis and, 156, 172, 246n. 28
Parker and, 25
*Risorgimento* and, 119–20
Gatley, Alfred, 84

gaze
Akers and, 104
gender and, 102
Hosmer and, 82, 108–10, 134
Lander and, 73
in *The Marble Faun* (Hawthorne), 97, 106
neoclassicism and, 41, 49, 51, 57, 153
in "On the Medusa of Leonardo da Vinci in the Florentine Gallery" (Shelley), 129
Ream and, 190, 195
sexuality and, 235n. 48
Stebbins and, 106
Whitney and, 111, 115–16, 141, 160
Gemme, Paola, 238n. 2
gender. *See also* manhood; womanhood
abolitionism and, 161–62, 169–75
Ames and, 185–86
artists and, 2–3, 26–27, 27–28, 32, 33, 61, 63, 80, 84–85, 131–32, 134, 203–5, 211–12
autonomy and, 53–55, 100–102, 129–30
beauty and, 189–90
clothing and, 18, 29, 31, 35, 65
domesticity and, 173–75
emancipation and, 169–75, 180, 195–96
Enlightenment and, 6–7, 27, 55
expatriation and, 3
gaze and, 102
Italy and, 28, 116
Lewis and, 167–75
literature and, 27–28, 124–25
marriage and, 61
morality and, 8–9, 102, 106, 110–11, 174–75, 189
neoclassicism and, 6–7, 53–55, 160–66, 180
nudes and, 97, 102–10, 110–11, 244n. 110
painting and, 24
professionalism and, 189–90, 196–99, 203–5
race and, 99–101, 150–55, 157–66, 169–75
Ream and, 189–90
*Risorgimento* and, 124–25
Rome and, 27–28, 99–102, 116
sculpture and, 6–7, 22, 24, 26–27, 32, 211–12
slavery and, 161–62, 169–75, 216n. 11
studios and, 63
tomboy stereotype and, 15–17
womanhood and, 8–9, 31, 167–75, 189–90
*George Washington* (Greenough), 155
Gibson, John
Foley and, 88
Hawthorne and, 72
Hosmer and, 23, 46, 55–57, 57–58, 81, 82, 83, 84, 85, 109, 191
Ironside and, 242n. 72
*Narcissus*, 57
on *Nathaniel Hawthorne* (Lander), 73
*Oenone*, 55–57
Stebbins and, 103
*Tinted Venus*, 45–46, *45*, 57, 83
Giddon, George R., 120
Gigi's Academy, 102
Gilbert, Sandra, 240n. 45
Gilman, 247n. 41
Gioberti, Vincenzo, 117, 119
*Giuseppe Garibaldi* (Martegana), 123, *123*
Goethe, Johann Wolfgang von, 1, 19
Goodden, Angelica, 240n. 46
Gore, Governor, 229n. 44
Gorgons, 51, 130, 132, 134–35. *See also Medusa* (Hosmer)
"The Gorgon's Head" (Hawthorne), 225n. 64
Grant, Ulysses S., 181, 200
Great Britain, 93
Great Exhibition, 46
Greece, 150
*Greek Slave* (Powers), 57, 69–70, *70*, 134, 161–62, 164
Greely, Horace, 19
Green, George Washington, 223n. 5
Greene, Dr., 230n. 64
Greenough, Horatio, 5, 7, 40, 155
Greenough, Louisa, 7
Greenwood, Grace
on Hosmer, 31
in Paris, 212
Ream and, 197, 198, 199
*Risorgimento* and, 119
Rome, arrival in, 28, 32, 220n. 74
Gregorovius, Ferdinand, 121, 123, 136, 239n. 32
Gregory XVI, 20, 117
Grey, Sibyl Mary, 59–60
Grimes, Leonard A., 150, 172
Griswald, Almond, 247n. 54
Groseclose, Barbara, 127
Guerrazzi, F. D., 128–29
Guinness, Benjamin, 236n. 76
*Guy Mannering*, 29

Hadwen, Lizzie, 90
Haiti, 141–44
Halberstam, Judith, 29
Harper's Ferry, 122–23, 137
*Harper's Weekly*, 82
*Harriet Hosmer in Her Studio*, 63–65, *64*
Hatt, Michael, 244n. 110
Hawthorne, Julian, 80, 229n. 42
Hawthorne, Nathaniel
Akers and, 103
authenticity and, 85
in Boston, 17
*Faun of Praxiteles* and, 113
Fuller and, 20
"The Gorgon's Head," 225n. 64
Hosmer and, 63–65, 72, 75, 76, 77, 82, 101, 134, 229n. 40
Lander and, 65–67, 72–73, *74*, 75–78, 78–80, 235n. 40
*The Marble Faun*, 4, 72, 73, 75, 79, 96–99, 101, 104, 106–8, 110, 153
*Nathaniel Hawthorne* (Lander), 72–73, *74*, 80
P.P. Caproni and Brother, bust by, 228n. 28
in Rome, 72–78, 93, 96
Stebbins and, 106
Hawthorne, Rose, 229n. 41, 229n. 42
Hawthorne, Sophia Peabody
Akers and, 103
*Beatrice Cenci* (Reni) and, 125
*Corinne, or Italy* (de Staël) and, 1, 220n. 71
Fuller and, 19
Hosmer and, 82
Lander and, 77

in Rome, generally, 72, 73–75, 76, 96
Hawthorne, Una, 74–75, 76
Hay, John, 250n. 7
Hays, Matilda, *30*
Cushman and, 28, 29, 34, 35
Hosmer and, 59
mannish woman stereotype and, 29, 31, 55
Heade, Martin Johnson, 117–19, *118*
*Head of Perseus*, 225n. 55
Healy, George Peter Alexander, 194, *194*
Heckscher, August, 222n. 106
Heckscher, Richard, 222n. 106
Heckscher Museum, 222n. 106
Helen, 57
Herbert, T. Walter, 229n. 49, 230n. 59
Hercules, 140
*Hesper* (Hosmer), 22, *23*, 49
*Hestia Giustiniani*, 225n. 55
Hicks, Thomas, 20–21, *21*, 24–25, 40, 238n. 7
Higginson, Thomas Wentworth, 162, 246n. 36
*History of the Roman Revolution* (Fuller), 232n. 113
Holmes, Oliver Wendell, 17
horseback riding, 15–17, 18, 33, 55, 101–2, 167
Horton, James Oliver, 173
Hosmer, Harriet, *16*, *64*, *82*, *87*, *210*
abolitionism and, 131, 149–50, 166
*African Sibyl*, 178–80, *179*
Akers and, 103
authenticity and, 67, 81, 83–86, 132, 208
autonomy and, 101–2
Barrett Browning and, 57, 59, 67, 125, 149, 242n. 76
*Beatrice Cenci*, 125–31, *126*, *128*, 141
Benton statue, *210*
in Boston, 26–27, 85–86, 130–31
"Boston and Boston People," 26–27
Brackett and, 222n. 102
cameo carving and, 233n. 131
Carr and, 22, 28, 35, 59, 134, 237n. 76
Catholic Church and, 128, 129, 130–31, 144–45
Cavour and, 242n. 82
Child and, 132, 134, 149–50, 232n. 117, 241n. 66
class and, 3
clothing of, 18, 31, 65, 74–75, 82, 86, 102, 167, 190, 191, 208
Crawford and, 57, 67
Crow and, 22, 28, 55, 61, 81, 101, 106, 129, 144, 149, 208
Cushman and, 28–29, 31–32, 35, 83, 208, 222n. 110, 237n. 76
*Daphne*, 46–51, *47*, 59–60, 71
"Doleful Ditty of the Roman Caffè Greco," 84–85, 86
education of, 15–19, 45, 46, 67–69
emancipation and, 176–78, 178–80
Falconnet memorial, 60–61
Foley and, 88
*The Fountain of the Siren*, 86
*Freedman's Memorial to Abraham Lincoln*, 176–78, *177*
Gibson and, 23, 46, 55–57, 57–58, 81, 82, 83, 84, 85, 109, 191
*Harriet Hosmer in Her Studio*, 63–65, *64*
Hawthorne and, 63–65, 72, 75, 76, 77, 82, 101, 134, 229n. 40
*Hesper*, 22, *23*, 49
horseback riding by, 15–17, 33, 55, 101–2, 167
*Hosmer and Her Men*, 86–87, *88*
Jameson and, 81, 131–32
Lander and, 76, 77, 81
latter years of, 212
Lewis and, 166, 167, 249n. 87
marriage and, 31, 49, 59, 61
*Medusa*, 46–49, *48*, 51–55, 59–60, 71, 83, 129–30
Minerva and, 134–35
morality and, 67, 108–9, 128
neoclassicism and, 22–23, 35, 41, 46–61, 106–10
nudes and, 55–59, 67, 106–10
*Oenone*, 55–59, *56*, *58*, 67
personality of, 25, 33
professionalism and, 193, 207
*Puck*, 26, 60, *60*, 83, 231n. 93
race and, 8, 100, 116, 120, 132, 166
Ream and, 187, 189, 191–92, 197, 208
residences of, 28, 29, 31–33, 35, 54, *54*, 111, 130, 167, 191, 231n. 96
*Risorgimento* and, 17–18, 125–37, 138, 144–45
Rogers and, 78
in Rome, generally, 2, 4, 28, 29–32, 33, 35, 54, 55, 59–61, 63–65, 74–75, 81–87, 100, 101, 144–45, 184
sculpture and, generally, 22–23, 32, 33, 35, 41, 46–61, 81–86
sensuality and, 46–55, 57–59, 67, 106–10
sexuality and, 31, 59, 65
*The Sister Sculptresses Taking a Ride*, 101–2, *102*
slavery and, 131, 149–50, 176–78
*Sleeping Faun*, 106–10, *107*, *108*, 113
Stebbins and, 33, 83
studios of, 46, 63–65, *64*, 74–75, 81–82, *82*, 86–87, 167
Sumner memorial and, 200
tomboy stereotype and, 15–17, 31, 49, 55, 86
*The Waking Faun*, 109, *110*, 113
Whitney and, 111, 193
womanhood and, 46–55, 63–65, 71, 125–37, 178–80
women's rights and, 18, 83, 120
workmen and, 81–87, 89
*Zenobia in Chains*, 55, 67, *68*, 72, 81–86, 89, 125, 131–37, *133*, 166, 208
Hosmer, Hiram, 15, 17, 28, 55, 231n. 94
*Hosmer and Her Men*, 86–87, *88*
*Hospital Sketches* (Alcott), 184
Hottentot type, *154*, 155, 160–61
*The Hour and the Man* (Martineau), 243n. 105
How, Charles, 243n. 102
Howard, Jacob, 188
Howe, Julia Ward
in Boston, 67
Foley and, 25
on Hosmer, 86
*improvisatrice* and, 28
on poverty, 138
race and, 101
*Risorgimento* and, 244n. 113
on torchlight viewings, 37, 40
Howe, Samuel Gridley, 101
Howitt, Mary, 32, 90, 145
Hoxie, Richard Leveridge, 208, 210

Hutchinson, Thomas, 200
"Hymn for the Celebration of Italian Unity" (Howe), 244n. 113

*Ideal Head of the Water Nymph* (Lander), 26
idealism
  Ames and, 184, 185
  Canova and, 42
  in *Corinne, or Italy* (Staël), 1, 2
  Crawford and, 40–41, 99
  Foley and, 89
  Gibson and, 45, 46
  Hawthorne and, 79
  Hosmer and, 23, 35, 49–50, 51, 53, 55, 58, 106–8, 109
  Lander and, 69
  Lewis and, 173, 175
  neoclassicism and, generally, 5–6, 19
  Ream and, 189
  Story and, 153, 155
  Thorwaldsen and, 44
  Whitney and, 111, 115, 140, 143, 160–66, 202
  womanhood and, 8–9
imperialism, 93, 99, 116, 117–22, 135–37
*improvisatrice*, 1, 4, 27–28
*Incidents in the Life of a Slave Girl: Written by Herself* (Jacobs), 173
*The Indian* (Crawford), 99, *100*
*Industry* (Stebbins), 222n. 106
Inman, Henry, 33
"In Memorium A. H. H." (Tennyson), 22
International Exposition, 82–83
Irigaray, Luce, 226n. 71
Ironside, Adelaide, 242n. 72
Italy. *See also Risorgimento*
  clothing in, 94
  expatriation and, 93
  gender and, 28, 116
  imperialism and, 93, 116, 117–20
  Lincoln assassination and, 175–76
  literature and, 2
  maps of, *121*, *122*
  race and, 93–99, 116, 120
  tourism and, 7, 93
Ives, Chauncey, 4, 63, 192

Jacobs, Harriet, 173
James, Henry, 2–3, 5, 22, 145
Jameson, Anna
  in Boston, 17
  on Cenci, 128
  Cushman and, 32
  death of, 135
  Hosmer and, 81, 131–32
  *Lives of Celebrated Female Sovereigns and Illustrious Women*, 128, 131
  *Tinted Venus* (Gibson) and, 46
  women's rights and, 131–32
Jarves, James Jackson, 33, 131
Jefferson, Thomas, 223n. 24
*Joan of Arc* (Frémiet), 202–3
Johnson, Andrew, 189
*Journal of a Residence on a Georgian Plantation* (Kemble), 216n. 11
Judaism, 96, 153
Juno, 134
Jupiter, 134

Kaplan, E. Ann, 235n. 48
Kauffmann, Angelika, 1, 27, 28
Kellogg, Minor, 195
Kemble, Frances Ann
  in Boston, 17, 18
  clothing of, 31
  Crow and, 218n. 39
  *Journal of a Residence on a Georgian Plantation*, 216n. 11
  in Rome, 32, 59
  Sedgwick and, 18, 226n. 88
  tomboy stereotype and, 18, 31
King, Edward, 235n. 50
King, Rufus, 242n. 88, 249n. 80
Know Nothing Party, 130–31
Krafft-Ebing, Richard von, 215n. 44

Ladies Great National Sanitary Fair, 186
Lander, Edward, 26
Lander, Elizabeth, 77
Lander, Frederick W., 25
Lander, Louisa
  *America Defending Her Children*, 80
  American Civil War and, 81, 184
  in Boston, 22, 23, 25–26, 75, 76, 80–81
  class and, 3
  clothing of, 65
  education of, 67–69
  *Edward Lander*, 26
  *Evangeline*, 65–67, 69, 75, 80
  Gore, bust of, 229n. 44
  Hawthorne and, 65–67, 72–73, 75–78, 235n. 40
  Hosmer and, 76, 77, 81
  *Ideal Head of the Water Nymph*, 26
  morality and, 65–67, 69–71, 73, 75–78, 80, 83, 84, 101, 106, 189
  Mozier and, 85
  *Nathaniel Hawthorne*, 72–73, *74*, 80
  neoclassicism and, 69–71
  nudes and, 65–67, 69–71, 78–80, 106
  race and, 101, 166
  *Revolution* celebrates, 253n. 69
  in Rome, generally, 2, 4, 61, 63, 65–71, 72–73, 76–80
  sensuality and, 78–80
  sexuality and, 67, 75–78, 80
  studios of, 63, 65–67, 72–75, 77, 80, 81, 167
  *To-day*, 67
  *Undine*, 78, 80
  *Virginia Dare*, 65–67, *66*, 69–72, 75, 78–80, *79*, 80–81, 134, 166, 230n. 69
  womanhood and, 65–67, 69–71
  in *Women Artists in All Ages and Countries* (Ellet), 33
  workmen and, 73, 80–81
Landucci, Teresa Bandettini, 27
*Laocoön*, 6, 26, 37, 140, 224n. 28
Lateran, 96
*Le Donne Romane*, 217n. 31
*Le Modèle* (Whitney), 203, *203*
Lennox Academy, 17, 18–19, 22
Leo XII, 24
*Letters from Abroad to Kindred at Home* (Sedgwick), 17
Lewis, Edmonia, *167*
  abolitionism and, 149, 150, 155–57, 169–75
  in Boston, 155–57, 166
  Brackett and, 222n. 102
  *Bust of Colonel Robert Gould Shaw*, 156–57, *157*, 166
  clothing of, 167–69
  domesticity and, 173–75
  *Edmonia Lewis* (Rocher), 167–68, *167*
  emancipation and, 169–75, 180

*Forever Free*, 169–75, *170*, *172*, 249n. 87
*Freedwoman and Child*, 169, 171
gender and, 167–75
Hosmer and, 166, 167, 249n. 87
latter years of, 212
patrons and, 156, 171–73
*Preghiera*, *168*, 169
race and, 3, 156–57, 166, 169–75
Ream and, 190
residences of, 175
*Revolution* celebrates, 253n. 69
*Risorgimento* and, 138
in Rome, generally, 2, 29, 166–68
studios of, 167
Whitney and, 138, 157
womanhood and, 167–75, 180
Lewis, Frederick Christian, *154*, 155
*Liberator*, 119, 156, 169, 173–74, *174*
"The Liberator, an African Slave, who is free and aspires to Greatness," 144
*Liberty Bell*, 149
*The Libyan Sibyl* (Michelangelo), 153–55, *154*, 179
*The Libyan Sibyl* (Story), 150, *152*, 153–55, 160, 162, 179
*Lily*, 18
Lincoln, Abraham
*Abraham Lincoln* (Ames), 183, *183*, 184–86, *185*, 198
*Abraham Lincoln* (Gardner), 185, *186*
*Abraham Lincoln* (Ream), 181, *182*, 183, 186–90, *187*, *188*, 192, 194–99, 200
American Civil War and, 122, 137
assassination of, 175–76, 242n. 88
*Emancipation Monument* (Ball), 178, *179*
Emancipation Proclamation and, 157, 195
*Freedman's Memorial to Abraham Lincoln* (Hosmer), 176–78, *177*
Lewis and, 246n. 28
*Lincoln Monument* (Brown), 195, *196*
*Model for a Monument to Lincoln* (Brown), 195, 196
Lincoln, Mary Todd, 253n. 54
*Lincoln Monument* (Brown), 195, *196*
Lippincott, Sarah Jane Clarke. *See* Greenwood, Grace
literature, 1–2, 27–28, 124–25
*Little Women* (Alcott), 17
*Lives of Celebrated Female Sovereigns and Illustrious Women* (Jameson), 128, 131
*London Daily News*, 124
*London Times*, 84, 106
Longfellow, Henry Wadsworth, 69, 150
Longworth, Nicholas, 197
"The Lotos-Eaters" (Tennyson), 104, 106, 114, 115
Lott, Lucretia, 239n. 12
*The Lotus Eater* (Stebbins), *105*
generally, 33, 104–6, 109–10
Whitney and, 111, 113, 114
*Lotus Eater* (Whitney), 114–15, *114*
Louis Napoleon, 20
love, 18, 31, 34–35, 59. *See also* friendship; marriage
Lowell, James Russell, 31–32
*Lowell Offering*, 24
Lyman, J., 175, 249n. 80
Lynn Museum and Historical Society, 250n. 8

*Machinist* (Stebbins), 222n. 106
*Machinist's Apprentice* (Stebbins), 222n. 106
malaria, 4–5, 76, 96
manhood, 173–74, 176–78. *See also* gender
Manifesto of Excommunication, 117
Mann, Horace, 34
Manning, Adeline
in France, 202, 212
*Roma* (Whitney) and, 243n. 102
in Rome, 111
Whitney and, 157, 162, 179–80, 203
mannish woman stereotype. *See also* tomboy stereotype
Cushman and, 29, 31, 35, 55, 86
Hays and, 29, 31, 55
Kemble and, 31
Stebbins and, 86
womanhood and, 10, 55
Manoguerra, Paul, 238n. 6
*The Marble Faun* (Hawthorne)
classicism in, 79
*Cleopatra* (Story) in, 153
*Dead Pearl Diver* (Akers) in, 104
*Faun of Praxiteles* in, 110
generally, 4, 72, 75
Hawthorne, Sophia Peabody, in, 73
*The Lotus Eater* (Stebbins) and, 106
race and, 96–99, 101
*Sleeping Faun* (Hosmer) and, 106–8
*Margaret Fuller* (Hicks), 20–21, *21*, 24–25, 238n. 7
Mariani, Andrea, 236n. 70
Maria Sophia, 135–37
Mario, Jesse White, 8, 124, 125
Markus, Julia, 59, 221n. 100
marriage. *See also* friendship; love
artists and, 61
Cushman and, 29, 34–35
domesticity and, 29, 31, 34–35, 59
gender and, 61
Hosmer and, 31, 49, 59, 61
professionalism and, 31, 73, 208–11
race and, 156, 165–66
womanhood and, 49, 59
women's rights and, 18, 156
Mars, 143
Marsh, George, 140
*Mars Ludovisi*, 143, *143*
Martegana, Giuseppe, 123, *123*
Martineau, Harriet, 17, 243n. 105
Mazzini, Giuseppe, 7, 19–20, 117, 121, 124, 217n. 31
McDowell, Joseph Nash, 22
McGann, Jerome J., 241n. 58
McIntire, Samuel, 25
Medusa, 132, 134–35
*Medusa* (Hosmer), *48*
*Beatrice Cenci* (Hosmer) compared with, 129–30
generally, 46–49, 51–55, 59–60, 83
*Virginia Dare* (Lander) compared with, 71
*Medusa Rondanini*, 226n. 72
Melville, Herman, 6, 17
Mengs, Anton Raphael, 27
Mercer, Sallie, 28, 32
Merrill, Lisa, 221n. 100
Merrimack Corporation, 24
Metropolitan Museum of Art, 225n. 60
Metternich, Klemens von, 8
Meunier, Constantin, 203

Michelangelo, 110, 153–55, *154*, 179, 236n. 70
*Midsummer Night's Dream* (Shakespeare), 60
Millet, Jean-François, 203
Milli, Giannina, 27–28
Mills, Clark, 186, 187, 188
Mills, Fisk, 186–87
Mills, Sara, 234n. 10
Milmore, Martin, 200
Milmore Brothers, 237n. 85
Milroy, Elizabeth, 222n. 110
Minerva, 55, 129, 134–35, *135*, *136*
miniature painting, 24
Missouri Medical College, 22
Mitchell, Maria, 83
*Model for a Monument to Lincoln* (Brown), 195, 196
morality
  beauty and, 5, 128–29
  Cenci and, 127–29, 131
  domesticity and, 8–9, 24, 77
  emancipation and, 174–75
  gender and, 8–9, 102, 106, 110–11, 174–75, 189
  Hosmer and, 67, 108–9, 128
  Lander and, 65–67, 69–71, 73, 75–78, 80, 83, 84, 101, 106, 189
  neoclassicism and, 5, 6–7, 40, 69–71, 79–80, 184, 189
  nudes and, 65–67, 69–71, 79–80, 102, 106, 108–9, 110–11
  professionalism and, 181–83, 188
  race and, 160, 174–75
  Ream and, 188, 189
  sexuality and, 67, 76–78
  Stebbins and, 106
  studios and, 63, 65–67, 73, 77
  Whitney and, 181–83
  womanhood and, 8–9, 65–67, 69–71, 160, 174–75, 181–83
Morelli, Maria Maddalena, 1, 27
Morse, Samuel F. B., 131
Mozier, Joseph, 4, 63, 72, 85, 192
Murray, Freeman Henry Morris, 245n. 17, 248n. 62
*Murray's*, 94
Musée Napoleon, 224n. 28
Museum of Fine Arts, Boston, 219n. 60, 237n. 76
Naples, 121, 122, 135–36
Naples Museum, 236n. 74
Napoleon, 42
Napoleon III, 239n. 32
*Narcissus* (Gibson), 57
Nast, Thomas, 122
*Nathaniel Hawthorne* (Lander), 72–73, *74*, 80
*Nation*, 240n. 41
National Academy of Design, 33, 143, 160, 162, 171
*National Anti-Slavery Standard*, 15
National Sailor's Fair, 160
National Women's Suffrage Association, 198, 200
National Women's Suffrage Convention, 199
Native Americans, 69, 97–99, 166
naturalism. *See also* sensuality
  Ames and, 184, 185
  Hosmer and, 46, 49, 51, 55
  Praxiteles and, 223n. 22
  in *Roman Fish Market, Arch of Octavius* (Bierstadt), 234n. 8
  Whitney and, 144, 202–3
Necker, Germaine. *See Corinne, or Italy* (de Staël)
Nelson, Charmaine, 247n. 50, 247n. 52
neoclassicism
  *Apollo Belvedere* and, 6
  beauty and, 40–41, 51–53
  in Boston, 26, 37–41
  domesticity and, 69–71
  Enlightenment and, 5–7, 7–8, 55
  expatriation and, 5–6
  Fuller and, 19
  gaze and, 41, 49, 51, 57, 153
  gender and, 6–7, 53–55, 160–66, 180
  Hosmer and, 22–23, 35, 41, 46–61, 106–10
  idealism and, generally, 5–6, 19
  Lander and, 69–71
  morality and, 5, 6–7, 40, 69–71, 79–80, 184, 189
  naturalism and, 202
  nudes and, 5, 37–41, 55–59, 69–71, 78–80, 103–16
  originality and, 41, 164–65
  race and, 153–55, 160–66, 169–75, 180
  Ream and, 189, 194–95
  *Risorgimento* and, 5–6
  in Rome, 37, 41–46, 53–57, 59–61, 71
  sensuality and, 37, 42, 44, 45–55, 57–59, 103–10
  Whitney and, 141–44, *142*, 160–66, 202
  womanhood and, 46–55, 59, 69–71, 160–66
Neptune, 51, 129
Nesmith, James Willis, 187–88
*New York Daily Tribune*, 119, 239n. 37
*New York Evening Post*, 84, 150
New York Garibaldi Fund Committee, 122
*New York Illustrated News*, 122
*New York Times*, 120–21, 212
*New York Tribune*, 19
Nicolay, John G., 250n. 7
Nochlin, Linda, 234n. 8
*North American Review*, 219n. 54
*North Star*, 161
Norton, Charles Eliot, 121, 122, 153
Nott, Josiah C., 120
Nucci, 84
nudes
  autonomy and, 109–10
  beauty and, 40–41
  Catholic Church and, 102
  education and, 102
  Enlightenment and, 5
  gender and, 97, 102–10, 110–11, 244n. 110
  Hosmer and, 55–59, 67, 106–10
  Lander and, 65–67, 69–71, 78–80, 106
  in *Margaret Fuller* (Hicks), 21
  morality and, 65–67, 69–71, 79–80, 102, 106, 108–9, 110–11
  neoclassicism and, 5, 37–41, 55–59, 69–71, 78–80, 103–16
  race and, 109, 110, 144
  Stebbins and, 103–6, 109–10
  tourism and, 103–4
  Whitney and, 110–16

Oakey, Maria, 255n. 17
Oberlin College, 150
Octavian, 150
Odysseus, 104
*Oenone* (Gibson), 55–57

*Oenone* (Hosmer), 55–59, *56*, *58*, 67
"Oenone" (Tennyson), 57
Olimpica, Corilla, 1, 27
"On the Medusa of Leonardo da Vinci in the Florentine Gallery" (Shelley), 129
originality
  Canova and, 44
  Hosmer and, 32, 58, 81
  neoclassicism and, 41
  torchlight viewings and, 45
  Whitney and, 164–65
*Orpheus and Cerberus* (Crawford), 26, 37–41, *39*, 67, 111
Ossoli, Giovanni Angelo, 20

painting, 4, 24, 212
Pakenham and Hooker, 4, 63
Palazzo Barberini, 125, 240n. 47
Palazzo Patrizi, 63
Palmer, Erastus Dow, 70, *71*, 134, 228n. 20
Pantheon, 96
*Paolina Borghese as Venus Victorius* (Canova), 161, *161*
*Papal Conspiracy Exposed* (Beecher), 130
Paris (France), 3, 57, 202–3, 212, 236n. 76
Paris (mythological), 57
Parker, Theodore, 25, 165, 230n. 64
*Pascuccia* (Foley), 89, *90*
patrons
  Canova and, 42–44
  Gibson and, 224n. 44
  Hosmer and, 55, 59–61, 129
  Lander and, 78
  Lewis and, 156, 171–73
  Whitney and, 113
Peabody, Elizabeth
  *Corinne, or Italy* (Staël) and, 220n. 71
  Fuller and, 19
  Hawthorne, Sophia Peabody, and, 228n. 33
  Lewis and, 156, 172–73, 174
Peabody Essex Museum, 228n. 28
Pellegrini, Isabella, 27
Peneus, 49
Pennsylvania Academy of the Fine Arts, 33, 110, 185
Perseus, 42, *43*, 51–53, *52*, 129, 225n. 55
Peter, Sarah Worthington King, 24
Petrarch, 27
phallus symbol, 51, 53, 78, 108
Philadelphia School of Design for Women, 24
Phillips, Wendell, 141, 150, 246n. 28
*Pietà* (Michelangelo), 236n. 70
Pius VII, 42
Pius IX
  Antonelli and, 193, 194
  *Risorgimento* and, 20, 117, 119, 136, 144
Pluto, 40
*Poems Before Congress* (Barrett Browning), 124–25, 134
Potts, Alex, 42, 49
poverty, 25, 93, 94–96, 138–41. *See also* class
Powers, Hiram
  *Greek Slave*, 57, 69–70, *70*, 134, 161–62, 164
  Lewis and, 167
  Mozier and, 232n. 113
  Ream and, 189, 196–97
  *Risorgimento* and, 5, 7
  studios of, 75
P.P. Caproni and Brother, 228n. 28
Praxiteles
  Canova and, 42
  *Chaldean Shepherd* (Whitney) and, 115
  *Cupid*, 46
  *Faun of Praxiteles*, 97, *98*, 104–6, 109–10, 111, 113
  *Sleeping Faun* (Hosmer) and, 108
  *Venus de Milo*, 58
*Preghiera* (Lewis), *168*, 169
Preston, Robert, 224n. 44
*The Prince of Wales at Miss Hosmer's Studio*, 82, *82*
"The Prisoner of St. Joux" (Whitney), 141
Proclamation of the Republic, 20, 117
Proctor, Nancy Elizabeth, 2, 80
*Prodigal Son* (Mozier), 85
production processes. *See also* workmen
  of Canova, 42–44
  of Foley, 89
  of Gibson, 45–46
  of Hosmer, 83, 85, 109
  of Lander, 80–81
professionalism
  Ames and, 183–84, 186, 187, 193, 207
  beauty and, 189–90, 192–93
  in Boston, 15, 18–19
  class and, 207
  clothing and, 31
  Cushman and, 207
  domesticity and, 18–19, 59, 61, 63–65, 80, 191, 192, 207
  gender and, 189–90, 196–99, 203–5
  Hosmer and, 193, 207
  marriage and, 31, 73, 208–11
  morality and, 181–83, 188
  Ream and, 181–84, 187–90, 191, 192–93, 194, 196–99, 207–11
  in Rome, 2, 5, 10, 29, 55, 63–67
  salons and, 207
  Stebbins and, 193, 207
  studios and, 63–67
  suffrage and, 211–12
  Whitney and, 181–84, 193
  womanhood and, 2, 5, 8–9, 10, 18–19, 29, 31, 33, 55, 67, 181–84, 186, 197–99, 207
  women's rights and, 8–9, 10, 211–12
*Progress of Civilization* (Crawford), 99
Protestantism, 130–31
psychoanalytic theory, 53
*Puck* (Hosmer), 26, 60, *60*, 83, 231n. 93
Pygmalion, 37, 55, 80, 189

*Queen: The Lady's Newspaper and Pictorial Times*, 84
Quiner, Joanna, 219n. 54

race
  abolitionism and, 149–50, 150–55, 156–57, 159–60, 161–62, 165–66, 195
  beauty and, 165
  Boston and, 166
  class and, 160
  domesticity and, 173–75
  emancipation and, 195–96
  Enlightenment and, 153, 164
  expatriation and, 8
  gender and, 99–101, 150–55, 157–66, 169–75

race (*cont'd*)
- Hosmer and, 8, 100, 116, 120, 132, 166
- imperialism and, 99, 120
- Italy and, 93–99, 116, 120
- Lander and, 166
- Lewis and, 156–57, 166, 169–75
- manhood and, 173–74, 176–78
- marriage and, 156, 165–66
- morality and, 160, 174–75
- Native Americans and, 97–99
- neoclassicism and, 153–55, 160–66, 169–75, 180
- nudes and, 109, 110, 144
- patrons and, 171–73
- Reconstruction and, 178
- *Risorgimento* and, 120
- Rome and, 93–101, 116
- sexuality and, 160–61
- slavery and, 97–99, 120, 149–50, 161–62
- Story and, 150–55
- Whitney and, 116, 120, 150, 157–66
- womanhood and, 3, 157–66, 169–75, 178–80
- women's rights and, 120

Radcliffe College, 237n. 76
Rantoul, Robert, 219n. 54
Raphael, 193, 194
Read, Thomas Buchanon, 72
Ream, Robert, 251n. 13
Ream, Vinnie, *187*, *194*, *211*
- *Abraham Lincoln*, 181, *182*, 183, 186–90, *187*, *188*, 192, 194–99, 200
- age and, 3
- American Civil War and, 186
- authenticity and, 186–87, 192, 197, 202
- beauty and, 189–90, 192–93
- Catholic Church and, 193–94, 208
- clothing of, 192–93, 194, 208, 210, 220n. 71
- *Corinne, or Italy* (de Staël) and, 1, 220n. 71
- domesticity and, 191, 192, 207
- emancipation and, 194–99
- *Farragut Memorial*, 207–11, *209*, *211*
- gender and, 189–90
- Hosmer and, 187, 189, 191–92, 197, 208
- morality and, 188, 189
- neoclassicism and, 189, 194–95
- professionalism and, 181–84, 187–90, 191, 192–93, 194, 196–99, 207–11
- in Rome, generally, 2, 190–94
- salons of, 207
- studios of, 189–90, 192–93
- suffrage and, 195–96, 197–99
- womanhood and, 181–84, 189–90, 197–99, 207
- women's rights and, 195–96, 197–99, 211
- workmen and, 192, 197, 202

Reconstruction, 178, 195, 198, 199. *See also* emancipation
relief medallions, 88, 89
Reni, Guido, 125–27, *127*, 129
*Resting Satyr. See Faun of Praxiteles*
*Revolution*, 181, 197, 199
Reynolds, Joshua, 41
Richardson, Marilyn, 255n. 14
Rimmer, William, 110–11, 237n. 87
Rinehart, William Henry, 192
*Risorgimento*
- abolitionism and, 119–20, 122–23
- Barrett Browning and, 124–25, 130, 131, 134, 135, 137
- Catholic Church and, 99, 117–20, 123, 130–31, 134, 138, 140–41, 144, 193
- Cushman and, 123
- Enlightenment and, 7–8
- expatriation and, 5–6, 7–8
- Fuller and, 19–20, 117, 119, 124, 239n. 37
- Garibaldi and, 20, 119, 121–23, 135–36, 138
- gender and, 124–25
- Hosmer and, 17–18, 125–37, 138, 144–45
- imperialism and, 117–22, 135–37
- Lewis and, 138
- Lincoln assassination and, 175–76
- neoclassicism and, 5–6
- Pius IX and, 20, 117, 119, 136, 144
- race and, 120
- Rome and, 7, 123, 124, 137–45
- slavery and, 120, 122–23, 137, 141–44
- United States and, 119–23, 130–31
- Whitney and, 138–44, 145
- womanhood and, 125–37
- women's rights and, 124–25

Riviere, Joan, 252n. 27
Rocher, Henry, 167–68, *167*
Rogers, John, 76, 77–78, 80
Rogers, Randolph, 63, 72, 192
Rollin, James, 186
*Rollo in Rome* (Abbott), 37, *39*
*Roma* (Whitney), 138–41, *139*, *140*, 193
*The Romance of the Republic* (Child), 165–66
*Roman Fish Market, Arch of Octavius* (Bierstadt), 94–96, *95*, 108
*The Roman Goat Herd* (Heade), 238n. 1
Roman National Committee, 123, 175–76
*Roman Newsboys* (Heade), 117–19, *118*
Roman Republic, 7, 19–20, 117–20, 124
Rome
- artists in, generally, 1–5, 27–28, 116, 120, 144–45
- autonomy and, 100–102
- domesticity in, 5
- Enlightenment and, 27
- expatriation and, 1–2, 3–5, 93, 137, 144–45
- gender and, 27–28, 99–102, 116
- Lincoln assassination and, 175–76
- literature and, 27–28
- map of, xvi
- neoclassicism in, 37, 41–46, 53–57, 59–61, 71
- poverty in, 93, 94–96, 138–41
- professionalism in, 2, 5, 10, 29, 55, 63–67
- race and, 93–101, 116
- *Risorgimento* and, 7, 123, 124, 137–45
- studios in, 63–67, 72–75, 86–90, 111–13
- tourism in, 4–5, 63, 72, 73–75, 93, 96–97, 97–99, 103–4, 138, 144–45
- womanhood and, 2–3, 5, 28–35, 63–67, 71

*Romeo and Juliet* (Shakespeare), 29
Roos, Jane Mayo, 2
Ross, Edmund G., 189
Rousseau, Jean-Jacques, 5
Rowe, John Carlos, 236n. 53

Royal Academy School, 81
Ruane, Joseph, 234n. 17

Salon (Paris), 202–3
salons
of Barrett Browning, 124
of Cushman, 32
of Fuller, 19, 67
of Kauffmann, 27, 28
of Ream, 192, 207
of Sartoris, 31
*Samuel Adams* (Whitney), 200, *201*, 202, 204, 205
Sand, George, 28, 29
Sanitary Commission Fair, 247n. 54
Sanitary Commissions, 86, 137, 176, 184, 232n. 128
Sant'Andrea delle Fratte, 60–61
Sappho, 125
*Sartjee, the Hottentot Venus* (Lewis, Frederick C.), *154*, 155
Sartoris, Adelaide, 31, 59
School of Design for Women, 19, 24, 26
Schriber, Mary S., 73–74
Scott, Charlotte, 176
sculpture
cameo carving, 24–25, 26
education and, 22, 24, 33, 41, 44, 45, 46, 67–69, 102, 103–4, 110–11, 113–14, 150, 186, 189–90, 202, 212, 219n. 59
gender and, 6–7, 22, 24, 26–27, 32, 211–12
originality and, 32, 41, 44, 45, 58, 81, 164–65
production processes, 42–44, 45–46, 80–81, 83, 85, 89, 109
relief medallions, 88, 89
torchlight viewings of, 37, 39, 42, 45
workmen and, 42, 73, 80–81, 81–87, 89, 111, 192, 197, 202, 236n. 61, 243n. 102
Sedgwick, Catharine
on colonialism, 99
on Crawford, 44
Hosmer and, 247n. 55
Kemble and, 18, 226n. 88
*Letters from Abroad to Kindred at Home*, 17
as mentor, 17–18, 24
on Orpheus, 40
Sedgwick, Charles, 17
Sedgwick, Elizabeth, 17, 216n. 11
sensuality
Hosmer and, 46–55, 57–59, 67, 106–10
Lander and, 78–80
neoclassicism and, 37, 42, 44, 45–55, 57–59, 103–10
Servius Tullius, 175–76
Severe style, 42, 49, 58, 132
sexuality
clothing and, 29, 31, 65
Cushman and, 29, 34–35
domesticity and, 9, 29, 31, 34–35, 59, 69–71, 77
friendship and, 9–10, 59
Fuller and, 20–22, 217n. 17
gaze and, 235n. 48
horseback riding and, 235n. 44
Hosmer and, 31, 59, 65
Lander and, 67, 75–78, 80
morality and, 67, 76–78
psychoanalytic theory and, 53
race and, 160–61
womanhood and, 3, 9–10, 31, 34–35, 49, 59, 65, 67, 69–71, 160–61
women's rights and, 254n. 72
Shakespeare, William, 29, 60
Shaw, Robert Gould, 156–57, *157*
Shelley, Percy Bysshe, 51, 128, 129
Shepard, Ada, 229n. 41
Sherman, William Tecumseh, 181, 208, 211
Shortall, John, 237n. 76
Sicily, 121, 122, 136
Siddons, Sarah, 18
Siegel, Jonah, 41
*The Sister Sculptresses Taking a Ride*, 101–2, *102*
Sistine Chapel, 153–55, *154*, 179
"Sketch of Sojourner Truth" (Gage), 155
Skillin brothers, 25
Slack, Charles, 203–4
slavery
gender and, 161–62, 169–75, 216n. 11
Hosmer and, 131, 149–50, 176–78
Parker and, 25
Powers and, 69–70
race and, 97–99, 120, 149–50, 161–62
*Risorgimento* and, 120, 122–23, 137, 141–44
Story and, 153
Whitney and, 141–44, *142*
womanhood and, 161–62, 169–75
women's rights and, 156
*Sleeping Faun* (Hosmer), 106–10, *107*, *108*, 113
Smith, Edwin, 25
Society of Lady Artists, 233n. 136
Spain, 121, 136
spheres, private and public
domesticity and, 211
gender distinctions in, 9, 53, 80, 125, 130, 181, 183–84, 190, 197, 199, 200, 208, 212
Italy and, 116, 125
neoclassicism and, 6–7
sexuality and, 9, 10
women's rights and, 8–9, 181, 183–84, 196, 197, 199, 200, 204–5, 207
Stanton, Elizabeth Cady
"Declaration of Sentiments," 8–9, 61
Parker and, 25
Ream and, 181, 198, 199
suffrage and, 253n. 70
Stebbins, Caroline, 222n. 104
Stebbins, Emma, *34*
*Angel of the Waters*, 34, *34*
authenticity and, 83
autonomy and, 101–2
Cushman and, 34–35, 111, 221n. 94, 236n. 61
*Faun of Praxiteles* and, 113
Foley and, 87–88
Hawthorne and, 72, 77
Hosmer and, 33, 83
latter years of, 212
Lincoln assassination and, 175
*The Lotus Eater*, 33, 104–6, *105*, 109–10, 111, 113, 114
mannish woman stereotype and, 86
morality and, 106
nudes and, 103–6, 109–10
professionalism and, 193, 207
Ream and, 190

Stebbins, Emma (*cont'd*)
Rogers and, 78
in Rome, generally, 2, 4, 29, 32, 33–35, 54, 61
*The Sister Sculptresses Taking a Ride*, 101–2, *102*
studios of, 190
Sumner memorial and, 200
tomboy stereotype and, 17
Whitney and, 111, 243n. 102
workmen and, 236n. 61, 243n. 102
Stebbins, Henry, 34
Stephenson, Peter, 22
Stevens, Thaddeus, 187, 189
Stevenson, H. E., 248n. 62
Stone, Lucy, 161, 198, 199
Story, Emelyn, 20, 149
Story, William Wetmore
abolitionism and, 149, 150–55
Boston Athenaeum and, 219n. 59
*Cleopatra*, 72, 150–53, *151*, 155, 162, 166
Cushman and, 31–32
Fuller and, 217n. 21
Hosmer and, 84, 101
Lander and, 78
*The Libyan Sibyl*, 150, *152*, 153–55, 160, 162, 179
in *The Marble Faun* (Hawthorne), 97
on poverty, 234n. 11
race and, 150–55
Ream and, 187, 190, 192
residences of, 125
*Risorgimento* and, 20
in Rome, generally, 4, 72
in Siena, 75
slavery and, 153
*Venus de Medici* and, 230n. 72
Stowe, Harriet Beecher, 149, 155, 157, 159, 247n. 55
St. Peter's Cathedral, 96, 144, 190, 236n. 70
*Street Scene in Rome* (Heade), 238n. 1
studios
of Akers, 65
of Ball, 202
of Canova, 42, 167
of Crawford, 44
domesticity and, 63–65
of Foley, 63, 87–90
gender and, 63
of Gibson, 46
of Hosmer, 46, 63–65, *64*, 74–75, 81–82, *82*, 86–87, 167
of Lander, 63, 65–67, 72–75, 77, 80, 81, 167
of Lewis, 167
morality and, 63, 65–67, 73, 77
professionalism and, 63–67
of Ream, 189–90, 192–93
of Stebbins, 190
tourism and, 63, 72, 89
of Whitney, 111–13, 193
womanhood and, 63–67, 86–87
suffrage
emancipation and, 179–80, 195–96
professionalism and, 211–12
Ream and, 195–96, 197–99, 211
womanhood and, 197–99
women's rights and, 179–80, 195–96, 197–99, 203, 205
Sulgher, Fortunata, 27
Sumner, Charles
Brackett and, 150
*Charles Sumner Memorial* (Whitney), 200–202, *202*, 203–5, *204*
Crawford and, 223n. 5, 223n. 7
Lewis and, 246n. 28
on Orpheus, 40
Ream and, 187–88
Story and, 149, 153, 187
women's rights and, 179–80, 253n. 70
Surratt, John H., 242n. 88
Swisshelm, Jane Grey, 184, 188–89, 199

Taddei, Rosa, 28
Tarnowska, Valeria, 51
Tasso, 27
Tempietto, 140
Tennyson, Alfred, Lord
"In Memorium A. H. H.," 22
"The Lotos-Eaters," 104, 106, 114, 115
"Oenone," 57
Terry, Luther, 238n. 7
theater, 29
Thompson, Cephas Giovanni, 72, 76, 77–78
Thorndike, Augustus, 26
Thorwaldsen, Bertel, 42, 44–45, 224n. 30, 247n. 54
"Thos. Nast, Esq., Our Special Artist," 122, *123*
Ticknor, Anna, 86
Ticknor, William, 73
Tilden's Book Shop, 25
Tilten, John Rollin, 222n. 104
*Tinted Venus* (Gibson), 45–46, *45*, 57, 83
*To-day* (Lander), 67
tomboy stereotype. *See also* mannish woman stereotype
Cushman and, 17
gender and, 15–17
Hosmer and, 15–17, 31, 49, 55, 86
Kemble and, 18, 31
marriage and, 49
Stebbins and, 17
womanhood and, 10, 55
torchlight viewings, 37, *39*, 42, 45
Torlonia, Alessandra, 242n. 72
tourism. *See also* expatriation
Catholic Church and, 144–45
Italy and, 7, 93
nudes and, 103–4
in Rome, generally, 4–5, 73–75, 93, 96–97, 97–99, 103–4, 138, 144–45
studios and, 63, 72, 89
*Toussaint L'Ouverture in Prison* (Whitney), 141–44, *142*, 150, 200, 202
Transcendentalism, 19
Treaty of Villafranca, 121
*Triumphant Perseus* (Canova), 42, *43*, 51–53, *52*
Truth, Sojourner, 155, 157, 159–60, *159*, 173, 180
Tubman, Harriet, 159
Tuckerman, Henry, 70, 239n. 24, 247n. 55
Twelfth Baptist Church, 172
*Types of Mankind* (Giddon and Nott), 120

Uffizi Gallery, 58, 79
*Uncle Tom's Cabin* (Stowe), 149
*Undine* (Lander), 78, 80
United States, 93, 99, 119–23, 130–31
U.S. Capitol
*Abraham Lincoln* (Ames) at, 183, 250n. 9
*Abraham Lincoln* (Ream) at, 181, 183, 195, 196–97

in American Civil War, 184
*Giuseppe Garibaldi* (Martegana) at, 123
race and, 69, 99
*Samuel Adams* (Whitney) at, 200, 204, 205
Story and, 155
U.S. Congress, 187–89
U.S. Constitution, 179–80, 198, 207
U.S. Supreme Court, 254n. 72

Vanderbilt, Cornelius, 254n. 71
Vasari, Giorgio, 42
*The Vatican by Torchlight*, 37, *39*
Vatican Museum
Akers at, 103
*Belvedere Torso* in, 99
Canova at, 42, 51
Crawford at, 44
Gibson at, *43*, 82
permits required for, 144
torchlight viewings at, 37, *39*, 45
Vaughn, Virginia, 28
Venice, 121
Venus
*Paolina Borghese as Venus Victorius* (Canova), 161, *161*
*Tinted Venus* (Gibson), 45–46, *45*, 57
*Venus de Medici*, 26, 78–79
*Venus de Milo*, 46, 58
Vicinus, Martha, 9
Victor Emmanuel II, 121, 137, 138
Victoria, 24, 231n. 96
Vigée-Lebrun, Élisabeth, 27
*Vindication of the Rights of Women* (Wollstonecraft), 215n. 42
*Vinne Ream* (Healy), *194*
Virgil, 6
*Virginia Dare* (Lander), *66*, *79*
generally, 65–67, 69–72, 75, 78–80, 80–81
race and, 166
Rogers on, 230n. 69
*Zenobia in Chains* (Hosmer) compared with, 134
Voltaire, François-Marie, 5

*The Waking Faun* (Hosmer), 109, *110*, 113
Wales, prince of, 82, *82*, 83, 236n. 76
Ward, George Cabot, 219n. 59
Ward, John Quincy Adams, 143, *143*, 189, 202
Ward, Louisa, 67
Ware, William, 241n. 65
Warren, Mary, 78
Washington, George, 121, 155, 223n. 24, 239n. 21
*Washington Evening Star*, 181, 195
Washington Monument, 175
Waterston, Anna Quincy, 156, 246n. 28
Weedon, Chris, 223n. 21
Weld, Theodore Dwight, 119, 120
West, Benjamin, 25
West, Cornel, 153
West Church, 246n. 35
Western Sanitary Commission, 176
Westphal, Carl von, 10
*White Captive* (Palmer), 70, *71*, 134
Whitney, Anne
abolitionism and, 141–44, *142*, 149, 150
age and, 3
authenticity and, 202
in Boston, 110–11, 137
*Chaldean Shepherd*, 111, *113*, 115–16, *115*
*Charles Sumner Memorial*, 200–202, *202*, 203–5, *204*
Child and, 246n. 32
*Ethiopia Shall Soon Stretch Out Her Hands to God, or Africa*, 157–66, *158*, *163*, *164*, *165*, 171, 179, 180, 200
Foley and, 233n. 135
in France, 202–3
Hosmer and, 111, 193
latter years of, 212
*Le Modèle*, 203, *203*
Lewis and, 138, 157
*Lotus Eater*, 114–15, *114*
morality and, 181–83
neoclassicism and, 160–66, 202
nudes and, 110–16
"The Prisoner of St. Joux," 141
professionalism and, 181–84, 193
race and, 116, 120, 150, 157–66
Ream and, 181–83, 190, 192, 193, 202
residences of, 167
*Risorgimento* and, 138–44, 145
*Roma*, 138–41, *139*, *140*, 193
in Rome, generally, 2, 111–13, 137–38, 144
*Samuel Adams*, 200, *201*, 202, 204, 205
slavery and, 141–44
Stebbins and, 111, 243n. 102
studios of, 111–13, 193
*Toussaint L'Ouverture in Prison*, 141–44, *142*, 150, 200, 202
on Vatican Museum, 144
womanhood and, 157–66, 180, 181–84
women's rights and, 120, 179–80, 199, 203–5
workmen and, 111, 243n. 102
*The Youth*, 111, *112*
Whitney, Edward, 203
Whitney, Sarah, 203, 254n. 76
Whittier, John Greenleaf, 166
Williams and Everetts Gallery, 80
Williams College Museum of Art, 250n. 9
Winckelmann, Johann, 242n. 72
Winterer, Caroline, 6
Wollstonecraft, Mary, 215n. 42
womanhood. *See also* gender
abolitionism and, 161–62, 165–66, 169–75
age and, 3
Ames and, 183–84, 186
artists and, generally, 2–3, 10, 18–19, 73–75
autonomy and, 49–51, 53–55
beauty and, 189–90
captivity and, 69–71
class and, 3, 171, 199
clothing and, 65, 86–87, 167–69
domesticity and, 5, 8–9, 10, 29–33, 34–35, 69–71, 90, 174–75
education and, 18–19
emancipation and, 169–75, 178–80
gender and, 8–9, 31, 167–75, 189–90
Hosmer and, 46–55, 63–65, 71, 125–37, 178–80
Lander and, 65–67, 69–71
Lewis and, 167–75, 180
marriage and, 49, 59
morality and, 8–9, 65–67, 69–71, 160, 174–75, 181–83
neoclassicism and, 46–55, 59, 69–71, 160–66

womanhood (*cont'd*)
  professionalism and, 2, 5, 8–9, 10, 18–19, 29, 31, 33, 55, 67, 181–84, 186, 197–99, 207
  race and, 3, 157–66, 169–75, 178–80
  Ream and, 181–84, 189–90, 197–99, 207
  *Risorgimento* and, 125–37
  Rome and, 2–3, 5, 28–35, 63–67, 71
  sexuality and, 3, 9–10, 31, 34–35, 49, 59, 65, 67, 69–71, 160
  slavery and, 161–62, 169–75
  studios and, 63–67, 86–87
  suffrage and, 197–99
  tomboy stereotype and, 10, 55
  Whitney and, 157–66, 180, 181–84
*Woman in the Nineteenth Century* (Fuller), 19, 128
*Women Artists in All Ages and Countries* (Ellet), 33, 65
women's rights
  Child and, 15
  class and, 199, 200
  "Declaration of Sentiments" (Stanton) and, 8–9
  domesticity and, 8–9
  education and, 81
  emancipation and, 179–80, 195–96
  Fuller and, 19
  Garrison and, 156
  Hosmer and, 18, 83, 120
  Jameson and, 131–32
  marriage and, 18, 156
  Parker and, 25
  professionalism and, 8–9, 10, 211–12
  race and, 120
  Ream and, 195–96, 197–99, 211
  *Risorgimento* and, 124–25
  sexuality and, 254n. 72
  slavery and, 156
  suffrage and, 179–80, 195–96, 197–99, 203, 205
  Whitney and, 120, 179–80, 199, 203–5
Woodhull, Victoria, 198–99
*Woodhull and Claflin's Weekly*, 196, 198–99
Woodmere Art Museum, 250n. 9
workmen. *See also* production processes
  Canova and, 42
  Hosmer and, 81–87, 89
  Lander and, 73, 80–81
  Ream and, 192, 197, 202
  Stebbins and, 236n. 61, 243n. 102
  Whitney and, 111, 243n. 102
World's Columbian Exposition, 243n. 102
Wreford, Henry, 248n. 62

Yeatman, James, 176
Yellin, Jean Fagin, 247n. 52
*The Youth* (Whitney), 111, *112*

*Zenobia, or the Fall of Palmyra* (Ware), 241n. 65
*Zenobia in Chains* (Hosmer), *68*, *133*
  authenticity and, 67, 81–86, 89, 132, 208
  Hawthorne and, 72
  Medusa in, 55, 132, *133*
  race and, 166
  *Risorgimento* and, 125, 131–37